DE[V]
GENERAL PH[YSICAL]

SCALE (

0　　　　5　　　　10　　　　　　　　20

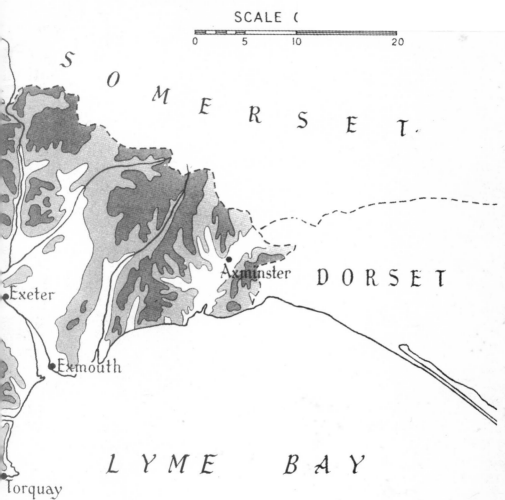

S O M E R S E T.

D O R S E T

•Exeter

Áxminster

•Exmouth

L Y M E   B A Y

Torquay

2000 Feet	
1500 ,,	
1000 ,,	
500 ,,	
250 ,,	

A New Survey of England

★

DEVON

The Mouth of the Dart : on the far side is Dartmouth Castle with St. Petrock's Church; on the near side is Kingswear Castle

A NEW SURVEY OF ENGLAND

DEVON

by

W. G. HOSKINS

DAVID & CHARLES
NEWTON ABBOT · LONDON

To
HOPE BAGENAL
Poet and Topographer

British Library Cataloguing in Publication Data

Hoskins, W. G.
Devon.—New ed.—(A New survey of
England)
1. Devon (England)—History
I. Title   II. Series
942.3´5   DA670.D5
ISBN 0-7153-5577-5

First published 1954
Second impression 1954
Third impression 1959
Fourth impression 1964
New edition first published 1972
Second impression 1978

Printed in Great Britain by
Redwood Burn Limited, Trowbridge, Wilts.
for David & Charles (Publishers) Limited
Brunel House   Newton Abbot   Devon

CONTENTS

CONTENTS

PART TWO

ILLUSTRATIONS

Illustrations are from old prints or recent photographs.

ILLUSTRATIONS

viii

ILLUSTRATIONS

MAPS

*An endpaper map showing the physical features of Devon
will be found at the front of the book.*

MAP REFERENCES

In the gazetteer which forms part two of this book the map references (B4, G9, etc.) can be found on the Ordnance Survey quarter-inch map (sheets 10 and 11) by means of the National Grid. Each square on the national grid is identified by the reference number of its western and southern boundaries; and the map references in this book are to the same squares. (Thus B4=31 and G9=86.)

N

	2	3	4	5	6	7	8	9	0	1	2	3	
4	A1	B1	C1	D1	E1	F1	G1	H1	J1	K1	L1	M1	
3	A2	B2	C2	D2	E2	F2	G2	H2	J2	K2	L2	M2	
2	A3	B3	C3	D3	E3	F3	G3	H3	J3	K3	L3	M3	
1	A4	B4	C4	D4	E4	F4	G4	H4	J4	K4	L4	M4	
0	A5	B5	C5	D5	E5	F5	G5	H5	J5	K5	L5	M5	
9	A6	B6	C6	D6	E6	F6	G6	H6	J6	K6	L6	M6	
8	A7	B7	C7	D7	E7	F7	G7	H7	J7	K7	L7	M7	
7	A8	B8	C8	D8	E8	F8	G8	H8	J8	K8	L8	M8	
6	A9	B9	C9	D9	E9	F9	G9	H9	J9	K9	L9	M9	
5	A10	B10	C10	D10	E10	F10	G10	H10	J10	K10	L10	M10	
4	A11	B11	C11	D11	E11	F11	G11	H11	J11	K11	L11	M11	
3	A12	B12	C12	D12	E12	F12	G12	H12	J12	K12	L12	M12	

W ... *E*

S

A NEW SURVEY OF ENGLAND

EDITOR'S INTRODUCTION

THIS NEW SURVEY OF ENGLAND has two main objects. It is intended
in the first place to describe the local history of England, relating
it to the history of England as a whole; and secondly to give some
account of the country as it is to-day, linking past and present together.

Massive labour has been devoted to English local history during the
past four hundred years—by the early masters, like Leland and Camden
and Dugdale, by the eighteenth-century topographers, by the contributors
to the publications of our local antiquarian and historical societies. The
evidence that has thus been accumulated for the history of our counties
and towns is much too bulky for the ordinary reader to absorb; and it
often presents serious difficulties of interpretation. A sustained effort
is being made to analyse and expound it in the *Victoria History of the
Counties of England*. But that great project, though it has been in progress
for over fifty years, is not yet half completed, and its scale is far too large
for the ordinary reader. Where is he to turn for a compendious account
of the subject? Back to the old histories, which—however excellent in
their time—are inevitably out of date; and from them to the vast and
fragmentary evidence that lies buried in the *Transactions* and *Proceedings*
of the county societies and in monographs, greatly varying in value.

. The time has come to summarise our present knowledge of English
local history in a form that can be understood by an intelligent reader
without an academic training, and within the manageable compass of a
single volume for each English county. Such a synthesis is perhaps even
more urgently necessary than fresh research, the discovery of new evidence. We are in grave danger, in this field as in many others, of
accumulating more knowledge than we can absorb; and one result has
been a widening separation between local and national history. That
separation is surely most unfortunate, for it leads us to write English
history too much in terms of the central government, of London, and to
base it too exclusively on the central records. Above all, it leads to
unsatisfactory generalisation. The national historian tends to overlook

the abundant variety of provincial life, with the significant exceptions it constantly offers to the accepted verdicts of history.

The NEW SURVEY aims first at synthesis, at the summarising of evidence that is already available. But it is designed also to extend our knowledge, by the use of new material and by enlarging what has generally been regarded in the past as the proper field of English local history. Very much new evidence is available. Some of it is still in manuscript, in the hands of private persons, of business firms and public corporations, in the record offices that have been established with such admirable zeal by local government authorities in recent years, in the greatest Record Office of all in Chancery Lane. But there is much more historical evidence waiting to be worked that is not in manuscript. Local historians, to take one example, have made slight use yet of the vast stores of information that are contained in the Parliamentary Papers of the past two centuries. Our provincial newspapers, too, have been little explored for this purpose. As long ago as 1914 Mr. James Townsend showed, in his *News of a Country Town*, what a valuable contribution *Jackson's Oxford Journal* could make to our knowledge of Georgian Abingdon; but there are very few other works of the same kind.

Nor is this additional evidence to be found only in books. The one-inch Ordnance Survey map, and its eighteenth-century predecessors, have a good deal more to tell us about English history than has yet been realised, especially when the study of them is linked with the technique of air-photography, which has been developed so remarkably in the past thirty years, and with the careful study of place-names. There is, too, a great body of pictorial evidence that is almost entirely unworked by local historians. Topographical art has a long and distinguished history in England, beginning well back in the seventeenth century and continuing down to the present day. A single drawing will sometimes help to illuminate the whole history of a street or a piece of landscape: Cornelius Varley's " Market-Place at Ross," for instance, or any one of Cotman's Yorkshire drawings of 1803-1805. Tens of thousands of such pictures exist. They are not always of that high artistic quality, but they describe for us, in a way that no words could achieve, buildings that have now been destroyed and scenes that are changed for ever.

Local history must always be largely a visual study. It can never be based wholly on books, on written evidence, as constitutional history— for example—can. But if its methods are largely visual, if it is based on the actual examination of the relics of the past that remain, then another consequence follows: it is concerned with the present as well as with the past. To the true local historian it will not be enough to reconstruct a sixteenth-century street from its surviving buildings, from their deeds, from the wills and papers of their occupants: he must inevitably be led to consider what has happened to the street between that time and this, why and how it came to assume its present form. The erection of the tram-standards and the arrival of the chain-stores are just as much a part of its history as the building of a half-timbered town hall or of the parish church.

Surely local historians should above all others be conscious of the continuity of present and past. Yet this is hardly borne out by their practice. Looking through the publications of the county societies, one notices that they seldom deal with subjects nearer to us in time than the seventeenth century. The industrial, the social, the political history of modern England—the England whose power has extended throughout the world: these are matters they hardly touch on. There are exceptions to this broad statement, especially in the publications of the county societies of the North: but even there they are not numerous. This was not the way of the scholars who founded the study of local history in this country. They were interested closely in the history of their own age, as well as in the past. One can see it all through Leland's *Itinerary* and Camden's *Britannia*: beside Dugdale's *Antiquities of Warwickshire* stands his *Short View of the Late Troubles in England,* an account of the Civil War of his own time.

★   ★   ★   ★   ★

These are some of the considerations that lie behind this NEW SURVEY OF ENGLAND, which has been in preparation since 1947. It is designed to provide for each county, within a single volume, a connected account of its history and its present state, together with a brief description of the monuments of the past that it still has to show.

This general plan has been subject to two modifications. Treated in this way, Yorkshire is too big for a single volume, even a very large one: plainly it requires three, one for each of its Ridings. Here the NEW SURVEY will be following a well-established precedent. But another of its practices will be new. It is a consequence of the general neglect of the local history of modern England that the English towns have received far less than their due share of attention. In the early history of England they occupy a subordinate, though increasingly important, position. But modern England is an urbanised country. At least since 1851 a majority of Englishmen have lived in towns: only one fifth of our population today lives outside them. We may like that fact or deplore it; but we cannot run away from it. If a survey of this kind is to achieve its true purpose, it must therefore give full and prominent attention to the history of our towns.

For this reason it has been decided that about a dozen important

English cities shall be treated in separate volumes of this NEW SURVEY. London is in a class apart: it is intended that it should eventually have four. The others that have been selected for this purpose are either cities with a long and exceptionally rich history, such as Bristol, York, Exeter, and Oxford, or cities like Liverpool and Manchester and Newcastle, which have played a great part in the economy and the politics of modern England.

Such treatment inevitably presents difficulties. It is not easy—at some points it is impossible—to separate the history of Devon from that of Exeter, which has always been its capital. The treatment of the history of Devon in this SURVEY will not be complete until both volumes have been published. But not all the cities that have been chosen raise such problems:. for five centuries and more Bristol, York, and Newcastle have stood almost wholly outside county administration, and the same is largely true of the great modern industrial cities like Liverpool and Manchester. The most important thing is to secure adequate space for the treatment of the history of these cities: to describe it within the framework of a county volume would extend the volume to an impracticable length. Moreover, as communities they are, and have long been, quite distinct from the counties that adjoin them.

Many towns will compete to be dealt with in this way; but the number of such volumes must be strictly limited. Those that are not so treated will also receive careful attention, fuller in proportion than that usually given to them in previous histories of the kind.

One other general decision has had to be taken. Should a co-operative method be adopted, splitting the work up into subjects and topographical divisions and allotting each one to a separate author? Or should each volume be left in one author's hands? There is much to be said for both solutions: but my decision has been clear from the outset. I am anxious that each of these volumes should be the product of a single mind and a single pair of eyes: that, in a literary sense, it should be the work of one man and not of a committee. To say this is not to impugn the other method. What I would claim for the NEW SURVEY is this: that it presents a summary of the history and a brief description of each of these counties and cities as it appeared to one intelligent observer in the twentieth century.

This method must involve differences of emphasis and treatment, both in subject and in material, between one volume and another. It is the editor's business to try and see that they are not unduly great, involving serious discrepancy. Certain common practices and standards will be adopted throughout the series as a whole; but there will be as little rigid uniformity as possible. Though the NEW SURVEY stands as a single project, under one general direction, the most important part in it is played by the authors, each of whom has his own outlook, ideas and style—as highly individual as the county or city he is describing.

Lastly, it should be emphasised that the illustrations and maps in each volume are to be regarded as an integral part of its text. They have not been chosen merely to adorn it. The pictures include examples of the topographical art that has already been mentioned, together with modern photographs, a great many of which have been taken expressly for the NEW SURVEY. The line-maps, too, have all been drawn to the authors' specifications. They include, for example, geological maps and plans of towns and streets, which will, it is hoped, assist the reader to understand better not only the past but also the face of modern England.

In its scope and objectives this SURVEY represents something of a return to the methods of the earlier English local historians. Though Leland—to name the Father of them all—was the King's Antiquary, interested primarily in the past, the account given in his *Itinerary* of the revolution he saw in progress around him is still of high value to us, four centuries afterwards. The NEW SURVEY OF ENGLAND attempts a task similar to his, in the social revolution of our time.

DEVON

AUTHOR'S INTRODUCTION

NO comprehensive history of Devon has appeared since the year 1822, when Daniel Lysons published the sixth (and last) volume of his *Magna Britannia*. This volume was devoted to the history and topography of Devon. Ever since that date it has been a quarry for all later writers including myself. With all its faults, it was the most useful—and in general the most accurate—of the histories of Devon, which do not rank among the best of their kind. But as the scope of English local history widened, notably in the development of the social and economic field as a great new branch of History, and as the mass of records, both in the public archives and in private hands, became more generally accessible and grew in bulk to formidable proportions, it no longer appeared feasible for one man to attempt the history of a whole county over a long period of time. As long ago as 1877 the Sidmouth antiquary Peter Orlando Hutchinson (one of the thorough old school of local historians so noticeably missing to-day) told the Devonshire Association that the task could only be accomplished by " a committee of literary persons." Fortunately, knowing what we do of committees of local antiquarians, nothing came of this proposal. Two more generations have passed since then, and the task has in the meantime become still more formidable. As the field of English history widened, so also has that of the local historian. Nevertheless, a book covering as well as may be the history of the county from its beginnings on Bronze Age Dartmoor down to the present day, within the compass of a single volume of manageable size, is badly needed; and I have attempted to write it here.

Clearly, this book is *a* history of Devon, not *the* history. Others would have written it very differently, with a different emphasis. No man can claim an equally detailed knowledge of all branches of history, not even of English history, or of the sources for writing them. Where my own knowledge was weakest I have sought the advice of others more learned in that field. In particular I owe much to my friends Hope Bagenal and Herbert Finberg. Much of this book has been discussed with them and

I gratefully acknowledge their help in matters of interpretation and of fact. If errors and erroneous opinions remain, in spite of their advice, I am alone responsible. I am grateful, too, to Sir Cyril and Lady (Aileen) Fox, whose recent arrival in Devon is a great piece of good fortune for the serious study of its archaeology and early history. If only they could have come sooner, this book would have been better in its earlier chapters. I am conscious that I have not benefited as much from their liberal help as I might have done. If, as a mere historian, I have stumbled about a little in the darkness of prehistory, they are in no way to blame. Nor is Mr. Ralegh Radford, who has been equally generous in his help, and who produced in particular the map of the prehistoric antiquities of Dartmoor which may be, I believe, the first of its kind, and is certainly an enhancement of this History. Work upon the prehistory of Dartmoor, and of Devon as a whole, is going on all the time; views change; and it may well be that what I have written here upon the subject is already out-moded in some detail. I think, however, that the general picture will stand untarnished for a considerable period, and I hope that it may contribute to the intelligent enjoyment of Dartmoor in particular, one of the most mysterious and fascinating regions in all England, through the understanding of its four thousand years of history. A definitive study of the prehistory of Devon has yet to be written, and until that time the historian must do the best he can in a peculiarly difficult field.

A more serious problem, for it is of wider consequence, has been the problem of references. In a work of this kind, based as it is upon material collected, things seen, and books read, over a period of thirty years— for I made my first notes at the age of fifteen—the references should have been many times more numerous than they are. But to have given adequate references to each page of this book would have meant the sacrifice of many thousand words of text, and on balance I felt that in a book primarily intended for the enjoyment of the general reader the text would be more welcome than the apparatus behind it. Hence the references have been reduced to a minimum. I have given my references wherever I make use of manuscript or unprinted material; and, so far as the printed sources are concerned, wherever they are difficult of access or only to be found in unlikely places, and where also in my judgment they were vitally necessary for other reasons—where, for example, I might be advancing a new view or controverting an old one. I cannot hope that specialists, if any should chance to read this book, will not find this selectiveness exasperating at times; but I hope that in the main justice has been done in this respect and that wherever I have made use of the work or conclusions of others the fact is clearly acknowledged by a suitable reference.

There are other matters which should be made clear to the reader at the outset. Most important is the omission of the city of Exeter from this history of Devon, apart from a summary account of its history and principal " antiquities " in Part Two of the book, and apart, of course, from many incidental references throughout Part One where the history of the county as a whole would be unintelligible without them. The county of Devon is so large and so rich in every aspect of human history that to compress it into a single volume is itself a task of some magnitude. To have added to this task the history of one of the most ancient and exciting cities of England, a city which has been the capital city of a province for nineteen hundred years, and whose magnificent collection of archives begins well back in the twelfth century, would have been disastrous to my object. The result would have been an inadequate history of both county and city: two fine subjects ruined in one book. Wherever the history of the city has affected, or been affected by, the history of the county it has been woven into this book; but the history of Exeter as an individual civic community remains to be written separately upon a scale adequate to the theme.

Considerations of space, even in a book of this size, have obliged me to adopt expedients which may not commend themselves to all readers. I refer in particular to the apparently cursory treatment of Plymouth in Part Two, where it receives less space, for example, than the little town of Tavistock. This is as painful to me as it will be to the people of that noble and historic city, for which, as an Exonian, I have a great admiration. The discrepancy of treatment is to a considerable extent lessened in the course of Part One, where Plymouth is treated again and again in its various aspects. But I had also to take the view that it already possesses a number of good histories of its own—unlike such towns as Tavistock and Totnes—to which the attention of the reader is directed in the Bibliography, and that I ought therefore to devote more of my limited space to those places which have been less well served by their local historians. Further, so much of the history of Plymouth belongs to the history of England as a whole, and is more fittingly written there. I hope, therefore, that I may be acquitted of any charge of injustice to a great city.

Now and then, in dealing with the smaller places, I have allowed my own enthusiasms to dictate the amount of allotted space. No one will suppose that the amount of historical interest is to be measured by the size of a place, or that there can be any agreed criteria in matters such as this. I must confess that I have occasionally spread myself over a place that has always possessed for me a special fascination, where I have felt the *genius loci* in its fullest power, as for instance in the little riverside town of Topsham.

The writing of this book has been an immense pleasure as well as a heavy labour. It has compelled me to visit every parish, however remote, in my native county, to penetrate deep lanes in search of ancient houses that had been only names to me until then, to wade across rivers and to scramble over hedgebanks following Saxon boundaries—seeing the lie of the land as the Saxons saw it and the reasons why they did things as they did—to acquire a detailed knowledge of a county which I thought I already knew tolerably well. In doing all this, and little else for the space of five years, I have learnt a vast amount about the topography and the history of Devon, two things so often inseparable, but I realise also how little one really knows even at the end of all this. There is so much in the smallest and the simplest scene, in the detail of every land-scape however restricted, and I can only hope that something of this secret history has come through in this book, in the descriptions of certain places at least.

In a county so full of zealous antiquaries, at least one watchdog in every parish and sometimes several, I can hardly expect to escape criticism or correction. With all one's care over the facts, some may well have defied my efforts, and I shall be grateful for any corrections that may be felt to be necessary. All I can claim to have done is to have sketched in the outlines of the history of this county. Little more was possible in the allotted space. Even now much remains to be unearthed: there are enough problems for a regiment of antiquaries and a score of research students, and enough, I am glad to feel, to keep me quietly busy in the intervals of other work until the great age to which Devon-shire antiquaries usually attain, somewhere just short of ninety.

I have always wanted to write such a book as this, indeed I had vowed as a schoolboy that I would one day do so. It is a premature book, of course. In twenty or thirty years' time I should be better qualified to write it, but in the sort of world one lives in today one cannot take this generous view of time. One hears every day, not so much " Time's winged chariot hurrying near " as the loathsome hum of other winged chariots devised by insensate man for his own destruction, and one is all too aware of the other gifts of modern science to wish to delay one's books indefinitely. Moreover, even in happier days local historians have been known to die leaving behind a generation of illegible notes and no more, the book unwritten. Here, then, is a history of Devon, with all its faults and imperfections, written by a native whose ancestors have all lived in the county since Elizabethan days and most of them since a time " when the memory of man runneth not to the contrary."

My ancestors were men and women of no particular eminence even in local history, farmers nearly all of them until the collapse of local communities all over England in the early nineteenth century drove them off the land and into the towns and across the water to the American continent. But they were the sort of people who form the foundations of any stable society. I may perhaps be allowed to resurrect one of them, a characteristic figure from a more humane England. Baring-Gould, in *A Book of Dartmoor*, published in the year 1900, says, " I recall the church before modern ideas had penetrated to Chagford. At that time the clerk, who also led the orchestra, gave out the psalm from his seat under the reading-desk, then, *whistling* the tune, he marched slowly down the nave, ascended to the gallery with leisure, and the performance began." This clerk, I discover, was my great-great-grandfather Richard Thorn, who became parish clerk in the year 1800 at the age of twenty-four and held the office all his long life until he died at the age of seventy-seven. He farmed thirty-two acres of his own land at Thorn, a hamlet in the parish from which his ancestors had long ago taken their name, where Thorns had lived since Robert atte Thorne back in 1332, back no doubt to the first moorland peasant who broke up the ground around the solitary thorn-tree, perhaps in the closing years of the twelfth century or the first years of the thirteenth. First the ancient tree gave its name to the farm, then the farm gave its name to its first owners; and still there are Thorns in Chagford. Richard Thorn was succeeded as parish clerk by his son John Thorn, who is described in the directory as " Saddler, Harness-maker, Postmaster, and Parish Clerk "—a man of many useful parts. Father and son were parish clerks of Chagford for eighty-two years between them.

These things delight me when I come across them. This is the immemorial, provincial England, stable, rooted deep in the soil, unmoving, contented, and sane. Those are my forebears, who have made me what I am whether I like it or not; and I have enlarged upon them a little because they have really determined what sort of book this is.

W. G. HOSKINS

Steeple Barton Vicarage,
Oxford
9 January 1953

DEVON

Hic amor, haec patria est

PART ONE

CHAPTER I

GENERAL DESCRIPTION

THE MAP OF DEVON

TOPOGRAPHY is the foundation of local history, and the one-inch map of the Ordnance Survey is the foundation of topographical knowledge in England. It is with the one-inch map of Devon that we begin this history of the county, for the map, as the curious and affectionate eye wanders over its intricate pattern, speaks an historical language of its own, though a language mostly of questions. It asks some questions and answers them almost at once—though the immediate answer is not always the right one—but it asks far more and leaves them unanswered. And these unanswered questions lead us back to the other records, to the immense wealth of documents from Anglo-Saxon times onwards, both local and national, so great a store that one man alone can no longer cope with them even for a single county.

The earliest maps of Devon, beginning with Saxton's map of 1575, are only of limited value as records: the information they give is meagre and sometimes misleading, though sometimes they may settle a small historical point. Donn's great map of 1765, on a scale of one inch to the mile, takes us much further and was a triumph for one man working single-handed; but it necessarily had large blank patches between the chief roads and therefore still failed to give the complete text of the Devonshire landscape. With the first edition of the one-inch Ordnance map, published in 1809, we have as near a full text as any map on that scale can give. It gives no contours, it is true, but it delineates the variations of surface by a skilful hachuring which portrays the physical appearance of the county with great clarity. The absence of contour-lines and of certain other details (such as parish boundaries and footpaths) also throws up the details of town and village plans in a manner unrivalled by any modern map. Its only near rival as a clear picture of the landscape is the fifth (relief) edition of the one-inch map published in 1931-3, an edition which was abandoned before Devon was completed.

If we spread out on the floor all the sheets of the first edition of the one-inch map of Devon we need a space of more than six feet each way to cover this large county from sea to sea. And as we survey this immense canvas of Devon, what sort of picture do we get?

The first impression beyond all doubt is of the extraordinary mass of *detail* on the map, much more so perhaps than in any other county. There is not a square inch of the map (except in the wilder recesses of central and northern Dartmoor and on the higher slopes of Exmoor) that is not studded with detail of fascinating interest to the local historian. The map is so thickly crowded that one discovers new things on it, new entertainment for the mind, even after years of use. It is like a painting by Breughel or a major symphony. No one book can do justice to the historical richness of such a canvas: one could write a book about every few square inches of it, about nearly every one of the 430 or so parishes that make up the county.

Roads and lanes wind and twist abruptly in apparent confusion all over the landscape. Off the turnpike roads of 1809 there run smaller branch-roads, making a close network in the intervening country; and off these smaller roads there run, every few hundred yards, yet narrower lanes that penetrate along remote combes or deep into the flanks of some massive hill, to end in a nameless farmyard, with the unpathed fields beyond and all around. So many farmsteads in Devon lie alone at the end of a deep-sunken lane thick with mud in winter, stony and rutted in summer. Every lane has its own history: it is not there by accident: and every twist it makes once had some historical meaning, which we can sometimes decipher to-day, but not often.

Dispersed over the map of 1809 are the clear black outlines of numerous small country towns and of large compact villages, closer to each other in the country east of the Exe than to the west, yet never so close together as the compact villages of the midland counties. West of the Exe, that fundamental dividing-line between the old rocks and the new (as we shall see in due course), these little market towns and nucleated villages are fewer. They may be anything up to seven to ten miles apart: and the wide intervening spaces are all the more thickly studded with isolated farms and hamlets, laced together by a fine network of lanes. Even east of the Exe, on the newer and more fertile rocks, this dispersion of human settlement between the villages is very noticeable.

Then we observe the variety of the names on this crowded canvas: that many farms and hamlets are called *hayes* or *hayne* in the south-east of the county: that many are called *worthy* in the west and north-west: that scores have the suffix *cott*, especially in the north: that in nearly every parish there is at least one farm called *barton* (plate 36), sometimes two or three: that in some parts of Devon the village as it is understood elsewhere in England hardly exists at all (plate 24). Only a lonely hill-top church with a single farmstead beside it gives its name to the thousands of upland acres that make up the parish. And the names of these parishes: the larger, more compact, settlements so often called after the river they stand on, like Crediton and Tawton, the smaller and more dispersed ones after the saint to whom the parish church is dedicated, as at Virginstow or Mariansleigh; and how, in the west of the county above all, these dedications are to Celtic saints—such as Germansweek, Petrockstow, and St. Budeaux. The names of the towns, villages, hamlets, and farms, either reveal some detail of history at once or suggest questions that call for an answer.

On the map of 1809, too, drawn before the revolutionary changes of the 19th and 20th centuries had obscured their ancient pattern, the plan of the market-towns and the larger villages sets the mind working im-

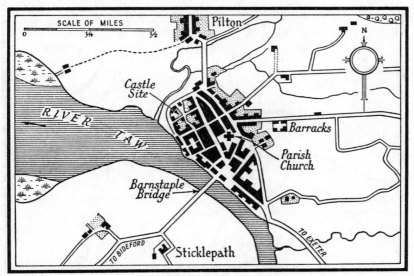

FIG. 1—BARNSTAPLE IN 1809

A town that grew up inside medieval walls (redrawn from the 1st edn. of the Ordnance Survey, 1809)

mediately. So often they are gathered around a large rectangular space (as at Bradworthy and North Lew) with the parish church on one side and roads entering this open space from all points of the compass. Why that particular plan? To what age does it belong?

And how neatly the little towns lie in that early 19th-century landscape! There they are, compactly gathered together within a small compass on an intelligible site, their streets beginning and ending abruptly and cleanly on the edge of the country, with not a trace of that shapeless mess of building on all sides that heralds their approach to-day. There is a most striking contrast, for example, between the neat, contained shape of Paignton in the year 1809 and the formless chaos of the seaside town of 1953, stretching back westwards in ribbons and clots for miles towards Totnes, and equally shapeless north and south along the ravaged shores of Tor Bay. On the older map one can see exactly why the village grew on that site, half a mile or so back from the shore for safety and shelter, at the foot of the inland hills as they die away into the coastal flats.

On the same map and on the same bay one sees the tiny settlement of Tor Quay, a few houses around a minute harbour in the shelter of Warberry Hill, completely protected from the lashing south-easterly

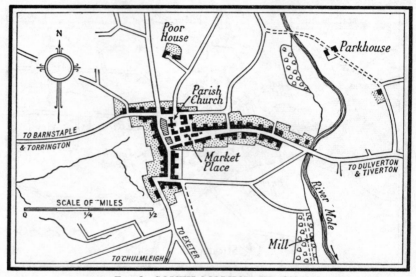

FIG. 2—SOUTH MOLTON IN 1809

*A town that grew up in open country (redrawn from the 1st edn.
of the Ordnance Survey, 1809)*

gales to which the bay is open. And one sees also what is obviously the original settlement at this end of the bay, about a mile back from the sea, the village of Tor Mohun, at the southern end of the hill (*tor*) which gave it its name. Where the drives and terraces of mid-Victorian Torquay now coil endlessly round the hills and headlands, the map of 1809 shows only open hills with an occasional farm in the warmer hollows—Ilsham, Hope Farm, and Torwood. The site of Exmouth is equally interesting on this early map, before the town had begun to expand as the seaside outlet for the city of Exeter. Over and over again one notices how the flourishing seaside towns of to-day originated as villages a mile or so inland and how, in the course of the 19th century, they have grown towards the sea and left the old village high and dry (as it was intended to be) around the parish church, as at Dawlish or Seaton, for example, on the south coast, or at Ilfracombe and Combe Martin on the north.

These are all comparatively new towns, the creation of the 19th century. The oldest towns of Devon lie safely away from the sea, at the head of a navigable estuary or the lowest bridging-point of the river, depending on one's viewpoint, some seven to ten miles inland. Such ancient towns are the mother-city of Exeter—*Isca Dumnoniorum*—at the head of the Exe estuary and its lowest bridging-place until modern times;

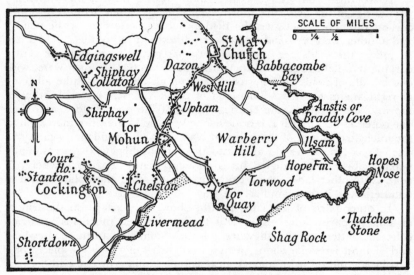

FIG. 3—TORQUAY IN 1809 (AFTER DONN)

Totnes, in the same position on the Dart; and Barnstaple likewise on the Taw. The map of 1809 shows with remarkable clarity the plans of these early towns. Though their medieval walls had all but disappeared by that date, the influence they had had upon the shape of the town is still discernible. And in 1809 one could still see that the walled towns had quite a different shape from the unwalled inland towns that had grown up as market-centres in the post-Conquest period, as witness the contrast between the shapes of Barnstaple and South Molton (figs. 1, 2), or between Exeter and Crediton. These contrasts in the shapes of the old towns, so very evident still on the early 19th-century map, are striking enough to impel one to seek out the causes forthwith, and so from the map we find ourselves fairly launched into the unexplored seas of urban history.

Where we find old towns on or near the open sea—as at Plymouth or Dartmouth—they are nevertheless comparative newcomers as towns go, creations of the 12th century. They were founded when the great age of the pre-Conquest migrations and invasions, an age when sudden attacks came oftener from the sea than overland, was over and done with; but even so they were not originally built on the sea-coast but a mile or two inside some estuary or bay. And even so they have suffered periodically and heavily from later attacks across the Channel.

If we turn from the one-inch map to the 6-inch, on which the boundaries of the fields are shown, yet other questions arise. We notice curious differences between the field-patterns of one part of the county and another, and often indeed between different parts of the same parish. In places the fields are long and very narrow, with straight or gently curving parallel hedges, and they are grouped in bundles as it were, with one bundle of fields all lying one way and an adjacent bundle all lying at right angles to them. This kind of pattern closely resembles that of the midland counties, the classical home of the open fields; and then one observes also that it is best developed on the Devonshire map around the nucleated village of the midland type. Near such villages, again, one often finds long lanes running into the surrounding fields, occasionally making abrupt right-angled turns and apparently leading nowhere, in contrast to other lanes which run purposefully from one isolated farm to another, even if they wind all the way.

In other parts of the same parish, above all perhaps on the fringes of a large parish covering several thousand acres, the fields make no coherent pattern at all: they are generally smaller than those elsewhere and of most irregular shape, fitting into each other like the pieces of a vast jigsaw puzzle, with ancient little coppices filling up the odd corners. Between these two contrasting types of field-pattern on the 6-inch map of Devon there lie profound differences of economic and social history whose roots go back to the dark centuries following the Saxon settlement in the 7th and 8th centuries. It will be one of our tasks to uncover this history so far as it can be done.

Turning from the 6-inch map to the 25-inch map, our interest passes from the fields to the plan and lay-out of the farmstead itself. Here we are confronted with the single house, the smallest unit of human settlement, and here, too, just as much as in the plan of an old town or a compact village, the long process of human history is partly revealed to the inquiring eye, seeking to decipher the palimpsest of the Ordnance map. What is the age of this solitary habitation, lost among the trees in some little combe and far removed from the parish church, or high up

on the frontier of the unbroken moor? Why does the farmstead follow
this particular plan—sometimes a courtyard completely enclosed on all
sides, sometimes an open space with buildings grouped around three sides
but not joined together in a continuous series, sometimes a single rectangular building with dwelling-house, barns, and stables all under the
same line of roof? Why is it here at all, far removed from the human
warmth and security of the village? Often the name of this solitary farm
will suggest part of the answer to these questions, if we know how to read
it aright; but in the main the map asks questions that we cannot answer
at first glance. We must pass on to the other records and seek the answers
there.

THE MEANING OF "DEVON"

The earliest reference to the shire by name is to be found in the Anglo-
Saxon Chronicle under the year 851, when " the Alderman Ceorl with
the men of *Defenascir* fought the heathen army at Wicganbeorg and after
making great slaughter obtained the victory." In 894 the form *Defnum*
occurs, *Defenum* in 897, and *Defenun* in a charter of 955. Somewhat
earlier, in 823, the Chronicle speaks of " the men of Devon " as *Defnas*.
This tribal name was transferred, as in several other English counties,
to the territory inhabited by the tribe.

The *Defnas*, to trace the name further, derived their name from the
British *Dumnonii*, the name of the Celtic inhabitants of south-western
England, which was transferred to the Anglo-Saxons who conquered
them.[1] And the Dumnonii in turn got their name from a Celtic root
dumno- or *dubno-*, used adjectivally in the sense of " deep " and as a noun
meaning " world " or " land." The tribal name therefore meant " the
people of the land."[2] The theory that the old name for south-western
England—Dumnonia—meant " deep valleys," which would suit the topography of the county well, rests solely upon the modern Welsh form for
Devon of Dyfnaint, which has this meaning. This is a piece of folk-
etymology but it has no other authority.[3]

Thus the name of Devon is derived ultimately from a Celtic tribal
name—" the people of the land." Both the modern forms—Devon and
Devonshire—are equally ancient, dating from the earliest days of the
shire in the 9th century. Neither usage is more correct than the other.
The form we use to-day is governed largely by the euphony required in a
phrase and partly by custom. Thus we speak of Red Devon Cattle, and
we used to speak of Devonshire cream.

BOUNDARIES OF DEVON

On the east Devon is bounded for the most part by the county of Somerset, with a few miles of Dorset at the southern end. The exact date of the fixing of this boundary is not known, but it has been suggested with considerable authority that Devon was one of the seven shires known to have existed in Wessex during the second half of the 8th century. Charters attested between 757 and 778 have the names of seven men, who are evidently the ealdormen of shires, of whom one Scilling was most probably ealdorman of Devon.[1] But the boundary with Cornwall was probably not finally determined until the time of Athelstan (925-39), when it was fixed on the Tamar.[2]

The eastern boundary of Devon to-day is not the historic boundary. In 1842 and again in 1896 considerable changes were made, which took the parishes of Stockland, Dalwood, Chardstock, and Hawkchurch away from Dorset and added them to Devon, and transferred the parish of Thorncombe from Devon to Dorset. In addition, the parish of Church-stanton was transferred from Devon to Somerset. Before 1842 the two parishes of Stockland and Dalwood, deep in the Blackdown Hills, formed an outlier of Dorset surrounded by Devon, and Thorncombe was a Devonshire island in the county of Dorset.[3] The Stockland, Dalwood, and Thorncombe transfers were made in 1842, the others in 1896.

The western boundary of Devon has a curious history.[4] If we begin at its southern end, we follow the Tamar for half its length, to a point just north-east of Launceston. Here a great tongue of Devon, two or three miles wide and seven miles long, thrusts deep into Cornwall; but three miles farther upstream the river becomes the boundary again and so continues (except for negligible breaks) to within a few yards of its source near the north coast. From this point a direct four-mile line down a steep, wooded combe brings one westwards to the Atlantic coast at Marsland Mouth.

The great tongue of which we have spoken covers some nineteen square miles and consists of the two large parishes of North Petherwin and Werrington. These parishes have always been included in the archdeaconry of Cornwall for ecclesiastical purposes, but are still in Devon for all other purposes. They were already included in Devon in 1086, and as they were entirely owned by the Devonshire monastic house of Tavistock it has been suggested that the abbot saw to it, when the boundary was drawn, that the whole monastic endowment on both sides of the Tamar was conveniently included in the one county.[5] But until 1066, or shortly afterwards, this large estate had been included in the Cornish hundred of Stratton and was a part of the royal demesne which descended to Gytha, the wife of earl Godwin.[6] Some time between 1066 and 1068, when Gytha left England for ever, she had transferred the estate to Tavistock abbey. There is evidence that it was still reckoned to be in Cornwall as late as 1084, but by 1086, when Domesday Book was compiled, the abbey had been deprived of it and it was included under Devon, where it has remained ever since.

It is almost certain that the Tamar had been the original boundary along its whole length, except for the parish of Maker at its mouth, and that the transfer of these nineteen square miles from Cornwall to Devon took place silently when Baldwin de Brionne, sheriff of Devon, held the farm of Harold's and Gytha's lands in Devon. As Werrington (the political name of this territory) was Gytha's only considerable Cornish estate, it too fell under his administration. Such an arrangement suited the sheriff of Devon financially, for he paid an inclusive rent for the farm of the Devon lands and should have paid a further rent if Werrington had been officially known to be in Cornwall; and since the Exon Domesday returns were drawn up at Exeter under his supervision he had the opportunity also to set the official seal upon a deliberate fraud of the exchequer. The estate was therefore described under Devon in the final Domesday return, and as recently as 1929 a Cornish bill to restore the *status quo* of 1066 was defeated in a committee of the House of Lords.

The parish of Maker, at the mouth of the Tamar and now so obviously a part of Cornwall, was in fact a part of Devon until 1844, when it was transferred. There can be little doubt that this curious enclave of Devon in Cornwall embodied a piece of history stretching back to the earliest days of the Saxon occupation (*c.* 700), to a time when it was necessary to have a unified control over this important estuary.

AREA AND DIMENSIONS

The geographical county of Devon is the third largest in England, exceeded in size only by Yorkshire and Lincolnshire. It is, indeed, the largest single administrative area, covering (in 1939) 1,660,948 acres— nearly 36,000 acres larger than the administrative county of the West Riding and more than 300,000 acres larger than Norfolk or the North Riding, the next largest.

The population of the geographical county in 1951 was 798,283. Of these, 284,000 live in the two county boroughs of Exeter and Plymouth, and a further 80,000 in the urban concentration of Torquay-Paignton on the shores of Tor Bay. Thus a total of 364,000 people live in the three largest urban concentrations. Outside these are three towns with 16,000 to 17,000 people each (Barnstaple, Exmouth, and Newton Abbot) and half a dozen smaller towns with 9,000 to 12,000 people. A number of small but historic boroughs, such as Totnes and Honiton, contain from 3,000 to

6,000 inhabitants. Finally, there are six more old towns which, though not boroughs for administrative purposes, have all the other attributes of a town, such as Ashburton and Crediton, whose population is between 2,500 and 6,000. Outside the three largest urban concentrations, however, one can say that the county is almost entirely rural, with large stretches completely uninhabited on Dartmoor, and wide areas in mid-Devon and west Devon only thinly peopled (25 to 100 per square mile).

The greatest length of the county from north to south is about 75 miles, from the lighthouse on the Foreland, that tremendous cliff that commands the entrance to the Bristol Channel, down to the southern look-out on Prawle Point, where Lloyd's signal station reports all passing ships. Prawle, thrust well forward into the narrowing English Channel, has been a look-out station for well over a thousand years. To the first Saxons who made the rough passage round its point it was " lookout hill ": its Old English name was *Prawhyll*. In Domesday the hamlet behind the headland is called *Prenla*, but the form of *Prahulle* in 1204 is more recognisable. The modern English word " pry " has the same Old English root.[1] In Victorian London, before the days of the radio and the aeroplane, the message " passed Prawle Point " was the first news of many a ship homeward-bound from the other side of the globe.

Near the Foreland the Romans had established two signal stations to watch the Bristol Channel, one on either side of the headland. One was at Old Barrow Hill, to the east, and the other at the Beacon, in the parish of Martinhoe. These commanded the whole sea across to the Welsh coast.

From east to west, Devon is nearly as wide: 73 miles from the Cornish border near Canworthy Water to the extreme eastern point by Birdsmoor Gate, that typical Dorset name—600 feet up on the downland, only two miles from the great Dorset landmark of Pilsdon Pen and all the Hardy Country below. The extreme western point of Devon is, however, not in the Petherwin-Werrington tongue, but on the Atlantic coast south of Hartland Point, on the cliff just north of Welcombe Mouth, with Hawker's country all around and his parish of Morwenstow immediately to the south.

Within this great expanse of country lay some 450 ecclesiastical parishes, varying in size to a degree not found perhaps in any other English county.* We may broadly contrast the six square miles of the average Devon parish with the two square miles of the average Suffolk parish or the twelve square miles in Northumberland, but these bare averages are misleading. If we look at a map of Devon which shows us

---

*A return made in 1563 of the deaneries and parishes in the diocese of Exeter gives the total number of parishes in Devon as 454, with one chapelry in addition. We may regard this as the historic figure, before modern boundary changes had begun to operate (BM Harl. MS. 595, ff. 21b-22).

the skeleton of parish boundaries—and for this purpose the modern map showing civil parishes will serve adequately—we see beneath our eyes a pattern of lines that sets the mind asking one question after another. Such a map is as near a palimpsest as any map can be: its wavering lines, fitting together like a jigsaw puzzle, reveal to a patient scrutiny a good deal of early history which is nowhere else recorded. Averages conceal the truth; it is the variations that reveal it and kindle the historical imagination.

In Devon the parishes range in size from tiny Landcross, whose 331 acres are almost wholly contained within a bend of the Torridge above Bideford—so small that a curlew calling on the tidal mud can be heard all over the parish—up to the 17,650 acres of the parish of Tiverton which lie in two enormous halves on either side of the middle Exe valley.* There was at one time, indeed, a parish of only 52 acres—Broad Nymet, with its own rector, which was absorbed into Nymet Tracey hardly more than a century ago. At one end of the scale, eight rural parishes have fewer than 500 acres, and 36 have fewer than 1000 acres. At the other end, 12 parishes undulate across more than 10,000 acres, and these are by no means the wild and empty moorland parishes. Half of them are, but half are not, and to that extent they are historically interesting, in their very size and shape, before we begin with their recorded history. The way parishes fit together, the way they group themselves into compact blocks suggesting an older unit of settlement before parish boundaries were drawn, the relationship between tiny parishes and giant ones, the shape of parish boundaries and the way they run, all these matters of observation furnish clues to the early history of the colonisation of England in the centuries before written evidence becomes available, if only we knew how to decipher it all.

TOPOGRAPHY AND GEOLOGY

Devon is shaped like a trapezium, with its shortest side washed by the Bristol Channel and its longest by the English Channel. It is one of only three English counties—Cornwall and Kent being the other two— to possess a north and a south coast, and with the exception of Cornwall it has the greatest proportion of coastline to area of any county. The sea thus plays a large part in the climate and the history of the county from the Bronze Age onwards, the more so historically because Devon is connected with the rest of England only by a narrow neck of land between the mouth of the Parrett on the north coast and Lyme Regis on the

*The parish of Lydford, which includes the whole of Dartmoor and claims to be the largest parish in England (56,333 acres), is a special case, and need not be considered in this context.

south, a distance of 35 miles. From the top of Windwhistle Hill, almost on this narrow neck, one can on a clear spring evening discern the sea shining to the north and to the south. Beyond this neck, the peninsula of south-western England thrusts westwards into the Atlantic for 130 miles or so, widening into a solid block in Devon, more than 70 miles across, and then tapering rapidly down the length of Cornwall.

Not only was the connecting link with the mainland a narrow one; it was also difficult to traverse. The Somerset levels were always deeply flooded in winter, and beyond them to the west one saw (as one sees to-day from the Great Western railway near Taunton) the long dark mass of the Blackdown hills to the south-west and the less massive but wilder hills of Brendon to the north-west, almost meeting to block the way into Devon. There were, historically, only two narrow gateways into Devon from the rest of England: the northern gap between the Blackdowns and the Brendons, and the southern gap, less conspicuous, through the Axe valley. These are the historic landward entrances into Devon from Saxon times onwards; and in the 19th century the two main railway lines from London to Exeter tunnelled their way through the same gaps at Whiteball tunnel (G.W.R.) and Honiton tunnel (L.S.W.R.).

The contoured map of Devon makes an intricate picture, one which appears at first sight to defy any reduction to simple statements, with thousands of little streams in their combes, hills tumbling away in all directions, ragged and indented coasts, and a variation of surface every mile or so.

There are, however, a few fundamental facts which help to reduce the tangled mass of topographical detail to a semblance of order. Most important of all—the master-key to the topography of Devon—is the granite boss of Dartmoor, a broken tableland some twenty miles from north to south and fifteen from east to west. There are 300 square miles of visible granite, but if we add to this the aureole of altered rocks affected by the granitic pressure the central core covers some 400 square miles.

This core is all that remains of an antique volcanic region which once formed either a single volcano or a series of cones. If the former it must, from the extent of its site, have constituted a Devonian Etna some 18,000 feet high—a *massif* even grander than the Etna of to-day. If the latter, its active peaks, rising from the coastal waters of the Devonian Sea, may very well have resembled the Lipari Islands as we know them. In either case the underlying granite was itself lifted or thrust upward in course of time, and at all periods it was penetrated by veins and dykes of fresh intrusive lava, forming the elvans. The sequence of eruptive periods is thought to have continued into Carboniferous and post-Carboniferous times. The last act was a long process of denudation during which wind, frost, and rain (and possibly ice also),[1] wore down the superincumbent rocks, through thousands of feet, to the granite itself—down to the original magmatic reservoir. The present average height of the Moor is only 1200 feet above sea-level. It is likely that Brentor, so like a volcanic cone as one sees it from afar off rising from the surrounding plain, is a fragment of a crater of this old volcanic region. Further evidence is given by the tufas or volcanic ash of western Devon, by the lavas of the Exe and Teign valleys, and by the far-carried *ejectamenta* found in the breccias. The deep-seated granite had cooled under enormous pressure, thus causing the wide-spaced joint planes which, on exposure, bring about the weathering into giant blocks. The more resistant of these form the tors which to-day rise from the whale-backed tableland (plates 27, 28). At times their demonic silhouettes resemble the man-made statues of Easter Island, most notably at Bowerman's Nose near Manaton.

Dartmoor is the Great Source. Its granite produced the stone for votive columns, propitiatory altars, and sacred avenues; for huts and houses and barns; for burial chambers; for the walls of man's earliest cornfields and cattle pounds; and long afterwards for his soaring church towers and his Christian tombs, and for London's streets and bridges. Its lavas went to the building of the dark basalt walls of Roman Exeter in the third century, to the vaulting of Exeter cathedral in the thirteenth; its tufas to the making of Tavistock abbey and to the creation of modern Tavistock town, built of the green volcanic ash of Hurdwick. And its limestones have been altered here and there by heat and earth pressures, and contribute building-stones, marble monuments for churches, and the glistening rainswept pavements of Plymouth:

> Never hath anger so much beauty made.
> Behold his passion into marble cooled,
> His burning ashes into fields allayed,
> His frowns fair streams. . . .

From Dartmoor flow in all directions the chief rivers of Devon—all except Tamar, Exe, and Torridge, and even they are abundantly fed by Dartmoor streams. These radiating rivers enriched the fertile lowlands and attracted early farmers. Towns grew up where the rivers broke out of the Moor, as at Tavistock and Ashburton; and where they widened into estuaries little ports arose as early as the 10th century, as at Totnes and Barnstaple.

Not only did the Moor yield stone for the expression of man's religious beliefs—his pagan avenues and his Christian monasteries and churches—over a space of four thousand years, and for the building of his houses and the shelter of his animals. It collected on its broad back nearly all the water of Devon and dispersed it down the deep valleys at every point of the compass. And there was, too, the rich mineral treasure, produced by the acid vapours once given off by the granite at high temperatures. These vapours, penetrating the lodes and rifts, gave rise to tin and other metals, and also over large areas altered the granite itself by a process known as *kaolinisation*, thus producing china-clay. Mining has been carried on, from the 12th century down to our own day, on the Moor and its foothills.

And on the Moor dwelt, in a kinder climate than to-day, the earliest settlers of whom we have any real knowledge, the farmers of the Early Bronze Age with their little corn-plots and their flocks and herds. Apart from the lone, nomadic figure of palaeolithic man, in numbers quite unimportant, we may regard Dartmoor as the earliest home of man in Devon, the beginning of forty centuries of continuous human occupation in the south-western peninsula of England.

The other fundamental fact about the topography of Devon is the dividing-line between the old rocks and the new—the so-called Tees-Exe line—which reaches its southern terminus on the shores of Tor Bay. The ancient city of Exeter stands at this great geological junction: and from the city walls one looks westwards over the Exe to the high, rolling, pastoral and wooded hills of the old Culm Measures, and eastwards over the lower, more gentle and more richly cultivated Permian and Triassic sandstones. It is sometimes said in jest that the Midlands begin at Exeter, and there is a geological sense in which this provocative remark is true: but it is truer to turn these words around and to say that the West begins at Exeter, with that steep climb out of the city into the emerald-green hills, from whose summit, only two or three miles from the cathedral, one sees the dark bastions of Dartmoor ahead; from Dartmoor the jagged outline of Bodmin Moor lies against the western sky; and from Bodmin Moor one looks on towards " dark Bolerium," to where out of sight the Atlantic surges unrestingly against the granite of the land's end.

This junction of the old and the new rocks is also the boundary between the Highland zone and the Lowland zone, a division of fundamental importance in the prehistory of Britain. The country west of the Exe closely resembles Cornwall in structure and topography, increasingly so as one goes farther westwards. In the Hartland peninsula of north-west Devon the landscape is almost purely Cornish in its appearance and feeling. East of the Exe, the new red rocks link Devon geologically with the Midlands, just as the cretaceous rocks of the extreme east of the county link it with southern and south-eastern England.

The Exe is, however, only an approximate boundary between the two great zones. A narrow band of the red rocks runs down to the shores of Tor Bay, at Paignton, where the red cliffs end; and immediately west of this band is the Haldon plateau, which is a detached remnant of the

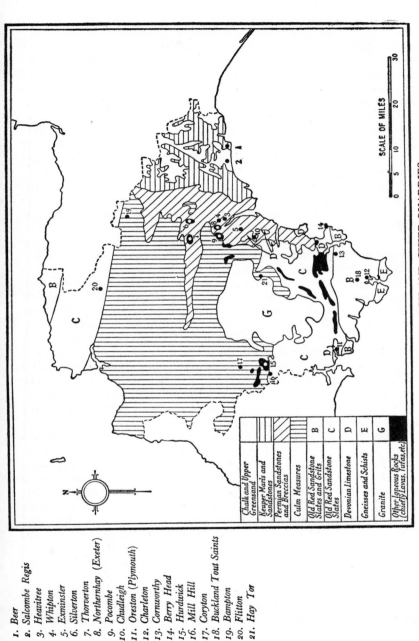

1. Beer
2. Salcombe Regis
3. Heavitree
4. Whipton
5. Silverton
6. Thorverton
7. Northernhay (Exeter)
8. Pocombe
9. Chudleigh
10. Oreston (Plymouth)
11. Charleton
12. Cornworthy
13. Berry Head
14. Hurdwick
15. Mill Hill
16. Coryton
17. Buckland Tout Saints
18. Bampton
19. Flitton
20. Hay Tor

Chalk and Upper Greensand	
Keuper Marls and Sandstones	
Permian Sandstones and Breccias	
Culm Measures	B
Old Red Sandstone Slates and Grits	C
Old Red Sandstone Slates	D
Devonian limestone	E
Gneisses and Schists	G
Granite	
Other Igneous Rocks (chiefly Lavas, Tufas, etc.)	

SCALE OF MILES

0 5 10 20 30

N

Fig. 4—GEOLOGY AND CHIEF QUARRIES

The sources of Dartmoor moorstone (granite) and Roborough elvan have not been indicated,
as these were surface stone until recent times

cretaceous plateau of east Devon. Moreover, the new red rocks thrust two
tongues westward into the older landscape, one to the west of Tiverton
and another, much larger, for over twenty miles through Crediton and
North Tawton, as far as Hatherleigh. On the other hand, the older rocks
appear some miles east of the Exe at Holcombe Rogus (near the Somerset
boundary), south of Cullompton at Ashclyst Forest, and in the wooded
hills immediately to the north of Exeter. These intrusive tongues have
the effect of dovetailing together the old and the new rocks in Devon, and
also produce some interesting local variations of scenery and of human
settlement.

When we pass beyond this elementary division of the old and the
new rocks, to look more closely at the details of the geological structure
of Devon—for it is quite fundamental to an understanding of the prehistory and early history of the county—we are faced with a most complicated scene. The coloured geological map of Devon is a delight to
the geologist and the topographer, with an eye to the infinite variety of
its detailed changes and their effect on scenery, human settlement, and
land-use. The historian, too, must face its complexities as resolutely as
he can. Much of the pleasure and value of local history and topography
remains beyond reach if one is content to remain ignorant of geology.
There is hardly a single aspect of local history, whether we are looking at
documents or the landscape itself, that is not illuminated to some degree,
sometimes completely explained, by a knowledge of the underlying
rocks. At times like these the arid jargon of the geologist, which we
have laboured to understand, is transmuted into a kind of poetry. The
carving of a Norman doorway in a small country church, still bold and
clear because the Normans knew so well how to select the best stone from
the quarry, gives us all the more pleasure if we recognise also the stone
they chose and if we know its nearest outcrop, so that we can go on down
the very lane up which they brought it when Henry II reigned at Westminster and Bishop Bartholomew reigned at Exeter, and push through
the tangled undergrowth to the deserted pit itself. Here the red or
purple or green rock still glows with colour in the afternoon sunlight,
birds fly in and out of the trees and bushes that nearly fill the hollow,
and sulphur-coloured butterflies flutter against the warm rock face. Out
of this pit, we reflect, came the east gate of medieval Exeter, or the blood-
red tower of the great collegiate church at Crediton, or the simple Norman
doorway at Loxbeare, or the green and vanished splendour of Tavistock
abbey. There are a score of building stones in Devon, and there are
several hundreds of deserted quarries, in fields or hidden in woods, and
their history is mostly written only in the buildings within a short radius
of them. Very occasionally the stone came from outside Devon: to find
the quarry out of which the noble 14th-century arcades of Bratton Clovelly

came, or that dove-grey south arcade of Sampford Courtenay, we have to cross the border into Cornwall and penetrate to the Polyphant quarry in the parish of Lewannick: but such a pilgrimage outside the county is not often necessary.

Nor is the importance of geology to the historian by any means confined to the visual. As one travels from church to church, noting the stone used in fonts, arcades, walls, mullions, towers, or in the larger houses and farm-buildings, one sees how far afield some particular stones were carried —especially granite and Beer stone—and one is led to speculate on the economics of the medieval building industry which could move such weights (often by road) over considerable distances, and on the economics of the society which could meet the cost of all this building, a burden far beyond the means of the impoverished 20th century. A working knowledge of geology is indispensable for any study of the medieval building industry, for any detailed study of the settlement and colonisation of the countryside, and for its subsequent agrarian and mining history.

One may say, in the broadest outline, that north and south Devon consist almost entirely of slates and sandstones of Devonian age, which occupy altogether one-quarter of the area of the county. The whole of central and west Devon is covered by the carboniferous series known as the Culm Measures,[1] which occupy rather more than two acres out of every five in Devon; and the granite boss of Dartmoor occupies one acre in nine.

These three regions together constitute the " old rocks " and cover about four-fifths of the county. East of the Exe we find the Permian and Triassic rocks, mostly red sandstones and marls, covering about 15 per cent; and east of these again is the cretaceous formation (mostly a high greensand plateau) covering rather less than 5 per cent. Small post-Tertiary deposits make up the remainder of the surface. South-western England was never covered by ice-sheets, and the drift deposits which are so important in other parts of England are wholly absent in Devon and Cornwall.

Altogether, the " new rocks " make up only one-fifth of the total area of the county. The scenery which is so commonly regarded as typically Devonian—the deep and fertile red earths contrasted with a luxuriant green vegetation—occupies in fact only one-seventh of the total area. The greater part of the county shows landscapes that are strikingly different in their scenery and their agricultural possibilities from the " red land." Large tracts of Devon were, and still are, relatively infertile, and their entire history has reflected this geological fact.

One other fundamental geological fact is less obvious: it is the existence of three great platforms at 1,000 ft., 750-800 ft., and 430 ft., respectively. All these platforms are of unknown age, arising from marine erosion of older surfaces over a wide area, the wearing-down of ancient hills and mountains, with the worn and levelled surface subsequently uplifted to its present height. The 1,000-ft. platform is best seen around Moretonhampstead. Some of the waste material from this area has filled the deep basin around Bovey Tracey, which yields brown coal like that of Germany, but is more important for its valuable ball-clays, used in local and distant potteries.

The 750-800-ft. platform is seen most clearly on the western side of Dartmoor, where the famous Lydford Gorge has been cut deep into it. The 430-ft. platform is most evident in Cornwall, but is traceable in many parts of Devon, especially in the coastal topography. The subsequent uplift of this plateau led to the rejuvenation of the drainage, with the result that the rivers rapidly deepened their valleys, so giving the characteristic steep-sided gorges of Devon and Cornwall (best seen in Devon at Lydford Gorge and Lustleigh Cleave). Successive uplifts also led to the drowning of the lower valleys of many rivers, so producing a number of magnificent, sheltered deep-water inlets of which those of the lower Tamar and lower Dart are the most notable.

The existence of these high-level platforms, particularly those at 430 ft. and 750-800 ft., has had a profound effect upon land-use in Devon and upon agrarian history. Over large tracts of the county the flat surfaces of these platforms are responsible for the bad drainage of the land, despite its elevation, above all on the poor soils of the Culm Measures. Then, too, the deep valleys incised in these platforms are generally too steep for arable cultivation, which is restricted to the drier plateau areas between the valleys. On the other hand, the depth of the valleys protects them from the strong winds, especially from the west, and produces thick woods. Trees are infrequent on the plateau, more and more so as one goes westward towards the Atlantic coast, and most farmhouses and villages seek the valleys or some sheltered dip in the plateau. And finally, the drowned valleys carry the moderating influence of the sea far inland, giving relative security from frosts in the valley-bottoms and encouraging the growth of flowers and fruit, as, for example, in the extensive plum-orchards at Dittisham on the Dart estuary, and the large strawberry fields of the lower Tamar valley. One should go to Tavistock in June to appreciate this best.

Once again we see that the generally accepted ideas of the topography of Devon do not bear close examination. It has often been argued or implied, for example, that the open-field system, so characteristic of Midland agriculture, never existed in Devon—or certainly not on any appreciable scale—because the hilly surface of the county precluded it. But, in fact, great stretches of the Devon landscape are plateau-like, either flat or gently undulating for miles, intersected—sometimes closely but often only at great intervals—by steep-sided river valleys. This is particularly true of the Culm Measures country, which stretches from the Somerset boundary on the east to the Atlantic coast on the west, and from the shores of Barnstaple Bay southwards to the foothills of Dartmoor. Many other tracts of the county are also plateau-like, such as parts of the South Hams, where wide views disclose remarkably level horizons. We shall see, in fact, that the open-field system of agriculture was widely established in all parts of medieval Devon, though possibly in not quite the same form as the classic Midland pattern. It would indeed be truer to say that the topography of the greater part of Devon presented not the slightest obstacle to the development of the open fields. Neither the Culm Measures nor the Permian and Triassic landscapes offered any serious physical obstacle beyond those to be found in most parts of England.

CLIMATE

The climate of Devon is as complex as its topography when we look into it closely. In general, however, it is governed by the geographical position of the south-west peninsula of England, thrust well forward into the mild, rain-bearing winds of the Atlantic. The county has two long coastlines, and a number of river estuaries running far inland, all of which help to spread the climatic influence of the sea. The other major physical fact is the existence of masses of high land in the peninsula which attract a heavy rainfall. In central and south Devon the great mass of Dartmoor, rising to summits of just over 2,000 ft., and in north Devon the tableland of Exmoor, rising to over 1,500 ft., both have more than 60 inches of rain a year. The high tableland of north-west Devon, so near the sea, gets over 50 inches, and the Blackdown plateau of east Devon over 40. The peninsular position of Devon, coupled with its highlands being so near the sea, gives it in general a mild, wet climate, with rapidly changing weather.

Within the county the climate varies greatly from place to place, according to height above sea-level, situation in relation to open water, and comparative shelter or exposure. There are such local sayings as " as cold as Challacombe ": Challacombe is nearly 1,000 ft. up, in a fold of Exmoor, and its Old English name means " cold valley ". Or they say that " the devil died of the cold at North Lew." Now, North Lew is only 400 ft. above sea-level; but the wind pours for uninterrupted miles across the plateau of cold yellow clays round here, bringing fifty inches of rain with it. At the other extreme are the sheltered south-coast towns between Sidmouth and Torquay, mildest of all being Salcombe in the extreme southern tip of the county.

The highest parts of Dartmoor receive more than 80 inches of rain a year. At Princetown the average annual rainfall is just under 82 inches, but a fall of over 100 inches is not uncommon. In 1882, 115 inches were recorded. At the other extreme, the estuary of the Exe, from Exeter down to the sea, gets slightly under 30 inches a year, and the greater part of the red-earth lands in the Vale of Exeter less than 35 inches. In general, however, a great part of Devon receives 40 inches or more annually, including a belt which stretches from the north coast at Clovelly almost to the south coast at Dartmouth, and thence westwards to the high ground at the back of Plymouth. All the high ground of north-eastern and east Devon similarly receives over 40 inches. Most of Devon can therefore be classed as a wet area, with something like twice the annual rainfall of the Thames valley (20 to 25 inches).

Temperature and sunshine are the other climatic factors which are historically important. The south-western peninsula is the mildest area in Britain, its climate being tempered almost everywhere by the sea all the year round, though there is a greater range of temperature as one goes inland. The mean annual temperature inland is 50.5 degrees Fahrenheit, and 51.5 degrees on the coast, at sea-level in both cases. The mean annual temperature for January at sea-level is 42 to 44 degrees, as compared with 38 to 39 degrees over most of eastern England. The difference is slight numerically, but very real indeed to Devonians transplanted to eastern or midland England, and the winter landscape of Devon, still full of colour and life when the midlands are bleached with cold, speaks vividly of the difference of temperature between the two regions.

Though the Devon climate is generally equable, extreme temperatures occur, as in all parts of Britain. In January 1940, 30 degrees of frost were recorded at Cullompton, and 16 degrees even at Torquay. The severe frosts of the winter of 1946-7 ruined many fine sub-tropical gardens on the sheltered south coast. In summer, temperatures of over 90 degrees have occasionally been known: at Killerton, in the Vale of Exeter, 94 degrees were recorded in July 1923. Generally, however, a heat-wave in Devon is many degrees cooler than a heat-wave elsewhere in England.

Snow is rare over most of lowland Devon: it lies less than five mornings a year on low ground, rising to more than twenty days on the higher parts of Dartmoor, and perhaps to more than thirty days on the 2,000-ft. summits of the Moor. Memorable falls of snow have occurred in January 1881, March 1891, Christmas 1927, and February 1929. In the great blizzard of 1891, still a vivid memory to old men all over Devon, which they resurrect in detail whenever the young exclaim at some modern snowstorm, many trains were embedded in snow all round Dartmoor, and the Princetown train was out of sight, except for the funnel, for several days on end.

The south coast of Devon is one of the sunniest regions of the British Isles, though not quite so sunny as that of Sussex. On the north coast the daily average of sunshine all the year round is 4¼ hours; on the south coast it rises to 4.90 hours at Salcombe and 4.87 hours at Torquay. Even Plymouth, with nearly 37 inches of rain a year, averages nearly 4.6 hours of sunshine daily. At Ilfracombe, on the north coast, the corresponding figure is 4.22 hours. Fog is rare everywhere in Devon, except on Dartmoor.

The humidity and cleanness of the air all over the south-western peninsula encourage the growth of lichens and mosses, even more so in Devon than in Cornwall owing to the great variety of the geological strata, and this adds to the colour and tone of buildings in any kind of stone. Much of the rich winter colour of Devon arises from the brilliantly coloured lichens, which stand out all the more prominently when the trees are more bare.

The climate of Devon has been an important historical influence in various ways, above all in determining the kind of farming that has been carried on for centuries, and hence the kind of settlement over wide areas; and later in attracting a considerable class of people of independent means along the whole of the mild, southern coast, and well inland in the Vale of Exeter. The influence of this class upon the architecture and social life of the county during the past 150 years has been very marked, and they are still an important and characteristic element in the population, much more so in the south than in the north; though even in the north the towns of Bideford and Barnstaple have a little of the flavour of Sidmouth and Torquay. And the holiday resorts of the south coast, especially, are almost the creation of the Devon climate, and have now become the major industry of the county.

CHAPTER II

PREHISTORIC AND CELTIC DEVON

A LTHOUGH Devon possesses some of the most striking evidences of prehistoric man in Britain—notably the palaeolithic caves at Torquay and Brixham, the great complex of Bronze Age monuments on Dartmoor, and many fine examples of Iron Age hill-forts—its prehistory is full of unsolved problems and of formidable *lacunae*. Moreover, the county lay far to the western side of Britain, for the most part away from the main streams of influence, and its problems are the peculiarly difficult problems of a frontier region. This, indeed, is true not only of its prehistory but of the whole of its early history, through the Roman period and the succeeding Dark Ages, and well on into the years of the Saxon Conquest in the seventh century.

The shadowy figure of palaeolithic man need not detain us long, though he himself roamed over what is now Devon for immense periods of time. It is in the limestone caves of south Devon, on the shores of Tor Bay and of Plymouth Sound, and perhaps inland at Torbryan, that we find traces of his presence. In Kent's Cavern, about a mile due east of the harbour at Torquay, we have (with the Pin Hole in the Derbyshire limestone at Creswell Crags) the oldest recognisable human dwellings in Britain. Here Neanderthal man sought a winter refuge from the cold of the last Ice Age, and here have been found a quantity of Mousterian implements deposited round about a hundred thousand years ago. Aurignacian and later palaeolithic implements have also been found in different parts of the cave. Kent's Cavern was sporadically occupied at later periods, into Romano-British times.[1] Across the bay, the Windmill Hill cave at Brixham, discovered in 1858, has produced some evidence of palaeolithic occupation. The inland caves of Torbryan have yielded remains of later Pleistocene animals, but the evidence of contemporary human occupation (palaeolithic) is dubious.[2] The limestone caves near the junction of the Plym with Plymouth Sound—particularly at Catte-down—have produced human remains of the palaeolithic period. On the opposite shore, the Oreston caves are said to have yielded human bones of similar age, but they were thrown away as of no importance.[1] Elsewhere in Devon, on the border of Dorset, the Broom gravel pits near Axminster have long been known for their wealth of palaeolithic implements, ranging back possibly into the eolithic period. Palaeoliths from Broom have been found at several places in Devon, as far west as Tavistock. The cutting of the new road from Seaton to Beer also produced a number of early Mousterian implements.[2]

But the whole palaeolithic population of Britain was probably no more than a few hundreds, a primitive economy of hunters ranging over great tracts of country. Even right on into neolithic times, there is little to look at in Devon.[3] The most impressive of all the Iron Age hill-forts of Devon, that of Hembury Fort on a great southward-reaching spur of the Blackdown plateau, has been shown by excavation to be imposed upon a neolithic causewayed " camp " which occupied the southern half of the present earthwork. The pottery found on the site showed that the occupants had equal affinities with the " Windmill Hill " culture of Wiltshire and Sussex and with the neolithic culture of northern France. This dry site on the greensand plateau was probably occupied for a long period down to at least 1800 B.C., as there were undoubted evidences of contacts with the Bronze Age. At Hembury the neolithic occupants lived in huts on the inner margin of their rampart. One hut-site revealed stake-holes for the support of a circular wall of wattle and daub and contained a cooking-hole, a hearth for heating stones, and much household débris.[4] Hembury is the most westerly of the neolithic causewayed camps in Britain.

Eighteen miles south-west of Hembury, on the summit of the high greensand plateau of Haldon, an isolated neolithic house-site has been excavated. This was a fair-sized rectangular house with stone foundations, about twenty feet long and varying in width from $14\frac{1}{2}$ to 17 feet. The roof was gabled and probably thatched, and the walls were of timber or wattle. The site is important as showing that the western neolithic people were familiar with timber frame construction. The pottery found at Haldon showed that the neolithic settlers here were in contact with those at Hembury. Indeed, the two sites are visible from each other across a wide expanse of east Devon. Apart from this site, it is remarkable that the high tableland of Haldon should be archaeologically so unimportant, though it may be that further sites of this kind still await discovery.[5]

It is remarkable, too, that the upland expanse of Dartmoor, heather, bare granite, and bog, so thickly strewn with remains of the Bronze Age, should have produced no certain evidence of neolithic occupation. Not a scrap of neolithic pottery has come from the hundreds of hut-circles on the Moor, nor is there evidence of a single long barrow here or anywhere in Devon.

Just off the Moor is the most tangible memorial of early man, the so-called Spinster's Rock, about two miles west of Drewsteignton village and close to a farm called Shilstone—" shelf stone " or " ledge stone," referring to the capstone of the structure. This is a megalithic burial chamber akin to the Cornish dolmens, and is the best of the four left in Devon.[1] It seems probable, however, that the six other Shilstons and Shilstones in Devon represent the sites of destroyed burial-chambers. These lie in the parishes of Bishop's Tawton, Brendon, Chittlehampton, Exbourne, Modbury, and Throwleigh. Three of these sites, like Drewsteignton, lie not far from the foothills of Dartmoor, and suggest that neolithic man settled within sight of the Moor but not on it, and that he used it for summer pasturage and for hunting though not for permanent habitation. Neolithic celts, hammers, and other implements have been found at many places in Devon but these are not evidence of settlement except where they occur in large numbers, as at Hembury where thirty-six have been found. The caves at Torbryan, and Kent's Cavern at Torquay, also show traces of neolithic occupation.

Even taken all together, the evidences of neolithic man in Devon are not to be compared with those of the chalk and limestone uplands to the east and north-east; but with the coming of the early Bronze Age (c. 1900-1500 B.C.) it is vastly different. Here, in Devon, we not only have the remarkable, and in many ways unique, complex of prehistoric monuments of Dartmoor, ranging forward well into the Iron Age; but there are, too, the scores of barrows scattered over the Exmoor plateau and its foothills, and on across the dreary moors of mid-Devon as far as the Atlantic coast; and the notable concentration on the southern end of the Blackdown plateau in east Devon. Few of these burial-mounds have been scientifically excavated, but such as have been have proved to be of Bronze Age date.

The prehistoric monuments of Dartmoor number several thousand: the map is thick with them. But they are by no means evenly distributed over the Moor, and their distribution supplies a clue to the probable origin of these Bronze Age settlers.[2] There are alignments or stone rows; stone circles; cists (burial-chambers), cairns, and menhirs (standing stones); and hut-circles and pounds. The latter cannot strictly be called monuments, but they belong to the same complex as the sepulchral monuments. In some ways, too, they are more interesting, as they enable us to study the living—however sketchily—rather than the dead.

Whether some marked climatic change took place towards the end of the neolithic period and the beginning of the Bronze Age, leading to the actual settlement of the Moor in place of a seasonal visitation, we do

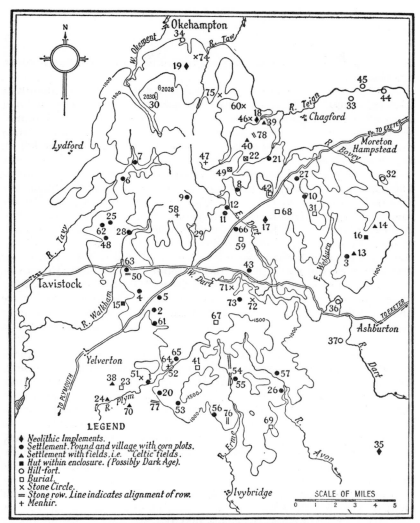

FIG. 5—PREHISTORIC DARTMOOR

Only the most important sites of each type are shown. Some modern roads are shown in order to facilitate the location of sites on the ground

1. Legis Tor. 2. Raddick Hill. 3. Blackslade Down. 4. Yes Tor Bottom. 5. Harter. 6. Standon. 7. Watern Oak. 8. White Ridge. 9. West Dart Head. 10. Grimspound. 11. Broad Down. 12. Broad Down Ring. 13. Foale's Arrishes. 14. Grea Tor. 15. Rountrundle. 16. Holwell Tor. 17. Runnage. 18. Gidleigh. 19. Cullever Steps. 20. Trowlesworthy Warren. 21. Metheral. 22. Fernworthy. 23. Wigford Down. 24. Dewerstone. 25. White Tor. 26. Ryder's Rings. 27. Shapley Common. 28. Langstone Moor. 29. Wistman's Wood. 30. Black Tor Beare. 31. Hamel Down. 32. Hunter's Tor. 33. Cranbrook Castle. 34. Promontory Fort, Okehampton. 35. Hazard Hill. 36. Holne Chase Castle. 37. Hembury Castle. 38. Wigford Down. 39. Kes Tor. 40. Shovel Down. 41. Langcombe Bottom. 42. Hurston Ridge. 43. Huccaby. 44. Wooston Castle. 45. Prestonbury Castle. 46. Gidleigh Circle. 47. Quintin's Man. 48. Wedlake Farm. 49. Grey Wethers. 50. Merrivale. 51. Brisworthy. 52. Drizzlecombe. 53. Shell Top. 54. Stall Moor. 55. Erme Pound. 56. Dendle's Waste. 57. Dean Moor. 58. Beardown Man. 59. Lakehead Hill. 60. Buttern Hill Circle. 61. Raddick Hill. 62. White Tor. 63. Merrivale. 64. Drizzlecombe. 65. Drizzlecombe. 66. Lakehead Hill. 67. Childe's Tomb. 68. Soussons Down. 69. Corringdon Ball. 70. Shaugh Moor. 71. Sherberton. 72. Hexworthy. 73. Hexworthy. 74. Nine Stones. 75. White Moor. 76. Staldon. **77. Trowlesworthy. 78. Shovel Down**

27

not yet know. What is clear is that the southern and, to a lesser extent, the western sides of the Moor were occupied by a considerable population very early in the Bronze Age. These settlers were predominantly a pastoral people, though in some settlements they occasionally grew crops in small enclosed plots.[1] There is not the slightest evidence that they came in search of tin. No traces of tin have ever been found in or near their huts and the density of their settlements does not correspond with the tin-deposits.[2]

Such evidence as there is suggests that the Bronze Age population of Dartmoor was composed of two elements: one coming directly across the Channel from Brittany, the other coming along the coast and up the Devon rivers from south-eastern England. The Dartmoor people had few or no affinities with those either of north Devon or of Cornwall. Exmoor shows no monuments similar to those of Dartmoor; nor is there much evidence of Bronze Age life around the headstreams of the Taw and Teign, on the northern side of Dartmoor. A Cornish origin can be ruled out. Though there are some affinities with Cornish culture, notably in the common practice of cremation throughout the Bronze Age, there are also important differences. The beaker-culture of the early Bronze Age is almost completely absent from Cornwall, whereas Dartmoor was a focus for it.[3]

The great concentration of antiquities on the southern moor, above all in the upper Erme valley, the upper Plym and Walkham, between East and West Dart, and round the sources of the South Teign, the Wallabrook, and the Bovey, points to a southern origin for the Bronze Age settlers on Dartmoor. And since the only other area in Europe where alignments or stone rows are at all common is the Carnac district of Brittany (and there are other parallels between the two regions), we may safely assume a migration across the hundred miles of water from Brittany to Devon *c.* 1900 B.C.: the first of many such cross-channel migrations down to the Breton " onion-boys " who used to make their cheerful and loquacious way from house to house in Exeter before the war of 1939.

There is every reason to believe that the Bronze Age population of Dartmoor settled and lived permanently on the moor, and no suggestion that they were nomadic. The country immediately surrounding the moor is devoid of Bronze Age settlement; while up on the Moor itself the extraordinary number of sepulchral monuments (cairns and cists) and of hut-circles, some with corn-plots, points to a numerous population living on the spot. It is incredible that such people should have lived elsewhere, and carried their dead up to the Moor and erected great monuments there. Moreover, the siting of the early Iron Age hill-forts, in a ring around the outskirts of the Moor, implies a permanent population on the

Moor at the end of the Bronze Age, and somewhat later, against whom these forts or " camps " were a protective barrier.

Let us take the habitation-sites of these people first, rather than their sepulchral monuments. It is difficult for any but prehistorians to feel a passionate interest in the visible remains of the hut-circles on Dartmoor, which are the walls, or the ruins of walls, of dwelling-houses, store-sheds, and cattle-sheds. Nevertheless, certain sites are impressive even to the layman and give him some sense of kinship, however dim, with his prehistoric ancestors. Such a site is that on Standon Hill, on a hillside between eleven and thirteen hundred feet above the sea, tumbling down through the boulder-strewn heather to the eastern bank of the infant Tavy. From here we command an enormous view, far down into Cornwall, where the outline of the alien hills of Brown Willy and Rough Tor meets the western sky. Below us the Tavy leaps on down its rocky valley; past the lonely grey Dartmoor farmsteads of Nat Tor, Bagga Tor, Willsworthy, and Wapsworthy, the homes of medieval farmers who had colonised the Moor again after a long silence: leaps on down to the first small hamlets—Cudlipp Town and Mary Tavy and Peter Tavy— down to the first town, beautiful green Tavistock. In the silent Bronze Age village in which we stand, among the tumbled walls, with the wheatears jerking from stone to stone and the larks spiralling overhead, we are among the oldest houses that we know, built on a hillside where a spring emerges from the interstices of the granite in the dry, short turf. Standon village contains the remains of over seventy hut-circles, some of them with substantial walls still *in situ* and standing to a height of three or four feet. Some, however, appear to have been rebuilt to form modern shelters for sheep and shepherds.[1] Many of the huts are connected by stone walls which form a complicated system of small enclosures of irregular shape. These are corn-plots of early Bronze Age date.[2]

The large village at Standon was not surrounded by a wall: it lay open and unprotected. Other village-sites, and notably those of Grimspound and Broadun, were enclosed within a more or less circular wall of dry, unhewn masonry.

Grimspound covers about four acres and contains the remains of twenty-four hut-circles, some of which have been excavated and well restored. A half of the huts showed signs of human habitation; they had hearths and their floors were strewn with charcoal. Four miles away, almost due west, is the equally impressive pound at Broadun (Broad Down), on the hillside above the right bank of the East Dart. This encloses an area of $14\frac{1}{2}$ acres and some forty hut-circles.[3] These pounds, of which about 155 can be traced on Dartmoor, were probably constructed for the protection of flocks and herds. They have weak defences and are often in an indefensible position, as at Grimspound and

Broadun. Such pounds, especially the larger ones, usually contain hut-circles.

The total number of hut-circles on the Moor has at times been greatly exaggerated. A careful survey over many years has revealed some 1,330, not all of which are yet marked on the Ordnance Survey maps. Allowing for those still to be discovered, the total is not likely to exceed 1,500. An unknown number must have been destroyed in areas enclosed in medieval times to form the " ancient tenements." They would have been hindrances to agriculture, and their stones were useful for the making of boundary walls and fences. The making of roads on the Moor in later times has led to further destruction, even within the present generation.

The surviving hut-circles are numerous enough, however, to give a good picture of the original distribution of settlement. This is very markedly concentrated in the valleys of the southern part of the Moor, and to a lesser degree on the western slopes of the Moor as far north as the upper Lyd valley. The northern part of the Moor, higher and wetter than the southern half, was very thinly settled, in places not at all. The central and eastern Moor shows a thin distribution, denser than the north but much less dense than the south or west.[1] The eastern side of the Moor is lower than the remainder, and much drier. Round Moreton-hampstead and Chagford the annual rainfall of 36 to 37 inches is less than a half that of the northern Moor. One would expect to find many more traces of hut-circles here. But for these very reasons the eastern side was settled and cultivated earlier than the rest—some farms were already occupied at 1,100 to 1,200 feet above sea-level in the eleventh century—and this must have involved a greater amount of destruction of hut-circles and other monuments than round the remote headwaters of the Erme, Plym, and Yealm. In recent years remains of hut-circles have, indeed, been found on the high ground in the parishes of Christow and Hennock, only eight or nine miles from Exeter. These were not on the granite but on the metamorphic aureole.[2] One may reasonably expect more such sites to be discovered in the future on the eastern slopes of the Moor, and on the lower moors between here and the Teign valley.

The densest settlement is found in the upper Yealm valley, at and above Hawns and Dendles, where there is an average of twenty-seven huts to the square mile. Round Trowlesworthy and Ditsworthy Warrens in the upper Plym valley there are twenty-three huts to the square mile. The upper valleys of the Avon, Erme, and Tavy also show a fairly dense distribution. The average number of huts, over the whole area of the Moor, is a little over five per square mile.

The walls of the huts are constructed of large vertical slabs of granite, presenting a smooth face inside, and backed outside with a bank of turf. The entrance doorway is usually on the south-west and is frequently protected against wind and rain by shelter-walls. Although this meant facing the Atlantic rains—sixty to seventy inches a year—it was infinitely better to turn one's back on the north-west wind, which could kill in a moorland winter. The floors are rarely less than eighteen inches below the surrounding ground, having been excavated to reach the gravelly subsoil of decomposed granite or " growan," which was firm to the tread. In some huts the floor was paved.[1] The average diameter of the huts was between 15½ and 17 feet, although considerable variations are found. At Grimspound, where the huts are rather smaller than the average, the diameters vary from 6½ to 15½ feet. Hearths and cooking-holes are found in the inhabited huts. Other huts, where the doorways are unusually wide, were probably cattle-stalls, and yet others were simply store-houses. The conical roofs of all these buildings were probably thatched or turfed over a wooden frame: certainly stone was not used.

The sepulchral monuments on Dartmoor require some remark, though the purpose of some of them is still a matter for speculation. Stone rows or alignments, of which sixty-two are known on Dartmoor, are very rare elsewhere in Britain.[2] They may be single, double, or multiple rows of stones; they are usually associated with a burial (and probably always were originally); they may be only a few inches high and are rarely more than two or three feet (though many on Stall Moor are 6 to 8½ feet high); and they vary greatly in length. A row at Merrivale is only forty-six yards long, but that on Stall Moor, running northwards to a barrow on Green Hill, is 2¼ miles long and is the longest known stone row in the world. Another row on Butterdon Hill is over a mile long. The rows tend to run roughly east-west, but the Erme valley group all run north-south. The significance of these rows is open to conjecture. It has been surmised that they mark the resting-place of a great chief and that the number of stones represents the size of his retinue.[3]

There are over ninety known stone circles on Dartmoor, the best being the quadruple circle near Yellowmead Farm, one mile due east of Sheepstor village. Other good circles occur at Brisworthy, Fernworthy, Scorhill, Sherberton, Cosdon, and the " Grey Wethers." Their purpose is unknown but might be sepulchral.

Kists or cists are stone coffins, probably originally covered by a barrow or a cairn. Ninety examples have been recorded.[4] They are almost invariably made of large slabs and vary in size, but they are usually about three feet by two and lie at an average depth of 2½ feet. In addition there remain on Dartmoor several hundreds of cairns and barrows, originally covering cremated remains. No inhumations (e.g. crouched skeletons) have been found; but inhumed bones would not survive in this acid soil in any event. And finally, there are the *menhirs* or standing stones, of which there are thirteen recorded, some associated with stone rows as at Drizzlecombe (a fine example) and some standing free and alone, such as " Bairdown Man " near Devil Tor.

From this vast number of sites, the datable finds are small. Most of the pottery from the hut-circles and cairns is undatable; but all the evidence points to the fact that Dartmoor was occupied from the beginning of the Bronze Age (c. 1900 B.C.) onwards and that it was largely abandoned early in the Iron Age (perhaps in the 3rd century B.C.), possibly for climatic reasons. Six beaker sites on Dartmoor have produced the earliest type of pottery on the Moor, and another type can be assigned also to the early Bronze Age. Moreover, the typical Dartmoor monument of a cairn enclosed in a circle is common throughout the Highland zone of Britain during the early Bronze Age. Gordon Childe considers, however, that some of the Dartmoor examples may belong to the late Bronze Age (c. 1000-500 B.C.). Hut-circles at Foales Arrishes have produced early Iron Age pottery.[1] It is becoming possible, too, to distinguish at least two types of huts: a small, early type which goes with small garden plots for corn growing, and a later and larger type, confined to the edge of the Moor and below the 1,000-foot contour, which goes with a recognisably Celtic field system.

Dartmoor is not the only scene of Bronze Age settlement in Devon. There are considerable traces of such settlement in east Devon, represented by groups of barrows. A number of these lie on the dry, pebbly Woodbury ridge between the Exe and the Otter valleys; but by far the most remarkable concentration is on the summit of the greensand plateau from Gittisham Hill, across Farway Common south-eastwards to Broad Down, all between seven and eight hundred feet above sea-level. No fewer than fifty-seven barrows occur in a distance of two miles, and none elsewhere on this plateau. Such a site, where a number of ridgeways meet, has aptly been termed " a Bronze Age necropolis."[2] There were no inhumations, only cremations, and the pottery suggests a date of c. 1400 B.C.—the early phase of the Middle Bronze Age. The Farway barrow-builders came from the Dorset area, and were a link between Devon and the early Bronze Age culture of Wessex. A mixed group of communities used this necropolis, including later Beaker invaders who came by sea. There was also penetration up the Exe. A double axe of early Bronze Age date has been found at Topsham, and on the other side of Exeter an isolated group of barrows of the same date is to be found between Upton Pyne and Thorverton.

In north-west Devon there is another series of barrows on the extensive plateau of the Culm Measures, beginning near the Atlantic Coast (Bursdon Moor in Hartland), continuing through East Putford, where there are eight barrows, and eastwards to Huntshaw parish on the hills beyond the Torridge. The excavation of two of the East Putford barrows suggested an early Bronze Age date,[1] while one of the Huntshaw barrows produced a grooved dagger of the Wessex type. On the high plateau between the Taw and the Exe and extending northwards to the top of Exmoor, many more barrows occur; and again in the poor upland country west of Okehampton almost to the Cornish border. But the study of the Bronze Age in Devon, apart from Dartmoor, is only beginning; and even on Dartmoor there is a multitude of unsolved problems.

The occupation of Dartmoor continued into the early Iron Age. A few sherds of pottery of this date (perhaps 3rd century B.C.) have come from the hut-circles at Foales Arrishes ($1\frac{1}{2}$ m. S.E. of Widecombe-in-the-Moor). This group of huts was once enclosed within a circular pound almost as large as Grimspound; most of the walling has been destroyed for road mending since 1851.[2] One of these huts was of great size—30 to 31 feet across—with a cooking-place outside the main building in a sort of " outshot." Such a hut may represent a late type, belonging to the early Iron Age. The hut-circles at Merrivale, above the eastern bank of the Walkham, are of various ages and types. Only the early types have so far been excavated, none of the later period.

It seems likely that the abandonment of Dartmoor and of the uplands of western Devon was brought about by a marked deterioration of climate (mainly an increased rainfall) at the end of the Bronze Age and the beginning of the Iron Age—say about 500 B.C. Most of the upland country of west Devon where Bronze Age barrows are found consists to-day of wet " moors " which are generally useless except as rough grazing, and which could never support much settlement under present climatic conditions. It is conceivable that Dartmoor was abandoned piecemeal from west to east, as the western side gets nearly twice as much rainfall as the eastern, and that evidence of human occupation continuing into the early Iron Age may be confined to the eastern side where it has already been found.

The earliest Iron Age invaders, whose culture is now known as Iron Age A, were small groups of peasant farmers. They used iron, lived in small settlements and tilled the soil, and practised a bare subsistence economy.[3] Traces of this culture have been discovered at Foales Arrishes, Kes Tor, and possibly on the limestone plateau at Dainton, now being excavated, where some of the pottery may be of this period. Some sherds of similar pottery have come from Kent's Cavern, five miles away.

The most striking evidence of the continued occupation of the Moor into the early Iron Age, and of the arrival of another people from elsewhere to colonise the lower ground, is the great ring of Iron Age hill-forts around Dartmoor, which are designed to guard against attack from the Moor and not by Dartmoor people against an attack from outside. Such a system of defences argues that the eastern side of the Moor was considerably more populated than the few remains of pottery at present suggest.

These hill-forts are especially noticeable on the north-eastern and eastern outskirts of the Moor, above all in the upper Teign valley where Cranbrook, Prestonbury, and Wooston tower above the wooded gorge of the river. On the east, the hill-fort of Holne Chase commands the gorge of the Dart where it begins to leave the Moor for the lowlands. Farther back from the Moor lie the impressive " camps " of Posbury (near Crediton), Castle Dyke (near Chudleigh), Denbury, and Milber; and, to the south, Stanborough (near Halwell) and Slapton Castle.[1]

East of the Exe, on the Blackdown plateau and the long finger-like ridges that spring from it, is another remarkable series of hill-forts. Hembury is the grandest earthwork in Devon, an Iron Age fortress enlarged from, and superimposed upon, a neolithic causewayed camp. Other fine examples of fortified hill-settlements (to describe them more truly) are to be seen on Dumpdon Hill, a notable tree-crowned landmark near Honiton, at Stockland, and at Membury. To the south-east a chain of such settlement dominates the Axe valley, of which Hawkesdown (near Axmouth) and Musbury lie in Devon. On the hills and ridges associated with the east Devon plateau, too, are the settlements of Blackbury (near Southleigh), Sidbury, and Woodbury; the fragmentary remains of Belbury, commanding the Otter valley near Ottery St. Mary; and the vanishing cliff-top " camp " at High Peak, just outside Sidmouth.

In mid-Devon, Cadbury and Cranmore (just outside Tiverton) command the Exe valley. From Cadbury, especially, there is a tremendous view: one of the most beautiful in England. One looks over the greater part of Devon, all except the heart of Dartmoor and the South Hams beyond, and far away into Dorset, Somerset, and Cornwall. In north Devon is a small group of hill-forts of which Clovelly Dykes, on the plateau above Barnstaple Bay, looking across to the coast of south Wales, is the most striking: an immense series of ramparts covering a greater area than any other hill-fort in Devon except Milber. On the edge of Exmoor are the forts of Countisbury and Shoulsbury (near High Bray).

Few of these earthworks, in which Devon is so rich, have been scientifically excavated—only Hembury and Milber in recent years, and Cranbrook some fifty years ago (1900).[2]

The neolithic occupation of Hembury ended about 1800 B.C., perhaps a little later. Then followed some sixteen centuries or so during which it was desolate, until it was repeopled by Iron Age B people who constructed the main ramparts of the fort not before the first or second century B.C., and probably in two stages. The re-occupation of Hembury brings us just into historic times, for there is evidence that it was lived in by the *Dumnonii* until about A.D. 50-75,[3] so linking up chronologically with the earliest archaeological traces of human occupation on the site of Exeter. With the Dumnonii, too, we reach the first fringes of documentary history.

Cranbrook has produced pottery of the first century B.C., nothing earlier. Its occupation was only of one stage, perhaps not earlier than 50 B.C., when it was first constructed with a stone-built rampart. Milber was excavated in 1937, but only an interim report is yet available.[1] This great earthwork, which commands the eastern and southern flanks of Dartmoor as well as the Teign estuary, was a fortified settlement constructed by Iron Age B people in the first century B.C. It stands on the brow rather than the summit of the hill; its triple defences with wide spaces between them compensate for this military weakness. Clovelly Dykes is a similar but more elaborate type of settlement of the same period which has not yet been excavated. Milber seems to have been occupied until well into the first century A.D.

Cadbury, five miles SSW. of Tiverton, is probably a settlement of the same date, constructed by the Iron Age B people, and there is the evidence of casual finds that it continued to be occupied well into Romano-British times.[2]

The hill-forts of Devon and Cornwall suggest a ruling race, who had overcome the Iron Age A people. The Iron Age B culture, of which the hill-top settlements are an expression, was brought to south-western England by immigrants from the other side of the Channel, most probably from Brittany. It is these people who mainly constitute the *Dumnonii*, "the people of the land," and it is they who constructed the great majority of the fortified hill-settlements of Devon in the first century B.C. Their tribal territory covered the greater part of Devon and Cornwall.[3] In Roman times Exeter was their capital—*Isca Dumnoniorum*—but the whereabouts of their tribal capital before the foundation of Exeter is unknown. Possibly it was the great fortress of Hembury, fourteen miles to the north-east, which they are known to have occupied up to the date that Roman Exeter was founded.

The coastal settlement at Mount Batten, on the eastern side of Plymouth Sound, where pottery of Iron Age B type has been found in quantity, suggests a native trading settlement, as also does the riverside settlement at Topsham, on the Exe, of somewhat later date. Neither of these sites has yet been adequately explored. The discovery of a hoard of iron currency bars in Holne Chase " camp "—the earliest type of currency in Britain—and the later discovery of two coins of the 4th century B.C. and 1st century B.C. there, are also evidence of trade at that date; but, tempting as it is to associate these finds with Dartmoor tin, it must be said again that there is no evidence that tin was worked on the Moor before the 12th century.

ROMANO-BRITISH DEVON

There is no real break in Devon at the Roman conquest and it is perhaps misleading to suggest it by this heading. The Romans did not occupy the land to the west of the Exe; Exeter was their frontier-town, the most westerly of their towns in Britain. This suggests that the *Dumnonii* were not hostile to Rome—there is no evidence of conflict at Hembury as there is at Maiden Castle in Dorset—and it has been surmised that the Celtic kingdom of Dumnonia may indeed have entered into an alliance with Rome.[1]

The Romans made little impact anywhere in Devon, except at Exeter, which they founded in the reign of Nero (A.D. 54-68), and which became the south-western terminus of their great frontier road, the Fosse Way. Despite many attempts to prove the existence of Roman roads west of Exeter (and attempts *inter alia* to establish Totnes as a Roman town) there is as yet no evidence of Roman occupation beyond the Exe. The sum total of Roman or Romano-British occupation is meagre. Apart from Exeter, there is Topsham, which was possibly a port for the capital or a naval base. The two were joined by a straight road four miles long— the present South Street of Exeter, merging into the Topsham road. Then there is Mount Batten, on Plymouth Sound, already mentioned, probably a native trading settlement; and there are four villas, all in the extreme east of the county (two at Seaton, one at Uplyme, and one at Membury).

Although Exeter was the terminus of the Fosse Way, the exact course of that road is still not known for certain between Dinnington, in south-west Somerset, and Honiton in Devon. The intervening country is mostly that of the massive Blackdown ridges separated by deep valleys, country in which even a Roman road could not go dead straight. The likeliest line seems to be from Dinnington straight on to the summit of Wind-whistle Hill, at the western end of which the road forked. The left-hand fork led, by a fairly well-authenticated road, via Street (a significant name) and Perry Street down the present Axminster road to Millbrook. It is not clear whether the road turned here to go into what is now the town of Axminster: all we can say is that it ran on along the eastern edge of the Axe valley, past Ashe and through Musbury and probably terminated at Axmouth, which may have been a small harbour. The Axe estuary was probably much wider in Roman times, since it is almost certain that the marshes on both sides represent estuarine land reclaimed at a later date. At Axmouth the river was perhaps half a mile wide in Roman times and would have formed a far better harbour than it does to-day. Almost opposite Axmouth, on the eastward-facing hillside behind Seaton, were two Roman villas within a short distance of each other. The only other known villas in Devon were similarly sited on easterly or south-easterly slopes, near Holcombe Farm in Uplyme, and just behind Membury Court in Membury parish.[1]

The right-hand fork of the Fosse Way, making for Exeter, is more difficult to disentangle from the present road-system, but the line of the present Chard-Stockland road may represent it; then over Stockland Hill, past Cotleigh into Honiton, whence the present Honiton-Exeter main road undoubtedly follows the line of the Fosse all the way. The original frontier road of the Fosse Way probably terminated at the mouth of the Axe and represented a stage in the conquest of Britain, completed by the autumn of A.D. 47. The road to Exeter was possibly constructed as a branch a few years later, after the foundation of the town (c. A.D. 50).

The Celtic kingdom of the Dumnonii continued to exist all through Romano-British times: it existed indeed as late as the 10th century; but there is not much evidence of native life in Devon—certainly nothing to compare with such native Cornish villages as Chysauster and Porthmeor.[2] Outside Exeter, which we are not concerned with in this book, the most interesting settlement so far discovered is that at Topsham.

Topsham to-day stands on a broad gravel plateau between the estuary of the Exe on the west and that of the Clyst to the east. It now lies at the head of the Exe estuary, which narrows suddenly, just below the town, from a width of a mile to about three hundred yards or less. Here, too, there is good reason to believe that the river was considerably wider in Romano-British times and that the wide Exminster marshes were then mud-flats covered at spring tides. If so, the estuary was still a mile wide at Topsham, and I am inclined to think its head lay much nearer to Exeter—at Higher Wear or perhaps even as far up as where St. James's Weir now is—so that Exeter and not Topsham lay immediately at the head of the estuary.

But the greater part of the estuary between Exeter and Topsham was shallow, a narrow channel flowing between wide flats uncovered at low tide, and very probably fordable. The advantage of Topsham was that here the deep river channel flowed close to the gravel ridge on which the little port grew up. It gave close access to dry land, a good landing place, and shelter from the wind. A number of small dry valleys ran up from the shore to the gravel ridge, on which the light soil and vegetation further encouraged early settlement.[3]

Excavations begun in 1936 have told us much about this fascinating little riverside town, though much yet remains to be unearthed. The evidence of prehistoric occupation is slight and uncertain, but there is no doubt about the existence of a settlement here in the first years of the Roman conquest in Devon. The earlier of the two sites which have been excavated at Topsham produced pottery indicating an initial occupation under Claudius—i.e. before A.D. 54. This was associated with a large timber building, and there is some reason to believe that this early site may have originated as a naval base and continued as the port of Exeter, which appears (on present evidence) to have been founded late in the reign of Claudius—about the same time as Topsham. It has been pointed out that the Exe was the last safe harbour in the west, and that the ships required in the campaign against the tribes of Wales and Scotland, which had to round Land's End to enter the Irish Sea, would naturally have started from a western harbour.[1] The beginnings of Topsham may be associated with the south-western advance of the Second Legion under Vespasian, which we know to have been stationed at Seaton, the southern terminus of the Fosse, from the legionary tile found there.

Not many yards from this very early site there is evidence of a small agricultural community tilling the open gravel plateau in the 2nd century and later. A large sandstone building excavated in 1938—nearly 52 feet long and 23½ feet wide—proved to be a combined corn-mill and bakehouse which had operated from about A.D. 250 to 400. It had not been destroyed but had fallen into gradual decay. Its size suggests that it may have supplied merchant vessels putting in at Topsham as well as the local community.[2] There is evidence, then, of more or less continuous occupation at Topsham throughout the Romano-British period from the middle of the 1st century until the end of the 4th or perhaps beginning of the 5th, though there may have been decay during the 4th century as there was in Roman Exeter.

With the departure of the Romans early in the 5th century the native rulers took over. This is the last phase of the Dumnonii, but it lasted more than three hundred years. Geraint was attacked in 710 by the kings of Wessex and Sussex together and with him the kingdom of Dumnonia almost certainly perished in Devon—though in Cornwall a shadow of Dumnonian royalty lingered on until the early 10th century.

CHAPTER III

THE ENGLISH SETTLEMENT

DEVON was only thinly peopled during the Romano-British period, and more thinly still during the centuries between Romans and Saxons (400-650). A great part of the county still consisted of moorland, not only Dartmoor and part of Exmoor, but also the extensive wet moorland of mid-Devon stretching from the high ground west of the Exe right away almost to the Atlantic coast, and the Blackdown plateau and its outliers to the east of the Exe. It should not be forgotten that the term " moor " was often applied to low-lying ground, where it was wet and useless, and not only to the wild uplands so called to-day.

The lower slopes of the uplands and plateaux, and the deep valleys that intersected them, were thickly forested with oak and ash (both common elements in Devon place-names), while the beech, too, was a familiar sight in ancient Devon, growing anywhere except on water-logged soil. Beech-pollen has been found in peats of the Bronze Age in Devon.[1] Many of the beech trees seen to-day, especially in the higher and more exposed country of the north and west of the county, where they act as wind-breaks for old farmsteads and as avenues leading in from the nearest road, were planted from the 16th century onwards, and above all in the 18th; but others may well be self-sown descendants of trees that flourished in the landscape of the Bronze Age, three to four thousand years ago. The holly, which gave its name to Holne in Anglo-Saxon days, still flourishes in the hedges of that parish. The elm also is an ancient tree in Devon, on the lower ground, for both the Lemon, which flows into the Teign at Newton Abbot, and the Lowman, which reaches the Exe at Tiverton, derive their names from a Celtic word meaning " elm."[2] In the warmer river valleys the tall elm was as familiar to Celtic men as it is to us to-day: in these trees, beech, elm, holly, and the primeval oak, we are linked in feeling with our pre-Roman forebears. But the burnished sycamore, which shelters so many an ancient house in Devon, is not a native tree in Britain. It was not known here before the

16th century and was probably planted extensively in Devon in the latter part of that century when most houses of any consequence were rebuilt or substantially improved. It was a quick-growing tree. Above all it resisted the Atlantic wind that drives across the upland country, and its wood was useful for several purposes.

Besides the moorlands and the woodlands, there were extensive tracts of marshland along the river estuaries, often covered at high tide, so that the estuaries were then even wider than they are to-day. There is good reason to believe, as we have seen in the previous chapter, that the Exe, the Otter, and the Axe, were in Roman times considerably wider than they are to-day—in places at least—and the same must be true of the Taw estuary in north Devon.

If one could imagine a land utilisation map being compiled in Celtic Devon, as late as the eve of the Saxon occupation in the middle of the 7th century, we should find that uncultivated moorland occupied the largest area—perhaps larger than all the others put together—with woodland, ranging from thick forest to scrub, a good second. Whether the area under cultivation would have come third we cannot say for certain. On the whole, perhaps, one might hazard the guess that it exceeded, adding together all its scattered pieces, the area under marsh; but both these categories were only a fraction of the size of moor and wood.

Devon had been more populous, and its cultivated area greater, in the Romano-British period than subsequently, for we know that there were considerable migrations of Britons from south-western England across the Channel to Armorica, which consequently became known as Brittany. These migrations reached their height most probably in the first half of the 6th century, though their cause is not clear.[1] By the 7th century, then, much land had gone out of cultivation and had reverted to waste. One wonders whether this is not the meaning of the many farmstead names in Devon which speak of former cultivation, names bestowed on land where the English recognised that someone had been before them. Such names are Yalland in the parish of South Brent, which appears as *la Yoldelande* in 1291, or Yellaton in Berry Narbor, on the other side of the county, or the seven Yellands, all meaning " old farm " or " old land." It is noteworthy that many of these significant names are found in or very near parishes where Celtic place-names or some other evidence of Celtic habitation, such as a dedication to an early missionary-saint, survive. Even where land had been abandoned in the 5th or 6th century, and prolific Nature had overgrown the tilled fields again, the signs of older cultivation must have been apparent enough to the settlers of the 7th and 8th centuries in contrast to the untouched moor or the virgin woodland. There would have been no mistaking it.

The Dumnonian kingdom was thinly peopled, perhaps almost de-populated in places, when the Saxons established themselves in western Somerset after their great victory at Penselwood in 658.[1] Large tracts of relatively open lowland country, in part perhaps already cleared, lay open for the taking; and we cannot ignore the possibility that some of the undoubtedly ancient nucleated villages which lie near the southern coast—so different from the hamlet and farmstead settlement of most of Devon—may represent colonisation from the sea, from points farther east, peaceful settlements in fertile country which preceded the political and military conquest by a number of years. Such early villages are Axmouth, Colyton, Sidbury, Dawlish, Paignton, and Brixham. Even if they do not represent settlements ante-dating the Saxon Conquest—and that can only be a tentative hypothesis at present—they are undoubtedly amongst the earliest places founded by the Saxon invaders.

THE CHRONOLOGY OF THE SAXON SETTLEMENT

The chronology of the Saxon settlement of Devon, late though it was, still remains a matter of considerable uncertainty. The documentary evidence is meagre in the extreme, only three entries in the Anglo-Saxon Chronicle and the *Annales Cambriae*. The earliest of these records the victory of the West Saxons over the Britons at Penselwood, on the borders of Wiltshire and Somerset, which opened the whole of Somerset to the Saxon advance at one blow. We cannot, therefore, put the beginning of the Saxon conquest of Devon before 658. Then, in 722, the *Annales Cambriae* record the West Saxons fighting—unsuccessfully—as far west perhaps as the river Hayle, within a dozen miles of the tip of Cornwall.[2] This must almost certainly be the other limiting date, particularly since the creation of a new see at Sherborne in Dorset in the year 705 argues that most (if not all) of Devon was English by that year. Intermediate between these two limiting dates of 658 and 722 is the entry which records the decisive victory of Centwine over the Britons in 682 at an unspecified place, when he " drove the Britons in flight as far as the sea."

There is one other piece of evidence that helps us so far as the conquest of the eastern part of Devon is concerned. The life of St. Boniface, probably born at Crediton about the year 680, tells us that a monastery existed at Exeter at that time.[3] Exeter, and much of the country to the west and north-west, must have been in English hands some years before 680 since the abbot of its monastery bore an English name.* Moreover, since there is no strongly defined natural frontier west of Exeter until one reaches the Tamar, nearly forty miles away, the first stage of the conquest

---

*The possibility that the monastery at Exeter was a Celtic foundation cannot, how-ever, be ruled out.

must, for reasons of security, have gone many miles beyond the city. Possibly the upper Taw, the largest river in mid-Devon, formed the frontier at this date (*c.* 660-70), linking up with "the great wood" (*mor-cet*) which ran from Morchard Bishop to Cruwys Morchard, and beyond to the Exe near Tiverton.

The most eminent local historian of this period in Devon has made a careful study of all the evidence and arrived at a chronology for the whole conquest, but it is not easy to accept some of his conclusions.[1] He puts the beginning of the Saxon conquest of east Devon, operating along the old Roman road from Dorchester to Exeter, at 665-70, and regards Centwine's victory of 682 as merely completing this stage of the conquest.[2] Then there is a pause in the conquest from 682 until 695, when Ine launched an attack from Taunton on Geraint or Geruntius, the king of Dumnonia. This phase saw the conquest of north Devon by about 720, and possibly of the eastern part of south Devon.[3] Finally, the conquest of the remainder of south Devon—so completing the conquest of the whole county—was begun from Exeter about 753-7 and concluded about 765. Under this chronology, the Saxon conquest of Devon occupied just about a hundred years (*c.* 665-*c.* 765), years not of continuous warfare but of three great campaigns in which the east, north, and south of the county were subjugated in that order.

There are many difficulties in this chronology. Chief of these are the significance of the decisive victory of 682 and of the setting up of a new see at Sherborne in 705, and the identification of *Hehil* where Ine's men were repulsed in 722 by a force of Britons.

It is hard to believe in the first place that the victory of 682 merely completed the conquest of east Devon when we know a monastery already existed at Exeter. No identification can be offered for the site of this battle: not a single clue is offered by the chronicle. All we can say is that it took place far to the west of the Parrett, and almost certainly in Devon. But one can see no reason for accepting the observation of the editors of the *Place-Names of Devon* that "the configuration of the country suggests that it took place in the south of the county."[4] Indeed I would draw the very opposite conclusion from the same evidence. The configuration of the coast of Devon beyond Exeter is such that the Atlantic coast is surely the only likely terminus of the great pursuit of the Britons. A pursuit "as far as the sea" along the south Devon coast could have little military meaning, as the merest glance at the map will show, unless we assume that it reached the extreme south of Devon somewhere round the Kingsbridge estuary. Of these two possibilities, a pursuit to the Atlantic coast is the more likely, certainly would have been the more decisive. With a temporary Saxon frontier somewhere west of Exeter, and the dark, forbidding wall of uninhabited Dartmoor all along the southern horizon, a further drive north of the Moor would be the most obvious next stage in a piecemeal conquest, in order to establish a tenable western frontier.

Such a westward drive " to the sea " is not the pure theory of an armchair map-reader. It is strongly supported by the evidence of place-names, which are almost entirely English as far as the Atlantic coast itself, from the present county boundary down the Cornish coast for a dozen miles to Poundstock. There is a clear frontier between English and Cornish place-names from Poundstock down the Ottery to the Tamar. A few—but very few—names stray across this frontier from their proper homes; but the one-inch map showing the Ottery valley leaves no shadow of doubt in the mind that the river was at one time a racial frontier.

Moreover, it must have been a frontier for a long period, long enough for scores of English farmsteads and hamlets to be founded and settled, before the Tamar was established as the county boundary between Devon and Cornwall in the early part of the 10th century.

I therefore suggest that the battle of 682 was fought somewhere in mid-Devon, north of Dartmoor and many miles west of Exeter, and that it resulted in a pursuit of the defeated Britons as far as the very edge of the Atlantic for the simple reason, as the map will show, that the country all the way from the Taw to the coast offered not a single natural line of defence. As a result of this victory, a Saxon frontier was probably established as far west as the Ottery, below the high ground of Bodmin Moor, before the end of the 7th century. East Devon was in English hands by the third quarter of the 7th century, and the whole of north and west Devon by 682. Dartmoor was uninhabited, or only sparsely peopled at its edges.

Nor can one believe that Exeter was on the southern frontier when its monastery was founded: the Exe estuary and the coastal fringe as far as the Teign estuary at least must have been in English hands also before *Escanceaster* could be regarded as safely held. Thus most of Devon had been conquered by the Saxons by the end of the 7th century. If any part remained unconquered at that date, it was only the country between the Teign and the Tamar estuaries and below the Moor.* This was a substantial area, it is true, but it was hardly more than a fifth of the habitable land of Devon. Even this stretch of country was probably thinly populated by the native British and there may well have been Saxon settlements on or near the coast (as at Paignton and Brixham, for example) before the formal act of conquest.

If we accept this view of the chronology of the Saxon conquest, the establishment of a new see at Sherborne in 705, which implies a great

---

*At Denbury, SW. of the Teign estuary, is a large hill-fort, the name of which means " the *burh* of the men of Devon." Possibly this strong fort was held for a time against a Saxon advance into South Devon (*Place-Names of Devon*, xivn).

extension of a settled Saxon culture far to the west, becomes more intelligible. Moreover, the creation of this see, and the consequent organisation of ecclesiastical activity in the south-west, resulted in the establishment of monastic communities at *Axminster* and *Exminster* shortly afterwards. Both were founded, in all probability, during the episcopate of Aldhelm, first bishop of Sherborne (d. 709), or that of his immediate successor Forthhere.[1] The establishment of such a monastic community at Exminster as early as this argues, too, that the country to the south and west was securely in English hands at this time.

The chronology suggested above also makes sense of a grant of twenty hides of land at *Linig* by the Tamar, made by King Ine to Berwald, or Beornwald, third English abbot of Glastonbury, between 705 and 712.[2] No details of this grant are known, as the abbey had lost this land again long before the Norman Conquest, and consequently did not trouble to preserve any record of it beyond a note of the initial grant. Though the whereabouts of *Linig* cannot therefore be known with certainty, the likeliest identification is the territory between the Tamar and its tributary the Lynher, now in Cornwall. The two rivers flow parallel with each other for several miles and make a large peninsula, almost indeed an island at its southern end. *Linig* is probably " Lin-island," the territory between Tamar and Lynher, a piece of country closely studded with English names to this day, while to the west of the Lynher the Cornish names begin immediately. It looks as if the Lynher, too, had once been an early frontier.

Such an identification presupposes that Ine was in a position to grant land to the west of the Tamar by the year 712. There is good reason to believe this may have been so. The kingdom of Geraint was already greatly contracted when Ine, together with his kinsman Nunna, king of Sussex, attacked him in 710. This attack probably completed the conquest of Devon and established a temporary western frontier along the Lynher by 712 comparable with that along the Ottery established thirty years earlier.

This western frontier must have been difficult to hold against British raids, for neither the Ottery nor the Lynher was as formidable an obstacle as the Tamar. Nevertheless, the numerous Saxon place-names in the country bordering upon them to the east make it certain that these rivers remained the frontier for an appreciable length of time. We must probably regard the war between Cuthred and the Britons (under the year 753 in the Anglo-Saxon Chronicle) as marking some disturbance in eastern Cornwall rather than the beginning of the conquest of south Devon, and Egbert's devastation of Cornwall from east to west in 815 as a reprisal for British raids into the West Saxon kingdom.[3] In 825 there was further warfare, ending in a British defeat at *Gafolforda*, which has been identified as Galford in the parish of Lew Trenchard.[1] Finally, in 838, Egbert decisively defeated a combined force of Britons from Cornwall and marauding Danes, who were together preparing an invasion of Wessex, at Hingston Down, on the heights immediately above Callington.

There is no further evidence of trouble from Cornwall. It must have been about this time that Cornwall was incorporated into England as a shire, and the boundary between it and Devon fixed along the Tamar. Athelstan is known to have fixed the Tamar as the diocesan boundary, and probably made that river the shire boundary at the same time. It is possible that in these generations of sporadic fighting on the West Saxon frontier the Glastonbury estate of *Linig* was lost to the monastery for ever, although another estate of five hides on the Torridge, given by Egbert to the abbey in 802, was lost between then and the Norman Conquest.[2] The whereabouts of this estate on the Torridge is not known, but it is perhaps significant that Monk Okehampton is so called in the 11th century although it was in lay hands in 1066 and 1086. The name may well commemorate its former ownership by Glastonbury. Petrockstow and Jacobstow (*stow* is a " holy place ") may represent other parts of this old estate. If so, the estate granted in 802 lay somewhere on and near the great northward bend of the Torridge and ran some way up the Okement.

To sum up this discussion of the chronology of the Saxon conquest of Devon: it is unlikely that it took a whole century (665 to 765) to overcome the resistance of the thinly-peopled kingdom of Dumnonia, certainly so far as its eastern end (Devon) was concerned. Cornwall proved to be a longer and a tougher proposition. Here the conquest seems to have taken a century or more (710-838). In Devon the country east of the Exe and well beyond, perhaps as far as the upper Taw, had been taken over by about 675. By 682 the whole of Devon was in English hands as far as the river Ottery (now in Cornwall), except perhaps the southern fringe from the Teign around to the Tamar. By 712 this, too, had been overrun, and a frontier established well beyond the Tamar again, this time along the Lynher. So far from taking a hundred years, the Saxon conquest of Devon may be telescoped into the space of fifty years (*c.* 660-*c.* 710) and that, too, into three short bursts, *c.* 660, *c.* 682, and *c.* 710.

SAXON SETTLEMENT AND CELTIC SURVIVAL

The Saxons overran Devon rapidly: there was little opposition. It is indeed conceivable that to speak of a " conquest " is to exaggerate the importance of the military and political events. It is not unlikely, as has already been hinted, that much peaceful penetration of the lowland districts, especially along the southern coast from Axmouth onwards, took place without any opposition from the scattered Celtic communities that remained in Devon in the 7th century. There was plenty of land for all, especially in a countryside that had been largely deserted by its natives. It is possible that armed clashes, breaking into open warfare, took place only when there were " incidents "—as we have learned to call them in the 20th century—like those between the early American colonists and the native Indians.

There is no record, we may observe, of any battle resulting in the Saxon occupation of east Devon as far as Exeter and beyond: nothing until the battle of 682, by which date all east Devon was securely in English hands, securely enough for monastic life to be established. It seems likely that the whole of east Devon was peacefully occupied as a result of the Saxon victory at Penselwood in 658, the few Celtic settlements left undisturbed, and Exeter taken over without resistance. One would have thought that the capture of an important city like Exeter after armed resistance would have called for record in the Anglo-Saxon Chronicle, if there were a capture and not a peaceful taking-over. As it is, the first mention of the city in the Chronicle comes as late as 876, in the Danish troubles.

The possibility of a widespread, peaceful penetration over most of Devon, with only two sharp conflicts when British resistance was met towards the west, must be seriously considered. It is natural that battles and political upheavals should find a place in the records, while the peaceful founding of villages and hamlets in unoccupied country would call for no comment at all.

The fact that fewer than one per cent of the place-names of Devon are pre-English is not evidence of a wholesale extermination of the Celtic occupants by the newcomers, but more probably of Saxon settlement in what was largely an uninhabited landscape, though bearing considerable marks in a score of places of former habitation and tillage, as we have seen. Such Celtic names as survive speak fairly clearly of British life going on in isolated districts, notably on the fringes of Exmoor, where Charles, Landkey, and Wallover (in Challacombe), and perhaps Countisbury, speak of Celtic life continuing into English times; and in the hilly, remote country between the Exe estuary and the Teign valley, where we find names like Trusham, Dunchideock, and Marshall (in Ide), and Treable not so far away, in Cheriton Bishop.

The moorland valleys and foothills harboured more Celtic clusters, as we might expect, particularly notable being Walreddon, near Tavistock, which seems to signify a small community of Britons (*Wealas*) living independently in a free condition. The Walla Brook, a tributary of the Dart, is *Weala broc*, " Welshmen's brook"; and so, too, is the Walla Brook which flows into the Tavy past the site of a former Celtic hamlet now known as Trendle.[1] In the western hundred of Lifton there is a notable concentration of Celtic names.

Scattered about the county are isolated Celtic names which show that the Romano-British population of Devon were not entirely upland dwellers. There are two Crookes, one in North Tawton, the other in Combe Raleigh, both in low-lying country.[2] The hamlet of Aunk, in Clyst Hydon parish, certainly has a Celtic name: it lies on a low spur of land in the valley of the Clyst, about two miles north of Whimple, which is also a Celtic name (" White pool "). There can be little doubt that most of these Celtic names designate hamlets and farmsteads which were continuously occupied from Celtic times into the period of the Saxon settlement, when they were left undisturbed, and so down to the present day. When we stand in such places as this we are in the presence of a remote antiquity, going back to the days of the Celtic kingdom of Dumnonia. On this spot farmers have lived and tilled the soil since the 5th, 6th, or 7th centuries, if not earlier in some instances, for Aunk and Whimple lie in the shadow of Hembury, that great fortress of the early Iron Age which was abandoned for the lower ground in the first century of the Christian era, and Treable has produced a coin of the second century.

The number of Celtic names to survive in Devon is few indeed; but it is probable that the number of Celtic settlements that continued an unbroken life into the Saxon period and so down to the present day is considerably greater than the evidence of place-names alone would indicate. There is, above all, the evidence of the predominant physical types one finds among the native Devonian population to-day, a high proportion of whom clearly reveal a pre-Saxon ancestry. " On the coasts of Devon there may be several coastal patches with dark and broad-headed, stalwart men," who are found also in nearly all the Cornish fishing harbours. Popular belief derives these very Mediterranean-looking people from marriages between Spanish survivors of the Armada, wrecked on the shores of south-western England in 1588, and the native Devon women. This belief may be dismissed at once, but it is correct in so far as it recognises the Mediterranean origin of these coastal types. They are most probably the descendants of the Iberian migrants who brought the Megalithic culture to Western Britain and who traded for Irish gold in the early Bronze Age.[3] Such groups, in formerly isolated clefts in the south-western coast, tended to inter-marry and to perpetuate their type, a notable example in Devon being the hamlet of Bucks Mill, between Clovelly and Appledore, where nearly everybody was said, not so long ago, to be called Braund. Around Dartmouth, too, there is a notably dark type of Iberian ancestry.

Other pre-Saxon types abound on the fringes of Dartmoor, short, dark long-heads.[1] A very common type all over Devon, especially perhaps in the east of the county, is the short dark round-head, with dark-brown hair, a quick hazel eye, small hands and small feet. The Saxon type, taller, with fair hair and grey eyes, is also conspicuous in Devon as we might expect in the light of what has been said already, but the older stocks form a high proportion of the native population and suggest that many pre-Saxon groups survived the English settlement and went on undisturbed in their hamlets and farmsteads.

Around the estuaries of the Taw and the Torridge in north Devon, and the Tamar and perhaps the Exe in south Devon, Beddoe found a large proportion of blonds which he attributed to Frisian or Danish settlements.[2] Danish settlement in Devon was negligible, however, and we must attribute this blond type in general to the Saxon settlers from the 7th century onwards. Beddoe's observations, made seventy or eighty years ago before " the extension of railways and the altered conditions of society " had led, as he says, to ever-increasing rapidity of local migration and intermixture, confirm strikingly what the map tells us about the foundation of large Saxon villages on or near the estuaries of the Devon rivers.*

SAXON VILLAGES AND FIELDS

The Ordnance map of Devon, especially the first edition published in 1809, which is free of the mass of detail that the 19th and 20th centuries have added to the landscape, tells us a good deal about the nature of the Saxon settlement. When we combine it with a reading of the Devonshire Domesday we obtain a pretty clear picture of what happened in the sparsely documented centuries between 650 and 1066. We notice first of all, if we read the map carefully and without preconceived ideas, that the landscape of Devon is not merely one of hamlets and isolated farmsteads —as historians like Maitland once thought[3]—but that there are many villages as large and compact as any of the Midland Plain, which has long been regarded as the classic home of the nucleated village. In north Devon we may point to Braunton and Hartland, Pilton and Northam; in east Devon to Colyton, Sidbury, and Woodbury; in the west to Bradworthy and North Lew; in the south to Paignton (as it once was), Kenton and Exminster, Ugborough and Yealmpton. And there are many others, some of them since grown into small towns like Bideford and Modbury.[4]

*One ought to resurrect Beddoe's remark about " the singular beauty of the women " in Devon, which he attributed to the very soft and mild climate, whence " a peculiar delicacy and softness of outline and complexion." The modern habit of plastering the face with chemicals has probably done a good deal to reduce the Devon women to the common level since Beddoe's day.

The Saxons who planted these large villages at intervals all over Devon, but more frequently perhaps in the lowlands which had been almost ignored by earlier farmers, also brought with them their large open fields. These were cultivated in common, like those of the Midlands, which survived in great part up to the time of George III. It used to be thought (and is still so stated in many books) that the open field never made its appearance in the extreme south-west, but we now know from abundant documentary evidence that it was widespread in Devon and in Cornwall also.[1] These open fields disappeared very early in the south-west, mostly (as far as we know) in the 13th and 14th centuries, though a few remnants survived into Tudor times. It is this early disappearance that led to the belief that they had never existed, but it is in fact almost certain that every one of the Saxon villages in both Devon and Cornwall originally had its open fields.

Whether or not these fields were set out precisely like those of the Midlands and cultivated in the same way is not clear: probably they were not. In the south-west the typical method of cultivation was that known as infield-outfield, in which a limited area around the village or the hamlet or farmstead was permanently under cultivation in some sort of rotation (the *infield*) and beyond it lay a much larger area—the *outfield* —parts of which were broken up and cultivated for several years successively, then let down to rough grazing again, while another patch was broken up and treated in the same way. The farming over the infield was more or less intensive; over the outfield it was extensive and intermittent. Land was as abundant in Saxon Devon as it was in 19th-century America, but as the population of Devon grew, above all in the 12th and 13th centuries, more and more of this outfield was appropriated to permanent occupation in individual ownership and hence to a more intensive cultivation.

Even in Saxon times, however, beyond the compact villages and their open fields, and on across the " waste " of their outfields, one would have come across hundreds of small hamlets and of single farmsteads, each lying alone in a clearing of the oak and ash woods or upon the edge of the moorland. Here farming was carried on in small fields separately held (like those of to-day). A close reading of Domesday Book reveals many such little farms in outlying areas, cultivated by a single villein or a serf working for a distant lord, as at Bradworthy in the far west of Devon.[2] Many of these small, isolated farms were pastoral: they had no plough. And many, though we cannot prove it, may well have been Celtic farmsteads whose owners had remained undisturbed through the Saxon occupation, though their farms had gradually acquired an English name from the people who lived in the central village of the territory.

Another very interesting and significant fact is revealed by Domesday

Book, throwing a backward light into the darkness of the preceding three or four centuries, and revealing however dimly to us something of the nature of the original Saxon colonisation. It is that a high proportion of these large villages, in Cornwall as well as Devon, appear as royal estates in 1066 and probably had been so from time immemorial. Many others, such as Bishops Tawton, Paignton, and Sidbury, belonged to the bishop of Exeter in 1066 but had formerly belonged to the king. It looks as though all, or nearly all, of the original Saxon villages in both Devon and Cornwall had been deliberately created as the centres of large royal estates, whose Teutonic inhabitants lived under direct royal protection in what was, in the first generations at least, an alien land.

Once more we are led back to the possibility that the Saxon occupation and settlement of Devon was a juridical process rather than a military conquest. The English settlers lived under Wessex law, paid dues to the kings of Wessex, and as royal tenants enjoyed their direct protection. Their Celtic neighbours, isolated and scattered, lived under Celtic law, paid dues to the kings of Dumnonia, and were under their protection for what it was worth. From time to time hostilities broke out, followed usually by a Saxon victory and the extension of Wessex jurisdiction. This is surely what William of Malmesbury means when he says that the Britons and English inhabited Exeter (and presumably also the rest of Devon) *aequo jure*, until Athelstan made an end of their " equality " and caused Wessex law to reign supreme.

Long before Athelstan, however, Devon had been incorporated into the political organisation of Wessex. By the third quarter of the 8th century it had been recognised as a shire, though the boundary with Cornwall may not have been fixed or may have been, at that date, as far west as a line along the Ottery and the Lynher.[1]

Each shire in southern England was " divided into smaller districts known as hundreds, for the adjustment of taxation, the maintenance of peace and order, and the settlement of local pleas "[2] but the hundred does not make its appearance before the reign of Edmund (939-46). In its origin it was in Wessex a subdivision of a larger *regio*, answering for a hundred hides " when the king took his farm or called out his fyrd." The hundred varied greatly in size between one part of England and another: there were more than fifty in Sussex and only five in Staffordshire.[3] In Devon there were thirty-two in 1086, but four had already disappeared— Hurtesberie (Berrynarbor), Molland, North Molton, and South Tawton.[4] The identity of the *regiones* in Devon from which the hundreds were created is almost completely lost. Nearly three hundred years had elapsed between the first Saxon settlements and the beginnings of the hundreds—as long a time as separates us from Charles II's reign—and there must have been numerous territorial changes in that long period

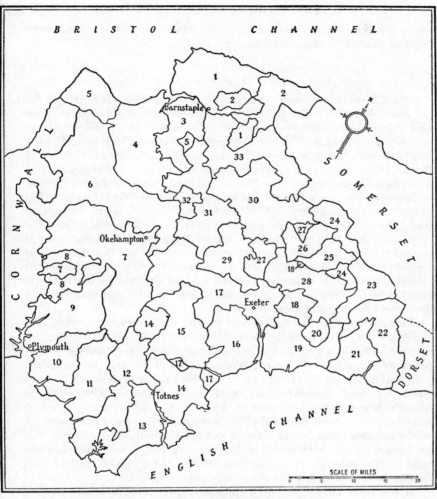

FIG. 6—THE HUNDREDS OF DEVON

*1. Braunton. 2. Sherwill. 3. Fremington. 4. Shebbear. 5. Hartland. 6. Black Torrington.
7. Lifton. 8. Tavistock. 9. Roborough. 10. Plympton. 11. Ermington. 12. Stanborough.
13. Coleridge. 14. Haytor. 15. Teignbridge. 16. Exminster. 17. Wonford. 18. Cliston.
19. East Budleigh. 20. Ottery St. Mary. 21. Colyton. 22. Axminster. 23. Hemyock.
24. Bampton. 25. Halberton. 26. Tiverton. 27. West Budleigh. 28. Hayridge.
29. Crediton. 30. Witheridge. 31. North Tawton. 32. Winkleigh. 33. South Molton*

51

when the countryside was being colonised and populated, and large areas of land were changing hands by charter.[1]

The Danes began visiting the English coasts for plunder early in the 9th century, the first known raid being on Sheppey in 835. During the next thirty years they made more than a dozen descents on different parts and did great damage. In 851 they came as far west as Devon, but the Anglo-Saxon Chronicle records that the ealdorman Ceorl and the men of Devon defeated them after great slaughter at a place called Wicganbeorg. This place, almost certainly in Devon and probably near the south coast, has been variously identified,[2] but Wickaborough or Weekaborough, less than four miles from the shores of Tor Bay at Paignton, seems the likeliest site. The whole of Tor Bay was wide open to sudden attack from the open sea before help could arrive—history repeated itself in the tip-and-run air raids on Torquay in 1943—and the large village of Paignton was a good prize for plundering. From the shores of the bay old trackways led inland over the hills to further plunder and pillage, but by the time the invaders were four miles along the lanes Ceorl and his men had reached the scene and defeated them decisively.

Twenty-five years later, however, in 876, the Danes captured Exeter and spent the winter there, but were thrown out by Alfred in the following summer. Within a year Alfred was obliged to withdraw into the Isle of Athelney in the face of a fresh Danish invasion of Wessex. In the meantime a nameless viking crossed to Devon from south Wales with twenty-three ships and besieged Odda, ealdorman of Devon, with many of Alfred's thegns, at a place called by Asser *Arx Cynuit*. Here he was killed with more than eight hundred of his men, and the resistance movement in the Somerset marshes received a powerful stimulus. *Arx Cynuit*, too, has been variously identified, but Countisbury Hill, where there are the remains of a considerable earthwork between the gorge of the Lyn and the sea, is very probably the site of this important battle.

In 893 there were renewed Danish attacks, one force attacking Exeter, another " a fort in Devonshire by the north sea " (so says the Chronicle) which can probably be identified as the *burh* of Pilton. These attacks were beaten off. Thereafter the south-west was left more or less in peace for nearly a century: then came a renewal of Danish raids towards the close of the 10th century. Devon and Cornwall were attacked in 981, Dorset in 982. The south-western coasts were harried again in 988, " when the thegns of Devon met the attack with a gallantry which became famous throughout the country."[3]

In 997 a more formidable force attacked the coasts of Wessex, beginning with the northern coasts of Cornwall and Devon, as well as south Wales. Then they turned back around Land's End and went up the Tamar " burning and slaying everything that they met," says the Chronicle, as far north as the *burh* of Lydford. Here they were repulsed and they returned to their ships in the river with incalculable plunder, some of it from Ordulf's new abbey at Tavistock—founded less than twenty years earlier—which they had burned to the ground. Then they moved eastwards to Dorset, Hampshire, Sussex, and Kent.

In the year 1001 they were back in Devon, " where Pallig came to meet them with the ships which he was able to collect; for he had shaken off his allegiance to King Ethelred, against all the vows of truth and fidelity which he had given him, as well as the presents which the king had bestowed on him in houses and gold and silver." So says the Anglo-Saxon Chronicle. Pallig, whoever he was, was what we to-day should call a quisling. The Danes sailed up the estuary of the Teign, burned the large village of Teignton (probably Kingsteignton), and crossed the few miles of water to the mouth of the Exe, where they landed.[1] Their intention was to take Exeter unawares, but the citizens defended their walls valiantly. At Pinhoe, just east of the city, a force of militia from Somerset and Devon assembled to relieve the town and fought with the Danes. The battle was probably fought on the slopes of the hill by Cheynegate, beside an ancient ridge-road. Not far away to the north, beside another old road, is Danes Wood, and in the parish of Plymtree, further on, Danes Mill. We are told that the morning after the battle the victorious Danes, unable to take Exeter, burnt the villages of Pinhoe and Broadclyst (*Clist*) " and also many goodly towns that we cannot name " before they departed eastwards again.

The uneasy truce of 1002 was ended by Ethelred's massacre of the Danes, in which the sister of King Swein of Denmark is traditionally supposed to have perished. Swein, probably to avenge his sister's death, invaded England in 1003. The south-west felt the first blow. The *burh* of Exeter was betrayed to the Danes by a French reeve of Queen Emma, who held Exeter in dower, and the whole town was destroyed and plundered. Thereafter the burning and the killing moved to other parts of England, and in due course (1016) Devon passed with the rest of Wessex into Danish rule under Cnut.

The Danes, during all this time, had made no settlements in Devon: they had attacked the south-west solely for plunder. Lundy is the only pure Scandinavian name: the Old Norse *lundi* means " puffin." It was " puffin island " to the Danes, who possibly used it as a base at times from which to harry the coasts of Wales and south-western England. On the mainland of Devon there is not a single Scandinavian place-name, in contrast to the opposite shores of Pembroke and Glamorgan. The few examples of Anglo-Scandinavian names, like " Cnut's stone " which gave its name to Knowstone, probably date from the 11th century, from the time of Canute or later, when Scandinavian names were popular. In the South Hams the names of Grimston, Oldstone, and Gripstone lie near each other and may represent a small Scandinavian settlement of this period.[1]

SETTLEMENTS IN 1066

Domesday Book (1086), with its backward look to a time when Edward the Confessor was on the throne, is our great authority for the extent of settlement in Devon on the eve of the Norman Conquest. It is not an easy record to use, but the detailed work of local scholars—notably Reichel and Whale—upon the fundamental task of the identification of the 1,200 or so entries has provided a fairly easy road for later workers. Nevertheless, there is still a great deal of topographical and economic information waiting to be extracted from the Devonshire Domesday. Such work must necessarily fall to local scholars who have a minute knowledge of the countryside and of its later manorial history.

Apart from the work of identification, there are further obstacles to the study of Domesday, in Devon as in many other counties. The most serious of these is the omission from the record of places that we know from other evidence were already in existence before 1066. A recent writer on "The Domesday Geography of Devon "[2] gives the total number of settlements that can be identified by name and location as 1170, while about forty places recorded in earlier charters are not mentioned in Domesday. There is, however, good reason to suppose that a far greater number of Saxon settlements than this escaped notice. Some of these are considerable villages, like Sandford and Thorverton, dating back in all probability to the earliest days of the Saxon occupation, but most are hamlets and single farmsteads which are silently included in the description of some large central manor to which they were appurtenant.

It is this which accounts for the empty spaces around nearly all the large villages on the Domesday map of Devon—around Sidbury, Crediton, Paignton, and Bishop's Tawton, to name only a few. Each of the large villages and valuable manors embraced a number of outlying hamlets and farmsteads. The more one studies the topography of a small piece of countryside in detail the more one is convinced that hundreds of small settlements which are first recorded in the 13th century had in fact existed much earlier. It is significant, for example, that many of the undoubtedly Celtic place-names do not appear in the records until the assize rolls of 1219-1249, or the Book of Fees in 1242, or the early 13th-century fines. Clearly, these places were not given Celtic names in the

12th or 13th centuries: they had already existed for centuries but Domesday includes them silently under another heading. The best informed local scholar on the subject has said that no fewer than 3,000 of the place-names of Devon are earlier than the 11th century.[1] If this is so, the map of Devonshire settlements should have more than 2½ times as many names on it as Domesday allows us to record. And we must suppose, too, that a considerable proportion of these small unrecorded places were Celtic in origin though they nearly all have English names when they are first written in the 13th century. How else can one account for the high proportion of pre-Saxon stocks who still populate Devon, even allowing that the ancestors of many of them were merely labourers on Saxon farmsteads in 1066?

Even if we plot only the 1,200 or so places which we can locate in 1066 we find that after four hundred years of Saxon occupation there is a very even spread of settlement over the entire county, on good and bad soils alike, except on the bleak waste of Dartmoor, which—probably because of climatic changes since the early Iron Age—could no longer support human existence. As a whole, Devon was much poorer than Somerset, though richer than Cornwall, and this remained true all through medieval times.

What is surprising is to find that, even on the cold, thin soils of the Culm Measures, settlement is as thickly dispersed as on the deep, warm soils of the New Red Sandstones, though on the former the villages are generally smaller and poorer. It is also striking to find that by the middle of the 11th century the Devonshire farmer was getting a living at heights we have not exceeded since, from which we have even retreated. On the western side of Dartmoor one finds in 1066 farmsteads like Willsworthy, nearly nine hundred feet above sea-level, cultivated by Siward, the Saxon owner, with small enclosed arable fields and much pasture. There was (in 1086) enough land at Willsworthy for four ploughs, but only one plough: in other words, a small infield and a large outfield which was broken up in patches, cultivated, and then abandoned again. But livestock were obviously much more important than grain.

On the eastern side of the Moor, with about half the rainfall of the west, small farms were to be found up to 1,000–1,200 feet. A number of farms called Shapleigh indicate that sheep were the most valuable stock on this drier side. At Natsworthy, north of Widecombe, one Edward was farming 1,200 feet up by the middle of the 11th century, and even growing grain, for there were (in 1086 at least) two ploughs on the manor.

Farming was being carried on in equally difficult places on Exmoor. At Radworthy, 1,200 feet up at the head of a small combe below Chapman Barrows, some pioneer called Raeda had made a clearing and a homestead, where in 1066 Alric was in possession. There was enough land for six ploughs, but only one plough—again we must envisage a large outfield—and two leagues of pasture on Challacombe Common. Radworthy was a tiny hamlet in 1086, in which three villeins and a slave clustered together for company, but some miles away over the top of the moor Edwin farmed in complete isolation at Lank Combe (*Lacoma* in 1086), in the " long valley " running westwards up from Badgworthy Water, below Brendon Common, with only the ravens and the eagles to keep him company.

Lank Combe was abandoned very early: it does not appear in any records after Domesday, and it is now only a name on the map. Radworthy seems to have been abandoned in more recent years. One wonders why such places were ever occupied, what brought these Saxon colonists so far out into the wilderness away from their fellows in the 10th and 11th centuries. " Wilderness " is perhaps a misleading word, for nearly all these lonely farmsteads lie near ancient ridgeways, along which the Saxon colonists penetrated the Devonian backwoods in all directions. These ridgeways were the Saxon equivalent of " a good bus-route " to-day. But it may also be that many of these lonely tenements had been Celtic homesteads which acquired a new name—as was natural enough—when in the course of time a Saxon owner or tenant took over the place. The good soils of Devon were far from being fully exploited in 1066, and yet the poor thin soils, and the exposed moorland fringes, were being farmed in hundreds of lonely places, before the " village lands " in the fertile lowlands were fully taken up. May not the explanation be, in many instances, that the isolated homestead and the remote hamlet below the moorland edge were there first: that they go back to the days of Celtic Devon before the villages were founded and the lowlands opened up? The local historian and topographer has much to do before we can answer such questions as this at all definitely.

CHAPTER IV

THE ECONOMIC BACKGROUND

AFTER four centuries of occupation and colonisation by the Saxons, the population of the whole of Devon was still no larger, in 1086, than that of modern Exeter. We may put it at somewhere between sixty and eighty thousand people. Of these, all but two or three thousand lived in the villages, hamlets, and isolated farmsteads. The city of Exeter contained some 1,500 people inside its walls; the " towns " of Barnstaple, Totnes, and Lydford had three or four hundred people each at the most. Okehampton, a new town, was only just struggling into existence. Such " towns " were distinguished from the purely agricultural villages only by the fact that they contained a more noticeable trading element and, where they had a navigable river, that they engaged to some extent in overseas trade. Neither Plymouth nor Dartmouth yet existed: the tides rose and fell along an empty strand. Nor did many of the places that ranked as market-towns in the 16th century exist, except perhaps as small villages. The site of some was still under grass or corn, or simply outlying waste where a track crossed a river.

In the countryside there were vast uncolonised stretches between the villages. From the old hill-forts that rose clear of the wooded valleys one would have looked across, not a patchwork of hedged fields dotted with white farmsteads, but miles of undulant tree-tops, apparently unbroken, though here and there a column of smoke would reveal the whereabouts of a clearing, of a cluster of three or four farmsteads or a single isolated farm lost among the trees. Only around the compact villages, grouped around their great " squares," was there much open ground to be seen. After three or four hundred years of occupation and hacking at the surrounding waste, as long a time as separates us from the Tudors, the villages of Domesday Devon had cleared a few hundred acres round about them, and here they practised some kind of open-field farming. A mile or two away, smaller groups of families—possibly all related to each other originally—lived in hamlets which had " hived off " the parent villages a century or two earlier. And deeper in the woods, or high up on the moorland edge, were hamlets and single farmsteads of even greater age, some of which had probably been continuously occupied since Romano-British times, perhaps even a little longer than that, the homes of Celtic farmers which had been ignored by the Saxon colonists of the 7th and 8th centuries. Here much of the farming was carried on by individual farmers, working in small, enclosed fields, and mainly concerned with cattle and sheep.

There was no industry in Devon, other than the small household industries such as pottery and cloth-making; there was little or no mining; trade was negligible; probably half the county lay " waste " in moorland, woodland, heath, and marsh. With only about 27 persons to the square mile at the end of the 11th century, Devon stood thirteenth in the list of English counties in order of density of population. Large areas were completely uninhabited. At the other extreme the vale of Exeter and the country behind Tor Bay had about 32 people to the square mile. But as a whole the county was poor, under-populated and under-developed. If we rank the counties in order of their assessment (acres per £1), Devon comes out nineteenth on the Domesday figure (though third largest in area), and twentieth in the levy for Danegeld made about 1150.[1]

The 12th and 13th centuries saw immense changes, comparable in magnitude and kind only with those of the 19th century. It was the great age of colonisation, which took the form of the spread of settlement and of the cultivated area in the countryside, and of the creation of new towns on a considerable scale. We may assign this remarkable movement broadly to the period of 1150-1350. In the countryside, some thousands of new farms came into existence, cultivated in severalty with small, enclosed fields from the beginning, and often named after their creator. Nearly all of the thousands of place-names on the modern one-inch map of Devon would have been found on a map drawn in 1350. Much, perhaps nearly all, of this colonisation of the moorland, the woods, the riverside marshes and the heaths, was the work of free peasants, armed with a charter from the lord of the manor which granted them a piece of territory within specified boundaries. This numerous class of free peasantry, as they extended their holdings field by field, then farm by farm, and rose to the ranks of yeomen and gentry, coloured much of the political and social history of the county down to the 19th century, and even to the present day.

The other aspect of the colonisation movement was the creation of " boroughs " by lords of rural manors, places where tenements were held in free burgage, by payment of a money rent. In most of these, if not all, there was a borough court, and not the manorial court that characterised the truly rural manors. All of them had a weekly market, many of them an annual fair. Indeed, the grant of a market and a fair normlly preceded the granting of a borough charter by the lord. Altogether we can find nearly seventy places in Devon which had the attributes of a " borough."[1] Some of these were created in the 12th century (e.g. Ashburton, Plympton, Tavistock, South Molton, Torrington), many more in the 13th century, and more in the 14th. The great majority of these boroughs had appeared by the middle of the 14th century. We must regard them all as hopeful speculations by the lords of rural manors who hoped to see a town grow, through markets and fairs and daily road traffic, and to reap substantial benefits from tolls and burgage rents in place of a modest income from agricultural land.

Many of these speculative ventures came off, especially in those places where the tin and cloth trades developed, to provide a solid backing for the more transitory trade of markets and fairs. But others, like Rackenford and Noss Mayo and a score of others, never got under way, never acquired the slightest appearance of an urban community. It took much more than a market, a fair, and a seignorial charter to create a " town," and a good half of the seventy Devon " boroughs " never developed beyond the stage of villages. It was, however, a remarkable aspect of the colonisation movement while it lasted. No other county can show, so far as we know, such a number of medieval " boroughs."[2] And once again it was the free peasantry, by and large, who were the means by which charters were translated into physical reality. It was they who peopled the new towns, put up the houses and the shops, the workshops and the mills, built the ships in the estuary towns like Dartmouth, Plymouth, and Bideford, developed the trade. They were recruited from the younger sons of the free tenants of rural manors, for whom there was no prospect of succeeding to the ancestral farm. The Hawleys, who built up Dartmouth in its early days, and made it one of the leading seaports in medieval England, originated in this way. The first John Hawley came down from Allaleigh in the neighbouring parish of Cornworthy to the riverside shortly before 1340, and became a shipowner and a merchant. He is probably the original of Chaucer's *Schipman*.

In these years, too, important new industries appeared. From the middle of the 12th century the rich and hitherto untouched deposits of tin-ore were worked on Dartmoor. For a couple of generations Devon was the largest European source of tin: there was a veritable " tin rush " on the Moor, and neighbouring landowners took advantage of it to create towns at strategic points. The abbot of Tavistock created a borough at Tavistock in these years; Ashburton was made a borough by the bishop of Exeter before the year 1200; and Plympton by the Earl of Devon about 1194. All became stannary towns at a later date, i.e. towns where tin was brought to be weighed and stamped. Elsewhere in Devon the rising cloth industry, of which there are signs at Exeter and Totnes before 1200, was responsible for the development of towns like South Molton, Honiton, and Tiverton, among others. Most of the small towns of Devon were the centre of a cloth industry by the middle of the 14th century, and it is probably to this that they owe their successful emergence from the general ruck of " village boroughs." The spread of the industry outside the ancient towns into the countryside is well evidenced by the location of the early fulling-mills.

Markets and fairs sprang up all over Devon during the 13th century and the early 14th, supplementing the few that had existed in the 11th and 12th, most thickly in the fertile country of the Vale of Exeter, and all the country from the Exe around to the Plym.[1] Agriculture was still the basis of internal trade, despite the growth of mining and industry.

The late 12th and early 13th century also saw the rise of Dartmouth and Plymouth as seaports and as bases for naval and military operations against the Continent. Dartmouth was the more important of the two in the early days, especially under the Hawleys. Plymouth's great days were to come in the 16th century, when the Hawkinses played the part here that the Hawleys had done at Dartmouth in the 14th. The acquisition by Henry II of the rich provinces of south-western France, through his marriage with Eleanor of Aquitaine in 1152, was the chief factor in the rapid growth of the south-west of England ports, especially as it coincided with the growth of the Dartmoor tin trade and of the cloth industry generally in Devon. Cloth and tin went out; wine came back, and these staple trades continued, with interruptions, for some centuries. In 1334 the four leading towns of Devon were all places with a considerable over-seas trade: Exeter, Plymouth, Barnstaple, and Dartmouth.

The 12th and 13th centuries were also the great age of church-building in Devon. In these years, especially perhaps between 1160 and 1220, the building of a new church set the final seal upon the work of colonisation. It was the visible symbol of the new community that had come into being all around, in hamlets and farmsteads, the centre of a new parish. Very little survives of this age except Norman fonts and occasional Norman doorways, for there were two waves of rebuilding after that. The visible remains in the churches, especially in western Devon, suggest that a great deal of rebuilding took place in the period 1300-50. The last great rebuilding, and the one which characterises the Devonshire churches to-day, took place between about 1400 and 1540. It swept away most of the earlier structure on each site, though once more the Norman font was carefully preserved and installed in the new church, for it was evidence of the right to baptize.

The Devon of 1348, on the eve of the Black Death, was very different from that of two centuries earlier. Thousands of new farms had come into being; the woodlands were greatly diminished. In the 12th century the cleared areas had been islands, some large and some minute, in a sea of trees or of moorland. Now it would be truer to say that the cleared areas were more conspicuous than the uncleared: that, apart from the upland waste of Dartmoor, still hardly scratched by the peasant's plough, it was the " waste " that now formed large islands in an encroaching sea of cultivation, which lapped all round their edges, reaching ever higher and higher. This was the high-water mark of medieval farming before the long ebb-tide that was ushered in by the Black Death. Estuarine marshes had been ditched and drained, and cattle now grazed where the tides had once flowed twice a day over the saltings. Inland heath and marsh had given way to the plough and livestock, as witness the number of farms called *Heathfield* or some variant of it, and *Venn* and *Marsh*.

The successive epidemics of the Black Death, from 1348 onwards, brought about, or coincided with, a period of comparative depression in industry, mining, and perhaps in farming. Mortality was very high, not only in the crowded little towns but also in the open country. The tin trade was brought to a complete stop, and all over Devon in the ensuing years we hear of lands left unoccupied for want of tenants. The poll tax receipts of 1377 suggest that the total population of Devon was barely 73,000: it had been brought back from its peak of 1348 to the level of the 11th century. Exeter may have had some 2,400 people, Plymouth about 2,000, Barnstaple and Dartmouth about 1,000 each. These were the four largest towns. Other boroughs, like Totnes, Plympton, and Modbury, had only 300-450 inhabitants. Some of the rural manors were considerably more populous than the market towns, and this remained so well into the 17th century. In the tax assessments of the period 1275-1503 Devon comes out somewhere near the bottom of the list—generally 33rd, 34th, or 35th among the English counties[1]—though there is good reason to believe that these assessments may have become increasingly conventional and did not reflect the real changes in taxable capacity that were taking place. Certainly we find that when Plymouth, Totnes, and Crediton are excused a good deal of their tax quota in the 15th century on grounds of impoverishment, they are simultaneously engaged in building the noble parish churches that we see to-day.

Certainly, too, Devon began to recover quickly from the heavy losses of people inflicted by the bubonic plague. From the last years of the 14th century onwards we find parish churches being rebuilt all over the county; stone bridges being built across the larger rivers; manor houses rebuilt in the deep country. There are few signs of depression in 15th-century Devon, whatever may have happened in the Midlands. By the last quarter of the century the cloth trade had fully recovered from a temporary setback, and the Dartmoor tin trade was developing a boom in production such as it had not known since the great days of the late 12th century and the early 13th. The widespread building activity of the years between 1400 and 1540, evident everywhere one goes in Devon to this day, must itself have supported a major industry, beginning with the quarrying of the stone and ending with the wood-carvers who produced the magnificent rood-screens, pulpits, bench-ends, roof-bosses, and wall-plates, and the richly carved woodwork of the larger houses. The building industry, with all its auxiliary trades and crafts, must have been as important in the economy of Devon as the cloth trade, and possibly more important than the tin-working. One tends to forget its magnitude because it is scattered among small units, often single men, and because its products do not enter into the export markets, of which we have fuller records.

By the middle of the 16th century Devon had emerged from the comparative isolation of a frontier region into the main stream of national politics, and from being a generally poor, under-developed region economically into one of the most valuable counties in the English economy. The rise of population in the county, which meant both manpower for wars and the full exploitation for the first time of her rich natural resources, was dramatic. In 1377 Devon had been one of the most thinly populated counties in England. Though third largest in area, she had stood eighth in population, with only half as many people as Lincolnshire or Norfolk, and considerably fewer than Kent or Suffolk. In the Elizabethan muster returns for 1569 and 1570 she comes out second only to Yorkshire in numbers of able-bodied men.

The earlier boom in the tin trade fell away, and production dwindled throughout the remainder of the 16th century, but the cloth trade rose steadily all the time in more than compensation. New cloth-towns appeared on the map, most notably Tiverton, which in the 15th century had been an insignificant market-town largely dependent on the Courtenay household at the castle, and by 1600 was the largest and most flourishing industrial town in Devon. There is, too, the remarkable growth of the Devonshire fishing industry, one of the most important around the English coasts. By the 1560s this had extended across the Atlantic to the rich cod-fisheries of the Newfoundland Banks. During the 17th century the Devonshire ports, whose fishing was based on private enterprise and not on a restrictive company organisation, came to dominate this valuable trade.

The growth of the cloth and fishing industries brought about a marked revival of many of the Devonshire towns. Others—more purely market towns—were greatly stimulated by the rising population, by the growing productivity of Devonshire farming on the one side and by the growing demand for foodstuffs on the other. The expanding industrial towns, populated more and more by a wage-earning class which had to buy food instead of growing its own, provided one great market. The navy and the merchant and fishing fleets provided another.

All this had its effect on the countryside. The rising level of population brought about a renewal of pressure on the land, a pressure which had slackened during the late 14th century and throughout the 15th, and this led in turn to a renewed attack on the waste lands, especially on the higher grounds, between six and nine hundred feet above the sea. It is possible that some of these uplands had been cultivated during the agricultural boom of the 13th century and the early 14th, and that the frontier of cultivation had retreated with the subsequent fall in population: we do not know. It is certain, however, that new farms came into being in the 16th and 17th centuries on the upland wastes, and that on the lower ground the long-settled farms extended their tillage over the appurtenant moors and commons and brought a larger acreage into permanent use, in place of the extensive and intermittent cultivation of " outfield " which had characterised an under-populated countryside. In the 12th and 13th centuries the creation of new farms had been the characteristic form of colonisation; in the 16th and 17th it was the enlargement of existing farms by the taking in of land for tillage and sheep from the surrounding waste.

The great rural prosperity of these generations is borne out not only by a study of contemporary tax assessments, in which many rural parishes show a higher taxable capacity than some of the market towns, but also by the visible evidence of the countryside to-day. As we walk around the county, studying the farmhouses of every parish, one fact emerges over and over again: that the great majority were rebuilt or at least substantially modernised in the period 1560-1640. Such an expensive capital investment, involving the farm buildings as well as the house itself, presupposes at least a generation or two of high prosperity beforehand, and of considerable savings. It is true that such rebuilding may have been paid for out of mortgages, but a sound mortgage is itself a sign of some financial strength. The substantial fines paid by 16th- and 17th-century farmers for their three-life leases, very often amounting to several hundred pounds, certainly point to real monetary savings on a large scale.

We are impressed, too, by the evidence of the stability of rural society between the 16th century and the early 19th. The ownership of land, though concentrated (as always in England) in a minority of families, was more widely diffused in Devon than almost anywhere else. The resident squire was much more common than in the Midlands, and there were besides at least two or three families of minor gentry in each parish, occasionally as many as half a dozen. One can see this in the mural monuments and the floor-slabs in the parish churches, or in the bench-ends with their coats of arms, without knowing anything of the parish records. In the main these are the descendants or representatives of the free peasantry who had colonised the waste between 1150 and 1350: in their coffers at home they kept the original charter, in its crabbed medieval Latin, which had started them off so long before, and to this they had added the charters and deeds of other farms which they had accumulated by marriage and purchase in the course of centuries. Below these gentle families, owner-occupiers more often than not, were the tenant-farmers whose leases for three lives gave them the security and outlook of free-holders. This was the time of " high farming " in Devon, when it was, according to Cromwell, the best-farmed county in England; and this golden age extended well into the 18th century.

There is, however, another side to this happy picture, one for which the evidence is not so easily come by. This is the growth of a propertyless wage-earning class both in the countryside and in the industrial towns, with all its attendant poverty and insecurity. As early as Henry VIII's time, before the cloth towns had developed to anything like their full extent, the wage-earning class formed a large element in the population. If we count the numbers of those assessed on " wages " in the all-embracing subsidy of 1524 we find that they amount to well over a third of the total population. In forty-four parishes scattered about the county, 833 assessments out of 2,333 were on wages—36 per cent—and the pro-portion is fairly constant throughout the county. In thirteen parishes of Axminster hundred it is 32 per cent; in nine parishes of Colyton hundred it is 39 per cent. These are the extremes, though there are naturally wider variations between the individual parishes which reflect purely local circumstances. Even in the deep country the labouring class con-stituted fully one-third of the whole population; in the larger towns, like Exeter and Plymouth, they were round about a half of the population.[1]

The numbers of the wage-earning class grew steadily after this. In the countryside, the throwing-together of small farms—a process that had been going on since medieval times but was now accelerated—made it difficult for small men to get holdings within their means, and they sought work in the industrial towns or as labourers on the land. In the towns, the growing scale of the cloth industry called for yet more wage-labour. There was little opportunity for the small independent producer in the south-west, where merchant capitalism had grown strongly from the 16th century onwards. John Greenway and Peter Blundell had started life with nothing, and had built up great fortunes in the cloth trade of 16th-century Tiverton, but those had been the early days when profits were high and able men could make their way in a new and fluid trade. By the 17th and 18th centuries the merchant class had solidified, trading connections had been established, much more capital was needed to make a start, and the career of Blundell or Greenway could not be repeated.

The specialisation of industry, and its growing dependence on overseas markets, so vulnerable to sudden closure by continental wars, made unemployment and under-employment an increasingly normal feature of town life. The burden of poverty, and of the poor-rates to relieve it, consequently grew all through the 17th and 18th centuries. Even in a remote country parish like Hennock, with no industry to speak of but agriculture, we find a remarkable rise in the cost of poor relief in the space of two centuries.[1] In the ten-year period 1598-1607 the average amount spent on poor relief was £5 17s. a year. By 1670-9 it was £38 2s. a year, and by 1780-9 no less than £164 8s. 4d. A good deal of this simply reflects the rising level of general prices over a long period, but the numbers relieved also rose greatly. In 1613 thirteen paupers were relieved during the year; in 1791 the number was forty-seven. No one has yet worked out the cost of poverty in the Devonshire woollen towns in the same period, but it must have been even worse than this.

We get some idea of the extent to which pauperism had grown from the numbers classed as too poor to pay the hearth tax in the 1670s. The list of those exempted in each parish is usually bluntly headed " Paupers." In the rural east Devon parishes of Membury and Upottery, 40 per cent of the inhabitants were paupers. In north Devon, typical parishes were Berrynarbor (43 per cent), West Down (41 per cent), and Clayhanger (43 per cent). At Bishop's Nympton, 35 of the 63 households are described as " poor," and 39 out of 83 at Zeal Monachorum. In south Devon, nearly 60 per cent of Revelstoke's 59 families were paupers, and in the adjacent parishes of Wembury and Brixton the paupers formed half the population. In Exeter, the largest town in Devon, 40 per cent of the city's 2,365 households were poor. At Honiton, a small cloth and market-town, the proportion was 37 per cent. On the other hand, the very small parishes had few paupers: Butterleigh's ten families included no paupers, Bittadon had one pauper family out of a total of seven. At Thornbury, six out of 47 families were paupers.[2]

We should expect that the larger and more populous a parish was, the greater the number of its poor. In all probability, Devon was now an overpopulated county: too many people for the available natural resources, especially as the land, the industries, and the mines, were falling increasingly into the ownership of fewer and fewer families. In simple terms we may say that by the middle of the 17th century there were too many people looking for land and too many looking for work in Devon: the results were low wages, unemployment and under-employment, poverty, bad housing, insecurity, and emigration to New England. But at the other extreme of the social scale, fortunes were being made, and successful merchants were buying country estates (as they had done on and off ever since the 12th century) and founding new county families.

The Devonshire woollen industry, which had risen to greatness on the kersey trade, moved over to the serge trade during the 17th century.[1] At Exeter, serges were being made by the 1630s, but Tiverton, grown rich on kerseys, did not feel impelled to introduce the new manufacture until 1690.[2] For a generation or so at the end of the 17th century and the beginning of the 18th, the Devonshire serge industry was the most important branch of England's export trade in woollens, with Holland, Germany, and Spain as its biggest customers. Tiverton was the largest industrial town; Exeter the great market and finishing centre. But the continual wars of the 18th century gradually killed the overseas markets for serges, and the Norwich stuffs captured a large part of the home market. Later in the century, the rise of the Yorkshire woollen industry, more highly mechanised and earlier organised in factories, knocked out both East Anglia and Devonshire. The Devonshire trade began to go perceptibly downhill by the middle of the century: Dean Milles's MSS. (c. 1755) are full of references to the decay of spinning and weaving in the country parishes. The Napoleonic Wars were the death-blow of the dwindling Devonshire woollen industry, though an artificial monopoly —exercised through the East India Company—kept the Chinese market open until the Company's monopoly of the trade was ended in 1833.

The long story of mining in Devon had virtually come to an end also during the 18th century. The tin trade, indeed, had been worth very little since James I's time, but periodically throughout the 17th and 18th centuries speculators worked copper, iron, silver and lead mines, bringing a passing flash of prosperity to localised areas. For a few decades in the mid-19th century the rich lodes of the Devon Great Consols Mine (opened in 1844) revived the greatest days of Devonshire mining. In the mid-fifties Devon and Cornwall were producing more than half the world's supply of copper, just as they had produced most of Europe's tin in the 12th and 13th centuries, but for Devon it was a transitory gleam of the old days. Devon copper production reached its peak within twenty years (1862) and from then onwards fell away steadily. By the end of the 19th century Devonshire mining had become a subject of antiquarian interest.

In the first census, that of 1801, Devon was the fourth largest county in numbers of people. Middlesex, and the two industrial counties of Yorkshire and Lancashire, were the most populous. Plymouth and Dock, now nearly joined, had flourished on the wars of the 18th century, and together massed more than 43,000 people on the peninsula between Tamar and Plym. Exeter, gently loosening its hold upon industry and overseas commerce, was a residential city of 20,000 people, including its Georgian suburbs, and far behind came a score or so of old market towns with two to four thousand people each. Another score, smaller still and more moribund, had between one and two thousand inhabitants. The remainder of the population lived in the villages, the hamlets, and the isolated farms. The bulk of the population depended on farming for a living; the industries of the county had reverted to the scale of the small local industries that characterised country towns anywhere in England.

Down to 1831 Devon remained fourth in numbers among the English counties; after that she fell farther down the list with each successive census—seventh in 1861, ninth in 1881. In 1901 the county was less than half as densely peopled as England and Wales as a whole (254 persons to the square mile). Agriculture was by far the largest occupation; mines and quarries (chiefly the latter) employed about 3,000 men; fishing about 2,000 men; and lacemaking about 1,850 men and women. The remnants of the woollen industry employed a few hundred people.

The 19th century saw some major economic and social changes in the county. First there was the continued growth of greater Plymouth as a naval base, a fishing port, and a commercial port. Together with Devonport it had nearly 180,000 people in 1901—well over a quarter of the total population of the county. Exeter, growing more slowly and comfortably, more peacefully residential, still had fewer than 50,000 people at the end of the century. But the main changes had been the great exodus from the countryside, and the rise of a new major industry —the holiday industry.

From 1841 onwards, each census showed large tracts of deep country losing people to the towns, especially the relatively poor and isolated west Devon parishes. Most of the country towns began to go downhill in the 1840s and 1850s. The spread of railways and the advent of cheap postage accelerated this exodus all through the century. Most of the migrants went no farther than Plymouth, Exeter, or the seaside towns. Of those who left the county altogether, most went to London and some did well there. Although a few " watering-places " had made their appearance in the 18th century—Exmouth being the oldest, and Teignmouth next—most took their rise after the ending of the Napoleonic wars. Of these, Torquay was the most notable, growing most rapidly, but decorously, in the mid-Victorian decades following the arrival of the railway in 1848. A moneyed class of annuitants and retired professional people had discovered the climatic and scenic amenities of Devon at the end of the 18th century; then came the invalids who sought a mild climate; then the middle classes who needed a quiet month or two by the sea; and finally, with the coming of Bank Holidays, the excursionists who swarmed in for the day.

By the 1920s the holiday industry, with all its ancillary shopkeeping and other trades, had become Devon's largest and most lucrative industry. The census of 1931 showed that the " personal service " trades employed nearly 10 per cent of the total population over the age of fourteen years. They were even more important than farming ($7\frac{1}{2}$ per cent). Commercial and financial work employed about $6\frac{1}{2}$ per cent, and transport rather less than 5 per cent. The rest of the occupied population were scattered over a wide variety of minor industries and trades. Of the historic industries of Devon, there was hardly any trace: only one person in a hundred was a textile worker, only one in 250 worked in the mines or quarries. Fishing, the third of the historic industries, had been ruined by the war of 1914-18 and the fundamental change in the industry itself to deep-sea fishing in Arctic waters. It now employed only one Devonian in 400. The rise of the " holiday industry " came just at the right time both in Devon and in Cornwall. As families were driven off the land for various reasons from the 1820s onwards, they set up as shopkeepers and lodging-house keepers in the towns. In the north of England and the Midlands the dispossessed were forced to enter the pulsing factories. In Devon they had a more pleasant if less remunerative outlet, and they had the satisfaction of keeping their roots intact in their native county, of not having to join the army of those who tramped the sterile road to London.

CHAPTER V

THE LAND

THE MAKING OF THE LANDSCAPE

BY the end of the 11th century the Devonshire landscape had already taken on something of its appearance to-day; but in other respects it was still vastly different. All the large villages existed which were to give their names to ecclesiastical parishes or had already done so, and they were now three to four hundred years old. Nearly all the multitude of hamlets or small villages—some 1,600 or more[1] in addition to the large villages—had also come into being by 1086, though a great number of them are not separately recorded in Domesday. And a considerable number of single farmsteads also existed in all parts of the county, more particularly perhaps towards the wetter and more pastoral west. It is possible that some of these farms had been continuously occupied since Celtic times. At Bradworthy, for instance, we find the nucleated village that gave its name to the parish, a sizeable hamlet away at Dunsdon, and no fewer than eleven single farmsteads scattered about the 22 square miles or so of the Bradworthy territory. Such a pattern is repeated all over Devon.

Around all the nucleated villages and many of the hamlets stretched open fields, cultivated in common and held in intermixed pieces; but around the single farmsteads, lying alone among the " waste," lay small fields of irregular shape, enclosed by massive hedge-banks several feet high and crowned with timber. These fields were cultivated or grazed over in severalty. Two distinct field systems existed in Devon in the 11th century, and for some two or three centuries afterwards. Both the open-field settlements and the single farmsteads practised an infield-outfield system of farming, which has already been described. The essence of it was the shifting cultivation of the outfield in parcels or blocks that were broken up and cropped for three or four successive years, and then abandoned to rough grazing once more. Beyond this again lay large tracts of land

which were even more wild and untouched—dense woodland, high moorland, wet lowland " moors," sandy and infertile heaths, undrained fen or
marsh, and wide belts of salt marsh along the river estuaries over which
the tide flowed twice a day.

It is impossible to say—though attempts have been made—how much
of Devon was still " waste " in 1086. The word itself is ambiguous. We
do not know, except in isolated instances, the area of the ploughland,
which is the basis of Domesday measurement. And even if we did, we
should still not know how much of the so-called waste was in reality subject
at intervals to intermittent cultivation as part of some outfield. We only
know that on the western side of Dartmoor the frontier of cultivation had
reached nearly 900 feet above sea-level, and on the eastern side 1,200 feet.
In isolated pockets on Exmoor some farmers struggled on the 1,200-foot
frontier. On the other hand, a great deal of the lower and more
rewarding country remained untouched. The proportion of untouched
waste rose rapidly as one went westwards in Devon, and also as one went
higher up the hillsides. The relationship between the number of Domesday
ploughlands and the number of plough-teams available would suggest
this,[1] as well as the topography to-day.

Few towns existed in 1086. The great majority that appear on the
14th-century map were still only small agricultural or fishing communities in 1086, such as Tavistock, clustering round the abbey gates, or
Sutton (the germ of Plymouth) a mere hamlet sheltering behind the
limestone cliffs of the Hoe, a few hundred yards from a bay rich in fish.
And some towns did not exist at all: they were as yet a nameless site in
the fields or waste of a rural manor.

Even if we allow that as many as 3,000 settlements existed in Devon
by 1086, the map was far from filled with names. The total number of
medieval farms was round about 15,000, as near as we can tell.[2] This
leaves a matter of some 12,000 settlements to be accounted for, nearly all
single farmsteads, since the villages and hamlets had come into being,
by and large, before Domesday. There is abundant evidence from the
volumes of the *Place-Names of Devon* that the great majority of these farms
had come into existence by 1350, in the great colonisation movement
that began in the 12th century and reached its peak in the 13th, though it
remained active in Devon until the coming of the Black Death.

This colonisation took many forms. The moorland was attacked,
and new farms created in a granite-strewn wilderness, such as Cholwich
—" the coldest farm "—which appears as a habitation and a name
soon after 1200. Or there was Lapflode (now Laployd), on the eastern
edge of the moors, where the Lapflodes were in possession by the time
of John.[3] These, and scores of others, created by 1200 or soon after,
were on the moorland edge, but the recesses of the Moor were not reached

until the early 14th century and then only in sheltered places. All over
Devon, the virgin woods were felled; hundreds of farm-names embodying
wood or *beare* testify to the widespread nature of this type of clearance.
The heaths were attacked—several *Heathfields* speak of this—but were less
rewarding. The waterlogged land was ditched and hedged, as witness
the many farms with the element *venn* (" fen ") and *marsh* in their names.
And along the estuaries, the tides were held at bay by means of embank-
ments, behind which long ditches were dug and the salt marsh conquered
from the sea for the fattening of cattle. The achievement of the extraordinary Sokespitch or Suckbitch family at Marsh Barton, beside the
saltings of the Clyst estuary, I have told at length in *Devonshire Studies*.
They came here towards the end of the 12th century with a charter
granting them about thirty acres of arable on the dry slopes above the
tidal river, and as much of the marsh (within certain wide bounds) as
they could win from the sea at their own cost. With banks and ditches
they created a rich farm of some 185 acres, mostly before the 13th century was out, and then lived comfortably here until the year 1803.[1] They
were only an extreme example of a common type of colonist.

This vast clearing of the " waste," in all its forms, was largely if not
entirely the work of individual colonists, armed with a charter from the
lord of the manor. The charter granted them what we should call to-day
a freehold estate, within certain boundaries set out in detail, to be held
by socage tenure at a small annual money rent, perhaps with the obligation also to attend the manor court at stated intervals, to grind corn at
the lord's mill, and to pay a relief when an heir succeeded to the estate.
Thus the Aclands held their ancestral nest of *Akkelane* (plate 35) by socage
tenure and 10s. rent, of the bishop of Exeter's manor of Bishop's Tawton;
the Monks held Potheridge in free socage at a rent of 1d. a year; the Lapflodes held the small estate from which they took their name by the same
tenure and at the same nominal rent; the Cholwiches, the same at ½d.
rent; and so on in nearly every manor in Devon. The colonisation
movement created a new class in Devon, who coloured the whole of its
social and political life in later centuries, and whose history can be
traced almost down to the present day.

It also brought into being a new kind of landscape, or rather, one
which had been rarely seen in earlier centuries: a landscape of small,
enclosed fields (often hardly more than an acre or so in size) surrounded
by hedge banks that resembled the walls of a fortress. On and around
the Moor, especially, the massive boulders and blocks of granite—strewn
about as though by a giant hand—were picked up and carried to the
boundaries of the new fields to form titanic walls of rubble masonry. The
long lane from the highway into the farmstead was lined on either side
by such walls, as at Cholwich Town to-day; the little fields of pasture

and corn were bounded by them; and the farmhouse and its buildings
were constructed of the same natural unhewn material:

> The old well-trodden lane
> Shadowed with broad-leaved sycamore, and hung
> Along its rocky sides with soft green moss
> And sunny stonecrop: at whose farther end
> The open porch, beneath o'er-arching boughs
> Gleams like a welcome.

Between these thousands of new farms ran narrow lanes, winding,
climbing and falling, linking farm to farm, or farm to highway, each
parish having a network almost completely independent of the next.
It is in these generations between 1150 and 1350 that the characteristic
Devonian landscape was born: the lanes, the small irregular fields,
the great hedge-banks, the isolated farmstead at the end of a track, and
the little parish church, alone among the trees, with its late-Norman or
Early English font.

The new farmsteads, by the nature of their creation and their site,
were held in severalty from the first. Many hundreds of Devon farm-
names embody a medieval personal name, compounded with some
topographical element. To the existence of this large area of enclosed
farm-land in almost every parish we must attribute the remarkably early
enclosure of the open arable fields in Devon. There is evidence that this
enclosure was going on in many places in the latter part of the 13th
century and the early part of the 14th. By Tudor times only a few
remnants of open field remained, though one of these—the Braunton
Great Field—has survived to the present day. The superior advantages
of individual farming over the communal farming of the open fields must
have been everywhere apparent (farmers quite rightly demand ocular
proof of theories first); and the abundance of "waste" for common
pasture meant that rights of common pasture over the fallow field—so
important where other pasture was scarce—were not the formidable
obstacle to change that they proved to be elsewhere.

This medieval enclosure of the open fields produced its own type of
landscape: generally one with large fields, hedges as straight as those of
a Midland parish enclosed in George III's time, and broad lanes and
tracks that run out from the village and end abruptly somewhere in the
fields for no apparent reason. These lanes are much straighter than the
winding tracks one finds in parishes enclosed directly from the waste,
though they may make a number of right-angled bends, but they do not
link together any habitations. They are simply the former "occupation-
roads" from the village where the farmers lived into the open fields where
their strips lay. In a low, clear evening light one can sometimes see after

so many centuries the faint lines where the old strips ran. There is a great deal we do not know about this early transformation of the village fields in Devon. In some places whole *furlongs*, covering several acres, seem to have been enclosed by the same massive hedge-banks as the single colonist threw up on his isolated farm; in other places, single strips seem to have been enclosed in the same way, and we can see the " fossilised " strips on the 2½-inch or 6-inch map to this day. But the reasons for this difference of treatment, and the exact process by which the redistribution of the land was effected at the enclosure, these—and many other related questions—still await a detailed inquiry.

By 1350 nearly every name was written on the map of Devon, nearly every line was drawn. Only on the highest ground were there blank spaces still waiting to be filled: on the Moor itself, on the Blackdown Plateau, and to a smaller degree on the high wet moors of mid-Devon between Tiverton and South Molton. In these upland areas we find new farms being created out of the waste during the 17th century. Among the estate papers of the old families are many leases for three lives or 99 years of a piece of the manor waste at a nominal rent, on condition that the lessee should put up a farmhouse and buildings, and make his habitation there while he toiled to make new fields out of the rough moorland.[1] Then, in the next lease, we find that a new farm has been born, and the entry fine and rent are proportionately high. In the main, however, the colonising process—which had halted after the Black Death for perhaps two hundred years—took the form of the enlargement of existing farms rather than the creation of new ones, especially again in the higher and rougher country. Much taking-in of the " waste " was still temporary. The practice of enclosing parcels of the " waste " belonging to a particular farm, and of ploughing it up and taking crops for three or four successive years, went on into the early 19th century.

Fraser, in 1794, reckoned that one-fifth of Devon was still waste land —about 320,000 acres.[2] Dartmoor and Devonian Exmoor accounted for a good half of this; the remainder was to be found mostly in the middle and the west of the county. In south Devon, Fraser found no extensive wastes or commons: many parishes had only 18–20 acres of common pasture left. But when Carrington came to Bridford, within sight of Dartmoor, as the new rector in 1805, he found hundreds of acres of furze-clad waste in his parish. Few people crossed these " barren lands," and there was little intercourse between farms. Much of this land was brought under cultivation in the next thirty years or so; much still remains intractable. And between 1802 and 1874, some seventy enclosure awards dealt with the public commons and wastes all over Devon as far as they were amenable to rescue.[3] Even so, most of Dartmoor remained useless for farming, and many of the enclosed wastes were useful only for rough grazing. In 1939, Devon still had more than 364,000 acres of rough grazing and moorland—22 per cent of its total area, nearly twice the average proportion for England as a whole.

THE LANDOWNER

When Fraser made his report to the Board of Agriculture in 1794, he remarked that freehold property was very much divided in Devon, more so than in any other county. There were few great proprietors, but " a great number of gentlemen of easy, independent fortunes, who pass their time chiefly on their own estates, and live in great harmony with each other, and with the respectable yeomanry in their neighbourhood." He goes on to say that this extreme division of property was excellent from a social standpoint, but bad on purely economic grounds.[1]

The pages of the county topographers, notably those of Pole, Polwhele, and Lysons, amply bear out Fraser's remarks, for all of them are much concerned with tracing the history of hundreds of freehold estates as well as the descent of the manors. There are many parishes with half a dozen such estates, the homes of small gentry or " squireens." In hundreds of instances the history of the estate begins in Henry III's time, often in the time of John or Richard I, and occasionally as far back as Henry II.

There were, indeed, a few great landowners in Devon by the time Fraser, Polwhele, and Lysons wrote, whose estates rivalled in size those of the Midland aristocracy. One of Lysons's correspondents, writing in 1821, gives the names of eleven landowners whose Devonshire estates were worth upwards of £10,000 a year, and a number of others worth between £5,000 and £10,000.[2] Lord Clinton's estate was reckoned to be worth £30,000 a year when all in hand, and even so was exceeded in value by that of Lord Rolle. Nevertheless, these figures do not alter the general picture of a landed society which consisted to a remarkable degree of squires, small gentry, and large yeomen. Devon was a vast county— nearly 1,700,000 acres—and a few large landowners made little impression on it. Certainly they did not dominate its social and political life as they might have done elsewhere. When Benjamin Donn published his fine map of Devon in 1765, he prefaced it with a list of " seats " in the county, and they number more than six hundred. This alone is a good confirmation of Fraser's view. It was reckoned, too, that in the early 19th century there were about 8,000 freeholders in Devon entitled to vote in the parliamentary elections.[3] As late as 1873, the picture of a fairly widely distributed property in land had hardly changed: the return of the owners of land in that year shows that nearly two hundred landowners had estates of a thousand acres or more, and another three hundred or so lived comfortably on estates of four hundred to a thousand acres. This class of gentry, large and small, which had numbered over six hundred in Donn's day, still mustered over five hundred in the closing years of the 19th century. What are the origins of this remarkable social pattern?

THE ORIGINS OF THE GENTRY

The first definite statement we can make about the origins of the Devonshire gentry is that they begin to appear in force during the second half of the 12th century. The Pipe Rolls for the period 1160-1200, and the Red Book of the Exchequer, give us the earliest reference to nearly a score of historic Devon names, some of which still survive. By 1166 we hear of Ralegh, Cruwys, Kelly, Coffin, Dinham, Champernowne, Speke, Pine, Dennis, and Bonville. Within a few years more we hear of Fortescue, Monk, and Speccott. From other sources than these, we hear of the Aclands, the Fulfords, the Worths, the Giffards, and the Ayshfords; all before the end of the 12th century. The illustrious family of Courtenay, who take their name from a small town to the south of Paris, crossed from France to England with Queen Eleanor, wife of Henry II, in 1152.

The Courtenays established themselves immediately among the most eminent families in Devon, by the marriage of Reginald de Courtenay with Hawise, the heiress of the barony and honour of Okehampton. This honour, the largest in Devon, was formed of the enormous estates of Baldwin de Brionne, Sheriff of Devon at the time of Domesday. By this marriage, too, Reginald de Courtenay became Baron of Okehampton, and hereditary sheriff of Devon in right of his wife.[1]   The honour of Plympton also, second only in extent to that of Okehampton, came to the Courtenays when Hugh de Courtenay succeeded in 1293 as the lineal descendant of William de Vernon, fifth earl of Devon. The two largest honours in Devon were united in Hugh de Courtenay, upon whom the earldom of Devon was bestowed in 1335. The Courtenays were now pre-eminent in the West; no other family challenged them until the rise of the Bonvilles in the 15th century.

The sudden appearance of nearly a score of the old county families during the second half of the 12th century is partly the result of the increasing volume of public records in this period. If we had more early monastic records than we in fact possess in Devon, we might well have carried the origins of some of these families back a little further.* But it seems improbable that any of them, except the Kellys and the Ful-

---

*The early charters of Tavistock Abbey take the Giffards back to c. 1130-40 when Robert Giffard built the church at Brentor, and the Modbury cartulary gives us Ralph Fortescue c. 1140. Both families survive to this day, though not in their original homes.

fords, can trace their descent directly from a Domesday tenant of their estates; and there is not a single family in the county which can reasonably claim a pre-Conquest pedigree. The hackneyed jingle

> Crocker, Cruwys, and Copplestone
> When the Conqueror came were all at home

has not a word of truth in it. There seems little reason to doubt that the first Cruwys came into Devon about the middle of the 12th century, probably from Flanders whence other Devonshire families originated (e.g. the Flemings). Most of those who crossed at the Conquest and during the ensuing hundred years arrived in Devon from Normandy—such as the Bonvilles, the Pomeroys, and the Grenvilles, to name only a few of the greater; but a sprinkling came from farther to the north-east, and a number came from Brittany, such as the Helions (from Helléan) and the Dinhams (from Dinant).[1] To revert to the jingle, we hear nothing of the Crockers before the early 13th century; and the first recorded Copplestone is found, according to Pole, at Copplestone in Henry II's time. They may well be older than this, but a pre-Conquest pedigree is far from established on these facts.

There are, indeed, certain instances among the smaller freeholders in Devon where one may reasonably suspect a pre-Conquest descent (though none of these families survives to-day). On the Tavistock abbey estates, a farm called Milemead, abandoned and overgrown to-day, gave its name to a family of freeholders who were certainly at home in 1186, and who are described in surveys drawn up for the abbey as holding " by ancient tenure." They had no charter from the abbot, for they had been there from time immemorial. The Colmestors, a little lower down the valley from Milemead, were of similar status and antiquity. It may well be that the free ancestors of the Milemeads and the Colmestors are to be sought among the *villani* of the Exon Domesday, not all of whom, by any means, can be regarded as of servile status[2]. There are certain small estates elsewhere in Devon where the Saxon owner was allowed to remain in possession after 1066, and where in the early 13th century we find free tenants installed with every appearance of antiquity, who have taken their names from their holdings. Such are Wadham and Shapcote, both in the wilds of Knowstone parish. We may suspect that the Wadhams, who from this unpromising start were later to found a college at Oxford, were descended from the Ulf who held *Wadeham* in the time of King Edward, and that the Shapcotes could claim as their primordial ancestor the Algar who held their estate before 1066.

Most of the old families above the rank of freeholders, those who were squires, so to speak, from the beginning, held their estates by knight service, under some great lord who had enfeoffed them in their lands in return for military service when it was demanded. Many of these endowments had been made by the time of Domesday. Thus the abbot of Tavistock, heavily burdened by the Conqueror with the obligation to provide and maintain fifteen knights, had probably carved territorial endowments out of the abbey lands for most of them by 1086.[1] The bishop of Exeter, who was obliged to find 15½ knights, had granted away some of his great manor of Crediton to a number of knights by the time of Domesday. An even greater number of such endowments were made during the 12th century, as the vast Domesday estates of the King, Baldwin the sheriff, the bishop of Coutances, the count of Mortain, and others, were granted away in blocks to lesser men, who re-granted in turn smaller parcels to the military followers whom we recognise as the ancestors of the Devon squires. So we find the Kellys holding the manor of Kelly for one knight's fee under the Courtenays, the Fortescues holding Whimpston for a knight's fee under the Valletorts, the Cruwys holding Cruwys Morchard for a knight's fee from the Tracys, the Fulfords holding Fulford for half a knight's fee under the Courtenays,[2] and so on all over the county. The oldest of the Devon squirearchy have their origin in the military class who followed the greater Norman lords in the late 11th and the 12th centuries. Some, like the Fulfords, have maintained this military tradition down to the present day.

These are the core of the old squirearchy. There were, of course, scores of others settled on their medieval manors all over Devon, whose names survive only in the village-names like Sampford Peverell and Cheriton Fitzpaine, or in the pages of the county topographers. But the ranks of the squirearchy were continually being replenished, and indeed grew as the centuries passed, for they drew upon a variety of new blood. There was, in the first place, the army of ancient freeholders, the most numerous source of recruitment, rising by a series of judicious marriages to a higher social class. There were the lawyers, a remarkably successful class in Devon from the 13th century to the 19th; there were the great town-merchants and the clothiers, and the successful yeomen from the countryside; and, not least, there were the immigrant landed families from other counties who were brought to Devon by marriage with a local heiress.

Something has been said already of the ancient freeholders as a class. Their social history—their diverse origins and fortunes through the centuries—constitutes one of the most fascinating aspects of the local history of both Devon and Cornwall, could it only be told at length. They seem to originate in a number of ways. Some are pretty certainly represented in the Exon Domesday under the misleading label of *villani*; others are in the same record among the King's thanes, such as Algar and Ulf, already mentioned. But the great majority of them undoubtedly originated in the 12th and 13th centuries, and possibly for two distinct reasons. We find in later centuries, in studying the inquisitions post mortem of these families, that they hold their aboriginal estates, those from which they take their name, by a fraction of a knight's fee or in socage. Examples of those holding by socage and a small annual rent have already been quoted. Many of the historic Devon families—Acland, Edgcumbe, and Pollard, for example—begin in this way; and this tenure is, I think, generally to be associated with the colonisation of new land in the post-Conquest period.

Where, on the other hand, we find the ancient freeholders holding their small estates by a fraction of a knight's fee, we are probably dealing with land cleared and cultivated before the Conquest. For example, the Bremridges held Bremridge in Sandford (about 75 acres) for an eighth of a knight's fee and an annual rent of 7s. 5d., and we may suspect that Bremridge was not just a piece of the waste land (" bramble ridge ") when the first Bremridge took up his habitation there, but that it was part of an older estate that was being divided into small endowments in order to spread the burden of knight-service over an ever wider class. Dowrish, not far away, is an example of the same kind. It, too, was held for one-eighth of a knight's fee and a nominal annual rent. A number of knight's fees had been created by the bishop of Exeter on his vast manor of Crediton, both before and after Domesday, one of which was held by William de Tracy in 1166. Four small estates made up this Tracy fee, Dowrish being one of them. At some date, certainly by the time of John and perhaps rather earlier, the Dowrish land was granted away, as a fraction of the whole fee, to a man who subsequently took his name from the estate. Both Bremridge and Dowrish were the homes of freeholders by the end of the 12th century, but both had probably existed as cultivated land on the episcopal manor of Crediton before 1066.[1]

Freeholders could also originate when an unfree man purchased his freedom and some land. Thus, on 1 July 1238 Geoffrey de Leya paid Nicholas de Molis, lord of Kingskerswell and Diptford, sixty marks of silver and for this " Nicholas acknowledged the said Geoffrey to be a free man, and remitted and quit-claimed for himself and his heirs the said Geoffrey, and Sexburga and Damrona his sisters, and their issue and heirs, from all manner of neifty and secular service for ever." A week later, Geoffrey bought from Ralph de Abbe half a knight's fee in Horsewell and Middleton (in South Milton parish) for twenty marks of silver. Again, in 1270, we find William de Bosco buying an 84-acre farm in Stockleigh Pomeroy from Henry de la Pomeroy, for £10 sterling, a price which included the release of William and all his household and their issue from all servitude for ever.[2]

Thus, by the end of the 13th century, we find an extraordinary number of free tenants wherever we look in the county. We have no means of estimating what proportion of the total tenant-population they constituted, but that they held a very substantial proportion of the total acreage of most manors the 16th-century surveys leave us in no doubt. Indeed we sometimes find small manors which had been entirely dismembered and sold off to the free tenants as early as the 14th century.[1] In general the free tenants owned a considerably greater proportion of the land than their numbers would suggest, for the free tenements tended to be larger than the unfree. The free tenants also tended to become more numerous as one went westwards in Devon, and especially in the parishes on the moorland fringe, where their ancestors had been the first settlers on the "waste." By successive marriages with the heiresses of neighbouring ancient freeholds, they added farm to farm, generation after generation, and gradually raised themselves to the point at which their estates rivalled those of the old squirearchy, whose daughters they could aspire to marry. The pedigree of the Aclands, as recorded by Vivian, is an illuminating lesson in the value of marriage with heiresses between the 13th and the 17th centuries. Robert Furse's account of his family's rise from "a little twig," written in 1593, gives one the details of a similar slow and steady accumulation of property through several centuries.[2] If one could avoid the disaster of a failure of the male line, and keep within one's income in each generation, the little twig would in the fullness of time become a great oak. It was a matter of some three centuries or so; ten or twelve generations for the ancient freeholder to establish himself in the ranks of the squirearchy—Acland, Furse, Monk, Edgcumbe, Arscott, a whole host of them succeeded—and marriage was the greatest single cause of their advancement.

Many large estates were accumulated in Devon by lawyers with a rich practice, more so perhaps than anywhere else in England. Fuller tells us that Devonshire men seemed to be "innated with a genius to study law," from Henry de Bracton, who was born at Bratton Fleming, onwards. Among the lawyers and judges who built up fortunes and raised an obscure family to eminence and landed wealth we find Sir John Cary and Sir John Wadham in the 14th century, and Sir John Fortescue and Sir Lewis Pollard in the 15th and early 16th. Among the remarkable number of successful Devonian lawyers in the 16th century were Drewe, Harris, Glanville, Sir William Periam, and Sir Edmond Prideaux. Right down to the 19th century we find these landed lawyers, the last of them on the grand scale being Richard Preston, Q.C. (1768-1850), the eminent conveyancer, who bought over eleven thousand acres in mid-Devon, from Chulmleigh right across to Broadwoodwidger.

The transition of the successful town merchants to the ranks of the landed gentry is a well-worn theme. All the Devonshire towns produced

such men, in the 16th and 17th centuries above all, and their ample
estates could be found everywhere. Westcote, born among the minor
gentry on a modest estate, disliked them intensely:

> Such upstart golden asses, whose niggardly covetous fathers have
> infatuated with an insolent arrogancy, by leaving them a mass of ill-
> gotten wealth; possessing, as their own, neither valour, learning, wit,
> nor ordinary discretion; but swollen hugely with that intoxicating
> venom of riches, and thereby wooing with the powerful persuading
> argument of a great jointure, inoculated into some generous family,
> and then by that grown high in their own imaginations, will presently
> be esquires; when their gentility (God wot) hangs as ill on them as
> if they had borrowed it of some near-like name, or bought it with
> their pennies; and then fret if they be not saluted with, your worship;
> vouchsafing faint salute to their honest poor kindred; casting a
> squinting eye on their equals; yea, vaunting themselves above their
> betters: crowing over the commonalty, their father's equals. . . . If
> some able pen were at leisure to undertake against such mushrooms,
> dipped in strong satirical ink, it would soon embowel these wind-
> puff bladders, and pluck off the loose periwig from their bald pates,
> and restore worship to his right seat and habitation, and those stolen
> titles to their just and true owners; and like another Aretine, strip
> these golden asses out of their gay trappings. . . .

There speaks the old-fashioned country gentleman of the time of Charles
I. The house where he wrote these passionate words, as he neared the
end of his *View of Devonshire*, may still be seen at West Raddon, below
the undulant sweep of the Raddon Hills, and much of the house is as
he knew it. It is a good farmhouse in the middle of a fertile " red-land "
farm. That, at least, would please Westcote, could he return to it to-day.
Probably the successful yeomen of the 16th century—the golden age for
farmers whose expenses were fixed and whose selling prices rose every
year—offended Westcote less. There were many of them, like the
Quickes who farmed in a biggish way at Kennerleigh and bought land
at Newton St. Cyres where they rose to be squires; and the Balls, who
rose to own Mamhead. The successful yeomen were, I think, less con-
spicuously successful here than in the Midlands, for they had too many
competitors in Devon among the cloth merchants, the lawyers, and the
old gentry themselves. And there was, lastly, the constant influx of old
landed families from other counties, brought to Devon by a good marriage.
So the Chichesters came into Devon from Sussex in the late 14th century
when they married the heiress of Raleigh, near Barnstaple; and the
Carews from South Wales when they married the Peverell heiress in
Edward I's time. Both families survive to-day.

THE RISE OF THE GENTRY

The eve of the Dissolution makes a good point at which to stop and survey the pattern of land-ownership in Devon. There were few large landowners—only the Courtenays, earls of Devon, and some of the ecclesiastical landlords. When Henry Courtenay, Marquess of Exeter, was attainted in 1536, the accounts of his officers, and the inquisition on his lands, showed that he was by far the greatest landowner in south-western England. He had estates in Devon and Cornwall, Somerset and Dorset, Berkshire, Buckinghamshire, and Hampshire, with a total rental of more than £2,100 a year.[1] The " eastern parts " produced just over £605 a year, the fourteen estates in Cornwall a little over £177, and Devon yielded £1,320 18s. 3¾d. Devon and Cornwall produced about £1,500 a year between them. In terms of modern money (pre-1939) we may say that the Courtenay income was round about £60-£70,000 a year. The inquisition taken in 1539, after his execution, gives the details of his vast estates. In Devon he had six boroughs, of which the most important were Plympton, Okehampton, and Tiverton; three castles (at the same places) and two other great houses—Colcombe, near Colyton, and Columbjohn, just north of Exeter; eight hundreds and two honours; thirty-six manors and nearly eighty farms in some twenty-five parishes in addition; and about twenty advowsons and various feudal offices that brought in fees.[2]

The bishop of Exeter was the next most powerful landowner in the south-west. His net income from temporal and spiritual sources was just under £1,600 a year, of which less than £84 came from his properties outside Devon and Cornwall (mainly in and round London). His Cornish estates were producing about £436 a year net in 1535, the Devon lands about £864 a year. He had two boroughs in Devon (Ashburton and Chudleigh), a palace at Exeter, another near Bishop's Teignton, and a dozen manors. His fat manors of Paignton, Bishop's Tawton, and Crediton were each worth more than the whole endowment of several of the Devonshire monastic houses.

The Dean and Chapter of Exeter had fourteen manors in Devon, a borough (East Teignmouth), and a number of farms in various parishes, producing altogether about £654 a year, but their spiritual income—a misleading word, for it consisted of very tangible income mainly from tithes—brought in another £470 a year clear. Their Devon income from rents and tithes and manorial courts was worth about £1,072 a year in 1535.[3] Other great ecclesiastical estates in Devon were those of Tavistock abbey (£986 gross) and Plympton priory (£837 gross). The Cistercian abbey of Buckfast came next with £486 gross.[4]

Among the lay families, about a dozen owned between six and twelve manors in Devon. The Courtenays towered over all. Their formidable rivals, the Bonvilles, had perished in the Wars of the Roses, and the inheritance had come to Cecily, great-grand-daughter of Sir William Bonville, who in 1476 married Thomas Grey, first Marquess of Dorset. Her large estates were centred upon Shute, in south-east Devon, not far from the Courtenays' splendid house at Colcombe. In north Devon, William Bourchier had married the heiress of Lord Fitzwarren, and so came into the large estate centred upon Tawstock, just outside Barnstaple. A son of the Fitzwarren heiress had married one of the Dinham heiresses, the last of whom had died in 1501. The Dinhams had been accumulating property in Devon since the early 12th century.[1]

In 1522-3 a special levy was made on all lay persons worth £40 a year or more in land or in personal estate, whichever assessment yielded most to the national exchequer.[2] Only 50 persons are assessed on lands out of a total of 476. The three branches of the Courtenays were assessed at some £1,600 between them; the next greatest assessment is that of Dame Anne St. Leger, at Annery, near Bideford (£402). She was one of the co-heiresses of the earl of Ormond, and had married Sir James St. Leger. The most wealthy of the Devon squires were the Bassetts, the Trevelyans (at Yarnscombe), the Bampfyldes, Hacches, Carews, Wydeslades, Whytinges, and Halses (of Sherford). All these were assessed at £100 a year or more. Rather less wealthy were the Monks, Stucleys, Tremaynes, Yeos, Grenvilles, and Burys. Most of the Devon squires had only one or two manors, and several freehold estates in addition.

Some of the wealthiest Devon squires are missing from this part of the list. They are among those assessed on personal estate, probably because they farmed on a big scale and also had extensive interests in tin-works and sometimes in shipping. The Courtenays, Copplestones, Edgecumbes, Fulfords, and Champernownes were all financially interested in Dartmoor tin. The Fulfords and the Drakes, and doubtless many others, owned a ship or two each. Several squires are assessed on their goods as highly as all but the richest merchants in Exeter. John Copplestone, at 700 marks, was surpassed only by two merchants in the whole of Devon. The Fortescues were rich also. As wealthy as the big Exeter merchants were the Coffins, Drakes, Prusts (of Hartland), Chichesters, Arscotts, Carys, and Gilberts. These were the bigger families. The general run of the squirearchy owned less land, farmed on a smaller scale, and had no interests in tin-works or shipping. They lived obscurely on incomes of £50–£100 a year, content to know only a small corner of the wide landscape of Devon, never moving outside it except perhaps occasionally to visit Exeter, the seat of government for the south-west of England.

The monastic houses, taken together, held a vast amount of property in Devon. Only Tavistock and Plympton, it is true, were of any size—the only houses with more than £500 a year. Ten houses—well over a half—fell into the £100–£300 group. Three more—Carswell, Cornworthy, and Pilton—had less than £100 a year gross. Not all this property actually lay in Devon, though most of it did. On the other hand, some 24 " outside " monasteries owned property in the county. We may summarise the figures as follows:[1]

Gross Value of Monastic Property in Devon, 1535
(per annum)

Devon monasteries	£4,967	0 6
Non-Devon monasteries	£1,013	16 1
Hospitals, priories, collegiate churches, etc.	£758	11 6
TOTAL	£6,739	8 1

The largest " outside " house holding property in the county was the Middlesex abbey of Syon, whose Devon property was worth more than that of many of the Devonshire houses (nearly £275 a year). Sherborne had much Devon property also (nearly £151 a year), having succeeded to the estates formerly held by Horton abbey. Several Somerset monasteries held valuable properties in Devon. These were Montacute, Barlynch, Cleeve, Taunton, Glastonbury, and Buckland.

The total value of the property, in Devon alone, which fell into the hands of the Crown in 1536-9 was well over £6,700 a year, the equivalent of about five times the extent of the great Courtenay domain in Devon. The Courtenay inheritance was also in the hands of the Crown by 1536.

The changes which took place in Devon as a result of the disposal of most of these lands, the greatest transference of property since the Norman Conquest, would provide material for a whole book in itself. It must suffice to say that they altered the picture of local society very considerably. They brought in powerful newcomers—chiefly the Russells and the Rolles. They raised one or two of the old Devon families from a competence to a fortune—chiefly the Dennises and the Petres. And they enlarged the estates of a great number of the old squirearchy to a notable degree without making them spectacular.

The grant of ex-monastic lands to John, first baron Russell, to support his viceregal authority as President of the Council in the West, was on a princely scale. In 1539 he was given the site of Tavistock abbey (the richest house west of Glastonbury) and most of its possessions, temporal and spiritual, two rectories belonging to Dunkeswell abbey, together with nearly 6,000 acres of its lands, and other fat tit-bits. As nearly as can be reckoned, Russell's new property was worth about £1,050 a year,* well over one-sixth of all the monastic property in Devon. No wonder Edmund Burke later called the Russells " the leviathan of all the creatures of the Crown." Such a grant was " so enormous as not only to outrage economy, but even to stagger credibility."

The Rolles were second only to the Russells in the extent of their monastic and other lands, and in time were to surpass them. George Rolle, the founder of the family in Devon, was a Tudor lawyer in the best of times. He had bought the estate of Stevenstone before the Dissolution, so establishing a footing in Devon, and in later years we find him trafficking in the lands of Frithelstock, Pilton, and Barnstaple priories, all in north Devon. When he died in 1552 his lands were to be found over most of north and west Devon, from Ilfracombe on the north coast down to the edge of Plymouth at Egg Buckland, and from West Putford right across the county eastwards to Tiverton and Crediton.[1]

The pre-eminence of the Rolles dates from their union with the Dennis family and their inheritance, early in the 17th century, of the large Dennis estates in south-east Devon. These had been built up mostly from monastic spoils by Sir Thomas Dennis (c. 1480-1561), privy councillor, chancellor of Anne of Cleves, frequently sheriff of Devon, and an eminent time-server. His monastic spoils were probably second only to those of John Russell. Sir William Petre, the son of an ancient freeholder at Tor Newton in Torbryan parish, was another Tudor official who profited greatly by the redistribution of monastic property in Devon and elsewhere. In 1555, fearing that Queen Mary might be disposed to restore the monastic lands to their former owners, he obtained a special papal dispensation to keep his twelve ex-monastic manors and three rectories.[2] The old landed families of Devon contented themselves with picking up a manor or so to round off their estates. So the Fulfords bought in 1544 the manor and rectory of Dunsford, which had belonged to Canonsleigh priory; the Drakes of Musbury bought the Glastonbury manor of Uplyme (1544); the Bluetts bought Holcombe Rogus (1540); the Arscotts bought the Hartland manor and rectory of Abbots Bickington (1545), and so on. Merchants and clothiers sometimes had a look in also: Robert Davie, the Crediton merchant, bought the manor of Canonteign in 1542, and William Wotton of Harberton, clothier, and John Wotton of Totnes, merchant, clubbed together to buy the Buckfast manor of Engleborne in 1546 for £324 10s.[3]

Not all the gentry profited by these changes, and not all the freeholders bothered to extend their ancient patrimony by marriage and

---

*The grant was not entirely a gift, for the Crown reserved an annual rent of £284 5s. on it, roughly £8,000-£9,000 a year to-day (in 1939 values).

purchase. Westcote tells us about 1630 that the Bremridges, already referred to, had " enjoyed that place [Bremridge] . . . with such a temperate moderation in every succession, that greedy desire of riches hath neither much increased, nor prodigality decreased, it." And on the remote farm of Westcott, in Bridford parish, he found a freeholder of that name whose ancestors had been there above three hundred years: " it is not great, but a competency; and therewith the tribe contented itself these many years . . . never putting themselves into public offices to get, perchance, fame, but assuredly envy; nor ever endeavoured to enlarge their possessions; yet with a careful frugality to preserve the main chance and not to lessen it. Of them and their like the poet speaks thus:

> The vain desires of Indian treasures great
> Made ne'er his ship to sail or oar to beat;
> The greedy hope of gain with vent'rous danger
> Made ne'er his sword be drawn to serve a stranger;
> He never sold, within the wrangling bar,
> Deceitful clatters causing clients' jar;
> But quietly manured his little field,
> And took th' increase thereof that time did yield."[1]

Not for them the rewards and hazards of the merchant, the lawyer, and the soldier.

Throughout the 17th century the successful merchants and the lawyers continued to found landed families. Many of them were the younger sons of old landed families for whom, under the custom of primogeniture, there was no estate at home, and many of them accumulated new estates that eclipsed those of the parent stock, like Roger Mallock, who bought out the Carys at Cockington in 1654. High political office, especially combined with a legal practice, was still a sure way to great lands. Sir Edmond Prideaux (1554-1629), a younger son of a west Devon squire, was bred a lawyer like so many younger sons, and was successful enough to raise his family in both title and estate. His second son, also Edmond (1601–59), was even more successful as a lawyer and a politician. He became solicitor-general, then attorney-general (1649-59), and also postmaster-general, where he made important reforms in the postal services. " He grew up," says Prince, " to great wealth and dignity: He was made commissioner to the great seal, worth 1500*l.* per annum: By ordinance of parliament, did practise with the bar as one of the King's counsel, worth 5000*l.* per annum: After that, he was attorney-general worth what he pleased to make it: And then post-master general for all the inland letters, which at sixpence the letter, as they went in those days, was worth 15000*l.* per annum."[2] Out of these rich employments, he acquired another great estate, including the site

of Ford abbey " where he built a noble new house out of the ruins of
the old." Prideaux's enormous income from his political offices may be
compared with that of Sir John Rolle who, about the same time, was said
to have an estate of six thousand a year and was " one of the richest
gentlemen in the country."[1]

The Civil War and the Interregnum impoverished the royalist gentry
very considerably, but did not break them. The county was much
fought over, country houses sacked, farms devastated and robbed, and
in addition the royalist landlords were heavily fined for their " de-
linquency " according to the degree of their support for the King's cause.
Sir Henry Cary of Cockington—whose great-uncle Sir George had greatly
increased the Devon estates out of the profits of political office, first as
Lord Treasurer and later as Lord Deputy of Ireland—was savagely fined
£1,985. The fine was paid, but further persecution followed, and one
result was that in 1654 he was obliged to sell the old family estate of
Cockington. Many of his sequestrated estates were, however, recovered
at the Restoration.[2] Some of the heaviest fines were:

Sir Edward Seymour	Berry Pomeroy	£3,133 (reduced to £1,200)
Sir Humphrey Tracy	Bovey Tracey and Stanway, Glos.	£1,500 (reduced to £1,300)
Richard Culme	Canonsleigh	£2,906
Sir John Acland	Columbjohn	£1,727
Henry Ashford	Ashford	£1,150
Sir Peter Ball	Dawlish	£1,250
Thomas Carew	Stoodleigh	£1,085
John Gifford	Brightley	£1,136
Sir Thomas Hele	Flete	£2,834
Sir William Pole	Colyton	£1,142

Many of the gentry were fined between £500 and £1,000.[3] Sir Francis
Fulford, a notable royalist, was fined £590 6s. 8d., reduced by £160 a
week later, because he had only a life interest in some of his lands. James
Courtenay of Molland, recusant as well as royalist, was fined £750;
Sir Hugh Pollard of King's Nympton £518; John Davy of Sandford
and Ruxford £800; John Fortescue of Fallapit £861 4s. 10d. The fines
were paid by raising money on mortgage, or by borrowing from relatives
and friends all over the countryside. It was difficult, if not impossible, to
sell lands because of the entails, and in any event, most landowners would
do everything to avoid selling. It meant that the next generation or so

had to live hard on heavily mortgaged estates, but they lost little if anything of their lands in the end. The Fulfords were typical: twice they have been turned out of their house and their lands forfeited or sequestrated (in 1461 and 1645) and twice they have returned (1465 and 1660), and still they are there. In 1873 they still held the average Devon squire's estate of just under 3,000 acres.

Nor did the 18th century see any spectacular changes. The merchants, clothiers, and lawyers were less conspicuous: few such outstanding names and fortunes as there had been earlier. Some of the great landowners steadily increased their estates by marriage and purchases. Sir John Rolle died seised of more than forty manors in Devon in 1706.[1] The Fortescues proliferated all over the county and added to their lands. But, with two or three exceptions, no great accumulations were built up: the old families threw up new shoots all over the place, and each throve independently on a more or less modest estate. Thus there were seven different branches of the Fortescues, and no fewer than eleven branches of the Chichesters, all with their own properties. Several families had produced five or six branches, many more two, three, or four.[2] The younger branches might not possess even one manor, but they had a substantial ancient freehold estate of three or four hundred acres, and perhaps two or three other farms in addition, and on this competence they lived easily and harmoniously with their neighbours. Now we begin to see why, in Benjamin Donn's day, there were more than six hundred " seats " in the county; and many more had already ceased to be so. These are the houses marked to-day in such numbers on the 2½-inch maps as *Mansion* (*remains of*), sometimes a ruin and sometimes incorporated into a farmhouse, where the richly decorative ceilings, linen-fold panelling, plaster mantelpieces with coats of arms, and pieces of armorial glass in the windows, all betray a former degree of gentility. There must have been a thousand or more such mansions lived in during the 16th and 17th centuries, each supported by a small freehold estate in land, and each originating in an ancient freehold of the 11th, 12th, or 13th century.

THE LANDOWNER IN 1873

The Return of the Owners of Land, made in 1873, gives us the first complete picture of the distribution of landed property since Domesday. It is a picture, moreover, of the landed class at the height of its opulence and political influence, in those rich and placid days of the early seventies when there was not even a depression in farming to worry about. There were 10,162 owners of one acre of land and upwards in Devon. The 21,647 owners of less than an acre apiece need not detain us, for they held rather less than three thousand acres all told.

At the top of the scale were five great estates of more than 20,000 acres each: the Hon. Mark Rolle with 55,592 acres in Devon (not an acre outside the county) with a gross rental of £47,170 a year,[1] the Duke of Bedford with 22,607 acres and a gross rental of nearly £46,000 a year, the Earl of Devon, 20,589 acres with £31,000 a year gross, and Earl Fortescue, at Castle Hill, with 20,172 acres worth rather more than £17,000 a year. The fifth great landowner was the duchy of Cornwall, whose 48,457 acres on Dartmoor were worth less than £5,000 a year. In the next group (10,000-20,000 acres) the largest owners were Lord Poltimore with 19,883 acres according to Bateman's revised figure,[2] the Earl of Portsmouth (16,414), Sir Thomas Dyke Acland (15,019), and Lord Clinton (14,431), who had inherited one of the great Rolle estates.

Leaving these detailed figures on one side, the general picture is of a county in which one-fifth of the land was owned by sixteen families (counting all branches of the same family—e.g. the Chichesters—as one). Below this topmost level, property was more widely distributed. One half of the county was held in estates of 1,000 acres and upwards, and owned by 150 families.

Ownership of Land in Devon 1873[3]

Size of Estate (acres)	No. of Owners	Total acreage held
Over 10,000	16	309,000
5,000–10,000	28	177,000
1,000– 5,000	154	303,000
500– 1,000	209	142,000
100– 500	1,890	394,000
1– 100	7,865	189,000
TOTALS	10,162	1,514,000

We have seen, in general terms, how several of the largest estates had originated and been built up, but these were not typical even in mid-Victorian days. There were only some forty or so estates of more than 5,000 acres. Nearly all the ancient squirearchy of the county fall closely together into the 2,000-4,000 acre group with a curious uniformity. In this group we find such old families as the Bellews, Bullers, Champernownes, Coffins, Fulfords, Fursdons, Kellys, Leys, and Worths. The " squireen " class is still strong: some 320 families owned between 400 and 1,000 acres, and even below this level there were ancient freeholders still living on the farms of their ancestors. Most remarkable of all, perhaps, were the Seccombes and the Reddaways, who in 1873 (and still to this day) were farming the land from which they had taken their names in the 13th century, if not earlier. The Reddaways are named

in the *Book of Fees* in 1242 as holding their land of Reddaway, in Sampford
Courtenay parish, by knight service; and in 1873 Thomas Reddaway
still held the 133½ acres of his ancestors. The Seccombes had owned and
farmed Seccombe, in Germansweek parish, since the 13th century at
least; in 1873 Roger Seccombe still lived off its 125 acres. All around the
edges of Dartmoor, especially, in the solitary old granite farmhouses, these
ancient yeoman families persisted, holding their lands from a time
" when the memory of man runneth not to the contrary."

> The child who played
> Beneath the ash trees by the riverside,
> Saw the same quiet home his fathers knew,
> Save that a deeper shadow from the boughs
> Fell on him. . . .
> So the same life passed down from sire to son.
> To the same granite font-stone each was borne;
> And the same chime from out the time-worn tower
> Called them to prayer; and by the same dark bench
> Carved by rude hands of old, they knelt to God.
> Year after year they trod the same green path
> Over the moors with wild thyme thickly spread
> To the far valley, where the church lifts up
> Her pinnacles between the sycamores:
> And there, beneath the shelter of their boughs,
> Each, as he passed away, was laid to rest.

THE TENANT FARMER

The landowner, large or small, was important, but always in a
minority. Most of those who lived on the land were farmers—that is,
occupiers, for this is the strict meaning of " to farm " land—and not
owners. According to Burnard, whose analysis of the Devonshire Domesday figures is more accurate than Ellis's, the classes below the tenants-in-
chief, the mesne tenants, and the thanes (whom we may regard broadly
as the " owners ") rank as follows: *Villani* 8,508 (43 per cent of the
recorded population), *Bordarii* 4,667 (24 per cent), and *Servi* 5,177 (26
per cent).

The *servi*, whom we must regard as slaves, and who were more
numerous in Devon than in any other county in England, worked the
lord's demesne, but may be counted as occupiers in a broad sense, though
they did not profit from their own labours. Some of the *villani*, at least,
were relatively free men who owned some land of their own; but the
bulk of them and of the *bordarii* were the occupiers and not the owners

of the land they tilled. We should be not far wrong if we put the proportion of occupiers, excluding such owner-occupiers as the thanes and some of the *villani*, at nine out of every ten men in the countryside, but this is only a guess. When we come to the 16th century, with a considerable number of manorial surveys to go upon,[1] we are on surer ground. On twenty-four rural manors, with a total of 1241 tenants, we get these figures:

Free tenants .. 221 (18 per cent of the tenant population)
Customary tenants 925 (74 per cent of the tenant population)
Conventionary tenants 95 (8 per cent of the tenant population)

The numbers of free tenants had risen greatly between Domesday and the 16th century, for reasons we have already seen, and they now constituted about one-fifth of the rural tenantry. The occupiers, with little or no land of their own, numbered four in every five. The customary tenants, who were mostly the descendants of the *villani*, *bordarii*, and *servi* of Domesday, held their land according to the custom of the manor and generally, though not always, by copy of the manor court roll. They were copyholders, and they constituted three-quarters of the manorial tenants in the 16th century.

The leaseholder, or conventionary tenant as he is called in the surveys, was beginning to appear in not inconsiderable numbers on a few manors by the middle of the century. Leaseholders on the lord's demesne had of course been known for centuries, and on some manors they were numerous. On the Tavistock abbey manor of Werrington, in its western half at least, we find fifty-four leaseholders in 1486, as against only fifteen tenants-at-will (customary tenants).[2] At Stokenham in 1548 there were ten leaseholders, all holding parts of the demesne, but they were vastly outnumbered by the customary tenants, of whom there were 158. On the other hand, the leaseholders at Bishop's Clyst in 1588 outnumbered the customary tenants by thirteen to eleven.[3]

Leaseholders were numerically more important than the figures given above would indicate, for the simple reason that some of the freehold land was let to tenants and not occupied by the owners. Undoubtedly, too, many of the bigger leaseholders and copyholders sublet some of their lands as an investment. These under-tenants were a class of unknown size, and the statistics derived from manorial surveys do not reveal the entire truth about the nature of land-holding. At Thorverton in 1661, for example, Mr. John Berry—a substantial yeoman—held five farms and twenty-two houses and cottages in the village, leased from the Dean and Chapter of Exeter, who were lords of the manor. A later note, made in 1675 by the Dean and Chapter's surveyor, shows that Berry had sublet the whole of this property at yearly rents, and was getting £162 a year from it. We do not know what he had paid in fines for the original leases and copies, but the surveyor's note makes it clear that he was subletting as an investment.[1] A good number of substantial yeomen lived on investments of this kind.

Early leases were for a term of years, but by the late 15th century and the early 16th we begin to get leases for three lives—those of the lessee and of two other persons nominated by him. These were usually the lessee's wife and his eldest son, where only one farm was held. In 1575 we hear for the first time (though slightly earlier examples may come to light) of what was to become the universal mode of leasing land in Devon: the lease for three lives or 99 years, whichever was the shorter. In practice, the three lives always ran out well before the term of 99 years as all the " lives " named in the lease had to be those of living people: unborn or prospective children did not count. New " lives " could be inserted, however, as old ones dropped out, by the payment of the appropriate fine, and in this way the tenancy of the farm could be—and often was—continued for centuries, so much so that it was not at all uncommon for life leaseholders to be regarded as the owners of the farm and for the name of the real owner to be known only to the lawyers and the stewards.

The leaseholder for three lives paid a heavy fine upon entry and thereafter a very small reserved rent. On the Duke of Bedford's estates the fine for three lives was calculated in 1726 at twelve years' purchase,[2] or six years' purchase for two lives, and there were other rules to meet various contingencies. Once this fine was paid, the farmer " liveth as merrily as doth his landlord, but according to his calling." The advantages of these long leases both to the landlord and the tenant appeared so obvious that copyhold tenure steadily disappeared in favour of life-leasehold and was rare, except on the conservative ecclesiastical manors, by 1700.[3]

Among the advantages to the tenant was the long security of tenure. For good tenants this meant long-term farming, getting the land into fine shape over a period of years and keeping it so. The better farmers at least could experiment to improve their farms without fear that their improvements would accrue to the landlord's pocket within a short period. The most striking example of this kind, perhaps, is that of the Quartlys at Great Champson, in the parish of Molland. The Quartlys revolutionised cattle-breeding in the west of England: they were the Bakewells of the west: and they did this over a long period of years as tenant-farmers. The first of them took a lease of Champson for three lives from the squire—John Courtenay of West Molland—in 1703, paying a fine of £778 15s. for a farm with a yearly value of £80. The reserved rent was only £2 a year.[4] Here they produced the famous North

Devon breed of cattle after years of experiment, and here they were still tenant-farmers in 1890 though their landlords had changed more than once; and they were still winning prizes for their cattle.

This was the life-leasehold system at its best; but by the time of Marshall and Vancouver we find it being roundly condemned, mainly on the ground that in paying 18 years' purchase—the prevailing rate by then—for such a lease to gratify his " indolence and pride " the tenant beggared himself, borrowed from family and friends, and could not farm properly for lack of working capital. " Having little or no reserved rent to provide for, the efforts of himself and family are directed to the annual cultivation of so much of his land as will pay the parochial and other small disbursements, and supply the bare wants of the most comfortless life it is possible to conceive, leaving no brighter prospect to his children, than what the lapse of 99 years may do, by the termination of a lease so injudiciously purchased."[1]

There were many reasons why a system which had deservedly been so popular with landlords and tenants, and had originally possessed such great merits, should have become, by the end of the 18th century, an abuse crying out for abolition. Perhaps the most important was the fact that with the increasing competition for farms landlords were too often tempted to let them to the highest bidder, regardless of his resources and qualities as a tenant, who, having paid away all his capital, then robbed the fertility of the farm as hard as he could in order to make a living. Too many of the later leases were bought with borrowed money, whereas in the early days the farmer had paid the fine out of real savings already accumulated. He could take over free of all obligations, and with a reserve of working capital. A remarkable example is that of Walter Cox, yeoman, of Farway in east Devon, who took in 1660 a lease for three lives of a farm in a neighbouring parish at a fine of £570. The squire, Sir Courtenay Pole, records in his cash-book that he had reduced the fine to £555 " because he pd. 250 *l.* of his fine in Golde."[2] There is no doubt about the reality of these savings. The leases, the good farming, and the new farmhouses and buildings, were all paid for out of the savings of the golden generations of high prices after 1540;[3] the later leases and farming too often had not this solid foundation.

By the beginning of the 19th century, landlords were introducing short-term leases (usually 14 or 21 years) at a rack-rent equivalent to the full annual value of the land, but change was slow. Not only was Devon a conservative region, where old practices and customs died hard, but by its very nature the system of leases for three lives could only be extinguished piecemeal, as tenants died. Moreover, in many parishes the lands of different farms were intermixed and this made it still more difficult to effect changes in tenure.

On Church manors copyholders were still strongly represented even after 1800. Elsewhere, they had disappeared except perhaps in odd pockets, but it took a long time for the ordinary leasehold for a term of years to become general. Life-hold tenure, as it was sometimes called, persisted in places into the later years of the 19th century, though the practice of renewal of lives was then quite obsolete. But most land was probably being let at a rack-rent by the middle of the 19th century; the copyholders and life-lessees were by then mere survivals of an earlier economy.

FARMING PRACTICE

There was a noticeable specialisation of farming as early as the 11th century. The important arable districts—as reflected in the density of plough-teams per thousand acres—were then the Vale of Exeter, the country between the Teign and the Dart, and to a lesser extent the low-land parts of north Devon. The districts with the fewest plough-teams were the Dartmoor borderlands, the whole of western Devon, and the high ground of mid-Devon, and it is in these districts in general that we find the highest density of cattle.[1] The whole of the high ground of the Culm Measures country, between Hartland and the Somerset border, and the Blackdown valleys, was pastoral rather than arable. In many small Domesday manors, especially in the west, we find no plough. They are evidently small cattle farms, worked in severalty.

Sheep were most important between the Teign and the Dart. Here there were nearly sixty per thousand acres. North Devon had over forty.[2] The arable districts generally carried the most sheep, as we should expect. The degree of specialisation, elementary though it may have been, would come out yet more clearly if we examined the early records in closer detail. Thus we find a farm called Shapwick (" sheep farm ") in 1167, in the parish of Uplyme, in the only corner of Devon where chalk down-land appears. This district appears as a considerable sheep-rearing area in the 16th century: in 1535 the wool and lamb tithes of a group of five parishes here amounted to nearly as much as the corn tithes.[3] When my own ancestor, George Hoskins, died in 1625, he had a flock of over 700 sheep pasturing on the downs above Axmouth and Musbury, a remarkable number for Devon.

Of medieval farming in Devon we know little as yet. The Tavistock abbey estates have been studied in detail, and show a standard of farming comparable with the best elsewhere, though these estates may have been exceptionally well managed and not typical of peasant farming.[4] But it is fairly certain that the use of marl on some soils, and of sea-sand and ashes on others, was widespread in the 13th century, probably among the peasantry as well as the monastic landlords. The assize roll of 1249 speaks of one Richard Harding of Legh, who was suffocated to death in a marl-pit (*marlera*) somewhere in the hundred of Uffculme,[1] and there are many references in the late 13th and early 14th centuries to the traffic in sea-sand from the beaches to farms miles inland. Bude sand was especially esteemed for lightening and fertilising the heavy, yellow clays of west Devon, and is still in demand to this day.[2]

It is sometimes said that orchards were not known in Devon before Elizabeth's reign, and that cider-making is equally recent in origin. But there is evidence that cider was being made in some parts of Devon as a regular part of the manorial routine in the 13th century. On the Earl of Devon's manor of Exminster the bailiff's account for the year 1285-6 shows cider-making on a considerable scale. It was a regular source of revenue here. At Tiverton, in the same year, apples were being cultivated and sold (but no cider), and at Plympton a small quantity of cider is recorded as left over from the year before. The apples were grown in what was called the " apple garden " in each place.[3]

Hooker, in his unprinted *Synopsis Chorographical* (*c.* 1600), refers to the great abundance of all kinds of fruit in Devon, and to the careful management of orchards and apple gardens. In Elizabethan days cider— especially from the coastal parishes—was sold in large quantities for the provisioning of ships. A generation later, Westcote tells us that the Devonshire men had much enlarged their orchards of late, and " are very curious in planting and grafting all kinds of fruit." The *Compleat Cyderman* (1754) says that Devon then surpassed all other counties in the management of fruit trees; but by the end of the century this reputation had been lost, like so much else that had been good in the native husbandry.

Devonshire cream is also of great antiquity. We learn this incidentally from the fact that the dairies on the Tavistock abbey estates in the early 14th century had no churns for butter-making, but raised the famous clotted cream by scalding the milk.[4] The cream, when cold, was then stirred and butter produced in that way. The monks of Tavistock, and their tenants, were certainly familiar with clotted cream as a result of this process. Indeed, the process is so simple as to suggest that it was known in prehistoric times. It would save a good deal of controversy between Devon and Cornwall if one could say that it was discovered in the ancient and undivided kingdom of Dumnonia, but this is something we shall never know.

Like many other good things, clotted cream has disappeared from our tables in the last ten years. Shall we ever see it again? In our present lunatic economy, overpopulated and impoverished by great wars, we can no longer afford to buy it, though it was liberally consumed by our benighted medieval forefathers. Cider is, however, still made all over the county, and some of it must be as good as ever it was.

Devon to-day is predominantly a grassland county. In medieval times it contained much more arable. We can trace a slow transition from arable to pasture in the manorial accounts of the Tavistock abbey estates, which were almost entirely confined to the western part of the county. Out of 69 manorial accounts between 1298 and 1538, corn-sales predominate in 35, and this in a region largely devoted to grassland to-day. Down to 1427, pastoral sales take the lead in only four accounts out of 27. After that the picture is more confused, but by 1490 pasture farming begins to predominate, though " the equilibrium between the two branches of husbandry was never quite upset." The expanding cloth trade, especially in the later years of the 15th century, was bringing about " a gradual intensification of pasture-farming."[1]

There is no doubt that when Hooker wrote his *Synopsis Chronographical of Devonshire* sheep had become still more important. He remarks of the cloth trade that it depended very largely on local wool, and that the number of sheep in Devon was as great as, or greater than, in any other county in England, though they were not so apparent to the eye in the small hedged fields of Devon as they were in the more open country elsewhere.[2]

We must beware of assuming, however, that the multiplication of sheep meant anything like the wholesale and dramatic conversion of arable to pasture that we find in the Midlands at this time. Hooker implies on another page that the reclamation of the wastes, a movement that had been revived about 1500 with the renewed pressure of a rising population, produced additional ground for " tillage and keepinge of sheepe."[3] The sheep were probably grazed on the rough pastures, so abundant in nearly every part of Devon, and then folded on the newly reclaimed arable which their manure enriched and their feet trod down. Sheep meant a sound arable husbandry in Devon rather than an unbalanced pastoral economy.

Devonshire farming was well on the way, in Hooker's day, to earning the high praise that Cromwell bestowed upon it later: " I have been in all the counties of England, and I think the husbandry of Devonshire the best."[4] Not only could the county now feed itself, but it supplied the Elizabethan merchant and fishing fleets with great quantities of beef and pork, beer and cider, biscuits, beans, and peas. Hooker describes with what pains and labour new ground was brought into cultivation by the ancient process of " beating "—a process already well established in the 13th century, and probably much older than that[5]—and how the farmer suited his methods and manure to the nature of the ground. Besides the ashes derived from beating and burning the old turf, and the sea-sand, seaweed, straw, ferns, and other stable manure, the Devon farmer used marl and lime also. Low-lying and rushy ground—the " wet moors " that had been neglected until now—was reclaimed by drainage and then the application of soap-ashes and liberal liming. On the higher grounds, water was led in wherever possible. Wherever there were standing pools, they threw in dung and lime, stirred it with a staff, and carried the rich mixture through their fields and meadows. The " in-grounds " of every farm were wholly enclosed " with mightie greate hedges and dytches." This, too, was admirable, for the hedges yielded big timber and fuel, and the small hedged fields permitted the cattle to feed continually " upon a new springing grasse."[1] Moreover, the hedges gave good shelter to the stock, and the small fields meant that no cowherd or shepherd was required as in the open-field country.

THE STUART AND GEORGIAN FARMER

The typical farmer of Stuart times lived in an isolated farmstead, some distance from his neighbour, and a considerable distance from his parish church. His farmhouse, barns, and stables had probably all been rebuilt since 1580, and the buildings of his medieval predecessors swept away. He lived in the midst of his enclosed fields, arable and pasture, though his pasture was tending to become more important. In the higher parishes of mid- and west-Devon, extensive tracts of rough heath and moor separated him from his neighbours, and made social intercourse next to impossible for several months of the year. There were, however, more favoured parts, like the Vale of Exeter, the Torbay region, and the South Hams, where villages were more common, and where there was little isolating " waste." Here life was a more sociable business.

Apart from the industry and ingenuity with which the farmer tended and improved his lands, qualities which Hooker praises highly, the standard of Devonshire farming owed much to the terms on which the land was held. Hundreds of small gentry and substantial yeomen farmed their own freeholds, while for the tenant-farmer the lease for three lives or 99 years had become all but universal in Devon, giving him a security nearly equal to that of the freeholder. Indeed, the land-tax assessments of the 18th century and early 19th put him down as the owner and taxed him accordingly. It is true that farming " in severalty " like this made good farmers better and bad farmers worse than they would have been under a communal system of open-field farming, and the Devonshire system had its dangers. But in the 16th, 17th and early 18th centuries, anyway, it worked to the good, and Devonshire methods were copied elsewhere. Beat-burning as a method of reclaiming rough pasture was called " denshiring " in other counties. By the last quarter of the 18th century, however, critics of Devonshire farming had begun to make themselves heard, and it is apparent from the pages of Marshall, Fraser and Vancouver that it now left much to be desired.

The Milles MSS. in the Bodleian Library are full of valuable information about Devon agriculture in the middle of the century (c. 1755) given in the form of answers to a questionnaire. Dean Milles hoped to write a history of Devon, but never did so. Let us take a few parishes at random. Abbotsham, on the shores of Barnstaple Bay, was wholly enclosed except for some heath towards the sea. The fields were very small and almost all arable, worth about 10s. an acre. Not one acre in twenty was fit for meadow, but such meadow as there was fetched 20s. an acre. The manures used were lime, sand and dung. Wheat and barley did best, the greatest yields being twenty-five bushels of wheat per acre, forty of barley.

At West Alvington, in the extreme south of the county, the whole parish was enclosed. There were no downs or heath, and only twenty acres of coppice. Arable land was worth 14s. an acre, and meadow (excellent in this parish) 30s. For manure, 180 seams of sand and 160 of dung, per acre. The average wheat yield was fourteen bushels, of barley and oats, twenty. About 110 acres were under orchards, producing the famous South Hams cider.

At Ashreigney the changing order of rural society is revealed by the fact that the parish contained the ruins of three mansion houses and four medieval chapels. This had come about since the 16th century. In Hartland parish, too, we are told that Seckington was formerly a large village and now had hardly a house left. The same was true of the hamlets of Hendon and Firebeacon elsewhere in the parish.

Another change is brought out in the account of Egg Buckland, just north of Plymouth. "Manuring ground is the chief trade, and particularly in providing Cabbage, carrots, turnips, beans, and other Garden Stuff for Plymouth & the Dock." Of Bratton Clovelly, the rector knew next to nothing. He wrote up from St. Mabyn in Cornwall, after a long delay, to say he could give no information about his parish, nor did his curate know any more: a pretty pair of spiritual guides for a large parish to be encumbered with.

The general picture we get is that arable farming was still much more important than it is to-day, but one cannot detect from these accounts alone whether the standard of farming was going down. It is clear, however, that the consolidation of farms, which was one of the most obvious changes in the countryside during the 18th century, was resulting in a noticeable decay of " mansions," hamlets, and farmsteads in many parts of the county, and this may be part of the answer to the problem of what happened to Devonshire standards during that century. The abandonment of these large farms—for the " mansion " was usually the centre of a barton farm of two, three, or four hundred acres—by the actual owners in favour of life-lessees must itself have had some effect on farming standards, above all where the lessee had skinned himself to acquire the tenancy of such a large property. The consolidation of small farms generally must have meant, too, the abandonment of the intensive methods by which the small husbandman had cultivated his twenty, thirty, and forty acres, the methods that Hooker had commended so highly at the end of the 16th century. There must have been other causes, too, for this remarkable deterioration of standards, one of which —the taking of life-leases by men with inadequate capital—has already been touched upon.

The 18th century was by no means a tale of deepening decay. James Quartly (born 1720) and his three sons Henry, William, and Francis jointly perfected the famous North Devon breed of cattle.[1] To Francis Quartly falls most of the credit, in the forty or so years he ran the Great Champson farm (1793-1836). Arthur Young visited the farm in 1796 and formed a high opinion of the Quartly cattle. Fussell records that when cattle shows began at Exeter in 1831 other breeders carried off the prizes for a year or two, but then the aged Francis Quartly allowed his nephews to enter and they took the prizes in all the eleven classes. In the middle decades of the 19th century John Quartly farmed Champson and James Quartly West Molland, by far the biggest farms in the parish. The Davys were important breeders also, contemporaries of the Quartlys, and produced fine Devons at Rose Ash. One of the Davys edited the first volume of the *Herd Book* in 1851.

THE NINETEENTH CENTURY

The war years of 1793-1815 brought prosperity to the Devonshire farmers, as they did all over England, above all to the larger men who were able to buy their farms, where they did not already own them, and often neighbouring farms as well. In many parishes in these years we can trace from the land-tax assessments the steady rise in the fortunes of these big capitalist farmers.[2] The coming of peace altered all this. It meant the loss of the tremendous markets of the fleet and the army, the collapse of corn prices, and competition from imported wheat, Normandy butter, eggs, and poultry. All farmers had a bad time, but the big men had the capital reserves to weather the crisis of the 1820s while the smaller men had not.

Once more I may be allowed to say what happened to my own family in these years, for it is completely typical of so many family histories. They had farmed in east Devon since the 1580s, before that in west

Dorset for many generations. Often they had farmed on a considerable scale, and accumulated at times a number of leasehold farms besides their own smallish freeholds. George Hoskins (1773-1839) married well —the daughter of a big landowning yeoman at Payhembury—though he had no land of his own, and for many years he did well on a large farm just outside Sidmouth. Then came the great slump in farm prices after 1814. It hit him hard, with twelve children to feed and clothe. At last he was forced to give up his farm. In 1827 the parish register describes him as " Labourer " for the first time, and so he remained until his death twelve years later. His sons and daughters all dispersed. His eldest son, my great-grandfather, walked to Exeter, some time in 1825, learnt the baking trade, and set up in his own small business in 1834. This is the history of thousands of farmers and their sons in these years. When one looks through the census schedules of 1841 and 1851 at the Public Record Office, one sees how many of the shopkeepers of the Devonshire towns—especially of Exeter and Plymouth—had been born in the villages twenty miles about, but had been forced off the land into the towns, into an occupation which called for little or no capital, and no special knowledge or training.

The storm was weathered eventually, but Devonshire farming was not generally thought well of by Victorian observers. Henry Tanner, in a prize essay written in 1848, declared it was inferior to that of most other English counties. Caird, in 1850,[1] thought, however, that it had made great progress in recent years, although " the cumbersome and unskilful practices which rendered Devonshire farming a byword in the estimation of the great corn farmers of the eastern counties are still too frequently to be met with."

There is one voice that has not so far been heard, and that is the voice of the farm labourers, the largest class of all those on the land, but the most inarticulate; whose history is, therefore, the most difficult of all to write.[2] Not until 1843, in the *Report on the Employment of Women and Children in Agriculture*, do we hear the labourer and his wife speaking for themselves, telling of their hard lives from childhood onwards, apprenticed to farming even at the age of six. But no one in Devon noticed the degradation of a whole social class until Edward Girdlestone arrived at Halberton as vicar in 1863, from a living in Lancashire where the farm labourers were well paid, well housed, and well cared for.[3] At Halberton he found able-bodied, well-conducted men bringing up a family on a wage of 8s. a week, sometimes only 7s., with an allowance of cider so sour that no one else would drink it, and no privileges whatsoever in addition to their money wages. Wives were often employed as semi-slave labour, as a condition of giving the husband work. Meat was hardly ever seen on their table. At the age of forty-five or fifty, the man was crippled with rheumatism and feeble from years of under-feeding, and must inevitably end " on the rates."

The vicar tried private remonstrance, but to no effect. Then, one Sunday morning in March 1866, when the cattle plague was at its height, he preached in Halberton church to the hard-faced farmers and their wives from the text: " Behold the hand of the Lord is upon thy cattle." He asked them if they did not think that God had visited His judgment upon them for treating their labourers with less consideration than their cattle.[1] From that moment the battle was on. He was attacked by scurrilous and anonymous letters in the local newspapers, ostracised by local landowners and farmers. He and his family were persecuted and harassed in every conceivable way. Even his fellow clergy declared themselves against him. Only the Wesleyan minister of Halberton supported him. When the farmers seceded from the church, and turned to the chapel to continue their Christian devotions, the minister told them plainly they had better go back. So the farmers stayed at home on Sundays and thought up fresh mischief.

The upshot of all this was that the vicar began, with the aid of money and other practical help from sympathisers all over England, to organise a system of migration for the labourers. From October 1866 until June 1872, when he left Halberton, between 400 and 500 men, many with their families, were sent away to the north of England and elsewhere, some to the Manchester and West Riding police forces. From this small beginning, the work of one man and his family, a great movement grew. Men who prospered in the north got jobs for their relations and friends; and the flow from Devonshire stirred the labourers of the other south-western counties from their apathy. Soon they, too, were on the move; and to this migration system succeeded emigration to the United States and the Colonies.

Canon Girdlestone (as he afterwards became) was the pioneer of the agricultural labourers' movement. In 1872, under the leadership of Joseph Arch, they formed their first trade union, which took over from the canon the good work of organising migration and emigration; and within a few years the unspeakable farmers of Halberton were forced to behave like civilised employers. By 1880 wages in the village had advanced by 50 per cent, despite the depression in farming, the labourers' cottages were vastly improved, the National School had doubled its accommodation through the breaking of the farmers' grip on the rates, the whole village was more prosperous.[2] The work of Canon Girdlestone deserves to be better known: he was a Christian when so much of Devon was saddled with foxhunting " squarsons " who were only Christian in the sense that they had once been baptized. Yet these are the men whom the sentimentalists perpetually write about. Rarely does one see the name of Canon Girdlestone mentioned. For every one in Devon who has heard his name, there must be a hundred who know the names of the futile Parson Jack Russell and the infamous Froude of Knowstone.

FARMING AFTER 1870

Detailed agricultural statistics begin in 1866. From then onwards we can obtain an accurate picture of the state of Devon farming, and, moreover, during a period of great changes. In 1872 the arable of the county reached its maximum: just under 670,000 acres. There were just 400,000 acres under permanent grass in the same year.[1] Then came the great agricultural depression of the late 1870s and the 1880s. In Devon, as elsewhere, more and more arable was laid down to grass as prices fell; and in 1889 the area under grass exceeded that under the plough for the first time. But the total abandonment of land was not so marked in Devon as in most counties. Indeed, it was in 1894 that the area of " improved land," i.e. under crops and grass, reached its maximum of 73 per cent of the total area of the county. Thereafter it fell again, and in 1938 it was down to 67½ per cent.

When the statistics begin, wheat was easily the most important grain crop in Devon, occupying nearly four times its 1938 acreage. All over Britain the wheat acreage fell in the late 1870s and onwards, but it fell even more sharply in Devon. Most of the county is naturally unsuited to wheat, and it is now only grown where soil and climate are relatively favourable.[2] The barley acreage also fell, but that under oats—which is best suited to the damp climate of Devon—rose. By the early 1880s oats surpassed wheat in acreage and have remained ever since the first grain crop in Devon. The area of " improved land," too, began to slip back, above all in the Culm Measures country west of the Exe, where many improved fields were allowed to revert to moorland. A comparison of the first edition of the Ordnance map (1809) with that for 1933 shows fewer buildings on the Culm Measures, and more in the New Red Sandstone country.

Devon is unique in the number of its distinct breeds of cattle, sheep, pigs and ponies. The North Devon cattle—the famous " Red Rubies of the West "—are excellent dual-purpose animals. Those of South Devon— the " South Hammers "—are hardly less notable. Before the 1939 war Devon was the biggest cattle county in England and Wales, and second only to Northumberland among the English counties in numbers of sheep, of which the county had five distinct breeds.[3] Of ponies, the Dartmoor and Exmoor breeds had a fame far beyond the county boundaries.

At the beginning of the 20th century, Rider Haggard gives an excellent picture of the farming of the county in *Rural England*.[4] Farms

were generally small: large holdings were very rare. Often these farms
had been rented by the same families for generations, unlike the eastern
counties, but the sons were now being put to some other occupation, more
rewarding and less arduous. Farming had once offered big rewards in
the fertile lowlands. One 400-acre farm between Honiton and Exeter
had made a fortune of £40,000 for the tenant in the 1860s and 1870s;
but the man who followed him caught the draught of the great depression
and was reduced to ruin on the same farm.[1]

The yeoman class still survived strongly, owners of up to a thousand
acres apiece. Among the tenant-farmers, working 50–100 acres, were
many who had begun as labourers and had risen by the sheer hard work
which Rider Haggard found characteristic of most Devon farmers (as
Hooker had done long before). Though farming was depressed, things
were decidedly better in Devon than in the north and east of England.
With so much more pasture, labour costs were lower, and the fall in
corn prices not so crushing.

The acreage under arable in 1901-2 had in fact fallen by just over
100,000 acres since its peak figure of 670,000 acres in 1872.[2] From 1902
it continued to fall steadily, except for a slight rise in the war years of
1917-18. By 1938 the arable was down by another 150,000 acres, or by a
quarter of a million acres since the 1872 peak. Most of this had gone
over to permanent grass, but there had also been a lamentable increase in
the amount of rough grazing in Devon. Between 1894, when this figure
is first given, and 1938, the area under rough grazing trebled, rising from
124,000 acres to 366,000. These summary figures show the general trend
clearly enough:

	Arable (000 acres)	Permanent Grass (000 acres)	Rough Grazing (000 acres)
1870	642	372	[not given]
1880	641	510	[not given]
1890	593	615	[not given]
1900	576	634	157
1910	521	690	161
1920	522	640	197
1930	436	701	302
1938	415	710	366

On the eve of the Second World War, only one-quarter of Devon was
under tillage. The area under rough grazing was nearly as large as all
that under the plough. Out of every hundred acres, twenty-five were
arable, forty-two were under permanent grass, and nearly twenty-two
were rough grazing.

During the war of 1939-45 there was, in Devon as elsewhere, a large-scale conversion of permanent grass to arable of various kinds. By 1944 the total area under arable crops had risen to 596,000 acres (about 44 per cent over the 1938 figure), but it is notable that it still fell far short of the maximum arable acreage that the county had seen back in 1872.

In 1938 there had been rather more than 140,000 acres under grain crops, about one-third of all the arable. Oats, with 83,000 acres, were more important than all other grain crops put together; wheat was the second largest crop (30,000 acres); barley third (20,000 acres); and 8,000 acres of mixed corn made up the remainder. The war years saw large increases in all these acreages. That of wheat rose most: the acreage had more than trebled by 1943. The area under oats reached its maximum in 1942 at 145,000 acres. Barley did not reach its maximum until 1946, at 3½ times its pre-war acreage. The area under mixed corn continued to rise steadily in every year after 1939. With the rise in the arable area, there was a corresponding steady fall in the livestock population.

At the end of the war, the wheat acreage dropped dramatically. The first peacetime harvest was only one-third the acreage of that of 1944. Barley and oats fell more slowly, but the acreage under mixed corn continued to be extended. To-day the total acreage under grain crops is still half as high again as it was in 1938, but the total arable area has fallen by some 50,000 acres below its wartime peak of 1944.[1]

CHAPTER VI

THE TOWNS

THE EARLY TOWNS

THE towns of Devon demand a chapter to themselves. The vast area covered by the county, nearly eighty miles each way, called into being a multitude of market towns to meet the needs of each locality. Hooker speaks of thirty-eight market towns in Elizabethan days. Then again, Devon had more incorporated towns than the whole of Yorkshire by the end of the 17th century. And finally, there were the parliamentary boroughs of Devon, second only in numbers and political influence to those of Cornwall. In one way and another, as economic centres, as foci for local society, and as political communities, the Devonshire towns played a large part in the life of the county from the 13th century onwards, and every one had a peculiar and distinct history. We must, then, regard them as a special aspect of Devonshire history, worthy of separate attention.

The four *burhs* set up by Alfred in the late 9th century, for defence against the Danes, were Exeter, Lydford, Pilton, and Halwell. Pilton lay on a hill just outside Barnstaple, and Halwell lay six miles inland from the Dart estuary beneath the shadow of Stanborough Camp —a stone-walled Iron Age hill-fort. Within a century, Barnstaple had supplanted Pilton, and Totnes had supplanted Halwell. Each of these new *burhs* stood at the head of a navigable estuary and at the lowest crossing place of its river. This change probably reflects the growing importance of seaborne trade in the 10th century, especially as (like Exeter and Lydford) the new *burhs* were constituted as market towns and given mints of their own. Exeter coins are known from the reign of Alfred (871-99). The earliest known Totnes coin dates from the reign of Edgar (959-75), those of Barnstaple and Lydford from the time of Ethelred II (979-1016).[1] We may thus date the emergence of Totnes and Barnstaple as towns from about the middle or third quarter of the 10th century.

In all probability there had been a small settlement on each site before this date. At Barnstaple we know this was so, for the Burghal Hidage (*c.* 913), which refers to Pilton, says it was opposite *Bearstaple*. This identification suggests that Barnstaple was already a sizeable place. It was, however, indefensible on its flat site beside the river, and dangerously exposed to attack by water, whereas the village of Pilton on its steep hill commanded the whole estuary as far as the sea and could be defended against assault. Barnstaple had probably begun life as a small settlement where the crossing place of the Taw, fordable at low tide, was marked by a prominent *stapol* or post.

There is no documentary reference to Totnes before the coins begin. The name means " Totta's *næss,*" Totta being an Old English personal name, and the *ness* the ridge of hard ground that runs down from the castle site almost to the banks of the river. Such a site, just where the Dart begins to broaden out into an unfordable estuary, was almost certainly occupied before the 10th century.

The next town to appear was Okehampton. Here Baldwin, Norman sheriff of Devon, had put up a castle between 1066 and 1086, which he made his chief residence in Devon, and here he had just begun to create a borough when the Domesday survey was made. There were, in 1086, only four burgesses and a market, but the unmistakable marks of a borough were present. Lydford at the same date had sixty-nine burgesses, Barnstaple sixty-seven, and Totnes 110.

Probably none of these nascent towns was yet walled around. At Lydford, indeed, it is unlikely that stone walls ever superseded the earthen ramparts of the Saxon *burh*, which was decaying from the 12th century onwards (plate 11); its military importance had passed to Launceston and Okehampton, at both of which strong castles had been built soon after the Conquest; and most of its trade (such as it was in this bleak spot) had passed to Okehampton and Tavistock. Barnstaple appears to have been walled early in the 12th century and Totnes possibly about the same date.

There were in 1100, then, only five towns in Devon. With the 12th century we enter the great age of town-creation, the age in the main of the seignorial boroughs, not only in England but over a good deal of the Continent. In Devon the movement was as active as anywhere. By the middle of the 13th century no fewer than eighteen new towns had been created, more if we count the abortive creations. Altogether we can trace nearly seventy places in Devon which were called " boroughs " in the Middle Ages.[1]

The motive for the creation of a borough by the lord of a manor, at some commercially strategic spot on his land, was largely financial. He hoped, as trade increased in his new town, to enjoy an ever-growing sum of ready money in the form of burgage rents and of tolls from the markets and fairs held there. To have the command of liquid capital in the form of money—and more of it than he could hope to get from a similar area of farm-land—was becoming a necessity for any man of substance in the 12th and 13th centuries.

Not all these seignorial boroughs developed into towns. In the taxation lists of the early 14th century we find twenty boroughs regularly listed, but Bovey Tracey, Combe Martin, Kenton, and Colyford—though they had markets and fairs and burgage tenure—were never formally recognised as boroughs in the outside world. There were many other places which we find described as " borough " over a long period, such as Silverton, Sampford Peverell, Rackenford, and North Molton, in the northern half of the county, and Aveton Giffard and Chillington in the extreme south, to name only a few. These " village boroughs " are something of a puzzle. Mostly, perhaps, they represent optimistic speculations by the lords of rural manors which failed to come off. They had their markets, their fairs, and their burgesses from the 13th century onwards, but trade simply did not come their way. Either they were badly sited, or they had no productive hinterland.

Who populated the embryo towns? Who gave them a physical start, without which the foundation charter was an idle piece of parchment? The answer is that country people for miles around came in and took up burgage tenements from the lord, and engaged themselves in trade. The names of the taxpayers in the 1332 tax-rolls reveal this clearly. The larger the town, the wider the field it drew upon. Many of the Cornish flocked to the growing town of Plymouth and helped to fill it and found it securely. Most of the country people who filled the town were probably the younger sons of the numerous peasant-freeholders in the backwoods, who were free to leave the ancestral farm. Only the eldest son could succeed to the small peasant property: it was too small to divide up: and the other sons and daughters had to fend for themselves. The younger sons of the minor gentry (to use a rather anachronistic term) also went to town—there are Fulfords in Plymouth in 1332, Fursdons in Exeter, Aclands and Raleghs in Barnstaple, and Malstons in Totnes. Doubtless, too, many a man and woman of servile status slipped quietly away into the nearest town, escaped notice, and ultimately secured freedom and a living.

So, in the years before 1349, the great work of colonisation went forward: some pressing deeper into the woods, the moors, the heaths and the marshes, creating farms and fields out of the natural wilderness, others putting up shops and stalls, forges and mills and workshops, creating streets out of what had once been farmland. One son was up on the hillside a few miles away hacking at the edge of the waste; his brother was down in the town putting up a house and shop. They hailed each other on market-days and fair-days, when the town met the country on which its livelihood so often depended.

By the early 14th century, however, the four leading towns in Devon were all seaports—Exeter, Plymouth, Barnstaple, and Dartmouth in that order—though Exeter and Barnstaple were important market and fair towns also, drawing upon a wide and fertile hinterland. Both Plymouth and Dartmouth had developed rapidly after the marriage of Henry II with Eleanor of Aquitaine in 1152 had brought the rich provinces of south-western France under English control, a control which led to strong political and economic connections with south-western England. The Cornish port of Fowey also owes its rise to this marriage and its consequences; and Exeter, though farther away, felt the benefit in its oversea trade. The inward wine trade and the outward cloth trade were the city's most substantial support in the second half of the 12th century.

Inland lay a score or more of market towns, some—like Tavistock, South Molton, and Totnes—becoming centres of a cloth industry also, based upon the poor local wool. Most of these towns had fewer than 100 to 200 burgesses, that is, 500 to 1,000 people at the most. Lydford had only 200 or so people altogether, Bradninch perhaps 500. Totnes may have had something like 1,500 people in the early 14th century, Plymouth possibly 2,500. Exeter, the political, economic, and ecclesiastical capital of the south-west, is unlikely to have had as many as 4,000 people. These figures are bound to be approximate, but they serve to show in a rough and ready way how small the medieval towns were.

The successive epidemics of the Black Death hit Devon hard, as the fragmentary remains of the poll tax records in 1377 show. Exeter then had a taxed population of 1,560 persons. Its total population, including the clergy, who were separately taxed, was somewhere in the region of 2,400. Barnstaple and Dartmouth had slightly more than 1,000 people each; Totnes had shrunk to about 450, Plympton to 360, Modbury to 315, and Dodbrooke to as few as 170 inhabitants. And other epidemics had yet to come.

Despite the partial recovery of the Devonshire towns, the 15th century was on the whole a time of stagnation and difficulty for most of them. The country market towns were the most decayed: Crediton, Okehampton, Tiverton, Kingsbridge, Modbury, and Dodbrooke were all impoverished. Of the ports, Dartmouth was the worst hit, mainly because of the interruption of its overseas trade by the interminable war with France. The stannary towns of Tavistock, Plympton, and Ashburton, with the tin trade to help them out, suffered least of all, and all were able to rebuild or enlarge their parish churches during this time.[1]

This was the darkness before the dawn for the Devonshire towns:

the 16th century saw an astonishing rebirth for most of them, and the emergence of other towns that until now had been scarcely more than villages. This rebirth arose largely from economic factors—the complete recovery of the cloth industry and trade, a high level of tin production, the development of important sea-fisheries off the Devon coast, and the extension of fishing as far afield as Newfoundland; and to some extent it arose from the political situation. The emergence of Spain as the principal enemy of England gave an added importance to the Devonshire ports and harbours, above all to Plymouth, which had undergone a transformation by the end of the 16th century.

THE SIXTEENTH CENTURY

Industry and trade had begun to pick up in the 1480s from the long depression. By the early years of the 16th century the Devonshire towns were recovering some of the prosperity they had enjoyed two centuries before, though in many of them ruins were a conspicuous sight in the town scene. At Barnstaple, Leland saw, about 1540, the town walls " almost clene faullen " and the " manifest Ruines of a great Castelle " at the north-west side of the town. The chantry chapel at the town end of the medieval bridge was " profanid." But these were the ruins of an age that was passing away rapidly: town walls, seignorial castles, and chantry chapels, all were the relics of a vanishing civilisation. The suburbs at Barnstaple were now larger than the old town within the fallen walls. At Totnes, the town walls had fallen to their foundations, and most of Judhael's great castle was " clene in Ruine " except the massive circular keep we still see to-day rising above the clustered roofs of the town. In all the towns, too, there must have been tumbled-down medieval tenements, rubble-strewn gaps where houses had once been—how well we should recognise such scenes to-day!—for few of them had yet as many people as they had housed before the Black Death.

The tax levied in 1523 on all lay persons whose real or personal estate amounted to £40 a year or more[1] gives us some valuable information about the comparative wealth of the various towns at this time. Exeter still kept a long lead over the rest: it had sixty payers, nearly all wealthy merchants, whose assessments amounted in all to £6,520.[2] The next most wealthy town, surprisingly so, was Totnes, where there were thirty payers whose assessments totalled £2,965. Among them was the wealthiest merchant in all Devon—John Giles, assessed at £520, who was in the process of founding a landed family—three Saverys who were about to do likewise, and a number of other merchants who are clearly the younger sons of landed families making their way independently

—William Gilbert, John Bydlake, Richard Pomeray. Here the medieval pattern repeats itself.

Plymouth was the third wealthiest town. Though it was considerably larger than Totnes (about a third as large again as near as we can judge), it had only half as many wealthy merchants—fifteen of them, paying altogether on £1,734 a year. Among them were John Pownde, one of the biggest merchants in Devon at £410 a year; John Paynter (400 marks) in whose fine new house near the harbour Katherine of Aragon had been entertained on her arrival in England in 1501; and old William Hawkins, most renowned of all Plymouth men but not the richest, " worth in goods together with £140 in Spanish parts as merchandise . . . £150." It will be noticed that practically all of Hawkins's fortune was ventured on his trading enterprises. Three Plymouth men were richer than Hawkins, and another was as rich. But Plymouth did not compare with the compact wealth of little Totnes, founded largely on the cloth trade but derived in good part also from the moorland tin a few miles away.

The little east Devon town of Colyton comes fourth in this list with twelve assessments amounting to £660. Some of the names are possibly those of wealthy farmers in the rural parish around, but the biggest men —like the Strobridges—were merchants in the town. The same is true of Ottery St. Mary, where there were twelve payers.

Tavistock, flourishing on cloth and tin like Totnes, but with a great abbey also, came next with eight wealthy merchants. Richard Prideaux led with an assessment of £200, and next came William Hawkyns (£180) who is probably the father of " old William Hawkins " at Plymouth. And there was a Drake—Richard Drake—in this select list also. The association of Tavistock with Plymouth was very close: Plymouth was the port through which Tavistock cloth and tin reached the outer world. Similarly there was a close bond between Totnes and Dartmouth: five-sixths of Dartmouth's exports in Elizabethan days came from the Totnes merchants ten miles up the river.[1] Most of the money was up in Totnes. Dartmouth had five surtax payers compared with the thirty at Totnes, a perfect reflection of their respective shares in the export trade.

Barnstaple was somewhat larger than Totnes: its population was approaching 2,000 at this time, Totnes perhaps 1,600 or 1,700. But Barnstaple had only six well-to-do merchants assessed on £382 a year— barely an eighth of the Totnes figure. And Bideford, for all its ancient charter from the Grenvilles, had come to little. It probably had 700–800 people, and nobody of any wealth. Its great days, like those of Plymouth, were ahead. Most of the north Devon trade went through Barnstaple, but at Bideford the shipbuilding industry was already foreshadowed. Leland saw " a praty quik Streate of Smithes and other Occupiers for

Ship crafte beyond the bridge," and three miles down river the little town of Appledore—also destined to build ships—was just rising beside the wide, serene pastel-coloured pool where Taw and Torridge meet to flow outwards together over the thunderous Bideford Bar, out towards Lundy and the distant Americas whence the tobacco-ships were to come sailing in.

Inland, the old market towns of Tiverton and Crediton—so sadly decayed all through the 15th century—were coming up once more, their cloth trade slowly recovering. A generation of better times had produced three or four wealthy men in each. We recognise some of these names as those of large cloth merchants, such as John Greenway, the Tiverton merchant who so beautified the parish church there, assessed on £150 in the neighbouring parish of Huntsham where he must have bought a country estate. He, the new man, was much richer than the feudal squire of Huntsham.[1] And at Cullompton we find John Lane, assessed at 200 marks (£133 6s. 8d.), who was to glorify his own parish church with his munificence. Even so, these little woollen towns, that were destined to rise to wealth and renown on the " New Draperies " by the end of the century, were as yet only feeling their way.

There were other prosperous little towns, like the riverside port of Topsham, which acted as the outport of Exeter, still cut off by weirs from sea-borne trade. Topsham had four wealthy merchants, assessed at £300 between them—more than the four big merchants of Crediton. Like Appledore, it developed a shipbuilding industry; probably it had already begun to do so. But its chief source of wealth lay in the Exeter trade, just as Dartmouth depended on Totnes up the river, and Plymouth on Tavistock.

Newton Abbot, founded by the abbots of Torre in the early 13th century, was a busy market town, and so too was Plympton. South Molton had two or three rich clothiers, while in the neighbouring borough of North Molton Thomas Parker, assessed at 150 marks, was laying the foundations of a fortune that led on eventually to the earldom of Morley and to that great house of Saltram, just outside Plymouth. It is worth noting, however, that in 1524 many a purely country parish paid more in taxation than some of the smaller towns. Thus the fertile parish of Shobrooke, near Crediton, paid £19 6s. 2d., while the borough of North Molton paid £16 18s. 2d.; and Newton St. Cyres, in the red lands of the Creedy valley, paid £17 3s. 6d., as against the £11 6s. 6d. from Bideford or the £14 2s. 10d. from South Molton. The towns were growing prosperous, but the country parishes were still well populated and relatively still very important. Moreover, their prosperity was more evenly shared among the inhabitants of the parish, above all in the fertile districts where nearly every farm was fat and grateful.

The growing wealth and importance of the Devonshire towns brought about an increasing desire for complete self-government, for full incorporation as municipal boroughs:

" to be a free burgh; to have a free trade; to hold their town at ferme, that is, to receive all the issues of their town to their own use, and to pay the King a yearly rent for the same; to answer to the King for his dues *per manum suam*, by their own mayor bailiff or other compeer, without being subject to the distress and coertion of the sherif of the county, or other rough and powerful officer sett over their town; to have mayor bailiff and other officers, to be chosen out of their own body; to have a common-seal, a town-hall, a mace, fine gowns, and other gayeties; to have return of summonces and other writs, capacity to purchase lands to the common use of their town, and capacity for particular burgesses to bequeath or devise burgage-houses or lands by their last will."

These were the advantages of incorporation as Thomas Madox summed them up in his classic *Firma Burgi* (1726).[1] Later he puts them more concisely still: incorporation fitted the townsmen for a stricter union amongst themselves, for a more orderly and steady government, and for a more advantageous course of commerce: though he notes, too, that they sometimes " made ill use of these advantages. Their privileges and their prosperity did now and then dispose them to be insolent; and in particular to domineer over their weaker neighbours."

In Devon, Plymouth had been incorporated as far back as 1439, but it had been something of a special case—a vigorous, lusty town still held in bondage by the monastic house that had given it birth, until an act of Parliament set it free. Next to secure incorporation was Totnes, as we might expect, in 1505. The privileges conferred by King John's charter of 1206 were confirmed, and it was incorporated as the mayor and burgesses of Totnes, with various further privileges and no outside interference of any description.[2] The city of Exeter was next to be incorporated, in 1537. This, too, was substantially a recognition of its ancient status, but it was also erected into a county of itself with its own sheriff.

Torrington achieved incorporation in 1554, Barnstaple in 1557, Bideford in 1573, and South Molton in 1590, but the sequence does not stop there. Plympton followed in 1602, Bradninch and Dartmouth in 1604, Tiverton in 1615, and Okehampton in 1623. And then, after a long interval, Tavistock achieved incorporation in 1682.[3] Altogether, thirteen Devonshire towns were incorporated, only a small proportion of all the towns in the county but still considerably more than in most other English counties. Lincolnshire, somewhat larger than Devon, had only seven incorporated towns. The whole of Yorkshire had only twelve.

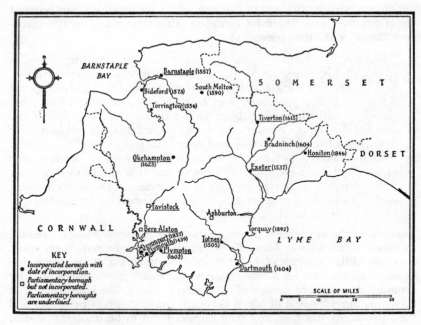

FIG. 7—PARLIAMENTARY AND INCORPORATED BOROUGHS

" Casual " parliamentary boroughs which returned occasional members at early dates and then ceased to do so have been omitted from the map

Tavistock was incorporated only for a brief period (1682-8) and has been excluded from the incorporated boroughs here

For the dates of parliamentary representation in each borough see the text (Chapter X)

Cornwall seems to have had fourteen incorporated towns, the most of any county in England.[1]

Most of the incorporated towns in Devon sent members to Parliament, though this was not a necessary consequence of incorporation. Bideford, Bradninch, South Molton, and Torrington sent no members. On the other hand, four boroughs—Ashburton, Bere Alston, Honiton and Tavistock—sent members but were not incorporated.* But sending members up to Westminster was much less important than the self-government of the borough by its own officers and the freedom from any interference by the sheriff of the county " or other rough and powerful

---

*Tavistock sent members to Parliament from 1295, but was not incorporated until 1682. Its charter of incorporation was annulled by James II in 1688, together with all other municipal charters granted since 1679.

officer sett over their town." There was, however, no pretence at democracy in the incorporated towns: the outstanding fact about their government was the complete control exercised by a small, self-perpetuating group.[1] This select group grew ever more shameless and corrupt, and out of touch with the burgesses at large, particularly during the 18th century and the early 19th. We see what a sorry state the government of the corporate towns had got into when we look at the report on municipal corporations published in 1835.

The Devonshire towns grew remarkably during the last generation of the 16th century and the first years of the 17th. The population of Barnstaple and its neighbour Pilton nearly doubled between 1560 and 1640; that of Bideford more than doubled in the same period. Tiverton doubled in numbers between 1560 and 1620. The city of Exeter was growing fast in the same years, while the parish register of St. Andrew's at Plymouth—the only parish in the town as yet—shows an even faster rate of increase. During the 1580s the number of baptisms in Plymouth averaged 141 a year; from 1600 to 1609 the average was 259. In the last quarter of the 16th century the population of Plymouth—now the most important English naval base for operations against Spain—more than doubled, rising from about 3,800 to about 7,800. Exeter had grown to about 9,000 people in 1600.

Tiverton probably had about 4,000 people at the same date and was the third largest town. It had emerged rapidly from its earlier obscurity as a feudal market town, dependent on the Courtenays' great castle, into the most vigorous of all the woollen towns. The " New Draperies " had transformed its life. Barnstaple, now a town of some 3,500 people, similarly owed its new impetus to the New Draperies, acting as the port for the clothing towns of South Molton, Torrington, and Chulmleigh in the adjacent countryside. Bideford, for all its fame under the Grenvilles, and despite its growth in numbers, still had only 1,100 people or so in 1600, but it was a busy little place and its shipbuilding industry was becoming notable. Already, in 1566, an Exeter merchant had had a ship of 250 tons built and furnished here, and in 1588 the port had sent merchant ships of 200 and 300 tons against the Armada.[2]

The flourishing towns of Elizabethan Devon were one of the chief glories of the county. Textiles, mining, fishing, and the provisioning of large areas around them: these were the economic foundations of the nearly forty towns that the county could now boast.

STUART AND GEORGIAN TOWNS

From about the middle of the 17th century we begin to get descriptions of the towns from various travellers, which help us to visualise better what they looked like. The tours of the Grand Duke Cosmo of Tuscany (1669), Celia Fiennes (1698), and Daniel Defoe (in the time of Anne), are particularly informative.[1] Exeter flourished as of old, and was only at the beginning of a new flowering of her merchant wealth. Plymouth was the largest and the wealthiest town after Exeter. In wealth she stood well under a half of Exeter, but in people probably well over a half. There were fewer rich men in Restoration Plymouth, and more poor.

The roaring Elizabethan days were over; the new naval dockyards that were to transform the town in the 18th century were still thirty years in the future. But Plymouth was far from being in the doldrums. Count Magalotti, who described Cosmo III's journey through England in 1669, puts it " among the best cities of England, having between twelve and fifteen thousand inhabitants." This is a great exaggeration—there may have been eight or nine thousand. " The buildings are antique," he goes on, " according to the English fashion; lofty and narrow, with pointed roofs, and the fronts may be seen through, owing to the magnitude of the glass windows in each of the different stories. They are occupied from top to bottom." Some of these tall Elizabethan and Jacobean houses still stand in the old part of the town near Sutton Pool, above all in New Street. This was called *Mr. Sperkes newe streate* in 1584 after the opulent Plymouth merchant, John Sparke, who was possibly responsible for building it. It was his grandson, Sir Jonathan Sparke, who had an estate of a thousand a year near the town, and who came in to pay his respects to the Grand Duke.

" The life of the city is navigation." Only women and boys were to be seen in the streets, most of the men living at sea. The town was well supplied with all the necessaries of life and several of the luxuries: " a great plenty of meat, cloth, and linen ": oysters from the sea in great abundance and of excellent quality, and salmon from Tamar and Tavy. And " silversmiths, watchmakers, jewellers, and other artists of this description are not wanting."

Celia Fiennes adds her own touch to the Plymouth scene thirty years later: " The houses all built of this marble [limestone] and the slate at the top looks like lead and glisters in the sun. There are no great houses in the town; the streets are good and clean, there is a great many tho' some are but narrow; they are mostly inhabitted with seamen and those which have affaires on the sea. . . ." She saw the very beginnings of Devonport, then called simply Dock. Work had begun on a new naval dockyard here, at the mouth of Tamar, in 1690: the first ship had used the dry dock in June 1695. When she saw it—having gone by water from Plymouth, the road being so bad—it looked " like a little town. The buildings are so many, and all of marble with fine slate on the roofs, and at a little distance it makes all the houses show as if they were covered with snow and glisters in the sun, which adds to their beauty." This was the beginning: within a hundred years Dock was to become the largest town in all Devon, surpassing even Exeter. The wars killed Exeter's commerce, but the naval base of Dock flourished, the dockyards extended farther north along the river front, and street after street went up outside the dockyard wall.

One of the most striking changes in the Restoration period is the decline of Totnes: second wealthiest town in Devon in Henry VIII's reign, by now somewhere about tenth, with less than a quarter of the taxable capacity of Plymouth. Neither Count Magalotti nor Celia Fiennes saw Totnes; Defoe's is the first description we have. " This is a very good town, of some trade; but has more gentlemen in it than tradesmen of note." Then follows a description of the salmon-fishing in the Dart, and of the subsequent dinner when they had six salmon-peal for a shilling. " This excessive plenty of so good fish (and other provisions being likewise very cheap in proportion) makes the town of Totness a very good place to live in; especially for such as have large families and but small estates. And many such are said to come into those parts on purpose for saving money, and to live in proportion to their income." Wise and sensible people: Totnes is still a good place to live in. Here we observe the early development of a " residential " town, now so common in Devon. One wonders when it began: perhaps after the Restoration when royalist gentry were nursing their depleted fortunes. Dr. Richard Pococke found it just as agreeable in 1750—" this town is a great thorow fare from Exeter to Plymouth, tho' not the post road; it abounds in good shops to supply the country, and has a cheap and plentiful market. The people are polite and generous."

In north Devon, Defoe reveals to us another interesting reversal of fortune. Barnstaple was going down; Bideford, of so little account until Elizabethan days, was coming up. " The first of these is the most ancient, the last the most flourishing," says Defoe, a change that had come about only of late years,[1] and mostly due to the silting up of the Taw at Barnstaple. " Biddiford is a pleasant, clean, well-built town "—so it is to-day, the most attractive town in north Devon, with its broad tree-shadowed quay fronting the lovely Torridge, the many-arched bridge, the emerald hills rising on the farther bank, the broad curlew-haunted estuary shining down to Appledore and above the bridge to the dark woods of Annery. Defoe saw it pretty much as it is to-day. " The more ancient street, which lies next the river, is very pleasant, where is the bridge, a very noble quay, and the custom-house. This part also is very well built and populous, and fronts the river for above three-quarters of a mile; but besides this, there is a new spacious street which runs north and south, or rather north-west and south-east, a great length, broad as the High Street of Excester, well built and, which is more than all, well inhabited with considerable and wealthy merchants, who trade to most parts of the trading world." This is Bridgeland Street, where several good houses of these ample years remain. Defoe also saw the usual large Dissenters' meeting house, a feature of most Devon towns at this time. The medieval bridge was so narrow—and apparently not wholly safe—that few carriages went over it. Laden carts and wagons preferred to wait for low tide and cross over the sand with greater ease and safety.

Bideford had more merchants, but Barnstaple had a greater inland trade. It was the chief landing place for Irish wool and yarn, which was sold in the great market to the serge manufacturers of Exeter and Tiverton, who came here to buy. Barnstaple " is a large, spacious, well-built town, more populous than Biddiford, but not better built. . . ."

There was little that was remarkable about the inland market towns. Ashburton was, to Celia Fiennes, " a poor little town—bad was the best inn." The borough of Colyford, founded so long ago by Thomas Basset, had only a shadow of life when Stukeley came upon it. Defoe would have passed it by disdainfully, but to Stukeley it was exciting as the probable site of the lost Roman station of *Moridunum*. " Here have been many inns and houses, and a considerable town. They talk of great stone vaults being found; so that it probably arose from the destruction of *Moridunum*, as Culliton adjacent, from it. Further, it was a corporation and they now keep up their claim by an annual choice of mayor, who has a mace too, but I suppose not of great elegance." As for Lydford, it is always a picture of decay in every century since Domesday. As far back as 1195 we find the Pipe Rolls recording payments " for making the king's market at Lydford as it used to be of old "—a vain struggle against the rise of Tavistock, Okehampton, and Launceston; and when Maton saw it in 1794 it had dwindled to " a small, shabby village."

A score of little market towns, places like Hatherleigh and Holsworthy, Chulmleigh and Chudleigh, all plodded quietly on for generation after generation, avoiding alike the ostentatious extremes of prosperity and of poverty. They were all about on a level—one or two thousand people, a good market, perhaps a big cattle fair once a year, a woollen industry that dwindled peacefully through Georgian days, some coach and wagon traffic if they lay on what passed for a main road in Devon, a collection of two, three, or four hundred houses of cob and thatch, mostly lined on either side of a very wide street or centred on a market square, with an uneventful history whose chronology revolved around the annual fair and at longer intervals the Great Fire: in earlier centuries it had probably been " the sickness time."

THE SEASIDE TOWNS

By the middle of the 18th century, travellers in Devon had begun to notice something new: the beginnings, though they did not know it, of what was to become the county's most important industry in the 20th century—the " holiday industry."

Exmouth was the earliest town of this new type. Dr. Pococke speaks of it in 1750 as " chiefly inhabited by fishermen and publicans, it being a place to which the people of Exeter much resort for diversion and bathing in the sea, and the situation is so pleasant, having beautiful little hills to the east finely improved, and a view of the fine country on the other side, that some persons of condition have come to live at the place, which they are improving by a gravel walk to the river, and they are going to make a bowling green." According to Polwhele the fame of Exmouth was spread by " one of the judges of the circuit, in a very infirm state of health [who] went thither to bathe, and received great benefit from the place ". This was somewhere about the beginning of the 18th century. The judge's praise brought Exmouth into repute with the well-to-do of Exeter, and thence the whole county. By the 1790s it was the most frequented watering-place in Devon. Mr. Rolle of Bicton—who owned the manor —began to build the houses on the Beacon in 1792, still the most attractive piece of Exmouth architecture, and an assembly room appeared soon afterwards. The houses on the Beacon were being let at from three to seven guineas a week in 1809, says Farington.[1]

Sidmouth began to come into favour in the last quarter of the 18th century. In 1794 it was " much frequented in the bathing season, and many families continue their residence even during the winter. The situation is certainly a delightful one." The mildness of the winter climate made Sidmouth especially popular among the upper and upper-middle classes during the Napoleonic Wars when foreign travel was restricted, and by 1809 a small house on the sea-front could be let for five guineas a week. This was considered moderate, however, when compared with the eight to ten guineas one paid for a house on the Kentish coast.[2]

To the west of the Exe, Teignmouth was the oldest watering-place. Lysons says it was " much frequented as a bathing place, and has all the requisite accommodation for invalids." It had become fashionable, and had begun to grow, about the middle of the 18th century. Dawlish, a much more attractive little place, began to draw summer visitors in the early 1790s. Maton (1794) speaks of it as " a neat, new village, not frequented by summer visitors until within the last two or three years."[3] The reason for the comparatively late start of Dawlish, as compared with Teignmouth, was that the old village lay the best part of a mile inland,

and there was no accommodation nearer the sea until lodging-houses
could be built down the little valley. By 1809, the first edition of the
Ordnance Survey shows that houses had been built all along the north
side of the stream (so as to catch all the sun) right down to the sea.
On the south side there were no houses as yet, except a small cluster
immediately behind the beach. There are still many attractive little
houses of this period along the Strand at Dawlish; and the parish
church has many memorials to strangers who came to seek health and
died here.

At the opening of the 19th century there were only four watering-
places on the Devonshire coast—Exmouth and Sidmouth to the east of
the Exe, Dawlish and Teignmouth to the west—and all were small and
select. Perhaps we should count Tor Quay as a fifth, for it had begun to
attract summer visitors about the same time as Dawlish. " Torquay far
exceeded our expectation in every respect," says Maton in 1794. "Instead
of the poor, uncomfortable village that we had imagined, how great was
our surprise at seeing a pretty range of neat, new buildings, fitted up for
summer visitors, who may certainly here enjoy convenient bathing, retire-
ment, and a most romantic situation."[1] But the parish of Tor Mohun,
in which Torquay lay, had only 800 or so people in 1801. The real
development of Torquay, as an all-the-year-round resort, dates from the
Napoleonic Wars. The fleet was often obliged to anchor in Tor Bay in
these years, before the building of Plymouth breakwater made the Sound
safe in all winds, and officers' wives sought accommodation on the
sheltered north side of the bay. By the 1820s it had developed into a small
town of about 2,000 people. The end of the war did not end its life
as a residential resort, for, when the officers' wives went, it was discovered
by the invalids who needed a mild winter climate, and along this lucrative
path the town developed rapidly in mid-Victorian years.

The north coast resorts were developed somewhat later. They were
cooler and less relaxing than those of the south coast. Ilfracombe seems
to have been discovered after the Napoleonic Wars: by the 1820s it was
much frequented for the bathing and made " an agreeable summer-
residence."[2] In the 1831 census the half-dozen seaside resorts showed a
curious uniformity of size—all except Teignmouth numbered between
3,000 and 3,600 people. Teignmouth, with some coastal trade to give
other employment, had 4,688 inhabitants. It is clear that the watering-
places of Devon were still more or less select preserves. Until the coming
of the railways and the wider spread of popular holidays there could be
no great transformation from the " watering-place " to the " holiday
resort."

Lynmouth was just beginning to be generally known, like Ilfracombe,
in Lysons's day. It was a small fishing village, but the herring fishery had

much declined in recent years. Otherwise it carried on only a small coastal trade from its little quay—coal, anthracite, and limestone coming in, oats and oak-bark going out. Fortunately, summer visitors began to replace the herrings. Here, too, a few well-to-do pioneers had found a quiet retreat when the Continent was closed to them. Among these were the Marchioness of Bute and Mr. Coutts the banker. Mr. William Litson, son of the local schoolmaster, saw the possibilities of the new development and began to furnish cottages for visitors. In 1807 he opened the first hotel; and visitors also began to build cottages for themselves.[1] The most rapid growth took place in the thirties and forties. White's *Directory* for 1850 reports that both Lynton and Lynmouth " have been much improved during the last twenty years " and now contained many neat villas and commodious lodging-houses (plate 13).

Clovelly had yet to be discovered. There, too, the herring fishery by which the village had lived since Elizabethan times had greatly fallen off by the 1820s: the fishing season now lasted only two months. Nor had visitors found it even by 1850. White makes no mention of them at that date. The population of the village was falling all through the 19th century, from the 1840s onwards. Murray's *Handbook to Devon and Cornwall* was recommending Clovelly to the discerning traveller from the 1850s, but only the solitary visitor is envisaged—" here the traveller should rest a day at the little inn, which will entertain him with great hospitality." The 1895 edition of the *Handbook to Devon* reveals that this solitude was ended: there were now three hotels and several lodgings. " The picturesqueness of the place is, however, not improved by the cards announcing ' hot water for tea ' and other refreshments which greet us at almost every step in the main causeway " and by the flood of excursionists just disgorged from the excursion steamer down at the old pier. In spite of Murray's pained remarks, Clovelly remained unspoilt and " undeveloped " by reason of the autocratic rule of the Hamlyns at the Court, and so it remains to-day. Romantic and picturesque are still the only adjectives that properly describe it, even in the crowded height of summer (plate 58).

The watering-places became transformed into holiday resorts with the increasing penetration of railways into rural Devon, and with the institution of the Bank Holiday and Sunday School " treats ". Discriminating visitors withdrew beyond the railways into remoter parts like Hartland Quay on the north coast, or Torcross on the south, where they remained undisturbed until the advent of the motor-car and the motor-coach.

Some of the seaside towns set out to develop this new industry of the summer visitor or the daily visitor (the " tripper "), especially those that lay near big towns, like Exmouth. Others, such as Torquay, offered no encouragement to these transitory holiday-makers and preferred to remain the more or less exclusive preserve of the middle-class invalid and the winter resident. Torquay in 1890 is described as " the Queen of Western Watering Places, and the Montpellier of England ". Now a town of nearly thirty thousand people, it had been developed in a seemly and orderly way by the fortunate Palks, who owned most of its soil, and it stretched back over the promontory to Babbacombe. It had swallowed up the old villages of Tor Mohun and Upton, and was about to engulf St. Mary Church and Babbacombe. Around the headland, facing south, had grown up those long winding drives, following the contours of the wooded hill, dotted with stuccoed mid-Victorian villas; a prosperous Victorian middle-class town.

A little farther round the bay, the village of Paignton had begun to develop in the 1840s as a resort for invalids, though it faced east and not south like Torquay, and was obliged to call its climate " bracing ". Perhaps it was this that led to the development of Paignton along different lines, as a family resort for summer holidays. Torquay was stuffy in summer (in more senses than one). Paignton was fresher and had a good beach. By the end of the century it had over 8,000 people and it welcomed the new holiday-making class from Exeter and Newton Abbot. During the sixties, seventies and eighties it was rapidly " developed " in building estates, the swamp and sand on the seashore were reclaimed to form public pleasure-gardens, and the old village, formerly half a mile or more inland, now stretched continuously to the sea. The popular seaside town of Exmouth had also been developed rapidly from the 1830s and had more than 10,000 people by 1900. Further eastwards, Budleigh Salterton, Sidmouth, and Seaton all remained small and quiet, chiefly because their pebble beaches attracted no families with children.

West of the Exe, Dawlish stayed small, despite its sandy beach. Exeter people went mostly to Exmouth, and Newton Abbot to Teignmouth and Paignton. Beyond Dartmouth the coast was more or less inaccessible, and right around to Plymouth one found only little fishing villages known to a few visitors and artists. Salcombe was the only place more generally known. On the north coast, Ilfracombe had grown to about the same size as Paignton. Already, by 1895, Murray's *Handbook to Devon* complains that " the railway from Barnstaple has given increased facility for reaching it; and those who desire quiet and comparative solitude will do better to pitch their tents at Westward Ho or at Lynton."

THE INLAND TOWNS IN THE 19TH CENTURY

The seaside towns of Devon flourished increasingly throughout the second half of the 19th century; the inland towns almost generally decayed. The woollen manufacture, which had helped to support so many of them for centuries, finally died, except in two or three isolated places where it was kept alive by the energies of a particular family, as at Buckfastleigh and North Tawton. Buckfastleigh was a prosperous little town all through the century. In 1890 there were still five woollen mills at work. Trade was so active that the railway traffic from Buckfastleigh station was exceeded only by that at Plymouth, Exeter and Torre, and was greater than that of Newton Abbot and Torquay.[1] Chagford also had the remnants of a woollen manufacture, but its Dartmoor tourist trade was already becoming more important by the 1880s.

The collapse of the mining industry affected other towns. Tavistock reached its maximum population in the 1860s and then lost more than 4,000 people in the next forty years as mine after mine closed down. Many went off to the coal-mines in the north of England, others to the mines of Australia and the United States. At North Molton the copper and iron mines were abandoned one by one, and the town fell into a torpor.

The coming of the railways killed many of the old market towns, though it gave a temporary stimulus to some by providing much-needed employment for a few years. So many of the little towns lay in hilly or inaccessible country. The railways kept to the valleys, and towns like Chulmleigh and South Molton and Ashburton were by-passed or tapped only by a branch-line at a late date, too late to do much good. Chulmleigh had lost its woollen industry by the end of the 18th century and depended on its three cattle fairs and a weekly market. It grew slowly down to the 1850s, reached a maximum of some 1,700 people, and then fell in the next two generations to fewer than 1,200. The North Devon Railway (opened in 1854) took away its cattle and sheep markets to Eggesford and South Molton Road stations, down in the valley.

Similarly, South Molton reached its peak in 1851, and then fell in numbers for the next half-century as new markets were opened up at Eggesford and Molland. In 1901 the town was back in numbers where it had been a hundred years before, and was less prosperous. Crediton in 1901 had a thousand fewer people than in 1801. The railway had brought the bigger markets of Exeter within twenty minutes' journey instead of two hours by road, and the local markets suffered at once. Ashburton, too, was smaller at the opening of the 20th century than at the beginning of the 19th.

All over Devon the ancient market towns decayed during the second half of the 19th century as the railways destroyed their *raison d'être*, their original function which had sustained them ever since the 12th century. Either the railways brought wholly new markets into existence in more accessible places, or they killed the local markets, which had had a hinterland of seven to ten miles, by bringing them into competition with the bigger markets and shops of places like Exeter, Plymouth and Barnstaple.

By killing, too, the coach and wagon traffic of the smaller towns, the railways ruined all the businesses that depended on it—the inns and public houses, the saddlers and harness-makers, the blacksmiths and wheel-wrights, the corn and forage merchants, and others. One has only to study *White's Directory* for 1850 or *Billing's Directory* for 1857 to see the variety and vigour of life in the little market towns before the railways had reached out towards them.

How different they are to-day, these silent little places with their peeling plaster, where cats bask on sunlit window-sills and prostrate dogs hardly bother to stir as an occasional car makes a détour around them in the road; the silence of a summer afternoon broken only at vast intervals by the short pang-pang of the church clock; the sun on the bleached blinds of the draper's shop, the wasps crawling wearily over the dried-up buns in the bakery and the sticky jars of sweets. No more three-day fairs, no more brisk markets every week for corn and cattle, sheep and provisions; no more cloth merchants and weavers, no more tin-miners and copper-miners; no more masons and quarrymen, ostlers and coachmen; no more the ring of the smithies up and down the street, the great stamping horses and the glossy cattle: but only the dusty black cats, the comatose dogs, and the eternal wasps.

Apart from the seaside resorts, only three towns grew noticeably during the second half of the 19th century—Plymouth, Devonport, and Exeter. Plymouth had about 22,000 people at the end of the Napoleonic Wars. Another 30,000 crowded into it in the next generation (by 1851) and in the following fifty years the population doubled again. Plymouth passed the 100,000 mark in the last years of the century. She had a variety of trades apart from shipping,[1] and the extension of the railway network made her a great market and shopping town for eastern Cornwall as well as south-western Devon. Hundreds of acres of dreary grey streets —cold grey limestone or drab-washed stucco—spread over the hills and hollows all the way to Devonport and Keyham.

The ending of the long wars slowed up Devonport's dramatic growth. In 1815 some 32,000 people lived here. The great naval dockyards, their ancillary trades, and the legions of small shopkeepers made up the economy of the town, by far the largest in Devon. Growth was slow up to the Crimean War; the population had only just touched 40,000 by that date. After this temporary stimulus, which brought numbers up to 50,000 by 1861, there was a fall through the peaceful sixties and seventies; and then, with the expansion in the size of the Navy and the growth in size of ships, came a great extension of the yards and a corre-sponding rise in the numbers employed there. In 1901 Devonport had just over 70,000 people, and was the second largest town in Devon. At Exeter, life went placidly on without any spectacular change: the population just about doubled in the first half of the 19th century, but then remained almost stationary through the 1850s, 60s, and 70s. In the late Victorian years there was a more noticeable increase; but in 1901 the city was less than half the size of Plymouth and only about two-thirds the size of Devonport.

CHAPTER VII

INDUSTRY AND TRADE

DOMESDAY makes no mention of anything that can be interpreted as an industry in Devon, but by the end of the 12th century it is apparent that both the cloth industry and the tin trade were well established. To these must be added the widespread medieval industry of quarrying, particularly important in a county so rich in building-stones. This industry was very active from the second half of the 12th century onwards, judging by the evidence of surviving buildings. The history of quarrying is best dealt with, however, in a later chapter.[1]

THE EARLY CLOTH TRADE

Of the cloth trade in Devon little is known before the closing years of the 13th century. Apart from purely local centres which met only local needs, the English cloth industry was concentrated almost entirely in the larger towns in the 12th century. In Devon, Exeter was the earliest centre. A record of payments made to the Crown by the cloth towns in the year 1202[2] shows that Exeter then ranked seventh in importance, equal to Stamford, Newcastle and Gloucester, and more important than Norwich and Coventry. Totnes also had a cloth manufacture at an early date. By 1253 its russet manufacture was sufficiently well known and reputable to provide the cover for the king's bed,[3] a fact which suggests that the manufacture may have been in existence for a generation or two before that date.

The invention of the fulling-mill, which made use of water-power, brought about a rapid dispersal of the industry into the countryside during the 13th century, a movement so pronounced that it has been called " an industrial revolution."[4] Devon was rich in tumbling streams, and by the early 14th century many of these were turning at least one fulling-mill. The earliest reference to fulling-mills yet found in Devon—where they were usually known as tucking-mills—occurs in an assize roll of 1238, which mentions a fulling-mill at Dunkeswell in a remote valley of the Blackdown Hills. This probably owed its origin to the influence of the abbey, founded here a generation earlier. In 1244-5 we hear of fulling-mills at Honiton and Tiverton; and before the end of the 13th century we find them at Chulmleigh, Sampford Courtenay, Hartland (two), Harpford, and Moretonhampstead. By 1327 others have appeared at Barnstaple, North and South Molton, Crediton, Chudleigh, Slapton, and Bovey Tracey.[1] Most of the small towns of Devon seem to have been centres of a cloth industry by the time of the Black Death, and some of the larger villages also. The appearance of the surname Tucker in the tax assessment of 1332 is good evidence of the existence of a fulling-mill wherever it occurs.

The accounts of the aulnagers, whose duty it was to examine all cloth offered for sale and to see that it conformed to the requirements of the law, throw some light on the distribution of the cloth industry in Devon at the end of the 14th century.[2] In the account of 1394-5 we find 75 sellers of cloth, who between them handled 6,738 " dozens " of narrow cloth. These " dozens " were small cloths, twelve yards long by one wide, whereas the " cloth of assize " was twenty-four yards by two. Four Devonshire dozens were therefore equivalent to one cloth of assize. The 75 Devonshire cloth merchants between them sold the equivalent of 1,684½ cloths of assize in this year; but the three leading merchants—all Barnstaple men—sold 615 of these, well over a third of the total trade. Exeter paid subsidy on 707 cloths of assize in the same year and was still the most important centre of production. The fourth largest merchant in the county seems to have been a Culmstock man, who disposed of 90 cloths.

Some idea of the magnitude of the Devonshire cloth industry at the end of the 14th century may be gathered from the aulnagers' totals for the years 1394-99. During these five years, the Devon merchants sold 8,235½ cloths, those of Exeter 2,828½; the whole of Cornwall sold only 205. This represents an annual sale of over 100,000 yards of cloth.[3] The industry was most active in north Devon and around Exeter to judge by these accounts. The two hundreds of Braunton and Sherwill, together with Barnstaple, accounted for half the Devon sales in 1396-97, excluding Exeter. Exports went chiefly to Gascony, Brittany, and Spain.

The early Devon cloths, known generally as " straits ", were rough and coarse, but during the late 15th century the manufacture of finer cloths, known as kerseys, was developed in addition. The production of the older and coarser cloths became confined to the western side of Dartmoor, where the wools were poorer in quality, Tavistock being the most important centre on this side. Totnes grew rich on the newer and finer cloths. It seems also that the introduction of the kersey manufacture led to the rise of the east Devon towns as cloth centres, particularly Tiverton, Crediton and Cullompton. At Tiverton John Greenway (d. 1529) was the most eminent of the early merchants, at Cullompton John Lane (d. 1529). Both beautified their parish churches by the addition of splendid aisles. At Crediton the Northcotes and the Davies made their fortunes in the cloth trade. From Robert Davie sprang the Davies of Creedy Park, just outside the town, where they still flourish.[1] From Walter and John Northcote sprang the Northcotes of Hayne in Newton St. Cyres, and ultimately the earldom of Iddesleigh. Their medallion portraits adorn the fine monument of John Northcote of Hayne (1570-1632), grandson of Walter and son of John, in Newton St. Cyres church. At Totnes, an incredibly wealthy little town in the 16th century, John Giles—the richest merchant in Devon—was laying the foundations of the family of Giles of Bowden; and Christopher Savery was founding the Saverys of Shilston.

In the late 15th century the Devonshire cloth industry seems to have contracted considerably in scale. The aulnagers' accounts for 1467-78 suggest that sales were well under half of those in 1394-99, and that Devon was as low as tenth among the clothing counties in order of importance. Suffolk, Somerset and Yorkshire were the first three, in that order.[2]

The introduction of the kersey manufacture towards the end of the century altered the whole picture. Within a hundred years Devon became one of the leading textile counties. The figures of the cloth customs from the various ports of the kingdom during the reigns of Henry VII and Henry VIII are the nearest reliable indication we can get of the increasing importance of the cloth industry in Devon, though it must be remembered that they reflect only the amount of cloth that entered into foreign trade and not the total output of the industry. London and her outport of Southampton between them accounted for over two-thirds of the national cloth customs between 1485 and 1509. Newcastle and Bristol were the leading provincial ports, with Exeter-Dartmouth only a little way behind Bristol.[3] Indeed, if we include the figures for the port of Plymouth-Fowey the total cloth customs of the Devon ports exceeded those of Bristol.[4] At Bristol the average of the cloth customs from 1485 to 1509 was £1,273 per annum; for the Devon ports as a whole it was £1,624. During the reign of Henry VIII the Devon cloth customs showed a slightly lower total, the annual average falling to £1,489, but Bristol was down, too, and the Devon ports ranked after London and Southampton. They formed the most important group of cloth ports in the provinces. On the other hand, it should be said that the cloth customs from Devon were only about 6 per cent of the national total between 1485 and 1547.

London's share was so overwhelming that none of the " outports " made much of a showing in comparison.

THE GREAT DAYS

About the year 1570, or shortly before, the " new draperies " made their appearance in England. These were light fabrics of the worsted type, which were first made in the Flemish towns. Flemish refugees, driven out by Alva from 1567 onwards, brought the new manufacture across to East Anglia, where the government welcomed it. It was exempted from the general regulations governing apprenticeship, and not until 1594 was it brought under inspection and taxation by the aulnagers. The new fabrics had reached Devon by the closing years of the 16th century, though probably only in and around Barnstaple at first, where Westcote tells us that bays were being made in his time. Elsewhere in Devon the kersey manufacture was too profitable to divert attention from it for a long time to come.

Soon after 1600 another valuable branch of the new draperies had appeared in Devon—the manufacture of serges or perpetuanos (so called for their long-wearing qualities). This trade was destined to oust all others by the end of the 17th century, but it seems at first to have been confined to Exeter and its immediate neighbourhood. Tiverton still concentrated on the kersey trade. Tiverton kerseys were known by that name all over the kingdom, and were chiefly sent to London for export. It was in this trade that Peter Blundell (1520-1601), the most eminent of all the great Devon clothiers, made a humble start and eventually amassed a fortune of some £40,000. His career was typical of that of many clothiers in the early days, when risks were great and profits high. Dunsford reckons that the profits on the kersey trade were little less than a hundred per cent in these years.[1] No wonder the successful merchants made a fortune in a few years, and were able to build up large landed estates, to which they could retire comparatively young.

Crediton also specialised in kerseys in the 17th century, and was pre-eminent for fine spinning. Totnes and the district around it went on making " a sort of coarse cloth which they call narrow-pin-whites; not elsewhere made ", and was dying out as a cloth centre. The civil wars seem to have finished it off as an industrial town. Neither kerseys nor the new draperies caught on at Totnes for some reason. Tavistock also kept to the older and coarser cloths, but developed something of a serge manufacture by the 18th century. In north Devon, Barnstaple and Torrington made " bays, single and double; frizadoes and such like."

A number of smaller towns concentrated on spinning for the weaving districts elsewhere in the county. By the end of the 17th century this specialisation was most pronounced. The principal spinning districts were to be found around Barnstaple and Bideford, the receiving ports for Irish wool; between Dartmoor and Bodmin Moor (as at Launceston, Liskeard, and Tavistock); and on the eastern side of Dartmoor around Ashburton. The manufacturing area proper (weaving, fulling, and dyeing) lay to the north, north-east, and west of Exeter, in a belt extending from Taunton across to North Tawton.

With the Restoration, the Devonshire cloth industry expanded vigorously, turning increasingly to the manufacture of serges for the Dutch, German, and Spanish markets. Holland had supplanted Spain as the most valuable customer for Devonshire woollens by the 1680s, perhaps a little earlier. Even at Tiverton the serge manufacture eventually killed the kersey trade on which the town had grown, since the late 1400s, to be the largest industrial centre outside Exeter. Dunsford records that serges were first made at Tiverton for the Dutch market about 1690 and within twenty years had completely ousted the kersey manufacture.[1] The whole countryside for ten or twelve miles around worked for the Tiverton trade, in spinning and weaving. In the town itself no fewer than fifty-six fulling-mills were at work in 1730. Defoe, of course, went out of his way to see such a triumph of commerce and rhapsodised over it in his usual manner.

For the space of a generation or so, down to 1715, the Devonshire serge manufacture was the most important branch of the great English woollen industry, certainly in the field of exports. Holland, Germany, and Spain were the biggest customers; Exeter—with Topsham—was the port through which nearly all this vast trade flowed.[2] Dartmouth had lost nearly all its woollen trade with the decline of Totnes, though some of the Ashburton serges went that way; and Barnstaple and Bideford mostly received the raw wool but exported few manufactured goods.

THE DECLINE OF THE CLOTH INDUSTRY

The long war that was ended by the treaty of Utrecht, in 1713, greatly damaged the Exeter trade upon which the woollen industry of the whole county depended for its livelihood. Both the Dutch and the Spanish trades were much reduced. By the 1720s the competition of Norwich " stuffs " was pushing the Devonshire serges out of the Spanish market; by the 1740s the same thing was happening in the Dutch trade; by 1750 the steady German trade was going the same way.[3] This reversal of fortune was largely due to a change of fashion. Just as serges had "come in " during the 1670s, so Norwich stuffs were coming in now. The Norwich manufacturers had learnt to produce a finer fabric and to sell it more cheaply than serges.

No real alarm was felt in Devon until the staple Dutch trade began to show signs of falling off in the 1740s. Unemployment now appeared in the woollen towns on a scale not experienced before. An enterprising Tiverton manufacturer, taking a weaver with him, went off to Norwich to learn the secrets of the " stuffs " trade. " About the time they had effected their purpose," says Dunsford, " the manufacturers of Norwich suspected their design; and it was with great difficulty and hazard that they escaped from the city. Had they fallen into the hands of their pursuers, it probably would have cost them their lives."[1] They returned to Tiverton, and a manufacture of Norwich stuffs and other fabrics was started in 1752. At first this was highly successful, giving employment to several hundred people, but it collapsed suddenly in 1761 (no reason is given) and produced great distress in the town and surrounding country. Attempts were made to reduce costs by importing Irish worsted yarn already combed and spun, but the woolcombers of Tiverton fought the masters who bought it and the weavers who used it.[2] The continual wars of the 18th century, by closing the overseas markets for years at a time, added greatly to the burden of adjustment to changed economic conditions.

The ending of yet another war in 1748 brought improved prospects for the moment, especially with the growth of a new trade to Italy in the middle years of the century. By 1763 this trade had taken first place; but the German trade was collapsing in turn, and the Dutch trade was worth only about a half of what it had been in the days of Queen Anne. At Tiverton, which had reached the height of its glory during the early years of the reign of George II, the poor rates more than doubled between 1720 and 1780.[3] All the woollen towns were suffering to a proportionate degree. Even in the remote country districts the spinners and weavers who worked for the merchant manufacturers of the town became an increasing burden on the parochial poor rates. A study of the overseers' account-books shows the rates rising steeply in parish after parish, almost without exception. As early as 1755 we hear of symptoms of decay in the answers returned to Dean Milles of Exeter for his projected history: at Ashprington " there were clothiers formerly, now none," and at Chulmleigh the woollen trade " did flourish here but is now much decayed," and similarly from many parishes.[4] The interminable wars of the 18th century were not the only cause of the decline in the Devonshire industry. To the competition of the Norwich stuffs, keenly felt by the middle of the century, was added the even more formidable competition of the Yorkshire trade, which by the 1780s was turning to steam-power based on cheap coal and organising itself in ever larger units. Simultaneously came the devastating competition of cheap cotton goods.

The War of American Independence delivered another heavy blow to the Devonshire trade; and then the prolonged war with France, beginning in 1793, gave the death-blow—or would have done had not the East India Company intervened at the most critical period. By buying Devonshire serges and dumping them in the Chinese market at a heavy loss for the best part of fifty years the Company kept the industry alive on a reduced scale.[1]

This artificial respiration was valuable. Even when the Company's monopoly was broken in 1833 and the China trade was thrown open— so putting an end to these uneconomic contracts—the woollen industry survived. In 1838 there were still thirty-nine woollen mills in the county, employing more than three thousand looms in weaving serges. Some 700 looms were at Buckfastleigh, another 660 in and around Ashburton, and 230 at Totnes. A half of the surviving industry thus lay in the middle Dart valley. Okehampton and district had 530 looms, Cullompton 500, Exeter 300, North and South Molton 200, Crediton and North Tawton 150, and Tavistock 100.[2]

These are, indeed, derisory figures when compared with those of the northern factory-towns, but the local historian does not view them in that light. To him each of these mills is a valuable part of the economy of a small town, helping to keep it active and prosperous, and alive with young people. The closing of even one mill in a small town was a disaster. Elderly people still recall these disasters as a landmark in the history of the town or village, changing its economic and social character completely as the younger people were driven elsewhere to find a living, either leaving their native place for good or being carried out of it every morning to work in a larger town some miles away, and using their homes only as places to sleep in. The local roots wither and the old community (in the true sense of that degraded word) decays.

As the 19th century went on, the woollen mills fell out one by one. In 1881 there were only about 1,200 people in the whole county employed in the woollen and worsted manufactures; but where the mills survived they were still important. To-day the industry survives only at Buckfastleigh; at Harbertonford, near Totnes; at Ashburton; in the new venture at Dartington Hall, and on a very small scale at Tavistock, Bovey Tracey, and North Tawton. Excluding the Axminster carpet industry, the woollen and worsted industry employs fewer than 500 people.[3]

THE TIN TRADE

Although Cornish tin has been worked since the Bronze Age, and was " the one famous product of ancient Britain ", not a scrap of evidence of prehistoric tin-working has been forthcoming in Devon. The find of iron currency-bars of late Celtic date at Holne Chase might indeed be interpreted as indirect evidence of trade of some kind on the eastern side of Dartmoor, but in the complete absence of any other evidence from the multitude of Bronze and Iron Age sites on the Moor one cannot suppose the existence of a trade in tin. Nor is there any evidence from the Roman period in Devon; and, a thousand years later, Domesday Book is silent about any tin-working, either in Devon or Cornwall.

The earliest reference to tin-working in Devon occurs in the Pipe Roll of 1156.[1] From then until the end of the century the rich alluvial deposits of south-west Devon produced nearly all the tin of Europe. Cornish production was negligible and came mostly from near the Devon boundary. The rich deposits of western Cornwall, worked so extensively in prehistoric times, appear to have been unknown to the tin-workers of Henry II's time. It looks as though tin-working virtually ceased in Cornwall about the middle of the 4th century and was recommenced in the middle of the 12th. We know this is what happened in coal-mining and in certain quarries of stone and slate. The knowledge of them was lost, and rediscovered in the 12th and 13th centuries. When tin was found again, it was on the south-western side of Dartmoor that the main deposits were located. Almost certainly we can put the date of the beginnings of the industry in Devon at about 1150, as the output for the years 1156-60 was small and rose rapidly in the following years. One would like to know what pioneer made this momentous discovery, what led him to search the wastes below the high moors, and where the first discovery was made.[2] The first specific places we find mentioned are Sheepstor, and Brisworthy, a hamlet about two miles away to the south over a shoulder of the Moor, near the waters of the upper Plym. At both these places we hear of tin-working going on in 1168.

For the first fifty years the bulk of the output of tin came from Devon. Probably they were virgin deposits and richer than anything known in Cornwall; but they were quickly exhausted and by the early 13th century the centre of production had shifted to Cornwall and remained there ever afterwards. Devon had produced over 600 thousandweight in 1189; by 1243 output had fallen to 74 thousandweight.[3] In 1220 the Devon stannaries were farmed out by the Crown for two hundred marks, but those of Cornwall fetched a thousand marks in the same year.

Throughout the 13th and 14th centuries, Devon production remained at about one-tenth of Cornish, and about an eighth of what it had been in the boom days of the late 12th century.[4] During the 15th century there was some slow recovery, with many ups and downs, production between 1400 and 1450 averaging about 100 thousandweight, rising to an average of 194 thousandweight from 1450 to 1500, probably as new deposits were opened up in different parts of the Moor. This is suggested by the variations in the amount of coinage duty collected in the four stannary towns, which divided the Moor between them. Tinners were obliged to carry their metal to the stannary town nearest the mine, there to have it weighed and stamped, and to pay duty on it. Chagford, covering the north-eastern quarter of the Moor, takes first place from 1385 until the middle of the 15th century, thereafter yielding to Ashburton, which covered the south-eastern quarter. Tavistock, which had led at times in the past, varied between second and third place during the 15th and 16th centuries.*

During the last years of the 15th century, and the early years of the 16th, the Devon tin-trade enjoyed a boom lasting for some thirty or forty years. Output reached a peak in 1515 at rather more than 470 thousand-weight (252 tons). The years 1523 and 1524 attained almost the same high level, and Devon production for a time averaged more than one-third of that of Cornwall, the highest proportion it had reached since John's reign. In these boom years the Ashburton stannary accounted for nearly 40 per cent of the Devon total, Tavistock for nearly 30 per cent. The magnificent granite tower of Widecombe-in-the-Moor church (plate 29), built in these years, is traditionally said to have been paid for by the tinners of the parish, and this may well be so.[1]

Thereafter tin production fell in Devon, at first slowly and then with increasing speed. Output fluctuated widely from year to year, but the general trend was downward, and by the 1590s the average output for the decade was only 124 thousandweight.

Production dwindled further during the early part of the 17th century: by the eve of the Civil War it was only about 15 thousandweight a year. The war stopped all tin-working for several years and we have no more figures for output until the 1670s. By this date Devon production was negligible—about ten tons or so a year as against some 1,500 tons from Cornwall in most years. In the early 18th century there was a minor and short-lived boom—output in Devon exceeded 55 tons in 1706—but it was a passing flash, and by the 1730s the industry was to all intents and purposes dead. A certain amount of tin-mining was, however, still being carried on in the 1820s.[2]

It had ceased to be of much consequence in the economy of Devon by the middle of James I's reign. Westcote scarcely bothers to mention it, except to speak of the extreme poverty of the working tinner—than whom, he says, "no labourer whatsoever undergoes greater hazard of peril or danger, nor in hard or coarse fare and diet doth equal him: bread, the brownest; cheese, the hardest; drink, the thinnest; yea, commonly the dew of heaven, which he taketh either from his shovel, or

*The earliest stannary towns were Tavistock, Ashburton, and Chagford. Plympton was added in 1328. Coinage took its name from the fact that after the weighing the assay-master chiselled a small piece from the corner (coign) of each block of tin and assayed it for quality before stamping it.

spade, or in the hollow of his hand. . . . He spends all day (or the major part thereof) like a mole or earth-worm underground, mining in deep vaults or pits, as though he intended (with noble Sir Francis Drake) to find a way to the antipodes; yea, a nearer, and so to surpass him: for it is sometime of that profundity, that notwithstanding the country (so they term the earth over their heads) is propped, posted, crossed, traversed, and supported with divers great beams of timber to keep them in security, yet all is sometimes too little; they perish with the fall thereof notwithstanding."[1]

Westcote copies this description almost verbatim from Hooker, who was writing in 1599 or 1600. It tells us that tin was being got by shaft-mining at considerable depths in the Elizabethan period, but of the beginnings of shaft-mining in Devon we have no direct information. It is said by Lewis to have begun in Cornwall not earlier than 1450, but the evidence is scanty, and Leland, in the early 16th century, throws no additional light on this important development, unless his distinction between wet and dry tin-works refers to shaft-mining and the traditional method of " streaming " respectively.[2] One is tempted to account for the sudden increase in the output of Devon tin round about 1500 by the introduction of shaft-mining in the immediately preceding period.

There is a marked rise in Cornish output at precisely the same period. From 1450 to 1490 the output from Cornwall fluctuated round 700–800 thousandweight. In 1495 and 1496 it suddenly jumped to well over 1,000 thousandweight, and in the early 1500s usually ran from 1,200 to 1,400 thousandweight. I am inclined to date the beginning of shaft-mining in both Devon and Cornwall to round about 1490-1500. In various places on the fringes of Dartmoor there must be the remains of these early mines with their shafts and timbered galleries. It is remarkable that Mr. Hansford Worth makes no mention of any of them in his papers on " The Dartmoor Blowing House "[3] and that no one else appears even to have noticed them.

Until the introduction of shaft-mining, the tin had been got by " streaming ": not a stream of water but a bed of detrital ore in the form of heavy black stones and sand. The bed varied in thickness from one to ten feet, and in breadth from six feet to most of the width of a valley. It was usually fan-shaped, narrowing as one went up the hillside towards the parent lode from which the tinstone had been carried down so long ago. It was this parent lode that the shaft-miners sought to find and to follow downwards,[4] but the earlier tinners contented themselves with shallow workings in the detritus down to a depth of thirty or forty feet.

The tin ore was smelted on the Moor in structures known as " blowing-houses ". This improved method of smelting seems to have been introduced at some time during the 13th century. The prepared ore was smelted on the hearth of the granite furnace by a charcoal fire, fed by a blast from a large pair of bellows, which were worked by a water-wheel. The molten tin, of a purity unsurpassed by smelters of to-day, was then cast into granite moulds to form blocks weighing two or three hundred pounds. The remains of more than forty of these smelting-houses survive on Dartmoor and have been listed by Mr. Hansford Worth. Some of the best examples are marked on the 2½-inch Ordnance maps.

Much more could be said of the organisation and working of the tin industry, but G. R. Lewis's book on *The Stannaries* must be left to answer most of the questions. One or two important aspects should, however, be briefly touched upon. Besides the four stannary towns, there was the grim prison at Lydford, to which transgressors against the elaborate code of stannary laws were committed. This great square keep was erected in 1195, at a cost of £32, and it was used from the beginning as the stannary prison.[1] It still stands at the west end of the church in the forlorn and decayed town of Lydford. And, in the desolate heart of the Moor, lies Crockern Tor, where that remarkable institution, the stannary parliament, assembled.

At Crockern Tor the bounds of the four stannaries met, and here, from time to time, the Warden of the Stannaries—an office that dated from 1198 and still continues—convoked a meeting of the ninety-six representatives of the Devon stannaries, presided over by the vice-warden. The earliest " parliament " of which the statutes have survived met on the summit in 1494, and it may be that these gatherings are not much more ancient than this. The last met there in 1730.[2] These parliaments enacted the ordinances that governed the working of the industry in all its detail, and imposed penalties for breach of these laws. The famous case of Richard Strode, M.P. for Plympton in the parliament of 1512, who was committed to the Lydford prison after conviction by the four local stannary courts, is sufficient illustration of the fact that the stannary statutes were meant to be obeyed, and that not even a member of parliament could treat them lightly. Strode's offence was that he introduced a bill at Westminster to restrain mining operations near the seaports, on the ground that their harbours were being choked with refuse from the mines. He was presented at all four stannary courts and convicted of conduct subversive of the tinners' liberties.

Many of the working tinners were small husbandmen who probably eked out their livelihood by searching for tin ore when the opportunity occurred. The only equipment needed was a pick, a shovel, and a bucket. The average output was so low that we cannot suppose anyone lived by this means alone. Thus in the 13th century the number of working tinners amounted to between two hundred and four hundred or so, producing all told only 25 to 45 tons a year. The wide fluctuations in the number of working tinners from year to year also suggest that it was a casual occupation for many men and not a full-time job.

As the tin could only be stamped twice a year at the coinage towns, and could not be sold before being stamped, the smaller tin workers inevitably fell into the hands of capitalist " adventurers " and tin dealers. As early as the 13th century we hear of wage-earners in the trade, working for others. By the early 16th century, indeed, the Devon tin trade had attracted a remarkable variety of investors from all ranks of society. The coinage roll of 1523 has 1177 entries on it, possibly seven or eight hundred different names.[1] The Earl of Devon himself had three hundredweight of tin coined at Plympton. The names of many well-known landed families appear—Copplestone, Prideaux, Cole, Edgecumbe—together with those of great town merchants like John Giles of Totnes, William Periam of Exeter, and William Hawkins of Plymouth. Bakers, tanners, and tuckers also figure in the list. But fewer than ten per cent of the entries record the coinage of a thousandweight or more at a time: the largest producer was Elis Elforde, who had rather more than $3\frac{1}{2}$ tons coined in two instalments at Tavistock.

It was still mainly a small man's trade. " The big capitalist has already appeared on the scene . . . but there is still ample room for small working partnerships, and even for the lone adventurer toiling with pick and shovel at his own claim ": the immemorial bowed figure of solitary man, working in the vast silence of the Moor as his ancestors had done in the Cornish wastes three thousand years before.

OTHER MINING

Next in antiquity to tin-working were the silver and lead mines. Like tin, they were discovered comparatively late, enjoyed a boom for the first fifty years, and then fell off, though later intermittent attempts to revive them brought about temporary increases of production. Like the tin-works, too, the argentiferous lead mines were a favourite field for royal enterprise. They were actively exploited down to the 16th century under direct royal supervision, exercised through a warden who had power to hold a court and to try miners for all offences. Each of the royal silver mines at Bere Alston, Bere Ferrers, and Combe Martin had its own court, presided over by the keeper of the mine, who with a jury of miners dispensed justice to the workers. Workers were obtained by impressment, they received the king's wage, they were free from ordinary taxes and tolls while in service, and came entirely under mine jurisdiction except for serious offences.[2] They were, in fact, industrial soldiers.

The early mines were located in the peninsula between the estuary

of the Tavy and the Tamar, known down to the 14th century as *Birlanda*
or *Birlond*, now the parish of Bere Ferrers. We hear of these mines in
1294, when 370 lb. of silver were sent up to London from Martinstowe
(now Maristow), where there was evidently a quay on the Tavy. The
mines had been discovered only a few years earlier, not much before
1290. During the five years 1292-7 they produced £4,046 worth of
silver, and about £360 of lead. In 1299 the king pledged the mines to the
Frescobaldi, the Italian merchant-bankers, who worked them for a time
but lost heavily on the deal.[1] The mines continued to yield well, however,
in the king's hands and in 1305 produced £1,773 of silver and £180 worth
of lead. By 1340 the boom was over, and a few years later the Bere mines
yielded only £70. During the boom years, 1290-1340, miners had been
drafted from the older lead-mining districts. Thus in 1297 the accounts
show that 384 miners from the Peak were working at Bere, and 35 from
Wales. It is in these years that Bere Alston developed into a market town
for the miners, and then became a borough.

The early " mines " were open diggings, at the most pits of varying
depth. Even so, water was a considerable nuisance and for a time the
Devon mines closed down in winter, until better methods of drainage
were found. Smelting-houses similar to the " blowing-houses " in the
tin works, their blast actuated by a water-mill, were in use as early as
1295.[2] The beginnings of shaft-mining are obscure, but the purchase of
" winding hooks " for the Bere Ferrers mine in 1480 may be a sign that
it had begun. The accounts for this mine in 1480 give us a good picture
of its working and organisation.[3]

From time to time in the 15th century the mines were leased to
private adventurers, but no great fortunes were made. At times the
yield was dismally low: in 1426 it was recorded that only 39 ounces of
silver had been produced in two and a half years. From 1445 to 1451,
however, the average yield rose to 4,000 ounces. The Bere mines were
apparently abandoned before the end of the 15th century, and by Westcote's day were forgotten. Neither he nor Risdon mentions them.[4] They
were opened up again by Sir John Maynard in Charles II's time, but
without success. About 1784 they were reopened and produced 6,500
ounces of silver in two years. The mines at Bere Alston, along the Tamar,
were reopened early in the 19th century, and were active enough to
employ about a thousand men in 1850. They seem to have closed down
finally in the early 1880s. The official returns show that in 1866 they
produced 13,017 ounces of silver; in 1876, 5,890 ounces; and in 1886,
none. Lead ore fell likewise, from 723½ tons in 1866 to 20 tons in 1886.[5]

The other silver-lead mines were at Combe Martin. These, too, seem
to have begun in the time of Edward I, when we hear of 337 men being
brought down from Derbyshire to work them. The history of these mines

is very little known. They seem at first to have been very productive: Lysons says that they furnished silver for Edward III's wars. According to Westcote, Henry IV also worked the Combe Martin mines profitably: " but most chiefly his son, King Henry V, for the better maintenance of his wars in France." In Westcote's day one could still see " divers monuments " of this period—the mine, store-house, blowing-house, and refining-house. The mines were apparently worked in 1485 also, and employed, together with those at Bere Ferrers, about a thousand men. According to Stephen Atkinson, the Bere Ferrers and Combe Martin mines were worked for five years, " and being then boothe deepe, and almost worne out, ceased."[1] This would be about 1490.

Although the Combe Martin mines were then abandoned, the king reserved the gold and silver mines when he sold the manor and borough of Combe Martin to Richard Pollard in 1537.[2] No more is heard of them for fifty years. They were opened again in 1587, when a rich new lode was discovered by Adrian Gilbert, of the famous south Devon family, and John Poppler of London, " a lapidary." But they found that they could not refine the ore, rich though it was. " Artists from sundry nations came to viewe it," says Atkinson, " but did no good at it " until it came to the ears of Mr. Bulmer " being then a great lead-man uppon Mendipp." Bulmer was successful where the others had failed; he rode to Combe Martin to see the mine for himself, and bargained with Gilbert for a half share in it. He was to take half the ore and meet all the costs of digging, refining, and so on, while Gilbert took the other half as a sleeping partner. For two years the mine yielded the partners £2,000 each; the next two years showed a falling off as the mine deepened. In its fourth and last year it yielded £1,000. Atkinson tells us it was called Fayes Mine. It reached a depth of thirty-two fathoms, and the same in length. With the last silver taken out of the mine, in 1593, Bulmer fashioned two rich and fair standing cups, one of which he gave to the Earl of Bath at Tawstock, the other to the Lord Mayor of London.[3] Both cups were inscribed with verses, that on the Earl of Bath's being as follows:

> In Martyn's Combe long lay I hydd,
> Obscured, deprest with grossest soyle,
> Debaséd much with mixéd lead,
> Till Bulmer came; whose skill and toyle
> Refinéd mee so pure and cleene,
> As rycher no where els is seene.
> And addinge yet a farder grace,
> By fashion he did inable
> Mee worthy for to take a place,

To serve at any Prince's table.
Combe Martyn gave the use alone,
Bulmer, the fyning and fashion.

Thomas Bushell took a lease of the mines in 1644, but their sequestra-
tion by Parliament shortly afterwards put a stop to any work. He
recommended their reopening to Parliament in 1659: again nothing
happened. They were apparently opened towards the close of the century
and soon stopped; opened again from 1813 to 1817; closed and re-
opened until 1848. They were reopened for the last time, and again
unprofitably, in 1875.[1]

Copper-mining has also been important in Devon. Some mining was
carried on at North Molton during the 18th century, but had been
abandoned before 1778. Polwhele speaks of copper-mines at Ashburton,
Woodhuish (in Brixham), and one or two other places. By the end of
the 18th century most of the profitable mines were in the Tavistock
district, but they rarely produced a hundred tons of fine copper between
them. Production rose after 1800, reaching a peak in 1812 of nearly 507
tons of fine copper, worth £40,340.[2] Wheal Friendship, in the parish of
Mary Tavy, was particularly productive. Opened in 1796 or 1797, it had
spread prosperity all around it, and had created a demand for additional
transport which was met by the construction of a canal from Tavistock
to Morwellham on the Tamar. This canal, a considerable engineering
achievement, was opened in 1817. It ended at the edge of a steep hill
240 feet above Morwellham Quay, which was reached by an inclined
plane down which the loaded barges were sent, fastened upon trolleys
and controlled by a windlass and chain. The quay was " a scene of busy
industry, with its unloading barges, and shouting sailors, and hammering
workmen, and trains of wagons ascending or descending the inclined
plane."

Mining activity reached its peak in the 1850s, chiefly as a result of
the opening of the richest mine of all—the Devon Great Consols at
Blanchdown, two or three miles up the river from Morwellham. In these
wonderful years of the mid-fifties, Devon and Cornwall produced more
than half the world's supply of copper. The population of Tavistock
parish rose dramatically; the shares of the company (with only £1 paid
up) were worth about £200 each in 1850; the mine employed 1,100 men
and extended over a vast area. Trollope stayed at Tavistock about
this time and visited the mine: he gives a spirited description of it in
The Three Clerks (1858).

The Devon copper lodes were rich but shallow: output soon began
to decline. But while it lasted the Devon Great Consols was one of the
richest mines in the world. Between 1844, when it began work, and 1878,

it produced over 622,000 tons of copper ore, worth £3,150,000, besides mundic (iron pyrites) and over 17,000 tons of arsenic. The royalties received by the Duke of Bedford, on whose lands this happy discovery was made, amounted to just under £270,000 in this period, an average of rather more than £8,000 a year.[1] The mine had also paid nearly a million pounds in dividends. By the 1880s, though still at work on a large scale, it had ceased to pay any dividends and production was concentrated on arsenic. The arsenic works were the most extensive in the world.

William Morris's father had held 272 of the 1,024 original £1 shares of the company. Within six months of the beginning of operations, the shares were changing hands at £800 each, and Mr. Morris's holding rose for a time to the value of over £200,000, an immense increase in the family wealth. Of this mine, J. W. Mackail says, in his *Life of William Morris*, that " its earlier fortunes, and its gradual decline, were not without importance in determining the course of Morris's life."[2] The Devon Great Consols has yet other literary associations, for it is probably these mines that Coventry Patmore is describing in *Tamerton Church-Tower; or, First Love*, published in 1853:

> On, on we toil'd amidst the blaze
>   From Dartmoor's ridges bare;
> Beneath the hush'd and scorching haze,
>   And through the twinkling air;
> Along the endless mountain-side,
>   That seem'd with us to move;
> Past dreary mine-mouths, far and wide;
>   Huge dross-heap, wheel, and groove;
> Dark towns by disembowell'd hills,
>   Where swarthy tribes abode,
> Who, in hard rocks with harder wills,
>   Pursued the crooked lode. . . .

It is not given to many mines to have such rich literary associations as these—William Morris, Trollope, and Patmore.

Devon copper production reached its maximum in 1862, when 41,513 tons of ore were produced. From then onwards the annual returns showed a steady decrease. In 1887 the six mines then at work produced only 5,182 tons between them, of which four-fifths came from the Devon Great Consols. Arsenic production was worth 2½ times as much as copper ore, again mostly from the Devon Great Consols.[3] By the end of the century this great activity was over. Morwellham Quays were deserted: not a ship on the river: the canal was unused, and the men were all away working in the fields or in mines some miles off. The Devon Great Consols closed down completely on 31 May 1901.[4] Now the Blanchdown mines lie silent, the great cogged wheels broken; and the vast slag-heaps rise and fall above and among the Tamar woods, a majestic scene of desolation and colour.

Iron was apparently mined in Elizabethan times near North Molton and Molland, on the southern foothills of Exmoor, probably as a result of the setting up of the Mines Royal in 1568, with powers to seek and exploit the mineral resources of England. In the early 17th century these mines had been superseded by others in South Devon, at Brent, Ashburton, and Holne.[1] From 1796 to 1802, nearly 10,000 tons of rich iron-ore was sent from the Combe Martin district across to the iron-works at Llanelly, in South Wales, but shipments ceased in 1802. In the late 19th century Devon was producing 2,000–3,000 tons of ore, chiefly from a mine at Brimley (in Molland parish) where it had been mined 300 years earlier.[2]

Manganese was first found in Devon at Upton Pyne, about 1770. This mine, with two smaller mines on the same lode in Newton St. Cyres, supplied the whole country for many years. It was used at first in the manufacture of Egyptian ware in the Potteries, and in purifying glass. Its later use in bleaching led to a considerable increase in output, some 2,000–3,000 tons being shipped annually from Exeter in the early years of the 19th century. When the older mines failed, new deposits were found in the hills west of Exeter—at Ashton, Doddiscombsleigh, and Christow—and about 1815 other deposits were found in west Devon, chiefly around Milton Abbot, Coryton, and Maristow.[3] By the end of the 19th century only the Milton Abbot mines were working, on a small scale. The old manganese workings now produce yellow ochre.

From time to time attempts have been made to find coal in Devon: mercifully all have been fruitless. Attempts were made near Exeter in 1698, in the 1760s, and again in 1818.[4] The lignite of Bovey Tracey was being exploited as early as Henry VIII's reign,[5] and intermittently at later dates. In Lysons's day it was used only by poor cottagers round about, because of its bituminous smell, and in an adjacent pottery, founded in 1772.

A number of other minerals have been exploited in Devon on a small scale, some of which, like barytes at Bridford, are still produced. But the only other minerals of any real consequence in the industrial history of Devon are china-clay and the ball-clays, which are best treated in the section on the pottery industry.

OTHER INDUSTRIES

In addition to the cloth trade and mining, a number of other industries have been of some importance historically in Devon, chiefly the lace, carpet, paper, and pottery industries.[6]

The lace industry is said to have been introduced into Devon by Flemish refugees in Elizabeth's reign. This is possibly true, as Westcote mentions it about 1630 as though it were not a new trade. Of Honiton he says: " Here is made abundance of bone lace, a pretty toy now greatly in request," and he further mentions that it was made at Bradninch also. By the end of the 17th century the industry had spread into all the east Devon parishes. A petition to the House of Commons in 1699 against the threatened repeal of the lace duties shows that there were over 4,700 people employed in lacemaking, the largest centres being Honiton (1341) and Ottery St. Mary (814). Colyton, Beer and Seaton, Sidbury, and Sidmouth each had more than 300 lace-workers. The hill-parishes like Luppitt and Upottery were also important centres.

The trade flourished all through the 18th century, until a profound change of fashion to simple muslins and gauzes, about the time of the French Revolution, brought about a slump. This was aggravated about 1810 by the introduction of machine-made net, which threw hundreds more lace-workers out of work. One of the largest machine-lace factories was, indeed, set up in Devon itself. John Heathcoat migrated from Loughborough, in Leicestershire, owing to the smashing of his machinery by the Luddites, and took over a defunct woollen mill at Tiverton in 1815, where he employed some 1,500 work-people.[1]

The slump in hand-made lace continued, despite some royal patronage, until Queen Victoria ordered her wedding-dress to be made of Honiton lace at Beer and Branscombe. This turned the tide, the demand for lace soon exceeded the supply, and quality began to suffer. The Great Exhibition of 1851 gave a further temporary impetus to the trade, but it never reached the level of its 18th-century activity, and by the 1860s was again declining. By 1887 the depressed state of the trade was sufficient to engage the attention of a parliamentary committee, whose report is a valuable document for the social and economic history of east Devon.[2] Although the numbers employed in the trade had fallen, some two-thirds of the remaining workers were then unemployed. They were mostly middle-aged women who knew no other trade, and their distress was abject and pitiful. At Beer there had been 400 lace-workers a generation earlier, now only sixty or seventy remained. At Exmouth, where twenty lace-schools had flourished, none was left in 1887. And so it was all over east Devon.

Children went to the lace-schools at five to seven years old. They were taught to read and to make lace by the dame who kept the school, boys as well as girls working twelve hours a day in summer. Grown men worked at lace-making as a side-line in the evenings, especially sailors back from long voyages. The Education Act of 1870 killed most of these schools, and the slump in trade (chiefly due to the competition of machine-made Nottingham lace) ended the rest. But the extinction of the trade was not all social loss: the lace-workers toiled at this close work in small unwholesome rooms for ten or twelve hours a day, and were recognised by their sallow complexions, rickety frames, and general appearance of languor and debility. Most of the workers were girls and young women, and after years of this confinement it was not surprising that they could produce only puny and short-lived children.[1] The lace trade was the Domestic System almost at its worst.

In the closing years of the 19th century the better-quality trade was revived, and continues to-day in some of the traditional centres, notably at Honiton and Beer.

A carpet manufacture was begun at Axminster in 1755 by Mr. Thomas Whitty, after many preliminary difficulties.[2] The industry took root and flourished to such an extent that the Sultan of Turkey himself ordered an Axminster carpet in the early 1800s at a cost of more than £1,000. Axminster carpets were to be found in the royal residences of Windsor and Brighton, as well as in many country houses. It was very much a luxury trade, the product was expensive, and only about a hundred workers, chiefly women, were employed in 1830.[3] The grandson of the founder became insolvent shortly after this date. In 1836 the machinery was sold, taken to Wilton, near Salisbury, and the manufacture of Wilton carpets begun. Since 1945 the manufacture of carpets has been revived at Axminster, and within the last two or three years Berry's woollen factory at Buckfastleigh—one of the few surviving woollen mills—has been taken over for the extension of the industry.

The paper industry of Devon has a long history and was formerly of some importance.[4] Altogether about fifty-two paper mills are known to have existed in Devon, concentrated to a large degree in the Culm and Creedy valleys, to the north-east and the north-west of Exeter. A smaller concentration was centred upon Plymouth. There were few mills before the middle of the 18th century, but with the ending of French dominance of the paper market the number increased quickly. Both Devon and Cornwall offered marked advantages for the industry: abundant and reliable supplies of suitable water (needed both for power and in the manufacturing process), cheap labour, ports for the landing of rags and other raw materials, and a large local market for paper. The earliest mills seem to have been two in or near Plymouth, set up by a Frenchman shortly before 1684. Another Plymouth mill is recorded in 1710. A paper mill was working at Countess Wear, below Exeter, by 1704; another at Halberton in 1703, and one at Uffculme in 1707. Colyton may also have had a mill at this time, or very shortly afterwards.

The number of mills increased rapidly during the second half of the 18th century and the early years of the 19th. The industry seems to have reached its peak in the 1830s, but as with so many other local industries the coming of expensive machinery and of railways proved fatal to the smaller and more remotely placed manufacturers. Several paper-makers installed machinery at an early date, and have survived to this day, with a considerable and a varied trade. Of the eight mills which are working to-day, six lie in the Exe and Culm valleys between Exeter and Cullompton, close to the route of the Great Western Railway. Of the remainder, one is Stowford Mill at Ivybridge, and the other is Tuckenhay Mill, near Cornworthy, the only " vat " mill left in Devon, which produces a high-quality hand-made paper.

Large deposits of pipe clay and potter's clay occur in south Devon, especially around Bovey Tracey and Kingsteignton, and in north Devon at Fremington and Peters Marland. China clay is also extensively worked on the south-western corner of Dartmoor. Despite these rich resources, no native pottery industry of any size has grown up in Devon, for lack of fuel. It has been cheaper to send the clays to the coal than to bring the coal to Devon.

Many medieval churches in north and west Devon contain embossed floor-tiles which appear to have been made at Barnstaple from Fremington clay. Though some of them may be 14th-century in date, the majority date perhaps from the period when the churches were rebuilt and refurnished (say 1450-1540). They continued to be made well into the 17th century and possibly later.[1] At Barnstaple, Cross Street was Crock Street in the 15th century, the street where " crocks " or pots were made. A pottery was established at Bideford in 1668 and closed down only in 1896, using the Fremington and the Marland clays. These local potteries of Barnstaple, Bideford, and Fremington turned out domestic and farm earthenware—harvest-jugs, butter-pots, cooking-pots, and so on. Small potteries survive at Barnstaple and Braunton, but the last Bideford pottery closed in 1916. Some fine specimens of the traditional North Devon ware may be found in the local museums.

The ball-clay deposits of south Devon are more important. They were first extensively worked about 1730[2]—at Knighton, then at Bishopsteignton, and later still at Kingsteignton. Teignmouth had a considerable export trade in these clays from the middle of the 18th century. About 20,000 tons a year left the port, mainly for Staffordshire, in the early 19th century. Three potteries were opened up, however, in and around Bovey Tracey between 1760 and 1800, of which one still survives. In the 1880s Kingsteignton alone was producing some 50,000 tons of clay a year for export from Teignmouth, besides supplying the large local pottery which had opened shortly before.[3] Potteries were also started at Aller Vale and Watcombe in the 1860s, which still continue.

Plymouth had three earthenware potteries at work in 1815, one of which continued until the last quarter of the century, but it was chiefly notable for the only china manufacture that Devon ever had, associated with the name of William Cookworthy. Cookworthy's discovery of china-clay and china-stone in Cornwall, and of the process of manufacturing true porcelain, belong to national history.[1] In 1796 he started the Plymouth china factory at Coxside, but in little more than two years it was transferred to Bristol, where Richard Champion carried it on. In 1773 Champion purchased the patent rights from the ageing Cookworthy, and so ended the brief manufacture of Plymouth China. Plymouth and Bristol wares are not of high artistic importance, but " their charm resides in their associations and in the impression they give to an informed mind of something new, achieved with great difficulty—the charm in fact of the true primitive." They are the fruit of more than twenty years' unaided search by one man.[2]

The china-clay deposits of Devon were not worked for some time afterwards, probably not until the 1830s. The Lee Moor works, now the largest in Devon (plate 26), opened up in the 'forties. Here, and to the east of the Erme, are vast reserves of china clay. The output from Devon has always been a fraction of that from Cornwall: indeed from 1900 to 1943 it was only about one-tenth.[3] Most of the Devon output is exported from Plymouth for the pottery, paper, and textile trades elsewhere. Near Plymouth the Plym flows almost milk-white with the washings of the clay, and the greyish-white mounds of waste " sand " form a striking landscape on the blue moorland edge to the north.

CHAPTER VIII

COMMUNICATIONS

ROADS

ONE glance at the map of Devon is sufficient to show the intricate mesh of roads and lanes that covers the whole county except the highest moors. Apart from Yorkshire, Devon has a greater mileage of roads than any other English county. Even a hundred years ago there were nearly 7,000 miles of roads capable of taking wheeled traffic.[1] An adequate study of these roads, and of the kinds of traffic that they carried, would require a whole book to itself. The story begins with the trackways that wind along the high ridges traversed by Bronze Age man, and ends with the pattern of bus routes that now links all but the remotest villages to the towns, breaking down their long isolation for one day a week, if no more.

The pre-Roman highways of Devon have been closely studied by Dr. G. B. Grundy.[2] These highways—literally so, for they mostly run along the bony ridges of the landscape—formed a network of very uneven density in different parts of the county. Great tracts of Devon are blank; other parts have a fine pattern of ridgeways. Dartmoor has no trackways nor has the wide stretch of country north of the Moor as far as Chulmleigh. The blankness of Dartmoor in this respect may furnish a valuable clue to the antiquity of most or some of these " ancient " highways. The Moor was fairly thickly settled, especially on its southern and western sides, throughout the Bronze Age, and largely forsaken during the succeeding Iron Age. This would suggest that the existing trackways are not as old as the Bronze Age, or they would surely have penetrated into the recesses of the Moor and not stopped short at its edges. The fact that they are often associated with hill-forts of the early Iron Age period (i.e. pre-Roman) adds further weight to the suspicion that most of these ancient trackways date from that time. Here and there it is possible that a ridgeway may be as old as the Bronze Age, especially where it appears to be associated with tumuli of that period, but in general an Iron Age date is safer.

There is a particularly close network of trackways north of Chulmleigh, as far as the coast, above all on the Exmoor ridges; and another between the western rampart of Dartmoor and the Tamar valley. Another interesting group of trackways runs down from the southern foothills of Dartmoor, along well-defined ridges, to the edge of the sea, especially between the mouths of the Dart and the Avon. These still form, in many instances, the most direct roads from the Moor to the coast after nearly three thousand years.*

The chief interest of these early trackways for us lies, however, in the fact that they form the first threads in that great mesh of the Devonshire road system. Grundy traces 679 miles of ancient ridgeways in Devon, of which no fewer than 665 miles are represented by modern roads and lanes. They have been continuously in use, most of them, since pre-Roman times, and right down to the early 19th century carried a good deal of the local traffic of the Devonshire countryside—the perennial traffic of pack-horses, carts, and wagons, and cattle-drifts, as distinct from the summer and occasional travel that followed the less ancient and less exposed roads catalogued by Ogilby in 1675.

The Romans added very little to the road pattern. They built about forty-five miles or so of roads in what is now Devon, of which the greater part remains in use in modern roads or lanes. But this gives us a total of hardly more than 700 miles in existence by the Roman period: only one-tenth of the mileage we find in the 19th century. It is possible, indeed likely, that the native Celtic population of Dumnonia added considerably to this total. In many places we recognise winding lowland roads that are undoubtedly of great antiquity—they may be followed by parish boundaries, for example—but which are demonstrably not prehistoric ridgeways, and certainly not Roman.

For all this, it is evident that the greater part of the complex road-pattern has come into existence since the Saxon occupation of the 7th century. Most, if not all, of the villages date from the period between the 7th and the 11th centuries, and the inter-village roads are of the same date. Many hamlets and isolated farmsteads may be pre-Saxon and the lanes that link them together correspondingly old; but again the vast majority are later in date. A number of hamlets and some thousands of single farmsteads came into existence in the great colonisation movement of 1150-1350; some thousands of miles of roads and lanes were marked

*The " great central trackway " across Dartmoor, the subject of many antiquarian theories for a long period, is almost certainly a fiction. The late Mr. Hansford Worth, who knew nearly every stone and path on the Moor, did not accept this trackway as a fact. There was, however, a medieval track over the Moor, from Chagford to Tavistock by way of Two Bridges.

out in these two centuries. Their winding nature, with many abrupt
and apparently meaningless turns between massive hedge-banks, is
evidence of their origin in a landscape directly enclosed from forest and
wood. It is certain that by the middle of the 14th century the immense
network of roads that we see on the modern map was already in existence,
with the numerically unimportant exceptions of certain main roads which
were deliberately planned along easier routes in the early 19th century,
and a few other roads on the high moors and plateaux that remained
uncolonised until a late date.[2]

The appearance of bridges, sufficiently important to be named,
affords good though necessarily sketchy evidence of the growth of the
early road system and of the direction of trade. A few bridges are well
evidenced in Anglo-Saxon times.[1] Creedy bridge, just outside Crediton,
is mentioned as a landmark in a charter of 739. Bickham bridge, over the
Avon, linking two parallel ridgeways on the heights above, is mentioned
in a charter of 962. So, too, is the " king's bridge " over the head of the
estuary where the town of Kingsbridge later grew up. This linked two
royal estates on either side of the estuary (hence the name) and also two
ridgeway systems on the plateaux to the east and west. There was a
bridge over the Tamar in the 11th century, at Bridgerule, which is called
simply *Brige* in Domesday. A pre-Roman trackway had crossed the
Tamar here. Bridges also existed in 1086 at Swimbridge and Thelbridge
(" plank bridge "), which throw some light on trade routes in their
respective districts. An important bridge crossed the Teign in the 11th
century: Teignbridge gave its name to a hundred in Domesday, and it
may well be much older than this. When the ruinous bridge was being
rebuilt in 1815 a remarkable sequence of bridges on this site was brought
to light. The earliest of the sequence, a bridge of fine white freestone,
ashlar laid, was found fifteen to twenty feet below the level of the meadows
and has been thought to be of Roman date.[1]

A considerable number of important bridges make their first appearance in the course of the 12th and 13th centuries as a direct result of the
growth of towns, both in size and number, the multiplication of fairs and
markets, and the general increase of internal trade. The Exe Bridge at
Exeter is referred to in 1196; the Dart was bridged at Totnes by the
time of John. The rapid rise of Plymouth from the late 12th century led
to the building of a number of bridges on the roads leading into and out
of it: Plym bridge appears in a record of 1238, Yealmbridge in 1249, and
Ivybridge (*Ponte Ederoso*) in 1280. The fact that the last-mentioned bridge
had had time to become covered with ivy suggests that it was already of
some age, and had perhaps been built in the earlier part of the 13th
century. The more important bridges over Exe, Dart, and Tamar
probably all date from the 13th century, though many of them were

rebuilt in the 15th century (e.g. Holne and Staverton bridges, in 1413). The rebuilding of bridges in the 15th century, a very noticeable activity, was often the replacement of a timber bridge by a stone one, as at Thorverton in 1415. Several of these 15th-century bridges survive in Devon, but only one, so far as we know, from the 14th century. This is Clyst St. Mary bridge, which probably dates from 1310. There are, too, some hidden land-arches of the Exe Bridge at Exeter which may belong to the first stone bridge, erected in the latter part of the 12th century.

Something recognisable as " main roads " must also have appeared during the 13th century, linking together more or less distant towns such as Exeter and Totnes, Totnes and Plymouth, Exeter and Plymouth, and so on. These " main roads " were not planned as such. They made use of stretches of old ridgeway and filled in the gaps with stretches of such inter-village roads as fitted into the general direction. Here and there, no doubt, a mile or two of new road may have been made to fill in blank patches; but over the greater part of their course these " main roads " must have resulted from the piecing together of a multitude of smaller and purely local roads, just as the 19th-century railway system evolved to a large degree out of a network of small lines built in the first place only for local traffic.

We know little of the speed of medieval travel in Devon. On urgent public business between Exeter and London it was possible to cover nearly sixty miles a day in the 15th century. Thus John Shillingford, the well-known Mayor of Exeter, left Exeter at 6 o'clock on a Wednesday morning in the May of 1448 and reached London at 7 o'clock on Saturday morning. In 1494 Bishop Redman rode from Torre Abbey to London in four days, averaging about fifty miles a day.[1] But these were most exceptional speeds over the best roads, and few men cared or bothered to travel so hurriedly. The itineraries of the medieval bishops of Exeter show a more normal rate of progress over the by-roads and lanes of Devon and Cornwall, though even these reflect at times the tremendous energies of a bishop rather than the pace of an ordinary trader or traveller.[2] Neither the temperament of the native Devonian nor the condition of the local roads encouraged undue haste. Risdon's description of the painful travel one must expect in Devon in the 16th century (for he copies from Hooker) is well known: " Rough and unpleasant to strangers travelling those ways, which are cumbersome and uneven, amongst rocks and stones, painful for man and horse." Few travellers from outside Devon or Cornwall wished to repeat their first experience of the local roads. It is, however, possible that the medieval main roads had been somewhat better. The frequent indulgences granted by the bishops to all who contributed to the repair of bridges and causeways suggest that some roads, at least, were well looked after. The disappearance of indulgences

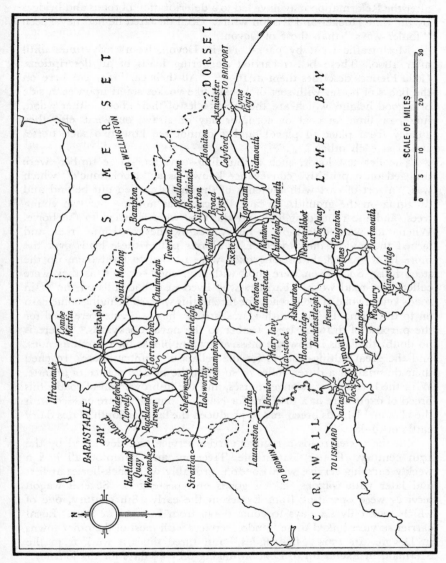

Fig. 8—MAIN ROADS IN 1765 (AFTER DONN)

after the Reformation may have led to a deterioration of roads and bridges by the time Hooker and Risdon wrote. Cecil declared he had never seen " fouler ways " than those of Devon.

Most traffic went by pack-horse in Devon, from early times until after 1800. These beasts carried staggering loads of all descriptions. Celia Fiennes describes them in 1698: " All their carriages are here on the backs of horses with sort of hookes like yoakes stand upon each side of a good height, which are the receptacles of their goods, either wood, furze, or lime, or coal or corn, or hay or straw, or what else they convey from place to place; and I cannot see how two such horses can pass each other. . . ."

The heaviest loads, such as building-stone and large timber, were dragged on a primitive conveyance known as a " truckamuck," which was " a sort of cart with the ends of the shafts carried out behind and dragging on the ground. In fact, the cart was nothing but two young trees, and the roots dragged, and the tops were fastened to the horse. When they wanted to move a heavy weight, they used four trees, and lashed the middle ones together."[1] Horses pulled these loads over the more level ground, but strong oxen were needed to haul them up the steep hills. Such oxen were shod with iron cues—or Q's, as they were called—for road work. Farmers who lived near bad hills on the main roads kept a yoke of oxen ready for hire in this way, so bringing some cash on to the farm. In the South Hams, strong, heavy beasts were bred for the purpose of drawing large timber to the naval dockyards.[2] There is no doubt that this is how the massive granite blocks for church arcades, and the great salting-troughs for the cellars of country houses, reached their destination a dozen miles or so from the nearest source of granite. With the breeding of stronger horses, and the improvement of roads, this breed of oxen were at a discount for haulage, but they were crossed with the Channel Islands breed and so produced the famous South Hams dairy cattle of to-day.

On the better roads a regular carrier service had developed by the 17th century. Exeter, Barnstaple, Tiverton, and Bampton all had a weekly carrying service with London, probably with pack-horses at first and later with wagons, taking goods and passengers. Several wagon services were operating from Exeter in the early 18th century, one of which took only six days to come down from London in 1722. Local carrier services linked these London services with most of the other towns in Devon. In 1764 " fly-wagons " ran three times a week from the Mermaid in Exeter up to London, taking only $4\frac{1}{2}$ days for the journey.[3]

The first passenger coach service into Devon started in 1658, taking four days for the journey from London to Exeter. Its average pace probably did not exceed three miles an hour.[4] A stage-coach from

Exeter to Bath and Bristol was started in 1727, running only in the summer, and taking three days to Bath—an average of less than thirty miles a day. In 1764 a London coach reduced the time for the Exeter journey to two days; in 1784 it was further cut to 32 hours. By 1828 the Devonport Mail was running to Exeter in 19½ hours from London. An average speed of ten miles an hour was now regarded as normal for a fast coach over a good road. The fastest timing came as a result of the duel between the " Quicksilver " (the Devonport Mail) and the " Telegraph " in 1835. Galloping hell for leather, with the fewest and shortest possible stops, as though Devonport were the only town that mattered, Quicksilver reached Exeter in 16½ hours from London, and Devonport—a punishing road nearly all the way beyond Exeter—in 21¼ hours. Riding on the top of the Devonport Mail at this cracking pace must have left an indelible impression on mind and body. The " Telegraph " actually made the Exeter journey in just over 16 hours' running time—slightly faster than Quicksilver—but allowed more time for meals *en route*: twenty minutes for breakfast and thirty for dinner! These were the fastest coaches out of London in the thirties.

Exeter was now connected by coach services with many of the great provincial towns. Most of the coaches ran through to Plymouth also. There was, for instance, a daily service from Plymouth to Liverpool, Manchester, and Birmingham, and three days a week to Southampton and Portsmouth. A number of coaches competed between Bristol, Exeter, and Plymouth, and one coach ran daily from Bath to Sidmouth.[1] From Exeter coaches ran three times a week to the watering-places of Exmouth, Sidmouth, Dawlish, and Teignmouth, and once a week to Bideford. North Devon was poorly supplied with local coach services. Apart from the Bristol and Exeter coaches, wagons were the only public vehicles plying between the towns.

This revolution in public travel had been made possible by the institution of turnpike trusts. The earliest of these in Devon were the Exeter, Honiton, and Axminster trusts, all set up in 1753, which covered the London road between them and a number of the important side-roads. The Tiverton trust began in 1757, the Okehampton trust in 1760, the Barnstaple trust in 1763. The roads of the Plymouth district began to be improved about 1758—high time, for land communication between Plymouth and Dock was so bad that it was easier to go by water. No carriages ran between these towns until 1775. In 1784 a turnpike road was made, and six years later a diligence ran from Fore Street in Dock to Old Town Street in Plymouth, the single fare being one shilling. Dock was, in fact, linked to Exeter by turnpike road before it was linked to Plymouth, so cool were the relations between the two neighbours. In 1780 one could go by turnpike road to Tavistock, and thence across the heart of Dartmoor by a new road to Moretonhampstead, and so to Exeter.[1]

The old main roads were gradually improved, and a number of new main roads cut along easier routes in the early 19th century. Until this date one could truthfully say that the course of the main roads in Devon was still largely determined by the location of the Saxon villages and of the seignorial boroughs of the 12th and 13th centuries. The old roads had struggled across the grain of the country, rising and falling steeply all the way, with hardly a level half-mile anywhere. Most important of the new roads were the Exeter-Barnstaple road along the Taw valley,[2] the Exeter-Tiverton road following the Exe valley, and considerable stretches of the Exeter-Plymouth road. A comparison of the main roads in 1765 (see Fig. 8) and those of to-day will reveal the principal additions, made in the early 19th century for the most part.

The twenty-nine turnpike trusts covered most of the inter-town roads in Devon, but very little more. In 1815 only 776 miles consisted of turn-piked roads and paved streets, about $11\frac{1}{2}$ per cent of the total mileage capable of taking wheeled traffic, as compared with 31 per cent in Middlesex or 28 per cent in Huntingdonshire.[3] Nearly 6,000 miles of roads in Devon had not been turnpiked in 1815—and these were all considered capable of taking wheeled carriages: Heaven alone knew how many thousand miles there were besides which carried farm traffic on packhorses and sleds. Coaches, wagons, and turnpike roads affected only a very small part of the county, that in the vicinity of the main roads. Away from these, villages and hamlets still remained isolated. The village of Bridford lay only nine miles south-west of Exeter by road, yet the rector tells us that when Napoleon's invasion of England was considered to be imminent the well-to-do families of Exeter made plans for flight to Bridford as though it were in another continent.[4]

The same parson noted that in 1818 he buried three very old men who had been born in the parish, never lived out of it, and died in it. This is a more authentic picture of the nature of communications in Devon than any statistics about turnpike trusts and stage-coach timing. There was not a cart in the parish in 1800; all carriage was by pack-horse. Within the next thirty-five years the wheel had superseded the packhorse, and there were some fifty carts kept in the parish by 1840—the transport revolution at Bridford coinciding roughly with the coming of railways in more progressive parts of England.

The history of the turnpike trusts in Devon has yet to be written. Devon came under the Highway Amendment Act of 1864, and one by one the trusts were dissolved. Nearly all had gone by 1890. The new Highway Boards spent more money on the roads and greatly improved surfaces and gradients. By the 1880s the principal roads of the county were said to be in excellent condition. The side-roads were, however, still narrow, with unnecessarily steep hills, and being shut in by high banks and timbered hedges did not dry quickly after the winter rains.

The railways killed the coach and wagon services one by one as they advanced into Devon, and penetrated into one valley after another; though there were remote districts where both lingered on—in the South Hams, on Exmoor, and in the lonely country to the west of Bideford, all badly served by railways. A coach ran regularly between Dartmouth and Kingsbridge until 1914, though it was an adjunct of the railway.[1] Carriers' carts were still an important means of communication all over the county, and remained so well into the 20th century. Even in 1935 there were more than a dozen regular carrier services from various inns in Exeter to neighbouring villages and towns, and nearly a score from Plymouth.[2] Barnstaple, Bideford, and a number of other towns all had a small nucleus of carriers. The carrier's cart gave one a good idea of the speed of medieval travel: the carrier from Bideford to Bude allowed a day for the journey of twenty-six miles, and a day for the return journey. Still, it was a social and friendly business, and plenty of time had to be allowed for conversations at every port of call—nothing like the grim, silent business that travel has become to-day, except on the deep-country bus and the remoter railway branch lines.*

The roads never went out of use in Devon to anything like the same extent as elsewhere. The railways took the through traffic and the heavy loads, but the distances in Devon were so great, the railway system so thinly spread as compared with many other counties, that the roads were still needed to carry most of the local traffic. They were important, too, in the social life of the county; when people called on each other they almost invariably went by road. So, when the motor-car came, and motor-bus services were started, there had been no real break in the continuity of road traffic.

FERRIES

Something has been said of the growing importance of bridges in Devon, from the early 13th century onwards, many of which replaced more or less dangerous fords, as at Bideford. But some river-crossings were too wide for anything but ferries. The numerous estuaries, particularly along the south coast of the county, were serious obstacles to travel, especially as the more important medieval towns of Devon were coast towns and were linked with each other by road. Doubtless all the estuaries had a ferry service of a sort, but the smaller passages, like those

*I have myself travelled in a carrier's cart from Exeter to Cadbury, nine or ten miles away, a journey which occupied an endless summer afternoon.

of Axe and Otter, probably did not require much more than the casual services of a boatman. The crossings of Exe and Tamar, and to a lesser extent Teign and Dart, were another matter, however, and here a regular ferry-service was maintained, for men and horses, from an early date.

Sherborne abbey, in Dorset, which from 1122 had possessed the manor of Littleham, on the eastern side of the Exe mouth, developed a regular ferry across the estuary from the fishing hamlet of Exmouth to a landing-place, now called Starcross, in the manor of Kenton. This ferry enabled travellers along the south coast to avoid a détour of twenty miles through Exeter, then the lowest bridging point,* and was therefore of some concern to the city through loss of tolls. So we find, as early as 1266, an agreement between the abbot of Sherborne and the mayor and commonalty of Exeter about the Exmouth ferry. When Sherborne was suppressed in 1539, the city took steps to acquire the ferry almost at once, in order to safeguard its interests, and the Chamber were letting it to a succession of Drakes at Exmouth throughout the rest of the 16th century at a rent of 26s. 8d. (later 20s.) a year.[1]

This ferry remained in regular use, and could take coaches, down to the 19th century. In 1846 it was sold by the Exeter corporation to the South Devon Railway for £1,000.[2] A small vessel now plies several times a day between Starcross and Exmouth, over the same route that has been followed since the 12th century.

On the Kenton side of the estuary, the Earl of Cornwall had certain ferry rights across to his fishery at Exmouth. We find this passage valued at 26s. 8d. a year in the closing years of the 13th century.[3] It is not clear how the respective rights of the earl on the one side, and the abbey on the other, were demarcated, but the ferry from the Kenton side appears to have lapsed quite early.

The earl also had a ferry across the Teign at Teignmouth in these years, worth only 6s. 8d. a year, and used by travellers making for Dartmouth. Hence, too, we hear of a regular ferry at Kingswear, across the Dart to Dartmouth, at an early date. The Kingswear ferry is first recorded in 1365, but is undoubtedly as old as Dartmouth itself. It probably goes back to the early years of the 13th century as a regular crossing, and still operates. The Teignmouth crossing was superseded by Shaldon Bridge in 1827, but foot passengers still cross to Shaldon by boat as of old.

The Tamar estuary was an even more formidable obstacle than that of the Exe. Until the 15th century the nearest bridge lay some thirty miles upstream—Polston Bridge, on the great highway from Exeter to Launceston. Hence there were two important ferries from Plymouth

*Countess Wear bridge, now the lowest on the river, was not built until 1774.

into Cornwall from the 12th or 13th century—the Saltash passage and the Cremyll passage.

The Cremyll passage was originally from Devil's Point across to Barn Pool, but was moved about 1730 from Barn Pool to the present landing-place at Cremyll because of the annoyance caused to the lords of Mount Edgcumbe by the traffic. Probably the Mount Edgcumbes were extending their park at this time, and the Barn Pool road lay in their way. The old passage was less than half a mile across, but Celia Fiennes, who used it in 1698, records that it took at least an hour because of the tricky tides, and that she caught a cold from the wet boat, which shipped water heavily. In 1788 Shaw tells us that the Cremyll ferry was worth £400 a year rent to Lord Mount Edgcumbe, and kept seven men busy.[1] It still runs, but from a pier some way north of Devil's Point.

Travellers used the Saltash crossing as much as the other. We hear of it in 1364 (it existed earlier) when the Black Prince granted it to his " porter " William Lenche, in consideration of services rendered, including the loss of an eye at the battle of Poitiers. Leland seems to have used the Saltash ferry, and so did Defoe. " The Tamar is here very wide," he writes, " and the ferry-boats bad; so that I thought myself well escaped when I got safe on shore in Cornwall."[2] This ferry also still runs.

A third ferry over the Tamar was started between Devonport and Torpoint before the 18th century was out, and in 1836 was supplemented by the Steam Floating Bridge when the new road from St. Austell to Devonport was opened.[3] This is now the Torpoint vehicular ferry, the most crowded and lucrative in Devon.

In north Devon the only ferry of note was that across the Taw-Torridge estuary from Appledore to the south end of the Braunton Burrows. Ogilby's map of 1675 shows the main road from Bideford to Ilfracombe going this way. A medieval chapel (St. Ann's) stood on the north shore of the estuary, and undoubtedly marked the site of an early crossing. No record survives of this ferry, but it must have been flourishing between the 16th and 18th centuries. The road over the Burrows is still marked on the Ordnance map of 1809, but it had been superseded by the new turnpike roads between Bideford and Barnstaple, and Barnstaple and Ilfracombe.

The Exmouth-Starcross ferry is now only of local importance, chiefly for summer holiday-makers, since it cannot take motor traffic. The Devonport-Torpoint ferry and the Kingswear-Dartmouth ferries take motor traffic and are more important, especially the former. There is a tendency for the smaller ferries across the other estuaries to lapse, as fewer people now walk and local traffic has dwindled. It is unwise to expect every ferry that is marked on the Ordnance maps, especially on the remoter routes, to be there when one reaches the bank of the estuary. Several seem to have disappeared quietly during the recent war.

CANALS

The Exeter ship canal, running from Exeter to Topsham, was the first canal in England to use the pound-lock. It was begun in 1564. Its history belongs properly, however, to the history of Exeter, since it was made at the initiative and expense of the Chamber of the city, and it will, consequently, not be treated here.

No more is heard of canals in Devon until the " canal mania " of the 1790s. This produced the usual crop of grand schemes, though perhaps fewer than elsewhere, for the county was rich in navigable rivers and seaports, and the advantages of canals were less obvious than in the midland counties.[1] On the other hand, there were certain localities in Devon with special needs that called for short canals, which became highly profitable undertakings. Such was the Stover or Teigngrace canal, for which an act was obtained in 1792. This was to run from the Teign tide-water at Newton Abbot for $5\frac{1}{2}$ miles to Bovey Tracey, with a branch cut to Chudleigh, of the same length. It was to tap the rich clay deposits of the district, and the Bovey lignite, and to bring in coal, sea-sand, and lime. The main canal was completed in 1794 at the sole expense of James Templer Esq. of Stover, and was immediately successful, but the Chudleigh cut, of four miles down to Kingsteignton, was not finished until 1843, at the expense of Lord Clifford of Ugbrooke.[2]

In 1820 George Templer added greatly to the value of the canal by the construction of a railway, of granite sets laid lengthways and cut with a flange to prevent the wagons leaving the track. This railway or tramway ran for $8\frac{1}{2}$ miles from Emsworthy Newtake, near Hay Tor, down to Ventiford, on the Stover canal, and was built to take the granite from Templer's quarries. It was said to have been occasioned by Templer's getting part of the contract for the granite for London Bridge.[3] To handle the granite at Teignmouth, where it was transferred from barges to ships, George Templer built the New Quay in 1821-5.

The next canal to be planned hung fire, and was never completed according to the original intention. This was the Grand Western Canal, for which an act was obtained in 1796. It was to run from Taunton to Topsham, with branches to Tiverton and Cullompton, and would have linked Devon with the national canal system. By 1820 the only part to be finished was that from Tiverton to Burlescombe, about twelve miles, which was chiefly used to carry limestone from the Canonsleigh quarries. It was subsequently extended to Taunton, but it never came farther west or south than Tiverton. Nor did it ever pay its way, and in 1865 it was bought by the Great Western Railway and abandoned from Taunton to Holcombe Rogus.[1]

Among other projects of the 1790s, which were frustrated by the outbreak of the French war and never afterwards attempted,[2] was a canal from Wear Giffard, on the Torridge, through Peters Marland, Sheepwash, and Hatherleigh to Okehampton, where it would have met a canal from Exeter and Crediton.[3] It was also proposed to link the Taw and the Exe by a canal from Barnstaple bridge to Stoke Canon and Cowley bridge. At Stoke Canon it would have met the Taunton-Topsham canal. The Taw-Exe canal would have necessitated a tunnel nearly $3\frac{1}{4}$ miles long at the summit level near Copplestone. The narrowness of the isthmus between the Bristol and the English Channels also attracted many schemes for making a navigable cut from one sea to the other. Vancouver reports one such plan to make a canal from Axmouth, through Chard, to Uphill in Somerset, which would facilitate the import of Somerset coal into Devon, but nothing ever came of it.

Another short canal, which proved immensely successful, was that from Tavistock, the centre of a rich mining district, down to Morwellham Quay on the Tamar, which could be reached by vessels of 200 tons, drawing fourteen feet of water. An act was obtained for this canal in 1803. It was to bring in coal and lime principally, and to take out mineral ores and slates from the Mill Hill quarries (reached by a two-mile branch). The formidable engineering difficulties which the route involved —including a tunnel nearly two miles long under Morwell Down and an inclined plane on the last lap dropping 240 feet down to the quay—were all overcome, and the canal was opened on 24 June 1817. For the next sixty or seventy years it carried a heavy traffic, and Morwellham Quay was the scene of intense activity, reaching a peak in the 1850s and 60s when the Devon copper mines were at the height of their production. The coming of the main line of railway to Tavistock shortly after 1890, and the rapid decline in the mining activity of the district at the same date, brought the usefulness of the canal to an end, and it ceased work before the end of the century.

The only other canal in Devon was the Bude-Holsworthy canal for which an act had been obtained in 1819.[4] This was originally planned to go on to Okehampton and to handle the vast traffic in sea-sand from the Bude beaches to the west Devon parishes, a centuries-old stream of packhorse traffic which was said to be ruining the parish roads wherever it passed. Although Lysons thought in 1822 that the canal would reach Holsworthy within twelve months, it did not arrive in fact until 1826, and it went no farther towards the Torridge. Shortly before the canal had been begun, the third Earl Stanhope, in conjunction with Robert Fulton, the celebrated American canal engineer and inventor of the submarine, had surveyed a route from Holsworthy to the Bristol Channel. Fulton died in 1815, and nothing came of this interesting project. The Bude-Holsworthy canal, fifteen and a half miles long, went out of use about 1885, but was reopened for a time to carry material for the building of the Holsworthy-Bude railway (completed in 1898).

RAILWAYS

The first railway in the modern sense did not penetrate into Devon until the spring of 1844, when the Bristol and Exeter Company completed its line to Exeter, but there had been three earlier projects which call for some attention. The Heytor Granite Railway, opened in 1820, has already been mentioned. It was the earliest railway in Devon, and was operated by horses. The trucks were slightly adapted road wagons, the leading truck usually had shafts, and a local jingle suggests that eighteen stalwart horses pulled a train of twelve wagons loaded with granite. This railway carried traffic for about fifty years. Murray's Handbook for 1865 speaks of its being in use then, but the edition of 1872 says it was then disused.

The Dartmoor Railway, from Plymouth to Princetown, originated about the same date.[1] The great prison having been built on the Moor, it became a problem how to secure the necessary supplies. Sir Thomas Tyrwhitt induced the Plymouth Chamber of Commerce to support a plan for a horse-railway, and in 1819 the first Act was obtained, authorising the construction of a railway from Crabtree, at the head of the Plym estuary, up to the prison. A second Act in 1820 authorised a two-mile extension from Crabtree to Sutton Pool, in Plymouth. On 26 September 1823 the line was opened for public use as far as King Tor (twenty-three miles), and the remaining two miles or so to Princetown were completed shortly afterwards. The object of the line was to carry granite down from the Moor, for building purposes in Plymouth and elsewhere, to carry up limestone, lime, and manure for the improvement of the moorland—a project that Tyrwhitt had been actively engaged in since 1785—and to take up coal to the growing settlement of Princetown, where it was badly needed to overcome the climate.

The railway never paid. It cost far more to construct than had been expected, and was heavily mortgaged from the first. Moreover, with the end of the war in 1815, the prison went out of use and houses in Princetown were left untenanted, with a consequent diminution of traffic. Some tenants returned with the railway, but traffic gradually decreased until 1880. In that year the Dartmoor portion was reconstructed to take locomotives, and the line opened to a junction with the Plymouth-Tavistock railway at Yelverton in August 1883.[2] Most of the remainder of the old tramway survives, winding in ample curves along the contours and through the woods, running from near Crabtree, past Higher Leigham (where there is a tunnel 620 yards long), thence high above the west bank of the Plym, through Holt Wood to Roborough. From here it follows approximately the course of the old Plymouth Leat to Yelverton.[1] These two historic lines run beside each other for some miles—Drake's leat to supply Elizabethan Plymouth with water, and Tyrwhitt's railway.

The third of the early projects is in some ways the most interesting, though it came to nothing. As early as 1831[2] the principal inhabitants of Okehampton and Bideford, and of the country between, raised funds for elaborate reports and surveys for the construction of a railway to join the two towns; and this at a time when much larger towns elsewhere in England were exerting themselves to keep the railways as far away as possible. Even in the backwoods village of Winkleigh " a large and enthusiastic meeting " was held in support of the proposed railway.

The engineer was to be Mr. Roger Hopkins, who had built the Dartmoor Railway, completed about two years before. It was to be a narrow-gauge line, worked by " two Locomotive Steam Engines," each making three journeys a day, and it was to carry passengers as well as goods. Thus in two important respects it marked a great advance on the lines that had already been constructed in Devon: it was to be worked by locomotives and not by horses, and it was to carry passengers. The principal revenue was to be derived, however, from goods traffic: from South Wales coal imported at Bideford and distributed along the line to Okehampton; from limestone, granite, and slate quarried mostly round Okehampton; from the vast beds of potter's clay and pipe-clay in the Peters Marland district; and from building materials, general merchandise, and agricultural produce. Hopkins's general reports, and the detailed parochial reports on the country to be served, are full of valuable information for the local historian and topographer.

Despite strong local backing, nothing came of this project. By 1836 some of its promoters had diverted their attention to a proposal for a railway that subsequently became the London and South-Western, to be constructed by George Stephenson. The idea was revived in 1845, when a prospectus was issued of " The Bideford and Tavistock Railway, with branches to Barnstaple and Crediton," the engineers to be Hopkins's two sons. The South Devon Railway had obtained powers to extend from Plymouth to Tavistock, and the Act for the Exeter and Crediton line had just been passed. The Bideford and Tavistock line would have forked at Okehampton, one branch going east to Crediton, the other continuing south to Tavistock. But the decision of the South Devon Railway not to extend to Tavistock after all led to the abandonment once again of the Hopkins's line. When the Tavistock extension came up again in 1852, the further extension to Bideford was revived once more, but still nothing came of it; and west Devon, which had been the first in the field with proposals for a steam railway in fact was the last part of the county to achieve it. Not until 1925 was a light railway opened from the Torrington terminus of the Southern Railway, through the Peters Marland clay country and Hatherleigh, rejoining the main line at Halwill Junction, and not at Okehampton.

The first steam railway to reach Devon was the Bristol and Exeter railway.[1] The construction of this line had begun from Bristol which was already linked with the Metropolis, in 1841. It had reached Taunton by 1 July 1842, and a further eight and a half miles to Beambridge was opened on 1 May 1843. At this point the line met the Exeter turnpike road, and coaches carried passengers on to Exeter as they had done from Bridgwater and Taunton in earlier months. The boring of the Whiteball Tunnel (1,092 yards), on the Devon-Somerset border, had been begun early in 1842, but the final stage of twenty-two miles from Beam Bridge into Exeter was not ready until the spring of 1844.

On 1 May of that year the first steam train reached Exeter, witnessed by vast crowds that had come into the city at an early hour from many miles around. " The happy and eager countenances," says the editorial in the *Flying Post*, " brightened with the glow of expectation, betokened that no ordinary event was to be witnessed, but something which would form the subject for many a curious tale, whereby the sightseers intended to astonish and delight their friends for years to come." Old people had walked many miles to see the latest wonder of modern science (for science then had no reason to be ashamed of its triumphs) and " the Juveniles, whose spring time of life was just budding forth in all the merry sportiveness of Childhood," were there in thousands. A mighty cheer went up as the first train of six carriages, drawn by the engine *Actaeon*, steamed in from Paddington at twelve-thirty after a journey of exactly five hours for the 194 miles. A great dinner was given in the goods shed at Exeter Station, and the return journey was begun at 5.20 p.m. Paddington was reached at ten o'clock precisely—in four hours forty minutes. Sir Thomas Acland, who had made the return journey from Exeter, was able to rise in the House at ten-thirty and to say that he had been in Exeter little more than five hours earlier.

The Bristol and Exeter Railway had been authorised by Parliament in 1836, at the instigation of a group of Bristol merchants. At once, a number of enterprising Plymouth men proposed a railway to Exeter, to meet the other line, and the great Brunel surveyed the country in the summer of 1836.[2] Nothing came of this, probably because the Devonshire people were slow to subscribe the required capital, and several further schemes were still-born. It is interesting to find that Brunel's original

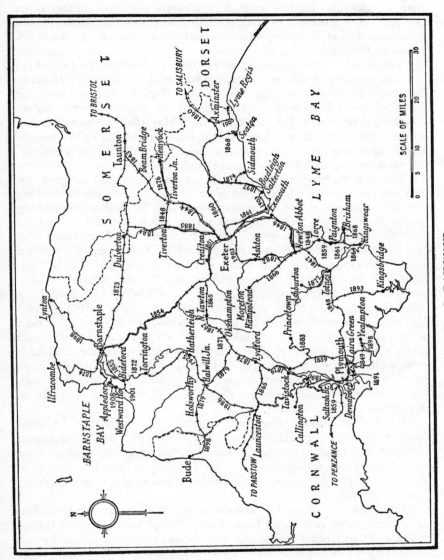

FIG. 9—RAILWAYS

The dates given show when the lines were opened

plan was to take the line from Exeter along the coast to the Teign (roughly on its present course), and thence over the Teign to the neighbourhood of Torquay, on across the Dart, and so through the South Hams to Plymouth.

The South Devon Railway was eventually authorised in July 1844; the first meeting of the new company was held at the Royal Hotel in Plymouth on 28 August 1844. By 30 May 1846 the line was open for traffic as far as Teignmouth, by the end of the year to Newton Abbot. Totnes was reached in July 1847, and on 5 May 1848 the line was open to the temporary station at Laira Green, within three miles of Plymouth. On 2 April 1849 the line was completed to the Plymouth terminus: Plymouth was joined to London, 246½ miles away.[1]

The first meeting of the company at Plymouth had adopted, on Brunel's recommendation, the idea of the atmospheric system for working the line. The pressure of the atmosphere was to be used as a propelling force.[2] Brunel was wholeheartedly in favour of the idea, and scouted the powerful opinions of George and Robert Stephenson on the other side. The experiment was tried and was a complete failure, mainly because of the decomposing action of water and iron on the vital leather component of the valves. In September 1848 the line was worked by locomotives, and the " Atmospheric Caper " was abandoned for good, after more than £400,000 of the company's money had been wasted. Brunel had made a tremendous mistake, but he was too great to suffer more than a temporary blow to his reputation. Until a few years ago, one could still see the last traces of this unhappy experiment in the Italianate campaniles at Exeter, Starcross, and Dawlish that disguised the large chimneys of the atmospheric engine-houses (plate 7). There had been ten of these structures between Exeter and Totnes, at intervals of approximately three miles.[3]

In 1850 the railway system of Devon was still confined to the main line from Taunton, through Exeter, to Plymouth, with a short branch from Tiverton Road (later Tiverton Junction) to Tiverton, and another from near Newton to Torquay (now Torre station). Both these branches were opened in 1848. The Exeter and Crediton Railway had been completed but not opened.

The Exeter and Crediton was authorised in 1845. It was to be five and three-quarter miles long, from Cowley Bridge junction on the Bristol and Exeter, to Crediton, and was to be leased upon completion by the local company to the Bristol and Exeter. The line had been ready early in 1847, but the manœuvres of local railway politics—a local skirmish in the great battle of Broad Gauge v. Narrow Gauge[4]—then caused it to be left derelict for four years. It was eventually opened on 12 May 1851 as a broad gauge single line (the other track being left narrow) and worked as a branch of the Bristol and Exeter.

So far the railways of Devon had all been constructed on the broad gauge favoured by the Great Western. The opening of the North Devon Railway from Barnstaple to Crediton in 1854 was another victory for this gauge. It was built by the famous engineer Thomas Brassey, who took a lease of it for seven years from the opening and worked it in connection with the Bristol and Exeter. The North Devon Railway was opened to Bideford in 1855, but the final extension to Torrington did not come until 1872.

Apart from purely local improvements in Plymouth, and the extension of the Torquay line as far as Paignton in 1859, the only other railway of any note to be opened during the 1850s was the Plymouth to Tavistock line. Two rival groups had contended fiercely in 1852-3 for the authority to construct this line, the " South Devon and Tavistock," led by Lord Morley, winning the day in 1854. The company's own engineer died soon after work had begun, and the line was carried through by Brunel, to be opened as far as Tavistock on 22 June 1859. It was leased to the South Devon Company until 1865, when it became their property (now the Western Region). A few weeks before this the Cornwall line had been opened as far as Truro, a difficult route which began with a major engineering achievement in Brunel's great Saltash Bridge.

The 1860s saw great additions to the railways of Devon. In 1860 itself, the London and South Western Railway (through the Yeovil and Exeter Company) at last reached Exeter. The project had been talked about ever since the early 1840s, but railway politics had been particularly fierce over this project to make a shorter route to Exeter than the Great Western through Bristol, and it was not until 1 August 1860 that the first train reached Exeter by this southern route. The inaugural journey took five hours ten minutes, longer in time than the G. W. R. over a route that was twenty-two miles shorter.

In 1861 the highly profitable Exeter to Exmouth line was opened. The Torbay line crept slowly down to the Kingswear terminus in 1864. At one time it had been proposed to make the terminus at Greenway, on the Dart, with a view to a subsequent crossing of the river and a line down the western side of the estuary directly into Dartmouth. Such a line might well have altered the whole course of Dartmouth's later history by saving it from the slow decay that set in as the railway network left it on one side. It was opposed in the Lords, however, by Mr. Harvey of Greenway, and the Kingswear route was taken instead, ending with a ferry across to Dartmouth. At Kingswear a large hotel was built in the hope that the terminus would become the landing-place for some of the Atlantic passenger traffic, but this proved an idle dream. The little

Brixham branch, opened in 1868, owed its existence solely to the public spirit and enterprise of Mr. R. W. Wolston of Brixham. After a sad financial history it was bought by the Great Western Railway in 1883.[1]

In 1865 the Plymouth-Tavistock line had been extended northwards to Lydford and then west to Launceston, worked throughout by the South Devon, which absorbed it in 1873. More important than this, the South Western began to lay' out its rival route round the northern side of Dartmoor to Plymouth, working through an apparently independent company, the Okehampton Railway.[2] The line began at Coleford Junction (on the Barnstaple line) and by 1865 was opened as far as North Tawton. Two years later it was opened to Belstone Corner, now Sampford Courtenay station, but Okehampton was not reached until October 1871.[3] Lydford was reached in 1874, a difficult piece of line which involved making the Meldon viaduct and climbing to 950 feet above sea-level (the highest point on the Southern Region railway system). Tavistock was reached in 1876.[4] The last section, from Tavistock, through Bere Alston, to Devonport was not opened until 1890; and in the following year the South Western gained access to Plymouth at Friary station.

Besides pushing on towards Plymouth in the 'seventies, the South Western had reached out to Holsworthy by 1879. Its final extension to the coast at Bude did not come, however, until 1898. North Devon saw most of the railway activity in the 1870s (see Fig. 9). The 1880s saw the completion of the second route to Plymouth by the narrow-gauge Devon and Cornwall line, and the opening of the Yelverton to Princetown line, using the old Dartmoor Railway route for most of the way. Only small pieces now remained to be added to the Devon network, the details of which will be found in Fig. 9.*

All the railways of Devon, like those elsewhere, had been constructed by more or less small and independent companies, though often they were substantially assisted by the engineers and capital of larger companies anxious to extend their spheres of influence. Many were also leased to the larger companies for working. But as railway groupings became larger and competition more powerful, the independent companies themselves felt constrained to seek the protection of larger companies. The sudden acquisition by the Midland of a share in the Somerset and Dorset Railway, bringing the powerful Midland well into the West, frightened the Bristol and Exeter, prosperous though it was, and in 1876 it came to terms with the Great Western. In that year the Bristol and Exeter ceased to exist, and the G. W. R. took over. Similarly, the plans of the South Western

*The Lynton and Barnstaple Railway was closed and dismantled in 1935. The Bideford-Westward Ho railway was closed during the war of 1914-18. The rails and rolling-stock were sent over to France, and the line was never re-opened.

to make an alternative route to Plymouth led to an agreement between the South Devon and the G. W. R. for ultimate amalgamation. The South Devon was dissolved in 1878. By 1876 the G. W. R. had extended its main line from Bristol to Penzance, and took over as well all the smaller constituent lines of those two railways. Further absorptions followed steadily. Similarly, the London and South Western took over the various companies operating in north and east Devon, and by the opening of this century only a few short lines remained outside the ownership of one or other of the two great companies.*

There remained the problem of the gauges in the West Country. Most of the Great Western system had been broad gauge, but the company had recognised since the sixties that the narrow gauge had won the day and that it would sooner or later have to conform. A mixed gauge had been introduced by laying a third rail: the whole main line from Paddington to Exeter had been so treated. But the line from Exeter to Plymouth was still all broad gauge, except the last three miles or so from Tavistock Junction, and a good deal of the main line in Cornwall, besides many of the Devon branch lines. The decision was made early in 1892 to end the broad gauge for good, and the gigantic task of conversion was carried through between the night of Friday 20 May and the following Monday morning.

The Great Western Railway dominated Devon, and indeed the whole of the West of England, and what a splendid railway it was. It was as solidly built, as spaciously efficient, as safe to use, as unimpeachable, as the Bank of England. Men were proud of working for it, and served travellers with the courtesy and pride of those who knew their jobs and their high reputation. And those who used the railway felt in turn almost a personal affection for it, its complete dependability and its foibles. The passing of the Great Western at midnight on 31 December 1947 was a sad day for the West Country. With pain its admirers have watched it being dragged down to the level of those other railways that cannot be named on the same page, its pride visibly decaying, even the once-incomparable Cornish Riviera Express running late; and no one cares. No one, that is, except those brought up on or near it, who still secretly hope for the return of the old love. The whistles and the hooters blew interminably at St. David's Station in Exeter on that December midnight, to welcome the birth of British Railways; but I fancy that they would blow with even greater fervour to-day if the old Great Western were coming back to the men who understood it and were proud of it.

*In 1912 only two independent companies were left within the Great Western territory: the Teign Valley, which remained in existence until 1923, and the Princetown Railway, absorbed in 1922. Both were leased and worked by the G.W.R., however, long before their absorption.

CHAPTER IX

POPULATION

THE study of population growth and change is fundamental to the understanding of a good deal of social and economic history. Without it our comprehension of much of the history of Devon will be superficial indeed. It is, however, well to have at all times some fairly precise idea of the orders of magnitude we are dealing with. How astonishing it is to find, for example, that the whole population of Devon at the time of Domesday was still no larger than that of modern Exeter: it helps to put the Saxon settlement in its proper perspective, and to show how vastly much still needed to be done in the colonisation movement of the 12th and 13th centuries. It is salutary, too, to contemplate what little towns in Elizabethan Devon produced its great men: we learn to reflect more on quality and individuality, and less on large numbers, contrary to all our modern way of thinking.

THE DOMESDAY POPULATION

The first estimate we can make of the population of Devon is one derived from Domesday Book (1086), and we run into difficulties at the outset of our inquiry. The totals of the *recorded* population arrived at by Sir Henry Ellis and more recently by a local scholar, Robert Burnard, differ considerably.[1] I accept Burnard's total here, on the ground that a writer who makes a close computation for one county is more likely to be correct than one who deals with the country as a whole. Moreover, Burnard was aware of Ellis's figures and wrote accordingly.

According to Burnard there were in Devon 8,508 *villani*, 4,733 *bordarii* and *cottarii*, 5,178 *servi*, and 436 miscellaneous persons, a total of 18,855. If to these we add the numbers of the tenants-in-chief (seventy-seven), the mesne tenants (402), and the burgesses (274)* we get a total

*These three figures are Ellis's, unchecked by Burnard. But they are small and do not affect the grand total noticeably.

approaching 20,000. Indeed, Ellis's figure for burgesses in Devon appears to involve a substantial underestimate. 250 burgesses are enumerated outside Exeter—Totnes 110, Lydford sixty-nine, Barnstaple sixty-seven, and Okehampton four—and at Exeter some 416 houses are enumerated on various pages of Domesday, each of which represents a household, whether burgess or not. This gives a " town " population, to use a loose expression, of 666 households, and brings our grand total of the recorded population of Devon to 20,000 exactly.

If we wish to know the actual population of the county we encounter two major difficulties: how many people shall we reckon to the " household," and can we legitimately count all the *servi* as separate householders? Russell, in his *British Medieval Population* (1948), boldly multiplies the recorded population by $3\frac{1}{2}$ in order to arrive at the actual total. If we do likewise, we get a total of 70,000 people for the county, rather fewer than live in Exeter to-day. There is no point in trying to refine this figure, since one can never arrive at certainty. The truth lies somewhere between 60,000 and 80,000, if we want to feel on safer ground.

Whatever the possible error may be in estimating total populations, it is minimised if we use our Domesday statistics for comparative purposes, to see how Devon stands in relation to other counties at the same date. Absolute figures have little merit in themselves, and are not very informative even if they are sometimes salutary. The local historian must always try to see his own field in perspective as a part of the national landscape— without, however, being so much influenced by the general view that he does not see the significant detail of his own—and not dig in his own little pit oblivious of all else.

On an average there were slightly fewer than eight recorded persons per square mile in Devon. If we adopt Russell's multiplier of $3\frac{1}{2}$ in order to make use of his comparative tables we get an actual population of twenty-seven persons per square mile. The highest densities in England are found in Suffolk ($46\frac{1}{2}$), Norfolk ($42\frac{1}{2}$), and Essex (thirty-five).[1] Only two regions in England had more than thirty persons to the square mile: a large block comprising the four east-coast counties from Lincolnshire down to Essex, and another block of three counties in the south midlands —Oxfordshire, Wiltshire, and Berkshire. Nineteen other counties had between twenty and thirty persons per square mile. Devon stands thirteenth in the list of English counties. To the east, Somerset was slightly more densely populated (though not so much as we might have expected) with $28\frac{1}{2}$ persons to the square mile; to the west, Cornwall had fewer than fourteen—only half the density of Devon. These figures must be treated as approximate in view of the nature of the record, but they tell us a good deal nevertheless.

An average figure for Devon, as for most counties, is misleading.

One has only to think of the great variations in soils and topography within a few miles almost anywhere in England to make one look behind all generalisations. In Devon we have the extremes of the uninhabited waste of Dartmoor, covering more than 200 square miles, and the deep red lands of the vale of Exeter almost immediately below. The densities of population in the different geographical regions of Devon have been worked out on a somewhat different basis from the figures given above. Morgan, in a paper on "The Domesday Geography of Devon",[1] adds together the recorded population and does not attempt to enter into the difficult questions of the relationship of this figure to the total population. Nevertheless, the results of this reckoning are interesting.

As we should expect, the moorland fringes of Exmoor and Dartmoor have the lowest density—only 4.7 recorded persons per thousand acres. The greatest density is found in the vale of Exeter, which roughly coincides with the New Red Sandstone soils, with 14.5 persons; and in the adjoining fertile area between Teign and Dart, stretching back to the foothills of the Moor, with 14.4.[2] Thus the most densely populated parts of Devon were about three times as thickly peopled as the least populous. The South Hams, between Dart and Plym, and the north Devon lowlands around the lower Taw and Torridge, had rather more than twelve recorded persons per 1,000 acres. Large tracts of Devon, particularly to the west of Dartmoor, had fewer than ten persons per thousand acres.

The average density over all the county was twelve recorded persons per 1,000 acres. The most densely peopled districts were only twenty per cent above the average for the county as a whole, a reflection of the even distribution of settlement in the 11th century which has already been referred to. Devon, as a whole, was a thinly populated county. Its richest regions were still only as densely peopled as Oxfordshire or Lincolnshire taken as a whole, a fact which must be attributed mainly to the difference of 200 years in the date of the English settlement of each county. Lincolnshire and Oxfordshire were being colonised and settled from the 5th century onwards; Devon only from the 7th. This difference of two centuries was of profound importance at such an early date as Domesday, and it took another five centuries to wipe it out.

POPULATION IN 1377

Our next population figures for Devon come from the poll tax returns of 1377, for it should be said right away that the tax assessments of the early 14th century are quite valueless for a count of population. Tax-evasion was widespread; nor do we know the number of exempted persons. The poll tax returns are not without their special difficulties, but they are valuable once more for comparative purposes.

None of the so-called Particular Accounts, giving the names of those assessed to the poll tax, parish by parish, survives for Devon. We have, however, an enrolled account which gives the total taxed population of the county.[1] Excluding Exeter and Dartmouth, the total of taxed persons (i.e. over fourteen years of age) is given as 45,635. Exeter's taxed population numbered 1,560, Dartmouth's 506. The grand total for Devon is therefore 47,701.* If we add to this a figure of fifty per cent to cover the children under fourteen years of age, we get a total of 71,550. And to this again we have to add 1,315 clergy of all kinds, who were separately taxed,[2] giving a final figure of 72,865 people, or just over twenty-seven persons per square mile.

The most densely peopled counties in England at this date were Norfolk (65.5 per square mile), Bedfordshire (63.4), and Northamptonshire (60.3). Devon came far down the list, about on a level with the starved northern county of Lancashire (twenty-six) and well below both Cornwall (thirty-seven) and Somerset (forty-eight). The net increase of population in Devon between 1086 and 1377 was the lowest of any English county. On the other hand, the jump in Cornwall (from fourteen persons per square mile to thirty-seven) is remarkable, and deserves the attention of the Cornish historian.

The net increase of population in Devon between 1086 and 1377—if indeed there is any increase at all—is so small as to suggest that the effects of the Black Death were more severe here than elsewhere, and there is, indeed, a good deal of evidence pointing that way. Dr. Lunn computed from the Exeter episcopal registers that the mortality among the Devon clergy was as high as forty-nine per cent in the first and severest visitation of the plague (1349-51). Exeter, Winchester, and Norwich were the worst hit dioceses in the country, and the deanery of Kenn, to the south and south-west of Exeter, was the worst hit deanery in all England. It lost eighty-six incumbents from its seventeen churches in those years. At Exeter it has been shown that the mortality among the lay population was very nearly as high as that of the clergy.[3]

Nor was the heavy mortality confined to the crowded medieval city. In the isolated parish of Templeton, with no village, we are told that the dead were collected by the cart-load from the scattered farmsteads, and taken by night to the mother-church of Witheridge for burial.[4] Even on Dartmoor the effects were felt. The bailiff's account for Dartmoor manor in 1350-1 gives a long list of the moorland farms "in the hands of the lord for want of tenants," and we find that as late as 1355 no tin was

*No separate figure for Plymouth appears on this account, as stated by Topham in *Archaeologia* 7 (1785), 344-7, who is followed by Russell. The Plymouth figure is a myth.

being produced on the moor. The output from Devon in that year was nil.[1]

There cannot be much doubt about the severity of the plague in Devon: the evidence from the city of Exeter, the deanery of Kenn, the parish of Templeton, the heart of Dartmoor, all points the same way. Nor can there be much doubt that the population of Devon had reached a peak on the eve of the Black Death. The widespread rebuilding and enlargement of parish churches during the first half of the 14th century is striking evidence of the expansion of those years. Such a general movement for larger and better accommodation is good evidence of a population-peak in those years, even if we do not fall into the elementary error of equating the size of a medieval church with the size of the parish population, as Cobbett was inclined to do. Still, we might not be far out if we put the population of Devon in 1347 at half as high again as that of 1377.

POPULATION AND PLAGUE IN THE 16TH CENTURY

Two hundred years later, when we can form our next estimate of population, the picture is strikingly different. The muster-books of able-bodied men between 1558 and 1588 reveal that Devon was now the second or third most populous county in England. Prof. Rich's table shows a total for Devon in 1569 of 14,610 able-bodied men between the ages of sixteen and sixty.[2] Essex comes next with 12,071, and then Suffolk with 10,512. Yorkshire is missing from the 1569 return, but in 1570 had 39,292 able-bodied men. In point of fact the Devon total is considerably more than 14,610 (which is the total entered on the record itself). The individual totals for the parishes add up to 15,359[3] and even then Plymouth and a dozen parishes of " tinners," who were separately mustered, are not included in this return. Exeter, returned separately, could muster 447 men. If we had all the necessary figures, the total for Devon would be in the neighbourhood of 17,000 able-bodied men.

Later returns show inexplicable variations in the county totals which cannot be pursued here. Yorkshire always comes out first, and Devon generally occupies second or third place, depending on the figure assigned to Kent. But whatever the minor variations between the standing of the counties, the rise of Devon from one of the most thinly and under-populated counties in 1377 to one of the most densely peopled in Eliza-bethan days is unmistakable. Not all this tremendous increase could have been natural: immigration from other counties and from across the Irish and English Channels undoubtedly played a large part. But these are subjects awaiting further inquiry.

This increase is all the more remarkable when one looks into the evidence of plague and other epidemics during the 16th century. A close study of the burial entries in the parish registers, often accompanied by the parson's own notes against the bad years, enables one to trace the march of the plague from house to house, and from family to family, culminating in the towns with mass burials when the plague was at its height.

At Crediton, for example, the plague of 1571 began in early April: there were five burials on the 9th. The death rate rose steadily through the warm months that followed. By 18 June there were 200 dead, by the end of July, 400. On some days in July there were as many as ten burials. Altogether 535 people died during this year. The average number of burials for the preceding normal years was forty to forty-five, so that nearly 500 people must have died of plague in this one small town, possibly a third of the total population. Some of these later visitations of plague were nearly as devastating as the first " black death " of 1349.

Plague came again to Crediton in the early autumn of 1590, brought in from the country round about, but it was slow in taking root. Not until September of the following year did it strike in earnest. Thirty-six people were buried in this month, including " Isabell Reeve a poore mayzed maide " who died in the street. The parson records that her clothing was buried with her. During October there were over eighty plague deaths, and only two normal deaths, one of these being " Joan Browne wydowe by report almost 120 years having a son eighty-four years of age living." One likes to think of old Mother Browne sticking it out to the end, plague or no plague. So it went on, month after month, into 1592, and then stopped suddenly in mid-August, after two years all but one month. 535 people had died of plague in that time. We have progressed since then: death by burning alive with napalm bombs has been substituted for death by bubonic plague.

Crediton lost over a thousand people by plague in the space of twenty-one years, nor was this exceptional. The small deep-country parishes show proportionate losses. At Newton St. Cyres in 1571 more people died of plague in three months than normally died in four years; and in the winter of 1604-5 there were thirty-five plague deaths and only one normal death. In the remote parish of Bridford, seven people of the same family name were buried in seven weeks between August and October 1591.[1]

Although some outbreaks of plague and other epidemics were widespread, it appears from an inspection of a great number of parish registers that most outbreaks were highly localised. One town might be burying its dead in scores; but ten miles away in the next town life went on normally. Perhaps the rigid quarantine regulations of the Elizabethan town authorities were successful to that extent; but Death was not mocked. A place that was smitten hard in one year seemed to gain some sort of immunity, but those that had escaped the first time fell at the second blow. And yet, with all this appalling total of deaths by pestilence, the population of Devon, as of England generally, grew remarkably.

THE SEVENTEENTH CENTURY

For the 17th century our best information comes from the Protestation Returns of 1642, and the hearth tax returns of 1662, 1664, and 1674.[1] Neither source, however, gives us a complete picture of the county, and each is subject to its own peculiar difficulties when we try to use it for counting purposes. Perhaps the simplest approach is through the hearth tax figures for 1674. In that year the total number of chargeable hearths in Devon was returned as 70,259, and of those exempt as 16,318, a grand total of 86,577 hearths. For Cornwall the corresponding total was 39,238 hearths.[2]

Now, a random sample of twenty-four parishes all over the county (but excluding the large towns of Exeter and Plymouth) shows that the average number of hearths per household was almost exactly 2.2.* If we divide this figure into the total number of hearths, we get a total of 39,353 households. We cannot be too precise about figures arrived at in this way, and we shall be near enough to the truth if we say that there were about 40,000 families in Devon in 1674. By 1801, when the first census was taken, this figure had risen to 73,391 families, an increase of eighty-five per cent in four generations.

This increase was not spread evenly over the county—Plymouth, Devonport, and Exeter probably grew faster than this—but a comparison, parish by parish, during this period still awaits the specialist student of population. Such an inquiry would by no means be purely statistical. One might find that certain deep-country parishes were losing people, and that behind this lay important changes in farming; and that some towns were gaining immigrants from the country because they offered new opportunities and new trades. The figures are only interesting as symptoms of deep-seated social and economic changes.

MOBILITY OF THE RURAL POPULATION

There was a remarkable amount of movement among all classes in Devon below the landed class. The squire and the big freeholder might remain rooted in the same parish for centuries, but the rest of the population measured its stay by generations.

*The sample is large enough to minimise the effect of " the great house " in some parishes. It covers exactly 1900 households, who between them had 4,218 hearths.

In a sample of seven parishes of various types, scattered all over the county, we find that between forty and seventy per cent of the family names disappear from the parish register within a hundred years.[1] The average rate of disappearance is nearly sixty per cent during the 17th and 18th centuries. Even allowing for the imperfections of our data the rate is so high that it would not be much affected by accidental omissions. Over a space of 200 years more than four families in five disappear from their ancestral parishes in most places. Branscombe and Huntsham show the lowest figures in the sample, and even here two out of three have disappeared in 200 years.

Anyone who has tried to trace the descent of an ordinary family—that is, below the level of the armigerous class—is aware of this extreme mobility. It is very rare to get a straightforward run through one parish register for more than a hundred years: one spends most time casting around the district to find where the migrants have gone. They have seldom indeed gone far. It would be impossible to follow up all the migrants from a given parish to see where and how far they had gone, but a long experience of searching for my own family and those related to it by marriage—all of them farming families for centuries—tells me that though most of them were moving about, almost from one generation to another at times, they did not move far. Between 1585, when they entered Devon from just over the Dorset border, down to 1825, they, and all the families they married with, only moved around within a radius of about ten miles in east Devon, although the records of their baptisms, marriages and burials are to be found in a dozen parish registers in this small area. People moved farther afield in the 19th century, especially after the great slump in farming of the 1820s, but in Devon they still did not move far. Certainly it was rare to leave the county altogether, unless one lived within a few miles of the Somerset or Cornish border. We may hazard the guess that before 1820 the average move was something under ten miles. It may have been up to thirty miles by the later years of the 19th century, when the railways and cheap postage had come to facilitate getting about, and to spread the knowledge of better jobs elsewhere.

These impressions of what happened to a few typical families in Devon during this century are borne out by the statistics of the 1851 census. In that year it was found that eighty-six per cent of the inhabitants of Devon had been born in it. Of the remaining fourteen per cent, more than a half had only come across the border from Cornwall, Somerset, or Dorset. Of the outward migrants in 1851, who amounted to thirteen per cent of those born in Devon, exactly a half went to London, but nearly all the remainder only went into Somerset and Cornwall. Fully eighty-seven per cent of those born in Devon were content to stay in it, but they were not static: most of them probably moved around in a radius of perhaps twenty to thirty miles during the course of the century.

POPULATION IN THE NINETEENTH CENTURY

In this discussion of mobility within the county we have been led far beyond the first census of 1801, and we must now turn back to it. In that year, there were in Devon 340,308 people and 57,955 inhabited houses.[1] Devon was third in size among the English counties, and still fourth in population, surpassed only by Middlesex, Yorkshire, and Lancashire.

There were only two large towns—Exeter and Plymouth. By a strict definition the largest town was Dock (renamed Devonport in 1824) with nearly 24,000 people. Plymouth had just over 16,000, Exeter rather more than 17,000. What we may call Greater Exeter, which included the suburbs of St. Thomas, St. Leonard, and Heavitree, had a total population of 20,543. Greater Plymouth, though not yet a continuous urban mass, numbered 43,194 people in Plymouth, Stoke Damarel (where Dock lay), and East Stonehouse. The roaring war town on Plymouth Sound was now more than twice as big as the stagnant industrial and commercial city of Exeter.

Far behind Exeter and Plymouth in numbers was a group of seventeen old market towns. The largest of these was Tiverton with rather fewer than 6,000 people,[2] and then came Crediton, Barnstaple, Brixham, Dartmouth, Tavistock, Cullompton, and Ashburton, all having between three and four thousand people. Another little group of nine towns— Bideford, South Molton, Topsham, Totnes, Ottery St. Mary, Honiton, Axminster, Torrington, and Teignmouth in that order—nourished between two and three thousand inhabitants. The growing seaside town of Exmouth—the oldest seaside resort in Devon—probably had about 2,000 people. No fewer than twenty of the ancient market towns of the county had only between one and two thousand people; and most of these could be regarded as decaying, or at the best moribund. Such a town was Hartland, which a traveller described in the 1790s as having " an air of poverty that depresses it to a level with a Cornish borough "— a damning comparison indeed.

Below the market towns was a considerable number of villages, each with a population of several hundreds and a large parish around dotted with outlying farmsteads and hamlets. Such villages had a great variety of trades and occupations—they were miniature market towns—and a considerable degree of community life. But beyond these again lay the deep country of nothing but hamlets, farmsteads, and lonely cottages with little or no community life, where the village settlement had never developed. Nearly one parish in three in Devon had fewer than fifty households in 1801; a great number had fewer than twenty.

Up to 1831 the population of Devon increased at about the same pace as the country generally: in that census year Devon was still fourth in total population and the same three counties led. The only significant changes inside the county were the continued growth of Greater Plymouth, which now had over 75,000 people, and the slower growth of Exeter which, with its suburbs, was a delightful little cathedral city of just under 35,000. The market towns had generally grown a little, though few exceeded 4,000 people. Much more important was the emergence of the seaside towns, which has already been discussed.

Since 1831 Devon has dropped steadily down the list of English counties. In 1861 she had fallen to seventh, by 1881 to ninth: the manufacturing and metropolitan counties were leaping ahead. This mattered not at all: there is no intrinsic merit in large numbers. But what was disturbing in Devon was the steady depopulation of the rural parishes which had been going on since the 1820s. Between 1841 and 1851 especially, hundreds of rural parishes lost people to the towns, above all to Plymouth, Exeter, and the seaside towns. Between 1861 and 1901 it has been calculated that 208 small parishes fell in numbers by anything up to sixty per cent.[1]

Most of the migrants went to the local towns, but some left the county entirely, like the Tavistock miners and the Halberton farm-labourers, who went to the north of England. Of those who left the county, most still went to London, but in the 1870s and 1880s there developed a steady trickle overseas to the colonies and the United States, helped to some extent by the cut-rates of the Atlantic shipping companies and by the railway rate-war on the other side. In my own family, men went out to New Zealand, Canada, and the United States in these years, just as one or two had gone out to New England in the early 17th century. Among the emigrants to Natal from 1849 onwards were a number of Devon and Cornish men. Natal's first organ-builder was George Vinnicombe, born at Sidmouth, who went out to join his brother, a ship's carpenter. Samuel Williams, son of a saddler of Winkleigh, migrated first of all to London and worked with the well-known saddlery firm of Peat. But all over England the railways were reducing the demand for saddlery, and Williams decided that the future of his trade lay in a colony where steam transport was as yet hardly known. The Acutt brothers from Torquay were among the most prosperous merchants of Durban in the 1850s. Edward Tyrell, son of the recorder of Tiverton, also went out to Natal. All sorts and conditions of men went out, and many of them rose to prominence in the commercial and political life of the infant colony.[2]

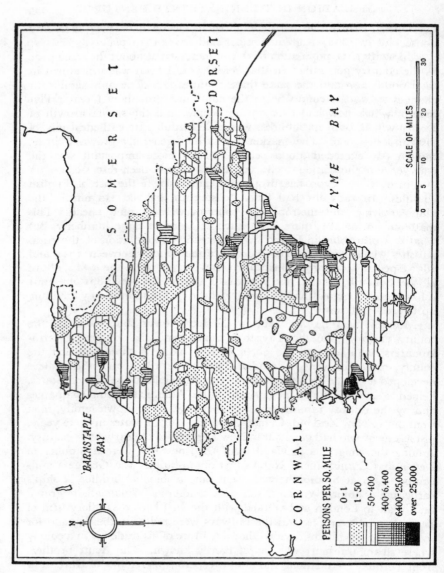

Fig. 10—DISTRIBUTION OF POPULATION (1931)

PERSONS PER SQ. MILE

0-1
1-50
50-400
400-6,400
6400-25,000
over 25,000

SCALE OF MILES
0   5   10   20   30

SOMERSET

DORSET

LYME BAY

CORNWALL

BARNSTAPLE BAY

N

The drain of the rural areas in Devon has continued to the present day. The map showing the decreasing and the increasing areas between 1921 and 1938 is almost identical with that for the years between 1841 and 1851. In more than two-thirds of Devon the population was falling. It was only increasing in the Plymouth dormitory area, along the south coast from Kingswear to Seaton, around Exeter and over east Devon generally (except on the Blackdown plateau), and in a small area around Barnstaple and Bideford. There were other small patches where population still increased, owing to quite local causes such as the large milk factory at Lapford, and the Dart valley which attracted a growing residential population by reason of its beautiful scenery. In general the towns were still draining away the country people, though even some of the towns were falling back, among them Dartmouth, Torrington, and Bideford. A recent report indeed speaks of north Devon in these pre-war years as " a land of static or decaying towns in an abandoned countryside."[1] Even Barnstaple was only standing still between 1921 and 1938. But the county as a whole was becoming more urbanised, as a result of the growth of the south Devon towns.

CHAPTER X

POLITICAL AND MILITARY HISTORY

PARLIAMENTARY REPRESENTATION, 1258-1603

THE early political history of the county has already been touched upon in the pages on the Saxon occupation, the Danish wars, and the early boroughs, and intermittently in other places. From the very nature of our sources, it is bound to be a disconnected story in these earlier centuries, with many unsatisfactory gaps. It is not until we reach the 13th century that the written records become sufficiently voluminous and explicit to enable us to produce a more or less continuous account of political development, and here we may most profitably begin with the history of the representation of Devon in Parliament, for which the records are naturally fuller and more detailed than most, and where, indeed, one or two local scholars have already worked out a good deal of the tangled story for us.

The long history of parliamentary representation in Devon begins with the parliament of October 1258, at which the shire of Devon was represented by four knights, drawn from local families. They were Sir William de Bickleigh (of Bickleigh, near Tiverton), Sir Roger de Cockington (of Cockington), Sir William de Courtenay of Musbury, and Sir Geoffrey de Dynham of Hartland. The next names we have for Devon are for 1290, when two knights were returned, again both Devon men. From the so-called " Model Parliament " of November 1295 onwards, Devon is continuously represented in every parliament down to 1832.[1]

The city of Exeter may have been represented in " De Montfort's Parliament " of 1265, and perhaps in others later, but we find no names before 1295. In that year a number of Devon boroughs were represented. Exeter, Barnstaple, Plympton, and Totnes may be regarded as " regular boroughs " as distinct from the transient or casual boroughs which make one or two returns and then drop out until a much later date. For example, Tavistock and Torrington returned members in 1295, and Dartmouth and Plymouth in 1298. But Tavistock did not begin to send members regularly until 1330, and Torrington never became a " regular borough." If we exclude the " parliament " of 1298 as not being a true parliament but a mere assembly, the parliamentary history of Dartmouth begins in 1351, and that of Plymouth in 1442. Ashburton returned members in 1298, but its regular history begins only in 1640.[1] Apart from Exeter, then, only three Devon boroughs have a continuous parliamentary history from 1295—Barnstaple, Plympton, and Totnes.

Eight other Devon boroughs returned members at some time or other during the 14th century, but of these only two—Honiton and Okehampton —were ever revived (both in 1640). The other six faded out altogether.[2] To this list of regular and casual boroughs in the medieval period we have to add Bere Alston and Tiverton, both of late creation. Bere Alston's parliamentary history begins in 1584; that of Tiverton in 1615. Altogether there were twenty constituencies in Devon (including the county itself), of which thirteen have a continuous and prolonged history.

A great many of the names of the medieval members in Devon are known to us, thanks to the labours of Mr. J. J. Alexander, whose work on the parliamentary history of the county is scattered through the volumes of the *Transactions of the Devonshire Association* from 1909 onwards. But it is difficult to invest these lists of names with life and movement.

Down to the 15th century, membership was regarded more as a disagreeable duty than an honour, more so in the south-west perhaps than elsewhere in England, except the extreme north. From Exeter to Westminster was 170 arduous miles; for many Devonshire members it was over 200. No wonder we hardly discover any Devon members over the age of sixty,[3] and no wonder members were paid to go. We find, too, many examples of " pluralists," usually lawyers, whose business took them to London and who were willing to represent two or more constituencies simultaneously. These pluralists were especially common in the three south-western counties of Cornwall, Devon, and Dorset.[4]

By the 15th century, however, membership of the House of Commons was becoming more attractive: it was beginning to offer social influence and opportunities of salaried office. So, by the middle of the century, candidates were seeking constituencies rather than the reverse, and with the increasing demand for seats came the patron of the borough. The county representation was another matter: Devon was far too large for the effective exercise of patronage and the shire representatives continued to be drawn from families of local standing.

Yet the Devon constituencies had far fewer " carpet-baggers " than the average. During the period 1439-1509, for example, only one member in eight came from outside the county. Devon had few parliamentary boroughs in relation to its size, and there was generally a good supply of local candidates—landowners, shipowners, manufacturers and merchants, and, above all, ambitious lawyers, of whom there were so many in Devon. Moreover, of the eighteen " carpet-baggers " in Devon during these years, no fewer than six represented Plympton and four Barnstaple. Plympton is the only undoubted example in 15th-century Devon of a nomination-borough, controlled by the Crown after the downfall of the Courtenays in 1461, though Barnstaple came very near the same description at times. On the other hand, there was a strong local flavour about the Totnes members. Half the members were connected with the town itself; the other half came from south Devon or were Exeter lawyers.[1]

Things were much the same during the 16th century. At Totnes the members were mostly either merchants of the town, like the Balls and the Haymans, or came from merchant families who had risen to the ranks of the gentry, such as the Saverys, the Gileses, and the Bogans. Sometimes they were local gentry of old standing, like Sir Arthur Champernowne and Richard Edgecumbe esquire, who sat for the borough together in 1563. And the mixture was much the same as Barnstaple: local merchants and local gentry predominated, with a very occasional " outsider " like William Gardener (1552-3), and Vincent Skinner (1572), a lawyer who sat for four other constituencies in the course of his career.[2] For the county representation, the most coveted and distinguished of all, only local gentlemen were ever chosen. There is no need to catalogue their names, for they include all the ancient families; but what is noticeable is that there is no sustained monopoly of the county seats by any one man or family. Only Sir William Courtenay sat as many as three times for Devon, during Elizabeth's reign. Twice was as often as even the more influential gentry could hope to sit. In all, seventeen of the leading families shared the county representation between 1529 and 1601, a considerable ringing of the changes.[3]

There were seven parliamentary boroughs in Devon down to 1584, when the new borough of Bere Alston was created, each returning two members. They were Exeter, Barnstaple, Totnes, Dartmouth, Tavistock, Plymouth and Plympton. Bere Alston, enfranchised by Elizabeth at the request of the two lords of the " town "—William, Marquess of Winchester, and William, Lord Mountjoy—made an eighth, also returning two members.[4] The distribution of these boroughs is remarkable. Six of the eight lay in the south and south-west of the county; the remaining four-fifths of the county had only two boroughs—Exeter and Barnstaple—forty miles apart.

The nature of the borough representation in 1584 will serve as some indication of the trends in Devon.[5] At Exeter, Barnstaple, and Totnes, all the members resided in their respective boroughs. At Dartmouth and Plympton, the four members resided in the county. At Plymouth, one member was a county man, but the other was a " foreigner." At Tavistock and Bere Alston, all four members were " foreigners."

Bere Alston was a pocket borough, under private patronage from the first, and its members were nominees of the two patrons. Tavistock had become the pocket borough of the Earl of Bedford, whose father had acquired the borough and a great part of the abbey lands at the Dissolution. He was all-powerful in the south-west, Lord-Lieutenant of Devon, Cornwall, and the city of Exeter, and later of Dorset also. Both the Tavistock members were consistently " foreigners," nominated by the Earl. In several Elizabethan parliaments one of the two members was a relative or connection by marriage. The Bedford influence may be detected also at Dartmouth and perhaps Plymouth.[1]

When the Earl died in 1585, his son-in-law, the Earl of Bath, became Lord-Lieutenant of Devon and Exeter. He lived in a great new house at Tawstock, of which only the massive gatehouse now survives as a hint of its splendour, and dominated the borough of Barnstaple two miles away. In earlier decades, Barnstaple had elected its mayors and ex-mayors as members; but from 1586 onwards the Earl of Bath nominated one member at each election. His Devon agent and former tutor, with two intermissions, represented the borough from 1586 until 1611. The Earl's dominance is laid bare in 1597, when the borough chose as its second member a man to whom the Earl objected. Another election was accordingly held, and an acceptable member chosen.[2]

Plympton, which became one of the rottenest of parliamentary boroughs during the 18th century, seems to have freed itself from powerful patrons until the 1670s, when the Trebys begin to emerge as the controlling interest. But from the early 16th century until then the local gentry—Strodes, Heles, Drakes, Slannings, Fortescues, and others—had the place pretty much to themselves.[3] Totnes, too, seems to have been free from patronage in Elizabethan times. In 1603, for example, it chose two local merchants to represent it, both ex-mayors. But the patron's hand is perceived a little later: in 1612 a letter was received from the Earl of Northumberland, the Lord Privy Seal, asking to be allowed to nominate one of the members for the borough. To this the corporation replied that they intended to return one of their own townsmen, and had promised their recorder, Sir George Cary, that he should nominate the other.[4] But the borough does not seem to have developed into a pocket-borough until the 18th century, and the same is true of Dartmouth.

The eighteen members from Devon had not been very conspicuous in the Elizabethan parliaments, but from the first parliament of James they became increasingly influential and were especially aggressive in the debates of 1621 and 1624. By the eve of the civil war, their numbers had been swollen to twenty-six, a formidable minority, with the enfranchisement of Tiverton in 1615 and the revival of the old boroughs of Ashburton, Honiton, and Okehampton, in 1640. There was more excuse for enfranchising Tiverton than Bere Alston. The latter must have been a poverty-stricken township in the 1580s, most of its mining at a dead end; whereas Tiverton had now become the largest and most active woollen town in Devon. Its first members, elected by the close corporation and no one else, were two Devon squires—John Bampfylde and John Davie—and until 1690 it seems to have systematically chosen local men, mostly gentry, with an occasional merchant.[1]

In the parliamentary debates of the 1620s, the Devon members were most aggressive and influential, particularly in the attack on the London trading companies—and above all the Merchant Adventurers—whose monopolies of certain overseas markets were of such moment for this industrial county. Among the most active of the members were John Glanville, Sir Edward Giles, Sir William Strode, John Pym, and such merchants as Neale (Dartmouth) and Delbridge (Barnstaple). And while they were mainly concerned with problems of trade, they also acted with the party opposed to the Crown on religious and constitutional issues. The Devonshire members played a significant part in the development of opposition to the Crown. In 1635, for example, all the then surviving Jacobean members—Giles, Strode, and Seymour—were summoned to answer before the Council for their opposition to Ship Money. In the Long Parliament of 1640, two of the Five Members, the leaders of the opposition whom Charles I tried to arrest, sat for Devon constituencies: Pym for Tavistock and Strode for Bere Alston.

THE COUNTY, 1603-1832

By the time of James I, there was no essential distinction between the county and the borough members, except that the latter occasionally returned merchants among the local landed proprietors.[2] There was a more important distinction between county and borough in the matter of patronage. The boroughs were becoming increasingly controlled by patrons, and at some elections a good deal of pressure was exerted to secure the return of members acceptable to the Court. The county was never controlled in this way: it was too large, and the electors generally too opulent to be amenable to bribery. In practice, however, as we shall see, the county representation tended more and more to fall into the hands of the territorial magnates, to be monopolised by a handful of great families. It was only patronage in another form.

Between 1603 and 1688, thirty-four families (all native to Devon) shared the county representation, but the choice was narrower than this would suggest. Out of seventy-six returns, the Rolles appear in twelve, and the Seymours in eight. One in four of the county members was a Rolle or a Seymour. And in contrast to the distaste in Elizabethan days for anything savouring of monopoly, Samuel Rolle of Petrockstow was chosen no fewer than seven times between 1679 and 1701. The Civil War and Interregnum had brought about a break with the past, in the personnel of the county members as in so much else. The parliaments of James and Charles had been reminiscent in their personnel of Elizabethan days; those after 1660 foreshadowed the 18th century. The entry of the Rolles is symptomatic. They first sit for Devon in 1641, in the person of Sir Samuel Rolle of Petrockstow, a notable parliament man. For the next 150 years, there were few parliaments without a Rolle in them.

From 1688 onwards we notice the increasing dominance of a few great families. Indeed, over the space of the next 144 years, down to 1832, the county members were chosen from only ten families, nearly all of them territorial magnates. The ordinary Devon squire very rarely had a look in. And out of these ten families, three are overwhelmingly dominant—Bampfyldes, Courtenays, and Rolles. Sir William Courtenay of Powderham sat no fewer than eleven times between 1701 and his death in 1735, and when he died his place was taken by a Rolle.

The county members from 1688 to 1760 were a particularly dull crowd. Of the fifteen, ten were named Rolle, Bampfylde, or Courtenay; and not one achieved sufficient eminence to be included in the *Dictionary of National Biography*. Of nearly every one we may say: " He belonged to a well-known Devon family; while in Parliament he made no speeches, held no office, and achieved no distinction of any sort; but whenever he is known to have recorded a vote, it was given against the government then in office."[1]

From 1701 onwards the great majority of Devon members seem to have been Tories. In the general election of that year, which went strongly in favour of the Whigs, the Devon electors returned two Tories, rejecting Samuel Rolle who had served them for over twelve years as a Whig. And until 1831 the members were invariably resident landowners. In that year Lord John Russell was elected, and even he had strong territorial connections with south-west Devon through his father, the Duke of Bedford.

Over the whole period 1485-1832, there were eighty-nine different county members, of whom only twenty are included in the *Dictionary of National Biography*, as compared with twenty-three from the pocket borough of Tavistock for the same years. Bere Alston had an even more remarkable record: no fewer than thirty-two of its members between 1584 and 1832 are included in the *Dictionary*. Few, if any, boroughs in

England could show a longer succession of eminent men. As compared with the pocket boroughs of the 20th century, returning their trade union nonentities so consistently, the " corrupt " boroughs of the 18th century had a good deal to be said for them.

THE BOROUGHS

In addition to the county, and the city of Exeter, there were eleven boroughs in Devon between 1640 and 1832, and their political history is complicated. Each requires a chapter to itself to do it justice, for in most of them one can distinguish clearly marked phases. Thus, at Dartmouth the years from 1660 to 1722 saw a series of election contests, a surfeit of petitions, and a struggle between Whigs and Tories for the mastery of the borough. There were seldom more than forty freemen on the list of electors, often fewer than thirty. Down to 1689 the elected members were nearly all gentlemen from the country round about. In that year the London merchant family of Herne established their influence, and for the next thirty years occupied one or both of the seats.[1] Then, from 1722 to 1780, follows the period of the placemen—" good subservient fellows, who were always ready to accept government appointments and the salaries attached to them." The merchant family of Holdsworth had taken over the political management of the borough from 1719. Indeed, the borough, with all its rights and revenues, was almost a family perquisite until the reforming acts of 1832 and 1835. From 1780 onwards, although Dartmouth remained a government borough, the Holdsworths and Bastards pretty well shared the representation.

Above the Arthur Holdsworth who first established the family stranglehold on the borough, there was Sir Francis Henry Drake, of Buckland, who managed affairs in south Devon for the Whigs; and he in turn was advised from London by Lord Chief Justice King. Drake and King, through their local managers in the boroughs, brought six of them into line as safe Whig seats: Plymouth, Plympton, Tavistock, Bere Alston, Totnes, and Dartmouth.[2]

The management of Dartmouth shows how it was done, with variations, in all the boroughs. Here, we are told in 1835,[3] there had been only two contested elections since 1790. The Holdsworths saw to it that the corporation and the freemen were of the same political views as themselves; but they also had numerous favours in their gift to distribute. There were jobs in the taxes and local customs, and the office of postmaster of Dartmouth was also in their gift. Two handsome livings in the neighbourhood—Brixham and Stokenham, worth about £400 per annum each —were in the gift of the government and were customarily bestowed upon the recommendation of the corporation. Indeed, in 1835, they were both held by members of the corporation. Dartmouth was one of the most corrupt of the Devon boroughs, and its tradition of venality died hard. As late as 1859 the member—Mr. E. W. H. Schenley—was unseated for corrupt practices.[1]

By 1832 all the Devon boroughs were controlled by patrons and all were rotten to a varying degree, exceeded in villainy only by those of Cornwall. It is difficult to know where to pick and choose. Ashburton was a Tuckfield seat for the first forty years of the 18th century. Then the parliamentary influence passed by inheritance to the earls of Orford;

November 1796   WALTER PALK ESQ.,
                DR. TO JAMES LLOYD

	£	s.	d.
Entertainment of sundry voters the day before election and morning of election	18	5	8
Dinner	36	10	0
Beer porter cyder and pop	4	5	0
Wine—612 *bottles red port @* 3/6	107	2	0
14 *bottles sherry @* 4/-	2	16	0
12 *bottles Madeira @* 6/-	3	12	0
2 *bottles claret @* 6/-	0	12	0
Spirits— 12 *bottles of brandy @* 6/-	3	12	0
7 *bottles of rum @* 6/-	2	2	0
15 *bottles of gin @* 6/-	4	10	0
Fruite	1	10	0
Sugar	1	15	0
Tea and Coffee	4	0	0
Cards	0	10	6
Supper—*porter and cyder*	3	0	0
pipes and tobacco	0	10	6
Store shut up at half-past 6 *o'clock after which the following liquor was consumed*—*grog and punch*	3	12	6
55 *bottles port wine*	9	11	6
Negus	2	12	0
3 *bottles of brandy*	0	18	0
Hay and corn	1	15	0
	£219	1	2
DEDUCT	5	19	6
	£213	1	8

Paid the 13*th February* 1797 *the contents*
By cheque on bank £213 1 8.   *James Lloyd*

and in 1774 to the Palks, who represented the borough continuously (except for one short break) until 1831. A bill for an election dinner in 1796 shows the least venal side of the business of patronage.[1] (See previous page.) But one can only wonder how many electors there were at Ashburton to pack away this intolerable deal of drink—for only freeholders having lands and tenements in the borough had the franchise.

At Tiverton, the right to elect parliamentary representatives was confined to the corporation of twenty-four " capital burgesses " and " assistant burgesses," who also chose the mayor and filled all vacancies on the council from their own ranks. The result was one of the rottenest boroughs in England. One of the two seats had come into the hands of the Ryders in 1735, who continued to fill it right down to 1832; the other was filled at the nomination of whoever ruled the corporation for the time being, i.e. the political manager. In return, the grateful government appointed him Receiver-General of the Land Tax for part of Devon, a position which, since the manager was usually a woollen merchant, enabled him to use large sums of public money as private capital over long periods, and thus to extend his business at the expense of other merchants. This connection seems to go back to 1703, if no further, when Robert Burridge, a considerable Tiverton merchant, sat for his native town and also enjoyed the receivership.

A succession of merchants filled the position of political manager, though they ceased to sit in the House themselves but nominated instead outsiders who were acceptable to the government of the day. Oliver Peard ruled Tiverton in this manner from 1744 to 1764, and when he died (by blowing off his head with a blunderbuss) even the mayor and corporation felt that tyranny had gone far enough. He had chosen the representatives for Parliament, filled every vacancy on the corporation, and had exercised unbounded power in every public concern of the town for the space of twenty years—a fascinating figure of American proportions, of whom one would like to know much more.[2]

When Peard died, with a shock felt all over the town, an Exeter merchant—one of the rising Baring family—attempted to fill his place. But his conditions were so rigorous that the mayor, fearing the renewal of the old tyranny, refused to consider his offer. Riots immediately broke out, for the townspeople only knew that Baring had offered to take the entire output of serges from the town, and thought that their livelihood was imperilled by the mayor's refusal. Moreover, they suspected him of holding out for a profitable bargain for himself. The riots were quelled, but at the next election another Exeter merchant—John Duntze—was chosen instead of the dangerous Baring, and a milder but no less effective patronage ensued. The political history of Tiverton is of exceptional interest, and deserves to be thoroughly explored.[3]

Tiverton was rotten enough under its oligarchic control, but the "democratic" borough of Honiton was blacker still.[1] Here "every inhabitant in the borough who had a family and boiled a pot there" had a right to vote, and there was consequently an electorate of over 500. There were only twenty-two boroughs in England with over 1,000 electors (Exeter was one), and another twenty-two with 500-1,000 electors. Honiton was thus among the largest franchises in the country, and therefore ruinously expensive to its parliamentary candidates.

When the borough was re-enfranchised in 1640, largely at the instance of Sir John Pole, its first representatives were William Pole, his eldest son, and Walter Yonge, the heir of a Colyton merchant, and the well-known diarist. The Poles sat for Honiton on and off until 1734, when Sir William, 4th baronet, wisely dropped out. It was becoming too expensive an honour. His will, drawn up in May 1733, makes it plain enough: "My request to my son John and other persons to whom I have limited my manors, etc., is that they will never stand as a Candidate or if chosen will never be prevailed upon to serve in Parliament for the Borough of Honiton."[2]

The Yonges stuck it until 1802 and ruined themselves to do it. Between 1640 and 1796, a Yonge sat for Honiton for 127 years: for twenty-seven Parliaments out of thirty-three. Sir George, the 5th baronet, used to say that he had inherited an estate of £80,000, had received another £80,000 with his wife, and yet another £80,000, from his government appointments; and Honiton had devoured the lot. When he stood again in 1802 without the money to bribe this noble electorate, it is said that one of the voters spat in his face and a woman set his wig on fire with her candle. No wonder Lord Cochrane, the celebrated admiral who sat for the borough in 1806-7, moved on to the city of Westminster, where he told the electors that Honiton was so rotten that "a Member who sat for it felt like a man in a dirty shirt." And so Honiton continued on its stinking way until 1832—and beyond—putting up its democratic price to six guineas per voter and throwing out the candidate who first tried to stop the practice after the 1830 election.

PARLIAMENTARY REPRESENTATION SINCE 1832

By the Act of 1832, the county was made into two divisions, each returning two members. Bere Alston, Plympton, and Okehampton were disfranchised, and Ashburton and Dartmouth were deprived of one seat each. On the other side of the picture, the borough of Devonport was created, with two members. It was only a mild dose of reform. Though the older electorate were now swamped by the new £10-householders, the tradition of corruption died hard in Devon. Thus in 1866 the Liberal member, Mr. John Pender, was unseated for corrupt practices at Totnes, and the Reform Act of the following year disfranchised the borough and ended another unsavoury history. At Dartmouth, the member was unseated in 1859 for corruption, and the borough disfranchised in 1868.

At Honiton the Act of 1832 had extended the boundaries of the parliamentary borough, with the result that for the next thirty-six years the lord of the manor could always secure one seat for himself or his nominee, regardless of the candidate's political views or " any d—d nonsense of that sort." For this reason Mr. Joseph Locke, a railway contractor who had been articled to George Stephenson and had helped to build the Liverpool and Manchester Railway, bought the manor in 1847 and represented the borough in his own person from then until his death in 1860. His conversion from Conservatism to Liberalism in mid-career caused the worthy electors of Honiton no heart-searching. In 1863 his widow sold the manor to Mr. Goldsmid, an opulent Jewish banker, for £110,000, with the result that Goldsmid *père* and *fils* sat for the borough from 1865 to 1868.[1] It was a bad investment, for the borough was totally disfranchised in 1868, together with Ashburton and Dartmouth.

There were allegations of bribery and corruption at Barnstaple in 1852 and again in 1864; at Totnes in 1852 and 1865; at Dartmouth in 1845, 1852, and 1859; and at Plymouth in 1852. Most of these allegations were the subject of parliamentary inquiries which make fascinating reading. At Plymouth, for example, the general election of 1852 brought down a Mr. C. J. Mare, a wealthy man with no Plymouth connections, who—to the surprise of the town—headed the poll as a Conservative. Plymouth had returned none but Liberals since 1832. Election day had been disorderly; an unusual proportion of the voters intoxicated. There had been treating on a large scale, promises of employment in the dockyard and elsewhere, and money had changed hands. " The *clou* of the piece was the revelation of the operations of ' The Man in the Moon,' who lived temporarily in a bedroom at the King's Arms Hotel in Totnes and passed out gold pieces in a gloved hand through an aperture in the curtains of the bed." Mr. Aitken Davies, who died a highly respected citizen of Plymouth in 1899, was that Man in the Moon. The petition against Mare's election succeeded, and he never took his seat in the House. He died later in extreme poverty in London, so poor that a few of his political cronies in Plymouth had to pay for his funeral.[2] One could write a whole history of electoral corruption in Devon *after* 1832; that magic date that is supposed to have ushered in the age of purity in politics.

In the redistribution of parliamentary seats effected in 1885 the boroughs of Barnstaple, Tavistock, and Tiverton were disfranchised, and Exeter's representation reduced to one member. Tavistock had already lost one of its seats in 1867. And lastly, in 1918, Devonport was deprived

of one of its two members. There were now only three parliamentary
boroughs in Devon—Plymouth (two members), Devonport, and Exeter
—and seven county constituencies, Honiton, Tiverton, Tavistock, South
Molton, Barnstaple, Totnes, and Torquay. In place of the twenty-six
members returned from Devon before 1832, there were now only eleven.

POLITICS SINCE 1832[1]

In 1832 political opinion in Devon was overwhelmingly Liberal, the
result of the pent-up feeling against the rotten boroughs and the close
corporations. The reports of the commissioners on municipal corporations
in 1835 show how bitterly the Devonshire townspeople felt about these
packed, oligarchic assemblies, how they hated them and all who sat on
them, and generally with ample reason. At any rate, only one Conservative was returned in 1832 among the twenty-two members from
Devon, and he sat for Honiton. It must have been tough work even
getting one Conservative in at Honiton: over 96 per cent of the new
electorate voted.

As the Reform issues died away, the Conservatives slowly recovered
ground at each election until by 1852 the two parties returned eleven
members each.[2] Devonshire Liberalism was, however, founded on something far older and deeper than the ephemeral Reform agitation. The
doctrines of Dissent had been widely supported ever since the mid-17th
century: Devon was one of the great chapel-going counties. We tend to
forget this in the face of the more noisy and militant Dissenters of neighbouring Cornwall. Chapel people voted Liberal as solidly as church-
people voted Conservative, right down to the present century, and
Liberalism died hard in the south-west. In east Devon there was the
Acland influence, in the south-west the Russell influence, weighing
heavily for the Liberals.

In the elections of 1857 and 1859 the Conservatives lost a good deal
of ground, but recovered in 1865, when they managed to return ten of the
twenty-two members. Devon was still predominantly Liberal at the 1868
election, but in 1874 the Conservatives took the lead for the first time
since 1832. There were now only seventeen seats in Devon, with the
disfranchisement of various boroughs and rearrangement of the constituencies, and of these the Tories captured ten. Until 1892 the Liberals
remained only as a strong minority; in that year they regained the lead
by seven to six. It was in 1892 that the young George Lambert (now
Viscount Lambert) captured the North Devon or South Molton division
and held it for the Liberals against all comers until 1945, except for one
break of five years (1924-9).

In 1906 came the great landslide which swept the Tories almost out of sight. Here in Devon only three members survived, all with strong local associations—Kennaway for the Honiton division, Walrond for Tiverton, Mildmay for Totnes. All over Devon the Conservatives felt like throwing themselves into the nearest river as the results became known. The county was now represented by ten Liberals and three Conservatives. But the two elections of 1910 completely altered the picture again. In the first election of that year the Conservatives took six of the thirteen seats; in the second, at the end of the year, they took no fewer than eleven. Of the Liberals, only George Lambert survived at South Molton, and Sir Geoffrey Baring at Barnstaple. Mr. Asquith's attack on the House of Lords—the occasion for this second election— had antagonised a county with a traditional deep respect for the landed aristocracy. Even the chapel-goers could not stand this sort of thing. They forgot their own ancient traditions of Dissent, and voted with the church people on the side of the House of Lords. So Devon entered the Great War, represented by only two Liberal members, a proportion which far from reflected the strength of Liberal principles among the electorate.

The first post-war election (1918) brought them no more comfort. The constituencies had again been rearranged and Devon now had only eleven seats. Of these only two returned Liberals—South Molton and Barnstaple again sticking to their principles. In 1922 Barnstaple turned Conservative, but Tavistock went Liberal (it had always had a strong Liberal feeling since the Russell days); and George Lambert still sat for South Molton. The election of 1923 saw the last brilliant flash of Devonshire Liberalism, when the party took seven of the eleven seats, but it was a lightning flash: another election a few months later (1924) swept them completely out of the county, all except Hore-Belisha at Devonport. Even George Lambert was rejected at South Molton, after thirty-two years. There could have been no greater measure of the political swing than this unbelievable defeat: one still remembers how it was discussed everywhere in Devon—even among the Tories—" George Lambert out at South Molton! " It was, it is true, an aberration on the part of the North Devon electors: they returned him again at the next opportunity (in 1929) and he sat as the Liberal champion without another break until 1945.

The 1929 election in Devon was notable, not only for the return of the North Devon electors to their senses, but for the emergence of the first Labour M.P. in the county. At Plymouth, one of the two seats went —rather shakily—Left. In the ignoble " scare " election of 1931, Devon could hardly have done otherwise than swing to the Right, and did so, leaving only two Liberal-Nationals—at South Molton and Devonport. The solitary Labour M.P. disappeared. Nor was the 1935 election any different, except for the recapture of the Barnstaple division for Liberalism by Richard Acland, a member of the great Liberal family with strong associations in north Devon.

The history of Liberalism in Devon is much the same as in England generally. This is no place to attempt an explanation of its failure to re-establish itself as a potential governing party. But it is relevant to observe that in Devon and Cornwall the Liberal voters clung to the sinking ship more tenaciously than any others in England, except perhaps in that other Border Country—Cumberland, Westmorland, and Northumberland. And where the choice had to be made between the two extreme parties, Devon chose to go right rather than left.

Even in 1945, which saw a massive swing over to Labour almost everywhere else, Devon stayed fundamentally Conservative. Plymouth, it is true, went entirely over to Labour—all three seats, including the old Liberal stronghold of Devonport; and in North Devon there was still a Lambert—son of the veteran—preaching now a sad, watery kind of National-Liberalism.* Exeter stayed Conservative, but only just. Seven of the eleven seats in the county as a whole returned Conservatives.

One can understand the recent political history of Devon in the light of national politics, but the violent political swings of the 19th century, from about 1860 to 1910, would repay a minute examination in the contemporary local newspapers. So, perhaps, would the astonishing election of 1923. The more recent parliamentary history of the county is left for discussion in the last chapter of this book.

COUNTY GOVERNMENT

By the beginning of the Tudor period, the great Anglo-Norman baronies, of which no fewer than ten had been centred in Devon, were of no political significance. The rancorous feud between the Courtenays and the Bonvilles, which had merged into national politics during the Wars of the Roses and had reduced the county to chaos, was ended. The Bonvilles had been wiped out in the wars, and were now represented in east Devon by Cecily—great-granddaughter of Sir William Bonville—who had married Thomas Grey, 1st Marquess of Dorset. Since the Greys lived mainly in Leicestershire, the Courtenays no longer had any real rivals in Devon. They themselves had not escaped lightly, however, for their earldom of Devon had been forfeited, together with their estates, in 1461, and the main line of the family extinguished. But among the many West Country men who fled to Brittany after the failure of Bucking-ham's rising in 1483 was Edward Courtenay of Boconnoc, in Cornwall, the next heir. To him Henry VII restored the earldom and all the former

*In 1950 this became " National-Liberal and Conservative," whatever this ungodly mixture may be.

Courtenay lands and honours. His son William married Catherine, daughter of Edward IV. The son and heir of this marriage, Henry, was therefore cousin to King Henry VIII: a dangerously close relationship to any Tudor monarch, for which the Courtenays paid in full during the 16th century. But all this is part of national history, and we must turn to the internal politics of the county.

Most of the leading Devon families of the 15th century had survived into the 16th, much as the Courtenays did. Thus though Sir Baldwin Fulford (sheriff of Devon in 1460) had been taken prisoner at Towton and beheaded later at Bristol, his son Thomas recovered the family estates and quickly re-established his position. It was probably his son William Fulford (d. 1517) who began the rebuilding of the ancestral house at Fulford, completed by his own son and heir Sir John Fulford (d. 1544). So by Henry VIII's time the Fulfords showed no signs of the trials they had passed through. They had one of the finest new mansions in Devon, a large estate in land, and interests in ships and tin-works.[1]

A notable feature of the Tudor period was the vastly increased use of local justices of the peace in the growing work of government. Without them indeed the whole machinery of Tudor administration in the provinces would have broken down, for there was no civil service to see to the performance of the " stacks of statutes," as William Lambarde, a Kentish justice, called them in 1581. In the 15th century the commission of the peace had included only a dozen to fifteen names in Devon, and those only of the magnates like the Earl of Devon, the Bishop of Exeter, Fitz-Waryns, Dynhams, and so on. The commission of 1491 included twenty-three names, that of 1514 thirty-two. The magnates are still on the list, but there are also the leading squires—Kirkham, Basset, Dennis, Strode, Stucley, Coffin, and others. In 1547 there were fifty-one names, but in later commissions the list is somewhat shorter.[2] By the end of the century the number had risen again.

On the first list which survives among the Devon county records (1592) we find fifty-five names. It is a valuable index to the social standing of the various county families, except that the Queen had just directed that all recusants, or husbands or fathers of recusants, should be omitted from the commission of the peace. For this reason some notable names are missing, but even so the list is a distinguished one.[3] It is headed by William Bourchier, Earl of Bath, Lord-Lieutenant of the county, followed by John Woolton, Bishop of Exeter, Sir Edward Seymour (eldest son of the Protector Somerset), Sir William Courtenay, and other magnates. Among the lawyer-members were Sir William Periam, chief baron of the exchequer, and Serjeants Harris, Granville, and Drewe. The latter was recorder of Exeter, and afterwards of London. Then there were Sir John Gilbert, brother of Humphrey and Adrian, and half-brother of Sir Walter Raleigh; the great Sir Francis Drake; George Cary of Cockington, later to be Lord-Deputy of Ireland; Edmund Prideaux, another notable lawyer; and Hugh Pollard who was sheriff of the county in the memorable year of 1588. We find, too, the names of William Pole, a distinguished lawyer but more notable as the first historian of Devon, and Richard Carew of Antony, the author of one of the earliest of all county histories (the *Survey of Cornwall*) and one of the most delightful to read. Besides these eminent figures, there were Aclands, Monks, Fortescues, Edgcumbes, Reynells, and all the greater squirearchy, many of them destined to be sheriffs of the county, or M.P.s, or already ex-sheriffs and ex-M.P.s.

What a galaxy! What a sight if one could have seen them all assembled in council together at Exeter Castle! There was not much room for a Justice Shallow in a county like Devon: the eminent crowded each other shoulder to shoulder in those days, or would have done had they all met together at once. In fact, they did not: the lawyers would be mostly away in London, and Drake had more pressing business elsewhere. But these were the greatest days of Devonshire genius: by the 18th century the Quarter Sessions would have accommodated more of the soporific Silences and Shallows.

The internal government of the county is far too vast a theme to be embarked upon here. An excellent idea of its working, and of the scope of the justices' duties, can be had from A. H. A. Hamilton's valuable little book *Quarter Sessions from Queen Elizabeth to Queen Anne*, which is based almost entirely upon the original records of the county.[1] The Tudor government had loaded task after task upon the creaking backs of the justices, who were slowly obliged to create their own elementary staff in order to get county business done at all. A permanent county treasurer seems to have been first appointed in Charles I's reign, a post filled by Mr. Treasurer Jones. A summary of his accounts over a period of eight years down to his death in 1639 shows that he had received in that time £3,283 and had spent £3,334, an average of about £400 a year. The justices resolved that he had been a " good husband for the county."[2] About the same time, besides raising the salary of one officer for good service, the justices also reduced that of another for idleness: a curious old-fashioned notion that would produce some revolutionary results if brought back into general practice to-day.

By the early years of the 19th century, county expenditure had risen to some £9,000–£10,000 a year, still only a trifling sum. In 1810 and 1815, it shot up to between £25,000 and £30,000, of which the greater part went on bridges. In the early 1830s it fell again to round about £15,000 a year. The evolution of county government during the 19th century has been studied by Mr. D. R. Tucker, from whose thesis these figures are taken.[1] For a time the old machinery nearly broke down under the new demands and needs of the 19th century, " but, after a period now of groping, now of sloth, the Bench moulded and altered and finally built up an efficient system of local government [which] was functioning as well in 1888 as ever it had done."[2]

Nevertheless, as the century went on and the scope of State interference widened, as new legislation brought new *ad hoc* authorities almost every decade, the complexity of administrative areas passed into chaos, in Devon as in every other county. Rates had been rising all the time, and the more enlightened ratepayers felt that the reform of this chaos of authorities and areas into one orderly structure would be one means of reducing the financial burden. Yet there was never any demand in Devon for an elected county authority. The ratepayers seem to have been satisfied with the old constitution. Though the Devon court of Quarter Sessions was preponderantly Conservative, it did not fear the elective principle and, under the chairmanship of Lord Clinton, took a patient and sensible view of the Local Government Bill of 1888. Elsewhere in England, chairmen were less co-operative. Sir Henry Halford, in Leicestershire, for example, declared the bill to be a bad one coming from a Conservative government.

The first meeting of the Provisional County Council took place on 24 January 1889. The *Devon Weekly Times*, a Liberal newspaper, commented that " the gathering looked much like Quarter Sessions . . . landlordism and squirearchy were in conspicuous force." Even so, when the first County Council proper met together on 1 April 1889, and all the elections were done with, it consisted of 104 men, of whom sixty-five were magistrates and thirty-nine were men who had never taken part in county government before.[3] Nearly all the prominent members of the Court of Quarter Sessions were back again, and the few absentees were co-opted as aldermen. Mr. J. C. Moore-Stevens had been the only magistrate of the old Court to be defeated at the elections by a non-magistrate, and he was peculiarly reactionary, evidently too much even for stolid Devon. At the Midsummer Sessions of 1882 " he confessed that his object was to get rid of traction engines altogether."[4] Still, if one substitutes the internal combustion engine for traction engines, one has a good deal of sympathy with Squire Moore-Stevens. At any rate, the new Council was under way, and, though there was a long way to go yet, democracy had been introduced into county government for the first time in its history.

MILITARY HISTORY

After the battles of the Saxon period, and the obscure conflicts of the

Danish age, Devon ceased to be the scene of any large military operations until Tudor days. The battles of the Western Rebellion of 1549 are referred to later (see Chapter XII); and the events of 1588 saw no actual operations in Devon. With the Civil War of 1642-6, however, it is otherwise, for there was much fighting in the south-west—more warfare indeed than had been known since the 9th century. Then follows a deep peace again for almost three hundred years, until in 1940 the first bombs of the German barbarians began to fall upon Devonshire towns and villages, culminating in the merciless destruction of Plymouth in the spring of 1941, and of Exeter a year later.

The Civil War began in 1642. In the south-west, as elsewhere, " it is broadly true to say that the peers and the greater gentry stood on the King's side, the lesser gentry and the townsmen for Parliament. Yet there were great exceptions. At Bristol and Exeter the townsmen were deeply divided: the royalists there represented a very large minority."[1] Exeter, the key to Devon, was indeed divided in 1642 exactly as she had been in 1549, when there had been a strong Catholic minority inside the walls, and the Prayer-Book rebels stood outside. Occasionally we find families divided, such as the Fortescues. Hugh Fortescue and his son Arthur, at Filleigh, were prominent parliamentarians, and so was John Fortescue of Buckland Filleigh. But the Fortescues of East Allington and of Spriddlestone were royalists. All the north Devon Fortescues were for Parliament, all in south Devon for the King. The Carews also seem to have been a divided family. Occasionally, too, a family changed sides. Sir George Chudleigh of Ashton took up arms for Parliament at first, and was one of their generals at the battle of Stratton. But he resigned his commission after his son James had been accused of treachery and subsequently went over to the King's side. His son, who had been a major-general in the parliamentarian army, was taken prisoner by the royalists in 1643, suspected of treachery in the action, and accepted a colonelship in the King's army in May 1643. Within a few months he was killed.

On the whole, Devon was more parliamentarian than royalist. The leaders of the local struggle against the king were powerful men like the Earl of Bedford, the Rolles, the Bampfyldes, the Drakes of Ashe and of Buckland, Martyns of Oxton, Strodes, Northcotes, and Calmadys. Tenants naturally sided with their landlords: it was difficult to do otherwise. But there were great landlords on the other side also—the Aclands, Seymours, Carys, Fulfords, Heles, Pollards and Poles. It is difficult to generalise about the squirearchy in Devon. The ancient names are found on both sides—Kelly, Bastard, Hatch and Speccott for Parliament; Fulford, Fursdon, Acland, and so on, for the King.

Although we have fuller contemporary accounts of the military operations in the south-west than in any other part of England, much of the intimate family history of the Civil War is still buried in the archives of the Devonshire country houses. We do not yet know what led these old families to take up arms on one side or the other, what strands of family history and of personal character determined the fatal choice. The history of the Civil War in Devon has yet to be written, as Miss Coate has written it for Cornwall. Besides the great landlords there were, too, the towns, so much more numerous and important in Devon and Cornwall than in other parts of England. Plymouth was strongly parliamentarian from the first, and the other seaports inclined the same way. But for the time being most boroughs remained shrewdly neutral, waiting to see which side would be better worth conciliating.[1]

In the south-west, Hopton had been left in charge as deputy to the royalist commander, the Marquess of Hertford. By the end of 1642 he had cleared the parliamentary leaders out of Cornwall, which was in any event so much more royalist than Devon. Devon was too strongly for Parliament to be subdued yet, and after a good deal of skirmishing as far east as Exeter, Hopton retired to Bodmin in the early months of 1643. His failure to take Plymouth was decisive. Indeed, the successful defence of Plymouth for Parliament was the deciding factor in the whole war in the south-west, as the defence of Hull was in the north.

The great royalist victory in May 1643 at Stratton, just over the Cornish border, opened up the whole of Devon to their advance. Nearly all the county fell into their hands: and the city of Exeter surrendered to Prince Maurice in September. But Plymouth still held out, under close siege, and held out until the final victory of Parliament in the spring of 1646. It was a series of sieges and blockades, lasting altogether three and a half years: the defence of Plymouth is an epic of the Civil War. Among the archives of the corporation is a remarkable record—the full accounts of the committee by whom the defence of the town was conducted during the final twelve months.[2]

By the end of 1643 the whole of western England, including the cities of Exeter and Bristol, was in royalist hands: all except the seaports of Plymouth, Lyme Regis and Poole: but the advance to London never took place. Partly because of local feeling once again—the Cornish had refused to cross the Tamar in 1642 and now they were even farther from home—and partly because of the loss of their beloved leader, Sir Bevil Grenville, at the battle of Lansdown, the royalist armies drifted home. And perhaps most important of all, Plymouth remained untaken and was a base for dangerous, plundering sorties. It was time to go back and defend their own homes in Devon and Cornwall.

In the summer of 1644, Parliament took the offensive in the south-west, but the Earl of Essex's invasion of Cornwall ended in disaster. In

Devon his route lay through Axminster, Honiton, Cullompton, Tiverton, Crediton, Okehampton and Tavistock, and so into Cornwall; and after him came the King himself. Charles was at Exeter on 26 July, where he saw his infant daughter, born at the Earl of Bedford's house in the city a few weeks earlier. On the 27th he reviewed Prince Maurice's troops at Crediton, and on the 29th resumed his march after Essex, sleeping that night in an alehouse at Bow. The house still stands—now Miss Riddaway's shop—in the main street.

In the end Essex was caught up and defeated at Lostwithiel. Many of his horse soldiers escaped back into Devon where they were dealt with in local engagements such as that on Hatherleigh Moor on 14 September. The second parliamentarian invasion of the West Country had failed dismally.

Nine months later came the crushing royalist defeat at Naseby, up in the Midlands, setting the New Model Army free to deal in formidable strength with the south-west. Under Fairfax and Cromwell they drove westwards in the late summer of 1645: Bristol, Bath, Bridgwater, and Taunton fell before them. By the middle of October they were in east Devon—Sprigg gives us the day-to-day movements in his *England's Recovery*—and trying to block up the royalist armies beyond the Exe. Tiverton Castle fell without much of a struggle on 19 October, and Fairfax took up his headquarters at Silverton on the following day. The main question now was whether " to straiten Excester," or to continue the advance westwards to the relief of hard-pressed Plymouth.[1] Winter was coming on, the men were weary and sickly, and it was decided therefore to halt and tackle the royalist stronghold of Exeter, where Sprigg says there were some 5,000 horse and foot soldiers in the garrison, a dangerous knot to leave untied in the rear of an advance. In the midst of one council of war, at Crediton on Friday 24 October, " Lieutenant-General Cromwell happily came in," his forces having freed Basing and Winchester, and now coming west to assist Fairfax.

Sprigg's account of Fairfax's movements around Exeter is full of topographical detail: one can walk over the very roads and lanes and see the military problems involved. One by one, a ring of country houses around the city was garrisoned by the parliamentarian forces: the blockade was now on. Then the plan was changed. Leaving a force to keep Exeter blockaded, Cromwell went on to Bovey Tracey, where he defeated the royalists, who were thoroughly surprised while playing cards, and a swift campaign ended in the recapture of Dartmouth by Fairfax in January 1646.

Fairfax now returned to resume the siege of Exeter, but was diverted from it a second time by the news that the enemy had turned up in north Devon, where another swift campaign followed.[2] The defeat of Hopton at Torrington gave the *coup de grâce* to the royalist cause in Devon, and after cleaning up in Cornwall Fairfax returned to negotiate for the surrender of Exeter at Poltimore House in the early days of April. Barnstaple surrendered a day or two later. On Saturday morning, 18 April, Fairfax marched away from Exeter towards Oxford. The war in the west was over. Not quite: down in the extreme south of the county, gallant little Fort Charles, on the Salcombe estuary, still held out under Sir Edmund Fortescue, and in far Cornwall Pendennis Castle still held firm. Fort Charles surrendered on 7 May. The governor was allowed to keep the key of the fort he had so well defended, and for 200 years the Fortescues treasured it at their house of Fallapit. It is said to have been sold eventually at an auction for half a crown.

The county suffered severe though localised damage in these periodic campaigns between the autumn of 1642 and the spring of 1646. Many country houses were burnt, such as Stedcombe and Ashe, or heavily damaged like Fulford. In the towns and their suburbs, some hundreds of houses were destroyed either in the fighting or in the necessary pre-parations for withstanding a siege, as at Dartmouth. On top of all this there had been years of plundering by both sides. The parish of Up Lyme had lost 3,000 sheep when the Parliament stronghold of Lyme Regis had been under siege.[1] The estates of the landlords, large and small, on either side had been stripped. And in the towns, the woollen merchants and the shopkeepers had lost large stocks of goods. No wonder most people in Devon wanted the war to move on somewhere else. It was a sad time, and long remembered. How often one reads on those rather rustic mural monuments to the old squires, ten, twenty, and thirty years afterwards, some reference to " The late Troubles."

Three hundred years later it all came again, more inhuman and more frightful, on a mounting scale. The first German bomb fell on Plymouth on 6 July 1940: the enemy had his airfields only a hundred miles across the water in Brittany. All through the winter fire and high explosive shook the city. Then, on 20 March, the barbarians began the systematic destruction of the town. In one week they killed over 1,000 men, women and children, wrecked the homes of 10,000; and so they continued. From far away down the Cornish coast, and far inland in Devon, that red, pulsing glow over Plymouth could be seen night after night, through late March and April. Help flowed in from all over the civilised world. Plymouth learnt then what it was to be " the mother of full forty Plymouths up and down the world"[2] (plate 44.)

So far the rest of Devon had escaped very lightly. It was Exeter's turn next: in late April and May of 1942 the city was burnt and shattered in a manner not known since the heathen Danes had destroyed the Anglo-Saxon town 900 years before. Then " tip-and-run " raiders began to sneak along the south coast in 1943, bombing and machine-gunning the seaside towns. Teignmouth suffered severely; so, too, did Torquay and Dartmouth. But even the harmless little fishing hamlets did not escape. Beesands, on Start Bay, was too easy a target: women and children were killed here too.

In the preparations for the Second Front, a large area of country behind Start Bay was taken over as a battle-practice ground, six parishes being completely emptied of civilian life and goods. It was a countryside that closely resembled that of Normandy, where the final attack was to take place, and for months the American troops fought over it. A memorial to them now stands on the middle of Slapton beach. Thousands of craft of all shapes and sizes were slowly gathered in the two great harbours of Plymouth and Dartmouth; and then in the first days of June 1944 they sailed, a formidable proportion of the whole vast invasion fleet that set out all along the south coast of England, over the grey water to Normandy.

Among this vast fleet were two battalions of the Devonshire Regiment—the 2nd and the 12th. The history of this great regiment is too good to spoil in a cursory survey and must be read in full elsewhere.[1] It had its origin in 1685, when the Duke of Beaufort raised a corps of musketeers and pikemen from the counties of Devon, Somerset, and Dorset. Shortly afterwards this corps was embodied as the 11th Regiment of foot, but not until 1782, when county titles were given to regiments in order to stimulate recruiting, was it designated the North Devonshire Regiment.

It had already fought in Flanders under Marlborough, at Dettingen and at Fontenoy in later years, but its greatest campaign was to come in the Peninsular War of 1809-14, in which it won seven battle honours. The bravery and terrible losses of the regiment at Salamanca (1812) earned it the title of The Bloody Eleventh. After that came service all over the world, including Afghanistan and South Africa; and in the first German War of 1914-18 the famous last stand of the 2nd Devons at Bois des Buttes on 27 May 1918 epitomised the ancestral obstinacy of Devonshire men. How far away now seems that figure of Colonel Anderson-Morshead, revolver in one hand and hunting-crop in the other, encouraging the remnants of his battalion to fight on against hopeless odds, a figure of chivalry in a pre-atomic age. In the Second German War of 1939-45 the regiment served with all its old distinction in Malta, Sicily, Italy, Burma, Normandy, Belgium, Holland, and Germany: the story of all their campaigns in these years is admirably told by Jeremy Taylor in *The Devons*.

CHAPTER XI

MARITIME HISTORY

THE long coast line of Devon on two sides, its many capacious estuaries and harbours, and its position in relation to the two ancient enemies of England—France and Spain—have combined to give it an important maritime history from the 12th century onwards. Before that date, there is little to be said. The Exe was regularly used by shipping in Romano-British times. Topsham originated as a naval base about A.D. 50, and probably maintained some commerce by sea during the following centuries. The existence of a Celtic trading settlement at Mount Batten, on the shores of Plymouth Sound, is also some indication of sea-trade, in all probability with Gaul. There were continual contacts between Brittany and south-western Britain from prehistoric times onwards, across the hundred miles of open water.

With the revival of commerce in the later Anglo-Saxon period, and the creation of new *burhs* at Totnes and Barnstaple, at the head of the Dart and Taw estuaries respectively, we may suppose that these estuaries and that of the Exe were all used by overseas shipping, at least from the early 10th century. Exeter, Totnes, and Barnstaple all had mints in the 10th century, as well as the inland *burh* of Lydford, and mints meant trade on a considerable scale. At each of these four places, too, we hear of a *burhwitan* in 1018, a kind of " borough council " capable of taking note of official transactions.

It is, however, in the 12th century that the maritime history of the south-west becomes important. The marriage of Henry II with Eleanor of Aquitaine in 1152, which brought the provinces of south-western France under English control, coinciding as it did with the rapid development of tin-working on the Devon and Cornish moors, brought the ports of Dartmouth, Plymouth and Fowey into existence almost simultaneously. All three make a recognisable appearance in the later years of the 12th century. The church of Fowey is first mentioned *c.* 1170, and a seignorial borough had been created here by the priors of Tywardreath *c.* 1190-

1220.[1] At Plymouth, the priors of Plympton created the borough of Plymouth out of their manor of Sutton, perhaps a little later than this: we do not know, for their charter has not survived as that of Fowey has.

The deep, sheltered estuary of the Dart, with the flourishing market town of Totnes a few miles up-river for the provision of supplies, was early used as a rendezvous for shipping. The second and third crusades sailed from here in 1147 and 1190. Within a few years we find a town growing here, chiefly concerned with the fitting out, repair, and perhaps building of ships. The first street we hear of by name in Dartmouth, in the 13th century, is " the street of the smiths." This lay parallel with and close to Mill Pool, a tongue of water (now filled up and built over) separating Clifton-Dartmouth from the suburb of Hardness, in which medieval ships lay up. Smith Street survives to this day.

Plymouth developed more slowly. Although it was used as a commercial harbour for the Gascony trade, and as a point of arrival and departure for military expeditions from the mid-13th century, it was much less frequented than Dartmouth in the early centuries, partly because of the natural disadvantages of its harbour, fine though it is, and partly because of its poor hinterland. The existence of Totnes, ten miles up-river, had a great influence on the origin and growth of Dartmouth; but Plymouth had no such centre of supplies behind it.

Most of the trade of the south-coast ports of Devon lay with south-west France—with Bayonne and Bordeaux above all—Exeter, Dartmouth, and Plymouth being the chief ports. The north-coast ports of Devon had some trade, though they were badly placed except for Ireland. For the Crécy and Calais campaign in 1346, a vast fleet was collected from all the English ports. The so-called Calais Roll, of which various late copies survive, differing in details, gives the following figures for the Devon ports:[2]

Dartmouth	..	..	31 ships	757 men
Plymouth	..	..	26 „	603 „
Exmouth ..	..	..	10 „	193 „
Tawmouth	..	..	7 „	120 „
Portlemouth	..	..	5 „	96 „
Sidmouth	..	..	3 „	62 „
Yealmpton	..	..	2 „	48 „
Seaton	..	..	..	2 „	25 „
Teignmouth	..	..	2 „	25 „

In spite of discrepancies in detail, the different versions agree about the order of the Devon ports in 1346. Of the eighty-eight ships collected from Devon, no fewer than fifty-seven were assembled from Dartmouth and Plymouth, and their members. Exmouth, of course, represents

Exeter and Topsham, and smaller places on the estuary. Tawmouth, the only sizeable port on the north coast, is Appledore, and includes Barnstaple and Bideford. Portlemouth, now a forgotten place on the Kingsbridge estuary opposite Salcombe, ranks surprisingly high. Other calls for shipping about this period mention Budleigh and Ottermouth, Kenton on the Exe, Combe Martin, Clovelly and Ilfracombe. All of these could produce a ship or two for military expeditions, if necessary, but their commercial importance was trifling.

The growing importance of Devon's overseas trade is shown by the great tax assessment of 1334.[1] In that year the four leading towns were all seaports—Exeter, Plymouth, Barnstaple and Dartmouth, in that order. Plymouth was used increasingly as a naval rendezvous from the late 13th century onwards. In 1330 forty of the largest ships (160-180 tons) were assembled here for an expedition to restore order in Aquitaine; and in 1356 the Black Prince assembled 300 ships here for his French campaign, returning to Plymouth in the following year with King John and other notable prisoners. Even so, Plymouth does not seem to have produced any seafaring family as remarkable as the three generations of the Hawleys at Dartmouth, who flourished there from the 1340s to the 1430s. It is almost certain that Chaucer met the first John Hawley when he visited Dartmouth in 1373, for Hawley was already a prominent ship-master and was to become mayor in the following year; and it is more than possible that he had him in mind in his well-known description of the " Schipman."

Cloth and tin going out, wine coming in: these were the main basis of south-western England's overseas trade in the 14th and 15th centuries. A record of 1408 gives details of the wine fleet of that year as consisting of 200 ships belonging to the English ports. Of these twenty-seven belonged to Dartmouth and nine each to Plymouth and Fowey.[2] The tin went mostly from the Cornish ports, the cloth (a poor quality known as white straits) from Devon. The Devon ports lost much ground in the 15th century, for local as well as national reasons. There was the gradual loss of the English possessions in south-western France (Bordeaux finally went in 1451); the growth of piracy in the Channel during a great part of the 15th century—an activity in which the West Country ports took a leading part, to their temporary advantage; and the development of regular warships by Edward IV and his successors, which reduced the importance of converted merchantmen.[3] Wars, too, reduced the trade of the south Devon ports. Plymouth was largely burnt by a Breton force in the summer of 1403, but another Breton attack, with a view to burning Dartmouth, was beaten off in the following year, a notable victory for which Henry IV ordered a *Te Deum* to be sung in Westminster Abbey. Apart from war and piracy, there was a great decline in English industry and trade during the greater part of the 15th century, which is reflected above all in the figures of cloth exports. The tax assessments of Dartmouth and Kingsbridge were reduced by 40 per cent in 1445, those of Plymouth and Exeter by nearly 30 per cent.[1]

There were local reasons also for this depression. At Dartmouth, for example, the Hawleys had died out (1436) and their accumulated estates in Devon and Cornwall had passed by marriage to the Copplestones, an inland family who took little interest in the affairs of the port. So, when the English began to visit Iceland waters for the rich cod fisheries in the 15th century, there was no one in Dartmouth with sufficient energy or resources to take part, the lead in the West Country passed to the great merchant family of Cannynge at Bristol, and the valuable Dartmouth trade in dried fish fell off seriously.

With the recovery of English industry and trade in the last quarter of the 15th century, the Devon ports revived also, but they had in the meantime lost ground to London, which was steadily increasing its share of England's foreign trade at the expense of all the outports. During Henry VIII's reign London accounted for just about one-half the total customs revenue, and its outport of Southampton for nearly one-fifth. Boston and Newcastle were the most active of the provincial ports, followed by Ipswich and then Bristol. The port of Exeter-Dartmouth, which included all the Devonshire ports except Plymouth, stood sixth among the outports from 1485 to 1547, accounting for about 3 per cent of the total customs during that period. The port of Plymouth-Fowey, which included all the Cornish ports, was far down the list with hardly more than 1 per cent of the customs revenue.[2] With the steady growth of the cloth trade in Devon during the 16th century, Exeter-Dartmouth rose to fourth place among the outports, surpassing the great port of Bristol. The total customs revenue from the leading outports for the period from Michaelmas 1577 to Michaelmas 1582 was as follows: Lynn (£9,971), Hull (£9,095), Yarmouth (£7,006), Exeter-Dartmouth (£5,974), Bristol (£5,411), Poole (£4,200), Chester (£2,626), and Plymouth-Fowey (£1,691).[3]

In cloth exports, Exeter-Dartmouth stood second only to Ipswich in the provinces, and in wine imports second only to Hull. The Devon ports were handling about 2½ per cent of the cloth exports, and about 4½ per cent of the wine imports. London dominated both trades (cloth 83 per cent, wine 63 per cent).[4] Perhaps one gets a truer picture for the purposes of local history if one says that Exeter-Dartmouth handled more than a quarter of the total cloth exports from the provincial ports, and about one-eighth of the wine imports. Plymouth was of very little importance for cloth or wine by Elizabeth's reign, but greatly interested in fish and tin. As fish paid no customs duty (after 1563) Plymouth's commercial importance is not properly brought out in these figures, and her growing importance as a naval port not at all.

Before we turn to this side of the picture, however, it may be as well to give the details of the limits of the Devonshire ports as they were constituted in 1565. In that year a closer administrative control over foreign trade was devised, a new series of detailed records of imports and exports, known as the Port Books, was begun, and lists were drawn up of all the harbours, creeks and other places at which goods might be loaded or unloaded, in order to minimise the evasion of customs duties. To the port of Exeter belonged the landing places of Exmouth, Topsham, Powderham, Dawlish, Lympstone and Kenton, which were all considered to be " within the river of Exmouth haven." Farther afield were Seaton and Teignmouth. Sidmouth and Ottermouth are no longer mentioned as harbours: they had long been silted up, and so had Axmouth. On the north coast of Devon, Barnstaple, Bideford, Appledore, and Ilfracombe were all reckoned to come within the port of Exeter, though separate port books were kept for Barnstaple and Ilfracombe. The port of Dartmouth extended from the south side of the Teign estuary around to the mouth of the Yealm, and included " Tore baye, Saltcumbe, and Yalme."[1] The port of Plymouth completed the catalogue of landing places in Devon.

From 1560 onwards we begin to get detailed information about the size and number of ships in the Devon ports. In that year, Devon possessed 1,268 seamen and eighteen ships of 100 tons and upwards. Of these, five belonged to Plymouth, the largest being of 150 tons; five to Dartmouth, the largest of 200 tons; four to Kingswear of 120-160 tons; two to Northam, one to Cockington, and one to Salcombe.[2] Devon was ahead of every other county, though London exceeded it by two ships and the average tonnage of the London ships is much higher. Another return, made in 1568, enumerates seventeen ships of 100 tons or more, one at Barnstaple, eight at Plymouth, and four each at Dartmouth and Exmouth. Dartmouth and Plymouth each possessed one ship of 400 tons.

In 1570 it was found that in Devon there were 1,264 seamen at home and 411 at sea. In the same return is a list of the ships belonging to " Hawkyns of Plymouth "—this is William Hawkins, the elder brother of Sir John, and son of old William Hawkins—who had a fleet of nine vessels in harbour and four at sea. Amongst them was one ship of 500 tons, one of 350, two of 200, and five of 100-150 tons. Mr. Oppenheim suggests that such a fleet belonged rather to a company of which Hawkins was " managing-director " and that not all were Plymouth ships. Certainly we find in 1585 that letters of reprisal were granted to William Hawkins, Humphrey Fownes " and company " of Plymouth.

Another return, made in 1577, shows that there were then 135 ships

in England of 100 tons and upwards, as against 77 in 1560; but the
number in Devon had actually fallen from eighteen to fifteen. One was
owned at Barnstaple, six at Plymouth, four at Dartmouth, and four at
Exmouth. We hear of a vessel of 250 tons being built for an Exeter
merchant at Bideford in 1566.[1] The four large ships credited to Exmouth
probably belonged to Exeter merchants, and had been built at either
Topsham or Bideford. Plymouth and Dartmouth also built ships.

Thomas Coleshill's register of trading ships, made in 1572, probably
includes coasters and others sailing only within the four seas, since the
largest vessel is one of 100 tons. The distribution of the 130 vessels
accredited to Devon is a valuable indication of the relative importance of
all the ports, large and small:[2]

Place	No. of ships	Largest in tons	Place	No. of ships	Largest in tons
Topsham	14	50	Northam	3	35
Kingswear	3	30	Bideford	6	80
Dartmouth	32	80	Exwater	1	20
Barnstaple	12	80	Plymouth	26	100
Kenton	6	30	Salcombe	5	40
Exmouth	5	50	Ilfracombe	3	30
Teignmouth	5	40	Powderham	4	52
Torbay	5	45			

The major importance of Devon's maritime history in the 16th
century lies, however, in the political field, in the realm of war and
exploration. Here the story is too vast to be told in anything but outline.
It belongs to the province of national history, and there it has been told
so often that one need not tell it again. The emergence of Spain as the
great enemy of England gave Plymouth a special importance as a naval
base. It had a magnificent harbour at the western end of the Channel,
and its fortifications had been repeatedly strengthened since medieval
times. Thus it became a clearing-house for the disposal of prizes captured
at sea in the Spanish war, partly because of its position, but partly also
because it was the home harbour of Drake and of John Hawkins, who
became treasurer of the navy in 1578 and comptroller from 1589 (plate
17). As a fishing town also, with important fishing towns and villages
all along the coast both east and west, it could muster able-bodied
seamen in large numbers, and quickly, for, instead of being transported
to the naval base at Rochester and then being brought down Channel
again, they could join their ships at once in Plymouth.

Dartmouth was as good a harbour; in some respects it was much better. Though it was less capacious, it was big enough for a large fleet, it was well fortified at its narrow entrance, and it did not face the prevailing south-westerly winds as Plymouth Sound did. It was also better protected against storms: Plymouth Sound could be a death-trap in a gale. If there had been a John Hawley at Dartmouth in these Elizabethan years, instead of a John Hawkins at Plymouth, there is little doubt that Dartmouth and not Plymouth would have been the western naval base in the war with Spain. As it was, while the war lasted, Plymouth grew spectacularly. People flocked into the roaring boom town, new streets went up all around Sutton Pool, the centre of shipping. The most memorable occasion in these days was the assembly of more than sixty ships at Plymouth—the greater part of England's navy and armed merchantmen—in July 1588, whence they sailed to meet the Armada of Spain.

What years these were! Old William Hawkins was already voyaging from Plymouth to Brazil and the Guinea coast of Africa in the 1530s, in the years when Stephen and William Burrough were growing up among the ships of the Torridge, while they were still " messing about in boats " at Appledore, or by the quay at Bideford. But they were not long over their play. At the age of twenty-seven Stephen Burrough commanded the first English ship to reach Russia (1553) and he had discovered and named the North Cape; at twenty-nine he had discovered the entrance to the Kara Sea; and at thirty-six he was Chief Pilot of England. His elder brother, William, who had sailed under him on his three Russian voyages, became comptroller of the navy after Hawkins's death in 1595.

While Stephen Burrough was still learning to manage boats in the fast tide-water of the Torridge, Humphrey Gilbert was born at Greenway, the house that looks down the widening Dart from its wooded slopes, and a year or so later Francis Drake was born at Crowndale Farm, just outside Tavistock, the son of a shearman. Within the next ten years John Davis, farmer's son, was born near Sandridge, above the Dart, and John Oxenham, born at Plymouth in all probability. Last of this constellation to appear in the Devonshire sky was Walter Ralegh, born about 1552 at Hayes, a large barton in the country behind East Budleigh, which was now a decayed old riverside port. Ralegh's mother was Katherine Champernowne of Modbury. She was already the mother of Humphrey and Adrian Gilbert by her first marriage, and not content with that she produced a genius by her second marriage with Walter Ralegh of Fardel, the great Sir Walter's father. One would like to have had a portrait, and to know more, of this remarkable woman.

The voyages of these sea-captains take us far beyond the scope of this book. The names of Devonshire men and places are to be found all over the western world from Davis Strait, discovered by John Davis in 1587, down the seaboard to Newfoundland, Maine, and Virginia. Humphrey

Gilbert founded the first British colony in North America in Newfoundland in 1583, and Devon families settled there from the first. Practically all the old families of Newfoundland are said to be of Devonian origin.[1] Gilbert perished in 1584, but Ralegh and Grenville carried on the work of discovery and colonisation. The real impetus to emigration from Devon came, however, in 1622 when Sir Ferdinando Gorges, governor of Plymouth, received a royal grant of extensive territories in what are now parts of New Hampshire and Maine. He founded New Plymouth in 1628, and became first governor of Maine in 1639. His nephew, Francis Champernowne, sixth son of Sir Arthur Champernowne of Modbury, went out to Maine in 1636 from Dartmouth and left several Dartmouth names on the map, as well as Dartington, which still survives.

Many of the younger sons of the Devon gentry migrated and founded families in New England, such as Tristram Coffin who emigrated to Massachusetts in 1642. By 1900 he had some 5,000 descendants in the United States and Canada.[2] Roger Conant, born at East Budleigh of yeoman stock, went out to Massachusetts in 1623, where he was the friend and associate of Governor John Endicott, himself of Devonshire descent, for the ancestors of this grim old Puritan had been settled at Endicott in South Tawton parish since the time of Henry III.[3] Humphrey Davie, the youngest son of the first Davie baronet at Creedy Park, emigrated to Boston in 1662. His son John graduated at Harvard College in 1681 and settled on a farm at Groton a few years later, where he became the first Town Clerk when the town was incorporated in 1705. The senior line of the Davies dying out without male issue in 1707, inquiries were made as to the next heir in America. The story goes that John Davie was working in his fields, barefoot, with sleeves and trousers rolled up, when the news came that he had succeeded to a baronetcy in England and an estate of four or five thousand a year. His old American neighbour, a farmer called James Packer, visited him years later at Creedy Park in Devon, where he was cordially received and shown around the estate. Upon their parting, the baronet said, " You see how I live, Packer, I have an abundance of this world's goods, and can gratify myself with a continual succession of pleasures, but after all, I am not so happy as when you and I changed work at threshing, and we had but one dish for dinner, and that was *cornbeans*."[4]

The full story of these Devonian settlers overseas, the motives that led them to emigrate, their numbers and whence they were drawn, has yet to be written. There will be much to say, for all over New England the Devonshire names are written by the score.

The opening up of the American " plantations " in the second quarter of the 17th century brought a fresh accession of trade to the Devonshire ports. The new plantations needed woollen goods and household stores of all descriptions, and they sent back tobacco and sugar. Bideford, which had had no foreign trade of any consequence before 1600, was in the forefront of this new development. Almost certainly this was due to Sir Richard Grenville's activities. He was lord of the manor of Bideford, and his expeditions to Carolina and Virginia were manned largely by Bideford seamen. From this it was a natural step for enterprising Bideford merchants like the Bucks and the Davies to acquire extensive possessions in the new colonies and to build up a growing trade in tobacco throughout the 17th century. By the 1720s Bideford and Barnstaple were among the largest tobacco ports in England.[1] Both Plymouth and Exeter shared largely in this trade. The port of Exeter sent out woollen goods in vast quantities to European markets as well as the American colonies, and imported chiefly wine, tobacco and sugar. Dartmouth, too, revived suddenly in the late 16th century and continued to flourish throughout the 17th and 18th. The development of the Newfoundland trade from the 1580s, and of the Plantations trade somewhat later, transformed the life of the town. Between 1583 and 1643 it enjoyed a prosperity it had not known since the days of the Hawleys. A large new quay was built, the two churches of the town reconstructed, a hundred new and handsome houses were built, of which the Butterwalk—built 1635-40—is the most notable survival. People came to settle at Dartmouth in large numbers in these years: by 1643 over half the families living there bore names unknown in the town a century before.[2]

The civil wars caused a temporary setback to the flourishing overseas trade of all the ports, but from the Restoration to the reign of Anne they enjoyed a further glory.[3] After that, the incessant wars handicapped their trade in all manner of ways—Bideford was never the same great place again after 1730—but trade continued at a diminished level until the American War of Independence. From this time onwards the Devonshire ports, except Plymouth, decayed rapidly and by 1800 they were of little consequence. Wars and the decline of the Devonshire serge industry killed them in the last quarter of the 18th century.

The almost incessant wars of the period 1689-1815 did immense damage to the legitimate trade of the Devon ports, but they created the great naval base of Plymouth, and it is to this that we must now turn briefly.

The main anchorage for naval assemblies was Cattewater, the mouth of the Plym, until the end of the 17th century. The site of Devonport, where the great dockyard was to grow, was until then marshland and river mud along the Hamoaze, as the mouth of the Tamar was called. It was Ralegh who first suggested that the fleet should be dispersed from the Thames estuary and Portsmouth, and divided between Portsmouth, Dartmouth, Plymouth, Falmouth and Milford. So long as Spain was

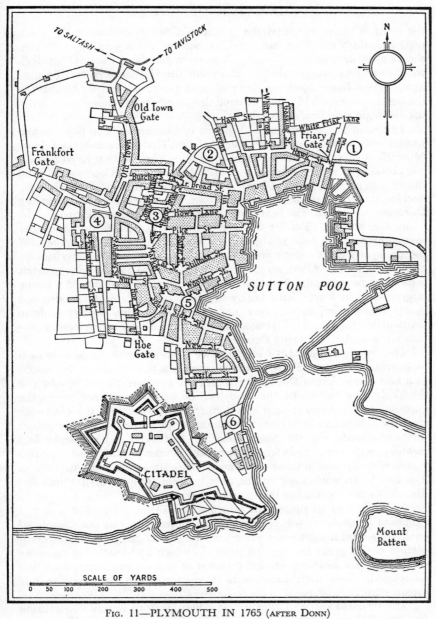

FIG. 11—PLYMOUTH IN 1765 (AFTER DONN)

1. Friary.   2. Charles Church.   3. Guildhall.   4. St. Andrew's Church.   5. New Quay.   6. Victualling Office

the enemy, there remained the problem of the prevailing S.W. wind, which would bring the enemy up-Channel and simultaneously bottle up the English fleet in the Thames. A western base was essential. Ralegh was the first to propose that at Plymouth the Hamoaze should be used as the naval base. Nothing came of these proposals, chiefly because as the century went on Holland became the prime enemy and the nature of the strategic problem changed.

The unimpeded landing of William of Orange in Tor Bay demonstrated once again the disadvantages of the Thames estuary as a base. More than that, the new strategic conditions after 1688 revived acutely the problem of a far western base, as a defence against operations from the French military ports of Brest and Rochefort. In 1690 the Admiralty decided on Plymouth as the western base, after surveying and rejecting Dartmouth.[1] Work was begun on a new government dockyard on the Hamoaze, and by 1696 the transfer of the naval base from Cattewater was completed. A new town, called Dock, began to spring up outside the dockyard walls. Each war brought it new life and prosperity. By 1733 it had over 3,000 people; by 1780, 10,000-12,000. Its greatest growth came with the Napoleonic Wars, and by 1801 Dock was the largest town in Devon with nearly 24,000 people (plate 4). Among the many who flocked to this war town in these golden years was John Galsworthy, the son of a Plymstock farmer, the founder of the Forsyte fortunes as a dealer in marine stores.[2]

The creation of a great naval base at Plymouth was not as easy as it looks from the map. There were many serious drawbacks to the Sound as a base. One formidable danger had been removed by the building of the Eddystone lighthouse (in 1698) on the terrible reef that lay in the entrance to the Sound; and the dangerous passage into the Hamoaze from the Sound had been buoyed by about 1730, and a body of competent pilots provided. But the Sound was still a dangerous harbour in bad weather, wide open as it was to the south-westerly gales, and Tor Bay was frequently used instead as an anchorage. It was the habitual use of Tor Bay as an anchorage for the fleet between 1793 and 1815 that led directly to the creation of the town of Torquay.

A breakwater to protect the entrance to Plymouth Sound was first proposed in 1806. It was begun by Rennie in 1812, but not completed until 1841, and a lighthouse placed on the end in 1844. With the completion of this great engineering work, in which $4\frac{1}{2}$ million tons of stone were used, the last stage in the creation of the western naval base was completed. Since then the fame of Plymouth as a naval base has only grown with each war.

The overseas trade of Devon had fallen away to practically nothing by 1800. When the war was over only the coastal trade and the fishing

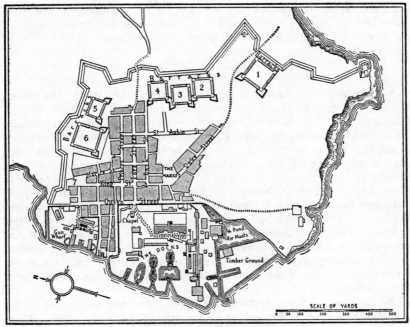

Fig. 12—DOCK IN 1765 (after Donn)

*1. Georges Square.   2. Cumberland Square.   3. Ligonier Square.   4. Frederick
Square.   5. Granby Square.   6. Marlborough Square*

trade were of any consequence, but the Bristol and English Channels were great highways for shipping heading for Bristol and Cardiff, Southampton and London, and the formidable headlands of the Devon coast needed lighting. The principal lighthouses were first lit as follows: Lundy (High light), 1820; Braunton, 1832; Start Point, 1836; Hartland Point, 1874; Bull Point, 1879; Lundy (North and South lights), 1897; The Foreland, 1900; and Berry Head, 1906.

The chequered history of the Eddystone light is well known. Winstanley's lighthouse was swept away, with its builder, in the terrible storm of 27 November 1703. John Rudyard, a silk mercer of London, was the architect of the second lighthouse, which was finished in 1709. This was burnt down on 2 December 1755. The first two lighthouses had been built of timber because it was believed that the greater elasticity of wood in yielding to heavy seas was a safeguard. But John Smeaton determined to build the third lighthouse of granite, and this was duly completed in 1759. It lasted until 1881 and was only abandoned then because of the undermining of the rock on which it stood. The new and fourth lighthouse was built by Sir James Douglas, the Trinity House engineer, and first lit in 1881. Smeaton's lighthouse was taken down as far as the solid base, and re-erected on Plymouth Hoe, where it still stands.

FISHING

We know little about the important fisheries off the Devon coast before the 16th century.* Plymouth—or rather its germ at Sutton—was a " fisher town " in the 12th century, having its principal market no doubt at the monasteries of Plympton, Buckland, and Tavistock, which all lay within easy reach by road. In the time of Richard II we hear of hake (presumably dried) being exported from Exeter. There can be little doubt that the rich fishing grounds off the south Devon coast were well known and exploited all through medieval times and that a small export trade had been developed. Richard II's grant of six years' customs at Plymouth in 1378 for the purpose of strengthening the fortifications of the town specifically mentions pilchards and hake among the principal articles of commerce. This, indeed, is the first reference to the valuable pilchard industry at Plymouth. The catching, salting, and exporting of this fish was one of the chief activities of the town down to the late 18th century.

By the early 16th century we learn more about the magnitude of the coastal fisheries from Leland and from the *Valor Ecclesiasticus*. Both Brixham and Kingswear are noted by Leland as fishing towns, and he tells us incidentally that net-fishing was carried on in Tor Bay at that time.[1] Other places which he particularly notes as fishing towns are Salcombe, Exmouth, Budleigh Salterton, Otterton, Seaton, Beer and Axmouth. He does not refer to any fishing town or village on the north coast. The *Valor Ecclesiasticus* (1535) enables us to be much more precise about the size of the fishing industry at the various ports, for the tithe of fish was an important item of ecclesiastical income in these places, and as such is separately given. The annual value of the fish tithes given in the *Valor* is as follows: Brixham (probably including Kingswear), £17; Paignton, £12; St. Marychurch, £12; Plymouth, £10; Dawlish, £6; Seaton, £4 10s.; and Clovelly, £1 6s. 8d. Although not all the places mentioned by Leland are given here, we have the most important figures. The south coast of Devon was one of the most productive English fishing areas in Henry VIII's time, and a great part of the industry was centred in and around Tor Bay. Plymouth was fourth in the list of Devon fishing ports, Dawlish fifth. Fishing was also important along the east Devon coast, but on the north coast the fishery of Clovelly was still very small.

*Among the customs of the manor of Stokenham, on Start Bay, in 1309 was the obligation on some of the bondmen to catch mullet and other fish for their lord.

The pilchard and the herring fisheries were the most valuable during the 16th and 17th centuries. By Westcote's day (*c.* 1630) Clovelly and Lynmouth were noted for their herrings—" the king of fishes "—while the pilchard fishery was mainly concentrated along the south coast, with Plymouth as the great centre for packing and export to the Mediterranean countries and Ireland. Bigbury Bay was long noted for its catches of pilchards; Risdon makes special reference to Hope Quay in this connection. Dartmouth, Teignmouth, and Dawlish were also much engaged in the pilchard fishery from the 17th century until the early 19th. By Lysons's day the fishery had greatly declined, however, at all these places. Plymouth was always the biggest centre. We find the Plymouth corporation making a number of by-laws relating to the pilchard fishery in 1565. Westcote says that one could often see 100 sail of the fishing fleet at Plymouth, sometimes 200, and that the dried fish was sent far inland as well as to the Catholic countries round the Mediterranean.

The herring was caught off both coasts, but was much the most important fish on the north coast. In contrast to the pilchard, which seems to have been steadily caught from the 14th century to the early 19th, the herring sometimes disappeared for years on end, causing great distress at Clovelly, Ilfracombe and Lynmouth. It was scarce about 1760, abundant again about 1780, and then scarce again about 1805. Clovelly had at one time sixty or seventy boats in the herring fishery, but had much declined by the time Lysons wrote. Again, large quantities were exported when they were available. On the south coast, Teignmouth had a large herring fishery about 1780. By 1820 this was insignificant, but it grew again later. Plymouth had no herring fishery in 1800, but a large one a hundred years later.[1]

By the middle of the 18th century the improved roads enabled flat fish such as turbot and sole to be landed at the Devonshire ports and sent up to Bristol, Bath and other fashionable inland places. This seems to have led to the invention of trawling along the bottom, as distinct from drift-fishing, a notable technical advance in the English fishing industry which appears at Brixham before 1800. The Brixham fishermen followed the fish up Channel, then through the Straits of Dover into the North Sea, and by the early 19th century some of them found it more convenient to settle in the east coast ports and carry on their trawling from there, particularly at Hull and Grimsby, which were poor places until the Devonshire men came and showed them how to fish.

In 1840 the chief fishing ports in Devon were Brixham (with Torquay and Paignton), Plymouth (with Cawsand), Bideford (with Barnstaple and Clovelly), Ilfracombe and Combe Martin, Exmouth and Topsham, in that order. Brixham was sending fish to London, Bath, and Exeter by the middle of the 18th century; fifty years later it was the most noted wholesale fish market in the west of England. Fish was carried up to fifty miles inland on pack-horses but the London fish was sent by sea to Portsmouth and thence overland. In 1843 Brixham had 165 trawlers and twenty hookers and seiners at work. Altogether this busy little place had more than 270 sail of vessels, comprising 20,000 tons of shipping, and employing about 1,600 seamen. The average weekly catch was about 150 tons but sometimes as much as 350 tons were sold on the Quay in a week.[1] The Brixham fishing fleet returning under full sail in the evening was one of the great sights of the west of England, and a sight we shall never see again. In 1900 there were 309 fishing boats at the port, with a total tonnage of 10,525, but the steam trawler had not yet made its appearance. The first steam trawlers had appeared at Plymouth in 1898 but the bulk of the Plymouth boats (360 of them by the 1870s) were drifters and not trawlers. Even after 1900 there were nearly ten times as many drift-nets as trawl-nets at Plymouth. By the 1870s, Plymouth had become the leading fishing port in Devon, and was tenth among the fishing ports of England and Wales, but Brixham was a close second.

The 20th century saw profound changes in the methods of fishing, however, which have reduced the Devonshire fishing towns to a melancholy state. The development of larger steam- and motor-powered ships and of the distant fishing grounds, especially in the Arctic, has altered the whole character of English fishing from predominantly small inshore and off-shore boats to large sea-going vessels whose catches are landed in the north of England and Scottish ports. The south-western ports are ill placed to share in this rich new trade, and have no deep-sea vessels. The full force of these changes was felt immediately after the war of 1914-18.

The experience of Brixham may be taken as typical of what happened in all the Devon and Cornish fishing ports in the twenty years after 1919. " In 1910 there were 213 trawlers of various sizes and types fishing from the port, and these boats were up to date and their crews young and keen. The women knitted underwear for the apprentices and wove nets; the older men were occupied in such industries as sail-making; 150 men worked in the yards of three shipwrights; seven firms made nearly 300 pairs of sea-boots yearly; and nine out of ten of the young men went to sea. Brixham men held a justifiable pride in their birth and town, and were respected in all the fishing ports of the coast from Bristol and South Wales round to Hull."[2]

The war came, the young men were called away into the navy for nearly five years. Those who came back found a very different town. Only eighty-six vessels, old and worn, were left, and these needed new equipment at inflated prices. Fish prices fell, losses of nets and gear were high in the wreck-strewn bay between Start and Portland; year by year boats went out of commission and the heart was slowly torn out of the old town. By 1935 only twenty-six boats were left on the register, and these were being sold at the rate of seven or eight a year at knock-down prices, mostly for conversion into private yachts. By 1939 not an apprentice was left, and the examination for skippers had lapsed for want of candidates. The famous Brixham fishing fleet was now practically extinct. In 1919 there had been 120 or so vessels in the sailing fleet; by 1938 there were only half a dozen. At Plymouth the sailing fleet was reduced from twenty-four to two in the same period. Some had, indeed, been converted to powered craft, but these were usually obliged to fish and land their catches far from home.

Among the minor fishing ports of Devon, Torquay comes first with an annual fishery of over £11,000. Beer fishery is worth about £7,000 a year, and Hallsands with its important shell fisheries £5,500. Dartmouth and Hope Cove come next in value (£2,000–£5,000). The east Devon and north Devon fishing ports are now all small, producing less than £2,000 worth each on an average. The corresponding figures for Plymouth and Brixham are £134,000 and £88,000 respectively.[1]

The almost total decay of the fishing industry at a score of little towns and villages around the Devon coasts is a part of the tragedy which was repeated all over Britain in a variety of forms during the 19th and early 20th centuries: a tragedy arising from the substitution of large-scale, extensive exploitation of world resources for the intensive and minute use of local resources in which the small man could find a living and work on his own account, in his own way and at his own pace. It was not only the decay of the fishing industry itself, but of all the other valuable trades and activities that catered for it, as we saw in the case of Brixham. The men are now driven to take town visitors out for what they call " fishing " in the bay during the summer holiday season, and their wives to let rooms to the same visitors during the season. It is a valuable function, no doubt, to cater for the wants of weary and jaded town-dwellers, but it is a poor way of living in more senses than one when one thinks of the life and vigour that once dwelt in these places, and of the glory that has departed.

THE SALMON FISHERIES

Although the salmon fisheries of the Devon rivers are not strictly a part of the maritime trade, this is the most convenient place to touch upon them. The salmon rivers have been locally important for a thousand years, but no one has yet written their turbulent and fascinating history. Mr. Finberg has devoted a valuable chapter to the Tavistock abbey fisheries in the Tavy and Tamar, but this necessarily covers only a limited time and a small district.[2] A great deal of the unwritten history is still buried in the central records of the law courts, now in the Public Record

Office, and much besides in the estate papers of the big families like the
Rolles (now Lords Clinton) who had important fishing rights in the Taw
and Torridge, and jealously guarded them. A good book is waiting to be
written on this subject.

As early as the middle of the 9th century the salmon of the Taw
estuary appear in the records. In 857 Ethelbald, king of Wessex, gave to
the abbot of Glastonbury ten hides of land at Braunton (*Brannocmynstre*)
for the taking of salmon for his house.[1] In the 13th century we find a
certain landholder at Braunton paying a rent in salmon. To this day
salmon fishing is carried on in the estuary on the Braunton side (though the
boats mostly belong to Appledore across the river) and the Taw and
Torridge together remain the most important salmon fishery in Devon.

Domesday records thirteen fisheries in Devon, almost certainly all
salmon fisheries, as they lie for the most part well inland. The Dart was
a notable salmon river (and still is), for at Dartington two fishermen had
to render eighty salmon yearly to the lord, and at Cornworthy, a few
miles lower down the river, the fishermen paid thirty salmon a year. At
Loddiswell, on the Avon, thirty salmon a year were also exacted by the
lord.

By 1086 the centre of the Taw-Torridge fishery had shifted to Bideford,
where it was valued at 25s. a year, the most valuable fishery in Devon.
There were also small salmon fisheries at Wear Giffard (Torridge),
Heanton Punchardon (Taw), and Northam (probably representing
Appledore). In south Devon the Exe was the most prolific river, as it
still is. Here the Exminster fishery was worth 20s. a year, and is the only
fishery named on the river. We know, however, that the important
salmon fishery of Topsham was in existence in 1141, when Baldwin de
Redvers, Earl of Devon, granted half the tithe of it to his new foundation
of St. James's priory just outside Exeter.[2] The Exeter city records contain
a great number of references to the Exe salmon, which were for centuries,
and in various ways, a valuable asset to the city. Celia Fiennes tell us
how, in 1698, she watched men at Exeter spearing the salmon as they
leapt the weirs above Exe bridge,[3] just as I have seen them many a time
and oft leaping through the boiling flood-water over the same weirs.

Domesday also records fisheries in the Tavy and the Plym, but neither
the Cornwall nor the Devonshire Domesday returns say a word about the
Tamar, which had valuable salmon fisheries towards the close of the
12th century.[4] There was, too, good fishing in the smaller rivers like
Erme and Teign at a later date.

Most of the travellers in Devon in the 17th and 18th centuries speak
of the abundance of salmon to be seen in the local markets. Indeed, the
taking of salmon by draft nets and weirs was so recklessly prodigal that
Lysons records about 1820 that the salmon fisheries of Devon, like those of

other counties, had much declined, mainly through the destruction of fish in the spawning season. To-day (1949 figures) the catches in the Devon rivers are as follows: Taw and Torridge, 4,300; Exe, 3,957; Tamar and Plym, 2,209; Dart, 1,711; Teign, 1,271; Axe, 83; and Avon, 10.[1] These figures are doubtless underestimates of the true catch, but they place the rivers in the right order. The Exe is the most prolific river in Devon. The commercial fishing is centred at Topsham (plate 54), where it has been since the early years of the 12th century. All the figures given above include salmon caught with rod and line, but it is usually reckoned that about 80 per cent are taken by draft nets in the estuaries. The Taw-Torridge fishery is centred at Appledore, that of the Dart at Stoke Gabriel.

THE NEWFOUNDLAND FISHERIES

The history of the great cod fishery on the Newfoundland Banks requires a page or two to itself. It began early in the 16th century. From the middle of the century English boats increasingly engaged in it; the Bristol company of merchants had organised annual voyages to St. John's by about 1560, and most of the south-western ports from Poole round to Bideford and Barnstaple also began to take part in the trade. During the 1570s the English fleet increased to fifty sail, and one catches glimpses of the growth of the trade in the customs and port books for the south-west.[2]

Little ships from the creeks and harbours of the Exe estuary—from Topsham, Exmouth, Kenton—were making the long, hazardous voyage from 1563 onwards. By the 1580s, Dawlish and Teignmouth occasiona'ly sent a ship. Most of these ships were only twenty-five to fifty tons, some (like the *Elizabeth* and the *John*, of Teignmouth) as small as twenty tons.[3] Plymouth was in the trade by 1570, but Dartmouth does not seem to have been much interested until a decade later. There are only four Newfoundland entries in the surviving Dartmouth port books of the 1570s. The first recorded ship from Newfoundland to Dartmouth is the *Gratias Deo* of Dartmouth, which came in from *Terra Nova* on 8 September 1565 with two tons of train oil, but it was not until 1580 that the trade was developed on any scale. In that year the Danes placed restrictions on the Iceland cod fishery that made it less attractive to the English fishermen, who turned westwards to Newfoundland.

The Bristol share of the trade was organised by a company, but that of Dartmouth at least was a matter of individual enterprise. Anybody could fit out his ship, get together a crew, and take a chance of fortune. The catch was divided at the end of the season into three parts: one-third to the ship owner for hire and maintenance, one-third to the merchant for fitting out and victualling, and one-third to the master and crew.[4]

The Newfoundland trade at the port of Exeter also seems to have been based on individual enterprise. Entries that suggest *ad hoc* " companies," headed by the master of the ship, occur frequently in the records. Probably the Newfoundland trade was free for all in all the south-western ports, and possibly as a result of this it became almost a monopoly of the Devon ports during the 17th century.

Topsham, on the Exe, became the leading centre of the trade in Devon; Bideford, on the Torridge, had taken second place by the end of the century. In 1699 Topsham had thirty-four ships and seventy boats in the trade, Bideford twenty-eight ships and 146 boats. Dartmouth then had seventeen ships engaged in it, Barnstaple eight, and Plymouth five. Outside Devon, only London and Bristol were of any importance, with seventy-one ships and twelve ships respectively.[1] The ships were now much larger, and generally armed. The Bideford ships, for example, ranged from 220 tons with sixty-five men and twenty guns to sixty tons, twenty men, and no guns.

Continual wars greatly injured the fishery in various ways, not least by the calling up of the seamen for the navy, for the hard Newfoundland trade was one of the finest schools of seamanship.[2] The trade was generally on a smaller scale throughout the 18th century than in the previous century. In the 1750s, some forty or fifty ships went from Bideford. Dartmouth also sent a considerable number of ships, but the trade had fallen into the hands of a few large merchants, like the Holdsworths, who had the capital resources to meet the more difficult conditions arising from wars and constant rumours of wars. Plymouth had very largely dropped out of the trade, but after the peace of 1763 her merchants again put considerable capital into the trade, and were successful until the American War put a stop to all commercial enterprise in the town. Indeed, in 1787, only Dartmouth and Topsham sent any ships to Newfoundland, and then only two vessels each. The trade revived after the war: in 1791 Dartmouth had 112 ships employed in it. By Lysons's day, only Dartmouth and Teignmouth had any substantial interest in it, with fifty-nine and thirty-five ships respectively engaged in 1820. At Plymouth only two ships were regularly employed in it, and Torquay had a small share also. At Bideford the trade failed as early as the 1720s, from the disastrous effects of Queen Anne's wars. Many attempts were made to revive it during the 18th century, but all failed.[3] The Topsham trade had wholly gone by 1820. It had been transferred to Teignmouth, possibly because of the greatly increased size of the ships. But even at Teignmouth and Dartmouth, the fishing voyages had been abandoned, and by the early 19th century the vessels were merely traders bringing home cod.

CHAPTER XII

ECCLESIASTICAL HISTORY

THE CELTIC SAINTS

THE early history of the Christian Church in Devon is a subject of peculiar fascination and difficulty. The mere thought of the Celtic saints wandering by the shores of Devon, or meditating in their little oratories in the primeval woods, seduces the imagination. Much, therefore, that has been written on this subject must be read with caution, and a good deal of it is best forgotten. Whoever approaches the Celtic saints walks all the time on the edge of a quicksand, but a quicksand that conceals some valuable treasure, if only we knew where to begin looking and which clues are worth following. All one can hope to do in the present state of knowledge is to avoid perpetuating old errors, and to clear away some of the speculative débris.

The Christian faith reached Britain towards the close of the 2nd century. The discovery of the XP monogram on a cooking pot at Exeter shows that it had reached the south-west by the late 4th century.[1] A dozen funerary monuments survive in Devon, dating in all probability from the period 400-650. Three of these are now to be found in the vicarage garden at Tavistock, all discovered in the immediate neighbourhood. Others have been found on the borders of Exmoor, one is on Lundy, and another stands on Sourton Down—recut as a medieval cross beside that lonely road out of Okehampton into Cornwall. These stones mark the graves of ecclesiastics and chieftains, none of whom can now be identified, and they are certainly Christian monuments.[2]

The Celtic church was monastic in pattern, but nothing has come to light in Devon comparable with the community at Tintagel, on the north coast of Cornwall, which was founded about 500 and survived until the 9th century. The archaeological evidence from this period is scanty, and we must turn cautiously to that of church dedications. Once again, Cornwall shows more abundant evidence than Devon, but some interesting facts come to light in Devon if we search carefully. Landkey, a parish just south-east of Barnstaple and not far from the head of the Taw estuary, is a suggestive name. It was " the church of St. Kea," a dedication also found in Cornwall and in Brittany. Here, in this warm fertile valley below the rounded sweep of Codden Hill, a monastic community was in all probability founded in the 6th century: a community of celibate clergy observing a religious rule and entrusted with the care of souls over a wide and ill-defined area. Landkey church is now dedicated to St. Paul, but this represents a re-foundation—probably in the 12th century—as a chapelry of the extensive parish of Bishop's Tawton. At some unknown date the Celtic community ceased to exist, as at Tintagel; the later church adopted another dedication, but the village name preserved the original.

Four miles farther inland is Filleigh, where the church is also dedicated to St. Paul to-day. But Canon Doble shows very plausibly that the place-name is derived from St. Fili, the companion of St. Kea, and that the original dedication was to that Celtic saint. St. Kea was probably a monk from Celtic Glastonbury, who had a Welsh companion named Fili. These two, perhaps with others from Glastonbury, were evangelising Devon during the 6th century.[1] Kerrian, too, was a disciple of Kea, and dedications to him are found in Devon (at Exeter) and in Cornwall.

Not many miles from Landkey and Filleigh, and within a couple of miles of the Taw estuary again, is Braunton, which is pretty certainly the *Brannucmunster* given (according to William of Malmesbury) by King Ethelbald to Glastonbury in the middle of the 9th century. Here the church is still dedicated to the 6th-century Welsh missionary, St. Brannoc or Brynach. Both William of Worcester and Leland tell us that Brannoc was buried in Braunton church, where his relics were certainly preserved until the middle of Elizabeth's reign. They now lie somewhere beneath the high altar.[2] Braunton was another monastic community of the same type as Landkey. It seems likely that the Taw estuary was a centre for the early Celtic saints, as we might expect from its position in relation to Wales and Ireland, whence so many of them came, and that a number of early churches were founded in the country behind.

Other churches dedicated to the Celtic saints—Breton, Irish, and Welsh—may be found scattered all over Devon, especially in the north, south and west of the county. The infrequency of Celtic dedications to the east of the Exe, in the Romanised part of Devon, is very noticeable. In all there appear to be about forty or fifty churches in Devon dedicated to the Celtic saints, to which must be added about sixteen medieval chapels which have now disappeared. The map suggests a close connection between the voyages of the early missionary saints, penetrating up the Devon estuaries, and the distribution of Celtic dedications, while there is also marked evidence in mid-western Devon of influence from Cornwall (as at Milton Abbot and Dunterton, for example).[1] No fewer than eighteen dedications to the Welsh saint Petrock are known in Devon: he was by far the most important of the western missionary saints in the 6th century. But the cult of St. Petrock continued vigorously throughout the diocese of Exeter down to the Reformation, and it would be a wild error to assume that all the churches and chapels dedicated to him were founded by him.

The evidence of church dedications is full of difficulties. Old dedications have been forgotten, or have been deliberately changed, or have been corrupted into something nearly unrecognisable—like St. Winwalloe at Portlemouth, now called St. Onolaus. Again, churches founded at a comparatively late date might still be dedicated to a Celtic saint. It is indeed possible that these were founded on sites already associated with early saints, sites marked perhaps by a holy well or a cross, but when we say this we are venturing well into the quicksands.

That the dedications of parish churches have a value as historical evidence is beyond question. They undoubtedly tell us something about Celtic Christianity in Devon. Especially is this true of the dedications to the more obscure saints, which are likely to be contemporary. But we must be cautious about tracing the footsteps of St. Petrock, for example, from the whereabouts of the churches that bear his name. Moreover, the Celts could and did dedicate churches to the apostles, and there may well be churches in Devon with such dedications that go back to Celtic times. In exceptional cases the study of church dedications may throw some light on the history of the early Church, as in the Barnstaple district we have just discussed, but taken as a whole it is a dangerous pastime for the historian.

All we can be certain of so far is that Devon was being fairly extensively evangelised during the 6th century by missionaries of Irish, Welsh and Breton extraction, that some of these came from the Celtic monastery at Glastonbury, and that a number of churches in Devon were founded at this time, notably on or near the estuaries and the sea-coasts.[2] There seem to have been close associations between Glastonbury abbey and ancient Dumnonia, as witness the early and extensive grants of land to the abbey in Devon and eastern Cornwall, and the connections of some of the missionary saints. It is possible, indeed, that the abbey which existed at Exeter in the 7th century—at which St. Boniface was educated —was a Celtic foundation and a daughter of Glastonbury, but there is no proof of this.

In ancient sunlight the Celtic saints sailed up the tidal waters of the Taw, and walked on its shores through " lorn autumns and triumphant springs." They knew by heart the shapes of the hills we see to-day, of

Codden above Landkey and the far purple sweep of the Exmoor edge below which they built their stone oratories and founded their churches. They knew the hill at Exeter—ancient *Isca* within its dark Roman walls—crowned by the abbey of St. Mary and St. Peter, and the wide glittering waters of the Exe down to the sea. They knew the Dart and founded a church on the rocks at its very mouth; and St. Brendan " the navigator " rounded the foaming Start and raised a chapel on the headland of Prawle. And they knew the noble Tamar well, for St. Indract and St. Dominic landed at the port of *Tamerunta* in the closing years of the 7th century,[1] which is Tamerton Foliot at the head of a forgotten creek to-day; and St. Budoc came here, too, when he founded a church at Budshead (*Budoc's hide*) on the shore of the same creek. Walking beside these estuaries and over these headlands, one treads on holy ground, where the Celtic saints once walked in " the freshness of the early world," and we breathe immortal air.

THE ENGLISH CHURCH

With the completion of the Saxon occupation of Devon, the southwest of England was brought within the new see of Sherborne, created in 705. Two hundred years later, in the year 909, this vast diocese of Sherborne was split up, and among the smaller sees then created were those of Wells, Crediton, and St. Germans, covering Somerset, Devon, and Cornwall respectively. About 1040, the dioceses of Cornwall and Crediton were united in the person of Lyfing. He was followed by Leofric, who also held the two bishoprics until 1050. In that year Leofric merged the two sees and moved his seat to Exeter,[2] probably because it was a walled city and Crediton only an open village. The see of Exeter thereafter included the whole of Devon and Cornwall, until the creation of the diocese of Truro in 1876, which brought the ancient bishopric of Cornwall to life again. There is no positive proof for the statement, often made, that the see was originally at Bishop's Tawton.[3] The medieval bishops of Exeter had a country residence there, from the early 14th century, perhaps earlier. The assertion of the existence of a pre-Conquest see rests upon the slenderest foundations, but some of the evidence is suggestive and we cannot rule out the possibility that Bishop's Tawton may have preceded Crediton as the seat of an assistant bishop under Sherborne.

After the absorption of Devon into the Saxon ecclesiastical organisation, parochial churches were built in increasing numbers, though we have no means of knowing how many existed at the time of the Norman Conquest. Domesday Book does not set out to give this information, and cannot be used for this purpose. Not a stone of Saxon building remains in Devon, except the crypt at Sidbury and possibly one or two fragments in Exeter. It is certain that the great majority of pre-Conquest churches in Devon were made of timber, for there were endless oak woods for the taking. All these timber churches were rebuilt long ago, and the archaeological evidence is now gone. The documentary evidence is slight, but here and there it helps us. The names of Exminster and Axminster (the only two *minsters* left in Devon) make it certain that churches existed here soon after 705. We know that a minster was founded at Crediton in 739, and that other early minsters existed at Braunton, Plympton, and Coryton. A considerable number of other churches had come into being before 1066. I am inclined to think that all, or nearly all, the true nucleated villages in Devon possessed a church by the 11th century. A list of all the churches which are the mother churches of a wide area would yield additional examples of pre-Conquest foundations, and in some instances a highly localised dedication, like that of St. Urith at Chittlehampton—a local saint and a unique dedication— would give a closer date.[1]

The 12th century was one of the most formative periods in ecclesiastical, as it was in political and economic, history. Let us pause for a moment, however, at the year 1100 to look over the diocese of Exeter as it was then. The bishop ruled over all the territory between Somerset and Land's End, a vast stretch of country, much of it difficult and almost unknown. (Even in the 14th century the newly-appointed bishops thought of themselves, as Grandisson did, as coming to the edge of the known world.) He was a powerful magnate, the third greatest landowner in the Devonshire Domesday. Figures are not easy to arrive at, but the episcopal estates in Devon alone have been reckoned at nearly 77,000 acres. The bishop had twenty-four manors in Devon, and another eleven in Cornwall. In Cornwall he was again the third largest landowner, possessing nearly one-eighth of the recorded ploughlands, with an acreage that may be tentatively reckoned at about 36,000. In all, the bishop's thirty-five manors in the south-west amounted to well over 100,000 acres.[2] In medieval times Exeter was the fourth largest diocese, and sixth in the value of episcopal revenues, being worth more than Lincoln or Norwich.[3]

Only the King and Baldwin, the sheriff, had greater estates than the bishop in Devon. Four monastic houses held nearly 40,000 acres of land between them in the county (Tavistock, Buckfast, Glastonbury and Horton). Altogether the Church held some 142,000 acres, nearly one-sixth of the recorded total of 907,665 acres, or about 232 hides out of a total of 1,129. The total holding of the Church was second only to that of the King.

The only two monastic houses in Domesday Devon were the Benedictine abbeys of Tavistock, founded about 974, and Buckfast, founded about 1030. A few others were founded before the end of the 11th century: St. Nicholas's priory at Exeter in 1087, St. Michael, a cell of Malmesbury, about 1066, and the two alien priories of Otterton, *temp.* William II, and Totnes, about 1088. Barnstaple priory was possibly founded about 1090, certainly before 1107. Ipplepen, a dependency of the Augustinian house of St. Pierre at Fougères, was founded about 1100.[1]

The parochial organisation of the diocese was just taking shape, but its origins and its development are equally obscure. Such churches as existed in 1100 exercised jurisdiction over a much wider territory, in most cases, than the modern parish. At first this territory was ill-defined, but with the increased building of churches by lay landowners for their dependents and their tenants it became necessary to define precisely the jurisdiction of their priests and the exact area from which they were entitled to draw tithes. On the Welsh border, for example, the bishop of Llandaff arranged in the 11th century for definite areas to be serviced by particular priests. In Devon the parochial organisation had probably been completed by the end of the 12th century, but of its beginnings we know nothing.

The 12th and 13th centuries saw a tremendous religious revival in England and in western Europe generally. In the far diocese of Exeter, on the edge of the western world, it was no less evident. A succession of powerful bishops reigned at Exeter throughout this period, and well beyond it. A magnificent cathedral arose on the site of the old Exeter abbey, which had perished at some unknown date (possibly in the burning of the city by the Danes in 1003); parish churches were rebuilt in stone throughout the diocese; hundreds of new churches arose in hamlets and at cross-roads where none had been before; and nearly a score of religious houses were founded in various parts of the county, most of them before the 12th century was over. Buckfast, which had probably become extinct before 1100, was refounded from Savigny in 1136. Plympton, Ford, Hartland, and Torre all arose before 1200, Dunkeswell in 1201. In the 13th century came Frithelstock, Newenham, Cornworthy and, last of all, the Cistercian foundation of Buckland in 1278. In the same century, too, the Dominican and Franciscan friars reached Exeter, and in the next they established themselves at Plymouth and Barnstaple.

As to the tremendous building activity in the parishes, the architectural evidence is abundant,[2] and it suggests, too, that this activity was at its height in the second half of the 12th century. At the same time the parochial system was perfected, parish boundaries drawn, and the rights of mother churches and their dependent chapelries carefully defined. We can probably attribute a great deal of this building and administrative activity to Bishop Bartholomew, one of the ablest bishops of the 12th century, who reigned at Exeter from 1161 to 1184 and who was called

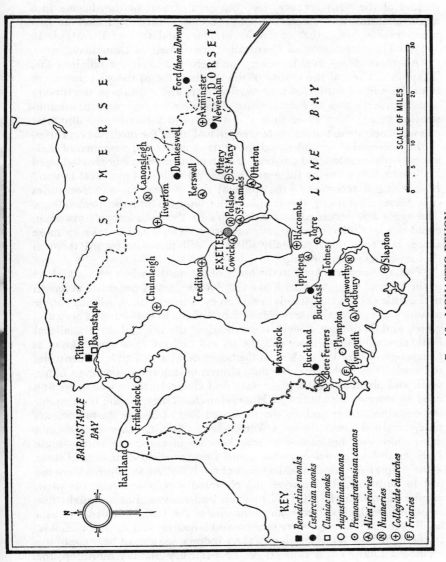

KEY
■ Benedictine monks
● Cistercian monks
□ Cluniac monks
○ Augustinian canons
⊕ Premonstratensian canons
Ⓐ Alien priories
Ⓝ Nunneries
⊕ Collegiate churches
Ⓕ Friaries

SCALE OF MILES
0 · 5 · 10 · 20 · 30

Fig. 13—MONASTIC DEVON

Hospitals, lesser cells, and granges have not been marked. The religious houses of Exeter
have not been recorded on this map

225

by Pope Alexander III " the luminary of the English Church." By the middle of the 12th century, too, the organisation of the diocese into archdeaconries was completed. The archdeaconry of Exeter is first mentioned in 1083, that of Totnes in 1140, and that of Barnstaple in 1143.[1] The archdeacon of Cornwall is mentioned in Domesday.

All these things are, however, the mere mechanics of religious life. They do not reveal the reality of the spiritual life of the past any more than the administration of a university bears any relation to the quality of its learning; and we must beware of treating the ecclesiastical administration as anything more than the mechanical substructure. But how can we penetrate to the reality of the spiritual life of the medieval centuries, to the unrecorded attitudes and thoughts of unlettered peasants, of their almost equally unlettered parsons, or even of the monastic houses wrapped in contemplation among the green woods and valleys of medieval Devon? If anything is recorded of the spiritual side of these far-away centuries it is almost invariably the scandals, the failures, and the backslidings. The *omnia bene* recorded at the bishop's or the archdeacon's visitation could not be duller or more uninformative. The scandals take up more space, but only the historically illiterate will therefore regard them as that much more important.

Perhaps we get nearest to the heart of the matter when we walk alone in the lanes of a remote parish like Honeychurch, and penetrate at length to the little church that stands beside an even quieter lane, with its rubble masonry from a local quarry softened by lichens to half-tones of grey and green, and its dumpy western tower housing the original three medieval bells, now silent. No more can the second bell say *Plebs omnis plaudit ut me tam sepius audit.* We push open the heavy door, and with it the centuries roll back: this withdrawn Norman church on the site of one even older, small and aisleless, only a plain nave and chancel: there was never any need to enlarge the church at Honeychurch. There, at the back under the curtained tower arch, is the mutilated font of Bishop Bartholomew's time, crowned unevenly by a worn, slightly comic, cover of Jacobean date; here are the leaning wormy benches of rustic carpentry—some 15th-century carpenter from Sampford Courtenay no doubt made them —the pulpit from which the doctrines of the Elizabethan Church were the first to be heard, the curtains, the plastered and bossed roof, the plain granite chancel arch. It is all so worn and uneven, not a straight line anywhere, soaked with so many centuries of the Latin Mass spoken to a small gathering of Devonshire farmers and labourers and their households. In the light from the clear glass of the windows, we almost hear again the mumbled Litanies and Collects on 18th-century Sunday mornings, the murmur of the Lord's Prayer and the Psalms spoken in broad Devonshire voices, the immemorial words of the English Sunday they knew by heart.

The buzz of flies in the sunlit windows, and the subdued farmyard sounds coming through the open doorway, the smell of the churchyard grasses, take us back immediately to those placid days when men and women worshipped in the midst of their work and their homes, among their numerous children and beside the graves of their ancestors. For a few moments we feel a little of the powerful forgotten rhythm that governed their lives, of the things that moved them inwardly year after year at the appointed times. Even so, it is difficult to think back beyond the barrier of the Reformation, that great wall between us and the medieval past. If at times we can feel imaginatively a kinship with the English men and women worshipping in their plain Protestant churches in Stuart and Georgian times, we can feel no imaginative link with those who went before them, except a faint pulse now and then. Four hundred years of Anglican religion have moulded and coloured the historian's mind also, and he finds it difficult to apprehend the inner life of pre-Reformation men and women, however linked he may be to the places where they lived.

Perhaps one gets nearest of all to it in the domestic chapels and oratories of which there were such numbers in Devon in the 14th and 15th centuries. The parochial system was complete. The ancient parish churches had produced daughter churches, dependent chapelries to give them their rightful name, in great numbers by the 13th century. As time went on, these dependent chapelries were elevated to full parochial status, though some did not achieve this status until late. Thus the chapelry of Welcombe, dependent on the mother church of Stoke at Hartland, was not given full parochial rights until 1508, and Bulkworthy and East Putford were still chapelries of Buckland Brewer at the time of the Reformation. But the Devon parishes, most of them, were large, and their houses scattered over an area of several square miles. Even a walk of a mile or two along the deep lanes in winter from home to church was a difficult proceeding, as anyone will know who has tried to reach a sequestered Devon farm after a wet winter. The high hedgebanks prevent the lanes from drying out, and for several months of the year there is deep and liquid mud everywhere. In these circumstances the practice grew up of applying to the bishop for permission to celebrate divine service in chapels or oratories attached to private dwellings. These chapels might be detached buildings (as at Bury Barton in Lapford) or a room in the house (as at Acland Barton), but only the well-to-do had them—knights, esquires, and franklins. From the 14th century onwards, the Exeter episcopal registers are full of references to such chapels and oratories.

The earliest of them appear in Cornwall in the late 13th century.[1] Bytton's register (1292-1307) is missing, but Stapeldon's register (1307-

26) contains more than a dozen licences for oratories or chapels in Devon, one of which was granted to his brother Sir Richard de Stapeldon, a judge of the King's Bench, on his manor of Stapeldon, in the parish of Milton Damerel. Milton already had a daughter church at Cookbury (now a separate parish), but Sir Richard still found it difficult to get to church. The earliest licence granted in Devon was that to Sir Simon de Montacute " to build an Oratory in his manor of La More in the parish of Luppitt " in 1308, and to have divine service celebrated there in his presence. The rector of Luppitt gave his consent provided that no injury was done to the rights and dues of the mother church. On the rector's cession or death, the consent of his successor was to be obtained, and in any event, the licence was only for Sir Simon's own lifetime.[1] Other early domestic chapels appear at Ilton in Malborough, Grimstone in Whitchurch, Way in St. Giles-in-the-Wood, all in the year 1309; and at Hartleigh in Buckland Filleigh and Dinsbear in Merton, in 1310. Various conditions were laid down to safeguard the rights of the parish church. Usually all other parishioners except the petitioner's own household were to be excluded, and the petitioner and his household were to attend the parish church on Sundays and the greater festivals. The licence to celebrate divine service was sometimes given for life, but often only for a term of years, or for one year.

By the closing years of the 14th century most houses of any consequence in south-western England had a private chapel or oratory. Bishop Brantyngham (1370-94) licensed more than 130 in Devon alone, and his successor Stafford (1395-1421) at least a hundred. Taking into account those chapels already licensed by earlier bishops, there may well have been 200 or so in Devon at any one time. Hartland not only had an abbey and a parish church, but ten chapels scattered about in various parts of the vast parish. Tiverton had six such chapels; several parishes had two or three.

The lists of these chapels are valuable in several ways. Not only are they an index of the extent of religious feeling—Hartland, for example, had only two churches in 1835 in place of the abbey and eleven churches and chapels in 1535—but they reflect also the social status of the families to whom the licences were granted. Many of the names are those we should expect to see, lords of manors and such like, but others are those of obscure franklins, emerging from the ruck of their unknown fellows, who in time will decorate the ranks of the Tudor gentry. Then again, a list of the places which had private chapels between 1300 and 1540 is also a list of those houses that had some pretensions to be called " mansions " in those years. The great majority of these are farmhouses to-day, a few so obscure as not to be marked on the one-inch map, but we are led to them, out of all the thousands of farmsteads in Devon, by their appearance in these lists; and we are frequently rewarded by finding a house of considerable architectural interest with traces of the former chapel in a hay-loft, a barn, or an outhouse. As one stands in such places, among the household débris or the hay, looking up at the arched oak-ribbed roof— the original roof of the chapel—or at the fragments of a traceried window, one is brought into immediate contact with the faith of pre-Reformation years. It is easier to apprehend something of its spirit, with the cows lowing nearby, as they must have done in the darkness of winter mornings while the mass was being said, where the whole thing was broken off so abruptly, than it is in a parish church where four centuries of Protestant worship have slowly buried all knowledge of the earlier faith. In such a cob-walled barn, dedicated to St. Katherine or St. Mary or to some one of a hundred medieval saints, the sense of the remote past is more immediate for all the incongruity of the surroundings.

One ought to speak of the medieval clergy and their lives, but they were much the same in Devon as elsewhere, and how can one speak of them briefly, or of the monastic houses, without falsifying their history? The fact is, we know so little of any of them. The records tell only of the black sheep or the weak. The Exeter episcopal registers have many pages about clerical misdeeds, even violent crimes and felonies. Stapeldon's Register is fairly typical.[1] Most of the misdeeds are those we are accustomed to read: fornication and all the variations of this eternal human frailty: but others reveal more peculiar habits among the medieval clergy. The eleven incumbents who burst open the door of St. Buryan church and so violently assaulted the Dean of St. Buryan and his attendants that the lives of some of them were despaired of have no counterpart in modern life. Or perhaps this was simply Cornwall, always a little peculiar and a law unto itself. The rectors of Broadwoodwidger and Tedburn St. Mary who poached for game in the Earl of Devon's park at Okehampton, and beat and wounded the earl's keepers, had their spiritual descendants in foxhunting ruffians like Froude and Radford in the 19th century. Even the bishop and the archdeacon of Exeter in their youthful days had, with the rector of Combe-in-Teignhead, led a rabble to attack the Dominican convent at Exeter, wounding some of the brethren, doing much damage, and stealing goods to the value of several hundred pounds.

Standards of morals and behaviour were not high. After all, many of the parish clergy were of peasant stock, as their names frequently betray, and if they were hardly distinguishable at times from their rustic parishioners, in their misplaced sense of humour and their human passions, it is no matter for surprise. They were ill paid, especially the vicars of parishes where the rectory was appropriated by a religious house, and those in charge of parochial chapels, and their intellectual attainments were correspondingly meagre. The best-paid vicars in 1291 got only £5 to £7 a year, and the average vicar's stipend was only £2 6s. 8d.[1] The average stipend of a rector was about £6 10s. The richest plum was the rectory of Axminster, worth £51 6s. 8d. Five other rectories were worth £33 6s. 8d. each. There were only 75 vicarages in Devon at the end of the 13th century, but the number was rising constantly as more and more benefices were appropriated by religious houses, and the number of the under-paid clergy grew accordingly.

Yet on the whole the parish clergy did their duty well. The visitation of the Dean and Chapter's benefices in 1301 probably gives us a fair sample.[2] At Sidbury the vicar was a good preacher and did his duty well, the only criticism being that he gave no teaching about mortal sin. At Branscombe, the vicar had given an organ to the church, and a new Antiphonary with Psalter. He preached frequently, he visited the sick, and he performed all his other duties well. The vicar of Colyton was a man of upright life, though his preaching lacked both quality and quantity, and he often failed to visit the sick. His curate at Shute, however, had nowhere to live and slept in the chapel, though the door was broken and the chancel unroofed. It is some measure of the man's devotion that he could be found there at all. Most of the vicars were good, some were spoken of in the highest terms. Only at Colebrooke and St. Mary Church were the incumbents really wanting. The former neglected his duties, preached only when he felt like it, taught little about the Faith, and his church and vicarage were badly in need of repair. The vicar of St. Mary Church preached well and performed his duties well when he was there, but he was often absent for a week or a fortnight, allowed his livestock to pasture in the churchyard, and his church and its furnishings were in a sad state.

This is the kind of picture we might find in any century down to the middle of the 19th, the same mixture of good and bad, of devotion and neglect, of wealth and poverty, learning and the lack of it. Except for its extremes of neglect and human badness, one may say it is true down to the present day. It is too easy—and unhistorical—to draw the picture in dark colours simply because of the nature of the records. When one considers the material conditions in which the medieval church and its clergy worked, the wonder is that the standards are generally so high. We must remember, too, that the medieval clergy constituted a much greater proportion of the total population than they do to-day. In 1377, for the purpose of the poll tax, the beneficed clergy in Devon were numbered at 559, the unbeneficed at 756, a total of 1,315.[3] There was about one clerk to every 55 people in Devon.

So far as the fabric of the churches is concerned, there appear to have been two major periods of rebuilding after that of the 12th and early 13th centuries. These were the early 14th century, and the 15th and early 16th. Nearly all the medieval work which remains in Devon to-day belongs to this last period of rebuilding, in which the earlier work was usually almost completely obliterated, but sufficient signs remain to show that the early 14th century must have witnessed a widespread reconstruction of yet older fabrics. The rebuilding of the Perpendicular period (1400-1540) was even more general and remarkable, and will be discussed in a later chapter.

Nor was it merely a reconstruction of the fabric, for most of these new buildings were simultaneously furnished with richly carved and coloured rood-screens, with complete sets of benches adorned with elaborately carved ends, sometimes with a lavishly carved and decorated pulpit (of which the dozen or so surviving examples are a sufficient revelation), and with coloured glass in the windows. Perhaps the village church of Torbryan gives us the most striking picture to-day of the richness of colour and the wealth of craftsmanship in wood, glass, and stone that characterised the late medieval churches in Devon. In contemplating such churches as this, or the even greater splendour of Cullompton, inside and out, we apprehend the intense reality of religious feeling on the eve of the Reformation, and we feel the strength of a faith that could devote so much of the material resources of relatively poor communities to the greater glory of God.

We can form a good idea, too, of how a small and comparatively poor country parish in Devon formed a large collection of vestments and plate from the churchwardens' accounts of Morebath, on the Somerset border, which run from 1520 to 1573.[1] These accounts contain innumerable references over many years to gifts of all kinds. There were no fewer than eight " stores " connected with the church, which attracted the gifts of different groups of parishioners, one store being run by the young men, and another by the young women. When, for example, a thief stole the chalice from the church on the night of 20 November 1534, the young men and women immediately met together and subscribed for a new chalice, so that no burden fell on the parish at large. When the church was reseated in 1534, all the timber needed for the work was given by one person and another. There were three, four, or five men who formed a kind of parish council, and who received the surplus from the eight stores for the general benefit of the parish. Substantial repairs to the fabric of the church were, of course, met by a special church rate. In many Devon parishes the adding or rebuilding of an aisle was often paid for by the squire or some substantial franklin in the parish.

THE REFORMATION AND AFTER

The religious changes of the 16th century can be told only in outline. The coming revolution was first made evident by the dissolution of the monastic houses in 1536–39. Some—the alien priories—had been suppressed by Henry V and their possessions mostly handed over to other monasteries, and to colleges and schools. In the suppression of 1536, seven small priories were swept away—Barnstaple, Carswell, Cornworthy, St. Nicholas at Exeter, Frithelstock, Pilton and Totnes. Polsloe Priory should have gone with this group of lesser houses, but the prioress compounded with the king to save the house, only for her successor to surrender it three years later. The ten remaining houses were suppressed in three weeks early in 1539, beginning with the surrender of Dunkeswell on 14 February and ending with that of Ford on 8 March.

At the time of the suppression the total monastic population in Devon was small. Tavistock was the largest house with an abbot and twenty monks (plate 15), and Plympton second with eighteen monks besides the prior. Of the remainder, only Buckland, Ford and Torre had more than a dozen monks all told. Canonsleigh held seventeen nuns besides the abbess, Polsloe thirteen nuns and the prioress.[1] Pilton Priory had shrunk to three occupants, Frithelstock to five, and Carswell to two. The total monastic population of Devon was well under 200, probably nearer 150, distributed among seventeen houses which enjoyed a gross income of £5,512 a year. Though some of the smaller houses were poor—like Carswell, with a gross income of less than £29 a year—most of the monastic population lived comfortable lives, buttressed and cushioned by large estates.

In this respect they did not differ from the great lay landlords, but they had departed a long way from the original high intentions of monasticism. Feeling was running against them for years before the final act of extinction, and not only among their secular enemies. They had made a great contribution to learning (Tavistock, for example, had set up the first printing press in south-western England by 1525), to good farming, and to the economic development of the county, if the story told by Mr. H. P. R. Finberg in his *Tavistock Abbey* is any guide to the Devon monasteries in general; but the privileged economic position of such a small minority could no longer be upheld. Their position was analogous to that of the country houses at the end of the 19th century, with a similar mixture of merit and demerit, and their reform was inevitable. But we may well wonder, like John Aubrey, and like the country people of Devon and Cornwall in 1549, if all need have been swept away so indiscriminately by the reformers: whether some monasteries could not have been saved as " receptacles and provision for contemplative men." And we may well wonder this to-day also, as we contemplate the downfall of the country houses in their turn.

The effect of the Reformation was not felt in the parishes for another ten years: the major changes in high policy during Henry VIII's reign passed over the heads of the mass of the English people. But the suppression of the chantries in 1547, followed by doctrinal and liturgical changes, brought the matter home at last to every parish in England. In the south-west the introduction of the new Prayer Book in English brought open rebellion immediately. There had already been a rising in Cornwall the year before, occasioned largely by the injunction concerning the removal of images from all churches and chapels. Though this had been put down with great brutality, the Catholic faith was strong enough in the West to produce a further outbreak in the summer of 1549. By the Act of Uniformity the new Prayer Book came into use on Whitsunday. The parishioners of Sampford Courtenay—that beautiful granite church on the northern edge of Dartmoor—heard it read and did not like it, and on the following day compelled their parish priest to return to the old ritual. They likened the new service to "a Christmas game," and would have no changes until the King was of full age.

Local justices came to remonstrate with the parishioners. A meeting took place in a field just outside the village, but the peasantry stood firm. William Hellyons, one of the gentry in Sampford parish, rebuked them too tactlessly, tempers were high already, and as he was going down the stairs of the church house—which still stands at the entrance to the churchyard—a farmer named Lethbridge struck him on the neck with a bill. Immediately, "notwithstanding his pitiful requests and lamentations, a number of the rest fell upon him and slew him and cut him in small pieces."

Now it was too late to do anything but go on. Gathering forces as they went, the rebels marched to Crediton, where they met a Cornish force which had risen independently a few days earlier. The Protector Somerset despatched Sir Peter and Sir Gawen Carew to go down and pacify the rebels, whose complaints were to be forwarded to the Council. The rebels barricaded the Exeter road and fortified themselves in the barns beside it. They refused to parley with the Carews, who were perhaps the wrong men to deal with the situation, for they were advanced Protestants: in the struggle and confusion the barns were set on fire and the rebels driven out. When the gentry entered Crediton, however, the town had been evacuated and they returned to Exeter having accomplished nothing. Indeed, they had accomplished worse than nothing, for so far from pacifying the rebels the burning of the barns inflamed the Catholic peasantry further.

With the sacred banner of the Five Wounds of Christ floating before them, and the pyx borne under a rich canopy, with crosses, banners, candlesticks, swinging censers, and holy bread and water " to defend them from devils and the adverse power," the procession of Devon and Cornish farmers and labourers, led by a few of the gentry, ignorantly pitting themselves against the whole power of the State, marched on to Exeter behind their robed priests, singing as they advanced: a pathetic, futile, and gallant rebellion. At Exeter they called upon the walled city to surrender, but though many inside sympathised with the rebels (including the mayor and many of the leading citizens) the gates remained closed, and the long siege began. The full story of the Rebellion has been best told by Mr. A. L. Rowse in *Tudor Cornwall*. The siege of Exeter gave the government time to send down Russell, with an army of Italian and German mercenaries: the battle of Fenny Bridges on the Honiton road, a few miles east of Exeter, resulted in the defeat of the rebels in the last days of July, and then, at Clyst Heath on 3-4 August came their crushing defeat after a bitter resistance which even the ranks of Tuscany could scarce forbear to cheer: Lord Grey said he had never seen the like in all his wars. It was all but over. The famished city of Exeter was relieved on 6 August, a day commemorated for about 200 years afterwards by an annual procession of the mayor and officials of the city to the Cathedral, where the mayor's chaplain preached a timely sermon.

Russell delayed at Exeter for ten days. In this space of time, the rebels regathered their forces for a last resistance at Sampford Courtenay, whence they had set out so bravely ten weeks before, and here on a Saturday afternoon and evening—17 August 1549—in a desperate stand in the village streets they were overwhelmed. Remnants who escaped into Cornwall and back into Somerset were caught up and captured; and then followed the long and barbarous reckoning, for the gentry and the priests most of all. There was, as Mr. Rowse says, no danger of Russell being too lenient.[1] After all, was he not the greatest receiver of monastic spoils in all western England?

The Western rebels had demanded that all the old ceremonies be restored, the Mass in Latin, the reserved Sacrament over the high altar, images once more, and all English scriptures to be withdrawn.[2] They also asked that the two principal monasteries in each county be restored —in Devon this would have meant the revival of Tavistock and Plympton —to be endowed with one-half of the monastic and chantry lands now held by laymen, however they had obtained them. In this at least, the common people of the south-west were moderate enough, anticipating John Aubrey's lament a hundred years later, anticipating, too, one might say, what has since been done all over England to restore monastic communities.

We do not know how many conservative and stubborn West Countrymen marched in that hopeless rebellion: a few thousands probably.[1] They spoke and fought for tens of thousands, no doubt, who disliked and detested the changes. But in most parishes the parson and his people accepted the orders from above and conformed outwardly. The church-wardens' accounts of Morebath, already cited, give us a picture of what must have happened generally: much more typical than the pathetic martyrdom of the Sampford Courtenay rebels.

The vicar—Christopher Trychay—was at Morebath during the whole period covered by the accounts (1520-73). We see how the Reformation affected this parish, uncomplicated by any change of parson, of new men coming in imbued with the new ideas. We find him buying a new suit of black vestments at Exeter, where they were blessed, some time in 1547, bought partly from the small gifts of his parishioners, and giving thanks to them and to God: no inkling of the changes about to break over them. The high cross was gilded at the same time, and the images cleaned. Then—at the end of the 1547 account—we read of three men and "the high Wardens" riding to Tiverton to meet the king's commissioners "to make an answer for chantry ground." In 1548 the vestments are put away, not sold or destroyed, but distributed among the principal farmers of the parish for safe keeping. The "boke of erassamus" is bought, and the "furst communion boke" in 1549. There is a good deal of riding to Tiverton and to Exeter "to answer for maters concernyng ye kyng."

In 1551 John Lowsmore is paid three shillings for taking away the side altars and the rood loft, the gold in the church images is sold, and three great brass candlesticks weighing eighty pounds sold to a brazier of Exeter. Then comes the blessed relief of Mary's reign: the vestments are returned from the farmhouses to the church, the images are brought out from their hiding places, and the vicar—who had allowed no word of regret to creep into his accounts as he detailed the stripping of his church year after year—now speaks from his heart at the restoration of the Catholic faith:

Item of John Williams of Bery we received again an image of Mary and the king and the queen concerning St. George. And of William Morsse at Lauton was received an image of John. And of the widow Jurdyn trails and knots. And of divers other persons here was rescued pageants and books and divers other things concerning our rood-loft. Like true and faithful Christian people this was restored to this church, by the which doings it showeth that they did like good Catholic men.[2]

This was in 1555. In the following year the side altar dedicated to St. Sidwell was replaced, and the rood loft put up again. Then, in 1562, it all goes again, and throughout the rest of the 1560s and 1570s we see the small changes taking place that were to produce the Church of England: the commandments put up on either side of the altar in 1568, the reference to the communion table in 1570—no longer the high altar with its gilded cross and the pyx hanging over it—the buying of Dr. Jewel's book, the English translation of his *Apologia pro Ecclesia Anglicana*, at Exeter, and of a chain for it. The old vicar still dozed in the vicarage, and pottered along to the church to perform his duties, but he was the only thing that had not changed during the half-century. It is idle to speculate on what he thought in his old age.

The south-west did not, like Lancashire, become one of the great strongholds of Catholicism, despite its resistance in 1549. But it remained stubbornly Catholic a little longer than most parts. Cuthbert Mayne, the first of the Catholic missionaries to be executed, was a Devonshire man: he had been rector of Huntshaw, near Bideford. Strype tells us that in 1579 Exeter College at Oxford, mostly filled with Westcountrymen, could show only four " obedient subjects " out of eighty members: " all the rest secret or open Roman affectionaries . . ." The cathedral chapter at Exeter had been purged by Jewel (also a Devonshire man) twenty years earlier, and the last Catholic bishop, James Turberville, deposed and sent away to an unknown fate. The vacant places were filled with radicals like William Alley (bishop) and Richard Tremayne (treasurer).[1]

Several of the old county families remained Catholic—most important being the Courtenays at Powderham, and their two branches at Upcott in Cheriton Fitzpaine, and at West Molland. The Courtenays of Powderham certainly remained Catholic until the 1640s, but it is not known when they ceased to be so.[2] Oliver says that the branch at West Molland remained true to their old faith until the end of their line in 1732, though John Courtenay certainly signed the Protestation Oath in 1642.[3] The Courtenays of Upcott were savagely fined and persecuted as recusants under the Act of 1581, which raised the fine for non-attendance at church to £20 a month. By 1592 James Courtenay owed £1,360 in fines, but the family remained Catholic to the end. The son-in-law of the last of them, who married the Courtenay heiress, turned the chapel at Upcott into a cider-house.[4]

Other notable families who remained Catholic were the Chichesters of Arlington (the rest of this numerous family conformed to the Protestant faith), the Carys of Cockington and Tor Abbey, the Cliffords of Ugbrooke, and a branch of the Coffins (that at Parkham). Oliver also lists the Kirkhams of Blagdon, the Pollards of Horwood, the Giffards of Halsbury, the Fursdons of Fursdon, the Rowes of Kingston, the Chesters of Bearscombe, the Knights of Axminster and Combpyne. By the end of the 17th century, however, only 298 Catholics remained in the diocese of Exeter. Another return, in 1767,[5] gives a total of 291 in the diocese, 134 men,

157 women. Of this total only fifty-six were to be found in the whole of Cornwall, and 235 in Devon. The return gives names, ages, and occupations. It contains only four county families—the Chichesters, Carys, Cliffords and Rowes, of whom the first three kept priests. Most of the rest were people of humble rank—the servants at the big Catholic houses, a few foreigners, some Irish, small tradesmen and workers. At Tiverton the Catholic ranks included "John Greenway, scrivener": one wonders if he was a descendant of the pious wool merchant who had founded that beautiful aisle in Tiverton parish church on the eve of the Reformation. Very possibly he was. The full story of the Catholic minority in Devon has still to be written: there are plenty of materials for it, and it is an appealing subject.

NONCONFORMITY

But Devon as a whole had become one of the most firmly Protestant counties in England within two or three generations of "the great commotion" of 1549. Much of this revolutionary change must be attributed to the powerful influence of Francis, second earl of Bedford, who had been appointed Lord Lieutenant of Devon, Cornwall, and Dorset in 1558. He and Cecil, the Spanish ambassador reported, were the two members of Elizabeth's council who busied themselves most to destroy the old faith. Bedford did not want for willing helpers in Devon—the Carews, the Tremaynes, and the like. Drake and Hawkins were Puritans also, and that must have carried some weight. In the discussions in Convocation in 1562, concerning the rights and ceremonies of the Church, the Puritan extremists included the Dean of Exeter (Dodds) and Tremayne, the treasurer of the cathedral.[1] By the end of Elizabeth's reign several important parishes had fallen into the hands of Puritan clergy. At the Hampton Court Conference of 1604 the chief Puritan champion was Dr. John Reynolds, born at Pinhoe just outside Exeter, and one of the translators of the Authorised Version of the Bible.

Puritanism grew steadily in Devon, both among the county families like the Strodes, Fortescues, and Yardes, and among the husbandmen and craftsmen. Among the many brought from Devon before the High Commission was George Churchill, yeoman of Rockbeare, a kinsman of Marlborough's ancestor. Strode's election as member for both Plympton and Bere Alston is some indication of the Puritan character of south Devon. He was a member of Exeter College, which from being a Catholic stronghold in the 1570s had now become a centre of Puritanism.

When Puritanism gained the upper hand during the Civil War and Commonwealth and set out to eliminate Episcopacy, about one-third of the clergy of Devon were ejected from their livings, mostly from the rural parishes. Episcopacy remained alive in the towns, except at Tavistock, Dartmouth and Plympton.[1] The return of Charles II ended the last hopes—or fears—of Puritan rule. The Act of Uniformity (1662) barred the Puritan clergy from the retention of their livings. Of the 2,000 clergy who resigned as a result of this Act, at least 132 were to be found in Devon. The sequestrated Episcopalians and the ejected Puritans were about equal in numbers in Devon, but it was not a simple reshuffle. Only in about forty-four places did both parties suffer in turn. Altogether, more than half the parishes of the county were affected by the ejections of one kind or another.[2] Only about fifty of the 128 ejected Episcopalians regained their livings: a greater number of Puritan intruders kept their livings by accepting the conditions imposed in 1662. The Presbyterians were cast out of the national church and went to swell the ranks of nonconformity outside it. Many of the ejected of 1662 founded congregations: by 1715 there were fifty-nine of these in Devon, with a total attendance of 21,750. More than a half of these congregations have continued in unbroken succession to this day, chiefly in the towns.[3]

Both Celia Fiennes (1698) and Defoe (c. 1714) have a good deal to say of the Dissenters in the Devonshire towns. At Bideford, for example, Defoe found

> a very large, well-built, and well-furnished meeting-house, and, by the multitude of people which I saw come out of it, and the appearance of them, I thought all the town had gone thither. . . . The person who officiates at the meeting-house in this town, I happened to have some conversation with, and found him to be not only a learned man, and master of good reading, but a most acceptable gentlemanly person, and one who, contrary to our received opinion of those people, had not only good learning and good sense, but abundance of good manners, and good humour—nothing sour, cynical, or morose in him, and, in a word, a very valuable man; and, as such a character always recommends a man to men of sense and good breeding, so I found this gentleman was very well received in the place, even by those whom he differed from in matters of religion, and those differences did not, as is usual, make any break in their conversing with him. His name, as I remember, was Bartlet. But this is a digression—I wish I could say the like of all the rest of his brethren.

This was William Bartlet, minister from 1700 to 1719. His grandfather, of the same name, had been intruded into the rectory during the Commonwealth and was ejected in 1662. He thereupon founded a congregation, and his son and grandson followed him as ministers.[4] The congregation has continued unbroken to this day, but the handsome meeting-house that Defoe saw (built in 1698) has been rebuilt.

Nonconformity was particularly strong in the towns. The early history of the meetings at Ashburton, Bideford, Exeter, Newton Abbot, Plympton, Seaton, Tavistock and Totnes has been written, but no comprehensive study of the subject has yet been made.[1] Dissent was, indeed, much stronger in Devon than in Cornwall until Wesley's coming. According to Defoe there were only four meeting-houses in Cornwall, but about seventy in Devon, " some of which are exceeding large and fine."[2]

The growth of Dissent was greatly helped by the increasing laxity of the Established Church. Under Bishop Lancelot Blackburne (1717-24) there were fewer candidates for ordination than at any other period in the history of the diocese, except at times of special trouble. He was away from the diocese for long periods, and of the few clergy he instituted to livings some were required to suit his convenience by appearing in London or Bath for the ceremony.[3] The growing use of faculty seats and family pews relegated the poor to the obscure corners of their churches, even ousted them altogether. A succession of feeble or slack bishops had its effect on the parish clergy. Bishop Keppel's visitations of his diocese, from 1765 onwards, show the low level to which Church life had fallen: pluralism and non-residence were common all over Devon and Cornwall. The rector of St. Mary Tavy, near Tavistock, was also vicar of St. Cleer in Cornwall, but he lived at neither: he had resided for thirty-four years at East Looe, whose church he served. The visitation of 1768 shows that nearly one-half of the incumbents of Devonshire parishes were non-resident, and a half of the benefices were held in plurality.[4] Shaldon had to be content with one afternoon service a fortnight, because the incumbent was also rector of Widecombe-in-the-Moor. The good man compromised, however, by living in neither parish, but at Teignmouth. The pluralist parson of Eggesford and Mariansleigh professed to conduct one service a Sunday at each, but he shut down altogether in winter " on account of the badness of the roads and shortness of the days." The rector of Bigbury, in south Devon, had been away in Spain for several years. The vicar of Hartland was believed to be living in London, but no one was sure. The vicar of Walkhampton was master of the grammar school at Exeter, forty miles away across Dartmoor, and served three churches in the city. In the deanery of Chulmleigh only three of the fourteen parishes had the undivided attention of the incumbent. Succeeding visitations show even lower levels of degradation: a number of the clergy in 1794 did not even bother to send replies to the bishop's visitation inquiries.

Such was the diocese where John Wesley (and his brother Charles) began their missionary labours in 1743. Yet, apart from Plymouth and Dock, they met with little success among the Devonians. John Wesley formed no high opinion of them: at Ashburton, " many behaved with decency, but the rest with such stupid rudeness as I have not seen for a

long time in any part of England." Of his Axminster hearers he observed
that he had "never seen a more unpolished people than these"; of
Plymouth, where he preached on the quay, he thought even less: "I
wondered at the exquisite stupidity of the hearers, particularly the
soldiers, who seemed to understand no more of the matter than so many
oxen." At North Molton, Wesley's followers suffered persecution: "A
neighbouring gentleman has threatened them much unless they will leave
this way, has turned many out of their work or farms, and headed the
mob in person." At North Tawton, when Wesley tried to preach, the
rector and several other gentlemen brought a huntsman and hounds,
and foiled his efforts.[1] Tiverton and Cullompton were more rewarding,
and John Wesley visited them regularly, but Methodism never took
anything like the hold in Devon that it did in Cornwall. With only one
or two exceptions, the clergy of Devon were indifferent to Wesley's
tremendous work; often they were openly hostile to it. It was only in the
middle decades of the 19th century that Methodism really took a hold in
Devon.

THE CHURCH IN THE 19TH CENTURY

When the redoubtable Bishop Phillpotts—"Henry of Exeter"—
succeeded to the see of Exeter in 1831, he found the diocese hardly
improved at all from the miserable level already described. It was said
that twenty parsons kept packs of hounds; scarcely a parson in the
diocese did not spend several days a week hunting. Nearly forty per cent
of the parishes still had no resident incumbent. Most of them had a
curate-in-charge, but there were seventy parishes with no resident clergy-
men of any kind.[2] The rule of Phillpotts (1831-69) brought immense
changes for the good, however lacking he was personally in some of the
Christian virtues. The Low Churchmen especially hated his discipline,
but the whole diocese needed a strong hand like his. He was feared
everywhere, and did not hesitate to go to law with his clergy to bring
them to heel, spending—it is said—some £20,000 to £30,000 on law-
suits in the course of his episcopate. But he steadily increased the number
of resident incumbents, improved the standards of divine service in most
parishes, restored the ancient and neglected churches, and provided a
great number of new churches for the growing towns and the outlying
country districts, often with the aid of generous personal subscriptions.
His famous law-suit with the Rev. G. C. Gorham, vicar of Brampford
Speke, over the doctrine of baptismal regeneration, is well enough known
as an example of his peremptory and vigorous methods, but at this distance
of time we may perhaps attach more importance to his work for the
diocese as a whole.[3]

But even Bishop Phillpotts had not had the time or the opportunity to bring the whole diocese up to a decent standard. There were still a few parsons like Froude, for forty-nine years vicar of Knowstone-cum-Molland (1804-53), of whom it could be said by his successor, who was also a magistrate, " I suppose he was guilty of every crime in the calendar."[1] Villains like Froude and his nephew Radford died out eventually, but there was much ineptitude and gross neglect in some parts of Devon as late as the 1890s, well within living memory. Prebendary Boggis relates many remarkable tales of these years in *I Remember*. He did duty at the remote church of Pancrasweek in October 1890 and noted:

> Exceedingly dilapidated church, 110 present; in the transept five pews together have the seats broken down; large holes in the roof, also in almost all the windows, some of which are boarded up; rain evidently pours in sometimes. A young woman played the harmonium: hymns " Ye servants of the Lord," " We love the place," and " Thy will be done," these being the only ones she could play.

Six months later he was there again:

> Walked to Pancraswyke (from Bridgerule) and at 3 I took Evensong. For 25 years there was no churchwarden till last Easter, when Mr. Hooper was appointed: he wishes to get the windows mended (some are boarded up, others are fragmentary), so we had a collection; one man collected in a pewter dish, and Mr. Hooper in his brown bowler hat, which he brought to me and I laid on the altar; about 125 or 130 people there; collected 8s. 6d.

He adds that of the population of 300, none was a communicant.

One by one, even the remotest and poorest of the little parish churches were restored. Those which had been too poor to undergo a thorough Victorian restoration, such as Hittisleigh and Honeychurch, fell farther into ruin, but were eventually rescued and restored when taste had improved. The old work, with all its hallowed associations, was conserved as far as possible instead of being blindly and indiscriminately swept away. And in hamlets, and by cross-roads in distant corners of the parish, the bleak little nonconformist chapels of various persuasions— ugly little brick boxes most of them—went up all through Victorian days to meet the spiritual needs of those who lived far from the parish church, or whose faith was more simple and direct. So, in the vast parish of Hartland, where there had been ten medieval chapels scattered about, there are now seven nonconformist places of worship instead. Ugly and misshapen as they usually are, they belong nevertheless to an ancient tradition of worship in these lonely places.

CHAPTER XIII

SOCIAL HISTORY

SOCIAL history, in its fullest sense, is a portrait of a whole society, but in this sense it would require a whole book to itself. Moreover, the general picture of Devonshire society should have emerged by now from a reading of the preceding chapters—the high importance of the squirearchy in Devon, giving employment in their own parishes, leading the social activities, governing the county at Exeter through the courts of Quarter Sessions, and representing the boroughs at Westminster; the bustling towns (until their industries decayed), with their merchants living in tall timbered houses on the narrow streets; the yeoman farmers on their freehold estates, living as comfortably as anyone; the crowded anonymous shopkeepers, craftsmen, and labourers of the towns; the industrial workers, the fishermen, and miners; and the small farmers on their dirty, isolated farms, hardly any better off than the labourers who worked for the bigger men. But some elements are still missing from this composite picture of teeming life, and we must now try to touch upon the more important of them.

THE VILLAGE COMMUNITY

Let us begin by opening White's *Directory of Devonshire* for the year 1850, and looking at the picture it offers us of a typical large village in east Devon—the village of Thorverton, on the edge of the Exe valley a few miles north of Exeter. There is no squire, for since the time of Edward I the manor had belonged to the Dean and Chapter of the cathedral at Exeter. They, and another big resident landlord, between them owned two-thirds of the parish, a large and beautiful parish of rather more than 4,000 acres of fertile land, dotted with hamlets and many scattered farmsteads and cottages. Of the 1,500 people, perhaps two-thirds lived in the village itself. Twice a year there were great fairs, the most exciting times of the village year: one on the last Monday in February, chiefly for fat sheep, and the other on the Monday after 18

July, for lambs, at which upwards of 40,000 were frequently sold at one fair.

The bare list of occupations given in the *Directory* is sufficient to tell us what a self-sufficient little community Thorverton was a hundred years ago. There were four bakers, three blacksmiths (one of whom was a part-time dentist), three butchers, four grocers, two saddlers, two shoemakers, four tailors, two wheelwrights, and two plumbers. In addition the village had a parson and a curate, a surgeon, a solicitor, an accountant, an auctioneer, and a veterinary surgeon; a builder, a corn-miller, an apple-nurseryman, an agricultural machine maker, a maltster, and a druggist; no fewer than three schools—an infants' school, a National School, and a boarding-school—and three inns. To those who have any imagination, the dry pages of the directory present a living picture of an English village a hundred years ago, a portrait of a now disintegrated society, that met nearly all its earthly and spiritual needs within its own boundaries, self-contained and self-sufficient, and provided its own amusements.

Thorverton was no exceptional place. Let us look elsewhere in the directory, at the large village of Ugborough in the South Hams, so very like Thorverton in its history and yet with its own individual flavour. It had just about the same number of people as Thorverton, again mostly living in the village. The remainder lived in houses scattered over a vast parish of more than 8,600 acres, which " includes several handsome mansions, and many respectable farm-houses." In this respect, Ugborough still presented the sort of picture that an Elizabethan village in Devon would have done, with several resident gentry living on their modest freehold estates, and a number of smaller farmer-freeholders. It still had two big cattle-fairs, but the old monthly fair had ceased. Four corn mills were still at work, and seven inns still brewed their own beer, and had connoisseurs for customers. Among the occupations of the village we find five blacksmiths, five boot and shoe makers, five masons, two bakers, a butcher and seven other shopkeepers, three carpenters, four tailors, two wheelwrights, and a saddler, not to mention the parson and the school-mistress. Fowellscombe, now an ivy-hung ruin all alone in the fields, was then the seat of Servington Savery, esquire (the descendant of the great merchant family of Tudor Totnes)—" a fine mansion with many large and elegant apartments."

Whichever village one looks up in the directory of a hundred years ago, it affords, for all its individual variations, the same essential picture of a compact, self-contained society: the parish church, the chapel, and the school; mills and fairs; mansions that gave employment and supplied the lead for village clubs and societies; and every kind of shop, craft, and trade that the village could need. For most of them, as for the country towns, the year 1850 saw them at their best, for each successive census thereafter saw their numbers fall. To-day, for example, Thorverton has fewer than half the people it had a hundred years ago, and most of the crafts, trades, and professions listed above have disappeared from the village, or are represented by one solitary follower.

As for the home-made amusements of the villages, one gets a good idea from those who can remember Victorian days, best of all before the railways came. At Silverton, for instance, about the same size as Thorverton and very like it in many ways, there were the church bell-ringers who regaled the village from time to time, the hand-bell ringers (for there were not enough church bells to go round), the Town Band, the Chapel Band, the Cricket Club, the Druids, and the Temperance Society. The man who could not find some niche in one of these was odd indeed. Then there were the great occasions, the national festivals when each village strove to outdo its neighbours with triumphal arches and hill-top bonfires, celebrated with village sports, and the Town Band at its best. Such occasions were the coronation of Queen Victoria, and greater than that, her Diamond Jubilee. At Silverton, there were medals, ribbons, and triumphal arches everywhere, sports in the cricket field, and the Town Band working tirelessly. Then teatime, and the traction engine lurching into the cricket field, its boiler specially cleaned out for tea-making on a gigantic scale, and small boys filling every receptacle inside and outside their persons with food; and later the bonfire on the highest point of the parish, watched for several nights beforehand lest the Bradninch men should set it off prematurely and score a mighty victory that would rankle for years. Or the relief of Mafeking, when the schoolmaster and his boys appeared on the rectory lawn before breakfast, before the rector had read the news in *The Times*, to summon him to the church for a thanksgiving service. Can one imagine this happening to-day? Or the funeral of the old Queen, with the whole church draped in black, and crowded with men and women in black. Those who had no black of their own were provided with coats by the Coats and Gowns Charity, made by the village tailor. Nobody stayed away because he or she was too poor to dress in a fitting fashion. The village was still a community.

The philanthropic impulse has been a deep sentiment in English life. For many centuries men and women have left money and lands for charitable purposes, for the relief of poverty in their own communities, for the education of children, the granting of loans to distressed tradesmen and craftsmen and labourers, for gifts of bread and money to the industrious poor, for the maintenance of the aged in almshouses, for the foundation of hospitals for the sick. In Devon no fewer than 380 parishes had charities of one sort and another. Only about fifty parishes had none, and they were mostly minute communities such as Bittadon and

Honeychurch where the problem of poverty, however it arose, could be dealt with by the even more ancient institution of the family.

Some parishes were exceedingly well endowed. Dunsford, the historian of Tiverton, lists no fewer than ninety-four benefactions to the town.[1] The earliest was made in the time of Henry III by Alice de Roos, who gave a common of 150 acres as a cattle pasture for the poor inhabitants of Tiverton. About the same time, the Earl of Devon gave " a constant supply of clear running water " from the country into and through the town, which was carried through the streets in open gutters, and still runs to this day. These open gutters of fast-flowing water are, indeed, a regular feature of east Devon towns and villages, and are perhaps of similar antiquity and origin.

From this time onwards the stream of private charity flowed copiously in Tiverton. Most notable were the almshouses and the schools, founded, nearly all of them, by the Tudor and Stuart cloth merchants. Of the almshouses there were those of John Greenway (1529), John Waldron (1577), and George Slee (1610); nor must we forget those of Thomas Ford, founded as late as 1891. Then there were the schools, beginning with Peter Blundell's noble benefaction in 1599 of a free grammar school for 150 boys, and for the maintenance of three scholars in the university of Oxford and three in the university of Cambridge. Ten years later, Robert Chilcott, merchant, founded " a free English school " for 100 boys; and in 1713 and 1714 came the first charity schools for boys and girls.

These were the greater benefactions. Scores of others were devoted to supporting poor weavers, fullers, and tradesmen, to lending money in times of distress, to paying apprenticeship premiums, to meeting every contingency and emergency that could befall the less well endowed. Blundell's greatest benefaction has obscured all his others, for he also left money to pay the apprenticeship premiums of four boys every year " for ever "; £400 to be lent to poor artificers of Tiverton at a low rate of interest; yet another £400 " to marry twenty poor maidens of Tiverton," each with a dowry of £20—what a pleasant light this alone throws on Peter Blundell's character!—and yet more money for the repair of the highways of the town and the body of the parish church.

Tiverton was, by reason of its history as a cloth town, exceptionally blessed with private charities, but hundreds of other parishes were endowed in proportion to their needs, with charity schools, almshouses, loans to poor artificers, gifts of bread, and so on, down to such small charities as that at Broadwood Kelly, where the twenty-four shillings interest on the " Poor's Stock Money " was distributed annually among poor labourers of the parish not receiving relief, in sums ranging from 1s. to 2s. 6d. according to the numbers in the family. At Silverton, Andrew

Ascott left, in 1659, the sum of forty-four shillings a year " to be made up in shirts and smocks, five of one sort and five of the other, forty yards of dowlas at twelve pence the yard, and the four shillings for making; and to be delivered every year at Christmas by the parson and warden, and the overseers of the poor, for ever."

With the widening incidence of poverty, as economic life became more complex and population increased, private benefactions became insufficient to deal with this problem, especially as charities left in the form of money diminished seriously in value with the passing of time. More and more the State was obliged to take over the relief of poverty, the provision of schools and hospitals, though private charity was, until recent years, still left with a large field in which to operate. In some parishes the old charities still play an important part in the relief of distress and poverty in old age; but in most it is probably true to say that the list in the parish church, the black board painted with gilt lettering so long ago, is now the only memorial to the long tradition of philanthropy, that noble word so despised and derided to-day. And so often even this one memorial is relegated to the tower, with all the other rubbish and débris, hidden behind thick dusty curtains, where, in fast-fading lettering, one reads with difficulty the names and good deeds of former parishioners who lived and died in a true community of people. " For ever " they had said, their charities should be distributed and they would be remembered; but in the 20th century they are almost all forgotten.

SCHOOLS

At Thorverton in 1850 there were three schools. One of them was already nearly 200 years old, for we discover its origin in another prosaic document—the report of the charity commissioners. The list of the Thorverton charities[1] begins with the gift of £60 by John Bury in 1618 " to be lent to poor tradesmen." There are half a dozen further charities —money to be lent to poor labouring men and widows, or shifts for poor women, or bread and money to be distributed to the poor at Easter. Then, in 1673, Thomas Adams left £100, of which one-half the interest was to be spent " for teaching poor children," and the other half on a distribution of bread. Five further gifts in the next seventy years brought the stock for teaching up to well over £300, including Margaret Tuckfield's gift of £30 towards providing " Bibles and coats for poor children " in 1710. So the village school began in a small way in 1673 and grew with the years; but by 1815 it had become inadequate for one reason and another. A petition to the court of chancery said that there were then about 140 poor children in the parish, of whom only a limited number could receive any instruction. The schoolmaster received a salary of £9 a year out of the trust fund. We are not told that he had any other source of income, but his successor was allowed to charge one shilling a quarter to the parents of each child under his care. In 1817 there were forty boys and thirty-six girls attending the school, only about a half of those who needed schooling. There had been no further endowments for the school since 1743, but the population of the village had grown greatly since then. Private charity had failed to keep pace with such a change, and in 1841 the National School took over the task of educating " poor children " that had begun in Charles II's day.

Thorverton school is typical of scores of village and small-town schools in Devon. Many were even older. Some thirty towns and villages already had schools by 1660, not only the towns, with their grammar schools (mostly of 16th-century foundation), but even small villages, some hardly bigger than hamlets.[1] One wonders, for example, how the minute community of Clannaborough, which had but seven families in 1801, came to possess its own school before 1603; or wild and lonely Knowstone, which also had a school in Elizabethan days.

Schools had, indeed, existed in some of the towns ever since the 14th century. Bishop Stapeldon had founded a grammar school at Ashburton in 1314 " for the erudition of children freely," and he had begun the founding of a school at Exeter which was brought into being by his successor Bishop Grandisson in 1332. Grandisson also founded the school at Ottery St. Mary in 1338, which lasted until chantry foundations were dissolved in 1545, and was refounded by Henry VIII as " the King's New School " two years later. At Barnstaple a grammar school was founded some time in the 14th century, and the village of Marldon, near Paignton, appears to have had a grammar school also.[2] Most of these early schools were dissolved as chantry foundations in 1545 and refounded later in the century. Ashburton, for example, was refounded in 1593, and Barnstaple before 1591. At Tavistock the monastic school, which had existed since Saxon times, was dissolved with the abbey, but was refounded in 1551, and endowed with the profits of three annual fair in the town, and with the income of the Market-house.[3]

By the end of the 17th century there were about fifty schools in the county, in 1800 more than 180.[4] No fewer than thirty-three endowed non-classical schools were founded between 1698 and 1800, and 106 charity schools. The most prolific period for the founding of new schools was the generation between 1710 and 1740, when nearly sixty were established—an average of two a year. By the middle of the 18th century few places of any size in Devon were without a school of some sort.

The Church exercised a more or less strict control over the appointment of teachers. Schoolmasters were required to be licensed, and the episcopal records at Exeter are full of trouble of one sort and another about inadequate teachers. At Northam in 1724, for example, teaching was carried on by three " infirm Sailors " who were discovered to be unlicensed and were consequently ordered by the bishop to desist from teaching. The parish thereupon petitioned the bishop on their behalf:

> We are situate, my Lord, at the very mouth of the two ports of Barnstaple and Bideford, and by that means abound with poor Sailors, whose Children are very numerous; by a moderate computation we have commonly four hundred within our Parish that want Education; the major part of the Parents are of the poorer sort, and many of their Children taught at the Expence of other people; and the above said persons who before their Monition taught part of these Children, we assure your Lordship, are each of them men of very sober life and conversation, and conformable to all the Rites and Ceremonies of the Church of England, and did and will (as we hope) contribute much to the good and welfare of those Little ones they had, and, by your Lordship's Indulgence, may have under their care. But the Circumstances of them, my Lord, especially of the Two latter, are too mean, the Reward of their Labour too little, and their Infirmities too great, to bear the Expence and Fatigue, of making their personal appearance for Licences. . . . Therefore it is humbly presumed [your Lordship] will not suffer this part of the growing Generation to be deprived of the Key of Knowledge, or of those other common Advantages whereby They may be better qualified to serve the Publick. . . .

At Ilfracombe in 1729 the only schoolmaster was also deputy-controller of the port and a boatman. These duties, together with other business, took up so much of his time that he had not taught school for the past ten or twelve years. Education had presumably collapsed altogether at Ilfracombe.

At Tavistock in 1721 an arithmetic master was badly needed, and a petition was accordingly addressed to the bishop.

> The bearer hath been for some years a laborious and reputable Tradesman in our Town, in the Woollen manufacture, 'tis now with us, as in other places, Trade is sunk, and a new method of living must be thought on.[1]

Most of the old schools taught reading, writing, and arithmetic, though occasionally a fine distinction is drawn between boys and girls. When Gertrude Pyncombe left £5 a year to provide a schoolmaster for Poughill and six neighbouring parishes, she stipulated that the boys were to be taught English and Arithmetic, and the girls English and the

Principles of the Church of England.[1] In most schools it is apparent that arithmetic meant " the casting of accounts."

To this curriculum the schools of coastal towns naturally added the teaching of the art of navigation. It was taught at Dartmouth from 1679, at Brixham from 1717, at Combe Martin from 1733. Even the little village school at Clyst St. George taught it from 1704, but then it lay next door to Topsham and many of the village boys went to sea as Topsham sailors. At Topsham itself a bequest was left in 1774 for teaching the girls to knit and sew.

By the middle of the 19th century several of the old grammar schools were in a poor way. A parliamentary inquiry of 1868[2] shows how deplorable some of them had become. At Totnes—that eminently rotten borough—the master of the grammar school was appointed by the corporation on political grounds, the school room presented the external appearance of a ruinous building, and there were only twenty boys. "The full value of the endowment of the grammar school is certainly at present not reaped or appreciated by the inhabitants, or properly cared for by those who are its guardians and patrons."

At Barnstaple there were only seven day-boys and twelve boarders. The headmaster had taught there for nearly half a century, and a more vigorous administration was badly wanted. The inspector goes on to say that the inhabitants of Barnstaple did not appreciate the school: only two in the whole town sent their sons to it. Barnstaple had three other schools at this date, all better than the grammar school.

Bideford grammar school (nineteen boys) was conducted over a cellar " in which a cooper practises his trade." At Ashburton the school (twenty-seven boys) was not considered by anyone to be a very useful institution. Two closed scholarships to Oxford had not been awarded for twenty years. Crediton and Honiton were both well reported on. The school at Ottery St. Mary, of which Coleridge's father had been master, and Coleridge himself a pupil, was hopelessly sunk—only four boys in a dilapidated room, the furniture out of repair: " The school is useless and cannot be said to be doing any work whatever." The famous old grammar school at Plympton, where Reynolds's father had been master and where Sir Joshua himself was educated, consisted of only two dilapidated rooms, with eight or ten boys. Its history during the 19th century was a series of calamities and misunderstandings. When the State took over the responsibility for secondary education in 1902, it was none too soon in most Devonshire towns. The Plympton school was at once closed down.[3]

From Elizabethan times onwards the brightest boys had gone on to Oxford and Cambridge. Most of them naturally went on to Bishop Stapeldon's foundation of Exeter College at Oxford, but a surprising number made their way as far east as Cambridge. The admission registers of four

Cambridge colleges between 1600 and 1660 show that no fewer than twenty-one Devonshire schools sent boys up in that period.[1] The sons of the gentry, who attended the nearest grammar school as a matter of course until the English public school made its appearance, generally went on, however, not to the universities but to the inns of court in London. Here they received the training which was so necessary for them in after life, and which they took to so readily. Not only were they destined, many of them, to be magistrates, but in an age that was furiously litigious they needed to know a good deal of law for the management and sure defence of their estates. Moreover, they were often called upon to act as trustees for one purpose or another, and to give advice on parochial affairs when law-suits might be threatened. A few years at one of the inns of court was the best vocational training a Devonshire gentleman could have. And if he were not an eldest son, with an estate to succeed to, then he studied the law for a professional qualification. No young Devon lawyer, if he had any *nous*, lacked business. Coming from a well-known family with social connections all over the county, he would be helped from the beginning in every practical way. The Devonshire lawyers had been renowned since the 13th century. Possibly there have been as many new estates built up in Devon out of the law as out of trade. The admissions to the Inner Temple alone, from 1547 down to 1660, contain the names of about 350 Devonians.[2] Pretty well every famous family name is represented and many eminent in the legal profession or in politics. The first half-dozen names on the roll include Sir John Whyddon of Chagford, a judge of the Queen's Bench from 1553, John Prideaux of Nutwell, King's and Queen's Sergeant 1557, and Thomas Williams of Stowford, Speaker of the House of Commons in 1563. But most of the Devonians returned from this university of London, for such it was, to their estates, and lived out their obscure and useful lives as country gentlemen and magistrates.

CRIME AND HUMAN FRAILTY

To speak of magistrates brings us to a less humane side of social history, the savagery of the law as dispensed in Quarter Sessions, and the cheapness of human life in earlier centuries. The records at Exeter Castle for the year 1598 leave us in no doubt about this. At the Lent Assizes, there were 134 prisoners, of whom no fewer than seventeen were hanged, and twenty others flogged. Eleven claimed " benefit of clergy " and were branded and set free. The clerk was too busy to write the death sentence in full: a laconic *s.p.* after a prisoner's name was all he felt to be necessary for the record—not even *sus. per coll.*—" hanged by the neck." At the preceding Epiphany Sessions, out of sixty-five prisoners eighteen were hanged. At Midsummer thirty-five prisoners, and eight hanged. At the Autumn Assizes, eighteen hanged out of eighty-seven. At the October Sessions, only one hanged out of twenty-five.

Altogether, seventy-four persons were hanged in this one year in this one county of Devon, more than a half of them condemned at Quarter Sessions. Nor was Devon unusually severe, as a Somerset justice tells us that forty were hanged in his county in one year (1596). Even so, he says, more felonies escaped punishment than were brought to trial, one reason being " the foolish lenity of the people."[1] No wonder: their humanity was in advance of that of the law, as it was generally down to the 19th century, when they witnessed so much hanging.

What were the offences that called for a barbarous hanging, flogging, or branding? They are not stated in the Order Books, but in many instances the depositions in the case survive and from them we learn the nature of the crime as well as much else. At the Midsummer Sessions of 1598, for example, when eight were hanged, the capital crimes were horse-stealing, cutting a purse, picking pockets (two charges), house-breaking (four charges), receiving stolen goods, picking a pocket and house-breaking (two charges), and sheep-stealing. Two women were hanged—Margery Pedell for cutting a purse, and Englishe Sanders for receiving stolen goods.

Among the seven who were branded, the crimes were stealing clothes and sheep-stealing. Thirteen were ordered to be flogged, six being women. In all cases the crime was stealing or receiving—clothes, sheep, cheeses, and so on.[2] At Easter 1598 it was ordered that every woman who had a bastard child should be whipped. In one case a woman was ordered to be whipped until she confessed the father of her child. Her gaoler may have been more merciful than the court, for it is noted that she escaped from custody.

We come very near the human life of the past in these crabbed depositions, and cannot help smiling, at this distance of time, over some of the ingenuous villains who found themselves before the court. There was John Knight who had acquired a love-charm which " he used to cossen wenches with." He was discharged upon confessing who gave it him. Or there was the traveller who turned up one evening at the Dolphin at Thorverton, sometime in the year 1650, and took a room for himself and his sister. The landlord, after a while, had reason to suspect their relationship, and taxed the traveller, who, confronted with some awkward facts, blandly said that as Adam and Eve were the father and mother of us all, the lady could truthfully be called his sister. On quite another occasion, William Shapton was committed for saying that there were not two honest women in Thorverton.

Prisoners could sometimes escape a more ferocious punishment by agreeing to join the army or to being shipped abroad. Four prisoners in Charles I's time were " by their own consent " to go to Dartmouth and thence to be shipped to Barbados. Among the milder punishments were the pillory and the stocks. Baldwin Whitfield was committed to prison for a year, and once each quarter to stand six hours in the pillory " for provoking the unlawful love of Mary Herder by witchcraft, charme, and sorcery."[1]

The strong Puritan tone of Devon comes out repeatedly in the Quarter Sessions records from the 1590s onwards. Church-ales, revels, maypoles, and all the cheerful goings-on of Catholic days were constantly being attacked. A maypole set up at Cullompton in 1631 was ordered to be taken down as the cause of great outrages, disorderly assemblies, and the like,

As long ago as July 1595, indeed, a sessions held in the Chapter House of Exeter Cathedral, with the detestable Bishop Babington (then newly arrived in Exeter) in the chair, had prohibited many of the old customs.[2] It declared that all " Church or parish ales, revels, May games, plays, and such other unlawful assemblies of the people of sundry parishes unto one parish on the *Sabbath day* and other times, is a special cause that many disorders, contempts of law, and other enormities, are there perpetrated and committed, to the great profanation of the Lord's ' Saboth,' the dishonour of Almighty God, increase of bastardy and of dissolute life, and very many other mischiefs and inconveniences, to the great hurt of the commonwealth." And it was therefore ordered that all such assemblies should be abolished on the Sabbath, that no drink should be " used, kept, or uttered" upon the Sabbath at any time of the day, nor upon any holiday or festival in the time of divine service or preaching of the Word, nor any time " during the night season." Nor—so these dreadful Puritans went on—shall there be " any minstrelsy of any sort, dancing, or such wanton dalliances " at the May games and at parish revels. No wonder William Shakespeare exploded in these same years—" Dost thou think, because thou art virtuous, there shall be no more cakes and ale? "

But the Puritans were rampant in Devon: nothing could stop them. In January 1599 the justices went even further than their predecessors of four years before and ordered that parish games, church ales, and revels should be utterly suppressed, for they were the occasion of behaviour " which with modestie cannot be expressed." This was true. The records of the ecclesiastical courts, housed in the diocesan registry at Exeter, reveal amply enough how many a virtuous girl met her downfall at some parish revel or May games, and such revels as persisted into the 19th century (for the Puritans achieved no permanent victory over human exuberance and love of living) still had the reputation of being all too human. The good Mrs. Tuckett, a farmer at Dunsford, told the commissioners of inquiry into the employment of women and children in agriculture in 1843, that she had never allowed her girl-apprentices to go to fairs and wakes. " There are no places so dangerous for girls. The girl whose time is now about expiring never was but at one fair in her life."[1]

Revels and parish feasts were restored after 1660, in so far as they had ever been effectively stamped out. The justices were now almost all churchmen and cavaliers, and it was the turn of the Puritans to suffer. Intolerance and a knowledge of Latin (for warrants) were the two essential qualifications for a justice of the peace, and the sessions records of the 1660s and 1670s are full of prosecutions of nonconformists, accused of attending conventicles. In the same period, transportation appears for the first time as a definite sentence, and the passion for hanging is correspondingly diminished. We see this in the petition of the inhabitants of St. Sidwell's, a suburb of Exeter, in 1667, begging that Peter Crosse, now a prisoner, be transported as " a terror to the City and Country, having committed many outrageous Crimes. . . . And it may please God this to be the means to save him from hanging, which undoubtedly will attend him without some wise prevention."[2]

In 1685 the justices had a busy time coping with the preparations to meet Monmouth's rebellion. Monmouth was generally popular among the common people in Devon, and the sheriff and under-sheriff were much perturbed at the possibility of having a rebellion on their hands. As it was, nearly 400 Devonshire men joined forces with Monmouth, most of them from the eastern parishes adjoining Dorset. Their names are given in a record now preserved in the British Museum.[3] They came from rather more than a score of parishes: Honiton, Axminster, Axmouth, and Colyton contributed most of the rebels, but a few came from as far west as Crediton and Tiverton. From all these parishes they marched to a hopeless end at Sedgemoor.

At the Exeter assizes, opened on 14 September, Lord Chief Justice Jeffreys announced that an unsuccessful plea of Not Guilty would be followed by summary execution. When the first two prisoners failed in their plea, James Foweracres of Axminster was immediately led out and hanged. The rest of the prisoners then pleaded Guilty. At these assizes thirty-three prisoners were sentenced: thirteen were hanged and quartered, seven were transported, and thirteen either flogged or fined. No fewer than 345 other Devonshire rebels were still at large and the sheriff was ordered to capture them for the next assizes.

Meanwhile, the boiled and tarred quarters of the hanged men were being sent around to twelve of the Devon towns, with warrants ordering the mayors to set them up. Altogether it seems that about twenty-six men were executed in Devon. After it was all over the under-sheriff,

Mr. Northmore, who had borne the brunt of the horrible work, went down with " a lurking fever." He wrote to Squire Coffin of Portledge, the sheriff of the county, that " another such year's trouble will I not undertake for 500 li. . . ."[1] One minor memorial to Monmouth still survives in Devon: after an interval a new street in Topsham was christened Monmouth Street.

TOWN SOCIETY

The early towns were hardly more than places in which to make money: there was little time or energy to spare for the cultivation of the intellect and the social graces. But with the inheritance of investment incomes by later generations, and the consequent growth of a " leisured " class in and near the towns, and above all, perhaps, with the growth of the professional class in the 18th century, accustomed to intellectual activity and the play of ideas, we get the beginnings of social and cultural activities in the larger towns like Exeter and Plymouth. The smaller towns, however, had little to show in the way of " society " even at the end of the 18th century.

Martin Dunsford, writing in 1790, tells us that " the inhabitants of Tiverton have long been characterised for a general disposition to social intercourse and conversation. The fine bowling green in the centre of the town, invites the gentlemen to associate there in dry summer evenings, for salutary exercise; and tea parties, etc., of ladies and gentlemen, are much encouraged in the same season of the year, by the many variegated walks near the town, and hospitable farmhouses in the parish. The adjacent hills and woods afford the means of much diversion to the lovers of the chace, in and about Tiverton. Regular assemblies, concerts, and card parties, are frequented in the winter. Many evening clubs and friendly societies have been likewise formed here, for mutual enjoyment and recreation after the business of the day; where the temperately circulating glass, and friendly offerings of tobacco, have, perhaps, had a happy tendency to promote good humour and good will."[2] There is, it is true, not much intellect here, but it is all very pleasant. A Book Club or Reading Society had, however, been formed in March 1775, composed of twelve members drawn from almost every sect, party, business and profession in the town. The Club met at each member's house in rotation, but we are not told any more about its activities.

·Nor had the growing seaside towns any more to offer at this date. Exmouth, the oldest of them all, had little in the way of social amenities about 1780. It " boasts no public rooms or assemblies, save one card assembly, in an inconvenient apartment at one of the inns, Monday evenings. The company meet at half after five, and break up at ten—

they play at shilling whist or twopenny quadrille. We have very few young people here, and no diversions—no *belles dames* amusing to the unmarried, but some *belldames* unamusing to the married. Walking on a hill, which commands a view of the ocean, and bathing, with a visit or two, serve to pass away the morning—and tea-drinking the evening."[1]

Early visitors to Exmouth took lodgings in the fishermen's cottages. The first " modern " houses to be built for all-the-year residents were on the Beacon, begun in 1792 (plate 42). By 1809 there was a small theatre, at which the great tragedian Edmund Kean appeared in Shakespeare, and also gave readings from Milton three times a week. The notorious Mrs. Clarke, mistress of the Duke of York, and the subject of a public investigation into the sale of government appointments, was living here about this time, and kept up a tremendous state at Manchester House (now the offices of the Clinton Estates Company). Lord Bute also resided in the town, and for many years two tragic women occupied houses on the Beacon—Lady Byron, the wife of the poet, and Lady Nelson, wife of the great admiral, who came to live at Exmouth after her separation from Nelson in 1801.[2]

In 1818 Exmouth acquired some new Assembly Rooms (there may have been others a few years earlier) and social life quickened considerably, with fortnightly assemblies for dancing and cards. These rooms still stand—also on the Beacon. They are now used as storage premises, but retain much of their original plan. In their heyday they were attended by a brilliant company from the big houses round about, such as Nutwell and Bystock, and by distinguished visitors like Lord Ellenborough and Lord Gifford in the season.[3] How long this exclusive social life persisted at Exmouth one does not know, but one suspects that the coming of the railway from Exeter in 1861 put an end to it, if it had not been dying before this.

At Exeter and Plymouth a vigorous intellectual and cultural life flourished during the 18th century and into the early 19th, for, like the self-contained villages, the larger towns had a rich social life of their own, of a quality that not even Londoners could afford to despise. The Lunar Society of Birmingham was perhaps the most distinguished of all the cultural societies in provincial England at this time, but other towns emulated Birmingham in one respect or another. Of the social and cultural life of Georgian Exeter we cannot speak here, but Plymouth was far enough away to have a completely independent and distinctive society of its own, revolving in its earlier days around the two families of Mudge and Reynolds.

A club already existed at Plymouth in the middle of the century, whose members met regularly for literary talk at the Pope's Head Inn. This club had grown out of the companionship of men who were accus-

tomed to meet at bathing parties off the Hoe.[1] One of the most eminent
of its members was Zachariah Mudge, vicar of St. Andrew's since 1731,
and formerly second master at Plympton Grammar School under Sir
Joshua Reynolds's grandfather. He knew well three generations of the
Reynolds family, and exerted a great influence on the painter, who
spoke of him as " the wisest man he ever knew." The formidable Samuel
Johnson, whom Reynolds brought down to Plymouth in 1762 for a visit
of several weeks, was impressed by Mudge's great learning and his
manners. When, in turn, Mudge visited London, he talked on equal
terms with the great men of the age, such as Edmund Burke, and Hazlitt
wondered that such a man did not leave the province of Devon altogether
for the metropolis.

Plymouth's greatest contribution to culture was her remarkable
succession of painters, " a regular line of master and pupil from Reynolds
in the 1740s to Eastlake who, when he died in 1865, was President of the
Royal Academy and Director of the National Gallery."[2] But she produced
no great work of pure literature, nor indeed did Devon as a whole.

By the early 19th century the literary and other clubs of Plymouth had
outgrown the accommodation of inns and other places and they were
establishing their own institutions and buildings. The Proprietary
Library, the Athenaeum, the Roya Theatre and the Hotel, all appeared
between 1811 and 1818.[3] The buildings, all by John Foulston, who had
come to live in the town, were in the grand classical manner, and formed
a group that dominated the architecture of Plymouth throughout the
19th century.

The Tourist's Companion to Plymouth, published in 1823, gives us a
good picture of the social and cultural life in these years of its
flowering. It is a not uncritical account. The Theatre was " open in
general during the winter months, at which time there are performances
here, and at the Dock theatre on alternate nights, by a company of
provincial comedians. It is occasionally made more attractive by the
appearance of some of the London performers." The usual prices of
admission were three shillings to a box, two shillings to the pit, and a
shilling to the gallery. There were public and private concerts during
the winter months, " at both of which the instrumental and vocal music
is of a description little above mediocrity."

The Companion has something to say of the painters in the town.
" Several able artists have lately sprung up: one of these is Mr. B. R.
Haydon, who excels as an historical painter; he has all the enthusiasm
and industry which are necessary to draw forth latent talents." Alas!
poor tormented Haydon! He was in this very year painting his great
unsaleable masterpiece, " The Raising of Lazarus," which is now in the
National Gallery, and though nearing the age of forty was so penniless

that he was arrested for debt while the work was in progress. And besides Haydon, there were Rogers, Prout, and Eastlake, all making their way.

Besides the lectures and the sermons, the concerts and the dancing, " a great deal of private visiting prevails in various circles; some partaking of the fashionable dinner, at five or six o'clock, whilst others are content to meet early in the evening, take their tea, play at cards, and retire at an early hour. There is not much dissipation among the higher classes, though private dances and concerts occasionally break in on the hours of the night. In their intercourse with each other, those who have not carriages of their own, and who refuse to use the public ones, are accommodated with sedan-chairs, of which there are about six in the town."

Most of this old self-contained social life and cultural activity has been exterminated by the changes of the 20th century. It survived to some degree until well into Victorian days, but it is not unfair to say that its high intellectual quality diminished with the passing generations. In the 18th century and the early 19th, men of ability and quality often preferred to remain where their roots lay and wisely eschewed the spurious charms of London. With the weakening of this powerful sentiment for one's native place, and the consequent increasing flow of able men to London, the rich cultural life of provincial England slowly withered. It now survives only in such metropolitan cities, far removed from London, as Manchester and Newcastle.

CHAPTER XIV

BUILDING AND BUILDING MATERIALS

BUILDING MATERIALS

DEVON has no characteristic building stone comparable in quality with the famous oolitic limestones farther east.* Only the Beer stone, quarried from the chalk close to the east Devon coast, and widely used for interior work, had anything more than a local reputation. But the complex geology of the county yields a remarkable variety of serviceable building stones, probably a greater number than any other county can show, and these do much to redress, by their varied colouring and use, the somewhat monotonous repetition of the Perpendicular style in the four hundred or so medieval churches of the county. Indeed, much of the vivid impression of colour that the Devonshire landscape makes upon the beholder arises in a large degree from the extraordinary variety of building materials that have been used in the past, and the brilliant lichens and mosses which they attract in the clean and humid air. Where the material is such as not to attract lichens, such as cob, artificial colouring is often employed as a wash, with striking effects in many villages.

The principal building stones of east Devon are the Beer stone, which is essentially a chalk rock, and the Cretaceous Sandstones found in the upper Greensand and chiefly quarried at Salcombe Regis and Dunscombe, to the west of Beer. This is sometimes known as *Malm* or *Malm Rock*. To the east of Beer, on the other side of the Axe valley, the Lias Limestone produced a building stone, nowhere really first class, which can be traced northwards, between Bath and Bristol, and thence into the Midlands. It was formerly much used in Gloucester, Stratford, Northampton, and Grantham, and may still be seen in the smaller Midland towns like Southam. In east Devon it was used locally for domestic building. A great deal may be seen in the older houses of Lyme Regis, just over the border. Its characteristic colour is a bluish-grey. Except in sunlight, and

* For a map showing the main geological formations of the county, and the location of the chief quarries, see fig. 4 (page 17).

amid grass and foliage, it has a sombre effect. Nor is it durable. It is readily attacked by frost, and where it was used in houses the chimney-flues were usually built of bricks as a safeguard.

On and around the margin of the Blackdown plateau, the greensand contains enormous quantities of flints which have been used for rough walling, for domestic building, and in a number of churches. The remains of the early 13th-century abbey church at Dunkeswell are of flint masonry; the 15th-century parish churches of Combe Raleigh and Cotleigh are built externally of dressed flints; and the Victorian rebuilding of Rousdon church also employed flint. Colyton and Axminster are the most notable medieval churches to make use of flints. Still east of the Exe, we find the New Red Sandstones used extensively from the early 15th century onwards, especially in and near the Culm valley, and to a much more limited degree the " trap rocks " quarried in and near Silverton. Thus in east Devon alone we find half a dozen distinctive building stones in use for churches and larger secular buildings, besides the cob used so commonly in the farmhouses and cottages of the vales.

THE EAST DEVON QUARRIES

The extensive quarries to the west of Beer were worked in Roman times. There is evidence that Beer stone was used in some buildings in Roman Exeter,[1] and in the Roman villa discovered near Seaton. It was used also for exterior work at Exeter Cathedral from the early 12th century onwards. It is a cream-coloured stone when freshly quarried, turning grey upon exposure, and has a crushing strength about equal to that of Portland stone. When fresh it can be easily cut with a hand-saw, but it hardens considerably on exposure, and when properly selected can be used for exterior work. It is, for example, used with striking effect in the quoins and buttresses of Kentisbeare church tower, and especially in the fine newel staircase to the tower where it is combined in a chequer effect with a rather rare cinnamon-brown variety of the New Red Sandstone from a local quarry (Upton, near Cullompton). In other east Devon churches, it has been used for external dressing and has generally weathered well. Where the mullions have failed, it is because the stone was not set in its natural bed. In large smoky towns it is generally not so successful. In the Carlton Club in London it has not stood well,[2] but in Beer village itself many houses are built of it, and it has proved completely satisfactory.

Beer stone was extensively used for interior work, not only in the cathedral at Exeter and the larger churches like Ottery St. Mary, but in nearly every parish church in east Devon, and in those parts of south Devon that could be reached by water. In scores of parish churches the arcades are of Beer stone. So, too, are the deeply-carved capitals, decorated usually with a naturalistic foliage, which are so characteristic of these Perpendicular churches.*

The stone was conveyed by water as far west as Tor Bay and the mouth of the Dart. Less frequently, we come across it even farther west, as at Blackawton, and in the churches near the Kingsbridge estuary, such as West Alvington and Malborough. But the cost of even water-carriage was high. When thirty-two cartloads were bought for Exeter Cathedral in 1429-30, the cost at the quarry was 64 shillings, but the cost of bringing it down to the shore, transporting it by sea to Topsham, and thence by carts to Exeter, amounted to a further £6 18s. 8d.[1] Nevertheless, the stone was in such repute that it was carried many miles inland. One finds it at Kentisbeare, used both internally and externally, and as far north as Burlescombe, some twenty-eight miles or so from the quarries by road. No doubt the Ayshfords paid, or contributed substantially towards, the cost of the arcades here. Westwards we find Beer stone arcades in the hill-country beyond Exeter, at South Tawton, Doddiscombsleigh and Ashton, and at Torbryan, all far from water. We even find Beer stone being bought for Tavistock church in 1448-49. In all these churches the munificence of the fittings suggests wealthy benefactors. In neighbouring churches with no rich local patron, we find plain granite arcades. But there is no doubt that where money was available, good building stone could be carried twenty or thirty miles by road. We need not assume that transport by river and sea was a necessity for the medieval building industry.

The Beer quarries were at their zenith during the 15th century and the early 16th, when so many Devon churches were being rebuilt or enlarged. The sudden cessation of church building after about 1540 must have brought about a dramatic decline at the quarries, especially as the stone was not generally regarded as suitable for external work and the industry could not benefit much, therefore, from the era of country-house building which followed that of church building. Bovey House, not far from Beer, was, however, built of the local stone when it was remodelled during the first half of the 16th century and so was old Shute House. It is possible that other country houses in east Devon have Beer stone beneath their stucco. Many houses in Beer itself were built of it down to recent times. At Exeter the Elizabethan portico of the Guildhall is built of Beer stone, except the pillars, which are of granite.

Leland speaks of Beer only as " an Hamlet of Fischar Men." He would surely have noted the quarries had they been at all active. Nor

---

*Beer stone gives a white background to the " heraldic " colours of the painted screens and monuments, and thus preserves for us to-day the right field for medieval polychromy.

do any 17th- and 18th-century travellers mention them. In 1822 Lysons speaks of some Beer stone being quarried and sent coastwise. De la Beche, in 1839, has a little to say about the quarry.[1] The stone was got out by a gallery or adit driven into the hill, its roof supported by large square pillars of workable stone left standing, but it does not seem to have been a large undertaking. Later in the century the rebuilding and restoration of churches seem to have provided a considerable market: the new church at Beer itself (1877) has external dressings of the local stone throughout. Sir Gilbert Scott favoured Beer stone for restoration work. The quarries closed down in recent years, though they are occasionally opened up when stone is required for a particular purpose. An open quarry is now worked for lime.

The other east Devon quarries were far less notable than those of Beer, but they were of considerable local importance in medieval and later times. The greensand quarries of Salcombe Regis were drawn upon for Exeter Cathedral, probably from the 12th century, and for Salcombe church itself. When Sidbury church was being reconstructed about 1445, the stone was drawn from the Salcombe quarry at Dunscombe. It was occasionally used for secular building: at Slade Farm in Salcombe are some splendid barns in this stone, and Slade House itself is built of it.[2] But like many quarries, those at Salcombe were practically untouched for centuries after church building ceased. Those at Dunscombe were re-opened about 1930 for the building of the modern church of Woolbrook, at Sidmouth, but are now desolate again.

The broad belt of New Red Sandstone, running from the Somerset border down to the south Devon coast at Paignton, produces serviceable building stones where sufficiently consolidated. There are old quarries near Poltimore and Broadclyst, but the most notable are those in the New Red breccias at Heavitree and Whipton, just outside Exeter, which were extensively worked for the rebuilding of the attractive little red city churches during the 15th century. The red sandstone was not generally used for building before the close of the 14th century, although fifty loads of Whipton stone were bought for Exeter Cathedral in 1341-2. The Wonford quarry at Heavitree was drawn upon, apparently for the first time, in 1390.[3] From this date onwards the red sandstone quarries were vigorously worked for ecclesiastical and secular building in Exeter, and also for the repair of the city walls. To the south of Exeter, the medieval quarries at Exminster, Kenn and Ugbrook were important, and give a fine series of red sandstone churches in the lowlands between Exeter and Paignton. The most notable of these are Kenton and Paignton itself.

The " trap rocks," a lava found in isolated patches to the north and west of Exeter, have long been known as a durable building material. The chief quarries were at Silverton, Budlake near Killerton, Raddon (just west of Thorverton), Posbury (near Crediton), Heazille (near Rewe), Pocombe and Barley (just west of Exeter), and Dunchideock. Most of these quarries were being worked by the end of the 13th century, some in the 12th. The red Posbury stone appears in the 12th-century work at Crediton church, and in late Norman doorways of parish churches round about. Stone from Silverton and Barley was being bought for Exeter Cathedral at the end of the 13th century. Probably most of these quarries of trap rock were being worked in the late 12th century; but the paucity of surviving work of that period in Devon makes it difficult to be certain. There are no documents to tell us; only the buildings can do that, and nearly all Norman work has been swept away in Devon. Indeed, the use of this basaltic stone is much older in places. The Romans quarried it at Northernhay, just outside the city, for the walls of Exeter, which were built about A.D. 200, and William the Conqueror used the same quarry for his castle of Rougemont, which he built to dominate the city in 1068-70.

Raddon quarry, west of Thorverton, was worked for church building from an early date, possibly from the late 12th century, but documentary references to it are few. We know, however, that Raddon stone was bought for the cathedral in the 1390s, and that in 1511 it was used for the rebuilding of the east gate of Exeter, when " Robert Poke of Thorverton, mason," contracted to complete the job for £28.[1] The quarry continued to produce building stone for the district until well into the 19th century. The " trap " stones are a rich, warm, ruddy brown in colour, with whitish veins, and are easily distinguishable from the red sandstones, with which they were often blended in buildings and walls. They may be seen in buildings of all ages from the 11th century to the 19th. In recent times the " trap " quarries produced great quantities of road metal. Those at Dunchideock are still in operation.

SOUTH DEVON QUARRIES

South Devon is almost equally rich in building materials, as one might expect from the exceedingly complicated geological structure of the region. The Devonian limestone produces a good building stone, varying in colour from almost white (near Ideford) to a dark grey, but generally a cool blue-grey as around Chudleigh and Plymouth. This stone may be seen in buildings and boundary walls of all dates from medieval times to the present day. The episcopal palace at Chudleigh was built of limestone from the bishop's great quarry, possibly in the 13th century. It was certainly a favourite residence of the bishops from the latter part of that century. The quarry was a valuable piece of episcopal property in 1535, when it was being leased for ten pounds a year. At this date the stone was mainly being used for the production of lime.

When Bishop Veysey was obliged to grant a 99-year lease to the Protector Somerset of the manor, town, park and palace of Chudleigh, the lease included the " Lyme Kylne, commonly called Chudleigh Calce."

The greater part of Plymouth, Torquay, and Newton Abbot is built of the Devonian limestone. So, too, was Plymouth breakwater. Many of the Devon limestones were sufficiently hard to take a high polish and ranked as marbles. These were produced chiefly at Torquay, Ipplepen and Plymouth, and widely used for interior decoration in church restoration of the last century. Usually the effect was overdone, and entirely disagreeable, especially in plain and simple country churches where such elaborate decoration was out of place.[1] Some monstrously ugly fonts were perpetrated in " Devonshire marble," which the reader will find for himself too soon. The production of these marbles goes back at least to Westcote's day, when they were used to a certain extent for building purposes[2] and also for the elaborate mural monuments of that time.

Around Totnes were various quarries in the " trap rocks " or basalts, of which the best known was that at Cornworthy. Some of the Cornworthy stone went to the building of Dartmouth Castle in 1488-94. From Stoke Gabriel, across the river Dart, came the red sandstone for the beautiful tower of Totnes parish church in 1451.[3] The magnificent stone chancel screen in the same church was carved from Beer stone in 1459-60. The roodscreen at Awliscombe is also made of Beer stone, and so probably was that at Luppitt, now destroyed.

In the extreme south of the county, the various slates and schists have provided good building material since the 12th century. Most of the medieval churches in the country west of Dartmouth are built of slate, which beds evenly with very fine joints, and can be readily dressed with an axe. Many of the towers, as for example Halwell and Stokenham, are noble. There were scores, if not hundreds, of small quarries for this stone, the best known perhaps being those of Charleton near the Kingsbridge estuary. These probably yielded slatestone for the late Norman churches that arose in such numbers. They are specifically mentioned as a valuable piece of property in an *inquisition post mortem* taken in 1439.[4] In 1488 it had been intended to build a round tower of Cornworthy stone at Dartmouth Castle, but this was abandoned in favour of a much stronger square tower of Charleton slate, brought round by water. Slate was used all over the South Hams for boundary walls and in the older farm buildings. It was easy to work, durable, and could be got in convenient sizes. There are magnificent barns built of it on most of the barton-farms of south Devon. It seems to have been the universal building material throughout the district from the 12th century to the 19th. During the 18th century great quantities of slate from the quarries at Buckland Tout Saints were exported to Holland. The outbreak of war in 1781 killed the trade. Slate from the great quarries at Mill Hill, near Tavistock, was similarly exported to the Channel Islands and France.[1]

Many quarries in south, west and north Devon produced tolerable roofing slates, and most of the older farmhouses and buildings are roofed in this way: most picturesque in their weathered irregularity and their multi-coloured lichens. The Devon roofing slates were, however, inclined to go soft with weathering, and by the mid-19th century were giving way to the more durable Delabole slates from Cornwall. Later, the spread of railways brought in the Welsh slates, a disagreeable and foreign material, and one by one the Devon slate quarries shut down.

In south-west Devon, two very characteristic building stones make a localised appearance. Hurdwick stone, from quarries about a mile out of Tavistock, is a loose-textured, free-working trappean ash, which was extensively quarried throughout medieval times and at intervals until the latter part of the 19th century. It is durable, and of a most pleasant colour: an under-water green. Tavistock abbey was built of it (the quarries were abbey property), and much of modern Tavistock during the 19th century, so giving the town that air of greenness everywhere that makes it so distinctively beautiful. Hurdwick stone can be found in medieval churches for miles north and south of Tavistock, where it may be recognised by its colour and its pitted appearance.

The other distinctive building stone of south-west Devon is the Roborough elvan, sometimes difficult to distinguish from granite unless one sees the two together, as one occasionally does in the two arcades of a 15th-century church, e.g. at Tamerton Foliot. The elvans are, indeed, granitic in character. Some make admirable building stone, others are worthless. The best was the elvan from Roborough Down, which was a favourite stone for dressings and carved work from the early 14th century onwards. It was widely used, in this part of Devon, in the arcades of Perpendicular churches, and for window mullions. In colour it is a warm buff, and it has little or none of the mica-sparkle of granite.

GRANITE

The granite of Dartmoor was not used as a building stone, except in the form of boulders for the rubble-masonry of medieval farmsteads, until the 15th century. It was used occasionally for fonts from the close of the 12th century, and might be carried for considerable distances, as we see at Bridgerule and Clyst St. Lawrence. As rubble masonry, usually in the form of dry walling, surface granite (known as *moorstone*) has been used from time immemorial. It was so used in the hut walls of the Bronze Age, and in the early Iron Age villages of Chysauster and Porthmeor in western Cornwall; and we cannot doubt that the earliest farmsteads on the Dartmoor fringes used it from the 8th–9th century onwards. The surface of the ground had to be cleared of its granite boulders, which were used to make boundary walls for the new fields, and for the farmhouse and outhouses. Dressed granite was used in the 14th century for quoins and buttresses, but not until the 15th century in window tracery and arcades.[1] In general, the interiors of the moorland churches are massively plain, for the moorstone did not lend itself to carving, but in the larger churches one finds a considerable degree of carving on the capitals. That granite could be magnificently carved at times the Cornish church of Launceston amply testifies.

In the great rebuilding of farmhouses and manor houses that began in Elizabeth's reign and lasted for nearly a century, moorstone was widely used all around the Moor and for miles beyond. Such buildings, of dressed blocks, survive in great numbers in all the parishes of the moorland fringe. The innumerable other uses to which the moorstone was put (e.g. gate-posts, stiles, bridges, querns, cheese-presses, cider-presses, and salting-troughs) have been fully described in Mr. Worth's admirable papers on " The Moorstone Age."[2] All this came from surface blocks. Quarrying for granite was almost unknown on Dartmoor earlier than the opening years of the 19th century, when the Heytor and Foggintor (Walkhampton) quarries were opened up. During this century the Devon and Cornish granites were in considerable demand for large building constructions, but the modern development of concrete has reduced this demand severely, and the granite is now quarried chiefly for pavement-stones, kerbs, setts, roadstones, and monumental purposes. A notable building to be constructed entirely of granite was Lutyens's masterpiece of Castle Drogo, at Drewsteignton (1911-30).

NORTH AND MID-DEVON

North of Dartmoor, the lone and level countryside of mid-Devon, based on the Culm Measures, is characterised chiefly by small plain churches built of a chocolate-coloured sandstone. This stone gives only a small rubble masonry and does not lend itself to decorative treatment. Here, in the poorest parishes, the absence of any building stone that could be carved led to the use of massive oaken arcades in churches, as at Nymet Rowland and Dowland, and to the use of oak window mullions in the older houses. We find these oak mullions also in the slate country of the South Hams. The wealthier parishes either imported Beer stone for their arcades, or brought down granite from the Moor. Either involved long and laborious journeys by road, the stone being loaded on sleds and pulled by oxen. Most of the older farmhouses and farm buildings are built of small rubble sandstones and limestones from innumerable local quarries.

The prevailing tone is a warm brown, but there is a wide variety of colouring in detail. Moreover, these stones readily attract grey and pale-green lichens, so that the original stone is completely disguised, and buildings appear at a distance to be a silvery-grey. Roofs are either deeply thatched or covered with local slates, the latter brilliantly coloured with orange lichens. Most of the older houses (before say 1850) in the towns are built of the same rubble masonry, though here it is usually covered with roughcast or stucco and the stone concealed. Leland noted, as early as Henry VIII's time, that " the Houses be of Stone " at Barnstaple, " as al Houses in good Tounes there aboute be."[1]

At various places between North Tawton and Hatherleigh a very good freestone was quarried at intervals for centuries. It is a sandy magnesian limestone, sometimes called Lee Stone, and was used in the dressings of Gidleigh Castle and Okehampton Castle in the late 13th century. In south Devon it was used for the 16th-century exterior of Boringdon House, near Plympton, and in the early 19th for the main front of Oaklands House, at Okehampton. Other houses in and near Okehampton are built of it.

In north Devon proper we find a variety of sandstones and slates used for building material in the medieval churches and the older farmhouses and town houses. Most of the upland churches are built of a dark, slaty stone, as at Challacombe, Stoke Rivers, and Kentisbury. At Kentisbury the 15th-century tower is a fine example of building in this stone. At Flitton, in North Molton, was a quarry of good sandstone, still worked in Lysons's day, from which the stone for the fine 15th-century tower of North Molton church was got. There was, however, no outstanding building stone in north or mid-Devon, nothing but small quarries supplying purely local needs, though sometimes the stone was of excellent quality and deserved a wider reputation.

BRICK BUILDING

Until Victorian days, brick was an uncommon material in the Devonshire countryside. Even in the towns it was not conspicuous owing to the liking for covering it with stucco. Brick as a building material was introduced into Devon by a Londoner—George Rolle, the Tudor lawyer, who amassed a great estate in the county. At Stevenstone, near Torrington, he had rebuilt the medieval house by the 1540s: Leland calls it " a right fair House of Bryke."[2] So far as we know, no other brick building was even attempted before the last decade of the 17th century. Possibly brick was unsuited to a damp climate. Carew tells us it was tried out in Cornwall in Elizabethan times and given up.[3] It looks as though the same thing happened in Devon. Moreover, building stone was abundant everywhere in the county, and in districts where suitable brick-earth was available the traditional building material of cob had obvious advantages over brick: it was cheaper and quicker to use and the thick walls gave a more even temperature all the year round.

Brick was not tried again until the 1690s, when it appeared almost simultaneously at Exeter, Topsham, Bideford, Tiverton, and in the new naval dockyard (later Devonport). At the latter, much of the new building was in brick, possibly because Nicholas Morrice would not sell his limestone to the Admiralty Commissioners at less than six times the normal price. Brick was an unfamiliar material: we are told that work in the dockyard was delayed by the bad quality of the bricks, and in 1697 some of the buildings had to be rebuilt because of defects in the brickwork.[1]

In the 1690s, when Holland was the greatest customer for the Devonshire serges, Dutch bricks often came back to Topsham as ballast, and it is to this—and to the personal contact between the woollen merchants and their Dutch customers—that we owe the so-called " Dutch houses " in the Strand at Topsham. There is also a pure Dutch house in the High Street of Exeter (c. 1690). At Bideford some early examples of brick-building (1690s) may be seen in Bridgeland Street.[2] Much rebuilding was done in brick at Tiverton after the great fire of 1731, and some fine examples survive. An early and interesting brick building is the Ayshford School at Uffculme, which is dated 1705.

A few country houses were rebuilt in brick in the time of Anne, the most notable example being Pynes, just outside Exeter, and other houses were enlarged in brick (e.g. Bradninch Manor House, c. 1740). At Great Fulford the stables were built in brick, 1750-75.[3] But it never became a popular material until the expansion of the towns in the 19th century, and even then Plymouth, the largest of them all, continued to use the local limestone almost invariably. At Exeter, however, and in the other east Devon towns, brick-building had become the recognised type by the latter part of the 18th century, usually (though not always) covered with stucco and painted. The old hand-made bricks were a deep warm red, as we may see in the Georgian crescents and terraces of Exeter, infinitely more attractive than the machine-made product that was to come later.

COB

Cob is a semi-wet mix of stiff clay and chopped straw which can be raised on a fork and placed in position. Walls are made vertical by the eye of the waller, and hence arises a characteristic and pleasing irregularity. It is a type of earth-building, of immense antiquity and widespread throughout the world in one form or another. Cob is akin to the Spanish *adobe* ("mud"), found in Mexico, California, and the south-western states of the U.S.A., and is distinguished from *pisé de terre*, another widespread type of earth-building, by the fact that it is a wet mix while *pisé de terre* is a dry mix. It is raised on a plinth or foundation of rubble-masonry or pebble stones, or whatever suitable material is found at hand, and so given a dry foundation. If protected against wet from above, preferably by a good thatched roof, it makes a first-class building material and will last for centuries. Many surviving Tudor farmhouses in Devon are built of cob, as for example Hayes Barton, where Ralegh was born in 1552. At Kentisbeare the old priest's house, known as Priesthall or Priesthill and built probably in the late 15th century, is of cob and remains in excellent condition. An even more remarkable example of age in cob-building is given by Cecil Torr in *Small Talk at Wreyland*.[1] Cutting through the cob wall of an old house, he found a silver coin embedded in the middle. This could only have got there when the cob was in a liquid state, and could be dated between 1216 and 1249. It had been in circulation for a good many years so that the wall was perhaps built in the late 13th century. The cob was well over six hundred years old when cut through in 1919, and found to be as hard as brass for cutting.

It is impossible to say when cob was first used in the south-west as a building material, nor do we know for certain what the word means. It has frequently been stated that the older form of the word is *clob*, quoting a 17th-century Devonshire reference,[2] but the *Oxford English Dictionary* gives a reference to cob in this sense in 1600, and Carew (1602) tells us that " the poore Cotager contenteth himselfe with Cob for his walls, and Thatch for his covering." Thus the word was certainly in use in Elizabethan days. It may possibly be derived from the Teutonic word *Korb*, meaning "basketwork," which would support the view that it originated in wattle-and-daub construction, perhaps a double-wattlework filled in between with mud. As the wattlework decayed it would be seen that the mud stood by itself, and so the cob wall was born. Henceforward the walls would be built without the wattlework.[3] In Devon, cob walling seems to have been known in the 13th century, as we have seen, and may be even older. Mud walls were in use for London houses as early as 1212.

The method of constructing cob walls has frequently been described in older books,[4] and need not be repeated. The great majority of farmhouses and parsonages in the eastern third of Devon were built of it before 1850. Cottages all over the county were generally built of it. The walls of cob houses vary considerably in thickness. They are usually about three feet, rarely less than 2 feet 6 inches. As a rule, we may say that the thicker the walls the older the building, and at times they run to as much as 4 feet 6 inches.

In the long tongue of the New Red Sandstone which runs westward as far as Hatherleigh, the cob is almost blood-red in colour. At Hatherleigh, where this tongue is only a few hundred yards wide, one find these red-walled cottages, but immediately to the north and south, on the Culm Measures, the cob is a disagreeable grey or buff colour. Fortunately, most cob buildings were plastered over and then whitewashed or cream-washed (sometimes brilliantly coloured) and the final effect is highly attractive. Vancouver tells us in 1808 that a three-roomed cottage, with larder and outhouse, could be built in cob, roughcast, and whitewashed, all for about £60. Thatch was the natural covering for a cob house in a peasant economy, which made good use of the humblest materials on the spot, and in Devon it was always wheat-straw that was used.* But whereas the art of building in cob has ceased for the best part of a hundred years, the art of thatching is still actively practised in Devon. There is a Devon Thatchers' Association, and the work of good thatchers is as distinctive as that of any other artists. To those who know the men and their work, it is as recognisable as a signed painting.

BUILDING—CHURCHES

Although a considerable number of churches had been built in Devon before the Norman Conquest, practically no traces of them survive. Only in the small crypt at Sidbury, and possibly in some traces in the tower walls at Branscombe, do we see anything of pre-Conquest work, in these instances of the 11th century. Nor does much work of the Norman period survive, although it is certain that nearly every medieval parish church in the county existed by the year 1220. The rebuilding or enlargements of the late 13th–early 14th century, and of the 15th–early 16th century, swept away, or disguised, nearly all the work of the prolific 12th century. Occasionally one can discover an original Norman plan embedded in later reconstruction; or Norman masonry in the nave walls of churches otherwise wholly Perpendicular in style; and much more often one finds a Norman doorway or a font in a later building.

The cruciform church, with or without aisles, and with a tower above the crossing, was common in Devon during the Norman period.[1] The large churches of Crediton, Colyton, and Axminster retain this basic plan, though the towers have been reconstructed. At Crediton, however, the arches of the crossing are still the original 12th-century work. Paignton was another important church of this type, though the Norman plan is more difficult to unearth here, and the original central tower was taken down and a new tower built at the west end in the 15th century. The cruciform plan survives very noticeably also in several churches in the

---

*Vancouver also tells us, however, that rye-straw had been extensively used in former times for thatching (*General View*, 170).

Ashburton and Newton Abbot districts. Lost in the folded country of mid-Devon, Honeychurch, though at first sight a 15th-century building, is essentially the original Norman building: apart from the tower, the masonry of the walls is clearly 12th-century in date, and there are other evidences of Norman work. Marystow, in west Devon, is largely a Norman building, though much altered at later periods. Brentor, in the same district, is almost entirely Norman. Norman doorways survive in later buildings at some forty places, but most numerous of all are fonts: more than 120 belong to the 12th century, nearly all standing in much later buildings.

There is structural evidence that a great number of Devonshire churches were enlarged or reconstructed in the late 13th century and the early 14th, though again not many escaped the later wave of rebuilding between about 1400 and 1540. Such older work tends to survive mostly in the remoter western parts of Devon where poverty precluded any later rebuilding. The land was generally the poorest in Devon; there was no cloth or tin trade to help out, no time of prosperity as there so evidently was in east and south Devon after 1400. Thus Cookbury remains a simple little 13th-century church of nave and chancel only (though badly restored), and Bradford, Thornbury, and Milton Damerel—all in the same district—all betray a complete rebuilding about 1330 without much alteration since. Bradford and Thornbury also retain good doorways from the earlier churches (*c.* 1150) on the site.

The Exeter episcopal registers, which begin in 1257, provide additional evidence of much rebuilding in the late 13th and early 14th centuries, though this evidence—chiefly that of dedications by the bishop—must be handled with care. Only in a limited number of cases, as at Tamerton Foliot and South Pool in 1318, where the bishop dedicated the high altars and three other altars in each, can we feel sure that there has been an entire rebuilding.[1] In a great number of instances the bishop's dedication follows some minor structural change, often long after the event. Among the later churches of the 14th century, that of Bratton Clovelly is a noble building, with almost cathedral-like arcades in the dove-grey stone from Polyphant in Cornwall.

Until the 15th century, the churches of Devon were, with very few exceptions, small and rather undistinguished buildings. There is little that can be remotely compared with the superb work of the period 1150-1350 that one finds so abundantly in the east Midlands and southern Lincolnshire. It is in the last phase of Gothic architecture that south-western England is so rich, Devon even more than Cornwall. Superficially, the unfailing recurrence of Perpendicular churches in parish after parish is wearying and disappointing, but " there is no English county in which a local type of late Gothic architecture can be studied with such undivided attention, or in which almost every church is so satisfactory a complement to the study of its immediate neighbour."[1]

The great rebuilding of the Perpendicular period affected nine churches out of ten in Devon, and in its fullest development produced a very characteristic local type: a continuous nave and chancel of five or six bays, with north and south aisles running the full length of the building, a western tower, and a south porch. Medieval spires are very rare in Devon. Occasionally the chancel projects slightly beyond the aisles. Internally, there is no structural division (in the form of a chancel arch) between nave and chancel. The division is marked by a rood-screen running the entire width of the church. To the east of this screen, the parts of the aisles so shut off form side chapels, divided from the chancel by parclose screens. These side chapels were often appropriated to particular families in the parish, and contain their monuments and pews. The absence of a chancel arch is almost certainly due to the development of screen construction, for above the screen was the rood-loft surmounted in turn by the crucifix: a chancel arch would have obstructed this towering glory. The fully developed plan is common throughout Devon, but much commoner in some parts than others. There are many exceptions, where only a north aisle or a south aisle appears. Generally the full plan appears in the more populous and wealthy parishes of the vale of Exeter (plate 48), the Tor Bay region, and the South Hams, though there are exceptions even here.

A clerestory is as rare in a Devonshire church as a chancel arch. The great church of Cullompton is exceptional in this respect. The roof of the church is usually unbroken from one end to the other. It is known as a cradle-, wagon-, or barrel-roof, and is generally ceiled. The timbers are frequently elaborately carved, especially the wall-plates and the bosses. One should never fail to raise one's eyes to the roof in a Devonshire church. Among the most notable roofs are those of North Bovey, Buckland Monachorum, Cheriton Bishop, Chulmleigh, Hatherleigh, King's Nympton, Lifton, Meavy, Milton Abbot, Ottery St. Mary, Sampford Courtenay, Stoodleigh, Tavistock, North Tawton, South Tawton, Thorverton, and Widecombe-in-the-Moor.[2] With the carved and coloured screens, which are the greatest glory of the Devon church (plate 53), and the carved roofs, went also a complete series of oak benches with elaborately carved ends. These, like the screens, have been made the subject of special study, and are far too numerous— even with all the destruction that has since taken place—to mention in detail. Like the screens, too, they are chiefly of late 15th- or early 16th-century date, though earlier and later examples can be found,[3] and they are the work of Devonshire craftsmen, not, as is so often said, of wandering Flemish craftsmen.

The handsome screen and rood-loft at Atherington, now reduced to the north-aisle section only, we happen to know from a contemporary law-suit was the work of Devonshire craftsmen from Northlew and Chittlehampton. John Parrys of Northlew apparently began the task of making the rood-loft but did not for some reason go on with it, and Roger Down and John Hyll of Chittlehampton were appointed as " carpenters, carvers, and joiners " to complete it. This they did at a cost of £14 7s. 7d., of which they had been paid only £10 by the nine parishioners who had entered into the original agreement. It looks as though the original estimate for the work had been £10 and that the parishioners were jibbing at the additional cost. At any rate, the two craftsmen were obliged to bring a suit about it in the court of Chancery some time between 1544 and 1547.[1]

The Atherington screen has features in common with those of Hartland, Marwood, Lapford, and Swimbridge, all in north Devon. The two Chittlehampton carvers may well have been responsible for all of these screens, and also for the screen at Chittlehampton itself, where the church was entirely rebuilt 1470-1520. Unfortunately, the Chittlehampton screen —which must have been magnificent if it accorded with the remainder of the church—was destroyed at some unknown date in the past. At Winkleigh, in mid-Devon, the churchwardens' accounts[2] record the first payment of twenty shillings to John Clement for making the rood-loft in 1512-13, and a second payment in the following year. The carpentry done, the parish called in John Kellegh, " kerver," in 1515 to adorn the work, and we find payments made to him for the next five or six years. The length of time and scale of the payments—nearly £48 in all—suggest that he was carving the screen as well as the loft. Here too, not a trace remains of all this craftsmanship. Altogether, however, no fewer than 140 medieval rood-screens survive in Devon, most of them unusually perfect, of which thirty-four retain their original vaulting. Of the twenty or thirty rood-lofts which remained as late as Lysons's day, however, only one is left—that at Atherington. Marwood still has the east balcony of its loft, but the rich western front was removed by a barbarous incumbent about the middle of the 19th century. The survival of the Atherington rood-loft has furnished an exquisite model for the restoration of other lofts in Devon, notably those at Staverton and Kenton.

The great period of rebuilding and refurnishing of the Devon churches lasted up to the 1540s, and then stopped except for minor changes internally. It seems likely that, for the next two or three generations after 1550, many churches were allowed to fall into serious disrepair. In view of the rising population and wealth almost everywhere in Devon in this century (1550-1650) such neglect is curious. The means were there, but the spirit was not so willing. The remarkable amount of reconstruction and even rebuilding that can be dated in the 17th century—particularly evident in towers, arcades and windows—argues a serious deterioration in church fabrics over a long period previously. The plain classical arch of such rebuilt arcades, especially where an intractable stone like granite is used, is frequently mistaken by the uninitiated for Norman work. At the same time the growing population of the country and town parishes necessitated the erection of western galleries, occasionally of galleries on three sides. We find many notable galleries of this period in Devon, as for example at Sandford, Silverton, Kentisbeare and Dartmouth, in which the great tradition of craftsmanship in wood is carried on. Charles Church at Plymouth is the only completely new church built in Devon during the 17th century (1640-57).

The Patent Books and Faculty Books in the episcopal registry at Exeter show that much structural alteration and refurnishing was carried out in the 18th and early 19th centuries. Galleries were put in at scores of places to accommodate the rising population; many churches got new seating throughout, and a decent new pulpit. Some old churches were enlarged by the addition of an aisle, as at Stoke Damerel (1750), Beer (1755), and Lynton (1817), but entirely new churches were rare. St. George's at Tiverton (1730) is the only notable 18th-century church in Devon. Filleigh, rebuilt in 1732, has since been reconstructed and Teigngrace (1787) has been spoilt. Sometimes there is evidence of a fall in numbers. At little Luffincott the church was taken down and entirely rebuilt in 1765, and the original two aisles reduced to one. At Horwood the south aisle was removed in 1791.

The Georgian period has left us a notable legacy of fittings and furnishings (particularly at Molland (plate 49), Cruwys Morchard, and Cornworthy) but the destruction of medieval rood-screens and lofts that this entailed is saddening. Cadeleigh lost its chancel screen in 1737, Blackawton its north and south aisle screens in 1751, South Molton all its screens and rood-loft in 1758. Other places that suffered in this way were Whimple (1777), East Worlington (1784), Stoke Fleming (1787), Highweek and Kingsteignton (both in 1801), Colebrooke (1805), and Tormohun (1812). At Langtree and Shebbear, both remote from the eye of the episcopal registry, the churchwardens had ripped out the old screens without any licence to do so, but a faculty was granted in each instance in 1815 to put the matter right legally. No one appears ever to have protested at this vandalism: it is always called an " improve-ment." Liturgically it may have been, at that time of Low Church goings-on, but aesthetically it was a disastrous change, for in the absence of any other division between nave and chancel, the " improved " church is too apt to look like an open barn to-day. There must also have been a vast unrecorded destruction of ancient painted glass. Very little medieval glass is left in Devon, except at Doddiscombsleigh and in the cathedral at Exeter, and an occasional panel here and there, but what remains shows how good it was. " In Devonshire . . . medieval work is often almost masterly in conception and design, and in technique and workmanship it is nearly always exceptionally good."[1]

It remained for the Victorians to complete the work of destruction in the medieval and Georgian churches. The melancholy tale of their vandalism, their complete disregard for the artistic achievements of the past, can be told in nearly every parish in Devon and is exemplified in Part II of this book. Devon suffered particularly heavily at the hands of the Victorian restorers. All that can be said in mitigation of their barbarism —how often in going around the parishes one has heard of the rood-screen being chopped up for firewood by the degenerate descendants of the old village craftsmen!—is that the mid-Victorian incumbents succeeded to the churches that their fathers and grandfathers had grossly neglected for the past hundred years, and there was not much they could do about it except to clear out a mass of mouldy or worm-eaten wreckage and start refurnishing all over again in new deal and pitch-pine. One has only to read some contemporary descriptions of the country churches in Devon in the 1840s to realise what a task faced Bishop Phillpotts and his clergy in rescuing something from the débris. Still, they went about their work in a heavy-handed and unsympathetic way. A good deal of the " restoration " work in Devon was done by Hayward of Exeter, and disagreeably done. Very rarely was a good architect called in, one with a national reputation (not that he was always a safe guide: look what Butterfield did to Ottery St. Mary). Fortunate indeed was the parish that was too poor to " restore " its church in the 1860s, 1870s and 1880s. Such were Hittisleigh, Molland and Honeychurch. By the time they came to be rescued the task of " restoration " had ceased to be synonymous with indiscriminate destruction, and the old work was conserved and cared for.

A considerable number of new churches were built in the Victorian period, in Devon as elsewhere, above all in Plymouth, Torquay and Exeter. The finest of these is St. Michael's at Exeter, by Rhode Hawkin. St. John's at Torquay is a notable work by G. E. Street, on an unusual site. Street also designed Holy Trinity, Barnstaple, and rebuilt Huish for the Rolles. Among the country churches, Yealmpton was completely rebuilt by Butterfield in 1850, an astonishing effort in local marbles. In the main the Victorian churches of Devon are not distinguished buildings: many are bad. Wherever there was plenty of money, as on the Rolle estates, " restoration " went mad. All the churches that the Rolles helped to restore in north and east Devon (except Huish) are depressing spectacles. One can only thank God that they never owned Molland or Honeychurch or West Ogwell, and that most of the old Devon squires were too poor to squander money on uglifying their ancestral churches.

CASTLES AND COUNTRY HOUSES

Devon is not rich in medieval castles and mansions. The more important castles were those of the Earl of Devon at Exeter, Tiverton, Okehampton and Plympton; Judhael's castles at Totnes and Barnstaple, and the castles at Lydford and Berry Pomeroy. At Exeter the early Norman gateway and a section of the curtain wall survive, at Tiverton a fine 14th-century gateway and other fragments of the same date. The remains of Okehampton Castle are substantial and impressive: a towering stone keep, the great hall and chapel, and some of the domestic quarters can all be identified. Of Plympton Castle, only the round keep remains. At Totnes the shell keep still survives largely intact, one of the best of its kind, but Judhael's other castle at Barnstaple has disappeared altogether. Only the mount remains at the western end of the old town. At Lydford the grim square keep, dating from the closing years of the 12th century, remains substantially unchanged, having long been used as the Stannary prison. Ranking with Okehampton for an impressive site, and even more impressive structurally, is Berry Pomeroy: a most romantic ruin embedded deep among the trees. It is an Edwardian castle (begun about 1300), of which the splendid gatehouse with two flanking towers is the most striking survival. The castle was converted into a country house by the Seymours in the late 16th century.

A number of smaller " castles," such as Hemyock and Bampton, also existed, though it is difficult to distinguish these at times from fortified houses. Powderham, the best-known of Devon " castles," probably falls into this category (plate 31). Originally built about 1390 by Sir Philip Courtenay, it consisted of a hall and kitchen strengthened by four angle towers and an entrance-tower commanding the estuary of the Exe. Nearly opposite Powderham, across the river, was another house of the same type—Nutwell—of which Hooker, writing about 1600, says: " It is reported that Nuttwell was sometimes a Castle of defence. . . ." Almost certainly this means a fortified house. Compton Castle, so called, is the finest surviving example in the county of this type of house, first built about 1320 and much enlarged about 1450. Like Powderham and Nutwell, it was built on low-lying ground with no natural defences, and relied on its own walls and towers for defence. Gidleigh Castle was also a fortified house, built about 1300, and Colcombe Castle (near Colyton) was of the same type and date. There are interesting remains of both. Affeton Castle, near Witheridge, was a fortified house with a gatehouse built by the Affetons in the 15th century on the site of an older house. Bickleigh Castle, below Tiverton, was a fortified house protected by a wet moat, like Hemyock, and by a formidable gatehouse which still stands. Many other houses of this type in Devon are known to have perished.

A considerable number of medieval manor houses were licensed to be crenellated or otherwise fortified, e.g. Bere Ferrers (1337) and Hatch Arundell (1463), and many medieval gatehouses survive to astonish the beholder in some quiet lane to-day, as at Bradstone, Morwell, Dowrish, and Wear Giffard. Some of the finest gatehouses are of 16th-century date —Shute (c. 1550), Holcombe Rogus (c. 1550), and Tawstock (dated 1574), to name only three. Thus, although Devon contains no striking castles to compare with those elsewhere in England, it is singularly rich in lesser castles, fortified medieval houses, and medieval manor houses generally (e.g. Bradley, Little Hempston, and Wortham).

Nor has the county any country house comparable with the palaces of the Elizabethan statesmen and officials in the Midlands. It is a characteristic of West Country building that it is almost everywhere on a small scale. The last of the great country houses, as one goes west, is Longleat in Wiltshire. Still, there is a notable amount in Devon of original 16th-century building by rising families. George Rolle's great brick house at Stevenstone (c. 1540) went long ago, but the house of another successful lawyer—John Haydon—built a few years later, still stands (restored) at Cadhay, near Ottery St. Mary. Great Fulford is another fine house of this period (temp. Henry VII–Henry VIII), rebuilt by the ancient family of Fulford on a wave of affluence (plate 32). It is the only house of this kind in Devon which still remains in the hands of the original family, who have occupied this site since at least the latter part of the 12th century, and who take their name from it.

Another ancient family, the Walronds, built themselves new houses during the 16th century, at Bradfield and Bovey (near Beer), the Carys rebuilt Cockington, the Tremaynes Collacombe, the Bluetts Holcombe. All over the county the squires were building, from Henry VII's time onwards. Scores of their houses survive, sometimes disguised by later work, sometimes largely unchanged. The pages of Risdon and Westcote, written in the first years of the 17th century, are full of references to the building of mansions during the preceding two or three generations, and the builders are either squires or successful lawyers. This remarkable fashion for building country houses continued into the first generation of the 17th century, Netherton (near Farway) and Sydenham (near Marystow) being good examples of this period. Other and older houses were much enlarged and transformed in the same century, especially perhaps in the last years of the century when the stringencies of the Civil War and its aftermath for royalist gentry were things of the past—"the Late Troubles." Dunsland is a notable example of a country house beginning in a small way about 1500 and successively enlarged and improved to its present size in the next two hundred years.

The wave of rebuilding, of the replacement of medieval confinement and discomfort by space and light, spread downwards through the social scale. By the third quarter of the 16th century the smaller gentry—the younger sons of old families on their own small inheritances—had caught the fever for rebuilding or modernising. By the end of the century most of them were engaged in costly improvements, and the yeomen had been infected too. Few parishes throughout the whole of Devon cannot show two or three small houses (often more) rebuilt or modernised between 1570 and 1640, their best rooms panelled with carved oak, their ceilings wonderfully decorated with all the art that the local school of plasterers could command. Sometimes it was a complete rebuilding, but equally often it was an internal reconstruction and enlargement of a medieval hall-house, as at Acland Barton, for example, in 1591. There are scores of such houses in Devon, of which the first and overwhelming impression one gets is of a house built about 1600, but which upon closer inspection internally reveal the undisturbed shell of a hall-house built perhaps two hundred years earlier.

Every landowner, even the smallest, had building stone somewhere on his land: the surface of the county is pitted with these little overgrown quarries that have produced only one house and its outbuildings and boundary walls. And he had ample oak timber for his new beams, his new floors, and his wainscotting. All this came off the estate and was lavishly used: how immensely gratifying it is to come across these buildings where nothing was skimped or measured to the last miserable inch, where even the non-essentials like the garden walls were treated on a generous scale. Such building is the product of a sane local economy, killed during the 19th century and now forgotten except when we contemplate its monuments like this. But the glass in the windows, now put in for the first time (as Carew tells us they were doing even in Cornwall), was a pure luxury, with its painted coats-of-arms, above all the amount of glass required for the enlarged windows that had now become fashionable. And the towering plaster mantelpieces with their coats-of-arms, and the ceilings covered with foliage, fruit, and all kinds of rich symbolism, all these were luxuries, too. More space, more light everywhere, more pleasant things for the eye to dwell upon: such were the new houses, set in their peaceful parks among the folds and trees of lovely Devon. These are the real architectural treasures of the county, reflecting more faithfully than anything else the kind of society and culture that had its being here, remote and withdrawn in the far south-west of England. The cold, ordered, sophisticated mansions of the 18th century—the Castle Hills, the Bictons, and the Saltrams—do not move us half as much as these smaller houses, lost among the lanes, among the pigeon-haunted trees at the end of decaying avenues of walnuts or beeches, or mourned over by desolate cypresses in the soft Devonshire rain.

By the 18th century something like a territorial aristocracy was emerging in Devon, though never to the degree we find elsewhere, and they built houses commensurate with their new position. The Fortescues began rebuilding Castle Hill from 1684-94, greatly enlarged and sophisticated it in 1730-40, and enlarged it yet again in the 1840s. The Rolles seem to have rebuilt Stevenstone on a grander scale in the 18th century, but little survives of this house for they rebuilt again in the 1870s and produced a villainously ugly house whose present dereliction need bring no tears. They also rebuilt Bicton, their east Devon house, towards the end of the century. Ugbrooke was rebuilt by the Cliffords in the 1730s, Killerton by the Aclands about fifty years later. A new and splendid Saltram arose in 1750-68, designed in part for John Parker by Robert Adam. Other notable 18th-century country houses are Clovelly Court, Maristow, Tawstock (1787—and hideous for its time), and Werrington, where an 18th-century house was added to an earlier one. But the huge house of Haldon, built for Sir George Chudleigh c. 1725-40 and modelled upon Buckingham House in St. James's Park, London, has been demolished (plate 14). Powderham, which had suffered severely in the Civil War, and was for a long time uninhabitable, began to take its present form from 1757 onwards. A number of smaller houses were rebuilt in the 18th century, some of them of great beauty. Puslinch (c. 1720) is "perfect Queen Anne," and belongs to the same group as Plympton (1700-20) and Antony in Cornwall. Pynes, near Exeter, is of the same date. Coryton near Axminster is dated 1754-56. Other houses, like Bradninch, were remodelled without being completely rebuilt.

The early 19th century saw a great deal of building. Kitley, an Elizabethan house already Georgianised, was remodelled about 1820 by G. S. Repton, who was also responsible for the new Follaton, near Totnes. John Nash built a number of houses in Devon, among them Luscombe at Dawlish for Charles Hoare (1800-4) and a new Sandridge for Lord Ashburton. He also built Stonelands, at Dawlish, in 1817, a house later occupied by the great civil engineer Sir John Rennie. Salvin rebuilt Mamhead about 1830. Later, the great house of Flete was remodelled by Norman Shaw from 1878 onwards; and Lutyens created a masterpiece on a new site—Castle Drogo (1911-30), the last country house that will ever be built in Devon.

TOWN HOUSES AND PUBLIC BUILDING

Except at Exeter, Totnes, and Plymouth, not a great deal of the domestic architecture of the 16th and 17th centuries is left. The Devonshire towns have, most of them, been devastated by fire on more than one occasion, and what was spared from fire has been destroyed by town councils, as at Dartmouth, which formerly had as remarkable a collection of merchant-houses as the sister-town of Totnes. The decorated plaster ceilings of the 16th–17th century houses, in Totnes and Barnstaple especially, bear witness to the existence of a remarkable school of plasterers in Devon at this period. Some of the smaller towns, like Ashburton, contain much 17th–18th century building behind the slate-hung fronts that are an architectural feature of the towns between Exeter and Plymouth. Most of the building in the older parts of the Devonshire market towns dates from the 18th century and the early 19th, often covered with a drab-coloured stucco or roughcast. The little riverside towns, like Topsham, Appledore, and Bideford, are particularly interesting architecturally (plate 41).

In the seaside towns, especially those on the south coast, there is much seemly small-town architecture of the period 1800-40, especially at Sidmouth, Dawlish, and Teignmouth, and to some extent at Exmouth and Budleigh Salterton. Torquay has some good building of this date, but more of the mid-Victorian years, some of it fine. Barnstaple is a somewhat disappointing town architecturally, though it has some good terrace building of the 1820s and 1830s, and some notable almshouses of the 17th century. Plymouth, Stonehouse, and Devonport were once rich in domestic and public building of the years between 1800 and 1840, almost all the work of John Foulston, in some ways the most remarkable of West-Country architects (plates 2, 3, 5). Most of his monumental public building in the centre of Plymouth, which must have turned Plymouth into the noblest town to look at west of Bristol, has now gone. War and ignorance between them have wrecked the grandest piece of town-planning in Devon. Foulston also did a good deal of very attractive building on a smaller scale, as in Albemarle Villas at Stoke Damerel (plate 5), and in parts of Stonehouse, and he did some monumental public building in the centre of Devonport (e.g. the Town Hall, and the Devonport Column). The Three Towns were everywhere stamped with his handiwork; and yet the *Dictionary of National Biography* does not devote a line to this most notable of Devonshire architects. Not far away, the naval dockyards afforded the opportunity for more monumental building from the 1690s onwards. Of this a good deal survives, despite the severity of air attacks, most notable being the truly grand Royal Victualling Yard at Stonehouse (1830) by Sir John Rennie, one of the greatest monuments of 19th-century architecture in England.

CHAPTER XV

LITERATURE AND THE ARTS

FEW English counties, if any, have produced more great men than Devon, but the Devonshire genius is strongly specialised. It is to be found pre-eminently among the lawyers, the sea captains, and the painters. The sea captains are readily explained, but the long roll of the Devon lawyers and painters has no obvious origin. Conversely, it is hard to explain the remarkable absence of great literary figures in Devon. Nor are there, with perhaps one or two exceptions in each case, any eminent musicians or architects in the history of the county. If one were to attempt a generalisation, one might say that the Devonshire genius has always taken a practical form, and that the Devonian mind is not, with the single and remarkable exception of Coleridge, in the highest degree imaginative. It has produced almost no poetry, music, architecture, or literature, of the first order, nor yet any great philosopher with the possible exception of Richard Hooker.

When we say this we are not, of course, forgetting the imaginative element in the work of the great painters, but even there we have to recall that the Devonshire painters produced their finest work outside the county and that most of them were painters of portraits. Again, the literature that Devon-born men have produced—such men as Hooker, Ford, Gay, Coleridge—has been produced outside the county for the most part. One might go even further and say that when men of literary genius found themselves embedded in Devon they found it uncongenial, if not positively hateful. Herrick at Dean Prior and Keats at Teignmouth are cases in point. Perhaps even Devonian geniuses have felt this, for it is also worthy of note that they nearly all achieved fame outside their native shire: the lawyers and the painters made their names in London, and the sea captains and explorers all over the western world. On the reasons for this it is perhaps idle for the historian to speculate, but the answer may lie in the climate, and in the isolation of Devon from the main streams of English life and thought.

In so far as genius is compounded, in part at least, of unusual energy, the climate of Devon is the least conducive of any to prolonged effort of any kind; and the isolation of the county, together with its great size, made it necessary for men who were conscious of exceptional powers to seek the stimuli to artistic expression elsewhere, above all in London.

PRINTING

The art of printing was introduced into south-western England by Thomas Richards, a monk of Tavistock, when he set up a press in the abbey in, or shortly before, the year 1525. This was the seventh press in all England, the others being at Westminster (the first), Oxford, St. Albans, London, York and Cambridge. Some twenty years earlier, Martin Coffin, an Exeter stationer and bookbinder, had published an edition of Stanbridge's *Vocabula*, printed at Rouen. Coffin may be regarded as the first publisher in the south-west, but he never set up his own printing press.[1]

Of the books issued from the Tavistock press, only two titles are known—*The Consolation of Philosophy*, translated from the Latin of Boethius and published in 1525, and *The Statutes of the Stannary*, published in 1534. No doubt there was a certain amount of ephemeral printing also. When the abbey was dissolved in 1539, the press came into the hands of an Exeter family named Williams, possibly through a kinsman William Williams, another Tavistock monk who may have been the printer after Thomas Richards had left Tavistock to become prior of Totnes. But what use was made of the press at Exeter is not known. No books were printed in Devon for another century and a half.[2]

Casual printing presses were at work in Exeter at various dates in the 17th century, but the first trace of a resident printer in the city occurs in 1683.[3] Since that date Exeter has never lacked a printer. According to Dr. Thomas Tanner, Exeter had a weekly newspaper by 1706, though no issue as early as this has been traced. Jos. Bliss's *Exeter Post-Boy* seems, however, to have begun in 1707, and was probably the third provincial newspaper in England. The earliest were the *Norwich Post* (1701) and the *Bristol Post-Boy* (1702).[4] Other newspapers followed in Exeter, and for a long time they had Devonshire entirely to themselves except for the formidable competition of the *Sherborne Mercury*, which was distributed by men on horseback throughout the four south-western counties.

Printing was introduced into Plymouth in 1696 by Daniel Jordaine, who may have been of Exeter descent,[5] and in 1718 the *Plymouth Weekly Journal, or General Post* was started. It lasted only until 1725. The *Plymouth Magazine*, begun in 1772, reached six numbers only. By the end of the 18th century a number of the smaller Devonshire towns had their own printing presses, and the first three decades of the 19th century saw more. In 1808 came the first Dock newspaper—the *Plymouth and Dock Telegraph* —and in 1824 the first newspaper in north Devon, the *North Devon Journal*. Torquay had a newspaper in 1839, and Sidmouth by 1849. In 1853 came the *Dartmouth and Brixham Chronicle*, and in 1860 the *Totnes Times*.

The county at large was served by Trewman's *Exeter Flying Post*, founded as *The Exeter Mercury* in 1763, and by Woolmer's *Exeter and Plymouth Gazette*, begun in 1772.[1] Both Trewman's and Woolmer's newspapers were Tory in complexion. So, too, was the third county newspaper, *The Western Luminary*, begun in 1813. In 1827 the *Exeter Weekly Times* was started as the first of the radical and reforming papers, by James Terrell at Exeter. It became the leading newspaper (as the *Western Times* from 1829) in the south-west, under the editorship of the fearless Thomas Latimer.

Newspaper circulations were still remarkably small. By 1850, the average weekly sale of the *Western Times* had climbed from its old circulation of a little over a thousand to 3,673 copies. That of the *Devon and Exeter Gazette* (Woolmer's paper) was 2,307, and *The Flying Post* figure was only 1,193. At this date the population of the county was some 567,000. In the 1850s, with the abolition of the tax on advertisements and the newspaper stamp tax, a number of additional newspapers started in various parts of the county—at Bideford, Ilfracombe, Dartmouth and Kingsbridge; and in 1860 the *Western Morning News*, which was to become one of the best provincial newspapers—as it still is—came to Plymouth as a powerful rival from the start of the older Plymouth and Exeter papers.

LITERATURE

The literary history of Devon may be said to begin with John Jewel (1522-71), born at Berrynarbor in north Devon, who became bishop of Salisbury and published his *Apologia pro Ecclesia Anglicana* in 1562. His protégé, Richard Hooker, born just outside Exeter, published his even more famous defence of the Anglican church—*The Laws of Ecclesiastical Polity*—in the 1590s, though the complete work was not printed until long after his death. But neither Jewel nor Hooker can be said to owe their inspiration to Devon. Their work can only be claimed by the accident of their birth. And similarly with John Ford (1586–after 1639), son of the squire of Ilsington, whose plays were written for the London stage in the 1620s and 1630s—" a powerful depiction of melancholy, sorrow, and despair." With William Browne (1590-1645), an almost exact contemporary of John Ford, we come to a poet whose work sprang

largely from his native soil. He was born at Tavistock, among some of
the loveliest scenery in Devon, and his poetry is full of images drawn from
this countryside:

> My muse for lofty pitches shall not roam,
> But homely pipen of my native home.

His *Britannia's Pastorals*, by which he is chiefly known, are too fluent
and desultory—he never knew when to stop—but they contain many
passages of beauty. They are among the earliest of topographical poetry
and can be read with special pleasure in Tavistock itself.

While William Browne was wandering by Walla Brook and Tavy,
Robert Herrick (1591-1674) was presented to the living of Dean Prior,
near Totnes (in 1629) and there he stayed for eighteen years until he was
ejected because he would not subscribe to the Solemn League and
Covenant. He was reinstated, however, in 1662, and eventually died at
Dean Prior in October 1674. Though he lived for thirty years in Devon,
it never touched his heart. London—" the blest home of my nativity "
always held him. His work is full of bitter words on Devon and Devonshire people. It is surely revealing that in more than a thousand of his
poems only one Devon place-name can be found.

Even so, all his most magical and haunting poems were written during
his first period at Dean Prior:

> More discontents I never had
> Since I was born, than here;
> Where I have been, and still am sad,
> In this dull Devon-shire:
> Yet justly too I must confesse;
> I ne'er invented such
> Ennobled numbers for the Presse,
> Than where I loath'd so much.

Several of his poems are clearly associated with the life of Dean Prior.
Porch Verse and *The Good-night or Blessing*, and above all, the charming
Thanksgiving to God for His House, are all intensely local in feeling. All
Herrick's poetry was written before 1648. When he returned to the
" loathéd West," he was a silent and lonely old man. He died at the age
of eighty-three, and is buried in an unmarked grave in the churchyard.
Somewhere near him lies Prudence Baldwin, his maid.

The Devonshire landscape has produced more bad poetry, perhaps,
than any other in England, and more sentimental ballads. But occasionally
the right note is struck, as in Coleridge's beautiful *Sonnet to the River Otter*:

> **Dear native brook! Wild streamlet of the West!**

The billowy, feminine beauty of so much of Devon does not lend itself to great poetry. It lacks austerity and the elements of nobility and sadness. Even Dartmoor has produced no literature or poetry of the highest order. No Hardy or Brontë has ever felt its power and translated it into immortal words.

Devonshire has been a playground rather than a workshop for writers. Fanny Burney came to stay at Teignmouth for several weeks in the summer of 1773, and is full of praise for the beauties of Devon, but they made no abiding impression on her mind.[1] She came again in 1788, in attendance upon Queen Charlotte, and is full of disillusion. Of Exeter she could only say it was " close and ugly," but Saltram impressed her as " one of the most magnificent houses in the country." Her last visit, in 1791, when she was free once more of the fatigues of royal service, was to Sidmouth, thence to Exmouth, and across to Powderham and Star Cross. At Star Cross she was shocked by the sight of some women " with feet and legs entirely naked, straw-bonnets of uncouth shapes tied on their heads . . . strolling along with wide mannish strides to the borders of the river, gathering cockles. . . ." And so back through Exeter, on to Cullompton Church, and away into Somerset.

Fanny Burney had praised Teignmouth. Keats loathed it, both the town and the people. The south coast of Devon has indeed inspired very little literature. Dickens laid the opening scene of *Nicholas Nickleby* at Dawlish, which he must have seen when he was arranging a house for his parents near Exeter, Praed wrote " Our Ball " about Teignmouth, and there is a view of Torquay in W. H. Mallock's *An Immortal Soul*— but that is all.

East Devon has been better treated. Thackeray used to stay, in his Charterhouse days (1825-28), at Larkbeare, a house not far from Talaton then occupied by his stepfather Major Carmichael Smyth, and he got to know the Otter valley well. The " Clavering St. Mary " of *Pendennis* is Ottery St. Mary, though it might be any small town in the south of England, while " Chatteris " and " Baymouth " no doubt stand for Exeter and Sidmouth. Stephen Reynolds lived at Sidmouth and wrote here his minor classic *A Poor Man's House* (1908) about the life of the fishermen. It is full of good descriptive writing of the coast. And W. H. Hudson has four chapters on the east Devon country in *Afoot in England*.

George Gissing's *The Private Papers of Henry Ryecroft* are set in the Exeter countryside. They contain few landscapes, but we can identify a number of his descriptive pages with the aid of his letters.[2] He lived in Exeter for two years (1891-3) and walked a good deal in the surrounding country, which he thought (like everyone else) beautiful in the extreme, But, like all other creative beings, he found that it did not excite the imagination. In April 1893 we find him writing: " On the whole, I fear that I have wasted two years here in Devon. It is obviously in London that my material lies, and I must work hard to recover lost ground . . ." and within a few weeks he was back in the teeming streets of South London. Devon is a good place to grow old in, as Gissing so well perceived in *The Private Papers of Henry Ryecroft*: to sit under some old wall, beside a broad estuary flooding with the evening tide, watching the boats move silently and the darkening hills beyond: but not while one is young and there is work to be done.

North Devon comes off by far the best in literature. Kingsley's masterpiece, *Westward Ho!*, published in 1855, is full of exact descriptions of Barnstaple Bay and its estuaries. Even now one cannot fail to be moved by this book, one of the greatest and most satisfying historical novels in the English language. One can only pity children who are more interested in jet engines and train numbers, who have never heard of Amyas Leigh, Salvation Yeo, John Oxenham, Will Cary, and the rest, who have never read those wonderful pages that describe the homecoming of the blinded Amyas Leigh. Blackmore's *Lorna Doone* (1869), another of the great English historical novels, does the same for the Exmoor country, but like *Westward Ho!* had, too, the incidental effect of destroying the beauty and solitude of the natural landscape by making it too widely known. In more recent years, John Fortescue's *Story of a Red Deer*, and the work of Henry Williamson, have drawn very largely on north Devon. The most notable of Henry Williamson's descriptive writing, exact, sharp and delicate, is to be found perhaps in *Tarka the Otter* and *Salar the Salmon*, the one centred upon the Torridge, the other upon the Taw, but the landscapes of his novels are hardly less affectionately done. They have warmed the heart and kindled the eye of many an exile from Devon, in London and the hard, northern towns.

In 1812 Shelley spent about ten weeks at Lynmouth, but he makes only one brief reference to the scenery. Once more, as with Fanny Burney and Keats, Devon made no permanent impression on the mind. Nor did it on the mind of Thomas Hardy, who visited the county and knew parts of it well. Apart from one or two passing references in his novels and poetry, he speaks of Devon not at all.

Dartmoor is best portrayed in Blackmore's *Christowell* (1881), and in the contemporary work of Eden Phillpotts, but the poetry it has inspired is mostly very bad indeed. Specimens of it by various writers will be found in *Devonshire Scenery*, edited by the Rev. William Everitt and published at Exeter in 1884. The most effective piece on Dartmoor is *The Hill Farm* by Richard John King, written with real feeling and exact description.

PAINTING

Leaving Middlesex aside, Devon has produced more notable painters than any other county in England.   Of the 438 painters in S. Redgrave's *English School of Painting* whose birthplace can be traced, Devon claims thirty-three.   Norfolk comes second with twenty-seven, Yorkshire and Somerset next with twenty-two.[1]   Of all English provincial cities, Plymouth (with its adjacent villages) stands first, represented by Reynolds, Prout, Haydon, Northcote, Eastlake and Solomon Hart.   It is unwise to be too precise about numbers, for Pycroft's list (*Art in Devonshire*) does not include Francis Towne and John White Abbott, both notable Exeter painters, but the pre-eminence of the Devon painters stands out on any reckoning.

The history of Devonshire painting begins with the figure-painting on the panels of the rood-screens and parclose screens of the parish churches. Though great numbers of these survive, they cannot for the most part be regarded as works of art, and they are generally inferior to those in the East Anglian churches.[2]   Nevertheless, some of the Devon paintings reach a high standard, notably those at Ashton and Plymtree.   A great number of other screens are worthy of close study, and often contain groups of considerable beauty.

The tradition of figure-painting on the screens continued up to the Reformation, well into the lifetime of the first known Devon portrait painter, John Shute, who was born at Cullompton, in all probability in the early years of the 16th century, studied in Italy in 1550, and died about 1563. He is called, by Walpole, the father of English miniature painting. Very little of his work has, however, been certainly identified.[3] He was also an architect, and the author of *The First and Chief Groundes oj Architecture* (1563). Nicholas Hilliard (1547-1619), the eldest son of an Exeter goldsmith, is usually regarded as the first important English miniature painter. He was goldsmith, carver, and limner to Queen Elizabeth and engraved her second Great Seal in 1586. He executed miniatures of his chief Elizabethan and Jacobean contemporaries. He lived most if not all of his life in London, but maintained a connection with his native city, for his father (who died in 1594) left him his lands in the parish of St. Pancras there, and the patronage of the church. Hilliard had done a portrait of himself at the age of thirteen, at a date (*c.* 1560) which overlaps with John Shute's life. One wonders if Shute could have been his earliest teacher.

The next two painters—James and William Gandy—are also Exeter-born. James Gandy (1619-89), member of an old Exeter family after whom Gandy Street is named, was a portrait painter, and a pupil of Vandyck.   He copied many of Vandyck's portraits for the Duke of

Ormonde. Most of his paintings are therefore to be found in Ireland, where he died, though at the end of the 18th century many remained in Exeter and its neighbourhood.[1] Reynolds admired Gandy's work, and when passing through Exeter never missed an opportunity of visiting the Hall of the Vicars Choral to see Gandy's portrait of Tobias Langdon. The picture is now lost, and the Hall destroyed in an air-raid.

William Gandy (d. 1729), son of James, was an itinerant portrait painter. Most of his pictures are to be found in the west of England. Though many are worthless, for Gandy was careless of his reputation as a painter, his best work was good enough to be much admired by Reynolds and Northcote. One of his best portraits (that of John Patch, sen.) may be seen at the Royal Devon and Exeter Hospital.

With Thomas Hudson (1701-79) we reach the first of the apostolic succession of Devonshire painters which extends down to Sir Charles Eastlake (d. 1865). Hudson (whose exact birthplace is not known) was the fashionable portrait painter in London until Reynolds displaced him. He had been Reynolds's master for two years (1741-3). A considerable number of Hudson's portraits remain in Devon. There is a series by him of local worthies in the Guildhall at Barnstaple;[2] a few in the Exeter Guildhall and in the boardroom of the Royal Devon and Exeter Hospital; one or two in the public art galleries, and some at Powderham Castle. It is probable that a number of others are to be found scattered among various country houses in Devon.

The facts of Sir Joshua Reynolds's career are too well known to require more than the briefest reference. He was born at Plympton in 1723, where he made his famous drawing of the old Grammar School. This persuaded his father to allow him to study art instead of medicine. For two years he studied under Hudson. He then returned to Devon and set up as a portrait painter at Plymouth Dock, where the naval officers and their wives were his subjects. There he met and worked for Lord Mount Edgecumbe, who recommended him to Captain Augustus Keppel (later Lord Keppel). Keppel took him to Italy for three years, during which Reynolds studied at all the great cities. Returning in 1752 he stayed for a few months in Devon, and then set up as a portrait painter in St. Martin's Lane, London. From then onwards his fame increased. He became the first President of the Royal Academy in 1768, was knighted in the following year, and was chosen mayor of Plympton in 1773—an honour which, so he told George III, pleased him more than any other which had come his way. Reynolds presented a portrait of himself to the corporation of Plympton as a mark of his esteem for his native place, but that poverty-stricken body was obliged to sell it about 1832 when the withdrawal of Lord Mount Edgecumbe's patronage shattered their already inadequate finances. This portrait is now at Orchard Wyndham in Somerset. The Plymouth Art Gallery contains several examples of his work, chiefly of the early period.

What is probably the finest collection of Reynolds portraits in Devon is, however, housed at Saltram, the seat of the Earl of Morley. Reynolds was very friendly with the Parkers from early days. It is said that Lady Catherine Parker presented Samuel Reynolds's children with the first pencil they ever possessed. No gift can have borne a richer fruit, for some of Reynolds's finest portraits—of the Parker family—hang here. Among the other portraits are those of Sir Thomas Acland and Sir John Chichester.[1] Reynolds was a frequent visitor at Saltram. He was here with Dr. Johnson in 1762, and his diary for 1770 refers to hunting and shooting here. In London he often dined with John Parker the younger (who succeeded to Saltram in 1768) and advised him about the purchase of Italian and other old masters.

One of Reynolds's most pleasant traits was his kindness to other Devon painters. Among these was James Northcote (1746-1831), the son of a Plymouth watchmaker who was apprenticed to his father's trade. He devoted all his spare time to drawing, made a little money from portraits, and found his way to London and the great Sir Joshua's studio in 1771. He returned to Plymouth four years later and there painted portraits. From 1777 to 1780 he travelled in Italy, then returned to Plymouth for a time, and thence moved soon to London where he painted a great number of portraits and amassed a fortune. He was one of the greatest characters of his day, as Hazlitt's *Conversations of Northcote* abundantly reveals. A number of Devon country houses contain portraits by him. The Exeter Art Gallery has one of his huge historical paintings, illustrating *A Scene from Shakespeare's Richard II.*

Northcote had followed Reynolds to London. In turn, Benjamin Robert Haydon (1786-1846), the son of a Plymouth bookseller, sought out James Northcote when he came to London in 1804, as a student at the Royal Academy. In vain did Northcote try to discourage Haydon from pursuing his ambition to be an historical painter. Haydon embarked upon the sad and stormy life revealed to us in his *Autobiography,* that led inevitably to his suicide in 1846, an embittered and a disappointed man. His *Raising of Lazarus* is now in the National Gallery, his *Agony in the Garden* at the Victoria and Albert Museum; and in the Tate Gallery is the remarkable *Punch and Judy* (1829). The Exeter Art Gallery has his *Curtius Plunging into the Gulf.* In the Plymouth Gallery is a good portrait of Haydon by William Nicholson (1781-1844).

Among Haydon's pupils were Charles Eastlake, the Landseers, and Thomas Bewick. Of these, only Eastlake (1793-1865) was a Devonian, and with him the long unbroken succession of Plymouth painters is ended. Eastlake studied at the Royal Academy and under Haydon, and returned to Plymouth to paint portraits. He made his name in 1815 when the *Bellerophon*, with Napoleon on board, put in at Plymouth. Hundreds of boats swarmed around the ship. Napoleon, gratified by the popular interest, showed himself freely on deck and in the gangway. Eastlake sketched " this Fascinating Monster," as the *Western Luminary* called him, from a boat, Napoleon posing for him and even sending parts of his uniform ashore so that every detail might be correct. The outcome was the dramatic picture of the brooding emperor that is known to every school-child. With the proceeds of this successful picture, Eastlake visited Italy and devoted himself to landscape painting. He later became President of the Royal Academy (1850-65) and the Director of the National Gallery (1855), which owes much to his wise taste and judgment.

Somewhat older than Eastlake was Samuel Prout (1783-1852), a fellow Plymothian who had attended Plymouth Grammar School while Haydon was a pupil there. Prout's father was a bookseller, like Haydon's. The Plymouth directory of 1823 gives him as " S. Prout, bookseller and tea dealer, Frankfort Street," an odd combination. The younger Prout became a topographical artist, began to exhibit scenes in the south-western counties in 1805, and contributed to *Beauties of England and Wales*, 1803-13. Some of his work will also be found in *The Antiquarian and Topographical Cabinet*. In 1818 he began the series of paintings of continental streets which made his name. Ruskin greatly admired Prout's work, but (as some think) overpraised it. The Plymouth Art Gallery has a small collection of Prout's water-colours, and some by Nicholas Condy the elder (1799-1851), who was born near Plymouth. His son Nicholas (1816-51), also a marine painter, died young and hastened thereby his father's death. One of the elder Condy's finest works was painted for Lord Mount Edgecumbe and hangs at Cotehele: *The Old Hall at Cotehele on a Rent Day.*

The pursuit of the Plymouth painters has caused us to pass by a number of earlier Devon painters. Among these were Francis Hayman (1708-76), born at Exeter, and chiefly known for his ornamental paintings at Vauxhall; Richard Cosway (1740-1821), born at Tiverton, where his father was master of Blundell's School, and notable as one of the best miniaturists of the 18th century; and Ozias Humphry (1742-1810), born at Honiton and one of several young Devonian painters in whom Reynolds took an interest. He was a painter of miniature and crayon portraits. A little later we have John Downman (*c.* 1750-1824),* whose charming miniature portraits may be found in several of the country houses of Devon. He was often in the West Country, visited Plymouth in 1806,

*Downman's birthplace is often given as Ruabon, but there can be little doubt that he was a Devonian. I have, however, sought his baptismal entry in vain so far. He drew numerous portraits of the Downman family of Exeter. The best study of Downman is by Dr. G. C. Williamson, *John Downman, A.R.A.* (1907).

and in 1807-8 set up at Exeter. He also painted some landscapes, which are little known.

Yet another miniature, landscape, and portrait painter was James Leakey (1775-1865), who was born at Exeter and lived there all his life excepting a few years spent professionally in London, where he knew Lawrence, Constable, Wilkie, and others. Francis Towne (d. 1816) lived much of his life in Exeter. Downman, who painted a portrait of him, described him as " Landscape painter of Exeter." His work remained unknown for nearly a century, until it was re-discovered by Mr. Paul Oppé. John White Abbott (1763-1851), an Exeter surgeon, was a pupil of Towne. He exhibited many times at the Royal Academy between 1793 and 1822, where his work was much admired by contemporaries like Ozias Humphry, but he never gave up his surgeon's practice to become a professional artist. He painted a good deal of Devon landscape, his work being of a more pastoral nature than Towne's. Many of his paintings remain in the possession of his great-great-grandson. A portrait of him was done by James Leakey.

John Gendall (1790-1865), also of Exeter, painted Devonshire scenery. He was employed in his early days by R. Ackermann and later exhibited many of his landscapes at the Royal Academy. His work was highly esteemed by the great Turner. There is a whole host of lesser, but still notable, landscape painters—T. H. Williams, J. W. Upham, A. B. Johns, Francis Stevens, William Traies, P. H. Rogers, F. R. Lee, Thomas Luny,* William Payne, J. S. Prout, and yet others. Of these, William Traies (1789-1872) was a delightful painter. His *Lime Kilns near Topsham* (in the Exeter Art Gallery) is especially pleasing. Several of his oil paintings and water-colours may be seen in the Exeter and Plymouth galleries. Traies was born at Crediton but lived most of his life in Exeter, in Holloway Street. The Exeter directory of 1828 lists a number of " Artists " living in the city. Among them we find the names of John Gendall, James Leakey, William Traies, and T. H. Williams, a remarkable and distinguished little group. It also included John White Abbott, the surgeon, who is not named among the " artists " as such, but who was still actively painting. Exeter had as many notable painters as Plymouth by this date. It is curious that neither town, with all this wealth of high talent, produced a school comparable with the Norwich School.

It only remains to add that three of England's greatest landscape painters did some of their work in Devon. Richard Wilson (1714-82) visited Okehampton on 1 August 1771 and painted a magnificent picture of the castle which now hangs in the Birmingham Art Gallery. This is

*Luny was probably born in London in 1759, but settled down at Teignmouth about 1810 and died there in 1837. The majority of his works (marine scenes) were painted in Devon, and apparently still remain there. See DA **18** (1886), 442-9, and **19** (1887), 107-90.

probably the painting of Okehampton Castle which is recorded as having been exhibited at the Academy of 1774, and which was at Powderham Castle in 1829.[1] Wilson also painted the waterfall at Lydford during this visit to Devon, a picture which was at Powderham for a time.

Thomas Girtin (1775-1802), the founder of modern water-colour painting, was in south Devon in 1800, when he painted the beautiful and well-known *Rainbow over the Exe* from a point just north of Powderham church. A dozen of his Devon water-colours are known, and three pencil drawings, dated from 1798 to 1801, so that he must have paid more than one visit to the county.[2]

J. M. W. Turner (1775-1851), whose father was born at South Molton, and whose grandfather was a saddler there, toured the south-western counties in the summer of 1811 in search of material to illustrate Cooke's *Picturesque Views of the Southern Coast of England*, and made many hundreds of drawings. He called on an uncle, Price Turner, who was a saddler at Exeter, and while staying at the Castle Inn at Barnstaple called on another uncle, John Turner, who was Master of the Poor House there.[3] In the Academy of 1812 he exhibited three Devon paintings—the river Plym, Teignmouth, and Ivy Bridge Mill. Ten years later he exhibited paintings of Ilfracombe, Tor Bay from Brixham, Dartmouth and Teignmouth. He exhibited a number of Devon scenes in 1833 also. His well-known *Rain, Steam, and Speed*, exhibited in 1844, is often said to have been inspired by the old South Devon Railway between Dawlish and Teignmouth. But the dates do not fit: this railway was not opened until 1846. It seems clear from the story told by Mrs. John Simon in a letter to Ruskin that it was inspired by a journey one stormy June night in 1843 which ended in " one of the loveliest June mornings that ever visited the earth " as the train neared London. The scene is somewhere between Bristol and London, and very probably near the Wharncliffe viaduct at Hanwell, not far from Paddington, so far as Turner had any precise landscape in mind.[4]

An artist whose work remains unexplored—P. W. Tomkins (1759-1820)—worked largely in Devon and Cornwall, and painted country houses.[5] One must also mention, if only in passing, the work of F. C. Lewis (1779-1856), one of the earliest discoverers of the scenery of Dartmoor, who published his *Scenery of the River Dart* in 1821. He published several volumes of plates illustrating the scenery of Devonshire rivers during the next twenty years or so. In the Sutherland Collection at the Ashmolean Museum in Oxford is a number of West Country drawings by George Shepherd, about whom very little is known. These drawings were done in the years 1819-25, and a list of them has been given by Professor Jack Simmons in *Devon and Cornwall Notes and Queries* (vol. 24, part 6) for April 1951. Shepherd's work is of more artistic merit than that of most topographical artists, and is of particular value to the student of local history for it is signed and dated, and is drawn with a care for accurate detail. Perhaps one should mention in this connection also the work of William Spreat, who was an Exeter bookseller. His *Picturesque Sketches of the Churches of Devonshire* were published in a number of parts by himself at 263 High Street, Exeter, and by Ackermann in London, in 1842. They are careful, painstaking drawings of a great number of country churches before they underwent " restoration," and as such are a valuable historical record, especially of interiors. Spreat also made a number of drawings of Exeter and other Devonshire places which, though of little artistic merit, are charming period pieces of about 1850 and are valuable for their careful topographical detail. He published *The River Scenery of Devon* in 1844, a set of eight prints of scenes on the Teign and its tributaries.*

MUSIC AND ARCHITECTURE

The contribution of Devonians to the arts of music and architecture is slight. Matthew Locke (*c.* 1630-77), born at Exeter, composed the music for Davenport's *Siege of Rhodes*, and for *Macbeth* and *The Tempest*, though that for *Macbeth* is sometimes attributed to Purcell. Mr. Blom finds Locke's music " aggressively modern."

Samuel Sebastian Wesley (1810-76), a grandson of Charles Wesley, is the most notable of all Devon musicians. He was born at Exeter and returned to Exeter Cathedral as organist from 1835 to 1841. He was a difficult man: it was said of him that he " disliked deans, scorned succentors, and persecuted precentors." Among his works are *The European Psalmist, Twelve Anthems and Responses*, and various well-known settings. He is in the first rank as a composer of English Church music. William Jackson (1730-1803) was a predecessor of Wesley as cathedral organist. He was the most popular composer of his day. His songs " Love in thine eyes for ever strays " and " Time hath not thinned my flowing locks " were warbled in every drawing-room, while his " Te Deum in F " reverberated through every cathedral in England. He also composed operas and madrigals, painted Devon landscapes, and published a volume of essays. Among his friends were Sheridan, Samuel Rogers, Gainsborough, Reynolds, and Goldsmith. In London he was, indeed, sufficiently well known to be called " Jackson of Exeter."

The Devonian contribution to architecture is meagre. John Foulston (1772-1842), whose work at Plymouth, Stonehouse, and Devonport has already been referred to, was not Devon-born, but he came to Plymouth as a young man and the whole of his professional life was spent there. Very little is known about him, a sad deficiency in our knowledge, for he

*He intended to deal with the other rivers of Devon, but no further prints appear to have been published.

gave a stamp to the architecture of Plymouth that lasted a hundred years
and made it one of the most good-looking towns in the provinces. Charles
Fowler (1800-67) is the only Devon-born architect of any stature. He
built Covent Garden Market (1830) in London; the Lower Market
(1835-36) and the Higher Market (1838), both at Exeter, and a few
churches in Devon (e.g. St. Paul's, Honiton). His Exeter buildings were
among the finest of the public buildings of the city. The Lower Market
was mostly destroyed in the air-raid of May 1942, but the Higher Market
remains, a noble building in the Greek style. It has been threatened with
demolition by the civic authorities—just as the civic authorities of
Plymouth blindly destroyed some of Foulston's magnificent public
buildings—but it should be preserved as a part of the new Exeter that is
now rising from its ashes.

One other great Devonian remains to be noticed briefly, and that is
Nicholas Stone (1586-1647), who was born the son of a stone-mason at
Woodbury, but who made his name entirely outside his native county.
He was, of course, chiefly notable for his tombs and sepulchral monuments,
and was famous in his day; but there is not in Devon, so far as we know,
a single example of his craftsmanship.

CHAPTER XVI

THE COUNTY TO-DAY

POPULATION

FROM 1801 to 1831 Devon remained the fourth largest among the English counties in numbers of people. There had been a time in the Elizabethan period when she stood second only to Yorkshire. Then throughout the 19th century she sank slowly down the list, and was ninth in 1881. In 1901 she was less than half as densely peopled as England and Wales as a whole. Now, in 1951, Devon is fifteenth among the English counties in order of population, with a total of 798,283 people,[1] and an average density of 304 persons per square mile. The average density for England and Wales is 750. During the past twenty years Devon's population has increased at only two-thirds of the rate for the country as a whole.

For the past half century the county has been growing progressively more urban. About fifty-seven people in every hundred now live in towns of 10,000 or more. Just over forty-five Devonians in every hundred live in the large urban agglomerations of Plymouth, Exeter, and Torquay-Paignton. Plymouth has, indeed, shrunk as a result of her heavy battering during the war and has nearly 12,000 fewer people than on the eve of the Second World War.[2] Exeter has added 5,000–6,000 people in the same period, despite extensive war destruction. Torquay and Paignton, though they retain very distinct characteristics of their own, and separate local government, have become a single town in effect. Since 1931 they have added nearly 14,000 people to their numbers, the Paignton end growing nearly three times as fast as the more sedate Torquay. The two together make up a seaside town of almost 80,000 people, and must eventually become a unified county borough despite the present differences. Together they form a town slightly larger than the capital city of Exeter, and they bear witness to what has become the largest and most important industry in Devon—the " holiday industry."

The ever-growing importance of this industry is brought out, though less strikingly, elsewhere in the county, and particularly along the more favoured (because warmer and less windy) south coast. Nearly all the largest increases of population since 1931 are to be found along this coast. Dawlish, indeed, has grown even more quickly than Paignton (by nearly forty per cent). Budleigh Salterton, Seaton, Sidmouth, and Exmouth all show large increases.

Of the inland towns, Honiton shows the largest increase of any town in Devon (over fifty-three per cent), mainly the result of a boundary change. Totnes shows the second largest increase among the inland towns (over twenty-two per cent). Ever since Restoration days, as we have seen, it has attracted a " residential " population, and it continues to do so as bus facilities improve in the surrounding countryside.

On the other hand, Dartmouth shows the largest fall of any town in Devon. It has lost nearly 900 people in the past twenty years—an eighth of its population—and it had been declining all through the 1920s also. Dartmouth presents the most serious urban problem in Devon. Its fishing industry went long ago, and unlike St. Ives in Cornwall it had no beaches to attract holiday-makers in compensation. It is difficult to get into and out of it: communications are bad: there is no bridge over the Dart below Totnes. The town is crowded on to a narrow site with precipitous hills limiting any further expansion; it attracts no new industries for these and other reasons. It " lives on the Naval College," on the yachting in the river and some holiday fishing, and on a small shipbuilding industry. It is sad to see the heart being eaten out of this ancient and beautiful seaport.

North Devon was spoken of in 1939 as " a land of static or decaying towns in an abandoned countryside." The census of 1951 shows that this decay has been to a large degree arrested. Barnstaple and Bideford have grown—not much, but at about the same pace as the county as a whole— and the Barnstaple rural district, which includes all the country east and north of the town, has increased considerably (twenty-seven per cent). This growth is mainly concentrated in the coastal and suburban parishes. Away from the sea, in the deep country where the main occupation is still farming, and poor communications prevent the development of the holiday industry except for travellers in search of peace and solitude, the level of population is either stagnant or still falling. The rate of fall tends to increase as one goes inland. Thus the Bideford rural district, which is partly coastal, shows a very small increase, but behind it the rural districts of Torrington, Holsworthy, and Broadwoodwidger, forming a solid block in west Devon, fell in numbers between 1931 and 1951 by nearly seven per cent. The town of Torrington itself continued to decline: the only town in north Devon not to increase its numbers. It presents much the same problem, though not so acutely, as Dartmouth in the south.

The Okehampton and Crediton rural districts also show a slight fall, and that of South Molton a considerable fall (five and a half per cent). The declining rural areas all lie west of the Exe and north of Dartmoor, in the Culm Measures country. Except for the coastal fringe around Barnstaple Bay this is everywhere a region of falling or stagnant population. On the other hand, the rural areas of east and south Devon continue to increase their numbers. This is mainly due to the increase of the " residential " population near the towns—the hinterlands of Plymouth, Exeter, Totnes, and Newton Abbot. This " retired " class is drawn by the softer climate of the southern half of Devon, and its better communications with the towns. North and west Devon are bleaker, towns and even villages are fewer, communications are poor. In the general picture of the county it is the holiday districts that are increasing in numbers, and the deep farming country that is dwindling all the time.

THE BIG HOUSE AND THE SQUIRE

The social revolution in the Devonshire countryside takes much the same form as elsewhere in rural England. The atmosphere of slow decay about the country houses is perhaps a little more noticeable, for so much of Devonshire society centred around the squire, and there are so many of these houses. What has happened to the big houses of a hundred years ago? If we look back to the largest houses and estates of 1850 and see how they fare to-day, what sort of picture do we get? The enormous Rolle estate is merged with that of Lord Clinton (who is now probably the largest landowner in Devon), and the Rolles' house of Stevenstone is an ugly ruin in a naked and devastated park. The Courtenays still keep up Powderham, but every few years see more sales of their land. The Aclands live in a corner of Killerton, and have given a great part of their estate to the National Trust. Most of Killerton now serves as a workers' holiday centre.

The earls and dukes of Bedford never had a mansion in Devon. They had a town house in Exeter (gone long ago) and a " cottage " at Endsleigh, deep in a park of some 3,400 acres above the wooded Tamar valley, which is still used by the family for fishing holidays.

The Bampfyldes' house at Poltimore is now a private hospital. The Earls of Portsmouth have left Eggesford (only built in 1832) to fall into ruin; the Carews have abandoned Haccombe in recent years; the Lopes (Lord Roborough) have gone from Maristow, which is now a home for aged clergy. Tawstock, once the home of the Earls of Bath, is a school. Only three great houses are still occupied by their old owners—Powderham, Saltram, and Castle Hill. This is the fate, then, of the ten largest houses and estates of 1850.

Of the squires' houses, the same melancholy tale can be told. Only two or three are occupied by ancient families: the Fulfords continue at Great Fulford, the Cruwys at Cruwys Morchard. But Kelly is a hotel, and so, too, is Portledge, the home of the Coffins since the 12th century. Bradfield, home of the Walronds since the time of John, is a public institution. Dartington and Tapeley are schools. The mighty tribe of Chichester, who once ramified over North Devon in ten or a dozen branches, are now narrowed down to Hall, in Bishop's Tawton.

But what atmosphere there is in these old houses where they are still lived in! The past is alive in every corner of them, in every piece of furniture, every turn in the stairs and every window-seat. They are

> Thronged with quiet, inoffensive ghosts,
> Impalpable impressions on the air—
> A sense of something moving to and fro.

There is the small collection of paintings up the staircase, mostly of the eighteenth century, pedestrian portraits of Georgian squires with hand tucked in ample, silken waistcoat, and their pudding-faced ladies; generally one attributed hesitantly and modestly to Gainsborough, but most of them, one suspects, done by painters like William Gandy on an off day.

In the library, looking out over the weed-enamelled drive and a park still timbered with walnut and oak and beech, the Victorian bookshelves rise to the ceiling and hold copies of Ovid and Horace used at Oxford by Georgian ancestors: dark, calf-bound, the faint, spidery brown hand-writing. On the bottom shelves is an early edition of the *Encyclopaedia Britannica* (an edition published before the Age of Steam but still occasionally useful). Somewhere nearer at hand is an old edition of Burn's *Justice of the Peace and Parish Officer*, perhaps an early run of the *Railway Magazine*, and row upon row of unreadable sermons, old botany books, bird books, fishing books, parish histories, the proceedings of the local antiquarian society of forty years ago, and a whole shelf on gardening. Papers cascade out of writing-desks as old as the room; dogs snuffle quietly in Queen Anne wing-chairs; photographs of cricket elevens may be observed in obscure corners, close to the stuffed corncrake, of Harrow, Winchester, and Eton long ago.

In the billiard-room, still occasionally used, are the nondescript paintings seconded to its walls about the year 1870 and since forgotten, and the assegais sent home from the Zulu wars by some great-uncle. And outside is the high-walled garden, warm in the sun, with its deep black earth spade-turned century after century; and the turret over the hall roof, with its silent bell. And just beyond the garden, among the tree-tops, one sees the pinnacles of the parish church, and one hears the clock striking the hours, day after day, season after season, for ever and ever, as they once thought. Here, where all is quiet, the lunacy of the outside world, the fate that has overtaken it, is an insoluble mystery. One ruminates over it for a few moments after the nine o'clock news, heard religiously each evening in the library on an antique and sizzling battery set. With relief the squire turns to the local newspaper, produced in the market town a dozen miles away, and reads the more intelligible and interesting news about the doings of his own countryside.*

In the parish church, the squire still sits in his own pew, with perhaps only three or four other people in the Sunday morning congregation. The service is simple and Protestant, in accord with the decent box-pews and the neat pulpit. In the chancel, or above the family pew, are the marble and brass memorials to his more recent ancestors—soldiers nearly all of them—commemorating every obscure war that Britain fought during the 19th century on far-away frontiers. Saddest of all are the memorials of the First World War.

The year 1914 marked the end of an age, the end of the country house, and the squire, and the old village life. So many of the sons and heirs of the old estates, following the traditions of their families, led those futile, hopeless attacks through the mud of northern France and Flanders, and fell there. One often reflects, looking at these plain, unassuming tablets on the chancel wall, or in some family chapel in the now deserted aisle, that the year 1916 above all gave the real death-blow to the country houses: when, on that terrible river the Somme, on that far-away July morning with the larks singing above the battlefield, so many young officers perished, leading their men. The Somme is commemorated on English chancel walls everywhere; and on the village greens, too, one reads the names of the men who followed, and perished likewise in that distant summer. At Upton Pyne, in the empty sunlight, where hardly a young man is to be seen to-day, the cross outside the churchyard gate records the names of sixteen men killed from this small parish alone. Hardly a family escaped. And so it was, to a greater or less degree, in every village. That year, and the two years that followed, did much to put an end to the traditional village life, the counterpart to the life at the great house, when the young men who would have carried on the trades and traditions of their fathers, and would have been the fathers of the next generation, failed to return. And now the tablets are going up for yet another war, mercifully with far fewer names on them, but often the same family names as those of the earlier years.

Nearly all the squires have gone. Even if the family has not died out, it has vacated the big house and usually left the parish to live elsewhere.

*The above description is a composite one. No particular house is intended, but every detail is authentic.

No one has taken the place of the squire. The smaller houses—the houses of the " squireens"—fall empty, too. Their old owners go, but these houses are quickly filled by retired military and naval officers (mostly the former) who buy them shorn of most of their land and treat them sympathetically. Occasionally one sees unfortunate and tasteless " modernisation," but it is rare. One can generally assume that wherever one sees a good Georgian or older house in a little paddock it is occupied by a colonel or a brigadier. The Devonshire countryside is thick with army men, who do not, however, and cannot, take the place of the squire. Here the vacuum remains.

VILLAGE AND PARISH

The departure of the squire is only the most recent of several important social changes. The majority of Devonshire villages have been falling in numbers ever since the 1850s, some for twenty years before that. Thorverton had 1,511 people in 1851, now (1949) it has 751. Cheriton Fitzpaine had 1,207 in 1851; now only 509. North Lew, too, has halved in numbers in a hundred years; Chittlehampton has more than halved; Culmstock has halved between 1831 and 1931. In the 16th century, we found the rural parish of Newton St. Cyres paying more tax than Bideford or South Molton,[1] but for all its ancient fertility it, too, halved in population between 1831 and 1931, falling from 1,317 to 670 people. It is much the same picture whether one looks at the unrewarding yellow-clay country of west Devon, or the village of the fertile " red-land " in east Devon. The only villages that do not show a great fall in population to-day are those that lie near towns, especially the holiday towns, for which they have become dormitories, or villages which have attracted large institutions of one sort or another, or where a large road-metal quarry has been opened up.

Where farming is still the sole or principal occupation, however, the village is a dwindling community. It would not be true to say of the larger villages that they are dead, but certainly they are only half as alive as they were two and three generations ago. The mere fall in numbers of people has had a serious effect on the range of social activities: with only half as many people as in mid-Victorian days, there are not enough to organise and to support the variety of village clubs and institutions there used to be. Then, too, the fall in numbers is even more marked among the younger men and women, many of whom now travel out of the village by bus to their work in a neighbouring town, and have not the same interest in their native place that their fathers and grandfathers had.

The former village community, for such it was in a way we can only dimly apprehend to-day from the talk of old men and women, is breaking up—has broken up in so many places—because there is no central figure to give it stability and continuous leadership. There is a world of difference between the parishes where the squire is still an active figure at the big house, and the parishes which have no squire; and country people know it, whatever town-born theorists brought up on false history may think, whatever fantastic rubbish they may talk about " despotism." Even if it sometimes was " despotism "—and the Victorian squire or his wife was sometimes unfitted to rule any community—it is better to have a personal despotism one knows of, and can attack, than an official many-headed despotism which can never be identified and brought out into the light of day. But there will always be an impassable gulf between the town-mind and the country-mind on this, as on other questions, and we must leave it there.

The stability of the village and parish community also derived in a great degree from the parson. Here, too, there have been changes making for the dissolution of the old order, principally two: the disappearance of the older type of parson with private means, and the union of two or three parishes under one man.

A large proportion of Devonshire livings were—and are—poor. A considerable number of small parishes came into being in Devon in early medieval times to link together scattered hamlets and farmsteads that had grown up through the colonisation of the wastelands far from the mother village. Most of these parishes were poorly endowed and were served by underpaid chaplains or by pluralist rectors. The rectories of Hittisleigh and Hollacombe are typical of this kind of late-colonised parish; their net incomes to-day are only £95 and £96 a year respectively.

In the 19th century the problem of the poor benefice was often solved by well-connected parsons with private means. Often, of course, they filled the fat livings, but they also filled a great number of the poorest benefices, and they stayed. That is the important point: they stayed till they died, for forty, fifty, and sixty years, and so gave a leadership and a personal focus to the parish (especially where there was no squire) which we can hardly begin to comprehend in these restless days. The passing of the old rector, after a rule of forty to fifty years in one place, was as shattering an event to the late Victorian village as the death of Queen Victoria was to the whole Empire. He had baptised nearly everybody in the village, married nearly all of them, watched them grow up and multiply through two whole generations or more, committed so many of them to the earth again, that he was the father—and a rather austere and unpopular father at times—of the whole community. With all his faults, and they might be many, he was a powerful cement for the parish community, and when he died something irreplaceable went with him.

Few people bother to read the rather tarnished brass tablet to the Victorian and Edwardian parson (" rector of this parish for forty-three years "): it is the most commonplace object in the restored and forbidding chancel, without a gleam of beauty in or near it. But what a vanished world it conjures up to those who have a sense of the past! Such parsons are now almost a vanished race—not quite—and are replaced by men of a different type. It would be impertinent to say whether these are better or worse spiritual guides than their predecessors, even if one could: they are simply different. Without private means they cannot remain in these livings for long, but must seek a more rewarding benefice after a few years. See how, on any list of rectors or vicars hung up in the parish church, the length of tenure tends to fall rapidly in the 20th century. And so they cannot acquire the authority that only the decades can give, and, with the best will in the world, can rarely become that cement binding the parish society together. It is not entirely the change of man: the Church itself has lost the authority it once had. So few people go near it nowadays.

The union of benefices, or the holding of benefices in plurality, is the inevitable result of the social and religious changes of the past two generations. A few such unions were made long ago (e.g. Satterleigh and Warkleigh), but most are recent. At the present day[1] some 185 country parishes are held in plurality. There are five groups of three, where the parishes are particularly small (e.g. Farway, Northleigh and Southleigh), and about eighty-five pairs of parishes. In effect, this means that nearly one-half of the rural parishes of Devon are held in plurality. The social effects of this arrangement upon the parishes which have no parson living among them need no elaboration. It is not, of course, anyone's fault: it is our ancient friend, the vicious circle. As the population of the parish falls, and as church-going falls faster still, the joining of two parishes becomes inevitable for reasons both of money and work. But this solution simply helps to accelerate the processes of decline, and raises fresh problems such as that of the dilapidated church which no one can afford to put into decent order again. The Victorians had the money to " restore " their parish churches, often too much to produce pleasing results, but with the squire gone and parishioners dwindling, there is no one to-day who can pay.

One must not, however, paint too dark a picture. Much still depends on the individual parson and, above all, on his parishioners. As one goes around the county, even in the remotest parts, one never knows, on opening yet another church door, what loving care may not be revealed in the most unexpected places. Hittisleigh, for example, the poorest rectory in Devon and held in plurality with Colebrooke, is a delightful well-cared-for country church; and so is Honeychurch, held in plurality with Sampford Courtenay; and there are scores of others that one looks back upon with pleasure, all over Devon, in poor country and rich country alike. There have been worse times than these, and the Church has lived through them.

Nor have the nonconformist churches escaped the poverty, economic and spiritual, of our times. They say that chapel-going has fallen off to a greater extent than church-going: it is hard to prove one way or the other. The experience of the Congregationalists, one of the largest of the nonconformist churches in Devon, is probably typical of them all. Back in 1898, there were 120 Congregational churches, with 5,513 members, and there were 11,346 Sunday school scholars under 1,148 teachers. In 1951, there were still 115 churches, with 5,302 members, but the new generation had fallen away. There were only half as many teachers in the Sunday schools (616) and not many more than one-third the number of scholars (4,460).[1] Very few Congregationalist churches have closed down during the past fifty years, any more than the Anglican churches have closed their doors, but the numbers interested in attending them have fallen everywhere.

The Roman Catholic Church, on the other hand, makes headway, though slowly. Here, too, reliable statistics are hard to find. The Roman Catholic diocese of Plymouth, created in 1850, comprises the counties of Dorset, Devon and Cornwall, and its estimated Catholic population is given as 33,275.[2] There are sixty-two Roman Catholic churches in Devon, and ten other places where mass is offered. The revival of the religious orders in Devon has also been remarkable. There are now five orders of men, with nine houses between them, and twenty-three orders of women with thirty-three houses. Of these houses, Buckfast (men) and Syon (women) are the most important. The Benedictine abbey of Buckfast, dissolved in 1539, was revived on its original site in 1902, when the first abbot of Buckfast since the Reformation was elected. Syon, a community of Bridgettine nuns, settled at Marley (in Rattery parish) in 1925. Though on a new site (the old Syon abbey was in Middlesex), this is the only English community of nuns with an unbroken continuity since pre-Reformation days.

FARMS AND FARMING

Four hundred years ago the ownership of large acreages of land passed from the monasteries to the landed gentry. Now the gentry are being dispossessed in turn by the State. Who are the new inheritors? They are the National Trust, the Oxford and Cambridge colleges, the Ecclesiastical Commissioners, and the Co-operative Societies. The Plymouth Co-operative Society owns and occupies over 3,000 acres in Devon, and is the largest farmer in the county.

There is another change about which it is more difficult to get accurate information. As the old estates are broken up, the number of owner-occupiers increases each year. In 1941-43 it was reckoned that forty-two farmers in every hundred in Devon were owner-occupiers, as against one in every three in England and Wales as a whole.[1] To-day, in the opinion of one expert, the owner-occupiers in Devon number about sixty in every hundred. The owner-occupier tends to be a rather smaller man on an average than the tenant-farmer, so that he may occupy, at an estimate, about one-half the total land under crops and grass. Indeed, if we had all the figures, we might well find that the ordinary farmer is the biggest single inheritor of land in the new agrarian revolution.

As to the size of farms, there is little significant change in the past two or three generations. The average Devon farm is small, round about sixty-five acres, and scarcely any bigger than it was back in the 1860s.[2] In 1944 there were 16,286 holdings, of which one in eight was less than five acres, and nearly one in three twenty acres or less. More than one-half the farms of Devon were fifty acres or less. At the other end of the scale, only one farm in a hundred exceeded 300 acres, as compared with five per hundred in England and Wales as a whole. The Devon figures are as follows:[3]

Above 1 and not exceeding 5 acres	2,005
Above 5 and not exceeding 20 acres	3,035
Above 20 and not exceeding 50 acres	3,312
Above 50 and not exceeding 100 acres	3,770
Above 100 and not exceeding 150 acres	2,111
Above 150 and not exceeding 300 acres	1,865
Above 300 and not exceeding 500 acres	169
Above 500 and not exceeding 700 acres	16
Above 700 and not exceeding 1,000 acres	2
Above 1,000 acres	1
TOTAL	16,286

On the poorer lands of the Dartmoor parishes and north-west Devon, farms are actually getting smaller. There are about 1,000 changes of occupier each year, a large proportion on the poorer lands. Here the tendency is to sell off part of the land with a cottage or so, and to keep the farmhouse and a few acres in hand, as a result of financial difficulties. On the good lands farms do not change hands so frequently, and in the main retain their identity.

There is more "improved land" in Devon to-day: that is, under crops and grass.[4] Since 1938 about 13,000 additional acres have been brought back from rough grazing. But the greatest change has been the expansion of the arable at the expense of permanent pasture. Arable is up by 131,000 acres over 1938; permanent pasture down by 118,000 acres. The difference between these figures is accounted for by the additional land brought in from rough grazing. Altogether, permanent grass covers 592,000 acres, and arable 546,000 acres (1950).

The total acreage of " improved land " to-day is about 1,138,000 acres. Rough grazings make up another 168,000 acres according to the 1950 return. This still leaves about 360,000 acres to be accounted for in the total area of the county, of which the built-up areas and roads, etc., account for a considerable part. But woodland is also very important. Devon has always been a fairly well-wooded county. In 1905 there were just under 90,000 acres in woods and plantations.[1] Two wars have devastated some of the woodlands, and the break-up of old estates has added to the toll, but there were in 1947-49 nearly 92,000 acres of private woodland in the county. Not all of this was suitable, however, for economic management. Of the area under High Forest, conifers covered about one acre in five, and broad-leaved trees nearly four in five. The oak outnumbers in acreage all the other trees put together. In addition nearly 16,000 acres have been afforested by the Forestry Commission, on which the conifers outnumber the broad-leaved trees by more than two to one. Altogether, there are well over 100,000 acres of land under woodland of one sort or another, an area greater than that of the whole of Rutland.

So far as grain crops are concerned, wheat and oats have fallen back, after the great war-time expansion, to their 1938 levels. Barley, however, is still double the 1938 acreage. The greatest increase is in mixed corn. Before the war only 8,000 acres were grown: now eight times as much. Rye is and was a negligible crop. Altogether, an additional 70,000 acres are under grain of one sort and another, an increase of 50 per cent over the pre-war acreage.

Devon was, before the war, one of the foremost livestock counties of England, with more cattle than any other English or Welsh county, and second only to Northumberland among the English counties for sheep. To-day the cattle population is up by more than 90,000 (432,000 to-day); but the sheep population has fallen by more than 20 per cent, and the pig population has fallen to well under a half of what it was. The days when every household in the village had its pig are gone: it is all too complicated and bothersome nowadays, too much " headwork " for those not used to the language of bureaucracy.

In Devon, as in all parts of England, the passing years see ever-growing encroachments by military and other Service Departments upon the available land. The total area held for various purposes by these departments now (1951) amounts to some 45,000 acres,[2] of which the greater part lies upon Dartmoor. The military have had a grip on the northern part of the Moor, near Okehampton, for the last fifty years or so, but have now extended their firing activities over a much wider area, covering 32,800 acres in the northern part, and another 5,540 acres on the south-western side, on Roborough Down and Shaugh Prior Moor. With their unfailing instinct for choosing beautiful places to wreck, they have now seized 1,680 acres on Braunton Burrows—a district of almost unique interest to the botanist and the ornithologist—and another stretch on Northam Burrows. Around Plymouth, various areas so occupied run to some 2,000 acres. Airfields cover about 2,000 acres in Devon. Mercifully there are not many large stretches of level land in Devon, and the low-flying aeroplane—the latest curse to be inflicted on suffering humanity—does not afflict Devon to anything like the extent it does Cornwall.

Against all this, Dartmoor was scheduled in 1951 as a National Park, the second area in England and Wales to be so protected. An area of 365 square miles, covering the Moor and its foothills on all sides, has been brought within the park. The battle with the military over their sixty square miles of occupied territory on the Moor remains to be fought out. Not only is Dartmoor of unique beauty as a stretch of natural landscape, but it is unequalled in southern Britain for its visible remains of human history during the past 4,000 years. The nearest comparable collection is on the western slope of the mountain mass of Merioneth in North Wales, but Dartmoor is more accessible and likely to yield the more valuable information. Already the military have done irreparable damage in the Tavy valley, and threaten to devastate the Ringmoor area, in the upper Plym valley, which embraces a range of antiquities of exceptional interest.[1]

The National Trust is one of the largest landowners in Devon. It now owns (1951) 13,746 acres of land and a number of notable buildings such as Bradley Manor, Buckland Abbey, Killerton, and the Church House at Widecombe-in-the-Moor. The greater part of the property is made up of the Killerton estate (6,210 acres), mostly given by Sir Richard Acland, and the Arlington Court estate (3,471 acres), given by Miss Rosalie Chichester. Another important property is the magnificent six-mile stretch of coast between Bolt Head and Bolt Tail (952 acres), the longest continuous coastline owned by the Trust. In north Devon, the striking headlands of Baggy Point and Morte Point are also in their hands.

THE POLITICAL SCENE

What have been the reactions of the electorate in Devon to the rapid social changes of the past few years? In the first post-war election (1945), seven of the eleven constituencies returned Conservatives, eight if we include the " National Liberal " returned for North Devon. The remaining three seats—all in Plymouth—" went Labour," following the prevailing trend in the country as a whole. Liberalism had been wiped out in Devon as a parliamentary force. In the great political choice of the inter-war years, between the two extremes of Right and Left, Devon chose to go Right rather than Left. The elections of 1950 and 1951 have shown the same tendency.

In 1950, eight Conservatives were returned, and two Labour members, both at Plymouth.* But this is not the entire story. There were nine Liberal candidates, and they polled 73,405 votes altogether, about sixteen per cent of the total poll. If we exclude Plymouth from the calculation, the Liberal vote in Devon amounted to twenty-two per cent of the whole and was second in strength only to that in Cornwall (twenty-six per cent) among the English counties. In the south-west of England as a whole (Cornwall, Devon and Plymouth), the strength of the Liberal vote was only exceeded by that of the border counties of Cumberland, West-morland and Northumberland.[1] These frontier parts of England were still the most resistant to the massive influences of the two big-party machines, still the most independent in their thinking. Liberalism was dying hard in these parts.

In the 1951 election, the Liberals of Devon—like Liberals all over Britain—were faced more than ever before by the choice between two extremes, for want of enough candidates of their own. The results showed that Devon had " gone Conservative " to a greater degree than ever before. Out of ten seats, the Conservatives took nine, and left Labour with only one (at Devonport). Plymouth was always only shakily Left. Down to the end of the First World War she had a powerful Liberal tradition, both members being Liberals from 1906 to 1918, and the Devonport end of the city maintained this tradition down to 1945.

The voting in the 1950 and 1951 elections reveals something of the most recent trends, though the historian must tread warily on such new-made ground as this:

	1950 *votes*	1951 *votes*
Conservative	236,420 (50%)	258,512 (56%)
Labour	160,200 (34%)	164,872 (36%)
Liberal	73,405 (16%)	35,834 (8%)
Total	470,025 (100%)	459,218 (100%)

The total Liberal vote, with only five candidates in 1951, instead of nine, fell by nearly 38,000: it halved. Of this missing 38,000 in 1951,

*The Plymouth constituencies were reduced in 1950 from three to two, so bringing the Devon total down to ten seats.

some 22,000 moved to the Right, fewer than 5,000 to the Left, and the other 11,000 or so wrestled indecisively with their consciences. Perhaps one cannot attach so much precision to these figures as they stand, but it looks as though the Devon Liberals, in the face of increasing pressure from the two giant millstones, moved Right rather than Left, and that Devon will—except for Plymouth at times—remain solidly Conservative.

About one voter in three in Devon votes Labour; but 60,000 out of the 165,000 Socialist votes are concentrated in one small corner of the county at Plymouth. The city is almost evenly divided between Right and Left. Here the old Liberal tradition has moved in the opposite direction to that in the rest of the county.

About one voter in every two is a Conservative. One in every six is still a Liberal, if we take the 1950 figures as more representative of the real strength of the party when it contested every seat except one.* As a whole, though, Devon is a great Conservative county and will continue— so far as the historian dare plunge into prophecy—to be so. It is only what one would expect in the light of its history, especially when one considers, too, the increasing weighting of the population by a large immigrant class of retired and elderly persons, living upon pensions and annuities, and with no mind for political adventures of any sort.

THE TOWNS

When Hooker wrote his *Synopsis Chorographical of Devon*, about the year 1600, there were thirty-eight market-towns in the county besides the city of Exeter. In the 18th century, and in Lysons's day, there were commonly reckoned to be forty.[1] The railways of the 19th century shattered many of these ancient and local markets and, combined with other changes such as the decline of local industries of all kinds, brought about the decay of many " towns " into overgrown villages.

There are to-day two cities in Devon (Exeter and Plymouth), ten municipal boroughs—what would in the past have been called " mayor-towns "—and about eighteen other places that can be called " towns," though some, like Holsworthy, are dubious cases and other places, like Topsham, with no recognised urban status, ought perhaps to be called " town." Without entering upon an inconclusive discussion, however, we may say that there are still some thirty places in Devon that are recognisably " towns." And we may also say that each of these thirty towns has a distinct individuality and a flavour of its own. Most of them are ancient, as we have seen, but even those seaside places that developed their urban character within the past century have a decided character

---

*Even in 1951, one voter in every six was a Liberal, in the five constituencies where Liberal candidates stood.

of their own: Dawlish and Exmouth are utterly different, Torquay and Paignton are different in almost every possible respect, Seaton and Sidmouth could not be more unlike each other.

The distinctive characters of the Devonshire towns are not only the result of differing histories, whether over one century or eight: they also arise from the largeness of the county and its own variety of people, topography, and climate. The county is so large that the towns do not get in each other's way: they have been free to grow in their own character. And the fundamental differences between north Devon and south Devon, and between west Devon and east Devon—which should have emerged in some degree in the course of this history—are marked enough to stamp themselves on the towns also.

Exeter, the former capital of the south-western province of England, still belongs to no one part of Devon. It is the meeting place for all four quarters of the county, but more particularly the north and east. Not only is it the seat of county and regional government, but it is the largest market in the south-west.[1] Though only one-third the size of Plymouth (rather larger since the recent war), its hinterland is slightly bigger than that of Plymouth, because of its converging network of railway and bus routes, its cafés and shops, its places of entertainment, and its " sights." Country people who travel thirty or forty miles " up to Exeter " want to see something as different as possible from their usual landscape. The Friday market at Exeter is a tremendous gathering of farmers and their wives over half the county. Cars pour into the city: the density of bus traffic on Fridays and Saturdays must be as high as anywhere in England, and it is heavy on all days of the week.

At special times, such as Christmas shopping, half the population of Devon may visit Exeter—perhaps the annual visit, the high spot of the year—or it may be for the Christmas pantomime afterwards. The heavy damage done to the shopping and entertainment area of the city by the air-raid of May 1942 diverted a great deal of Exeter's shop-trade to Newton Abbot, Tiverton and even Taunton, but with the slow re-building of the city centre all this lost trade is returning, and will return in full. Few cities in England occupy such a focal position as Exeter does, in the midst of a generally prosperous county. The city offers better-paid work to young people over a wide radius. Many travel daily from ten to fifteen miles into Exeter for their work. Even Exeter Prison has its own hinterland, though perhaps not a very effective one, for recalcitrant children as far away as west Somerset are told that " If you don't behave, you will go down the line."*

*One must not, however, exaggerate the mobility of the native population of Devon. One young woman of Cadbury, nine miles north of Exeter, had only visited the city once in ten years. When we reach the backwoods like the Holsworthy Rural District, this rarity becomes the average.

Plymouth is the Mecca for south-west Devon and south-east Cornwall, to which people travel regularly every week. On special occasions it draws people from the whole of Cornwall, an adventure which, for the older-fashioned Cornish, is known as "going up to England." Plymouth has good shops for all classes, a theatre (there is no theatre in the whole of Cornwall), large cinemas and cafés, and a professional football team. And it is fast rising from its ashes (plate 45).

Before the war, a five-shilling excursion train left Penzance whenever Plymouth Argyle were playing at home, and collected 2,500 to 3,000 Cornish people up to St. Austell. Whenever this train ran, a large multiple tailor's shop in Union Street at Plymouth had 200 additional orders for men's suits. Some of the cheaper pre-war excursion trains, by which one could reach Exeter or Plymouth for sixpence or ninepence, and which were much used by the thriftiest of the country people, were known as "The Scotch Express."

Plymouth and Exeter rarely come into contact, except when the two professional football teams meet at Christmas. Only then do the two cities become aware of each other's existence. They are $1\frac{1}{2}$ hours apart by train or car, $2\frac{1}{2}$ hours by bus, and their shopping and entertainment hinterlands are separated by the "buffer-town" of Newton Abbot. Their characters and interests are so radically different that there is no sense of rivalry or competition between them. Plymouth and Exeter people do not waste time arguing about the merits of their respective cities, for there are no points of comparison except the irrelevant one of size.

Newton Abbot has grown remarkably in recent years. It is now a lively town of some 16,000 people—the same size as Barnstaple—and is indeed sometimes called "a second Exeter." Like Exeter, it is a centre of rail and bus routes, and a good meeting place for friends with its shops, cafés and markets. The shops are cheap and good, specialising in country requirements like strong shoes, and when Exeter's trade dwindled after 1942 Newton Abbot took most of it. Its shopping streets are level, an important consideration for Devon country people who climb enough hills at home and like to give their legs a rest on the day off in town. Okehampton and Ilfracombe suffer as shopping centres for country people because their railway stations are at the top of a long hill. Among Barnstaple's many merits, its flat topography appeals to country customers sauntering from one shop to another, often on what they call "a shop fuddle," without wishing to buy anything.

Barnstaple is the capital town of north Devon, a bright, cheerful place with all the air of a good shopping and entertainment centre. It is an open question whether Barnstaple or Newton Abbot has the third largest hinterland in Devon and Cornwall. Bideford, with 10,000 people, is another excellent little town, with good shops and markets, and a tree-lined quay where something is always happening. It has also the special merit of possessing the best second-hand bookshop between Bristol and Penzance. Poor Torrington, on the other hand, suffers by comparison. Country people regard it as hopeless for serious shopping and for entertainment of any kind, and " there is nothing to see." They prefer to go to Bideford, only seven miles away.

The main reason for Torrington's decay seems to be the proximity of Barnstaple and Bideford. In either of these towns one could settle down happily for the rest of one's life. North Devon has a more bracing climate than the south, and has been far less spoilt, physically and mentally, by the consequences of a commercialised " holiday industry," except for the unseemly blot of Westward Ho! One might say that the difference is epitomised in the contrast between the bungaloid rash along Bigbury Bay, on the south coast, and the solitary, unravished loveliness of the Hartland coast on the north, which is still much as Hawker knew it a hundred years ago.

North Devon has few towns. The south coast has many. Torquay, a town of great natural beauty, with excellent shops, a theatre, and many cinemas, is regarded by native Devonians as having " a surface glitter and the highest prices," as catering mainly for summer visitors and retired residents. They prefer to go to Newton Abbot or Paignton for their ordinary needs, but like an occasional day at Torquay for a complete change of mental outlook.

Paignton, like Exmouth, caters for all classes of shoppers, and offers all the bustle and entertainment that country people expect of a day-off in town. For the less energetic, Paignton has—rather surprisingly—a good second-hand bookshop, tucked away up in the old village.

Totnes, a few miles back from Paignton, is a very attractive little town to be in at any time of the year. Its shops and markets cater more particularly for country people, it offers little in the way of commercial entertainment. It is older fashioned and easy-going. A cider made here goes down like a golden wine: there are good hotels and there is the flowing Dart: all that Totnes lacks for perfection is a good second-hand bookshop, that essential ingredient in any Paradise. Dartmouth, so beautiful to look at, has no attractive power. On Saturday afternoons the town is empty; everyone has gone to Paignton or Newton Abbot for shopping, just as during the week most of the young people go there for their work.

Tiverton, Tavistock, and Kingsbridge are each the local capitals for a small region. They are all far enough away from a big town to have a distinct hinterland for weekly needs, and to retain their own special character. Their markets are still important. But Crediton suffers from its nearness to Exeter, as it has done for the past hundred years since the railway was opened. Its young people flock to Exeter to work, and country people, who made Crediton their market town three generations ago, now travel on to Exeter. Crediton, like Bradninch and Modbury, and one or two other ancient market towns, lies asleep all the year round.

One of the great deficiencies in the whole of west Devon is a town large enough to act as a Mecca for the isolated parishes. Country people do not want to live permanently in a town, but they like—and need— the complete refreshment that an occasional day-off in town can give: the shops, the lights, the crowded pavements, the theatres and cinemas, the cafés, the exciting variety of things they do not want to buy. To be in Exeter or Plymouth on a winter afternoon just before Christmas is not just a useful or necessary trip to town: it is for country people a spiritual experience, an utterly satisfying re-creation, something to talk about afterwards for weeks, to look forward to for months. And there is no town in that great quadrant of western Devon between Dartmoor and Hartland Point, nothing to satisfy this deep need for a break from country isolation and hard toil.

The town of Okehampton does not meet this need: "You walk up the street and down the street, and then you have seen the lot." There is nowhere nearer than Bideford, Exeter or Tavistock, all too far away in a countryside with miserably bad communications. There are many villages where one has to cycle ten miles each way to reach even a poor local cinema. The wireless set has done a great deal to break down the intense mental isolation, but the physical isolation is still unbroken. So the young people of the western parishes leave home, and year by year the population falls as it has done steadily for a hundred years. There is no town of any size to hold them; and no town could ever develop in such an unrewarding land. Holsworthy and Hatherleigh, Lydford and Winkleigh, Hartland and Sheepwash, all were given the dignity of " borough " by their medieval lords, but not one developed a true urban character in this vast and lonely countryside " where all green things are crushed between the hammer of the west wind and the anvil of the yellow clay."

Addendum

THE CELTIC SAINTS IN NORTH DEVON

ON page 220 of this book I expressed the view that " the Taw estuary was a centre for the early Celtic saints, as we might expect from its position in relation to Wales and Ireland, whence so many of them came. . . ." The coast of North Devon consists almost entirely of towering hog-backed cliffs with few and dangerous landing-places, except the break in the cliff-wall afforded by the Taw-Torridge estuary and a few miles of level beaches on either side of it. This topography made the bay a natural point of entry for the missionary saints.

Since that page was written some further evidence confirming this view has come to light. It is possible to add to the number of sites in North Devon associated with these early saints, in particular with St. Endelienta and St. John, two of the twenty-four sons and daughters of Brychan of whom St. Nectan (at Hartland and Welcombe) is the best known in Devon. Mr. Pearse Chope (in *The Book of Hartland*, 13 n.) considers that the dedication of Instow church (*i.e.* John's *stow* or holy place) is to this Celtic St. John rather than to the evangelist or to any other of the name. The church is built on high ground, looking due west down the estuary to the sea, with Lundy and Hartland Point in full view.

As for St. Endelienta or Endelient, we have Nicholas Roscarrock's statement, made in the late 16th century in his MS *Lives of the Saints* (a reference which I owe to the kindness of Mr. A. L. Rowse): " I have heard it credibly reported that the chapel on Lundy was dedicated unto her and bore her name. Yet my good friend, Mr. Camden, saith the chapel was dedicated unto St. Helen, but, under correction, except he have better warrant than bare conjecture, I still hold the former report more likely, because her brother St. Nectan had a church dedicated at Hartland Point over against it, but fourteen miles from it, whereof it is not improbable that she did also sometimes dwell in that island. For many of St. Brechan's children planted themselves near one another. . . ."

There are only three known dedications to St. Helen, all in North Devon, close to the sea, and within sight of each other: the chapel on Lundy, the parish church of Abbotsham, and the ancient chapel (now ruined) on the high ground just W. of Croyde village. Abbotsham church was originally sited on the summit of the bold ridge that runs S. of Westward Ho, about 1½ m. N. of its present site, to which it was removed at an unknown date. Lundy is in full view from the old site. The church was dedicated, not to St. Helen or Helena the Empress (whose day was 18 August), but to St. Elen, whose day was 25 August. So said the Tavistock Calendar, and as Tavistock Abbey possessed Abbotsham from the 10th century we may regard this as a sound source. One is led to suspect at once that this St. Elen is St. Endelient, as on Lundy. Of the chapel at Croyde, which again is sited so as to have Lundy in view, we know nothing except that it was dedicated to St. Helen. But in view of the other two dedications, and its significant site above a good beach for landing, we can hardly doubt that it is the third of the small group of chapels founded by St. Endelient in the 6th century. On these now despoiled beaches of Westward Ho and Croyde, we stand linked with the early saints who landed upon them. It is curious to discover, too, that South Molton Fair always began on the Wednesday after the feast of St. Elen, though the parish church is now dedicated to St. Mary Magdalene. Can it be that we must add South Molton to the little group of original Celtic dedications in this district, such as Landkey and Filleigh?

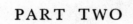

PART TWO

In the gazetteer which follows, references have been reduced to a minimum in order to save space for the text. Manorial descents are based on Lysons and on Reichel's *Hundreds of Devon*. References to chapels and oratories are taken from the Exeter *Episcopal Registers*. For church screens, Bond and Camm's *Roodscreens and Roodlofts* is the authority. Though I have personally seen every parish church and most of the interesting farmhouses in the county, many of the latter still await discovery by the enterprising traveller. For him I have tried to indicate wherever a farm is mentioned in Domesday Book or possessed a medieval chapel, for these are the best clues to a possibly interesting house. The earliest references to farms, wherever used, are taken from the *Place-Names of Devon* volumes.

ABBOTS BICKINGTON (B4) formed part of the original endowment of Hartland abbey *temp*. Henry II, which retained it until the Dissolution. Culsworthy was a small Domesday estate.

The church (St. James) is a pleasing little building, mainly of early 14th-century date. It has a small spire, most unusual for Devon. The tower is plastered outside, giving it the character of an old engraving, but concealing its true age. It is probably *c.* 1300.

The church was Victorianised in 1868 in a not unpleasing way. The E. window contains some medieval glass, and the chancel is floored with a considerable number of late medieval tiles, in common with many churches in this part of Devon. The only monument is one to Sir Amyas Pollard, bart. (1701) and his son Thomas (1710). Court Barton beside the church, where the Pollards lived and died, is so called because the abbots of Hartland held their manor courts here.

ABBOTSHAM (C3) takes its name from the fact that it formed part of the original endowment of Tavistock in the late 10th cent. The parish church (St. Helen) has a fine Norman font, but the fabric was rebuilt in the early 13th cent. and a tower added on the S. side *c.* 1300. A remarkably good set of carved bench-ends (early 16th-cent.) call for detailed study. Among the designs are the emblems of the Passion, two full-length saints, the Bourchier knot, and several ornamental initials. There is a good monument to John Willett, 1736. Abbotsham Court has some 16th-cent. work. Combe appears to be largely of early 17th-cent. date. Cornborough is Georgian and earlier.

ABBOTS KERSWELL (G9) was held by the abbot of Horton in Dorset in 1086. The church (St. Mary) is mainly 15th-cent. with some remains of 13th-cent. work in the chancel. Font and screen are 15th-cent. The screen, much restored but very good, has a beautiful vine-leaf enrichment of the cornice and excellent tracery. The attractive medieval statue of the Virgin Mary was found at the restoration of the church by Butterfield. The 16th-cent. Church House is a good example of its kind.

ALLINGTON, EAST (F11),

was one of the numerous homes of the widespread Fortescue family. Fallapit belonged to them from the early 15th cent. to the mid-19th. It passed to them by the marriage of Sir Henry Fortescue, Lord Chief Justice of the Common Pleas in Ireland, with an heiress. Sir Edmund Fortescue so gallantly defended Salcombe Castle for the King in 1645 that upon its surrender he was allowed to march out with the garrison, bearing their arms, to Fallapit and to take with him the key of the castle. When the Fortescues sold the house this key was knocked down by the auctioneer for half a crown. Fallapit was rebuilt in a pseudo-Elizabethan style *c.* 1810-15, near the site of the old house, and "enlarged and beautified" in 1849. The estate was sold to William Cubitt, a member of the famous firm of London builders. He restored the church in 1875 at a cost to himself of £2,500.

The church (St. Andrew) is an excellent 15th- and early 16th-cent. building with a rood-screen dated 1547, and a notable pulpit. There is a fine brass to John Fortescue (d. 1595) and Honor his wife (d. 1606), and another brass of a kneeling woman who may be Elizabeth, wife of Lewis Fortescue, Baron of the Exchequer in Henry VIII's reign. Another Fortescue monument is by Chantrey. Gilbert White once preached in this church. At Colehanger and Harleston are the remains of old manor houses. Coombe also is of some interest.

ALPHINGTON (H7)

has been suburbanised by its proximity to Exeter, but there is still much decent 18th-cent. and early 19th-cent. building. Mile End Cottage, beside the Exeter road, is the house in which Charles Dickens installed his parents in 1839. Facing the church is a good specimen of an early 17th-cent. Devon farmhouse.

The parish church (St. Michael) is almost entirely a 15th-cent. building, with a good tower. The 12th-cent. Beer stone font is one of the finest of its period in Devon. The rood-screen is 15th-cent. but the N. aisle screen is different in design and execution and may have come from another church. The screen across the tower arch was made up from the remains of the former Jacobean gallery (1625) demolished in 1875.

ALVERDISCOTT (D3)

(pronounced *Alscott*). The church (All Saints) stands high, with fine views all around. It is mainly a 15th-cent. building, heavily restored in the early 19th, when the N. arcade was rebuilt in a curious and unsatisfactory manner. There are medieval tiles of local manufacture in the S. porch, and a Norman font. In the N. aisle is a fine monument to Gilbert Hody (1686), and also an excellent altar-tomb with an alabaster effigy of a youth in Caroline costume— Thomas Welshe, son of James Welshe (1639). Webbery was a Domesday manor. The present house was rebuilt about 1820.

ALVINGTON, WEST (F11),

stands boldly on a hill overlooking Kingsbridge, commanding wide views towards the sea. This site determined its early occupation, probably not much later than 700. It was a royal estate in 1066 and was alienated from the crown by Henry I. The parish originally included all the land as far as the sea, for Malborough, Salcombe, South Huish, and South Milton were all chapelries of Alvington in medieval times. The present parish church (All Saints) is a noble 15th-cent. building in the hard green local slate, with a fine pinnacled tower. The lofty arcades are of Beer stone, brought by water. The church possessed until its restoration in 1866-67 a medieval rood-screen across nave and aisles, complete with rood-loft and a pulpit on top of that. In the chancel is a canopied Easter sepulchre, formerly a tomb.

Bowringsleigh was originally called Leigh. The Bowrings were here by 1332 but died out in the male line in the late 15th cent. After further changes Bowringsleigh was bought in 1696 by the Ilberts, who still live there. The present house is substantially Elizabethan and Jacobean in date, considerably Victorianised but still interesting and attractive. Battlements and dormer windows were added to the front by Mr. Roope Ilbert c. 1850. He also built the great tower in a 15th-cent. style. The ground floor of the tower, however, contains the chapel, which may date from the Bowring days. This has the richly-coloured rood-screen from South Huish church, which was rescued when that church fell into ruin. The hall of the house has a good Elizabethan plaster-work ceiling and an elaborately carved oak screen inlaid with ebony, c. 1620. The dining-room has a fine plaster ceiling (c. 1700) representing War, but a corresponding ceiling in the E. wing representing Peace was destroyed by fire in 1843.

Woolston and Bagton were Domesday manors. The remains of a manor house are to be seen at Woolston Court. Gerston, overlooking a creek of the Kingsbridge estuary, was a home of the Bastards for several centuries until 1773. Its gardens were famous for orange and lemon trees. There are some remains of the old mansion.

ALWINGTON (c3) church (St. Andrew) stands beside an ancient, grey barton. It is almost entirely 15th-cent. with a handsome tapered tower; the S. aisle and porch were rebuilt in the 17th cent. The nave arcade is of Lundy granite. The Portledge pew, at the E. end of the S. aisle, is made up of pieces from the Elizabethan minstrels' gallery at Portledge, and the reredos from old bench-ends taken out of Parkham church in 1806. The pulpit is made up largely from bench-ends in Alwington church itself; one of the remaining bench-ends is dated 1580. The mural monuments of the Coffins of Portledge are worth attention, especially that to Richard Coffin (1617) and Elizabeth his wife (1651) and their fifteen children.

Portledge was the home of the Coffins from the time of Henry II until recently, though the male line has failed twice. The house is now an hotel, but the Pine-Coffins still live in the neighbourhood. It is mainly a 16th-cent. house, much altered in the early 19th cent. Yeo Vale is a 15th-cent. mansion, of which the gatehouse survives, built into a large, square late Georgian country house. The ruined chapel beside the road up to Tuckingmill was formerly at Yeo Vale (licensed 1408), but was rebuilt here in the early 19th cent.

ANSTEY, EAST (G3), has a rebuilt church (St. Michael, 1870). The Barton was built in 1848 on the site of an old mansion.

ANSTEY, WEST (G3), has a 15th-cent. church (St. Petrock), much restored in 1880, with a Norman font. Ringcombe was a small Domesday estate.

APPLEDORE (see Northam).

ARLINGTON (E1) was until recently one of the principal seats of the ubiquitous Chichester family. They acquired the manor by marriage with a Raleigh heiress late in the 14th cent. Arlington Court, their residence, was handed over to the National Trust in 1947 and Chichester of Arlington is no more. There are fine grounds but the house itself, built 1820-3, is of little architectural interest. It is now open to the public. Amias Chichester (d. 1577), by Jane, daughter of Sir Roger Giffard of Brightley, had nineteen sons and four daughters. Kingsley refers to this noble sight of nineteen sons in *Westward Ho!* The church (St. James) was rebuilt by Gould in 1846, except for the tower. A number of mural tablets from 1622 onwards commemorate the Chichesters. Twitchen was a Domesday manor.

ASHBURTON (F9). The history of the quiet little town of Ashburton, by-passed by main roads and railways, is that of a score of Devonshire market-towns. It reached its maximum population in 1831, and then declined continuously for the next four generations. The census of 1951 shows the first increase of population (to 2,704) for 120 years, arising largely from the growing popularity of the Dart valley among retired persons.

Ashburton took its name from the stream on which it stands, the Ashburn, now called by the commonplace name of Yeo. It became part of the vast estate of the bishops of Exeter some time before the Norman Conquest, and remained episcopal property until the time of James I, when it was alienated to the Crown, and subsequently sold to laymen.

The town owed much to the bishops of Exeter, as well as to its natural situation in the midst of rewarding farmland and at the margin of the rich mineral wealth of Dartmoor. A market had already grown up before the end of the 12th cent. and a borough had been created by one of the bishops before 1238.

The Dartmoor tin trade developed spectacularly during the latter part of the 12th cent., and Ashburton became the natural collecting centre for the south-eastern side of the Moor. In 1305 it became one of the four official stannary towns. The tin trade remained important at Ashburton until the early 17th cent., and was carried on in a small way until well into the 19th.

Simultaneously with the rise of the tin trade, the cloth industry was established along the banks of the Ashburn, which supplied the power for a number of fulling mills. Ashburton became a considerable market for cloth, tin, corn, and cattle, and had two great annual fairs. It declined after the Black Death and not until about the 1580s did it experience a renewal of its old prosperity, arising from the development of the " new draperies." Many of its attractive old houses, some of them slate-hung in the South Devon manner, date from these years of prosperity up to 1640.

The great growth of road traffic after 1660 brought more inns and subsidiary trades, for the town lay on the main road between Exeter and Plymouth, about half-way between the two places. For some time iron-mining also was carried on near the town. An iron mill is marked on an Ashburton map of 1605, about two-thirds of a mile above Holne Bridge, on the E. bank of the Dart. The ruins of one furnace still exist, and the old shafts are to be found in the hillside immediately above.[1]

We catch a brief and unflattering glimpse of Ashburton in the pages of

Celia Fiennes (1698): " this Ashburton is a poor little town—bad was the best inn." Probably Ashburton's greatest days were in the 18th cent., before the cloth industry fell upon evil days and while the road traffic still clattered and thundered through its narrow streets.

The ending of the East India Company's monopoly of the China trade in 1833 brought disaster to Ashburton's trade, and the population fell as unemployed woollen workers drifted elsewhere. Then the opening of the South Devon railway in 1846, by-passing the town by several miles, killed the greater part of its coach and wagon traffic, except purely local trade, and so the decline went on. The arrival in 1872 of a branch railway from Totnes—one of the most picturesque little railways in England—did nothing to revive the dying town; and it mouldered gently on into the 20th cent., losing its young people to places like Torquay and Newton Abbot, and attracting only the elderly, looking for peace and quiet and reasonably cheap living.

Apart from the slate-hung houses and one or two picturesque parts like Kingsbridge Lane, the only notable thing to see in Ashburton is the parish church (St. Andrew). Its granite tower is one of the handsomest in Devon. Ashburton is essentially a 15th-cent. church, with unusual granite arcades and good bossed roofs. There are some traces of earlier work, the chancel being mostly 14th-cent. in date, but the church has been much altered and "restored." The fine rood-screen was chopped up for firewood. The present screen, designed by G. E. Street, who restored the church in 1881-3, is out of keeping with a Devon church, being more of the East Anglian type. Behind the organ is a memorial to John Dunning, 1st Lord Ashburton, who was born at Gulwell,

in the adjacent parish of Staverton, and educated at Ashburton Grammar School. Among others educated at the grammar school, which was founded in 1314 by Bishop Stapeldon, were William Gifford (1756-1826), the son of a glazier at Ashburton, who became the first editor of the *Quarterly Review*; John Ireland (1761-1842), son of an Ashburton butcher, who became Dean of Westminster; and possibly John Ford the dramatist, who was born at Bagtor in Ilsington, not far away. The grammar school is built on the site of the chapel of St. Lawrence, the tower of which may still be seen.

ASHBURY (D6) is little more than a church in a park. The church (St. Mary) was rebuilt in 1872-3 and is wholly uninteresting. Wadland Barton is a large and picturesque farmstead, built in 1668 (date in kitchen) on an ancient site which is first mentioned in 1244.

ASHCOMBE (H8) lies in a beautiful hollow below the Haldon Hills. Its small medieval church (St. Nectan) was largely rebuilt in 1824-5 and is charming. The character of the church is derived almost entirely from the early 19th-cent. work: it is perfect of its kind, with delicately colour-washed wagon roofs and walls. Baring-Gould, however, in the *Little Guide*, did not approve: "the fine screen was destroyed in 1820, and a good deal of money was then spent in making the church as hideous as the taste of that period could arrive at."

ASHFORD (D2) stands on a hill overlooking the Taw estuary. The church (St. Peter) was completely rebuilt in 1854, but the old woodwork, mostly of 16th-cent. date, was re-used throughout the church. The font is Norman.

ASHPRINGTON (G10) parish occupies a peninsula between the Dart estuary and the tributary Bow Creek, and is everywhere romantically beautiful. Most of its frontage along the Dart is taken up by the Sharpham estate, which has a river frontage of 2¾ miles, much of it hung with woods to the water's edge. The park is also finely wooded, and the gardens were laid out by "Capability" Brown. Sharpham House, high above the woods on a commanding ridge, is externally a plain, almost ugly, late Georgian house designed by Sir Robert Taylor (one-time President of the R.I.B.A.) for Capt. Philemon Pownall, R.N. Capt. Pownall had a distinguished and profitable career in the navy: his prize-money from one capture alone amounted to over £65,000, out of which he began to rebuild Sharpham in 1770. He was, however, killed in action in 1780—there is a monument to him in Ashprington church—and the house was not completed until 1826. The principal rooms are fitted and decorated in the Adam style.

The church (St. David) is mainly a 15th-cent. building with an earlier W. tower. The fabric underwent a drastic restoration in 1845 and again in the 1880s, but has since been vastly improved. The font is an excellent example of late Norman work. There are various 17th- and 18th-cent. mural monuments to local gentry.

Painsford had a private chapel (St. John the Baptist), licensed in 1400. This was rebuilt by John Kelland in 1683-7, and used for divine worship until about the middle of the 18th cent. Some small remains of it are to be seen N. of the rear court of the house. The house itself is of 16th- and 17th-cent. date, but its main front has been spoilt.

The by-road from Ashprington to Cornworthy through Tuckenhay is picturesque and interesting. The hamlet of Tuckenhay, at the head of Bow Creek, has extensive store-houses and quays, and formerly did a large trade in road-stone with London and other ports. It had also two paper mills at work in the mid-19th cent., as well as a corn mill, and was a thriving little place. One of the paper mills worked from 1832 to 1860. The other—on the Cornworthy side of the stream—began work in 1829 and is still active to-day. It produces a high quality hand-made paper, and is the only "vat" mill left in Devon.[1] One can also see the remains of an old gas-house, erected about the year 1806 for lighting the hamlet. Like so many of these remote riverside hamlets in Devon, Tuckenhay has a long and varied industrial history.

ASHREIGNEY (E4). The church (St. James) is 15th-cent., over-restored in 1889-90 and of little interest. Goodcott, Hook Farm, and Riddlecombe were all Domesday manors. Hansford Barton is mentioned as early as 1205.

ASHTON (G7) lies in singularly beautiful country on the W. slopes of Haldon, falling to the Teign valley. The scattered village is also most attractive. The parish church (now St. John the Baptist: original dedication unknown) is one of the most "atmospheric" village churches in Devon. It was begun before 1400 and completed with all its fittings by about 1485; and as it was restored at a late date(1900-5) it has conserved intact most of its ancient beauty. The striking rood-screen and parclose screens have some of the best panel-paintings in Devon, those at the back being even better than those at the front. The panel paintings in the Lady Chapel are particularly notable. Besides the screens, the church contains many carved medieval benches, medieval glass, a medieval wall-painting more intelligible than most, an Elizabethan pulpit with sounding-board and hour-glass, and a large wooden monument to Sir George Chudleigh (1582-1657). The original vaulting and loft of the rood-screen were destroyed soon after Rickman saw them in 1825; the present groined canopy was added in 1908. The roof-bosses are all restorations, except one. Such a bare catalogue cannot do justice to this really notable church, which ranks with Torbryan and Molland as one of the most beautiful village churches in the county.

Below the church is Place (now called Lower Barton) where the Chudleighs lived from the early 14th cent. until 1745, when Sir George, the 4th Bart., began to build the great mansion of Haldon (see KENN).

George Teign Barton is a large rambling farmstead of 16th- and 17th-cent. date for the most part, so called from the medieval chapel of St. George which formerly stood here.

ASHWATER (B6) is an attractive little village grouped around a green. The church (St. Peter) is interesting. It has a splendid Norman font of a Cornish type, with unique ornament, and a N. doorway of the same date. Otherwise the church is mainly 14th- and late 15th-cent. in date. Notice the curious S. arcade, which is said to date from a thorough restoration in 1676-7 when the churchwardens' accounts show that nearly £200 was spent on the fabric. Notice, too, the carved roofs. Some of the bench-ends are c. 1500, but most are the modern work of a local craftsman. The canopied tomb in the S. aisle with recumbent effigies is possibly that of Sir Hugh Courtenay (slain at Tewkesbury, 1471) and his wife Margaret. Near by are the royal arms in plaster, dated 1638.

ATHERINGTON (D3) stands high and commands magnificent views. The church (St. Mary), on the hill-top, is a landmark for miles. It is entirely a 15th–16th-cent. building, and is of exceptional interest for its contents. It is notable in the first place in retaining the only rood-loft left in Devon, though this is now confined to the N. aisle only. The screen and loft, of exquisite design and finish, formerly stretched across the church, but at some date (possibly about 1800) the chancel section was removed and a much poorer and simpler screen of an early type substituted for it. This early screen is said to have come from the chapel at Umberleigh, the home of the Bassets, when it was pulled down. We know that the rood-loft at least was the work of two Chittlehampton carvers c. 1530-40. They may also have been responsible for the aisle screen, which bears a marked resemblance to those of Lapford and Marwood. The church also has a fine series of carved and crocketed bench-ends, of a most unusual type for Devon, and of an early type (probably 15th-cent.). In the N. chancel aisle is a complete window of medieval glass. There are various effigies and tombs. The effigy of a 13th-cent. knight in armour in the N. chancel aisle is believed to be that of Sir William Champernowne of Umberleigh; and the two 14th-cent. figures in the chancel are said to represent Sir Ralph Willington, kt. (d. 1349) and Lady Eleanor (Mohun) his wife. These effigies were formerly in the chapel at Umberleigh, but were removed to Atherington church in 1818. The altar tomb on the N. side of the chancel has brass figures depicting a knight in armour, his two wives, and twelve children in two groups. It is the tomb of Sir John Basset of Umberleigh, and his two wives Ann (Denys of Orleigh) and Honor (Grenville of Bideford). Sir John died in 1529. Atherington church and screen were restored by J. L. Pearson in 1884.

Almost nothing remains of the great house at Umberleigh, beside the Taw. Umberleigh Barton contains some old work, possibly 16th-cent.

AVETON GIFFORD (E11) (pron. *Awton Jifford*) formerly had one of the oldest and most interesting churches in Devon (St. Andrew), built in the late 13th cent. for the most part, a cruciform building with a central tower. It was almost completely destroyed in a "tip-and-run" raid in 1943 and is still (1951) a ruin. The farms of Heathfield and Stadbury were Domesday manors; there are some traces of the former manor house at Heathfield. Harraton, beside the Modbury road, is a good example of an early 17th-cent. farmhouse. Court Barton, near the ruined church, retains some older features.

Robert Macey, who built numerous churches and theatres in London, including the Adelphi and the Haymarket, was born the son of a mason at Aveton Gifford in 1790.

AWLISCOMBE (K5) contains little of interest except the church (St. Michael), which is a typical 15th-cent. church in the East Devon manner. It has a good N. arcade of Beer stone, and a remarkable rood-screen, also of Beer stone, retaining much of its ancient detail. Thomas Chard, probably the titular bishop of Solubria and not the last abbot of Ford of the same name, was born at Tracey in this parish (now a

late Georgian house) about 1470. He was responsible for much excellent work in his parish church, notably the groined S. porch, and the chantry chapel in the S. transept with its beautiful early 16th-cent. window. He was prior of Montacute until 1532, and then prior of Carswell, a cell of Montacute (see BROADHEMBURY), and died in 1541. The church was mostly rebuilt in 1846, and was again restored by Medley Fulford in 1887.

AXMINSTER (L6) is a quiet little market-town, well sited on a bluff above the Axe. A *minster* or *monasterium* was founded here probably soon after 705, when the see of Sherborne was created to bring Devon within the Saxon episcopal organisation. The town itself lay on or near the Fosse Way, and was one of the earliest settlements in the Saxon occupation of Devon, founded in all probability soon after 660. It was a royal estate until 1204, when King John granted it to William Brewer. From the Brewers it passed to the Mohuns by marriage, and Reginald Mohun gave it to the Cistercian abbey of Newenham which was founded S.W. of the town in 1246. After the Dissolution the manor passed to the Greys, and then to the Howards. Lord William Howard sold it to Lord Petre in 1605 for £7,200. The Petres disposed of a good deal of the land during the next two centuries, and in 1824 sold the remainder, with the rest of their estates in the neighbourhood, for £43,000.[1]

A Sunday market had grown up at Axminster during the 12th century and in 1204 it was confirmed to William Brewer. A charter of 1209 is said to have made Axminster a free borough, and another in 1215 granted the burgesses an eight-day fair beginning on the feast of St. John the Baptist. This fair was still held in Lysons's day (1822) but has now ceased. Two one-day fairs are now held, one on the Tuesday after April 25, and the other on the Wednesday after October 10. At the October fair there is usually a good show of cattle, sheep, and horses.

The parish church (St. Mary and St. John the Evangelist), formerly prebendal, is the most interesting building in the town. It is a cruciform structure, with a central tower, its transepts enlarged into aisles at later dates; and the central tower was rebuilt in the 13th cent. above the old crossing. The chancel also is largely 13th-cent. At the E. end of the S. aisle is a good Norman doorway (c. 1150), originally the S. doorway of the nave. Among the fittings of the church are a handsome pulpit and reading-desk (1633) and a fine chandelier (1750).

Of Newenham abbey only small traces of walling remain. The farmhouse on the site (Higher Newenham) is of 16th- and 17th-cent. date. John Prince, author of *The Worthies of Devon*, was born here in 1643. Great Trill, first mentioned in 1173, was one of the properties of the Drakes of Ashe, and at one time a small manor house. There are remains of Tudor buildings in the yard. The house itself has been modernised to some extent. It is practically certain that the great Duke of Marlborough was born in this house on 24 May 1650, and not at Ashe House in Musbury, as is so often asserted.

Weycroft, "built on the rising of a hill," is largely of early 15th-cent. date. In 1417 Bishop Stafford licensed a private chapel here, and in 1426 a royal licence was granted to crenellate the mansion and enclose a park of 800 acres. The most interesting remaining feature is the great hall in the N.

section (c. 1400) which runs to the full height of the house and has a range of three large windows on each side. There is a contemporary gallery at the lower end treated like a rood-loft. The S. section of the house is mainly 17th-cent. and later, but the E. wing is probably 15th-cent.

Smallridge was one of the earliest homes of the Raleighs in Devon. They were here before 1242 and lived here for ten or eleven generations until Sir Wimond Raleigh, the grandfather of the celebrated Sir Walter, sold it *temp*. Henry VIII. Cloakham House, not far away, was built in 1732.

The Axminster carpet manufacture was started here in 1755 but failed in 1835. The original factory building may be seen NE of the church. The carpet manufacture has recently been revived in the town.

AXMOUTH (L6). One could spend a pleasurable week of exploration in and around this delectable little place, which always looks so inviting at any time of the year across the emerald marshes of the River Axe. The estuary of the Axe was formerly much wider than it is to-day, probably half a mile across, and extended considerably farther southward than the present coastline.

The hill-fort of Hawksdown dominates this estuary and a vast area beyond: the views up here are superb. It probably dates from the late pre-Roman Iron Age.

In Roman times, Axmouth appears to have been the southern terminus of the Fosse Way. In the Saxon occupation of the 7th cent., it was one of the earliest villages to be founded. It belonged to King Athelstan, later to Edward the Confessor, and then to William I. It was also the centre of an

early hundred, proof again of its antiquity and importance.

By Leland's time the mouth of the
Axe was almost barred by the high
pebble ridge which forces the river
through a narrow outlet on the E. side.
Attempts to reconstruct the harbour
from the Seaton side were made in the
15th cent., but came to nothing. At the
end of the 16th cent. the Earles tried to
remake the harbour from the Axmouth
side. For some reason this project also
failed. Early in the 19th cent., several
farmers of Axmouth and the neighbouring parishes attempted to dig out the
ruins of the ancient harbour. A pier
was built about 1803, behind which
vessels of 100 tons could unload, and up
to 1868, when the railway came, two
vessels traded regularly between Axmouth and London. Other vessels also
used the harbour. The railway killed
this trade, the harbour was allowed to
decay again, and a considerable part of
the pier was swept away in a gale on
Sunday, 31 January 1869.

Leland speaks of Axmouth as "an old
and bigge Fischar Toune." It was
much larger then than to-day, as is
proved by the foundations of houses
unearthed over a wide area.[1] By 1800,
it had shrunk to fewer than 400 people.
In 1871 its population had risen to
702, but since then it has been stationary or gently declining. The present
village is most attractive, with a number of excellent farmhouses and cottages
of 16th–19th-cent. date. Two or three
are notable examples of Elizabethan
domestic building. Axmouth is worth
careful exploration, and is indeed one of
the most unspoilt and delightful villages in Devon. To the N. of the village,
Stedcombe is a good William and
Mary house (1695), rebuilt near the
site of the older house which was
garrisoned for Parliament by Sir Walter

Erle and destroyed by the Royalists in
1644. Bindon, E. of the village, is a
former manor house, mostly 16th-cent.
in date, with some earlier remains.
The private chapel, still to be seen
in the house, was licensed by Bishop
Lacy in 1425.[2]

Axmouth church (St. Michael) is
structurally much more interesting than
most Devonshire churches, containing
work of almost every period from the
Norman to the Victorian. There are
substantial remains of the Norman
church (c. 1150); a narrow S. aisle was
added early in the 13th cent., and
further alterations made a hundred
years later. At the end of the 15th cent.
the fine W. tower was built, possibly
replacing a Norman tower at the E. end
of the S. aisle. In the chancel is the
effigy of a 14th-cent. priest, fully vested
in alb, stole, and chasuble. There are
memorials to the Erles of Bindon, and a
good 18th-cent. mural monument to
Hallett of Stedcombe (1749). The
church was restored by Hayward of
Exeter in 1889, who produced the
beastly Victorian font.

Axmouth lies in the chalk country of
Devon, and has some spectacular
coastal scenery. At Dowlands Farm,
the great landslip of Christmas 1839
may be seen: a chasm ¾ m. long, 300 ft.
wide, and 150 ft. deep, formed when
8,000,000 tons of earth crashed in one
night. The view from the E. end is
particularly fine.

Besides Axmouth and Stedcombe,
Bruckland and Charton existed as
separate estates before the Norman
Conquest. Bindon, though not separately mentioned until 1238, was a part
of Axmouth manor in pre-Conquest
times.

AYLESBEARE (j6) has an unexciting
15th-cent. church (St. Mary). On the

E. the parish rises to a heathy ridge (the Budleigh Pebble ridge), rather over 500 ft. above sea-level, from which there are fine views in all directions. Barrows on this heath have been excavated, revealing curious pebbled pavements, the date and purpose of which are not clear.

BAMPTON (H3) is a small market-town on the river Batherm near its confluence with the Exe, lying in beautiful hilly country. It was an early Saxon village and gave its name to a hundred, developing in the 13th cent. into a small town. It has two fairs and a weekly market, and by 1302 we hear of burgesses here. It was, however, never incorporated but continued to be governed by two portreeves until 1894. Like many Devon market-towns it had large cattle and sheep markets, and a cloth industry from early times. The latter had dwindled almost to nothing by the early 19th cent., but the two fairs remained among the largest in the west of England. The October fair is still famous for its cattle and sheep sales, and above all for the Exmoor ponies brought down from the moor.

The town is quiet and of no architectural interest. Most of the houses are covered with a rather drab stucco. The church (St. Michael, but formerly St. Mary according to Oliver) is mainly a building of *c.* 1300, much rebuilt and enlarged in the 15th cent. when the N. aisle was added. It is now all "scraped" and over-restored. The tall, plain tower is *c.* 1300 in date. John Bourchier, Lord Fitzwarren, created 1st Earl of Bath in 1536, and prominent at the court of Henry VIII, was buried in Bampton church where he endowed a chantry. As late as 1770 his tomb still stood in the N. aisle, with the effigies of himself, Cecily his wife, and their eight children.

Bampton Castle, so called, is at the E. end of Castle Street. It now consists of nothing more than a mount with some traces of outworks, and seems originally to have been a fortified house rather than a true castle.

S. of Bampton are extensive limestone quarries, of considerable interest to the geologist, commanding an excellent view of the town. Duvale Barton is probably a Celtic name from the British *du*, "black," and *bal* "peak, prominence," referring to the curiously shaped hill between the Exe and the Batherm. Dippford was a small Domesday estate.

BARNSTAPLE (D2), at the head of the Taw estuary, has been the most considerable town in North Devon since Saxon times. It is a lively and cheerful place with good shops and markets.

It began life, like Bideford, as a small settlement where the river estuary narrowed to a fordable width. This ford was probably marked by a *stapol* or post—" Bearda's staple or post."

Pilton, on a defensible hill to the NW., was the original *burh* in the early 10th cent., but the *burh* was transferred later in the same century to Barnstaple, which was constituted as a market-town and a borough, and given a mint. The earliest known Barnstaple coins date from 979-1016, and we may date the emergence of the borough from shortly before this. There is no authority for the statement that Athelstan gave Barnstaple its first charter in 930.

In 1086, Barnstaple was one of the four Domesday boroughs of Devon. It belonged to the King, and had belonged to Edward the Confessor before him. It is not clear whether a castle existed here at this date. The fact that there were thirty-eight houses " laid

waste" suggests that one had been
built, although the erection of the castle
is generally attributed to Juhel of
Totnes who received the manor in
Henry I's time.[1] Nothing remains of
this castle to-day except the mount,
sixty ft. high and forty ft. across at the
top. It is possible that the earthworks
dated from the Conqueror's reign, and
that Juhel of Totnes was the first to
substitute stone for the original timber
defences. Barnstaple appears to have
been walled around early in the 12th
cent. for a charter of Henry I's time
speaks of land "outside the walls
between the north gate and the east
gate," and a description of the north
and west gates of the town, demolished
in 1842 and 1852 respectively, clearly
suggests Norman work.[2] The town
walls were "almost clean fallen" in
Leland's day, but the four gateways
remained to be demolished in later
times.

Barnstaple was of considerable
economic importance throughout medieval times. In the early 14th cent. it
was the third town in Devon, Exeter
and Plymouth being the two richest, and
this position it has maintained until
recent times, except for a short period
from about 1680 to 1730 when Bideford
surpassed it as a port. Its great annual
fair, which now begins on the Wednesday before 20 September and continues
for three days, is of immemorial antiquity. This fair, always the largest in
North Devon, used to begin on the eve
of the Nativity of the Virgin Mary (8
Sept.) and last for five days. In Lysons's
day it began on 19 September (the
ancient date, if we allow for the eleven
days added to the calendar in 1752).
For centuries the chronology of North
Devon has revolved around "Barnstaple Fair," but like all these events it
is now largely a commercialised pleasure

fair. There were also two weekly
markets, which still go on—Tuesdays
and Fridays for vegetables and other
farm produce, Fridays only for corn
and cattle.

Not only was the town the largest
market in North Devon, unshakably
rooted in the local countryside, but it
had a considerable woollen industry for
several centuries, and consequently a
valuable overseas trade. A merchant
guild—the guild of St. Nicholas—appeared at a very early date. Barnstaple
was the most considerable textile centre
outside Exeter, and it remained so until
the rise of the New Draperies about 1600.
During the 17th–18th cents. it ceased to
be a woollen manufacturing town, and
became instead the principal landing
place for Irish wool and yarn which was
carried overland to the manufacturing
towns of east and mid-Devon. The
sands and mud of the Taw, however,
gradually blocked the harbour. Even
in Risdon's day "it hardly beareth
small vessels," and its foreign trade
gradually passed to Bideford where the
more powerful tidal currents of the
Torridge—see how they race in and out
to-day—kept the deep-water channel
clear. The Barnstaple merchants were
still considerable enough in Queen
Anne's day, however, to rebuild the
Exchange (1708-13) which still stands,
an open portico known as Queen Anne's
Walk, on what used to be the town
quay. The colonnade was rebuilt by
the corporation in 1798.

By Lysons's day only the coasting
trade remained, but some revival of
foreign trade took place after 1822,
when bonded warehouses were established here. The directory for 1890
speaks of trade with the Baltic, France,
Spain, Portugal and North America, as
well as an extensive coasting trade.
There is still a small coasting and over-

seas trade, and Barnstaple ranks as a Customs port.

Although Barnstaple was not incorporated until 1557, it has enjoyed the right to elect its own mayor from a much earlier time. The borough was chartered in 1154-8 by Henry II, who granted Barnstaple the customs of London, but the earliest known mayor occurs in 1303.[1] The borough also regularly sent two members to parliament from 1295 until it was disfranchised in 1885.[2]

Barnstaple grew fairly rapidly in the early 19th cent., especially from 1821 to 1851, a period which has left its mark upon the architecture of the town. Comparative stagnation in the second half of the century was followed by steady growth after 1901, so that it is now a lively town of some 16,000 people, the undisputed capital of North Devon. Behind the stuccoed middle-class terraces of the early 19th cent. are the narrower streets and lanes of colour-washed cottages, mostly of 18th-cent. date. Of the pleasant 1830-ish building, Union Terrace is a good example, though the best is to be found at Newport, a suburb to the SE. on the Exeter road. Here Newport Terrace, South Street, and Trafalgar Lawn are all noteworthy. Newport originated as a "new town" about the year 1295 when the bishop of Exeter obtained the grant of a market for it, and set it up almost at the gates of Barnstaple as a rival to the older centre. It never came to much, however, and is now incorporated as part of the borough of Barnstaple; but it contains more old building (16th–18th cent.) than the latter has managed to retain. Of the other early 19th-cent. building in Barnstaple itself, Bridge Buildings (at the N. end of the bridge), probably designed by a pupil of Soane; the Market Hall (1854); and Salem

Almshouses (in Trinity Street), built in 1834, all merit attention. The Guildhall (1826-8), in the Grecian style, contains thirty portraits of prominent 18th-cent. citizens, painted by Thomas Hudson in 1738-40.[3] Some other portraits are now hung at the Castle. Much of the work was done by Hudson's pupils and is conventional.

Of the churches of the town, the parish church (St. Peter) is the most ancient. The nave, chancel, and tower represent the church dedicated in 1318 by Bishop Stapeldon, though some of the masonry is older than this and is probably 13th cent. The N. and S. aisles are said to have been added c. 1670,[4] but presumably replaced older aisles. The lead-covered broach spire, which has twisted with the heat of the sun, is perhaps the best of its kind in this country. The whole church was heavily Victorianised by Sir Gilbert Scott in 1866-82, who left it dark and dull. It contains a great number of interesting mural monuments with sculptured figures, mostly of 17th-cent. date, the S. aisle monuments being especially good. Those in the S. chancel aisle are placed too high to see in this dim church; a pity, for taken as a whole the church monuments make a good gallery of 17th-cent. merchants and their wives.

Holy Trinity church, originally built in 1847 (Macintosh, architect), has a very handsome tower in the Somerset style, but the rest of the church had to be rebuilt in 1868 because of bad foundations and is dull. St. Mary Magdalene was built in 1844-6 by Benjamin Ferrey.

Barnstaple is fairly rich in almshouses as might be expected in a town of former commercial importance. Most notable are the Penrose Almshouses (1627) in Litchdon Street, a group of twenty dwellings around a charming courtyard, with a granite-columned cloister (somewhat similar to that at Moreton Hampstead) along the street frontage. Horwood's Almshouses (c. 1650-60) in Church Lane, founded by Thomas Horwood, merchant, stand beside the maids' school founded by his wife Alice Horwood in 1659, making a good group. Paige's Almshouses were founded in 1656. These almshouses, the monuments in the church, and the richly decorated plaster ceilings to be seen in various buildings in the town, leave us in no doubt that the 17th cent. saw Barnstaple's greatest and most prosperous days.

Many of the remarkable 17th-cent. ceilings, which were the work of a Barnstaple school of plasterers similar to those who worked at Totnes and Dartmouth in South Devon, have been removed or destroyed, but the Westminster Bank (formerly the Golden Lion Hotel) retains two good examples, that in the Banking Hall (dated 1620) being exceptionally fine. In Cross Street, No. 8 retains one good example.

St. Anne's chapel, near the parish church, is an early 14th-cent. building. It was endowed as a chantry in 1459, and suffered the fate of all chantries in 1547. It was afterwards (until 1908) used as a grammar school. John Gay the poet and dramatist (1685-1732), who was born at what is now No. 35 High Street and is Barnstaple's most well-known son, was educated here. So, too, was Sir John Doddridge, solicitor-general to James I. John Jewel and Thomas Harding, those great theological antagonists in later life, are also said to have had their schooling in this building in pre-Reformation days. On Sundays from 1685 to 1785 the room was used as a place of worship for Huguenots. It is now a museum.

Barnstaple bridge, of sixteen pointed arches and 700 ft. long, was first built in the late 13th cent. The present bridge was built about 1437, but has been considerably reconstructed, widened, and altered, and does not compare in beauty and interest with Bideford bridge. Nevertheless, it retains a good deal of medieval work.[1] Barnstaple has long been known as Barum, probably from the contracted Latinised form of the name.

BEAFORD (D4). The church (All Saints) is mainly late 15th-cent., but much restored and dull. The tower was rebuilt 1910; the font is Norman. Upcott, Warham, and Woodleigh (or Woolleigh) were houses of some consequence in this parish. They are worth visiting for their beautiful surroundings. Woolleigh still contains early 17th-cent. work but has been modernised in an unfortunate way. It was a Saxon estate, its name meaning " wolves' clearing." There are remains of a 15th-cent. chapel here.

BEAWORTHY (c6) has a small 14th-cent. church, practically rebuilt in 1871, and of no interest whatever. The S. doorway has small traces of Norman work. The church is the only one in Devon dedicated to St. Alban, the 4th-cent. protomartyr of Britain.

BEER (L7) is an attractive fishing village on a small bay, sheltered by the great chalk cliff of Beer Head (426 ft.), the first of the chalk headlands on the English coast as one comes up-Channel. Beer was made a separate civil parish in 1894, and an ecclesiastical parish in 1905, but the church of St. Michael dates from 1877-8. It was built on the site of an older chapel.

The famous Beer quarries lie about

¾ m. W. of the village. That to the S. of the lane is the Old Quarry, which was worked intermittently from Roman times to the late 19th cent. It is entirely underground, and one needs permission and a guide to explore its ramifications. To anyone who is historically minded, this quarry, out of which have come Roman villas and public buildings, cathedrals, parish churches, country houses and cottages, right down to recent times, is one of the most exciting things in Devon. One passes through the dark hole in the rock face into a Roman ante-chamber, in which the tool-marks are still visible on the walls; then on into the Norman quarry, like a cathedral itself with its massive square pillars of stone supporting the roof, and the dark aisles and side-chapels opening on either hand; thence along the great nave, through spaces that produced stone for those chalk-white arcades and carved screens in the Devon country churches, for Exeter cathedral and Rochester castle, for St. Stephen's at Westminster and Exeter Guildhall, and for beautiful Tudor country houses like Bovey not so far away; and finally through choirs and chapels to the blank rock-face where eighteen centuries came to an end in total silence and darkness. It is a deeply impressive place when one calls to mind what strength and what sunlit beauty have come from its heart over so many centuries.

On the N. side of the lane is the New Quarry, also entirely underground, first opened in 1883 and in extent equal to that of the Old. Most of this stone seems to have been quarried for church restoration work. This quarry is now closed except for the manufacture of lime in the open approaches. Beer village contains much building in the local stone, some used externally in 17th-cent. houses and still good. Bovey House lies NW. of the village beyond another group of old quarries. It came about 1300 to the Walronds (of Bradfield) who continued to own it until a marriage carried it to the Rolles by 1786. The present house, which is most attractive, is mainly of 16th-cent. date (early and late). Further work was done in the 17th cent., and some changes were also made about 1719. The house contains some notable 17th-cent. plaster work. After the death of the last Mrs. Walrond (1786) the house was left unoccupied. Both it and the lane leading to it were said to be haunted, with the result that smuggling was successfully carried on here. The house was rescued again in 1868, but reroofed with slate and the walls somewhat cut down.

Jack Rattenbury (b. 1778), one of the most notable of Devon smugglers, was a native of Beer and operated from here. He published late in life his *Memoirs of a Smuggler* (Sidmouth, 1837) when gout had caused him to give up his career, and he ended his days peacefully as a contractor for blue-lias lime for Sidmouth harbour, helped also by a pension of a shilling a week from Lord Rolle.

BELSTONE (E6) is a straggling village spoilt by some atrocious modern building since it was "discovered " fifty years ago. Nevertheless, the surrounding scenery is fine: Belstone Tor (1568 ft.) and Cawsand Beacon (1799 ft.) towering over the village, and the infant Taw hurrying through the gorge of Belstone Cleave. The parish contains much high moorland on which are some remains of hut circles and other traces of Bronze Age man.

The granite church (St. Mary) was deprived of nearly all its interest by a drastic restoration in 1881, when it was practically rebuilt except for the low 15th-cent. tower. It had been allowed to fall into a deplorable state, but the subsequent "restoration" swept away everything indiscriminately. The fine early 16th-cent. screen and the carved oak bench-ends disappeared, together with the gallery at the W. end of the S. aisle where the old village choir sat. The five bells "are somewhat light in tone, but very sweet, as they sound across the moor on Sunday evenings."

BERE FERRERS (c9) occupies the whole of the undulating and picturesque peninsula between the Tavy estuary on the E. and the Tamar on the W. This triangular piece of country was called *Birland* in Saxon times, from the Welsh *ber*, "pike, spit," or the Irish *bir*, "point," referring to the big spit of land between these two rivers. The Ferrers acquired the manor in Henry II's time and had a house near the water's edge on the Tavy, of which some remains can be seen in the present Bere Barton, chiefly the bottom stage of what was once a small keep-like tower.

The church (St. Andrew) is exceptionally interesting. It was rebuilt (except the tower) by Sir William de Ferrers *c.* 1330-33, who established a collegiate church here for an archpriest and four other priests and a deacon living as a community. The building was altered in the 15th cent. by the enlargement of the Decorated S. transept into a full aisle with granite arcades. Much excellent 14th-cent. work remains untouched, though some of the Decorated windows were altered in the 17th cent. (cf. the S. transept). The 14th-cent. glass in the E. window is reputed to be the oldest in Devon except one or two windows in Exeter Cathedral. Among the other notable features of the church are the vigorously carved Norman font (late 12th-cent., of Hurdwick stone); the 16th-cent. seats, carved bench-ends, and book-rests; the 17th-cent. fireplace in the N. transept; and the medieval tombs. The canopied tomb with effigies in the chancel is that of Sir William de Ferrers and his wife, the rebuilders of the church. In the N. transept is an earlier Ferrers tomb and effigy, and also a handsome table tomb which is almost certainly that of the 2nd baron Willoughby de Broke (d. 1522).

Bere Alston, now a small town and the principal part of the parish, originated in the time of Edward I as a mining settlement. The silver-lead mines were worked here from the 1290s intermittently down to the late 19th cent. Reginald de Ferrers obtained a market and fair here in 1295, and shortly afterwards set up a borough. As a parliamentary borough from 1584 to 1832, Bere Alston returned a remarkable number of eminent men, including Lord Chancellor King and Sir George Beaumont.

The parish has long been noted for its black cherries and its strawberry fields. The remains of the old mines are chiefly along the Tamar, and with the deserted quays on the river are very picturesque.

BERRYNARBOR (D1). The manor house of the Berrys, built *c.* 1480, still stands near the church, though the porch and one wing have been demolished. The porch and some elaborate carved work are now at Westaway, near Barnstaple.

The church (St. Peter) is largely a 15th-cent. building, but there are considerable remains of the 12th and 13th cent. The Beer stone arcade (*c.* 1500-10) has rather coarse detail on its carved capitals. Presumably this stone was brought all around the coast by sea from the East Devon quarry. The tower, built of the local red sandstone about 1480, is one of the grandest in N. Devon; its N. face is perhaps the best side, with the turreted staircase.

John Jewel (1522-71), bishop of Salisbury and author of the famous *Apologia pro Ecclesia Anglicana* (1562), which Queen Elizabeth ordered to be read in every church in her kingdom, was born at Bowden, a farmhouse in this parish. The present farmhouse, which retains an interesting 15th-cent. screen, may well be the very one in which Jewel was born. His great opponent, Thomas Harding (1516-72), who abandoned protestantism and retired to Louvain in the reign of Elizabeth, was born in the neighbouring parish of Combe Martin.

Watermouth Castle, a Gothic house in a lovely park, was built about 1825. East Hagginton was a Domesday manor.

BERRY POMEROY (G9) has been in the possession of only two families since the Norman Conquest—the Pomeroys and the Seymours. The great Norman family of de la Pomerai owned it from 1066 until 1548, making it their principal residence in Devon. It was then sold to Edward Seymour, Duke of Somerset, whose descendant still owns it. There is no evidence that a castle existed here before the building of the Edwardian castle by one of the Pomeroys in the early 14th cent. A survey of 1292 shows only the usual type of medieval manor house on the site. The 14th-cent. gatehouse, with its massive curtain-wall, leads into a courtyard in which are the ruins of the great house begun in all probability by the Lord Protector's son, who lived here from 1575 until his death in 1593. The Seymours lived at Berry for most of the 17th cent. Much work of this period is visible in the existing ruins, but the plan of the buildings has yet to be worked out in detail. John Prince, author of *The Worthies of Devon* (first published in 1701) and vicar of Berry Pomeroy, tells us that the Seymours spent upwards of £20,000 on the house " but never brought it to perfection." They had been strong royalists in the Civil War, and were heavily fined. Nevertheless, they were living here in some state in 1688 when Sir Edward Seymour, the 3rd bart., welcomed William, Prince of Orange, at Berry Castle. His son, another Sir Edward (1633-1708), who became speaker of the House of Commons and had a distinguished career in politics, made Maiden Bradley (Wilts.) his home and Berry was abandoned. When Prince wrote, it was already falling into decay and it is now one of the most romantically beautiful ruins in Devon, almost buried in deep woods on the edge of a cliff.

Berry Pomeroy church (St. Mary) is an attractive building, rebuilt in the time of Sir Richard Pomeroy (d. 1496). He is probably the occupant of the ornate tomb on the S. side of the chancel. The capitals of the S. arcade bear the names of other donors to the rebuilding, the scroll on the W. respond having the inscription *Et pro omnibus benefactoribus huius operis orate*. There is a fine Seymour monument to Edward, son of the Lord Protector (d. 1593), his son Edward (d. 1613), and the latter's wife, Elizabeth Champernowne.

John Prince was vicar here 1681-1723, and seems to have done a good deal of work on his church. The tower and S. porch look like a 17th-cent. rebuilding, and the old altar rails and altar table (now in the N. aisle) are of his date. So, of course, are the royal arms of William and Mary. The vicarage looks like Prince's handiwork also. Prince was succeeded by Joseph Fox, who was vicar 1723-81, so that Berry had only two parsons in 100 years.

At Longcombe, a farmhouse, William III is said to have held a meeting of his supporters in a house now called Parliament House, before moving on to Berry Castle.

BICKINGTON (G8) has a much restored 15th-cent. church (St. Mary), cluttered up with Victorian woodwork, and of no great interest. The 16th-cent. house E. of the church was formerly the Church House.

BICKINGTON, HIGH (D3), like so many villages in this part of Devon, stands on a summit commanding wonderful views NE. to Exmoor and S. to Dartmoor. This is one of the unknown and unspoilt parts of Devon. Lee Barton and South Heale are farmhouses of some antiquarian interest.

The church (St. Mary) is of exceptional interest. It is a 12th-cent. building, somewhat altered and enlarged in the early 14th, and considerably enlarged by two aisles and a W. tower in the late 15th or early 16th cent. The wagon roofs of nave, chancel, and N. aisle are worth attention, but the great feature of the church is a magnificent series of about seventy carved benchends. These fall into two main types: a late Gothic, with window tracery, etc., and a Renaissance, with figures, heads, etc., all *c*. 1500-30 in date. The modern carving on the choir stalls, portraying processions of animals and birds, is also very pleasing.

BICKLEIGH (D9) lies on the W. slopes

of the wooded Plym valley, here very beautiful. Bickleigh Vale was often visited by the historical painter Benjamin Haydon for inspiration. The manor was given to Buckland Abbey in 1278. After the dissolution it was sold to the Slannings, a local family. It was eventually bought (1798) by the notorious Manasseh Lopes, then M.P. for New Romney, who accumulated a vast estate in this part of Devon. The church (St. Mary) was wholly rebuilt, except the handsome tower, by Sir Ralph Lopes in 1829, and restored again in 1861.[1] It contains the remains of a memorial to Gamaliel Slanning, killed in a duel with Sir John Fitz of Fitzford in 1599. Above this are the helmet and gauntlet of his son, Sir Nicholas Slanning (one of the "four wheels of Charles's wain"), killed at the siege of Bristol 26 July 1643. There are also monuments to the Lopes family.

BICKLEIGH (H5) lies astride the middle valley of the Exe, here of perfect pastoral beauty with rounded green hills rising to 700 ft. or so on either side. Bickleigh Bridge, a noted "beautyspot" (but unspoilt), dates from the late 16th cent. In 1809 it was severely damaged by floods and was rebuilt.

Bickleigh Castle (so called), on the W. bank of the Exe, was a moated and fortified manor-house, of which the gatehouse range is the chief remnant to-day. A fortified house of the Bickleigh family existed here in the 12th cent. Work of this period may be seen in the bases of the imposts in the gatehouse, and in the small chapel immediately across the lane. Bickleigh came to the Courtenays of Powderham, who used it as an estate for younger sons, and it was they who rebuilt the Norman house early in the 15th cent.

There are traces of the former great hall, and N. of the gatehouse is a portion of the old moat, now mostly filled up. The gatehouse, which has a vaulted entry (*c.* 1400 in date), was reconstructed in the 17th cent. by the Carews. The house later degenerated into a farmhouse, but was rescued after the sale of the Carew properties in 1922, and restored to its present form. The Carews had acquired Bickleigh about 1510.

Bickleigh church (St. Mary) is a badly restored 14th-cent. building, with a 12th-cent. S. doorway and font. It is chiefly notable for the charming, though crudely executed, Carew monuments of 16th–17th-cent. date. Bampfylde Moore Carew (1690–1758) was the son of a rector of Bickleigh. He became a gipsy and was elected their king, was transported to Maryland but escaped back to England, followed Prince Charles Edward's army to Derby in 1745, and eventually settled down at Bickleigh where he died in 1758. There was still a Carew at the rectory in 1890; but the long association of the family with the parish was ended at the sale of 1922.

BICTON (J7) came to the Rolles, together with other large estates, by the marriage of Sir Henry Rolle of Stevenstone to Anne, daughter and co-heiress of Sir Thomas Dennis. By this marriage the Rolles became the largest landowners in Devon. They made Bicton one of their principal houses for several generations, and here they laid out a park and accumulated a fine library, now dispersed. The present house is said to have been built about 1730, but it was certainly not finished until the end of the 18th cent. It has been one of the great houses of the West of England, much visited by royalty. The gardens, laid out *c.* 1730, are some of the finest in the West of England, and employed forty gardeners early in this century. The arboretum, and especially the avenue of araucaria trees, is one of the best in England. The mansion is now an Agricultural College under the Devon County Council, but Lord Clinton (the present representative of the Rolles, now extinct in the direct line) retains the gardens and the arboretum, which are being slowly brought back to their former state after years of wartime neglect. The Obelisk, just outside the park, was erected in 1730 as a *point de vue* from the gardens, and the tower in the woods behind the house—known as the China Tower—was built about 1840 by Lady Rolle as a birthday gift to her husband. She later used it to house her magnificent collection of china, gathered from all over the world.

The present Bicton church (St. Mary) was built by Hayward of Exeter in 1850. It is dull. Near by are the ruins of the former church, of which little remains but the tower. It has been converted into a mausoleum for the Rolles, and contains a magnificent marble tomb of Dennis Rolle (1638) and his wife and child, which Oliver suggests may be the work of Nicholas Stone. If so, it is the only known work of Stone in Devon.

BIDEFORD (c3), the most attractive town in North Devon, lies on a hillside rising sharply from the W. bank of the Torridge where it begins to widen into its estuary (Plate 21). On the E. bank, joined to the town by a stone bridge of twenty-four pointed arches, is the suburb of East-the-Water, which is itself an old place. It probably arose when the bridge was built, shortly before 1300.

It is probable that both Barnstaple and Bideford bridges, the two most famous bridges in North Devon, were first constructed in the last quarter of the 13th cent. The earliest bridge at Bideford was of oak timber, and the first stone bridge (*c.* 1460) was built over and around this wooden bridge, which was used as scaffolding. Repair work before the widening of 1925 brought much of this timber to light from inside the masonry. The variation in the span of the stone arches from 12 ft. to 25 ft., and hence in the thickness of the piers, arises from their being built around the arches of the wooden bridge, which in turn varied according to the length of the oak-timber used in the lintels. The present bridge is substantially the 15th-cent. structure, though it has been widened more than once. It is managed by a body of trustees or feoffees, out of an income derived mainly from property in Bideford (cf. Bridgeland Street). Not only does the bridge maintain itself but its surplus revenue has from time to time enabled the trustees to initiate and support numerous schemes and improvements in the borough, above all, perhaps, the maintenance of the grammar school.[1]

Bideford was a place of little consequence until Elizabethan times. It grew up beside a ford over the Torridge, and was given by William Rufus to the Grenvilles. From this time until 1744, Bideford remained their property.[2] The town owes a great deal to the Grenvilles. Richard de Grenville made a borough of it before 1217,[3] and a later Grenville obtained a market and a five-day fair (probably a confirmation) in 1271. Bideford was, however, entirely overshadowed by Barnstaple until the late 16th cent., and was a place of no more than local importance, chiefly notable for shipbuilding (as Leland tells us) and fishing.

By 1573 the town had grown sufficiently to receive a charter of incorporation from the Queen, at the instance of the great Sir Richard Grenville. Sir Richard's colonisation of Virginia and Carolina led to the establishment of a considerable American trade at Bideford, which lasted for some 200 years until the American colonies achieved their independence. By Charles I's time the Bideford merchants were importing wool from Spain for the flourishing Devonshire textile industry, later extending their commerce to Holland, France, and the Mediterranean. Bideford Quay was first built in 1663 by the corporation. By the end of the 17th cent. the town had a large share in the Newfoundland trade, sending out more ships in 1699 than any other port except London and Topsham. Above all, it was the tobacco trade with Maryland and Virginia which made the largest Bideford fortunes, a trade which was at its height *c.* 1680–1730, and ceased about 1760. It was during this period that Bideford became the leading port in North Devon, far surpassing its ancient rival of Barnstaple. The handsome houses in Bridgeland Street (*c.* 1690-1700) and the Royal Hotel, at East-the-Water, formerly a merchant's house, testify to the wealth of these days. One after another, however, Bideford's overseas trades dwindled or collapsed, mostly as a result of the incessant wars of the 18th cent., and partly because of the collapse of the woollen industry in the county. By the early 19th cent. only a coasting trade remained.

The town revived during the course of the 19th cent. and grew steadily in numbers, more than doubling in size between 1821 and 1901. To-day it has rather more than 10,000 people, and is an active and cheerful town, with a good market and shops. Its foreign trade revived, on a small but useful scale, after the Napoleonic Wars. From the 1830s onwards it also developed a considerable emigrant traffic to America, with four first-class emigrant ships sailing regularly to America and elsewhere in the 1840s and 1850s.[1] The ancient shipbuilding industry was carried on vigorously throughout the century, down to the present day. Many of the local industries that flourished in the 19th cent. (potteries, lime-burning, breweries, etc.) have now gone or declined, but others have taken their place; and the town is now becoming known as a holiday centre and a good place to retire to in one's old age.

Although Bideford has such a long history and looks so attractive from any viewpoint, it is less interesting architecturally than might be expected. Much of the town is Victorian, built of the rather unpleasing local yellow brick, but there are some good things left. Most interesting of all is Bridgeland Street, which was laid out by Nathaniel Gascoyne about 1690–1700, planned from the start as a wide street lined with merchants' houses.[2] Several of these houses, especially Nos. 1, 4, 12, and 28, are good examples of their period; others have been refronted with stucco or rebuilt in the late 18th or early 19th cent. The other old streets contain little beyond some plain late Georgian building, of which the New Inn Hotel is a pleasant example. The old workhouse was built 1835-6 and is attributed to Sir Gilbert Scott.

The parish church (St. Mary) was rebuilt in 1865, except for its plain 14th-cent. tower, and has lost most of its character. It contains a fine late-Norman font, the canopied tomb of Sir

Thomas Grenville (1513), a tower screen of handsomely carved late 16th-cent. panelling, and some good mural monuments to the 17th–18th-cent. merchants of the town.

Across the river, the Royal Hotel embodies (at its N. end) the original town house of John Davie, an eminent merchant, built in 1688. The front has been altered, but the interior contains a good late 17th-cent. staircase and two fine plaster ceilings on the first floor. Charles Kingsley is said to have written part of *Westward Ho!* here.

BIGBURY (E11) probably takes its name from Borough Island which was known as *la Burgh* in the 15th cent. It is a miniature of St. Michael's Mount in Cornwall, and had indeed a chapel dedicated to St. Michael on its summit in 1411, of which there are now no traces. The coast here has been much spoilt by bungalow-building.

The church (St. Lawrence) is mainly a 14th-cent. building, virtually rebuilt in 1872-3 by J. D. Sedding, and good. The plain 14th-cent. tower has a short spire. The chancel retains its early 14th-cent. piscina and triple sedilia. The N. aisle and S. transept are said to have been added c. 1400 by the daughters of Sir William de Bigbury, whose fine brasses may be seen in the N. aisle. The pulpit and lectern were brought from Ashburton about 1777.

BISHOP'S NYMPTON (F3) was an estate of the bishops of Exeter. The church (St. Mary) is entirely 15th or early 16th-cent. in date, with a fine, well-proportioned tower. Restored in 1869 and 1877, the interior is Victorianised and unexciting. All the roofs have good bosses, especially the S. aisle. An altar-tomb on the N. side of the chancel without inscription is probably that of Sir Lewis Pollard (*c.* 1465-1540), king's sergeant in 1507, justice of the Common Pleas 1514-26, and one of the many eminent Devon lawyers to found a large estate. He lived at Grilstone in this parish, though he later bought a large estate in King's Nympton (q.v.) and made a park there. A window in the Pollard aisle formerly portrayed the judge with eleven sons kneeling behind him, and his wife with eleven daughters. About this Prince relates a pleasant tale: " That his lady, glassing this window in her husband's absence at the Term in London, caused one child more than she then had to be set there; presuming, having had one and twenty already, and usually conceiving at her husband's coming home, that she should have another. Which, inserted in expectation, came to pass in reality."[1]

There are some remains of the old house at Grilstone. Rawstone, Garliford and Hall are other farmhouses which were once the mansions of medieval freeholders and show some evidence of this origin. Whitechapel Barton was called *Blaunchechapele* in 1281, and *Whitechapel* in 1333, possibly from the colour of its stonework. The present house, which belonged to the Bassets for centuries, is an attractive building of 16th-cent. date, with some early 18th-cent. alterations.

BISHOP'S TAWTON (D2) is a large village, now almost a suburb of Barnstaple. There is a long-standing tradition that it was the site of the see of Devon before Crediton was chosen in 909, but conclusive proof of this is not yet forthcoming. Throughout medieval times Bishop's Tawton was, next to Paignton, the bishop of Exeter's most valuable property. He had a palace here, of which some remains are to be seen in the 15th-cent. building (next to the church) now occupied as a farm-house.

The church (St. John the Baptist), one of the few in Devon with a medieval spire, is substantially a 14th-cent. building, but has undergone sweeping restorations. The chancel, S. porch, and vestry were rebuilt in 1860. In the chancel are some mural monuments to the Chichesters of Hall.

Hall was the seat of the Halls, whose heiress brought it to a younger son of the Chichesters of Raleigh in 1461, so establishing a new branch of that formerly ubiquitous family in North Devon, and now the only one to survive in its old home. The present house, built in 1846-8 in the Elizabethan style, contains a galleried banqueting hall. A quantity of finely carved oak fittings, formerly in the private chapel at Hall, are now in a chapel of ease, erected at Herner in 1888. Little Pill, now a farmhouse, was formerly a "mansion," with a private chapel licensed in 1400. At Whitemoor farm some medieval work survives, including a 15th-cent. oak doorway, and an example of " cruck " building, rare in Devon.

New Bridge, over the Taw, existed in 1326 when Bishop Stapeldon left 60s. for its repair. The present bridge was probably built early in the 19th cent. The foundations of an earlier bridge can be seen 100 yards downstream.

Codden Hill (630 ft.), in this parish, is associated with W. N. P. Barbellion (born at Barnstaple), whose book, *The Journal of a Disappointed Man*, was a literary sensation of the early 1920s and contains much good descriptive writing about the Barnstaple country.

BISHOPSTEIGNTON (H8) is a large parish on the N. side of the Teign estuary. It belonged to the bishops of Exeter from before the Norman Conquest and was one of their richest manors. They had one of their numerous "palaces" or country residences here, at Radway just NE. of the village, but only a little 14th-cent. walling remains of this. The village is large, with a good deal of very pleasant early 19th-cent. building in white stucco.

The church (St. John the Baptist) was practically rebuilt in 1815 when the central tower was taken down and rebuilt at the W. end. The body of the church is 15th-cent. and of little interest, the removal of the screen turning it into a great barn. The N. aisle was the Lyndridge aisle and contains several memorials to the successive owners of the estate.

Lyndridge is a good 17th-cent. house, probably built in 1673 for Sir Peter Lear, bart., a Barbados merchant, who bought the estate from the Martins. It was formerly much larger. Two wings were pulled down about 1740, leaving the centre alone standing, and the house has been remodelled to some extent. It was refaced in brick in 1916. There are some sumptuously decorated rooms with magnificent plaster ceilings done *c.* 1673.

BITTADON (D1) lies in an unspoilt valley. On the hills to the E. is a group of eight large barrows, probably of Bronze Age date, and a few others to the N. again. The church (St. Peter) consists of nave, chancel, and dumpy W. tower with pyramidal cap. It was hideously rebuilt and ruined in 1883-7. The only objects of interest are a plain 13th-cent. font, and mural monuments to Edward Poyntz (1691) and Arthur Acland (1675).

BLACKAWTON (G10) is a large village in the unknown country that lies in the hills W. of Dartmouth. The exact significance of "black" is not clear, but it may be a reference to the colour of the local slate building-stone which is almost jet-black when wet.

The parish was formerly more extensive, running down to the shore of Start Bay, but the parish of Strete was carved out of it in 1881. A number of houses in the parish are of some interest. Fuge, first mentioned in 1269, was the "cattle-farm" of the royal manor of Blackawton, possibly from Saxon times. The present house was built in 1725. Oldstone was the seat of the Cholwiches for more than 200 years. It is probably an 11th-cent. estate, its name meaning "Ulf's farm." The mansion was largely rebuilt by the Cholwiches in the 18th cent. and is now a ruin. In the park are remains of a former house of unknown date. At Cotterbury Barton, Preston Barton, Lower Dreyton, and Hutcherleigh are the remains of what were formerly "mansions."

The church (St. Michael) is interesting both for its structure and its contents. It is essentially a 14th-cent. building, greatly enlarged in the late 15th. Of the 12th-cent. church there remains only the fine font, carved with honeysuckle ornament, the largest of all its type in Devon (except that at Paignton) and the most beautiful. The rood-screen bears the initials of Henry VIII and of Catherine of Aragon, with her badge (the pomegranate), and retains its ancient colours of vermilion and blue. There is a Jacobean pulpit, and a font cover of the same date; royal arms dated 1680; and a considerable number of inscribed floor-slabs and other memorials. Much of the window tracery appears to have been altered in the early 19th cent.

BLACKBOROUGH (*see* KENTISBEARE).

BONDLEIGH (E5) is in the pleasant,

unknown country of the upper Taw valley. The church (St. James) has some interesting Norman work, including a S. doorway with tympanum, and two richly carved portions of late 12th-cent. capitals built into the E. wall of the aisle. The Norman church was rebuilt in the late 15th–early 16th cent; and much reconstruction was done in the 17th cent. The fine tower is of granite below (probably 15th-cent.), but has been rebuilt above in the local brown dunstone. The 17th-cent. work included the remodelling of the windows of the aisle (except the E. window) and the insertion of a number of square-ended benches, some plain and some roughly carved. The nave and aisle have their original wagon-roofs with carved bosses, and there is some late 15th-cent. glass portraying figures of the Annunciation.

BOVEY, NORTH (F7), is an exceptionally attractive and unspoilt village around a green. It lies on a hillside above the river Bovey from which it takes its name, looking across to the eastern wall of Dartmoor. The parish runs far W. into the Moor, and abounds in hut-circles and other Bronze Age antiquities. These are best located on the 2½-inch Ordnance maps (sheets 20/68, 20/78). In the far W. of the parish, on Headland Warren, are numerous ancient tin-works dating from the days of "streaming," scoring the ground heavily, and a number of abandoned tin mines. The most notable is perhaps the Birch Tor and Vitifer mine, about ½ m. E. of Warren House Inn on the Moretonhampstead-Princetown road. The isolated farms of Beetor and Shapley were Saxon settlements and are referred to in Domesday Book.

The church (St. John the Baptist) is a 15th-cent. granite building of the moorland type, with a contemporary rood-screen of fairly good design though sadly mutilated. There are parclose screens N. and S. of the chancel, some plain 16th-cent. benches, and a modern pulpit in the medieval style. This replaced (in 1910) a Georgian pulpit. The wagon roofs have many carved bosses, those in the chancel being especially good and worth detailed study. There are many granite floor-slabs to 17th- and 18th-cent. yeomen of the parish.

The Manor House, so called, is a modern mansion on a new site. It was the seat of Viscount Hambleden and is now an hotel. The scenery of the entire parish is beautifully broken.

BOVEY TRACEY (G8) is a small and ancient market-town. Henry de Tracey created a borough here in the early 13th cent. and in 1259 obtained a grant (probably a confirmation) of a weekly market and a three-day fair at the feast of the Translation of St. Thomas. During the Civil War, Bovey Heath was occupied by part of Lord Wentworth's brigade. They were attacked on the evening of 9 January 1646, and completely surprised, by Lieut.-General Cromwell with a part of the parliamentary army under the command of Fairfax.

The church (St. Peter, St. Paul and St. Thomas of Canterbury) is mainly 15th-cent., with a tall and slender 14th-cent. tower. The nave arcades of Beer stone have delicately carved capitals of unusual design. It is possible that we have here an early 14th-cent. cruciform church (cf. the piscina of that date in the S. aisle), which was enlarged and reconstructed in the second half of the 15th cent. by the extension of the original transepts into aisles. The outer

N. aisle was added in 1858. The fittings of this fine church are notable, above all the excellent rood-screen of eleven bays. This was restored in 1887-8, when the missing vaulting was reconstructed, and the ancient colour and gilding renewed. The stone pulpit (with some excellent canopy work), the eagle-lectern, miserere seats in the chancel, and the font, are all of 15th-cent. date. In the tower arch is a finely carved achievement of the arms of Charles II, and an inscription by James Forbes, vicar 1628-65, about the execution of Laud " by the bloody Parliament " and the imprisonment of Bishop Joseph Hall in 1642. In the chancel are two Jacobean monuments, that on the N. being to Nicholas Eveleigh, on the S. to Elize Hele.

Near by are the Church House, built *c.* 1500, and the House of Mercy (by Woodyer, 1867). St. John's Church near the station (1853) has a richly decorated chancel with mosaics by Salviati.

Bovey Heathfield is a level expanse, of great interest to geologists. It is the bed of an ancient lake, and contains beds of lignite which have been mined sporadically since the early 16th cent. There are large potteries and brickworks here.

Elsford, Hawkmoor (now a large sanatorium), Pullabrook, and Woolley are all recorded as manors in Domesday Book.

BOW (F5) is a large street-village on the old Crediton-Okehampton road. The original centre of the parish was Nymet Tracey (for the meaning of *nymet* see KING'S NYMPTON) but in the 13th cent. a new settlement grew up on the main road. Henry de Tracey obtained in 1259 the grant of a weekly market and a three-day fair at the feast of St. Martin,[1] which would naturally be held down on the main road; and so Bow was born. Early in the 14th cent. an attempt was made to make a borough of it. We find four burgesses here in 1326;[2] but the place never developed any urban characteristics, though it retained its fair until about 1900.

Halse was a Saxon estate and is recorded in Domesday. Hillerton is recorded in a Saxon charter of 739. Here Mr. Reckitts, the starch magnate, built a mansion which is now completely demolished. At Hilldown, the Traceys are said to have had a castle (more probably a fortified manor house) of which some walls remained within living memory.

Nymet Tracey church (St. Bartholomew) is a 14th-cent. building, with a 15th-cent. N. aisle, all heavily restored in 1889-90, when the chancel was rebuilt. There are traces of Norman work in the S. doorway. An unusual early 16th-cent. rood-screen retains a good deal of the ancient colouring. The pulpit and altar rails date from 1680. There was formerly a chapel at Bow dedicated to St. Martin.

BRADFORD (c5) was the " broad ford " over the Torridge.

Besides Bradford itself, Dunsland, Henscott, and Lashbrook are all mentioned in Domesday. Dunsland descended to the Arscotts of Arscott, by marriage with the Battyn heiress, in 1522. They held it until 1634, when William Bickford married the Arscott heiress. The Bickfords held it from 1634 until 1817. It then passed to the Cohams, and subsequently to the Dickinsons, who sold it before 1939. Dunsland House is of considerable interest. Beginning with a small early Tudor house, it shows a succession of enlargements down to the late 18th cent. The original house (*c.* 1500) was added to about the middle of the 16th cent.: a record of 1580 refers to " the old parlour " and " the old kitchen," and suggests a house of some size.[1] It also refers to the chamber or chapel over the porch, a room which may still be seen. No earlier reference to a chapel at Dunsland has been found; but this suggests a pre-Reformation date for part of the house which is confirmed by the existence of linenfold panelling in one room. The house was enlarged in 1609; much of this work also remains. It was further enlarged and embellished by Arscott Bickford, who ruled at Dunsland 1659-93. The magnificent decorated ceiling and carving in the drawing-room, c. 1680, now restored, is part of his work. Lysons says that the house was further " much improved " by George Bickford, who had Dunsland 1771-95.[2] The house fell into considerable disrepair during the war of 1939-45, but has since been rescued and carefully restored. The remains of a moat and a large fishpond SW. of Bramble Wood probably represent the site of the medieval manor house of Dunsland, before the early Tudor rebuilding on a new site.

Henscott, now a farmhouse, was the home of the Henscotts from the early 13th cent. until 1572 when John Henscott died. Near the farm is a small earthwork of an irregular circular plan, overlooking the Torridge valley. Bovacott was a " mansion " in the 16th–18th cents. On the wall of the N. aisle of the parish church is an incised slate slab, of beautiful lettering and design, to the Maynards of Bovacott, 1666-88.

The church (All Saints) is essentially an early 14th-cent. building, with a good Norman S. doorway and a (restored) Norman font, preserved from the 12th-cent. church. The N. aisle was added early in the 16th cent. In 1550 the tower was repaired and raised, as appears by a dated stone, and the church probably reseated. A few remains of well-carved 16th-cent. bench-ends lie mouldering at the back of the church, together with a medieval chest. Many late medieval tiles remain in the floor. There are incised floor-slabs to the Arscotts, Bickfords, Henscotts, and other local families. The church, which had become ruinous, was restored in 1869 and again in 1875-89 when the chancel was rebuilt. Nevertheless, it remains an interesting and pleasant little building.

BRADNINCH (H5), lying in a fold of the hills that rise W. from the Culm valley to 850 ft. at Christ Cross, is a decayed borough and market town with a long history. In the 12th cent. it was held as an honour or barony with the earldom of Cornwall by Reginald, natural son of Henry I, who created a borough here by charter between 1141 and 1175.[3] King John's charter of 1208 granted the burgesses of Bradninch all such liberties and free customs as the city of Exeter enjoyed, together with a Saturday market and a four-day fair at the feast of St. Dionysius; and in 1238 King Henry III granted the borough a Thursday market and a three-day fair at the festival of the Holy Trinity. In 1337 Bradninch, with other estates, was absorbed into the Duchy of Cornwall, to which it still belongs. The borough was incorporated by James I in 1604, and given a mayor, 12 masters, and a recorder. The Municipal Corporations Act of 1835 removed Bradninch from the list of boroughs, although the report of the commissioners showed that it was far from being as scandalously corrupt as most of the Devon boroughs. Of the annual income of £64 10s., the corporation spent exactly one-half on feasting themselves.

Like many of the East Devon towns, it had a considerable woollen industry and was also noted for its lace manufacture. Both these industries decayed to nothing by the late 18th cent., and when Lysons wrote (1822) he tells us that all the fairs and great markets had long been discontinued; even the weekly market had not been held within living memory. Bradninch would, indeed, have sunk to the level of Plympton Earl and passed away in its sleep but for the timely establishment of paper mills on the Culm, whose water was eminently suitable for paper-making. A grist mill at Hele was converted to a paper mill in 1762, and in 1767 two more mills were started at Kensham, near by. The Hele Mills are still flourishing and produce high-grade paper. It was here that John Dewdney produced the first glazed writing-paper in England in the 1840s; he was called on to supply the paper for the catalogues of the Great Exhibition in 1851.[1] The mills were burnt down in 1821 and rebuilt. With the houses and cottages around, Hele makes an attractive group.

The town has little to commend it. It consists chiefly of one main street flanked by drab roughcast or red brick, lifeless and unattractive. The usual series of fires, so common in the cob-and-thatch country, has destroyed most of the old buildings, though away from the main street are one or two buildings in the old vernacular style. The church (St. Dionysius) is entirely 15th–early 16th-cent. in date, with an over-restored interior (1845). Only the rood-screen is of any interest. It is twelve bays in width, with fifty-two panels having painted figures or subjects. Two niches retain their ancient statuettes. The date of the screen is said to be 1528. Across the tower arch is a fine 15th-cent. screen, formerly the N. parclose screen.

The manor house was built by Peter Sainthill in 1547, but not much of this house is left. About 1712 the central block was rebuilt in brick. Though the house is somewhat plain externally, it retains a good deal of very fine carved Jacobean woodwork, most notably in the so-called "Job Room." This room has a splendid internal porch strongly resembling that at Bradfield; and the ceiling is a good example of the Devonshire school of plasterwork. The 17th-cent. library fireplace is also notable. Bradninch was the headquarters of King Charles's army on 27 July 1644, when the King slept at the manor house. In October 1645 the town was the headquarters of Fairfax.

BRADSTONE (B7) takes its name from some " broad stone," perhaps a boundary mark. The S. boundary of the parish is a prehistoric trackway down to the Tamar, where Greystone Bridge now is. This fine medieval bridge is mentioned in the Exeter episcopal registers in 1438 and by William of Worcester in 1478. There are superb views, all over the parish, of Bodmin Moor, Dartmoor, and the Tamar valley. The church, dedicated to St. Non, mother of St. David, is mostly an early 16th-cent. building with a good W. tower, boldly pinnacled. The 12th-cent. S. doorway was uncovered about 1888. Considerable portions of the S. wall of the nave appear to be Norman also. The medieval screen still survived in 1840; the later atrocity has been removed. The interior is plain, with no monuments. The Hall, now a farm-house, is a good Elizabethan house in local stone, with a gatehouse and fine ranges of barns and outbuildings.

BRADWORTHY (B4) is a large village in high remote country, built around an open square. In plan it is characteristic of a nucleated settlement founded early in the Saxon occupation (perhaps *c.* 700): the large open space, the houses grouped around the original water supply, and the parish church to one side. The latter (St. John the Baptist) is a dullish building, largely of early 16th-cent. date, containing an earlier font (*c.* 1200), a Jacobean pulpit, and some medieval tiles in the floor. Alfardisworthy was a small Domesday estate; the present farmhouse is of considerable age. Other Domesday estates were Ash, Brexworthy, Horton, Instaple and Kimworthy, while Limscott is recorded by 1196. On the outlying moors are a number of Bronze Age burial-mounds.

BRAMPFORD SPEKE (H6) is an attractive village, situated on a low cliff of red sandstone overhanging the Exe. George Gissing walked here from Exeter in February 1891 and wrote: " I have discovered a village called Brampford Speke on the Exe, which I seriously think is the most perfect I ever saw. One imagines that some lord of the manor must exert himself to keep it in a picturesque state." There is much excellent domestic building of cob and thatch, ranging in date from the late 16th cent. to the early 19th; but the church (St. Peter), although beautifully sited above the river, is disappointing on closer inspection. Except for the W. tower, it was entirely rebuilt in 1852-3 and is dull. This is the scene of the great struggle in 1847-51 between the bishop of Exeter (the formidable Phillpotts) and the vicar, the Rev. G. C. Gorham, over the doctrine of baptismal regeneration, in which the bishop was finally beaten. The vicar was

instituted and his first act was to rebuild the old church, Bishop Phillpotts assisting with some of his own money.

BRANSCOMBE (K7) is one of the most attractive places on the south coast of Devon—" Brannoc's combe," in a break in the high cliff wall. Eastwards the chalk cliffs rise to over 400 ft.; westwards to over 500 ft. Hooken Cliff, between Branscombe and Beer Head, is the first of the great landslips of Devon and Dorset. In one night of March 1790 nearly ten acres of land dropped 200-260 ft. vertically and moved 200 yds. seawards, breaking up into columns and pinnacles. On Berry Cliff, W. of Branscombe, is a large earthwork of unknown age, apparently of rectangular plan,[1] and to the W. a number of barrows.

There is no village of Branscombe. Hamlets and houses are planted inconsequently down the beautiful little combe almost to the very beach. Great Seaside Farm, the last of the chain, is a good specimen of an Elizabethan farmhouse. Dotted about the parish are other picturesque and interesting houses —the homes of medieval franklins and Tudor and Stuart gentry. Hole (recorded in 1249) was the home of the Holcombes for seven generations until the 17th cent., when it passed to the Bartletts. The present house is late 16th-cent. in date. Edge Barton, alone on a steep hillside, has some considerable traces of medieval work. Until the 14th cent. it was the home of the Branscombes, a distinguished family who produced three sheriffs of the county and one of Exeter's greatest bishops— Walter Bronescombe, bishop 1258-80. Edge passed from the Branscombes to another notable family, the Wadhams. Sir John Wadham, the judge, acquired it towards the end of Edward III's reign, and his descendants dwelt there until Nicholas Wadham (founder of Wadham College) died without issue. Lower House, N. of the vicarage, has been the home since the 16th cent. of the Fords, who still possess it. Church Living is a medieval house opposite the church. Barnells, not far away, was built by Capt. Ewell, Nelson's captain of Marines on the *Victory* at Trafalgar. It was known for some time as Trafalgar House.

The parish church is dedicated to St. Winifred, an obscure North Welsh saint who died *c.* 650. Such a rare dedication suggests that a church has existed here almost since that time. There is, indeed, pre-Conquest work to be seen on the inner side of the lower part of the tower walls, though it is possibly not earlier than the 11th cent. The church, besides being one of the most "atmospheric" churches in Devon, is of the highest interest, for it exhibits a process of continuous development from the 11th cent. to the 16th. Its architectural history is dealt with admirably in the local guide, one of the best of its kind, and is too complicated to be summarised in a few lines here, beyond saying that the massive central tower and part of the nave are Norman; the transepts and W. half of the nave 13th-cent.; and the chancel early 14th. Small changes were made in the 15th–16th cents. The woodwork of the church is highly interesting: an Elizabethan gallery, late 17th-cent. altar rails enclosing the altar on four sides, and a three-decker pulpit. There are numerous memorials to the Wadhams, Holcombes, and other local families, both inside the church and in the churchyard. One could spend a good week in and around Branscombe. W. H. Hudson and H. J. Massingham have both written lovingly about it.

BRATTON CLOVELLY (c6), a large remote parish, has one of the noblest churches (St. Mary) in Devon, and one of the least known. It is almost entirely of late 14th-cent. date—the date 1375 is traditionally given for its completion —with window tracery all of that date. The exterior is good but not exciting, but the interior view of the nave, looking from the chancel steps to the tower arch, is almost cathedral-like. The lofty arcades have moulded piers of the dove-grey Polyphant stone, so beautiful in colouring that one regrets there is not more of it in Devon (cf. Sampford Courtenay). The tower arch is especially lofty and grand. The contemporary chancel is small and mean for such a nave. There is also a magnificent Norman font, of the same type as that at Ashwater, and the N. wall shows traces of mural paintings.

The parish is large and contains a number of interesting old farmhouses, some with Celtic names such as Maindea and Breazle. Boasley occurs in a Saxon charter of *c.* 1050, and became a medieval "mansion." Chimsworthy is mainly an Elizabethan farmhouse, which has been turned around so that the original front door is now at the back. It is possible that the core of the house is medieval. Guscott was a Domesday manor. Bratton gets its second name from the Clavilles, who held the manor in the 13th cent.

BRATTON FLEMING (e2) is a large village along one street which climbs steadily up the foothills of Exmoor. The Flemings had their seat at Chimwell, now a farmhouse called Chumhill, which Risdon said was "one of the largest demesnes of this shire." Benton and Haxton were small Domesday manors. The great jurist Henry de Bracton was probably born at Bratton

Fleming, the first and greatest of the long line of Devon lawyers.[1]

The church (St. Peter) is a Victorian rebuilding of 1855-61, of the worst kind, redeemed by one good monument (to Bartholomew Wortley). At Chelfham the old Lynton and Barnstaple Railway, now dismantled, crossed the valley by a fine viaduct of eight arches, 400 ft. long and 70 ft. above the roadway.

BRAUNTON (c2) is an exceptionally interesting parish. One can only echo Preb. Chanter's words (in *The Church of St. Brannock, Braunton*) that with " its huge area of over ten thousand acres of rich cornlands, meadows, marshes, moorlands and rolling sandhills, its chapels-of-ease, ancient and modern, its many manors and manor houses, [it] is full of interest alike to the antiquarian, the ecclesiologist, the historian, and the botanist." The reader is referred to that guide for a detailed description of the church and the chapels, and for an account of St. Brannoc, the Welsh missionary-saint of the 6th cent. to whom the church is dedicated.

Braunton, which is the *Brannocmynster* of a 9th-cent. charter, owes its origin to St. Brannoc, who crossed from Wales and founded a chapel here, perhaps at Buckland where there is a St. Brannock's Well and where a chapel dedicated to the saint formerly stood. The saint is buried in Braunton church, possibly under the high altar; and his foundation became a *minster* or collegiate church by 857, when Brannocmynster was given to Glastonbury abbey " for the taking of salmon." The present church, of unusual plan, is mostly 13th-cent. with a great deal of later detail (15th–early 16th cent.). Its most remarkable feature is the wide nave, covered by a fine roof (*c.* 1500) enriched with bosses. The carved

bench-ends, of various dates between 1500 and 1600, are among the finest of their kind in England, and demand detailed inspection. There is a good deal of excellent Jacobean woodwork (esp. pulpit, reading-desk and gallery in the N. transept) and an early chancel screen of very unusual design, though rather meagre in character. There are many interesting 16th–18th-cent. monuments to the gentry of the parish, especially those of the Bellews of Ash and the Incledons of Incledon, and a curious palimpsest brass to Lady Elizabeth Bowcer (Bourchier), daughter of the earl of Bath (1548).

The village has grown greatly by reason of its nearness to Barnstaple, and has acquired a somewhat suburban character, but some excellent traditional building may be found in East Street, South Street and Church Street. In the latter, Nos. 33-5 (formerly one house) are dated 1579. No. 17 East Street and No. 7 South Street are similar in style. These houses, formerly good farmhouses, are a characteristic type of building in many North Devon villages, with their massive stone chimneybreasts on the street, beside the front door. Broadgate is an Elizabethan house, formerly a manor house called The Hall. It contains a plaster mantelpiece dated 1626. The S. block is medieval, with a fine roof of 14th-cent. date.

St. Michael's chapel is a conspicuous ruin on the top of a hill NE. of the village, built in the 15th cent. as a votive chapel for sailors and fishermen, where prayers were said for them and a look-out kept. It was a conspicuous landmark from the sea. St. Anne's chapel, at the S. end of the Burrows, stood somewhere near the present lighthouse and marked the ancient crossing of the estuary from Appledore. This route fell into disuse in the early 19th cent., the chapel decayed and is now quite gone, and the old road over the Burrows to Saunton has been lost.

There were formerly several families of gentry scattered about this large and fertile parish, their "mansions" being at Beer Charter, Buckland, Incledon, Saunton, Lobb, Fairlinch, Ash and Luscott. Most of these houses retain considerable evidence of their ancient status.

Braunton Great Field, to the SW. of the village, is one of the three surviving open-field areas left in England, still cultivated upon the "strip-system," but it is dwindling in area. Within living memory, some eighty-five small farmers cultivated this Field and the strips up on the Down to the E., but there are now only twelve.

BRAY, HIGH (E2), gets its name from its situation on the brow of a precipitous hill. The church (All Saints) stands on the summit and commands fine views. It was rebuilt early in the 16th cent. and thoroughly restored in 1878. The font is early Norman but the shell ornament on the lower part of the bowl was added later with a chisel.

The parish extends NE. to the Somerset boundary along a high ridge of Exmoor and includes Span Head (1618 ft.) and Setta Barrow (1556 ft.) There are numerous barrows on Whitefield Down, Bray Common and Fullaford Down. Gratton and Whitefield farms were Domesday estates, and Muxworthy is mentioned as early as c. 1100. The parish contains deep wooded valleys and fine moorland scenery.

BRENDON (F1) is a large parish with much beautiful valley scenery and moorland. Badgworthy, Cheriton and Lank Combe represent small Domesday estates. Lank Combe is now un-

inhabited. Cheriton means "farm by the church," but there is no church here to-day. At some date it was removed to its present solitary site about a mile away. It is dedicated to St. Brendan, the 6th-cent. Irish saint. The building is, however, of no interest except for its Norman font, having been almost completely rebuilt in 1873 when the N. aisle and N. transept were added. The churchyard, on a hill and surrounded by trees, commands very fine views of the rolling Exmoor foothills.

BRENT, SOUTH (F10), is an extensive parish running far on to the Moor. It takes its name from the steep hill (O.E. *brant* = "steep") just above the village, on the summit of which are the ruins of a small medieval chapel, built by the monks of Buckfast in the 14th or 15th cent. On the high moorlands are many hut-circles, enclosures, and barrows—all of Bronze Age date—the exact site of which must be located with the 2½-inch map (sheet 20/66). The manor of Brent belonged to Buckfast Abbey from the time of the foundation of the abbey in the early 11th cent. and was bought at the Dissolution by Sir William Petre, a large receiver of monastic spoils in South Devon.

The church (St. Petrock) is interesting. The massive Norman tower (now at the W. end) was apparently the central tower of a cruciform building, the W. portion of which was demolished at some date, perhaps in the early 14th cent. when the existing nave was rebuilt with two transepts. In the early 15th cent. these transepts were enlarged into aisles. The fine font, of red sandstone, is late 12th-cent. in date, and is similar in style to others in neighbouring churches. On the S. of the churchyard is the manor house, part of which is 15th-cent. in date.

Harbourneford was a Domesday manor. The old road from South Brent to Buckfastleigh goes this way, and there is a clapper footbridge with four openings alongside the ancient ford.

BRENTOR (G7) takes its name from the isolated conical rock, the remnant of a volcano, on the summit of which the parish church stands alone. The tor (1,130 ft.) is a striking landmark all over W. Devon; from its summit magnificent views are to be had, extending far over Devon and Cornwall. The church (St. Michael) was first built here c. 1140 by Robert Giffard at his own cost.[1] It was known in the 12th and 13th cents. as " St. Michael of the Rock "—"a church, full bleak, and weather beaten," says Risdon, " all alone, as it were forsaken, whose church yard doth hardly afford depth of earth to bury the dead; yet doubtless they rest there as securely as in sumptuous St. Peters, until the day of doom."

The small church consists of nave and chancel only, with a low battlemented W. tower, built of volcanic stone quarried on the hill. The S. wall of rubble masonry is probably the original early 12th-cent. work, the remainder early 13th-cent. The plain tower may have been added early in the 14th cent., as bishop Stapeldon came to consecrate the church on 4 December 1319.[2] In the following century the tower was raised and the battlements added. The church was restored 1889-90.

An earthwork of unknown purpose and date runs around the hill well below the summit, in the form of a massive, stone-faced bank. On 15 June 1232 Henry III granted to the abbot of Tavistock a three-day fair annually on the vigil, feast, and morrow of St. Michael (28–30 September) at the church of Brentor.[3] The manor belonged to Tavistock Abbey until the Dissolution and was then granted to John, Lord Russell, as part of his vast spoils from the Tavistock estates.

BRIDESTOWE (pron. *Briddistow*) (D7) is " the holy place (*stow*) of St. Brigid," the famous Irish saint (c. 450–c. 525) to whom the church is dedicated. The church, mainly 15th-cent. in date, was ruthlessly "restored" and practically disembowelled. One of its Norman arches now stands at the gateway to the churchyard. A fine screen was hacked to pieces, and every other enormity perpetrated.

There are a number of good houses in the parish. Bidlake, the home of the Bidlakes from 1268 until 1792, is a restored Elizabethan mansion, a good example of a squire's house of that time. Millaton, another ancient estate of the same type, had its house rebuilt c. 1700 and enlarged in the early 19th cent. Leawood is another small mansion, in a park. In addition, a number of farmsteads are recorded in Domesday Book: Battishill, Combebow, Ebsworthy Town, Fernworthy, Kersford, and Way. Battishill gave its name to a family who were flourishing round the edge of the Moor as late as 1890.

In Burley Wood, above the river Lew, is one of the strongest fortifications on the W. side of Dartmoor. It appears to be a large castle-site, with mount and bailey and extensive outworks, and is probably of 12th-cent. date. The manor of Bridestowe was held by the great Norman family of Pomerai (of Berry Pomeroy) in the 12th cent. and this may well have been a stockaded castle put up by one of them.

BRIDFORD (G7) is a wild, hilly parish, rising to over 1,100 ft. in places, and containing much beautiful scenery. The village is larger than usual in these upland parishes, mainly because of the granite quarries and the barytes mine. There are disused lead mines also. The older houses of the village are built of moorstone (i.e. surface granite) of which there was much in the higher parts of the parish. The church (St. Thomas Becket) is an early 14th-cent. building, reconstructed *c.* 1500. It contains many of its ancient fittings: some late medieval glass, carved stalls and bench-ends of the same period (early 16th-cent.), good wagon roofs, and a N. parclose screen. The chief glory of the church is, however, the rood-screen (plate 53). This retains its soft ancient colouring and is of high artistic merit. The carving is remarkably rich and lavish. Above the rood-loft door are the initials of Walter Southcote, rector 1508-50, who gave the screen. The double rose of Henry VIII and the pomegranate of Aragon appear on the screen, which can be dated at about 1530. The pulpit is said to have been made from pieces of the screen.

Laployd Barton (formerly Lapflode)' was the seat of the Lapflodes from the time of John until 1523 when the last of that family died. A chapel dedicated to St. Katherine existed here in 1409, but there are now no traces of it. The core of the present house, which is built of moorstone throughout, may be medieval, lengthened at both ends *c.* 1600, as is suggested by the NE. doorway. Weeke Barton and Woodlands are both good examples of old Devon farmhouses, possibly 16th–17th-cent. in date. Westcott was the home and property of the Westcotts, typical peasant freeholders, from the late 13th cent. (if not earlier) until the 18th cent.

BRIDGERULE (A5) was called *Brige* in Domesday Book, after the bridge over the Tamar here. It has a 15th-cent. church (St. Bridget) with an elegant granite S. arcade, a fine tower, and good wagon-roofs, especially that in the S. aisle which has carved bosses. A Norman font and stoup survive from the 12th-cent. church. The font is of the simplest type: a bowl hollowed out of a block of granite. The church seems originally to have been cruciform in plan, with N. and S. transepts. Tackbear was a Domesday manor, and a " mansion " in the 16th–18th cents.

BRIXHAM (H10), now a fishing port on the S. shore of Tor Bay, has a long history, much of it still awaiting exploration. Most of the parish consists of the dove-grey Devonian limestone, which gives fine cliff scenery (particularly at Berry Head); but from Sharkham Point southwards to the mouth of the Dart the slates and grits give even bolder cliffs and hills, from which one gets superb seascapes.

On Berry Head was a promontory fortress formed by a great rampart 18 ft. high constructed across the narrow neck of land, approximately where the outer wall of the Napoleonic Fort now stands. This rampart was said to have been constructed of masonry, and within the enclosed space a considerable number of Roman coins have been found.[1] The earthwork, probably of Early Iron Age date, was of the same type as the numerous cliff-forts on the Cornish headlands and elsewhere in Britain, about which little is known. Another was constructed on Bolt Tail, and there were apparently others on the Hartland coast in North Devon.[2] The Berry Head rampart was destroyed in the making of the Fort during the " invasion scare " of 1803, but it is commemorated in the name of the headland itself (from *burh*, " a fort "). Celtic pottery and bones have been found in a cavern named Ash-hole, near Shoalstone Point. About 3 m. SW. of the town, on a hill commanding the Dart estuary, is another Iron Age earthwork, of an irregular oval form, with a single rampart and ditch. The Berry Head earthworks, pottery, and coins suggest a late Celtic trading settlement, persisting into Roman times, as at Mount Batten (see PLYMSTOCK). The Windmill Hill cavern at Brixham, in the Devonian limestone, has produced evidence of occupation by palaeolithic man. This cavern, discovered in 1858, is now open for inspection by visitors.

The old harbour of Brixham formerly stretched about ½ m. farther inland than it does to-day, giving a fine natural estuary locked in and completely sheltered by the limestone hills on either side. The central part of Lower Brixham is now built over this harbour (plate 43). The original Saxon settlement was at Higher Brixham, where the parish church now is. It was an early nucleated village, possibly founded by colonists arriving by sea in the 7th cent., with its open fields, and its original territory included the whole of the great peninsula S. of the Galmpton neck, between the lower Dart and the sea.[1] That this was a royal estate in Saxon times, like most of these primary villages, is evidenced by the place-names of Kingswear and Kingston in this peninsula, names which go back to pre-Conquest times; but the estate had passed out of royal hands before 1066, when it belonged to one Ulf. A number of daughter-settlements had come into being by the middle of the 11th cent.—Kingswear and Churston (both now distinct parishes), Coleton, Lupton, and Woodhuish. The later

manorial history of Brixham is of no interest, merely the usual succession of great feudal names like Nonant, Valletort, Pomeroy, Bonville, and Grey. At a later date, the manor became divided into four parts, one of which was bought by a syndicate of twelve Brixham fishermen. Some of these shares became further divided, but "all the proprietors, be their shares ever so small, call themselves Quay lords."

The whole life of Brixham, for several centuries, was in fishing, shipbuilding, net-making, and all the subsidiary trades. William Brewer's foundation charter of Torre abbey (1196) shows that fishing with nets in Tor Bay was even then an established practice.[2] In the 16th cent. Leland refers to the net-fishing in Tor Bay, and the *Valor Ecclesiasticus* of 1535 shows that Brixham, Paignton and St. Marychurch were all important fishing ports. Brixham had probably taken the lead by this date, and it remained the foremost fishing port in Devon until overtaken by Plymouth in the 1870s. Lysons tells us that in his day the Brixham fish supplied the Bath and Exeter markets, and that great quantities were also sent to London, being taken by sea to Portsmouth and thence overland. About 100 trawlers were then employed at Brixham, sixty of which fished along the S. coast, and the others in the Bristol and Irish Channels. About forty smaller boats were occupied with inshore fishing during the summer season. By the 1840s there were more than 270 vessels in the port (20,000 tons in all) employing about 1,600 seamen. The subsequent growth of the Brixham industry, and its disastrous collapse from 1919 onwards, has already been related in Part I. The town more than doubled in population during the 19th cent.; it fell in numbers during the first quarter of the 20th cent. but has lately acquired a reputation as a holiday centre and is now growing again.

Though Brixham has a strong character of its own, there is little in the town of architectural interest. Lower Brixham church (All Saints) was built 1820-4, but has been considerably altered since. Its first incumbent was the Rev. H. F. Lyte, the author of the hymn *Abide with me*. He lived at Berry Head House, which was built as a military hospital during the Napoleonic Wars (1809), and is now a hotel. On the N. side of Berry Head are extensive limestone quarries which are eating into the headland, and on the summit is a diminutive lighthouse, erected in 1906, with a powerful light. On the Quay at Brixham is a statue, erected in 1889, to commemorate the landing of William of Orange at this point on 5 November 1688.

At Higher Brixham, the original parish church (St. Mary) is a late 14th–15th-cent. building of red sandstone, with Beer stone arcades, and a number of interesting monuments, especially that to John Upton of Lupton (1687). The altar tomb is that of a former vicar, William Hille, 1464-87.

At Upton, and near Sharkham Point, were iron mines, now disused. Upton Manor was built in 1768. Lupton House, now a school, was a seat of the Bullers for a time, and was rebuilt *c.* 1770. It has been gutted by fire and reconstructed in recent years. Nethway House, in a small park, was built in 1699 by John Fownes, and contains much work of this period. Coleton Fishacre is a modern country house by Oswald Milne (1925-6).

BRIXTON (D10) has a late 15th-cent. church (St. Mary), much restored in 1887 and 1894. Near it is a grove of elms, first planted in 1677 by Edward Fortescue of Spriddlestone, to be felled and sold for the relief of the poor of the parish. Immediately N. of the church is a late medieval house, probably the former parsonage or church-house. SW. of the church is a 16th-cent. house, and E. and W. a number of attractive cottages.

The parish contains a number of interesting "mansions." Apart from Brixton itself, no fewer than seven other estates are mentioned in Domesday Book. These are Chittleburn, Halwell, Hareston, Sherford, Spriddlestone, Winston, and Wollaton. At Higher Hareston is a very attractive early Tudor house with a good porch, and remains of a chapel licensed in 1408. Spriddlestone was the home of one of the numerous branches of the great Fortescue family from about 1355 to 1785. They built a large quadrangular house here (now gone) *temp.* Henry VI and enlarged it in Elizabethan times.

BROAD CLYST (H6) parish is exceptionally large, covering nearly fifteen square miles and including rich valley scenery, heath, and wooded hills like Killerton and Ashclyst Forest. Several of the farms date from before the Conquest (e.g. Ashclyst Farm, Clyst Gerred Farm, West Clyst, Mosshayne, Columbjohn, and Eveleigh.) Many, such as Killerton, Churchill and Southbrook, date from shortly after Domesday. The parish was for centuries full of ancient freeholders, of whom the most interesting (in view of their later history) were the Churchills, who took their name from Churchill in this parish as early as Henry II's time. This Churchill is almost certainly the original home of the present Churchill family.

The church (St. John the Baptist) has a fine 16th-cent. W. tower of the

Somerset type, said to have served as a model for Cullompton. The body of the church was probably rebuilt in the time of Bishop Stafford (1395–1419) as the Stafford knot appears on one of the capitals. The nave arcades of six bays are excellent, having graceful piers surmounted by beautifully carved capitals. In the chancel the fine 14th-cent. sedilia cover the effigy of a knight in armour, believed to be that of Sir Roger de Nonant, the last of the Nonant lords of Broadclyst, who died c. 1330-40. This monument, one of the best of its kind in Devon, closely resembles in style the Prouz monument at Widworthy.

There are good Renaissance monuments to Sir John Acland of Columbjohn (1620) and to Edward Drewe, Esquire, of Killerton (1622), as well as an attractive mural monument to Henry Burrough, gent., and his wife (1605).

Columbjohn, 2 m. NW. of the church, was a pre-Conquest estate, taking its name from the river and from one John de Culm who held it in 1235. It came eventually to the Earls of Devon, who had "a private retiring house" here, but they lost it by the attainder of Henry, Marquess of Exeter, in 1539. Late in Elizabeth's reign the estate was bought by Sir John Acland of Acland who built a new mansion on the site. Here the Aclands lived until Sir Thomas rebuilt Killerton, a mile away, about the middle of the 18th cent. Columbjohn was garrisoned for the king during the civil war, and in March 1646 it was the headquarters of Fairfax, whose army was then stationed at Silverton. Cromwell also stayed here. The old house was demolished when the Aclands moved to Killerton, but the arched Elizabethan gateway still stands among the trees. The chapel, con-

secrated by Bishop Cotton on Sunday, 11 September 1608, has since been rebuilt. The interior is of no interest, but the exterior and its surroundings are very attractive.

Killerton is now mainly a late 18th-cent. house in a timbered park. " Killerton Clump," the wooded hill behind the house, is a landmark for miles. Edward Drewe, sergeant-at-law, bought the estate late in Elizabeth's reign and built a mansion, only a mile from Sir John Acland's new house. Thomas Drewe, son of Edward, sold Killerton to the Aclands after his father's death, however, and moved to Grange in Broadhembury (q.v.) where the Drewes had built another mansion. The Aclands still live at Killerton, but Sir Richard Acland has handed over the house and park to the National Trust. The chapel in the park was built in 1842 in the Norman style, replacing that at Columbjohn. Round the summit of the hill (called Dolbury, " Dola's burh ") are the remnants of an earthwork, a simple, defensive enclosure with rampart and ditch, probably of Early Iron Age date.

BROADHEMBURY (K5) takes its name from Hembury Fort on a spur of the Blackdown Hills, the finest earthwork in Devon. A brief account of it will be found in Part I. It is an Iron Age fortress superimposed upon a Neolithic causewayed camp, and it continued to be occupied until the second half of the 1st cent. The name means " the high burh."

Broadhembury is one of the most attractive cob-and-thatch villages in Devon: it is rural East Devon at its best. The Drewe Arms, a notable example of village building, is an early Tudor house, and was probably the Church House originally.

The church (St. Andrew) is late 14th–early 15th cent., with a fine W. tower, good window tracery, and the usual pleasant Beer stone arcades. The S. chancel aisle was the chapel of the Drewes of Grange (in this parish) and there are two good early 17th-cent. Drewe monuments in the chancel. Notice also the excellent 15th-cent. font, the groined roof and inner doorway of the N. porch, and the nave roof which has kept a good deal of its original colour. The medieval rood-screen was removed to an outhouse about 1851, and there burnt: the determined " restorers " stuck at nothing. The Victorian interior of the church is pleasant, but it might have been beautiful had they been content to leave things alone. The Rev. Augustus Toplady, famous as the author of the hymn *Rock of Ages* (which he wrote in Somerset), ended his days here as vicar, 1768-78.

Near Kerswell, in the NW. of the parish, was a small monastic cell dependent on the Cluniac monastery of Montacute in Somerset, founded between 1119 and 1129. The Priory, about ¼ m. NW. of Kerswell, occupies the site of this cell.

Grange, SW. of the village, was another piece of monastic property, belonging to Dunkeswell Abbey. It was bought in 1603 by Edward Drewe, a successful Elizabethan lawyer who already possessed Sharpham and Killerton in this county, and he began to build here. He died in 1622 (and is buried in Broadclyst, q.v.), and the house was completed by his son Thomas. The latter was knighted at the coronation of Charles I, and d. 1651 (buried at Broadhembury). The house is still substantially the early 17th-cent. house, though it was much pulled about and altered in the 18th and early 19th cents. It is notable for its magnificent

plasterwork and carved woodwork, very similar in style to that at Bradfield (see UFFCULME). The Oak Drawing Room is the most elaborate room in the house, and one of the most beautiful in all Devon.

BROADHEMPSTON (G9) is a pleasant village with a fine church (St. Peter and St. Paul), which was rebuilt in 1401-03 except the tower and chancel (both c. 1300). The splendid late medieval rood-screen, formerly much mutilated and decayed, was restored by Herbert Read of Exeter in 1901-2.

Beaston was one of the "mansions" of the Rowes for 250 years, and the present farmhouse contains remains of the old building. Broadhempston is one of the small number of parishes to possess pre-Reformation churchwardens' accounts, beginning in 1519.

BROADNYMET (*see* TAWTON, NORTH)

BROADWOOD KELLY (E5) takes its suffix from the Kellys, who held the manor from the 12th to the 14th cents. Besides Broadwood itself, Brixton Barton, Ingleigh, and Middlecott were all Domesday estates. The church (All Hallows) is a 15th-cent. building, thoroughly restored in 1868. There is late medieval glass in one window.

BROADWOODWIDGER (C7) stands on a steep hill above the wooded valley of the Wolf, with splendid views of Dartmoor from the churchyard. The church (St. Nicholas) stands well and is interesting. Traces remain of the late Norman building, chiefly the font and the lower parts of the N. wall of nave and transept. An unbuttressed W. tower was added in the late 14th cent., the upper stage about a century later when the church was enlarged by the addition of a S. aisle. The granite arcade has good, boldly-cut capitals. The mutilated effigy in curious plate-armour in the S. aisle is said by West-cote to be that of William Shilston of Upcott, an old mansion in this parish, now a farmhouse of late 16th-cent. date. There is a good granite S. porch with roof bosses, a rood-screen of rather coarse detail (early 16th-cent.) and coarsely carved bench-ends of the same date. The S. aisle retains its original roof with carved bosses and wall-plates. Among the farms of the parish Downa-carey, Moor, and Norton were all recorded in Domesday Book. Witherdon was one of the mansions of the Bidlakes and retains a good deal of old work.

BRUSHFORD (e5) church (St. Mary) stands alone in the fields with the Georgian barton-farm below. Its tower of dunstone is weather-boarded in the top stage, and surmounted by a charm-ing slated semi-steeple. The three original medieval bells remain, but the body of the church was too much re-stored in 1876-7. The chancel screen is of almost unique design. A parallel to it is found in Brittany, at St. Fiacre-le-Faouet. Its cresting has been re-placed by some poor carpentry. The 12th-cent. S. doorway remains, but nothing else of the Norman church. In the reign of Elizabeth the Luxtons purchased the rectory and the manor from the Crown and remained here until early in this century as parsons and squires. The church is worth visit-ing for its air of remoteness, its beautiful situation, and its screen.

BUCKERELL (k5) has a pleasant little 15th-cent. church (St. Mary and St. Giles) with N. and S. transepts, plastered all over externally. It was completed in 1403, according to a stone in the vestry. The credence in the

chancel bears the same date. A fine chancel-screen of unusual type was brought from elsewhere and fitted here. The groining is perfect on both sides and the cornices are good. The church, which is attractive internally, is fitted with 18th-cent. box-pews, probably inserted in 1773 when the plan of the seating was made, and there is a W. gallery of the same date. The " sheaf pew " shown on the plan was the pew of whoever held the rectorial tithes (" the sheaf ") for the time being. In the N. transept is a monument by John Bacon, R.A. (1792), to Samuel Graves, Admiral of the White, who lived at Hembury Fort. The church possesses an Elizabethan chalice made at Exeter by John Jones in 1576.

BUCKFASTLEIGH (f9) is a small market town on the old main road from Exeter to Plymouth, close to the Dart. The original settlement was at Buck-fast, about 1 m. N. beside the river, where an abbey was founded c. 1030, and endowed by King Canute. It is possible that the house was founded somewhat earlier but no good evidence of this is yet forthcoming.[1] For some reason the abbey seems to have perished by the early 12th cent., and was re-founded by monks from Savigny in 1134-6. King Stephen ordered the restoration of all the former possessions of the abbey, which passed in 1148 under Cistercian rule and so remained until the Dissolution. The site of the abbey came to Sir Thomas Dennis of Holcombe Burnell, a great devourer of monastic lands in Devon; but the most valuable manors came to Sir William Petre (born at Torbryan not far away), Secretary of State to four Tudor monarchs. The great abbey buildings were stripped by Dennis, and were reduced to ruin. In 1806 a local woollen manufacturer, who had bought the site, levelled the standing walls and built a house and woollen mill here. The house now forms part of the reconstructed abbey. A community of French Benedictines acquired the site in 1882 and set out to rebuild the abbey. In 1902 they became an autonomous community once more, and elected the first abbot of Buckfast since the Reformation. The work of rebuilding the abbey church was carried on by the monks under great difficulties for twenty-five years and finally accomplished. On 25 August 1932, St. Mary's Abbey church was solemnly consecrated by Cardinal Bourne, archbishop of Westminster. The church follows the foundations of its 12th-cent. predecessor and is mainly in the transitional style between Norman and Early English. The tower was completed in 1938. There are some remains of older work, including the Abbot's Tower (15th cent.) and part of the Abbot's Lodging. The chapel of St. Anne in a vaulted undercroft is probably part of the 12th-cent. foundation. At The Grange, near by, the tithe barn is a medieval building. The woollen mills by the river are late 18th–early 19th cent. in date, and were working until recent years.

Buckfastleigh was "the clearing of Buckfast" and probably originated in the 13th cent. The parish church (Holy Trinity) stands above and away from the town, on a high limestone rock which commands a view of the abbey, the Dart valley, and the beautiful woods. It is a 13th-cent. building (tower and chancel) with a 15th-cent. nave. There is a fine Norman font. The church is pleasant despite the drastic restoration of 1845. In the churchyard are the ruins of a 13th-cent. chantry chapel.

Buckfastleigh never developed much as a town, chiefly because of the proximity of the woollen and stannary town of Ashburton (3 m. away), and it contains little or nothing of architectural note. Dart Bridge, which carries the main Plymouth road, is an attractive structure, perhaps of 15th-cent. date.

BUCKLAND BREWER (c3) is a sizeable village on a hill-top, visible from many miles away. The church has a curious double dedication to St. Mary and St. Benedict, but except for the fine tower, rebuilt in 1399 after being struck by lightning, is of little interest. It was rebuilt in 1879-80. A good Norman doorway (c. 1160) has, however, survived. In the Orleigh chapel are monuments to the Dennises of Orleigh (1641) and their successors, the Davies (1709-10). There is also an interesting monument to Philip Vening (1658), similar in style to that of John Downe at Instow (1640). The Church Room, in the churchyard, is traditionally stated to have been a chapel of St. Stephen.

Orleigh was part of the original endowment of Tavistock abbey c. 974, but was granted by the abbey to the Dennis family before 1200. Anthony Dennis (d. 1641) left no male heir, and in 1684 Orleigh was sold to John Davie, a successful merchant of Bideford. John Davie and his son Joseph between them altered and enlarged the house between 1684 and 1721, and gave it its present form; but the hall, with porch and room over, are part of the earlier house, which was rebuilt about 1580. Galsworthy, now a farmhouse of perhaps early 17th-cent. date, was a Domesday manor. It is the *fons et origo* of the family of John Galsworthy, the novelist.[1] Vielstone was a medieval manor, and retains traces of its former status in the house.

BUCKLAND, EAST (E2), lies high in the southern foothills of Exmoor. The church (St. Michael) was rebuilt, except the tower, in 1860. Brayley Barton was a Domesday estate. So, too, were Middlecott and Tossells Barton, both called Buckland in Domesday.[1]

BUCKLAND FILLEIGH (C5) is a small parish in remote unspoiled country, a great part of it occupied by the park and woods of Buckland House. It came to the Fortescues by marriage in 1454 and was held by them until the 1840s. The present house is a large early Georgian mansion, much altered about a hundred years later (1810). The small church (St. Mary) stands in the park. It was probably a 15th-cent. building but has been so rebuilt and "restored" that nothing is left of its original character. The N. aisle belonged to Buckland House and contains a number of mural monuments to the Fortescues (1622-1845), including one by Flaxman (1815).

BUCKLAND-IN-THE-MOOR (F8). The scenery of the parish is everywhere most romantic. The prevailing tone of the human landscape is a warm grey: grey thatched roofs, grey moorstone walls and buildings, and tall grey beeches around them. In the more sheltered combes the vegetation is luxuriant: mosses and lichens, fungi and ferns.

The church (St. Peter) is built of moorstone. The first church was put up in the late 12th cent. Of this building the fine font, and the S. wall of the nave and S. doorway, survive. In the 13th cent. the chancel was probably rebuilt, and in the 15th cent. or early 16th, more work was done on the fabric. A N. aisle was added with a granite arcade of three bays, and a W. tower.

The rich rood-screen probably marked the completion of all this work. The paintings on both sides of this are superior in quality to most in Devon. A wooden staircase for access to the rood-loft, elaborately carved and coloured, remains *in situ*. The church was further beautified in the 18th cent. when the pulpit and royal arms were added.

Buckland Court is a Georgian mansion.

BUCKLAND MONACHORUM (C9) occupies the undulating country between the Tavy, Walkham, and Meavy rivers, all of them exceedingly attractive. The meeting of Tavy and Walkham at Double Waters is excitingly beautiful even in this district of superb scenery. Buckland village contains much interesting old building from late medieval times onwards, and much modern unpleasing stuff also. Lady Modyford's School in the village square was built in 1702. Netherton Cottage, at the N. end of the village, is an attractive little 17th-cent. house.

The church (St. Andrew) is the best in the district, a complete 15th–early 16th-cent. rebuilding, with a lofty and fine interior. There are Drake monuments, and one by John Bacon to George Augustus Eliott who defended Gibraltar against the Spaniards 1779-83 and was created Baron Heathfield of Gibraltar in 1787. The early Norman font, now kept at the back of the church, was recovered from the foundations of the church in 1857.

One m. S. of the church is Buckland Abbey, founded in 1278 as a Cistercian house by Amicia, Countess of Devon, and colonised from Quarr Abbey (I.O.W.) which had been founded by Baldwin, 2nd Earl of Devon. At the Dissolution the site of the abbey with its demesne lands was sold to Sir Richard Grenville (1541) who probably demolished a considerable part of the conventual buildings. His grandson, the famous Sir Richard Grenville of the *Revenge*, sold the property, through intermediaries, to Sir Francis Drake in 1581, who made it his principal residence whenever he was in England. Grenville altered the house in 1576 and added the fine plaster ceiling to the hall. Either he or his predecessors converted the abbey church into a mansion, a very unusual (though not unique) arrangement, as might be imagined from the work involved. Drake's arms appear in plaster in an upper room. The house is now National Trust property and is leased to the Plymouth Corporation as a naval and Devon museum, with Drake relics. There are fairly extensive remains of other monastic buildings including the refectory and a magnificent tithe barn.

There are some picturesque old farmhouses in the parish, including Coppicetown (16th cent.) and Crapstone Barton (17th cent.). Bickham is a derelict 18th-cent. mansion in a park.

BUCKLAND TOUT SAINTS (F11),

in beautiful wooded country, takes its second name from the Toutsaints family who held the manor in 1238. The church (St. Peter) was rebuilt in 1779, but was thoroughly restored in the early 1870s, and is now uninteresting. Buckland House, in a well-wooded park, is a Georgian house on a much older site. Courtlands contains much 15th–16th-cent. work disguised by later alterations. Bearscombe, a large good-looking farmhouse of late 16th-cent. date, was formerly called Woodmanston and corresponds to the manor of Buckland held by one Odeman or Wodeman in 1086. Its present name derives from the

Beares who lived here in the 17th cent., of whom "Justice Beare," a notorious persecutor of nonconformists, was one. The extensive slate quarries in this parish, which had a large export trade to Holland before the war of 1781, closed down in the late 19th cent.

BUCKLAND, WEST (E2). The church

(St. Peter) was almost entirely rebuilt, except the tower, in 1863-4 and is devoid of interest. West Buckland School was founded in 1858 to provide a public school education for boys of the middle class. The Gothic buildings date from 1860-1. Furze and Stoodleigh were Domesday estates.

BUDLEIGH, EAST (J7). This large

and unspoilt village was formerly a market-town and a port, before the Otter silted up. According to Leland, ships were still using it in the 15th cent. There is much excellent building in cob and thatch, and a number of good farmhouses of the East Devon type. Hayes Barton, 1 m. W. of the village, was the birthplace of Sir Walter Raleigh in 1552, and remains a good example of a Tudor house.

The church of All Saints, built of red sandstone, rises boldly at the head of the village. It is largely a 15th-cent. building, with imposing arcades in Beer stone, well restored in 1884-7. The screen of five bays is of a simple 15th-cent. design, much restored. More than sixty ancient bench-ends survive, all vigorously and boldly carved. Most of them are 16th-cent. in date, but a few may be older. All of them are worth detailed study: almost certainly they are of local workmanship. The Raleigh pew, with the family arms and the date 1537 on the end, is the first on the N. side of the nave.

BUDLEIGH SALTERTON (J7), an

attractive little seaside town, has grown up almost entirely since the beginning of the 19th cent. as a watering-place. Since its beach is of pebbles, it has not attracted day visitors or family holiday-makers to anything like the extent of Exmouth, and has therefore remained small and residential.

Nevertheless, it has a long history. It is first mentioned in 1210 as *Saltre*, and as *Salterne* in 1405, its name being derived from the *salterns* or salt-pans which existed here by the mouth of the Otter at an early date.

It began to attract visitors during the Napoleonic Wars, among them James Lackington, the well-known London bookseller, who erected a chapel in the main street in 1811, known as The Temple, and later the Wesleyan chapel. This was, unfortunately, replaced in 1905. The town grew more rapidly after the peace of 1815: Lysons speaks of Budleigh as much frequented of late years in the summer season. It is now increasingly favoured by retired persons, and especially by old ladies. The town is very warm and sheltered, with myrtles growing freely. A number of attractive houses and cottages of the late Georgian and Regency period remain. The church (St. Peter) was built in 1893. Sir John Millais lived for a time at " The Octagon," at the west end of the parade, and painted here the famous picture " The Boyhood of Raleigh " which was exhibited at the Academy of 1870.

From West Down Beacon (400 ft.) one gets a magnificent seascape over Lyme Bay, extending on some days from Portland Bill to Berry Head.

BULKWORTHY (B4) is a small parish in the upper Torridge valley, formerly a chapelry of Buckland Brewer. The church (St. Michael) was largely rebuilt at the cost of Sir William Hankford (d. 1423), and a S. aisle added about a hundred years later. In 1873-4 the church underwent " a thorough restoration," when the remains of the rood-screen were cleared away and some of the carved bench-ends butchered to make the pulpit. The church to-day is dirty and neglected. It contains a much-altered Norman font.

Hankford, a large farm about 1 m. NW. of the church, gave its name to the Hankfords, of whom the most notable was Sir William, who was made a K.B. at the coronation of Henry V. He became chief justice of the King's Bench under Henry V, and is sometimes said to have been the judge concerned in the famous incident which culminated in the future Henry V being committed to prison. The present house is a good example of a barton-farm, *c.* 1600 in date.

BURLESCOMBE (J4) has a 15th-cent. church (St. Mary), which stands well and possesses a particularly charming interior. In the N. or Ayshford aisle are the coloured monuments of that family: (1) Roger Ayshford (1610) and his wife Elizabeth; (2) Elizabeth, wife of Arthur Ayshford (1635). These beautiful monuments hang like pictures on the plastered wall. The aisle has a wagon-roof with figures of angels along the wall-plates. In the chancel is the altar-tomb of William Ayshford (d. 1508) and his two wives. The tomb is coloured and is ornamented on its sides with ten standing figures under canopies. The 15th-cent. rood-screen has thin and poor detail and is crudely painted.

Ayshford, the seat of the Ayshfords from the time of Henry I to 1689, is now a diminished farmhouse, partly 16th-cent. in date. The private chapel of the family still stands near by, a 15th-cent.

building, thoroughly restored in 1860, with a poor screen and a mural monument to John Ayshford (1689), the last of the direct line. Ayshford was a Domesday manor. So, too, were Canonsleigh, Fenacre Farm, and Appledore.

At Canonsleigh Farm is the site of an Augustinian nunnery founded by Maud, Countess of Devon. A house of Austin Canons had been founded here by William de Claville between 1161 and 1173, but in 1284 the house and its property were made over to regular canonesses of the same order, the head of the nunnery ranking as an abbess.[1] A damaged gateway remains (the W. entrance to the priory) and part of a tower. There are also remains of the priory mill. At Westleigh, near by, are extensive limestone quarries producing lime and road-stone.

BURRINGTON (E4) lies on high ground, with beautiful landscapes in all directions. The church (All Saints) is entirely of early 16th-cent. date and is interesting. The granite S. arcade is lofty and severely beautiful, the tracery of the S. aisle windows good. The aisle also has a fine wagon-roof with two rows of angels along its entire length, carved bosses and wall-plates with trailing foliage, and moulded ribs. The nave roof, though not so good, is worth notice. The rood-screen, of eight bays, is early 16th-cent. in date, finely carved, with vaulting and cresting complete on the vestry side. It is an exceptionally beautiful screen, though badly painted, and bears some resemblance to those at Lapford and Atherington. The font is Norman, much restored; the altar rails are good Jacobean. Callard, 1¼ m. W., was the home of a family of that name for some centuries down to Elizabethan times.

BUTTERLEIGH (H5) is a small parish in remote, hilly country. Between 1161 and 1184 Brian de Boterlegh, lord of the manor, gave the church to St. Nicholas's priory at Exeter. The church was then newly built and the parish created at the same time. The font, a plain round bowl, dates from this time: it is the only relic of the Norman church, which was entirely rebuilt early in the 14th cent. and dedicated by Bishop Stapeldon in 1319. Early in the 17th cent. it underwent a further reconstruction by Peter Muden, a Dutch doctor of medicine who married a daughter of the Courtenays of Molland in 1600. He seems to have rebuilt the tower and probably the curious, unsatisfactory N. arcade. The church was badly restored in 1861. The tower retains its three pre-Reformation bells in their original cages or frames.

CADBURY (H5) is named after the high earthwork N. of the church—"Cada's burh." The parish is mainly on the new red sandstones and is hilly and strikingly beautiful, rising in Cadbury Castle to 829 ft. This is an Iron Age earthwork, commanding one of the most magnificent views in Devon. Dartmoor and Exmoor are nearly always visible; on a good day the hills of Somerset and Cornwall can be clearly seen.

Fursdon is a small estate which gave its name to the Fursdon family in Henry III's time, since when the family have lived here in unbroken male succession. The house is mainly an unexciting Georgian building with some older work behind the stucco. Great Bowley is a farm of pre-Conquest origin.

The church (St. Michael) is mainly a plain little 15th-cent. building, over-restored about 1860. There is little of note in it except a good panel of medieval stained glass (*c.* 1400) in the E. window of the N. aisle, and a carved Elizabethan lectern. The font is Norman, and some of the rubble masonry of the external walling may be also. Some old bench-ends converted into a stall show something of what was destroyed at the "restoration." Despite the great antiquity of the Fursdons there are no monuments of any note to the family.

CADELEIGH (H5), like Cadbury, lies in hilly and most beautiful country. The church (St. Bartholomew) stands on a high ridge, commanding fine views. It is mostly a pleasant 15th-cent. rebuilding of an older church (probably first founded in the 12th cent., in the time of Bishop Bartholomew of Exeter, 1161-84). The Leach monument in the N. aisle is magnificent. Made of Beer stone, with pillars and enrichments of Devonshire marble, it was erected by Sir Simon Leach (1567–1637) in memory of Katherine Turberville, his second wife. It shows Sir Simon and Lady Katherine as full-length recumbent effigies beneath a high canopy, together with the kneeling figures of their nine children. The monument commemorates other members of the family also.

CALVERLEIGH (H4) is a sequestered little place, though less than 3 m. from Tiverton, and near a main road. The church (St. Mary) has a 14th-cent. tower and font, and some 14th-cent. work in the S. aisle. The nave and chancel were over-restored in the 19th cent., but the S. aisle and arcade are better. The latter, rebuilt *c.* 1500, has well-carved capitals. The aisle has its original wagon roof, ribbed and ceiled,

with carved bosses, and its E. window contains some late medieval glass. Here are the memorials of the Southcotts, who held the manor in the 16th and 17th cents., including a curious mural monument painted with rustic portraits (1638) and an incised slate floor-slab to George Southcott (1654). There are considerable remains of a plain late medieval rood-screen, and a screen in the tower. The ancient mansion of the Southcotts was being demolished when Davidson visited the scene on 27 July 1843.[1] The present Calverleigh Court presumably took its place.

CHAGFORD (F7) is a little market-town on the edge of Dartmoor, set in a beautiful countryside. One could happily explore the parish for a full week, armed with the 2½-inch maps (sheets 20/68 and 20/78), and no mere catalogue of its charms and antiquities can do it justice. The name means "gorse ford" from the old dialect word *chag* (broom, gorse), the ford being that over the Teign which is now crossed by Chagford bridge. A bridge existed here before 1224, and one is mentioned by Leland. The existing granite bridge may, indeed, be the one Leland saw. The valley of the Teign, which is beautiful almost everywhere along its course, surpasses itself above and below Chagford bridge.

The parish climbs W. to high moorland, reaching 1432 ft. at Castor (or Kes Tor) Rock and 1279 ft. at Meldon Hill. There are hut-circles, stone rows, and kists scattered about these moorlands, particularly on Chagford Common, near Metherall, and on Shovel Down; their exact sites must be located on sheet 20/68 of the 2½-inch map. They were formerly far more numerous, especially on Chagford Common, but with the improvement of surfaces on the moorland roads the roadmenders have taken the stones from the hutcircles to metal the highway.[1]

The town stands upon a hill rising sharply from the Teign. It developed as a market centre for a wide moorland area as early as the 12th cent.[2] In 1305 it was made one of the three original stannary towns to which tinners had to bring their metal for assay and stamping (*coinage*), though it had been acting in this capacity for a considerable time before this. The stannary brought a fluctuating prosperity to Chagford until the end of the 16th cent., for the moorland tinners bought their household provisions here, and then the spinning of wool for the East Devon weaving towns took the place of the dwindling tin-works. In Lysons's time there was still a Saturday market for butchers' meat, vegetables, and earthenware, and there were four large cattle fairs annually. Though the woollen industry had by now sunk to nothing, Chagford remained an important little market-centre and continued to grow until 1831, when it reached its maximum population (1,868). After that it declined slowly: not much, for no railway reached out to it to disrupt its ancient local economy, nor ever will now: but by 1900 it had rather fewer than 1,400 people. In the early 20th cent. it grew again as a holiday and residential town for those who thrive on bracing moorland air, but in the past generation it has again contracted slightly.

There is much interesting small-town building, from *c.* 1500 to *c.* 1850, including a 16th-cent. granite house on the S. side of the churchyard which was probably the Church House, and another large early 16th-cent. house facing the churchyard—the Three Crowns Inn, in which Sidney Godolphin is said to have been killed. In February 1643, Sir John Berkeley attacked and dispersed some parliament forces, then quartered at Chagford, but in the action the royalists " lost Sidney Godolphin, a young gentleman of incomparable parts. He received a mortal shot by a musket, a little above the knee, of which he died on the instant, leaving the misfortune of his death upon a place which could never otherwise have had a mention in the world " (Clarendon).

The church (St. Michael) is a fine example of a 15th-cent. granite church. In the chancel is an Elizabethan monument to Sir John Whiddon, Kt., justice of the Queen's Bench (d. 1575), and a mural monument to John Prouz (1664) in the S. aisle. Sir John Whiddon bought the manor of Chagford and made himself a manor house and park at Whiddon Park 2 m. NE. of the town. The Park, at the entrance to the gorge of the Teign, is romantically beautiful, a place of rocks, ravens, and wild deer; the house is substantially Elizabethan in date, altered in the 17th and 19th cents., and attractive.

The ancient farmsteads of this parish, built of granite and generally very picturesque, are a study in themselves. Those mentioned in Domesday Book are: Rushford Barton, Middlecott, Shapley, and Teigncombe. Rushford is mostly Elizabethan in date. At Yardworthy are the substantial remains of an early moorland farmhouse (probably 14th-cent.) Hole is a good example of 17th-cent. rebuilding on an older site. Collihole and Waye Barton also have much old work; but there is ample scope in this parish for the wayfarer to make his or her own discoveries, especially in the tangle of medieval lanes to the S. and W. of the town.

CHALLACOMBE (E1) means "cold valley." It is a large moorland parish with scattered farms, of which Barton Town, Whitefield Barton, Radworthy, and Wallover Barton represent small Domesday manors. The last-named was "the farm of the Britons" and was probably a settlement of Celtic farmers which continued into Saxon times. The parish church (Holy Trinity) was completely rebuilt in 1850, except the W. tower, and again restored in 1874-5. It contains nothing of any age or interest except the font.

The upland moors of the parish have many groups of barrows, especially to the N. on Challacombe Common, where Chapman Barrows, extending into Lynton parish, form a group of a dozen large tumuli, some 12 ft. high and 300 ft. around. They are probably of Bronze Age date. In the SE. of the parish is Shoulsbarrow Castle (1,528 ft.), commanding magnificent views over North Devon. It is a square earthwork, protected by a second vallum on the N. and E. sides, but its age and purpose are uncertain. There is a tradition that Alfred held it against the Danes.[1]

CHARDSTOCK (M5) was transferred from Dorset to Devon in 1896. It was originally the *stoc* or cattle-farm of Chard. The valley in which it mostly lies is still given over to pasture. The church (St. Andrew) was rebuilt in 1863-4 except the S. wall and tower. A monument with kneeling effigies to Richard Symonds of Coaxdon and his wife (d. 1610), the grandparents of Sir Simonds D'Ewes, disappeared at this time. Coaxdon Hall was the birthplace of Sir Simonds D'Ewes (1602-50), the antiquary and author of *Journals of all the Parliaments during the reign of Queen Elizabeth*. Much of the old house still

remains. Chardstock Court, formerly Court House Farm, was a manor house of the bishops of Salisbury. It was crenellated by Bishop Erghum in 1377. Much of the present house dates from the early 14th cent., refashioned two centuries later. A long detached range with a magnificent 15th-cent. open timber roof was destroyed c. 1930. There are two picturesque old inns in the village, one of which is certainly 16th-cent. Besides Coaxdon and Tytherleigh, nearly all the farms up the valley—such as Woonton, Ridge, Cotley, and Hook—appear in records of Henry II's time.

CHARLES (E2) is probably a Celtic name. It seems to be derived from the Cornish *carn*, "rock," and *lis* or *les*, "court, palace." If so, it suggests the survival of a Celtic community here into Saxon times. The church (St. John the Baptist) stands on the brow of the hill overlooking the Bray valley. It was entirely rebuilt in 1875 and is of no interest except for the font (1727) and an inscribed brass to George Kellie, a former rector, and his wife Ursula (1649).

The novelist Blackmore stayed frequently with his uncle at Charles rectory and wrote much of *Lorna Doone* here. His grandfather John Blackmore was patron and incumbent here.

Mockham farm was a Domesday estate. On Mockham Down, about 2 m. NW. of the church, is a large oval earthwork, surrounded by a single rampart and of unknown age.

CHARLETON (F11) occupies the area between two arms of the beautiful Kingsbridge estuary. The parish was once notable for its quarries of finely-bedded slate, used for church-building all over the district from the 13th cent.

onwards. In 1488 the square tower of Dartmouth Castle was built of Charleton slate. The village shows much massive building of this material, including the church (St. Mary), which stands well. Its curious castle-like tower is probably of 14th-cent. date, but the body of the church was substantially rebuilt in 1849-50 and is of little interest. Charleton Court embodies some remains of the old manor house. The old slate quarries lie about ¼ m. S. of East Charleton and also about ¾ m. due S. of Charleton village, overlooking Frogmore Creek.

CHAWLEIGH (F4), on the upland between the valleys of Taw and Little Dart, was one of the many "village boroughs" of Devon in the 15th cent. The church (St. James) is entirely 15th-cent., with large windows filled with clear glass. It has a fine rood-screen with tracery of the Bradninch type and good vaulting. A parclose screen, also of 15th-cent. date, separates the chancel from the Chenson chapel. The chancel roof is notable for its great number of bosses, and some fine cresting similar to that on the screen.

Near the church is a late medieval building, possibly the old rectory. Chenson, on a slope above the Taw, was a medieval mansion with a chapel in 1400. Duckworthy was a Domesday estate.

CHELDON (F4) is a tiny, lost parish above the wooded valley of the Little Dart. The church (St. Mary) is small and attractive, mostly a rustic 15th-cent. building. The wagon roofs have some good bosses; there are 15th-cent. carved bench-ends and an 18th-cent. pulpit, altar-rails, and text-boards in the sanctuary. On either side of the chancel step are curious ironwork gates

surmounted by crowns, dated 1737 and 1743, perhaps brought from elsewhere.

CHERITON BISHOP (F6) is a small village in unspoilt country just N. of the Exeter-Okehampton main road. There must have been a church here in the 11th cent. as the name means "church town."

There were numerous small manors in the parish, of which Crockernwell, Eggbear, Lambert, and Medland are all recorded in Domesday Book. Treable is a Celtic place-name: there can be little doubt that it has been continuously inhabited since Celtic times. Grendon is mentioned in a Saxon charter of 739. Small pockets of Celtic people remained undisturbed in this remote, forested country long after the Saxon occupation, as witness also the adjacent *nymet* place-names (*nymet* derives from a Celtic word for a "sacred grove"). Easton Barton occurs in 1157 but is possibly a pre-Conquest site : the name means " Ethelric's or Elfric's farm."

Crockernwell is a hamlet on the Exeter-Okehampton road which has been the main route from Exeter into Cornwall from time immemorial. Parts of the road are undoubtedly on the line of a prehistoric ridgeway. A small settlement grew up at Crockernwell as early as Saxon times; and in 1390 Bishop Brantyngham licensed a chapel here.

Cheriton church (St. Mary) is an interesting building: plastered, whitened, and ceiled throughout, and altogether pleasant. The fine plain granite tower is 15th-cent., and the nave and N. aisle are of the same date; but the chancel is 13th-cent. with good lancet windows in red Posbury stone. The S. wall of the nave was rebuilt in the reconstruction of 1884, and the windows spoilt. The fittings of the church are noteworthy. The font is profusely ornamented Norman work. In the N. aisle is a fine medieval screen with most of its original colouring; old benches with carved ends, roof bosses, some 15th-cent. glass, the royal arms of Elizabeth on a hatchment (rare), and the royal arms of George II above. The upper part of the pulpit is elaborately carved 16th-cent. work.

CHERITON FITZPAINE (G5) is a

large village in unspoilt and beautiful country. Its name means "church-town" and indicates a church in pre-Conquest times. The Fitzpaines held the manor in the 13th cent. Of the farms in the parish, Chilton, Coddiford, Coombe Barton, and Lower Dunscombe appear as small estates in Domesday.

The church (St. Matthew)[1] is entirely a 15th-cent. building, spacious and light. The N. and S. arcades of Beer stone have good carved capitals of the Devon type; the original ceiled wagon roofs remain, with especially good bosses in the N. aisle; the royal arms are dated 1665. There are a number of finely incised floor-slabs (with coats-of-arms) mainly to the Moores of Upcott, and a particularly fine slab to Susanna Harris (1666). Upcott Barton, about 1½ m. N. of the church, was the seat of the Upcotts in Henry III's time. By the early 15th cent. it had come to Nicholas Radford, a lawyer, who was murdered in 1455 by Sir Thomas Courtenay, son of the Earl of Devon, and a band of followers. In Henry VIII's time Upcott belonged to the Courtenays and became the seat of a younger branch of that family. It is now a farmhouse, but retains considerable traces of its former status of "mansion."[2]

CHITTLEHAMHOLT (E3) was for-

merly a hamlet of Chittlehampton, having originated as a forest-clearing (holt) by people from that village. In medieval times it was a park of the Courtenays, Earls of Devon, but was disparked by order of Henry VIII. The church (St. John the Baptist) was built in 1838. Snydles, now a farm, was a Domesday manor.

CHITTLEHAMPTON (E3) is a large

compact village, originally built around an open square with the church on one side. It was one of the early villages in the Saxon occupation, c. 700 in date. The church is one of the finest in N. Devon. It has a unique dedication, to the Celtic saint Urith or Hieritha, who was born at East Stowford (about 1 m. N. in Swimbridge parish) and was martyred by the villagers of Chittlehampton who cut her to pieces with their scythes. St. Urith's well still lies at the E. end of the village, now called by the corrupt name of Taddy Well or St. Teara's Well. The ancient wall and building that stood above and around it have been removed, the well has been covered in, and a common pump fixed: but this prosaic object takes us back to the early days of Christianity in Devon, when an obscure Celtic maiden named Urith was slain by some heathen Saxons, probably early in the 8th cent.[3] She was buried near the site of her martyrdom, and a beautiful church was later raised above her. The exact burial-place was probably in the small chapel on the N. side of the sanctuary, which originally contained an image of the saint and was the scene of a pilgrimage on her day (8 July) until 1539. The small chapel has now been made into a passage leading to a vestry. It is floored by a stone with the inscription " Orate pro anima Joan Cobley," a medieval slab which there is some reason to believe may have been placed over St. Urith's relics. The removal of her image did not end her cult in Devon, for the Christian name of Urith or Hieritha was repeatedly bestowed on daughters in gentle and simple families for long afterwards, and is indeed still used in the Trevelyan and Trefusis families.

The church is entirely a rebuilding of (c. 1470–c. 1520), the magnificent W. tower being the last part to be completed (plate 1). It is unquestionably the finest church tower in Devon, combining the strength of Devon towers with the grace of Somerset. The medieval pulpit (c. 1500) survives, the figure on the N. side being that of St. Urith holding the palm branch of martyrdom and the foundation stone of the church. In the N. transept is a monument to John Giffard of Brightley with figures of his son Arthur and his grandson John (1602-66), a royalist colonel.

Brightley Barton, 2½ m. SW. of the village, occupies a medieval moated site. The park has long been given over to tillage, and the 16th-cent. house has been considerably pulled about.

Hudscott, SE. of the village, was one of the lesser seats of the Rolles. It was rebuilt in 1677 but is unexciting. Hawkridge Barton was a seat of a branch of the Aclands from the mid-14th cent. until the 17th cent. Externally there is nothing remarkable except a decaying avenue of ancient walnuts: so often the first indication of a 16th or 17th-cent. "mansion." The house may have been rebuilt c. 1615 as it contains a plaster coat-of-arms of Acland impaling Tremayne: Baldwin Acland married Elizabeth, da. of Tremayne of Collacombe, in 1615.

Among the other farmsteads of the parish, Whitestone, South Bray, and North and South Newton, were all Domesday manors. There is a good medieval stone cross at Brightley Cross, possibly erected as a guide post in connection with the widespread pilgrimage to the shrine of St. Urith.

CHIVELSTONE (F12) parish has magnificent cliff scenery along its whole coastline, including the fine headland of Prawle, the most southerly point in Devon. Prawle means " look-out hill " and must have been so used in Saxon times. A Lloyds signal station reports all passing ships. There was a medieval chapel at Prawle, dedicated to the 6th-cent. Irish saint Brendan, now quite gone.[1]

Chivelstone, Prawle, South Allington, and Ford were all Domesday estates and are now substantial hamlets. Much of the parish consists of a plateau of pre-Cambrian rocks, dissected by deep and beautiful combes of which Lanacombe is the best. Field-walls of grey slate on the plateau are an unusual sight for Devon.

The church, founded as a chapelry of Stokenham (q.v.), is the only one in England dedicated to St. Silvester, a 4th-cent. Pope. It is mainly a late 15th–early 16th-cent. building in local slate, with some granite. The chancel is 14th-cent. work (much rebuilt), as also are the tower arch and font. The altartable and rails, and font-cover, are 17th-cent. in date; but the richest features of the furnishings are the 15th-cent. roodscreen and the pulpit. The richly carved pulpit, similar to that at Holne, was carved from a single block of oak.

CHRISTOW (G7) stands on the W. hillside of the Teign valley. To the W. it rises well over 800 ft. to moorland where the two reservoirs of Tottiford and Kennick, supplying Torquay with water, lie. These cover nearly 74 acres; and here the scenery of the parish, which is everywhere of great beauty, reaches its loveliest.

Canonteign was the original Domesday manor. It was given to the canons of St. Mary du Val in Normandy *c.* 1125 and so acquired its prefix. Canonteign Barton or Old Canonteign was the Tudor manor house. It is a fine example of its period, built of local stone with massive granite quoins, window-frames, mullions, and doorways, and tall granite chimney-stacks. When Sir Edward Pellew bought the two manors of Christow and Canonteign in 1812, he built a new Canonteign House, in a beautiful timbered park SW. of the old house, and the old house was occupied as a farm. Some of its internal features remain, e.g. a fine early 17th-cent. staircase. The house was garrisoned for the King, and was taken by Fairfax in December 1645 (plate 33).

Sir Edward Pellew (1757–1833), first Viscount Exmouth, was a brilliant naval commander. Among his many exploits was the bombardment of Algiers in 1816, upon the refusal of the Dey to abolish Christian slavery, an action which brought him honours from all over Christendom and a viscountcy at home. He is buried at Christow, where a monument to him may be seen.

Christow church (prob. St. Christina) is a 15th-cent. granite building, except the chancel, which was rebuilt in 1862. The W. tower is one of the finest granite towers in Devon. It bears the date 1630, when it was either rebuilt in its old form or substantially repaired. There are some carved 16th-cent. bench-ends, a 15th-cent. chancel screen too garishly coloured, and some 18th-

19th-cent. Pellew monuments. The font is Norman.

There were formerly silver, lead, copper, and manganese mines in the parish. An abandoned lead mine may be seen near Old Canonteign. Pale Farm is of some antiquarian interest, and a farm near the church contains late medieval panelling.

CHUDLEIGH (G8) is a small market town on the main road from Exeter to Plymouth, to which it owed its rise in the 13th–14th cents. In the 11th cent. it formed part of the vast episcopal manor of Bishop's Teignton, and belonged to the bishops of Exeter until 1550, when Bishop Veysey was obliged by the King to alienate it. The bishops of Exeter had a medieval palace here, of which there are slight traces to the SE. of the town.

One of the bishops (probably Stapeldon) founded a borough at Chudleigh. Almost certainly its rise from a purely agricultural village to the rank of market-town and borough was due to the rise of Plymouth, 30 m. away, which brought greatly increased traffic along the road from Exeter. By Lysons's day there was a market and three fairs. As with so many Devonshire towns, Chudleigh reached its greatest size in 1841 and thereafter declined, though not as badly as most old market towns.

The town was largely destroyed by a fire in May 1807, and afterwards rebuilt. The church (St. Martin) is interesting, despite extensive 19th-cent. restorations. It is mostly an early 14th-cent. building, with a 13th-cent. W. tower of an unusual type for Devon. The S. aisle was added in the 15th cent. and has a good granite arcade. The rood-screen is unusual, probably of late date, and bears the arms of Courtenay. Sir Pierce (or Peter) Courtenay who died 1552 and whose tomb is in the chancel, may have had it made. There are ancient carved bench-ends, and numerous mural monuments, tablets, and floor–slabs to the 16th–18th-cent. gentry of the parish.

Next to the church is the old grammar school, now a private house, founded by John Pynsent in 1668. Scattered over the large parish are several interesting houses, of which the most notable is Ugbrooke, formerly the seat of Lord Clifford, in a fine deer park of 600 acres. The first mansion was built by the well-known Lord Treasurer Clifford of the Cabal, who died here (1673) before it was completed. This house was rebuilt about 1760 as a hideous "pseudo-Norman pile," but the interior decoration was by the Adam brothers. The Catholic chapel, built by the Lord Treasurer and consecrated by Bishop Sparrow of Exeter in 1671 (Clifford did not become an open Catholic until the year of his death), still remains, somewhat altered and enlarged, and magnificently decorated by the Adams. The Lord Treasurer is buried here.

The park, one of several which are claimed to be " the finest in Devon," contains a grove of beech-trees known as " Dryden's Walk." Dryden was a close friend of the 1st Lord Clifford, and often visited Ugbrooke. There is indeed a tradition that he completed his translation of Virgil here. At the topmost point of the park is an earthwork known as Castle Dyke, which commands a wide expanse of country N. and W. It is probably an Early Iron Age hill-fort.

. The great limestone mass of Chudleigh Rock was a favourite place of resort for "outings" from Exeter and other towns in days when people were more contented with the simple pleasures of life. The old quarries and lime-kilns are most picturesque. Hams Barton was the seat of the Hunts, and a good deal of their Elizabethan mansion survives. The fine banqueting-room is dated 1621. Upcott was the birthplace of the celebrated geographer Major James Rennell (1742-1830). Whiteway was acquired by the Parkers. The 1st Lord Boringdon began the present house, which was completed by his nephew.

CHULMLEIGH (E4) is a small decayed market-town, boldly situated on the top of a hill rising from the Little Dart river. It belonged to Baldwin the sheriff in 1086, passed to the Courtenays as part of the great honour of Okehampton before 1194, and remained in their hands until the attainder of Henry, Marquess of Exeter, in 1539.

Chulmleigh was made a borough by the Courtenays about 1253. It was a prosperous place throughout the 17th and 18th cents., with a woollen industry, a good market, and three cattle fairs. It also stood on the main road from Exeter to Barnstaple and shared in the road traffic. The Barnstaple Inn is dated 1633, and there is much other decent old building in the town. The woollen industry had practically gone by 1800, but the cattle fairs, markets and road traffic kept the town relatively prosperous until about 1850. Since then it has hardly moved. The causes of the decline were the making of the new turnpike road along the Taw valley (c. 1830) which took away a good deal of the wagon traffic from the old hill-road through the town, and the opening of the North Devon railway in 1854 along the same valley, which led to the setting up of new sheep and cattle markets at Eggesford and South Molton Road stations.

The parish church (St. Mary Magdalen) was formerly a collegiate church, with seven prebends founded at an unknown date. It was entirely rebuilt in the 15th cent., and has a very fine W. tower, restored in 1881. The interior is spacious, with lofty nave arcades and good wagon roofs with carved bosses and angels on the wall-plates. The chancel was rebuilt, and four memorial windows inserted, in 1860. A fine roodscreen, in perfect condition, with its vaulting and cornices complete, extends across nave and aisles.

In the surrounding parish are a number of interesting houses. Stone Barton, in beautiful remote country 2 m. E. of the town, has substantial remains of an earthwork on a promontory above the farm. There is said to have been a castle here, and in Westcote's day a ruined heap of stones could be seen. It may have been a small Iron Age hill-fort adapted later to an early medieval castle or fortified house.

Garland, a remote farm in the N. of the parish, was the birthplace of John Garland, grammarian, poet, and alchemist, who studied at Oxford and Paris, was professor at Toulouse University 1229-31, and wrote treatises on grammar, minerals, counterpoint, and plain-song.

Colleton Barton is architecturally the most interesting and attractive house in the parish. The present house was built largely by Humphrey Bury about 1612. This date appears in the diningroom. The gatehouse, with the chapel above it, remains from the medieval house. The chapel, dedicated to St. Edmund the Bishop, was first licensed in 1381. This is the period of the gatehouse, which probably gave access to a quadrangle round which the medieval house lay. The present house is E-shaped, the W. wing containing the

Hall and drawing-room. There are fine decorated plaster ceilings of early 17th-cent. date in the Hall, drawing-room and dining-room. The drawing-room is panelled with carved oak, adorned with the coats-of-arms of the Burys and allied families.

CHURCHSTOW (F11) is the parent of the market-town of Kingsbridge at its feet, for out of his manor of Churchstow the abbot of Buckfast carved his new borough of Kingsbridge (q.v.) soon after 1220.

A church was built on the apex of a high ridge, the place thereafter being known as "church-stow." This church (St. Mary), still a prominent landmark in the Kingsbridge country, may have existed before the Norman Conquest. The present building is a late 14th-cent. church, built entirely of the dark local slate, with a fine buttressed tower of the South Hams type. The S. aisle is early 16th-cent. The font is Norman, on a new pedestal and base.

The Church House Inn, near by, is a 16th-cent. building in green slate. About 1 m. NE. of the church is Leigh, still substantially a 15th-cent. building. The gatehouse is a striking object to come upon suddenly in this remote lane. Leigh was a Domesday manor, and later became a cell of Buckfast. It is now a farmhouse. Norton, also a Domesday manor, has remains of a mansion. Combe Royal is a Tudor house, much rebuilt, and now a school. It, too, is recorded in Domesday. Oranges and lemons were said to ripen in its gardens. The suffix " Royal " is derived from one William Royel, an early medieval owner. Sorley, which is mentioned in a Saxon charter of 947, has traces of a former manor house. Warcombe, recorded in 1228, is a cruciform building with a massive, central chimney stack, probably 16th-cent. or earlier in date.

CHURSTON FERRERS (H10) occupies the narrow neck of land between the S. shore of Tor Bay and the Dart estuary. Galmpton is a village in this parish, at the head of Galmpton creek on the Dart. Both Churston and Galmpton are recorded in Domesday Book. Churston Court, beside the church, is an attractive Elizabethan house. The church (dedication unknown) has a plain W. tower of early date (*c.* 1300) but the remainder of the fabric is 15th-cent. (restored 1863-4).

Greenway, overlooking the Dart, was the home of the Gilberts, and here Sir Humphrey was born about 1539. The present house is Georgian.

CLANNABOROUGH (F5) is a small parish with no village. The church, dedicated to the Celtic saint Petrock, lies just off an undoubted pre-Roman trackway, and commands a tremendous and beautiful view towards the northern ramparts of Dartmoor. It is an attractive little building outside, in a simple 16th-cent. style, but its interior was over-restored in 1858-9. The Barton was a Domesday manor; the present house was built *c.* 1800. Appledore and Walson Barton were Domesday estates also. Clannaborough gets its name from " the cloven hill " here—*Clouene-berge* in 1239.

CLAWTON (B6) lies in the cold yellow-clay country, so heavy that even in Risdon's day it was a local saying that " The Devil was clogged in Clawmoor." The church (St. Leonard) is mainly an early 14th-cent. building, somewhat altered in the early 16th cent. There is, however, a fine Norman font, and other 12th-cent. work in the chancel. The

chancel and aisle roofs retain many carved bosses. In the N. aisle is a mural monument to Christopher Osmond of Fernhill, gent. (1631). Fernhill, Blagdon, and Kempthorne, now farmhouses, were formerly mansions.

CLAYHANGER (J3) is a parish of rolling hills and many little combes. Donningstone Mill was a Domesday manor in this parish.

The church (St. Peter) preserves its original, simple aisle-less plan, with a W. tower. The church was completely restored in 1879-81 and partly rebuilt. The font is early 13th-cent. in date, and there are some remains of a 15th-cent. screen. There is also a considerable amount of early 16th-cent. seating with well-carved bench-ends of the West Country type. A number of floor-slabs and other memorials commemorate the Nutcombe family who owned Nutcombe estate from the early 13th cent. (if not earlier) until the middle of the 19th. Some of these memorials are excellently lettered. A marble monument commemorates Richard Nutcombe of Nutcombe, Esq. (1666-1736), sheriff of Devon in 1715-6 "who in an age both in principles and practice corrupt kept his faith entire and his morals untainted."

Nutcombe is a picturesque house, a rebuilding of *c.* 1600 on the old site. The kitchen block of this house has been demolished. Externally it presents no special features, but internally the original plan of the 1600 house is still clear. There are good plaster ceilings downstairs and more elaborate ones upstairs. The grotesque figures in the plaster mantelpiece of the hall were copied by the Elizabethan craftsmen from German and Flemish pattern books.

CLAYHIDON (K4). The church (St.

Andrew) is a 15th-cent. building. In the S. aisle is a recessed and canopied tomb, with the upper half of the effigy of a priest in vestments. Bolham and Hole were small Domesday manors. To the N. the parish rises to Buckland Hill (916 ft.) on the county boundary. An ancient trackway follows the edge of the escarpment here, from which there are magnificent views across the vale of Taunton to the Quantocks and Exmoor, and far up into the plain of Somerset.

CLOVELLY (B3) is one of the most notable of the many " beauty spots" in Devon. On either side there are tremendous hanging cliffs, with long and thickly wooded slopes; and the village street—so steep that it is stepped for the greater part—occupies the bed of an old watercourse, a mere cleft in this formidable coast. Seven generations of the Carys lived at Clovelly, from Robert (c. 1457-1540) to Robert (1697-1724), who died childless. It was George Cary (1543-1601), a Middle Temple lawyer and sheriff of Devon in 1587, who really created the village by building the massive stone pier we see to-day, so making the only safe harbour between Appledore and Boscastle in Cornwall (plate 58).

Until the middle of the 19th cent. Clovelly remained quite unknown to the outside world. In 1855 Charles Kingsley, whose father was rector here 1830-6, published his *Westward Ho!*, in which Clovelly and the Carys figured much. Then Dickens wrote of it in *A Message from the Sea* (1860), and it became known. Soon there were "artists and dustbins in every corner." Its subsequent history as a " tourist centre" has already been given in Part I.

Clovelly Court, situated above the village, was built c. 1740 by Zachary Hamlyn, who had bought the manor from the Carys. It was remodelled c. 1790-5 to make what Baring-Gould called " the present absurd Cockney Gothic erection," but it still contains a core of the Tudor house. Sir James Hamlyn landscaped the coast E. of the village before his death in 1829, making the 3-m. Hobby Drive, which is deservedly famous.

Clovelly church (All Saints) is somewhat restored but still very attractive. It is almost entirely 15th–early 16th-cent. in date, with a Norman font, and 17th-cent. benches and pulpit. The latter was given by William Cary in 1634, to whom there is a mural monument in the chancel. He is the Will Cary of *Westward Ho!*; the youthful Kingsley must often have gazed at this memorial. There is a good series of 17th-cent. mural monuments to the Carys and later monuments to the Hamlyns, besides floor slabs to the earlier Carys. Some of the windows are by Kempe and Comper. Clovelly Dykes, on the plateau behind the coast, is one of the largest and most impressive Early Iron Age hill-forts in Devon. It is a complex series of earthworks covering more than twenty acres.

CLYST HONITON or **HONITON CLYST** (H6) lies on the main road from Exeter to Honiton. It belonged to the Dean and Chapter of Exeter from pre-Conquest times. The village is poor (too much modern brick) and the church (St. Michael) was completely rebuilt and ruined in 1876. Only the early 13th-cent. font and some monuments escaped this devastation. The John Yarde commemorated by the 1575 monument in the church led the advance over Clyst Bridge against the rebels of 1549. Holbrook Farm was a pre-Conquest estate and was the home of the Holbrook family for centuries.

CLYST HYDON (J5)

lies in quiet red sandstone country. The church (St. Andrew) is a 15th-cent. building spoilt by restoration. The N. aisle was added in 1855. Aunk is a pre-Conquest estate with a possibly Celtic name, referring to the spur on which it stands.

CLYST ST. GEORGE (H7)

is the most southerly of the six parishes named after the Clyst. The church (St. George) was rebuilt in 1851-9 and completely spoilt. It was gutted by fire in an air raid in 1940 but has been again rebuilt (1952).

In this parish is Marsh Barton, granted by Henry de la Pomerai to the Sokespitches c. 1170-80 and held by them in unbroken male succession until 1803.[1] Kenniford Farm, an Elizabethan house, was formerly the home of the Osbornes.

CLYST ST. LAWRENCE (J6)

is in the placid, unspoiled country of the upper Clyst valley. The church (St. Lawrence) is the usual 15th-cent. rebuilding of an older fabric, of which the only evidence to-day is the plain granite font, c. 1200 in date.

The church contains a number of carved, grotesque heads, especially in the tower arch, and some good bosses in the wagon roof. Over the chancel arch is an interesting medieval painting, symbolising the Trinity, said to be the only one of its kind in Devon. Much of the furniture is also interesting (17th- and 18th-cent.), including the royal arms of Charles II. The glory of the church is, however, a chancel screen of five bays (c. 1480) which is beautiful even in its partial ruin.

CLYST ST. MARY (H6)

lies at the E. end of an ancient bridge over the river Clyst, the oldest surviving bridge in Devon, mentioned in a record of 1238. The raised causeway is 600 ft. long, and of the five arches the two westernmost probably date from 1310 when the bridge was substantially rebuilt.

The church (St. Mary) lies in the park of Winslade House. It was almost wholly rebuilt in 1870 and is the dullest Victorian work. Winslade House is a late Georgian mansion, now a school.

Clyst was one of the chief scenes of the Western Rebellion of 1549. It was here that the rebels were finally defeated and the village burnt by Lord Russell.

COCKINGTON (see TORQUAY).

COFFINSWELL (G9).

The great Iron Age earthwork of Milber Camp is partly in this parish, and partly in Haccombe with Combe. The church (St. Bartholomew) has a crude W. tower of 13th-cent. date; a nave and chancel probably of the same date; a small S. transept added early in the 14th cent.; and a N. aisle early in the 15th. The N. arcade of Beer stone has curiously carved capitals. On the capital of the W. pillar are the arms of the Scobhull, Holbeam, Leyton, and Gambon families. The font is a finely carved late Norman structure, with a bowl and shaft of Caen stone. Notice the wagon roofs and the fine oak lectern. Court Barton, near the church, was the manor house, and has much early 16th-cent. work, including some granite-mullioned windows.

COLATON RALEIGH (J7)

is an attractive village with much white-washed cob and thatch and many trees. Place Court is an ancient farmhouse, probably the former manor house, with an oratory. The church (St. John the Baptist) was rebuilt, all except the 15th-cent. sandstone tower, in 1875. It retains its Norman font.

COLDRIDGE (E5) church and village stand on the summit of a high ridge and are visible for miles. The houses are gathered round an open "square," from which there are wide views across to Dartmoor.

The church (St. Mary) is very interesting. It is almost entirely early 15th- and early 16th-cent., but there are distinct traces of Norman work inside. The special features of the church are (1) a good uncoloured 15th-cent. rood-screen; (2) a carved oak 15th-cent. pulpit; (3) some 15th-cent. glass, much smashed recently by wanton boys; (4) many late medieval tiles in the chancel and around the font; (5) some late medieval benches in the N. aisle; (6) some fine carved bench-ends in the S. aisle and S. chancel aisle, including the prayer-desk of Sir John Evans, probably all early 16th-cent.; (7) a parclose screen dividing the Evans chantry from the chancel; (8) a fine table-tomb and recumbent effigy of Sir John Evans under a canopy in the N. aisle; (9) the wagon roofs of the N. and S. aisles, with many carved bosses; (10) the font, probably early 13th-cent.; (11) the lofty and well-moulded arcades of elvan (not granite). The whole church is graceful and well proportioned, and has a good tower.

COLEBROOKE (F5) has a good 14th–15th-cent. church (St. Andrew) standing boldly on an eminence. It is probably an early 14th-cent. cruciform church, with a N. aisle opened out in the 15th cent., and S. transept c. 1300 in date. The W. tower is a fine example of Perpendicular building. There are some unusual carved bench-ends, somewhat crudely executed and probably of 15th-cent. date. Two bench-ends show the arms of Coplestone and Gorges, borne by grotesque men. As the Coplestone-Gorges marriage, which greatly enlarged the Coplestone estate, took place in 1472, this may be about the date of these benches. The priest's stall is early 16th-cent. work, contemporary with the fine rood-screen which has linenfold panelling. The E. end of the N. aisle (the Coplestone chapel) is enclosed by screens with an unusual curvilinear design, similar to those at Brushford and Coldridge, c. 1500 in date.

Coplestone takes its name from the 10th-cent. boundary stone, a carved granite pillar 10 ft. high on the main Exeter-Barnstaple road where three parishes meet. This *copelan stan* is referred to in a charter of 974. The Coplestones were seated on their estate of that name as early as Henry II's time, and still survive in the county, though they sold their ancestral home as long ago as 1659. The present house is unexciting Georgian.

Whelmstone Barton, an ancient freehold estate first recorded in 1249 but probably older, is now a house of c. 1600 with a stone-arched gateway to its courtyard. A chapel dedicated to St. Mary was licensed here in 1374, and remains of it, with a braced roof of 14th-cent. date, may be seen in a hay-loft in the farmyard. Landsend, a remote farm, was formerly a mansion, and had a medieval chapel. Combe is a late Georgian mansion.

COLYTON (L6) is a small and ancient town, grouped around a handsome church. It stands on the river Coly, near its confluence with the Axe, and at the mouth of a beautiful combe which runs back into the greensand outliers of the Blackdown Hills. The whole parish is singularly beautiful, with rolling green hills and deep combes dotted with ancient farmsteads. About a score of these farms have the suffix *hayne* or *hayes* in their name, from the medieval English *hay*, "enclosure." They are nearly all compounded with a medieval personal name which suggests that they were enclosed in severalty in the 13th or early 14th cent. Some of these farmsteads became "mansions" in the 16th–18th cents. and are architecturally interesting, e.g. Hooperhayne, Blamphayne, Cookshays, Heathayne. These and others were the homes of small squires, and are very characteristic of their period and status.[1] The combes of Colyton parish, with their network of medieval lanes linking farm to farm, make pleasant walking for several days on end.

Colyton was settled early in the Saxon occupation, probably before 700. It was a compact village of the Teutonic type surrounded by open fields, a royal estate, and important enough to give its name to a 10th-cent. hundred. In 1208 King John granted to Thomas Basset a seven-day fair at the feast of St. Michael. This Thomas soon afterwards set up a borough on a new site, where the old road from Exeter to Dorchester crossed the Coly by a ford; and a town quickly grew here. But Colyford faded out (probably during the 15th cent.) and when Stukeley saw it about 1724 it was only a remnant of its former size. Though it was never incorporated it somehow contrived to get itself a mayor and insignia. The mayor was still elected in Lysons's day, and had the profits of the large cattle fair. Colyford was the birthplace of Sir Thomas Gates, governor of Virginia 1611-14. There are a number of attractive buildings in the village, including the old Manor House. Colyford bridge is recorded as early as 1254, but the present structure is modern.

Colyton town retains a good deal of interesting building. The vicarage was built in 1529 by Dr. Thomas Brerewood, chancellor to Bishop Veysey, and is referred to by Leland as "a fair House." The Great House, on the Colyford road, was built by John Yonge, an eminent merchant of the town *temp*. Elizabeth. It was the principal residence of the Yonge family, who came into Devon from Berkshire *c.* 1500, and were baronets from 1661 to 1810. Walter Yonge (1579-1649), the author of the well-known diary for the years 1604-28 (published by the Camden Society, in 1848) was the son of the Elizabethan merchant. He lived for many years at the Great House, and wrote much of his diary here. Elsewhere in the town are some good 16th–17th-cent. houses.

The parish church (St. Andrew) is a large and handsome building, chiefly of 15th–early 16th cent. date but with some 13th-cent. work in the chancel and tower. The upper part of the tower, with its octagonal lantern, is late 15th-cent. The aisles were rebuilt in 1765 and 1816: hence the curious style of the arcades. The tombs and monuments of the church are interesting. Against the N. wall is a Courtenay tomb, with effigy. The heraldry and the costume indicate that the tomb is that of Margaret, daughter of John Beaufort, Earl of Somerset, who married Thomas Courtenay, 5th Earl of Devon, *c.* 1431. The shields of arms are those of Courtenay and Beaufort.

On the N. side is the Yonge chapel, where members of this family were buried from 1584 to 1812. There is a

Jacobean stone screen to this chapel. On the S. side of the chancel is the Pole chapel, containing some splendid Pole monuments, particularly that of Sir John Pole (1658) and Elizabeth his wife. It has been suggested that the monument is the work of Gerard Johnson of Southwark. Sir William Pole (d. 1635), the great Devonshire antiquary, whose *Collections* have been quarried by generations of local historians and genealogists, lies buried in this chapel but without a memorial. The stone parclose screen to the chapel was erected *c.* 1530 by Thomas Brerewood, who held the living 1524-44. On it appear the initials T. B. with the briar bush, a pun upon the name Brerewood. There are other monuments in the church, that to William Westover (d. 1614) being especially noteworthy. The parish registers of Colyton are perfectly preserved from 1538 onwards, and have been printed.

Colcombe Castle, ½ m. N. of Colyton, was one of the seats of the Courtenays, to whom the manor came in the 13th cent. A house was first built here by Hugh Courtenay, Earl of Devon, *temp.* Edward I, but Henry Courtenay, Marquess of Exeter, rebuilt it on a magnificent scale. After his attainder in 1539, the house fell into ruin. William Pole, father of the antiquary, bought it *temp.* Elizabeth, and settled it on his son who largely rebuilt it and made it his residence. Prince Maurice made Colcombe his headquarters in 1644, and from here attacked Stedcombe, Sir Walter Erle's new house, which he had garrisoned for parliament. The Poles later made their principal residence at Shute (q.v.), and Colcombe sank to the level of a farmhouse. The remains are, however, exceedingly interesting. Much work of early 16th-cent. date remains, including a splendid

kitchen with a fireplace nearly 20 ft. across, and a private room above. Some traces of pre-16th cent. work are visible, but the extensive additions by Sir William Pole in the early 17th cent. are more conspicuous.

Of the farms of the parish not already mentioned, Farwood Barton and Gatcombe were Domesday manors, and Yardbury was the mansion of the Westovers and then of the Drakes.

Colyton is a prosperous little town, founded securely upon a fertile countryside. It has sawmills, corn-mills, tanneries, and a small iron foundry.

COMBE MARTIN (D1) is a village of immense length, mostly a single street running down a long combe to the bay (plate 46). The valley is warm and fertile, and produces large quantities of fruit and vegetables for Ilfracombe and Lynton. Hemp was formerly extensively grown here, and large quantities of shoe-makers' thread spun from it in the village. In recent years, Combe Martin has become increasingly popular as a centre for summer holidays for those who like something less crowded and sophisticated than the neighbouring resorts. The cliff scenery E. of the village is superb, the Little Hangman and the Great Hangman (1,044 ft.) being especially notable. Holdstone Down, a little farther E., reaches 1,146 ft. From here and the Hangman cliffs there are wonderful views across the Bristol Channel to the Welsh coastline and mountains. Challacombe was a medieval mansion. The present house clearly shows that a 15th-cent. hall, open to the roof, was remodelled in the early 17th cent.

The silver-lead mines of Combe Martin have been worked at intervals since the end of the 13th cent. down to 1875, when they were finally abandoned.

The whole district is full of adits and shafts, some passing under the village street. Iron ore was found at Wild Pear Bay under Little Hangman, and considerable quantities were shipped to S. Wales in the late 18th–early 19th cent. Manganese was mined at Rawnes.

Thomas Harding (1516-72), the great opponent of Bishop Jewel, was born at Buzzacott, a farm in this parish.

Combe Martin church (St. Peter ad Vincula) is a most interesting building in a rose-coloured sandstone. The chancel is 13th-cent., but the remainder of the church is mostly 15th-cent., including the very fine tower (99 ft. to the battlements) which approaches the Somerset type, and is in the class of Chittlehampton and Cullompton. The S. porch was built in 1724. The 15th-cent. rood-screen and parclose screen are exceptionally fine. There is a most beautifully sculptured marble effigy of Judith Ivatt (1634) in the dress of the period. In the N. chancel aisle are some 16th-cent. carved bench-ends.

COMBE RALEIGH (K5) was owned

by the Raleighs in the late 13th cent. The church (St. Nicholas) is an attractive early 15th-cent. building of dressed flints, in wooded and park-like country. Near by is a medieval house called The Chantry, somewhat altered internally.

COMBE-IN-TEIGNHEAD (see Hac-combe-with-Combe).

COMBPYNE (L6) has an interesting

church (St. Mary the Virgin), mainly 13th cent., with a saddle-back tower. Some changes were made in the early 14th cent., and again in the 15th cent. when new windows were inserted in the nave. The fittings and glass are the result of the restoration of 1878. The church retains a chalice and paten of pre-Reformation date (c. 1500), still in regular use.

Rousdon, now united with Comb-pyne for all purposes, was a small parish on the cliff edge. The ancient church of St. Pancras having fallen into ruin, it was rebuilt at the cost of Sir H. W. Peek in 1872. It has nothing to commend it. The mansion of Rousdon was built for Sir H. W. Peek, and is a rich man's Tudor. Since 1937 it has been occupied by Allhallows School, who came here from Honiton. The cliff scenery is fine, with great landslips.

COOKBURY (C5) is a pleasant little

village in remote country. The church has an unusual dedication to St. John the Baptist and the Seven Maccabees. It consists of a nave and chancel of 13th-cent. date; a small N. aisle c. 1500, which replaced one of 14th-cent. date, of which there are traces; and a small S. transept added early in the 16th cent. Though the church has been restored, much interesting early work is left, including a floor of late medieval tiles in the chancel and a number of ancient benches in the nave.

Stapeldon, now a farmhouse, was the mansion of the Stapeldons in the 13th and 14th cents. and the birthplace of Walter de Stapeldon (1261-1326). He was professor of canon law at Oxford, chaplain to Pope Clement V, bishop of Exeter 1307-26, where he did much towards the rebuilding of the cathedral, founder of Stapeldon Hall (afterwards Exeter College) at Oxford, and Lord High Treasurer to Edward II. He was murdered by a London mob in 1326. The bishop stayed at Stapeldon for a few days in August 1315, when he dedicated Cookbury church.

CORNWOOD (E10) is a large parish

running far into the Moor. Of its total

area of 10,000 acres, more than 6,000 are moorland and wood. The high moorlands of the parish are intersected by the wooded valley of the Yealm, which is particularly beautiful at Hawns and Dendles where the river begins to leave the Moor. From here northwards to the parish boundary at Erme Head, the ground is studded with prehistoric, and later, antiquities of the highest interest. The detailed sites of these antiquities will be found on the 2½-inch Ordnance map, sheet 20/66. Around the headwaters of the Yealm we find the greatest concentration of hut-circles on Dartmoor—some 27 to the square mile—together with stone circles, and large and small enclosures or pounds. There is a particularly large pound about ½ m. NE. of Dendles Wood. Another fairly dense concentration of hut-circles and pounds is to be found all along the W. side of the upper Erme valley. Here also is the longest known stone row in the world, beginning at a stone circle near Erme Plains and running for 2¼ m. almost due N. to a barrow on the summit of Green Hill. For the possible significance of this monument, see Part I. There are barrows (Bronze Age burial mounds) on the top of Stall Down, and also a short stone row. At the very head of the Yealm are two blowing-houses of the old tinners, and another beside the upper Erme in Erme Plains.[1]

The domestic architecture of Cornwood parish is also exceedingly interesting. Much of the parish was "waste" in Domesday, and was colonised by free peasants in the 12th and 13th cents. whose farmsteads, from which they took their family names, will be found scattered about below the moorland edge. Best of these is Cholwich Town, where the Cholwiches began soon after 1200 and which remained in their possession

until the last of the family died in 1835.[2] The farmstead itself is one of the best examples of a moorland yeoman's house that one can find anywhere round Dartmoor, a rock-like structure of moorstone dating from the late 15th cent.– early 16th cent. Other farmsteads of this type which gave their names to medieval freeholders were Hanger, Stert, Wisdome, and Hele. Hanger to-day is a solid granite farmhouse of 17th-cent. date, Great Stert is late 17th-cent., Little Stert early 17th-cent., Wisdome and South Hele have some remains of 17th-cent. work.

Hele was the fountain-head of an important South Devon family, the Heles, who were considerable landowners in the 16th and 17th cents. Pole says they originated here in Henry III's time. The last Hele of Cornwood died in 1741. South Hele, now a farmhouse, was their mansion. Like so many of the old Devon freeholders, they owed their rise from yeoman obscurity to a successful lawyer, in this instance Sir John Hele (1565-1608). Other notable houses in the parish are Blachford, a Domesday manor, which became the seat of the Rogers family, who rebuilt the house on a grander scale in the 17th cent. and made a park.

Slade belonged to the Slades in the 13th cent., and then to the Coles from the time of Richard II until the early 17th cent. The present house is a composite structure of various periods from the 13th cent. to the 19th, with traces of quadrangular planning. It has a splendid great hall, with beautiful panelling of a Flemish character, and an open-timber roof with 60 well-carved bosses, a minstrel's gallery over the panelled screen, and a large granite fireplace. The entrance porch is 16thcent. There are other internal features of 17th–18th-cent. date. NW. of the house is a handsome old barn which retains its original doors.[1] Delamore House was rebuilt about 1819-20, but there are traces of the older mansion near Delamore Farm.

Architecturally, the most interesting house in the parish is Fardel, which was a Saxon estate and a Domesday manor. It came to the Raleighs (of Smallridge in East Devon) by marriage with an heiress early in the 14th cent. and continued in the family until Carew Raleigh, son of the great Sir Walter, sold it to the Heles. The house is a medieval mansion of 15th–16th-cent. date, with a well-preserved chapel and solar. The chapel was licensed by Bishop Lacy in 1432 and this is probably the date of the existing building. Near Fardel was found, in 1860, the first stone with an Ogham inscription to be discovered in England.[2] This stone is now in the British Museum.

Cornwood church (St. Michael) is of no great interest. It is mainly a 15th-cent. church, much restored, with a chancel and W. tower of c. 1300. There is a 17th-cent. pulpit, and there are a few mural monuments to local families, including one to Robert Bellmaine of Delamore (1627) and his wife Dorothy with a curious epitaph:

> Here's rest and peace
> Within this grave,
> Which we in life
> Could never have.

CORNWORTHY (G10) is one of the beautiful Dartside parishes. The parish church (St. Peter) is mainly a 15th-cent. building. It has a late Norman font, and a fairly good early 15th-cent. rood-screen. But the interior has all the feeling of the Georgian age, with its box-pews, pulpit and canopy, altar-piece, and windows of clear glass. A licence in the Exeter Faculty Books shows that it was entirely refitted in 1788, and it is now one of the most delightful church interiors in Devon, having entirely escaped the Victorian restorers. It is, however, now closed (1951) for public worship and awaiting urgent structural repairs. There is a good canopied tomb of Sir Thomas Harris, sergeant-at-law, in his lawyer's robes (1610), and Elizabeth his wife. The Rev. Charles Barter was vicar here for 71 years (1775-1846), the longest tenure of a Devonshire living that is known.

About ½ m. W. of the village are the remains of an Augustinian nunnery, founded between 1205 and 1238. A 14th-cent. gatehouse is all that survives. Allaleigh, now a farm, was the ancestral freehold of the famous Hawley family of Dartmouth.

CORYTON (C7) lies in a beautiful situation where the Lyd valley opens out (plate 23). The church (St. Andrew) has a pleasant exterior, with some 13th-cent. work in the chancel, but the interior is totally uninteresting as a result of thorough restoration in 1885. There was formerly a large quarry, opened in 1778, which produced excellent slates for roofing, tombstones, chimney-pieces, billiard tables, etc.

COTLEIGH (L5) is a small cluster of houses on a high ridge of the Blackdown Hills. The church (St. Petrock) is mostly 15th-cent., pleasant but of no great interest, with a rebuilt chancel (1867). The font and wagon roofs should be noticed.

COUNTISBURY (F1) has been identified with *arx Cynuit*, where Odda, the ealdorman of Devon, inflicted a decisive defeat on the Danes in 878. But a far more likely site is Combwich, on the W. side of the Parret estuary in Somerset, a better landing place altogether.

The parish contains superb coastal and moorland scenery, rising to 1,125 ft. at Kipscombe Hill and 1,136 ft. at Old Barrow Hill. Foreland Point is a hog-backed cliff rising to over 700 ft., with a lighthouse first lit in 1900. There was a Roman signal station at Old Barrow, somewhat NE. of the summit of the hill, commanding the Bristol Channel. It is a square enclosure with rounded angles, enclosed by a triple vallum and ditch, the outer vallum being a large circle.

Countisbury church (St. John the Baptist) is of little interest, having been rebuilt and enlarged at various dates between 1796 and 1846. It contains, however, a post-Reformation chancel screen upon which a classic pediment of late 17th-cent. work is superimposed.

CREACOMBE (G4) is one of the most remote parishes in Devon, completely lost in high and moory country. The church (St. Michael) was rebuilt in 1857, and only the font now remains of the original structure.

CREDITON (G5) is a bustling market-town situated in a large and mostly very fertile parish of more than 12,000 acres. The town and rural parish, known as Crediton Hamlets, were separated for local government purposes in 1894. Crediton first appears in history as the birthplace of Winfrith or (as he is more generally known) St. Boniface c. 680, who is in some respects the greatest man Devon has ever produced, the first preacher of Christianity in Central Germany and founder of the famous monastery of Fulda. In 739 a *monasterium* or minster was established here, King Aethelheard giving *Cridie* to Forthhere, bishop of Sherborne, for this purpose. A see was established here in 909 with Eadulf as the first bishop. Athelstan confirmed Crediton to the bishop in 933 as part of his endowment, and nine bishops ruled here until Leofric (1046-50) obtained papal permission to remove the see to the walled city of Exeter in 1050. The valuable manor of Crediton went with him to the new see of Exeter, and remained episcopal property until the Tudors despoiled the bishopric of most of its best estates.

The bishop of Exeter created a borough at Crediton shortly before 1238, but it never grew to much size or importance, probably because it lay too near to Exeter. The great revival of the Devonshire woollen industry in the early 16th cent. brought the most prosperous days. Among the Crediton merchants who made fortunes out of kerseys at this period, and founded landed families, were the Davies (later of Creedy Park), the Northcotes (later of Hayne in Newton St. Cyres and now Earls of Iddesleigh), and the Tuckfields, who enjoyed a large estate centred upon Fulford Park, in the neighbouring parish of Shobrooke, down to the early 19th cent. It remained a considerable textile town until the time of George III and then declined with nearly all the other Devonshire woollen towns. Like most old market-towns, Crediton began to decay seriously when the railway came (1851) and nothing has happened since to disturb its slumber. In late years it has become a dormitory for Exeter, helped by a frequent and cheap bus service.

The town, which consists mostly of one E.-W. street a mile long, has frequently been devastated by great fires, more so even than the majority of Devonshire towns. The fire of 14 August 1743 destroyed 460 houses in the West Town, and did £40,000 worth of damage. Other great fires occurred in 1766, 1769, and 1772. There remains, however, much decent building of late 18th–early 19th-cent. date and some pleasant old shop fronts. The blood-red local brick gives a warmth to the scene everywhere. On Bowden Hill some older buildings remain, including a Unitarian chapel rebuilt in 1729. Michaiah Towgood, the eminent Presbyterian divine, was minister here from 1737 to 1749.

The parish church (Holy Cross) is one of the finest town churches in Devon, a splendid red sandstone building with a tower strongly reminiscent of Exeter cathedral. When the see was removed to Exeter, the church was made collegiate and was perhaps the first of its class in Devon, with its stately chancel occupied by the stalls of 18 canons and 18 vicars. Edward VI dissolved the collegiate church in 1547, and the parishioners bought the church for £200. Nothing remains of the collegiate buildings, which must have been extensive. Twelve of the principal inhabitants (9 from Crediton, 3 from Sandford) were incorporated as the Twelve Governors of the church of Crediton, who keep the church in repair and have the gift of the living. The present handsome building is cruciform in plan, with a central tower, N. and S. transepts, an eastern Lady Chapel, and a three-storied vestry on the S. side of the chancel. It is in essence a great 12th-cent. cruciform church extensively remodelled in the late 14th–early 15th cent. The 15th-cent. clearstory is magnificent, an unusual feature in Devon churches. In the N. aisle is a muniment chest, c. 1420 in date. There are three notable monuments in the church: (1) John Tuckfield of Tedburn and Fulford (1555-1630), his son Thomas, and his daughter-in-law Elizabeth; (2) Sir William Periam (1534-1604), who sat on the commission for the trial of Mary, Queen of Scots, and became Chief Baron of the Exchequer; (3) Sir John Sully (1387) and his wife. He fought in most of the campaigns of the Black Prince. The grammar school was kept in the Lady Chapel from the time of Edward VI until 1859, when the present school buildings were completed. In the parvise chamber is a good parochial library.

The extensive parish contained a number of ancient mansions and fertile estates. The Bodleys, ancestors of the famous Sir Thomas Bodley, lived at Higher Dunscombe, beside the Exeter road, which shows traces of the mansion. Downes, not far away, is the seat of the Bullers who acquired it from the Goulds in 1726. The present house was built about 1692,[1] and was the birthplace of Sir Redvers Buller (1839-1908), who was sent to South Africa in 1899 in chief command, where after some initial reverses he relieved Ladysmith. He was immensely popular in Devon, and a statue to him was erected in Exeter with the inscription " He saved Natal." Other "mansions" in the parish were at Uton Barton, Court Barton at Venny Tedburn, Fordton Barton, and Spence Combe. The bishops of Exeter had a palace and a great park at Crediton, SW. of the town, of which there are now no traces.

At Posbury are the remains of an Early Iron Age hill-fort, an ancient quarry of volcanic trap rock worked since the 12th cent. and now disused, and a small Gothic chapel built in 1835.

CRUWYS MORCHARD (G4) lies high, in the unspoilt and unknown country W. of Tiverton. There is no village, the centre of the parish being the church and the manor house. The church (Holy Cross) is an attractive little building, of various dates. It is substantially an early 14th-cent. structure, the two lower stages of the W. tower and the chancel being of this date, and probably the nave also, with a S. aisle added in the early 16th cent. The top stage of the tower was rebuilt in brick after the disastrous fire of 1689 which gutted the church. The interior of the church is most pleasing: plastered, decent Georgian, with a remarkable chancel screen and S. parclose screen of Corinthian design, well carved and well kept. The chancel fittings are of exceptional interest as showing the continuity of traditional forms, the stalls running to the E. wall to inclose the communion rails, and returning on the other side in the ancient manner. The screen is early 18th-cent. in date.

Beside the church is Cruwys Morchard House, the seat of the Cruwys family since the reign of John and possibly a little earlier. They died out in the male line in 1804, but George Sharland married Harriet Cruwys the heiress, and his son took his mother's name by royal licence in 1831, so that the name of Cruwys continues at Cruwys Morchard. The house is a plain and modest Georgian to look at, but it stands upon an ancient site and incorporates much old work. One wing of the house may be medieval in plan, and the present hall is probably disguised Tudor. The present kitchen has a fine panelled roof of moulded oak timbers, c. 1500 in date or slightly earlier, and may have been the solar of the medieval house. The house and park are highly "atmospheric," as

characteristic as anything in Devon of the homes of the ancient squirearchy, the true deep-rooted squires who never made a fortune in law or in trade, and never produced anybody of note in Church or State.

The farms of Hill, Ruckham, and Yedbury were all Domesday manors.

CULLOMPTON (J5) is a cheerful little market town, mostly consisting of one main street with "courts" running off it. There are a few late Tudor buildings, most notable of which are The Walronds, begun by Sir John Petre in 1603 and completed in 1605, containing fine carved mantelpieces and moulded plaster ceilings of the period; and the Manor House (not so called until 1850) which is Elizabethan, enlarged c. 1718. In the main, however, it is an undistinguished 19th-cent. town, the product of frequent fires and rebuildings. The Great Fire of 1839 destroyed 264 houses, and necessitated much commonplace rebuilding.

Cullompton was one of the most important woollen manufacturing towns in Devon from the 16th cent. to the 18th, its greatest merchant, John Lane (d. 1529), being a contemporary of John Greenway of Tiverton. They rivalled each other in the magnificence of their additions to their respective parish churches. Although the woollen industry decayed, the parish still kept several large paper and corn mills, which carried on actively throughout the 19th cent.

The parish church (St. Andrew) is one of the grandest in Devon (plate 48). It was a collegiate church before the Conquest. William I presented the five prebends to Battle Abbey in Sussex, but at some early date the prebendal system was dropped. The present building is 15th–early 16th-cent. in date. The body of the church is *c.* 1450; the aisles were added *c.* 1500, the second S. aisle (Lane's) in 1526; and the majestic tower (in the Somerset style) 1545-9.[1] The church was restored in 1849 when the chancel was rebuilt and the chancel roof recoloured. A superb roof runs the whole length of the church: a panelled wagon roof of 24 bays, richly coloured, moulded, and carved. The 15th-cent. rood-screen extends the entire width of the church, of ordinary character but striking because of its great length and perfect condition. A Golgotha, or Calvary, which originally stood on the rood-loft, now lies at the W. end of Lane's Aisle, a gruesome piece of medieval carving. In Lane's Aisle the fan-traceried roof should be noticed, and the exterior carvings of merchants' ships, shears, and other symbols of the cloth trade. The pillars and capitals of the nave also call for study. At the W. end of the church is a massive Jacobean gallery.

The parish is large and fertile, full of beautiful pastoral scenery, and attractive farmsteads. Colebrook, Hillersdon, Langford, and Ponsford are all recorded in Domesday Book. Langford Court has some remains of old work. Moorehayes (originally Moor) was the seat of the Moores for sixteen generations from the 12th cent. down to 1711, when George Moore, Esq., the last of his line, died.

CULMSTOCK (K4) was once a small market town, but its population is now only one-half of that of 1801. The village is much uglified by red brick, but it has retained a good deal of traditional building of the 18th and early 19th cent. It had formerly a considerable woollen industry. Near the river Culm is an old woollen mill, and some 18th-cent. weavers' cottages.

The church (All Saints) is a 15th-cent. building of local flint, with a clearstory, an unusual feature in Devon. It has been too much restored from time to time, but retains a few interesting things. A fine stone rood-screen, standing in Lysons's day, was removed soon afterwards but rescued by Mr. Blackmore, the novelist's father, and replaced as a reredos. A 15th-cent. cope, of gold-coloured velvet with a central representation of the Assumption of the B.V.M., is preserved in a glass case in the N. aisle. Frederick Temple (1821-1902), who became archbishop of Canterbury (1896-1902), lived at Axon in this parish in his early years, and taught in the Sunday school here.

At the hamlet of Prescott is a Baptist Chapel, built in 1715, rebuilt in 1785, and renovated in 1892, which retains its 18th-cent. galleries and other furniture of the period. At Spicelands is a meeting-house of the Society of Friends, erected in 1670, rebuilt in 1815, also retaining much of its original simple character.

DALWOOD (L5) is not mentioned until 1195. Probably it was a late clearing in the forest, a hamlet settled from Stockland, with which it formed, until 1842, an outlier of Dorset inside Devon. The church (St. Peter) is entirely 15th-cent., restored in 1881 and of no great interest. At Loughwood Farm, just N. of the main Axminster-Honiton road, is a fascinating little 18th-cent. Baptist chapel with an unaltered interior.

DARTINGTON (F9) lies inside a great bend of the Dart, from which its name is derived, and was part of the possessions of the Martins from the early 12th cent. onwards. After some eight generations the Martin estates escheated to the Crown, and in 1384 Richard II granted the reversion of Dartington and other lands to his half-brother John Holland, created Earl of Huntingdon in 1387 and Duke of Exeter ten years later. The Duke made Dartington his principal seat in Devon, and the present Hall may be regarded for the most part as his work. The buildings, which were designed upon a splendid scale, originally enclosed a large quadrangle, nearly an acre in extent. The S. side was occupied by the great hall (some 80 ft. by 40 ft.), one of the finest buildings of its kind in England, and by the entrance porch, kitchen, buttery, and pantry. On the W. was the unusually long range of lodgings; on the N. stands a great barn, divided into two floors, with a fine timber roof of early 14th-cent. date. This is said to have been the great hall of the Martin house.

After various changes of ownership, the manor came to Sir Arthur Champernowne (d. 1578) who made the extensive alterations to the house which may still be seen; and in Georgian times further changes were made. The Champernownes continued to hold the manor until the 20th cent. but parts of the Hall were allowed to fall into ruin. Archdeacon Froude, who was trustee of the estate for a time, had the roof of the great hall removed for fear of its unsoundness, and made other changes. Some of the timber from the hall roof was used to construct the altars at Dartington, Holne, and Ottery St. Mary. In 1925 Mr. and Mrs. Elmhirst bought the derelict Hall and 1,000 acres of the estate for an experiment in the reconstruction of rural life. A company was formed which now controls many enterprises—farms, forestry, sawmills, a textile mill, builders and contractors, and the well-known Dartington School. It is impossible to convey adequately in a short space the scope and success of this remarkable experiment in rural reconstruction. Much restoration was done at the Hall; the great hall especially has been brought back to its original noble appearance, and the other ranges of building around the courtyard brought to life once more.

The old church of Dartington, which stood beside the Hall, was demolished in 1873, except the tower. This was left standing, and the Champernowne monuments placed in it. Some are, however, said to have been " lost," together with the medieval glass. The new church (St. Mary), designed by J. L. Pearson, stands beside the main Totnes road. The exact dimensions and style of the old church were followed, and much of the old materials, including the font, pulpit, roof, and chancel screen, was re-used. The church, completed in 1880, is a fine Victorian building, spacious and light, with lofty Beer stone arcades and clear glass.

At the old parsonage were born Robert Hurrell Froude and the historian J. A. Froude (1818-94).

DARTMOUTH (G10) is one of the most dramatically sited towns in Devon, built upon a steep hillside rising from the W. bank of the Dart estuary, about 1 m. from its mouth. The modern borough includes the parish and village of Townstall, on the heights 400 ft. above, which was the mother-village from which the town sprang in the 12th cent.

The name Dartmouth was first applied to the mouth of the river, but from the early 13th cent. onwards was given to the town, which resulted from the coalescence of two small riverside settlements—Hardness on the N. and Clifton on the S. These were originally separated by a deep pool—Mill Pool—which ran well back inland and was filled at high tide. This pool has been reclaimed and now provides the only flat land in Dartmouth, and an easier climb up to the Townstall heights.[1] In the older part of the town, in what was first called Clifton, the houses cling in tiers to the side of the hill, giving the town its very picturesque appearance from the sea or the opposite shore.

casual assemblage of houses and ship-yards, which had grown up along both banks of the Mill Pool to meet the needs of military and commercial shipping using the river.

The earliest street of which we have any record in Dartmouth is Smith Street—"the street of the smiths," who were concerned with ship-repairs. This

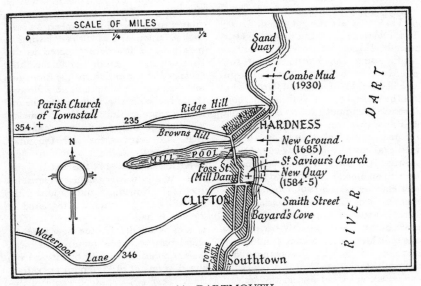

Fig. 14—DARTMOUTH

A sketch map of early Dartmouth showing the two ancient ridgeways running down to the waterside at Hardness and Clifton. The dotted line marks the present water-front (adapted from Russell, Dartmouth)

The importance of this magnificent, sheltered, deep-water harbour is brought out in the 12th cent., when it was used as the point of assembly and departure for the Second Crusade (1147) and the Third Crusade (1190). There are clear indications that by 1200 or soon after-wards a borough had been formally created by the Fitz Stephens out of the

originally lay along the water's edge, but later reclamation from the river, chiefly in the making of the New Quay from 1584 onwards, has left it some distance from the water today. As late as 1567 ships were still tied up to the churchyard wall of St. Saviour's, and the churchyard overlooked the harbour to the N. and E.[2] On such a restricted site, the town was obliged to expand S. along the water-front, overflowing its own boundary into the manor of Stoke Fleming and creating the suburb still known as Southtown, which is first recorded by name in 1328. In 1463 Southtown was brought within the borough boundaries, so that the mayor and burgesses of Dartmouth "may keep watch at a certain place called Galions Boure to guard against our enemies."

The acquisition of the SW. provinces of France as a consequence of Henry II's marriage in 1152 gave a great stimulus to commercial and military traffic using Dartmouth, and it rose quickly to be the fourth town in Devon, after Exeter, Plymouth, and Barnstaple.[1] All the cloth trade of Totnes flowed out through Dartmouth; wine from France and Spain was the chief import. Of all the merchants and shipmasters of the medieval port, John Hawley was the greatest. Chaucer visited Dartmouth in 1373 on official business and certainly met Hawley, who is probably the *Schipman* in the *Canterbury Tales*. After Hawley's death (1408) the port and town decayed sadly, partly because no one took his place as a leader and partly because of general economic and political conditions.[2]

The second great age in the history of the town fell in the period 1580-1643. Much building of this period remains and much more has been destroyed. In 1604 the town was formally incorporated, though it had elected its own mayor since 1340.[3] The great prosperity of these two generations arose from the development of the Newfoundland fishing trade, in which Dartmouth played a leading part, and from the renewed growth of the cloth trade—now the " New Draperies "—at Ashburton. Much ground was taken in from the river, a large new quay built, and valu-

able building sites created for the bursting town.[4] Some of the buildings put up at this date may be seen in the Butterwalk (1635-40) and along the frontage of the Quay, where they are sometimes concealed by later façades (e.g. the Castle Hotel, 1639, refronted in 1823).

Dartmouth was the scene of a good deal of action in the Civil War. It was first garrisoned for parliament, but after the capture of Exeter on 4 September 1643 Prince Maurice marched on and took it after a costly siege lasting a month. The town surrendered to the royalists on 4 October. Being rightly regarded as an important garrison, the fortifications were considerably strengthened on both sides of the river. In the final campaign in the West, Fairfax laid siege to Dartmouth on 12 January 1646. On Sunday the 18th the town was stormed and fell.

With the collapse of the textile trade in the inland towns, and the disappearance of the Newfoundland trade, during the 18th cent., Dartmouth stagnated as a port. It had been considered in 1689 as a possible site for the new western naval base that was required to meet the threat from France, but it was rejected in favour of Plymouth (or rather Dock, near by) mainly because of the hazards of the narrow entrance to the harbour. Similarly, in the 19th cent. it was hoped to make Dartmouth a terminus for the Atlantic and other overseas shipping routes, but that, too, came to nothing. For a time, indeed, from 1871 to 1891 the Cape and Natal Steamship Co. took up passengers and mails here, and Dartmouth had fast and regular steamship services to South Africa and Australia. In 1891 the Co. moved to Southampton, however, to suit the convenience of the General Post Office. Moreover, as steamships grew larger, no wharf at Dartmouth could take them.[1] Other shipping lines left Dartmouth alone because of its poor railway communication. The failure to bring the railway across the river at Greenway, and down the W. side of the Dart into Dartmouth itself, did untold damage to the town. From 1878 onwards the development of the coal-bunkering trade did much to bring about a revival of the port. The heavy destruction of steamships in the 1914-18 war, and the conversion to oil fuel after it, nearly killed this trade. Today, with the further destruction of 1939-45, it is virtually gone. Dartmouth suffered fairly severely from air-raids in 1942-43, partly because of the shipbuilding yards up the river, partly because of the use of the harbour by war-shipping. The presence of the Royal Naval College—built 1902-05 by Sir Aston Webb on a site dominating the harbour—no doubt helped to provoke enemy attention.

The stagnation of Dartmouth presents the most serious urban problem in Devon. The lack of proper railway facilities, and above all the strangulated site along the water's edge, discourage any large new industrial development, and the absence of beaches, golf-courses, and other amenities prevents its developing far as a holiday centre. It is an ideal centre for fishing and yachting, but these are select pastimes, and the town has become too largely dependent on the existence of the Royal Naval College. There are a number of small industries, of which shipbuilding is the most considerable.

Dartmouth was also a parliamentary borough. It returned members to the parliament of 1298, but its regular representation began in 1351 and continued until it was disfranchised in 1868.[2]

There is a good deal to see in the town. Beginning at the mouth of the river, the castle and St. Petrock's church make a most interesting and picturesque group. Edward III ordered special measures to be taken for the defence of the strategic port of Dartmouth against attack from the sea, but not until 1388 did John Hawley begin the building of a *fortalice* at the entrance to the harbour. In 1481 the strong, square tower, ever since known as Dartmouth Castle, was begun. Most of the surviving work dates from 1488-94.[3] On the other side of the harbour mouth, Kingswear Castle was begun in 1491 and finished in 1502 (Frontispiece).

St. Petrock's church, within the castle precinct, is on an ancient site. A record of 1192, referring to it as " the monastery of St. Peter," suggests that a *monasterium* or minster may have been established here in early Christian times. The present church was rebuilt in the Gothic style in 1641-2, and contains a pulpit, royal arms, and W. gallery of that date, and some fine brasses to Dartmouth merchants, especially that of John Roope (1609), who lived at Warfleet, an old house destroyed by the royalists in 1643. Before the altar is a floor-slab to John Newman of Dartmouth, merchant (1640), ancestor of Sir Ralph Newman, 5th bart., of Mamhead and Blackpool. The font is Norman (late 12th-cent.).

Above the castle is a Civil War redoubt known as Gallants Bower. At Bayard's Cove are the considerable ruins of a castle built in 1537 as a part of Henry VIII's coastal defence scheme. Here is the Old Quay at which most of the town's medieval shipping lay. Near by is the Custom House, rebuilt in 1739, of which the Long Room has a good plaster ceiling.

Many of the 16th–18th-cent. houses

at the S. end of the town, some of them splendid examples of merchants' houses, were swept away in 1864 to make Newcomen Road as a new exit from the town. Among the treasures that were demolished were the medieval house of the great John Hawley, long used as a guildhall, and the 17th-cent. house where Thomas Newcomen (1663-1729) laboured to produce the first industrial steam engine, surely one of the historic houses of England. Newcomen was a Dartmouth man, an ironmonger by trade, and his fame is commemorated today by a modest memorial in a public park. Newcomen's claim to be the chief begetter of the practical steam engine is recognised to-day by the existence of the Newcomen Society, with members all over the English-speaking world. Of the 17th-cent. houses that remain, those in the Butterwalk (damaged by bombs in 1943, but about to be restored) and on the new Quay, have already been referred to.

St. Saviour's church was dedicated in 1372. It was much altered in the late 15th cent. and extensively remodelled in the 1630s. The tower was raised in 1631, the N. aisle rebuilt 1634, the S. aisle in 1635. The magnificent W. gallery (1633) was made by local carpenters at a cost of £15, the royal arms being added in 1660. Among the many interesting features of the church are the extremely handsome 15th-cent. rood-screen, parclose screens, and stone pulpit. In the chancel are the brasses of John Hawley and his two wives (1408) and Gilbert Staplehill (1637). In the gallery is an early town fire-engine, of which the twin is now in the Science Museum at South Kensington. The S. door of the church is remarkable. It bears the date 1631, but the fine ironwork upon it is almost certainly of late 14th-cent. date. It depicts a tree in

full flower, with the trunk crossed by figures of two leopards.

In contrast to this exceptionally interesting church, the mother church of St. Clement at Townstall is dullish. It is mainly of 14th-cent. date (dedicated in 1318), with some traces of Norman work and an early 13th-cent. font, but was over-restored in the 19th cent. There are, however, some interesting monuments and memorials to the Roopes and the Boones (who lived at Mount Boone).

DAWLISH (H8) takes its name from the little stream that now flows through the town, recorded as *Doflisc*, " black stream," in a Saxon charter of 1044. The original village grew up nearly a mile back from the coast, for reasons of safety, and the parish church will be found here. Dedicated to St. Gregory the Great, and an ancient foundation, it is today a rather disappointing 19th-cent. building. The nave was rebuilt 1824-5, the chancel in 1875. Only the red sandstone tower is of any age (14th-cent.). The nave, in an early 19th-cent. version of Gothic, is pleasing with its slender columns and bowed ceilings. There are some late 18th-cent. mural tablets and many of the early 19th cent., including two by Flaxman on the S. wall. Most are unctuous and Victorian, but they have their own soothing flavour.

Dawlish began to attract summer visitors in the early 1790s. Among others, Charles Hoare, the banker, was attracted by its climate and scenery. In 1800-4 John Nash built Luscombe Castle for him, about 1 m. W. of the church, combining the external appearance of "our ancient baronial fortresses" with all modern comforts inside. The grounds were laid out by Humphrey Repton, and command fine coastal views. The chapel was unfortunately added by Scott in 1862. Nash also built the villa of "Stonelands" in 1817,[1] which became the home of Sir John Rennie, the eminent architect and engineer.

From about 1803 onwards the ground between the old village and the sea was being "landscaped," the stream straightened and broken by artificial waterfalls, and houses built along the N. side of the lawn. This street, the Strand, was practically completed by 1809, and still keeps a period flavour of Jane Austen, who knew and liked Dawlish very much. So also did Dickens, who placed the birthplace of Nicholas Nickleby here. In Old Town Street are the Manor House (c. 1800) and Brook House (c. 1800), and a relic of old Dawlish in a house dated 1539. At the upper end of the town is much excellent mid-Victorian villa architecture (e.g. Barton Terrace). In 1846 the railway came. Brunel was obliged to take his line along the sea-front (plates 6, 7), but he carried his railway across the mouth of the Dawlish valley on a small granite viaduct in the Egyptian style leaving free access to the beach, and built an ornamental station which is itself a nice period-piece to-day.

The railway did not bring large crowds to Dawlish, nor did Dawlish set out to attract them. Within the past generation, however, it has become more widely known, both as a delightful place to live in and as a place for summer holidays. It is now a bright, cheerful little town of some 7,500 people, and has grown faster than any other Devonshire resort in the past twenty years.

At Cofton was anciently a chapel dedicated to St. Mary, first heard of in the 14th cent. It fell into disuse after the Reformation, until Dr. George Kendall, the noted Calvinistic preacher, who had been intruded into the rectory of Kenton and was ejected in 1662, took it over for his own use. There is a memorial to him in the chapel, which was rebuilt (Charles Fowler, architect) in 1839. Cockwood is a picturesque hamlet near the chapel, on the shore of the Exe estuary. It probably originated as a fishing place in the 13th cent.

DEAN PRIOR (F9) is a parish with no village, on the SE. skirts of Dartmoor. The church (St. George) is disappointing: a large barn-like building, mainly of 15th-cent. date but considerably altered in the 17th, and enlarged and much restored in the 19th. The font is Norman. Dean is famous, however, for its association with Robert Herrick, who was vicar here 1629-47 and 1662-74 (he was ejected under the Protectorate and reinstated under the Act of Uniformity) and wrote all his poetry during his earlier tenure of the living. He and his maid, Prudence Baldwin, are buried in unmarked graves in the churchyard. Herrick hated Dean and Devonshire, but his poetry is full of local scenes and above all of the wild flowers that grow so luxuriantly in the woods and hedgebanks. The small hall, parlour, and kitchen of his vicarage remain, incorporated into the back of a more modern house. Near the church is Dean Court, said to have been built by Sir Edward Giles (1566-1637) whose monument, with an epitaph by Herrick, is the most interesting part of the church.

DENBURY (see TORBRYAN).

DEVONPORT (see PLYMOUTH).

DIPTFORD (F10) contains a number of ancient estates, of which Beenleigh,

Curtisknowle, and Farleigh were all Domesday manors. Crabadon became a "mansion" in medieval times. There are considerable remains of 15th- and 16th-cent. work, and a typical South Hams porch and doorway. At Diptford Court, the ancient court-house is now occupied as a farmhouse. Gara Bridge, over the Avon, on the old main road from Dartmouth to Plymouth, is probably not older than the 16th cent.

The church (St. Mary) is mainly 15th-cent. work, restored in 1870. It is one of the few Devon churches to possess a medieval spire.

DITTISHAM (G10) village is eminently attractive, and is noted for the wealth of its plum orchards. The church (St. George) is mostly a 15th–early 16th-cent. building, built of the local slate, a material which is found over most of the country W. of Dartmouth. There are a number of interesting things inside: an ancient red sandstone font, c. 1200 in date, a late medieval stone pulpit (plate 51), a rood-screen of the same date which has, however, lost its vaulting and cornice, and aisle windows by Pugin (brought here by Lord Henry Francis Kerr, rector 1827-52).

Bosomzeal is a medieval hall-house, "modernised" in the 16th cent. Downton appears to be mostly a 16th-cent. "mansion" built around a small courtyard. There is a good plaster ceiling in the Great Parlour. Lapthorne and Capton are also good examples of old farmhouse building in slate. A ferry crosses the Dart to Greenway.

DODBROOKE (see KINGSBRIDGE).

DODDISCOMBSLEIGH (G7) lies in a combe under the western slopes of Haldon. The Town Barton, formerly the manor house, is probably a 16th-cent. house, added to in 1604. The church (St. Michael) is almost entirely a 15th-cent. structure, with some slight traces of earlier work. The pulpit is 17th-cent., and there are some carved bench-ends, but the glory of the church is the medieval glass in the N. aisle, which is undoubtedly the best in the county. The five large 15th-cent. windows of the aisle preserve their original glass almost intact. Apart from four windows in Exeter Cathedral these are the only complete windows of medieval glass left in Devon. The E. window, showing the Seven Sacraments, is of exceptional interest.[1]

This part of the Teign valley, besides being very beautiful, is notable for the treasures of its churches, those of Ashton, Dunchideock, and Bridford being outstanding.

DOLTON (D4) is in a remote, little-visited part of Devon. The church (St. Edmund) has a remarkable font. It consists of two square blocks placed one on the other, the upper block being turned upside down and hollowed out. On three faces of this block the serpent motive appears, interlaced in the Scandinavian manner. The lower block is covered with another variety of interlaced work. These blocks were made out of a Christian monument (probably 10th-cent.) which may originally have stood at Halsdon (" holy stone ").

The church is otherwise uninteresting, mostly rebuilt in 1888. There are several inscriptions to the Stafford family, of Stafford Barton, from 1589 to 1835. At the E. end of the S. aisle are four 16th-cent. bench-ends one of which has the initials of John Stafford, Esq., and the date 1581. Stafford was a Domesday manor. The present house has been very much altered and enlarged, but the core may be of mid-16th cent. date or earlier. There was a chapel here in 1415.

Iddlecott and Cherubeer may be identified also as Domesday manors. Halsdon has been the seat of the Furses since about 1680, and is associated with William Cory (1823-92), the poet and writer, who lived here for a time.

DOWLAND (D4) has a very attractive little church (St. Peter), almost entirely unrestored. It has a good, plain 15th-cent. tower. The body of the church is roughcast and whitewashed, and therefore difficult to date; but the S. doorway is Norman and the nave and chancel may also be of this date. The N. aisle has a remarkable arcade of oak, i.e. oak arches and pillars, c. 1500 in date, which replaced an older arcade. The only other arcade of this kind in Devon is at Nymet Rowland. There are a number of carved bench-ends, probably c. 1500, some 18th-cent. box-pews, and floor-slabs to the Staffords of Stafford Barton.

Dowland Barton, beside the church, appears to be Tudor, remodelled in the 18th cent. At the entrance to the churchyard are two cottages of early 16th-cent. date with a number of windows having crudely carved oak mullions. This was probably the Church House originally.

DOWN, EAST (D1), is the ancestral home of the Northcote family, of which Sir Stafford Northcote, 1st Earl of Iddesleigh, was the head. Northcote, now a farmhouse, was a Domesday manor. The family owed its rise mainly to a fortune made in the cloth trade at Crediton in the 16th cent. Churchill and Bugford were also Domesday manors in this parish. East Down House, formerly the seat of the Pines,

later the Pine-Coffins, is a handsome early Georgian house.

The church (St. John the Baptist) was rebuilt, except the tower, in 1886-7, but is interesting for its fittings. There are carved Jacobean pews in the Pine chapel and a monument to Edward Pine (1663)—"lieutenant-colonel to Sir Hugh Pollard in the late unhappy wars." There are also a restored 15th-cent. screen, a Renaissance marble font on an elaborately carved shaft, an old Spanish lectern, an 18th-cent. pulpit, and an E. window by Kempe. The capitals of the S. arcade are carved with sporting scenes.

DOWN ST. MARY (F5). The church (St. Mary) was built in the 12th cent. at the crossing-place of two ancient roads, but only the tympanum over the S. doorway remains of this building. The W. tower, tall and plain, is a landmark; it was probably built c. 1413 after a hurricane had demolished its predecessor. The remainder of the church was rebuilt in 1871, but is worth visiting for its fine series of carved bench-ends (early 16th-cent.) and for its modern screen. Among the scattered farms of the parish, Chaffcombe was a Domesday manor. The present house is a rebuilding of c. 1600 with some slight traces of earlier work. Wolfin is another Domesday estate ("Wolf's Nymet" after the medieval owners) and Lammacott is mentioned as early as 1170.

DOWN, WEST (D1), is in open, undulating country, from which it takes its name. Besides Down itself, a number of hamlets and farms are of considerable antiquity. Aylescott, Bradwell, and West Stowford Barton are all recorded in Domesday. Crackaway Barton is first recorded in 1242, but the first element of the name may well be Celtic (*krako*, denoting "rock" or something similar).

The church is of unusual interest. It resembles Tawstock in being largely an early 14th-cent. cruciform church. The tower was, however, rebuilt in 1712 and the chancel was rebuilt in 1675 in its old style. The N. transept was the Stowford chapel and contains the wooden effigy, life-size, of Sir John Stowford (*c.* 1290-*c.* 1372), dressed in his robes of a sergeant-at-law. The colouring on the effigy was renewed in 1873. He was born and died at West Stowford Barton, and was a justice of the Common Pleas 1342-72. The transept has a fine early 14th-cent. oak roof of unusual shape. The dedication of the church is now said to be to St. Calixtus, but was formerly given as Holy Trinity. The manor house adjoins the churchyard. It dates from about 1580-1600 and contains a ground-floor room with a richly decorated plaster ceiling, an elaborate mantelpiece, and contemporary oak panelling.

DREWSTEIGNTON (F6)

has much semi-moorland scenery of great beauty. Fingle Bridge, over the Teign, is famous even in Devon as a " beauty spot." The bridge itself is of granite and is of 16th- or 17th-cent. date (plate 57). Towering above it to the E., on the end of a ridge, is Prestonbury Castle, one of the best of the Iron Age hill-forts that ring the edge of Dartmoor. At Shilstone, in the W. of the parish, is the best-known of the cromlechs or dolmens in Devon, known as Spinsters Rock, the remains of a Bronze Age megalithic tomb. Near by are remains of stone circles, etc., of the same age.

Drewsteignton village was formerly very remote, but buses now penetrate to it at intervals. Much of the village building is of granite. The church (Holy Trinity) is entirely 15th–early 16th-cent. in date, the chancel rebuilt in 1863, and is an attractive church of the moorland type with crudely cut granite arcades. The granite house S. of the church was left to the parish in 1546 by Peter Edgcumbe, and is an early 16th-cent. building with granite and oak-framed fireplace, a newel stair to the upper room, and some remains of an original screen.

On the end of a great promontory, about 1 m. SW. of the church, stands Castle Drogo, one of Lutyens's lessknown masterpieces. It was built for Mr. J. C. Drewe on a new site, begun in 1911 and completed in 1930, and is a granite castle: the last castle to be built in England and perhaps the last private building in granite. No other material but granite is used, and the massed effect is overwhelming. There is no comparable house in England.[1]

There were a number of small Domesday manors in the parish, now represented by farms—Coombe Hall, Fursham, Martin, Shilstone, and Thornbury. Drascombe and Parford are mentioned as landmarks in a Saxon charter of 739.

DUNCHIDEOCK (G7),

though so near Exeter, is a seldom-visited little place, buried among the foothills of Haldon. The name is Celtic and means "the wooded fort or camp," referring no doubt to the earthwork of Cotley Castle, 1½ m. NW.

The church (St. Michael) is of considerable interest for its fittings. It is a late 14th-cent. building, restored in 1875-7 and 1889, when the chancel was rebuilt. The chancel aisle was rebuilt in 1669 by Aaron Baker of Bowhay (in the neighbouring parish of Exminster). The nave arcade was re-modelled at the same time. There is a good font, *c.* 1400 in date; a number of carved bench-ends (some 16th-cent. and some modern); and a noteworthy series of carved roof-bosses. The re-stored rood-screen is of great beauty, the richly-carved pier casing being a notable feature. There is a mural monument to Aaron Baker (d. 1683), who made a fortune in the East Indian trade, and another to General Stringer Lawrence (1697-1775)—" the father of the Indian Army "—who commanded the East India Company's troops 1747-67. The epitaph is written by Hannah More.

Stringer Lawrence left all his fortune to his friend Sir Robert Palk of Haldon House, not far away (see Kenn), who erected a triangular tower in his memory, with a statue and an inscrip-tion in Persian, on the summit of the hills above. This tower, now known as Haldon Belvedere, is a landmark for many miles.

Near the church is a stone-built medieval house, now converted into cottages, which is probably the old rectory. In January 1396 Bishop Staf-ford invited the faithful to contribute towards the rebuilding of the rectory house.[1] Dunchideock House is a good-looking early Georgian house, but in parts much older. Thomas Birdall, who corrected Newton's *Principia*, was rector of Dunchideock.

DUNKESWELL (K5) lies on the Blackdown plateau, nearly 800 ft. up. The church (St. Nicholas) was rebuilt in 1865-8 and is wholly uninteresting except for the primitive Norman font, which has one of the earliest English representations of an elephant.

About 2 m. N. of the church are the small remains of the Cistercian abbey of Dunkeswell, founded in 1201 by William Brewer and colonised from Ford. The foundations of the building may be traced, but the only fragment above ground is a part of the gatehouse, and a flint rubble wall. Holy Trinity church, erected in 1842 by Mrs. Simcoe, occupies part of the site of the abbey. It is a plain building, not entirely with-out merit. The wood carving and the painting of the glass were done by the seven daughters of Mrs. Simcoe.

DUNSFORD (G7) parish has much diversified and beautiful scenery even by Devonshire standards, the wooded gorge of the Teign—deservedly famous for its beauty—being only one of its charms. The village stands on a hill above the Teign, and contains a good deal of whitewashed cob, and some 16th–17th-cent. moorstone building.

The church (St. Mary) stands well and dominates the village. It has a good W. tower, and is of 14th–15th-cent. date. The early 14th-cent. chancel was rebuilt in 1846. Though rather thoroughly restored, the interior is attractive and interesting. The pulpit, altar rails, and W. gallery are all late 17th–early 18th cent.-work. At the E. end of the aisle is the Fulford pew and an elaborate monument, with effigies, to Sir Thomas Fulford (1610) and his wife (1639). Hung above the tomb is a helmet of one of the Fulfords. The oak seating is modern (1933) and good.

Fulford, 2½ m. NW. of the village, was a Domesday manor. The Fulfords are first recorded here in the time of Richard I, and are today the only family left in Devon who can claim an uninterrupted descent in the male line since that date. Few Devon families have been more distinguished in the history of the county, above all as soldiers. Three early Fulfords were

Crusaders. Sir Baldwin Fulford fought at Towton for Henry VI, and was beheaded at Hexham in 1461. Sir Thomas Fulford came, with the Earl of Devon, to the relief of Exeter when it was besieged by Perkin Warbeck in 1497. In the Civil War, Col. Francis Fulford (later Sir Francis) garrisoned his house for the king. It was besieged by Fairfax in December 1645, and honourably surrendered to him after a bombardment from the park where two redoubts of this period may still be seen.

The present house, standing in an old park, is one of the most interesting in Devon (plate 32). It was built *temp.* Henry VII–Henry VIII, and probably completed about 1534 when much finely carved panelling of Renaissance type was put in. This has now been brought together in the Great Hall. Considerable remodelling was done internally *temp.* William and Mary: there is a fine staircase of that period. The house was altered externally and internally in the early 19th cent., when a garret floor was put in and the windows all Gothicised, but its quadrangular Tudor plan was left untouched. The chapel, licensed in 1402, was used intermittently as a chapel until well into the 19th cent. The pictures form a better collection than could be found in most of the Devon squires' houses. There is a bust portrait of Queen Elizabeth by Nicholas Hilliard. Sir John Fulford fought at Gravelines with Count Egmont in July 1558, and a huge canvas at Fulford depicts the scene. It is said to have been painted by the elder Franck and presented to Sir John by Egmont, whose portrait also hangs here.

Clifford Barton and Halstow were Domesday manors. The former is a fine old farmhouse with considerable traces of its former status as a "mansion." Clifford Bridge, over the Teign, is mentioned by Leland, but the present bridge may not be older than the 17th cent. Sowton Barton, recorded in 1244, also has remains of the old "mansion."

DUNTERTON (B8). There is a strong earthwork at Castle Head about ½ m. SSE. of the church, in the neck of a great loop of the Tamar, looking across to the earthwork of Carthamartha on the Cornish side. The date of these frontier earthworks is unknown but is probably Early Iron Age. Dunterton church (All Saints) stands alone. It is mainly a 15th-cent. building; some 14th-cent. work survives in the S. doorway and S. aisle. There is a bold W. tower with heavily crocketed pinnacles common to this district. The interior is plain and pleasant.

EGG BUCKLAND (*see* PLYMOUTH).

EGGESFORD (E4) has no village. The church (All Saints) stands alone in what was once the park of a great house. The estate belonged to the Coplestones in the 16th cent., an ancient Devon family with nearly as many branches as the Chichesters. Edward Chichester, afterwards Viscount Chichester, married the Coplestone heiress and inherited Eggesford through her in 1606. She died in 1616, he in 1648, and they lie under a noble monument in the church. This monument was begun by Edward Chichester, and completed by his son, Arthur, Earl of Donegal (1606-75). There is another "most sumptuous monument" to the latter, and his two wives, "where he standeth in full and just proportion, curiously cut out of pure alabaster, finely polished, between his two ladies, lying in effigy by." He was the nephew of Arthur Chichester, Baron Chichester of Belfast (1563-

1625), the Lord Deputy of Ireland, and made his own career in Irish politics. His two wives died long before him, and Arthur Chichester raised this magnificent memorial in 1650, 25 years before his own death. These two monuments are among the finest of their kind in Devon: only the Tawstock monuments of the Earls of Bath are comparable with them. Eggesford was bought by William Fellowes, Esq., in 1718, to whom there is a good monument (1723). The church was much rebuilt in 1867, but is still very pleasing both inside and outside.

The old Eggesford House was demolished about 1832 when the Hon. Newton Fellowes built the present Eggesford House, which is actually in the parish of Wembworthy. It probably stood in front of the large walled garden which remains on the hillside near the church.

ERMINGTON (E10) was founded early in the Saxon occupation of Devon, probably soon after 700, and appears as a royal manor in Domesday, giving its name to a hundred. The church (St. Peter) is a spacious 14th-cent. structure, enlarged in the 15th cent. by the opening out of the N. and S. transepts into aisles, with good arcades of elvan. It has a tall plain 14th-cent. tower with a twisted spire. There are a Jacobean screen in place of the usual medieval rood-screen, a brass with effigies to William Strachleigh (1583), and an Elizabethan monument to Christopher Chudleigh. The church contains much good modern woodwork.

Strashleigh was the seat of the Strashleighs from the early 13th cent. until the end of the line in 1583. The house, now a farmhouse, has some remains of the old "mansion." Strode

was the original home of the well-known Strode family. They were here in 1238, and probably earlier, though in the 15th cent. they acquired Newnham in Plympton St. Mary (q.v.) by marriage and have made that their principal residence ever since. The old Strode "mansion" was at Strode Farm, where there are traces of it. Worthele was a Domesday manor and there are traces of a medieval "mansion" at West Worthele. Hunsdon, not far away, is a picturesque farmhouse, c. 1629 in date. Woodland Farm, near Ivybridge, is 16th-cent. and later. Penquit, though not recorded until 1238, is a Celtic place-name (*pen coed*, "end of the wood"), and has probably been continuously inhabited since Celtic times. There are evidences of a former "mansion" here, and also at Higher Ludbrook, near the E. boundary of the parish.

EXBOURNE (E5). The church (St. Mary) is built of granite and is mainly c. 1500 in date. Its chief interest now lies in the rood-screen, which is of an interesting early type, well designed with good detail. The open traceried arcades are contained within rectangular heads, a feature of early screens. The Exbourne screen is probably c. 1420-30 in date. There are some excellent modern bench-ends, carved by Herbert Read of Exeter, and good bosses in the S. aisle roof.

EXETER (H6). (*The history of Exeter is treated fully in my Two Thousand Years in Exeter. The following account is no more than the briefest outline of the subject.*) Exeter, now a city of some 90,000 people, is one of the historic cities of England. The Romans halted their advance on the Exe: beyond lay the Celtic West into which they did not bother to penetrate. And here, on a steep-sided ridge rising a hundred feet above the river-frontier, they founded about A.D. 50 the town of *Isca*, which took its name from the river. Isca became the tribal capital of the Dumnonii, the people who occupied Devon and Cornwall, and at *Isca Dumnoniorum* their kings must have reigned for centuries. Ever since that time, Exeter has been the provincial capital of Western England, as well as the scene of many events important in national history.

Since 1050 it has been the seat of a bishopric; since 1068 it has had a castle; since the 12th cent. (if not earlier) there has been a guildhall in the High Street. Its mayors begin very shortly after those of London. Exeter had a mayor in 1205, second only to Winchester among the provincial cities.

From the 10th cent. to the 18th it was a considerable port, at times the third or fourth in the country, for it lay at the head of a fine estuary and also at the lowest bridging point of the river, where land- and sea-traders met. Even now, outpaced in industry and commerce, it remains the administrative capital of South-Western England, and has the largest hinterland west of Bristol. Its archives are among the richest in England, unsurpassed perhaps by any city outside London.

Though the history of Exeter has been closely interwoven with that of Devon from Roman times onwards, and can hardly be separated from it, the city has also had a rich, unique life of its own. A more detailed account of its origins, history, and buildings will be found in my *Two Thousand Years in Exeter* (1960). This contains a map showing the whereabouts of the chief places of historic and architectural interest.

Of the Roman period there remain considerable stretches of masonry in the city walls, which survive largely intact. The Roman portions (built about A.D. 200) are best seen in West Street, in Northernhay, and in Southernhay. Many Roman objects found in the city at different times can be seen in the city museum in Queen Street.

Of the Saxon period nothing survives except a few fragments of walling here and there. The Norman period is represented by the castle (Rougemont), built by William the Conqueror in 1068, of which the main gateway, the curtain wall, and one tower survive in Rougemont Gardens. It is also represented in the remarkable twin towers of the Cathedral (1114-33), and in St. Mary Arches church, perhaps the most complete Norman church in Devon.

The architectural history of the Cathedral is a complicated story of which fuller details will be found in the official guide-books. The main structure is as perfect an example of early 14th-cent. architecture as Salisbury is of the early 13th. Internally, Exeter may well claim to be the loveliest of all English cathedrals, with its vista of blue-grey Purbeck marble columns, soaring to a rich ribbed vault that is unique in England. The Cathedral Library, open to visitors on Tuesdays and Fridays, contains some of the greatest English treasures, notably the famous Exeter Book of Anglo-Saxon poetry and the Exon Domesday.

Next to the Cathedral, the Guildhall is the most interesting building in the city. The present hall was built in 1330, and remodelled in 1468-9, which is the date of the fine roof. The portico over the pavement of the High Street is Elizabethan (1592-5). The hall is hung with portraits, including two by Sir Peter Lely of Queen Henrietta Maria and General Monk.

The little medieval parish churches of the city are more picturesque than interesting, but the visitor should certainly see St. Mary Arches, St. Martin, and St. Mary Steps. Among the other noteworthy ecclesiastical buildings is St. Nicholas's Priory, in the Mint, founded in 1087 and retaining many 15th and 16th cent. features. Wynard's Alms-houses, founded 1430, make an attractive group of red sandstone buildings around a cobbled courtyard. The Tuckers' Hall (1471) is internally an interesting medieval building; so, too, is the Law Library in the Close.

The underground passages of the city, which run beneath the main streets, are a remarkable feature of its topography. They can be explored for considerable lengths by the visitor, who is strongly recommended to do so. These passages were originally made to bring water into the walled city from outside, and are probably early medieval in date. There is no reason to believe that they are partly Roman. A detailed description of them is given in an official pamphlet entitled *Exeter's Historic Underground Passages*, obtainable from the City Information Bureau.

Though the city was heavily damaged in the air-raid of May 1942, several good examples of Tudor and Stuart domestic building survive in and near the centre, especially in the High Street. The city was once rich, too, in Georgian architecture. It was Georgian Exeter that suffered most in the air-raids, many beautiful terraces and crescents—most notably Bedford Circus—being smashed up; but Barnfield Crescent, Southernhay West, and Colleton Crescent survive for contemplation. Regency architecture is best seen in Pennsylvania Park and Crescent, and in and around St. Leonard's Road. Scattered about the city are many individual buildings of great distinction, among them the Custom House on the Quay (1678-81), Rougemont House (*c.* 1820) in the bailey of the Norman castle, and the Higher Market in Queen St., a grand Greek revival building (1835-8).

Before the Germans wrecked it, Exeter was one of the most beautiful and appealing cities in England, full of colour, light, and movement. Even now, crowded as it is, it has an appeal unlike that of any other town in Western England. Exeter is the mother city and the tribal capital still.

EXMINSTER (H7) is a large village, somewhat suburbanised and spoilt by its nearness to Exeter. It is an ancient village, dating from the first days of the Saxon occupation of Devon and had a church soon afterwards—" Exe minster," probably shortly after the new diocese of Sherborne was set up in 705. The present church (St. Martin) is mostly of 14th-cent. date, with later windows inserted, and was too thoroughly restored in Victorian days. The fittings, however, are of some interest. The Peamore chapel is notable for its plaster ceiling dated 1633, depicting the apostles and the four evangelists, done by the Tothills of Peamore who probably reconstructed the nave arcade also. In the chancel is a good Renaissance monument to Otho Petre of Bowhay (now an interesting farmhouse), and a fine marble monument to John Cooke (1695), an Exeter merchant who bought the Kenbury estate, which is recorded as early as 1083. Kenbury House is mainly Georgian, in a pleasant little park. Peamore was a Domesday manor, and is now a hotel. Matford was a Domesday manor; the present Matford House is of considerable age.

EXMOUTH (J7) grew out of the two ancient parishes of Littleham and Withycombe Raleigh (q.v.). It is the oldest seaside town in Devon, having been frequented by Exeter people " for diversion and bathing in the sea " since the early 18th cent. It seems, like several other South Devon resorts, to have acquired a wider reputation among fashionable people when the Continent was closed to English visitors during the Napoleonic Wars. Until then it was merely a collection of fishermen's huts, with an occasional lodging-house or inn for the accommodation of summer visitors, though it had a small harbour and a not inconsiderable foreign trade in earlier centuries.

The manor of Littleham, on which Exmouth first grew up, belonged to the Rolles from the 17th cent. onwards, and it was they who did so much to develop the town as a watering-place from the 1790s down to the present day. The fashionable houses on the Beacon, still the most attractive architecture in Exmouth, were built in 1792 (plate 42). No. 6, now the U.D.C. offices, was occupied by Lady Nelson for a time; No. 19, now the Byron Hotel, by Lady Byron. A good deal of building followed, some of which is still preserved in Bicton Place, Bicton Street, and Louisa Terrace, and Exmouth continued to attract distinguished visitors down to the middle of the 19th cent. The building of the South Devon Railway on the other side of the estuary probably did a good deal to diminish Exmouth's position as a fashionable resort, for it gave direct access to Torquay by 1848, whereas Exmouth could only be reached by coach from Exeter or by a tiresome ferry from " Star Cross " station. Although a railway from Exeter to Exmouth was first projected in 1842, the scheme became involved in the great Battle of the Gauges and never materialised. A further attempt in 1854 failed for lack of capital (though an Act had been obtained), and not until 1861 was the line actually opened.[1]

By that time Torquay had become the fashionable Devonshire watering-place and Exmouth began to develop a different kind of life based largely upon the family holiday-makers from Exeter and the surrounding country. It has long sandy beaches and is attractively laid out as a " family holiday " resort. To the east of Exmouth the shingle beaches begin, from Budleigh Salterton onwards into Dorset, and being useless to children have never attracted families to them. Exmouth is the first of the sand-beach towns along the S. Devon coast.

Apart from the late 18th–early 19th-cent. building already referred to, Exmouth is not architecturally inspiring. It is bright, pleasant, and well tree'd; but red brick and the cold grey Devonian limestone are the dominant building materials of its age of expansion.

Holy Trinity church is a landmark for many miles. A medieval chapel of the Holy Trinity, licensed in 1412, stood on Chapel Hill, and was rebuilt in 1779. A new church became necessary with the growth of the town, and one was erected on the present site in 1823-5. In 1905-7 it was again rebuilt (G. H. F. Prynne, architect) in grey limestone.

The sea-wall was begun by Smeaton in 1841-2, greatly extended in 1870, and later extended to Orcombe Point, forming a fine promenade with views down the coast as far as Berry Head.

FARRINGDON (or FARINGDON) (J6) lies in pleasant, fruitful country. In Polwhele's day it was good cornland and "oak, ash, and elm grow to fine timber." Farringdon House, rebuilt in 1889 on an old site, is now an Approved School. Creely Barton was a Domesday estate.

The church (St. Petrock and St. Barnabas the Apostle) was completely rebuilt in 1871. The decorated brick interior is hideous; yellow pitch-pine pews commemorate the 1887 Jubilee.

FARWAY (K6) lies deep in the warm marly combes below the greensand plateau, which rises to over 800 ft. at Farway Hill. On the plateau is a large group of barrows, covering an extensive area, the most important Middle Bronze Age necropolis in Devon outside Dartmoor. Across the plateau runs an ancient ridgeway, followed by parish boundaries for miles, which is probably the *faer-weg* (" frequented road ") from which the parish takes its name.

Farway church (St. Michael) is attractively sited. It seems to have been a Norman church, much enlarged and altered in the early 14th cent., with a W. tower added in the 15th cent., the N. aisle in 1628, and the whole unfortunately Victorianised in 1877. The N. arcade has massive early Norman piers with scalloped caps. There is a good Elizabethan altar-table, and a monument in the N. aisle, with two recumbent effigies, to Sir Edmund Prideaux, Bt. (1554-1629). Below the effigy of Sir Edmund, in his lawyer's robes, is another effigy of a man in armour, possibly his grandson Edmund Prideaux (1618-43).

Netherton Hall was built in 1607 by Sir Edmund Prideaux, who bought the manor of Netherton, which had formerly belonged to Canonsleigh priory. Boycombe is a 16th-cent. "mansion," almost unaltered except for the demolition of one wing.

FENITON (J6) is a neat, well-cared-for village, set in park-like country. Feniton Court, a Georgian house, was the birthplace of John Coleridge Patteson (1827-71), first missionary bishop of Melanesia, murdered by natives in 1871. His father, Sir John Patteson, a distinguished judge, died at Feniton, 1861.

The church (St. Andrew) is entirely 15th-cent. work except the small N. transept. The fine 15th-cent. roodscreen to nave and S. aisle is of the Kentisbeare type, well proportioned and rich in detail, with its vaulting almost intact. The cornice is singularly rich. The S. parclose screen is also of beautiful design. In the chancel is a tomb with a striking naked and emaciated cadaver, probably that of one of the Malherbes (15th-cent.). A few 16th-cent. carved bench-ends survive, together with a number of modern ones of excellent design.

In Fenny Meadow, just N. of Fenny Bridge, the western rebels of 1549 were defeated by Russell's mercenaries. Curscombe Farm was a Domesday manor. Colesworthy is mentioned as early as 1219 and is probably of 12th-cent. foundation.

FILLEIGH (E3), on the main road from Barnstaple to South Molton, is a parish dominated by the great Fortescue mansion and park of Castle Hill. It probably derives its name from the original dedication of a Celtic church to St. Fili, companion of St. Kea who is commemorated at Landkey (q.v.), like Philleigh in Cornwall. The present church is, however, dedicated to St.

Paul. It was rebuilt in 1732, but most unfortunately rebuilt again in the Norman style in 1877. The interior is completely dull.

The Fortescues were by origin a South Devon family, but as with all rising families their younger sons married heiresses and founded new branches elsewhere. In 1454 Martin Fortescue, second son of Sir John Fortescue, who was Chancellor and Chief Justice to Henry VI, married Elizabeth, the heiress of the Denzil or Densell estates, and so acquired Filleigh, Wear Giffard, and Buckland Filleigh. The original estate was small, but it grew by slow degrees until in 1873 it amounted to rather more than 20,000 acres and was one of the four largest estates in Devon.

Castle Hill is one of the few country houses of any size or sophistication in Devon: "a prodigious string of golden-hued buildings, crowned here and there by little domes" rising from tiers of mown terraces and backed by lofty trees.[1] It faces a wide avenue running up the opposite hill, which is crowned by a "ruined" triumphal arch. The main road runs through the park on a level with the house, which "bursts entire upon the eye." The "Castle" is a sham ruin (early 18th cent.) on the top of the hill behind the house, answering to the triumphal arch on the opposite summit, but is now completely obscured by trees. This sham has given its name, however, to the mansion, which had previously been simply the manor house of Filleigh.

The original Tudor or medieval building had a forecourt looking N. into the hillside. In 1684 Arthur Fortescue of Penwarne in Cornwall proceeded to enlarge and turn the house around. This reconstruction was still in progress in 1694 when his son and heir Hugh Fortescue (1665-1719) petitioned the Bishop of Exeter for leave to make a new entrance to the church as he was "rebuilding his mansion."[2] He did not, however, spend much on building. The mansion as it stands today is mostly the work of his son Hugh, who succeeded to the estate in 1719, became Lord Clinton in 1721, and was created first Baron Fortescue of Castle Hill in 1746. He was, according to Hervey, "of mean aspect, and meaner capacity, but meanest of all in his inclinations." He retired from public life in the 1730s and began to transform Filleigh into Castle Hill, refacing the central block of 1684-94, and adding the low wings at either end, so giving the house an extraordinary length. This was required by the nature of the site, on a narrow ledge which prevented the normal projection of wings on either side of a forecourt. The Saloon of 1730-40 probably occupied the site of the great hall of the Tudor house, the Library that of the buttery. The Saloon rose to the full height of the façade and looked across the hanging terraces, over William Kent's formal lay-out of the park, to the distant triumphal arch. The greatest extravaganza of the Kentian plan was a complete "ruined" village, which a more economically-minded Fortescue later reconditioned into habitable cottages. Further internal and external changes were made in the late 18th–early 19th cent., when much of William Kent's early landscape gardening was deformalised. The most important changes were made by Edward Blore in 1842-3. He enlarged the house, and added the mansard roof, the cupola over the central block, and the flanking towers and domes. This roof and the domes obscured the fact that Castle Hill was an important example of early

Palladian architecture, contemporary with Holkham and Houghton.

The whole of the central block, including the Saloon with its magnificent plaster ceiling by a Parisian plasterer (c. 1735), was gutted by fire in 1934, and in the rebuilding of 1934-8 the opportunity was taken to restore the house to its original early Georgian proportions. Neither the Victorian mansard roof nor the Saloon were replaced, and the house was made more convenient inside. The main (S.) front is now much more pleasing, its true character once again revealed. The terraces, the " ruins," and the lay-out of the park survive to testify to "one of the most complete realisations of William Kent's conception of landscape gardening." The park is extensive (830 acres), well wooded, and very beautiful, making use of the sweeping undulations of the natural landscape with its streams, woods and hills, but also manipulating it on a grand scale. The parish church, for example, stood somewhere near the SW. corner of the present house before 1732, and was shifted to its present site because of the building and gardening operations of Lord Clinton at that date, just as the Morices shifted and rebuilt Werrington church (q.v.) for precisely the same reason in 1742. Probably the old main road from Barnstaple to South Molton was pushed S. at the same time, as the map suggests that it once ran below Oxford Down directly in front of the mansion.

The Fortescues have been one of the most distinguished families in Devon, and one of the most widespread. Since the 15th cent. few generations have passed without their name being prominent in county or national affairs. Between 1382 and 1702, 31 Fortescues were members of Parliament. In the parliament of 1592 there were no fewer than eight of them together. In Devon alone, their name is to be found in 46 parish registers, and in 20 more outside the county.[1] All the branches of the family but one have disappeared from their Devonshire estates (cf. the Chichesters), and that is the branch at Castle Hill, represented today by the 5th Earl Fortescue, now Lord Lieutenant of the county.

FREMINGTON (D2) has been spoilt by almost uninterrupted ribbon-building along the Barnstaple-Instow road, but a few old houses remain near the church. The latter (St. Peter) was " thoroughly restored " by Scott in 1866-7 and is uninteresting. Fremington was formerly a small port on the Taw, and also had a small pottery for which the local clay was peculiarly suitable. Hollocombe, beside the Taw, was a Domesday manor.

FRITHELSTOCK (C4) is notable for possessing the only remains of a religious house in North Devon. An Augustinian priory was founded here c. 1220 by Robert de Beauchamp, and dissolved in 1536. Only the W. and N. walls of the priory church remain, together with a portion of the S. wall. The W. wall contains three fine lancet windows. When Sir Stephen Glynne visited Frithelstock in 1845 he found much more of the priory standing. There were remains of a tower, at the SW. of the choir, nearly touching the parish church, and the refectory, which had "a fine open roof of the Suffolk type with collar and hammer beams."[2] There is no trace of the refectory now. The parish church (St. Mary and St. Gregory) is much restored and unexciting. It is mainly a 15th-cent. rebuilding to which a S. aisle was added c. 1500. Some good carved bench-ends (*temp*. Henry VII) display the crowned double rose of Henry VII, a single feather with label for Henry, Prince of Wales, the arms of Hartland Abbey (the mother-house of Frithelstock), and other figures and emblems. The royal arms, in plaster, are dated 1677.

GEORGEHAM (C2) was simply *Ham* in Domesday Book; the church is dedicated to St. George. Other Domesday manors in the parish were Croyde, North Buckland, Hole and Pickwell. The coastal scenery of the parish is attractive, especially at Croyde Bay, and at the fine headland of Baggy Point which now belongs to the National Trust. The parish church was rebuilt, except the tower, in 1876-7. It contains a number of interesting effigies and monuments. The effigy of a medieval knight is supposed to be that of Mauger St. Aubyn (d. 1294), who held the manor of Pickwell. In the Pickwell chapel also are some Harris monuments, and a good early 18th-cent. screen. In the old village of Croyde are a number of attractive cottages but the coastal end has been "developed."

GEORGENYMPTON (F3) is mainly an unexciting 15th-cent. church (St. George), with a tower rebuilt in brick in the 17th cent. The village is quiet.

GERMANSWEEK (c6) lies in the heart of a large unknown tract of clay-country, the pastoral nature of which is indicated as far back as the 11th cent. by the frequency of *wick* (i.e. dairy-farm) in its Domesday place-names. There were two Domesday manors called Wick in this parish, one now Germansweek (from the dedication of the church to St. Germanus of Auxerre) and the other now Southweek. The small village is on a hill rising steeply from the Wolf valley.

The church was drastically restored in the 1870s and is of little interest. The Seccombes have owned and farmed Seccombe since the 13th cent.

GIDLEIGH (E7) is a remote place on the edge of Dartmoor, not mentioned before the middle of the 12th cent.

The church (Holy Trinity) is a simple, granite building of the early 16th cent., with ceiled roofs and plastered walls, a good rood-screen, and a modern pulpit and lectern in granite (1853). Some medieval glass remains in the S. aisle. Slight structural changes were made in the 17th cent. (cf. the nave windows) and it is possible that the tower was rebuilt then.

Close to the church are the remains of Gidleigh Castle, a fortified manor house *c*. 1300 in date. It is contemporary with the later work of Okehampton Castle, and may well be by the same mason. It is a small " keep " consisting of a cellar below, and a solar above, and probably had originally a low-pitched roof covered with lead.[1]

Berrydown Farm is an attractive 17th-cent. farmhouse. Thule Farm is also interesting, modernised but not spoilt, and has the date 1566 carved on a beam in one of its rooms.[2] There are many hut-circles and other Bronze Age monuments on the high moors, especially on Buttern Hill.

GITTISHAM (K6) (pron. *Gitsam*) is an attractive village with some excellent cob and thatch building. A large stone-built farmhouse in the village is dated RS: 1600, and there are other good cottages and houses. Rapshays Farm was a Domesday manor. Combe House, in a beautiful park on the slopes of Gittisham Hill, is a good Elizabethan house (in parts probably older) in the Somerset rather than the Devon style. It was probably built by the Henry Beaumont (d. 1591) whose striking monument is in Gittisham church. He devised the manor to Sir Thomas Beaumont of Cole Orton (Leics.) "for the name sake," says Risdon, but it was sold to the Putts in 1615. They held it until 1792, when it passed by marriage to the Markers who still own it. The apple Tom Putt is named after Thomas Putt (1722-87), a barrister, who perfected it, and who planted the Beech Walk on Gittisham Hill.

The church (dedication unknown) is exceptionally attractive. It is a 15th–16th-cent. building. The S. aisle was probably built by Henry Beaumont between about 1528 and 1548. The atmosphere of the church is mostly that of the 18th cent.—box-pews, ceiled roofs, a collection of Putt hatchments, still freshly coloured, and a Georgian W. gallery. There are royal arms of Charles II, and some 16th-cent. glass in the N. chancel window. The chancel aisle contains several good monuments, besides that of Henry Beaumont already mentioned, including a beautiful mural tablet (1627) to the wife of a Beaumont rector, and an ornate marble monument to Sir Thomas Putt (1686) and his wife. There are other Putt and Marker memorials.

On the top of Gittisham Hill begins a large group of Bronze Age barrows, extending for 3 m. SE. to Broad Down. Most of these lie in Farway (q.v.) The deluded Joanna Southcott was born on a farm in Gittisham.

GOODLEIGH (D2). The body of the church (St. Gregory) was rebuilt in 1881-2, but is nevertheless very plea-sant, and lit with clear glass. A branch of the Aclands of Acland lived at Combe, now a farmhouse, and there is a small rustic monument in the church to James Acland (1655).

HACCOMBE WITH COMBE (G8) is a union of two ancient ecclesiastical parishes. Combeinteignhead (to give it its full name) is a village lying where a long valley (combe) opens out on to the estuary of the Teign. Coombe Cellars is one of those attractive old riverside inns (there are several in Devon) of which many townspeople have happy memories, of carefree summer evenings long ago. It was also a noted smuggling centre in the early 19th cent. Combe church (dedication unknown) is a 14th–15th-cent. church with transepts, too vigorously restored by Medley Fulford in 1887-8. There is a fine rood-screen, a notable 12th-cent. font, and some remarkable carved bench-ends (16th cent.) in the N. transept. In this transept also are the tombs and memorials of the Hockmore family of Buckland Barton. The chancel is small and dark, and looks rebuilt. Near the church are the almshouses, in red sandstone, given by William Bourchier, 3rd Earl of Bath, in 1620.

Buckland Barton was a Domesday manor. It was the seat of the Hockmores for many generations, and still retains much 16th–17th-cent. work though the old mansion has been curtailed in size. There are two fine plaster ceilings and a panelled room. Netherton was an ancient estate, probably dating from the 12th cent.

Haccombe consists chiefly of the church and the big house. The manor belonged to the Haccombes in the 12th–13th cents., passed eventually to the Courtenays, and thence by marriage to the Carews, who have held it since the mid-15th cent. The present house is a plain late Georgian mansion (*c.* 1805) on the site of the medieval hall.

Haccombe church (St. Blaize) is notable for its fine collection of medieval and later effigies. It is mostly a 13th-cent. building, of red sandstone rubble throughout. The date of the massive N. arcade is difficult to ascertain but it may be *c.* 1300. A college of six chantry priests, with an arch-priest at their head, was founded here in 1335. The rector of Haccombe still has the title of archpriest, which was used by the heads of a few similar foundations in the west of England, e.g. at Bere Ferrers.

The church has a great number of medieval tiles; some medieval English glass, later foreign glass, and good modern glass. In 1821-2 the building was fitted with a stone chancel screen, pulpit, altar piece, etc., by Nicholas Kendall, and given new pews.

The brasses and effigies in the church are among the best in Devon and can only be catalogued here: (1) Sir Stephen or Sir Jordan de Haccombe, a fine 13th-cent. effigy in red sandstone, formerly plastered and richly coloured; (2) and (3) are other Haccombe effigies; (4) and (5) are recumbent effigies on an altar-tomb in the N. aisle, possibly Sir Hugh Courtenay of Boconnoc and Haccombe (d. 1425) and Philippa his 2nd wife; (6) a small alabaster effigy of a child (14th cent.) of fine workmanship. On the chancel floor are five interesting brasses of the Carews: Sir Nicholas (1469), Thomas (1586), Mary, his wife (1589), Elizabeth, wife of John Carew (1611), and Thomas, with wife and six children (1656).

HALBERTON (J4) is a large village which gave its name to a hundred. Besides Halberton itself there are several hamlets and farms in the parish which were settled before 1066: Ash Thomas, Leonard Farm, East and West Manley, Muxbere, Sellake, Sutton, and Moorstone Barton. Watton Farm is mentioned in 1166, and most of the other farms of the parish appear by the 13th cent. A remarkable feature of the village is the large pond between Higher Town and Lower Town which is fed by warm springs and never freezes over. The Grand Western Canal, made by act of 1796, winds through the parish, derelict.

Moorstone Barton was so called after Morin who held it in 1086. In 1406 the Gambons were licensed to have a chapel at "their mansion of Morston." East Manley belonged to the Manleys from Henry III's time until well into the 19th cent.; there are still Manleys in the parish. The village contains a number of interesting houses, including one called The Priory. On the E. edge of the parish is the mansion of Bridwell, built in 1779 partly from the materials of a medieval chapel demolished at that time.

The church (St. Andrew) is of considerable interest. The tower and nave are early 14th-cent. in date. Of the fittings the rood-screen, the parclose screens, the pulpit, and the Norman font are all noteworthy. The rood-screen is fine and massive, with tracery of an early and plain variety and vaulting of an exceptionally interesting and rare type. There are few other screens in England like it. Its date is *c.* 1420. The pulpit, richly carved and excellently preserved, is of the same date as the screen.

HALWELL (F10), now a remote village, was one of the four *burhs* of Devon in the 10th cent. Within a century it had been superseded by Totnes. The church (St.

Leonard) is a very good late 15th-cent. building, with a fine W. tower built of the local slate. A good deal of granite is used in the church, notably in the vigorous N. arcade. The rood-screen was removed in 1810, which is perhaps the date of the decent box-pews.

Poulston and Washbourne were Domesday manors. S. of the village is Stanborough Camp, an earthwork consisting of a single rampart and ditch enclosing about 3½ acres. It is probably of Iron Age date and commands a vast stretch of country, including the open shore of Start Bay where hostile landings could be made. The camp was the ancient meeting-place for the hundred court of Stanborough. Halwell Camp, another earthwork of the same type, lies across the road to Dartmouth, but its S. half has been mostly destroyed. One of the finest examples of a prehistoric ridgeway in Devon runs by the W. side of Stanborough camp.

HALWILL (c6) church (St. Peter and St. James) was originally a 14th-cent. cruciform building, but was rebuilt, except the massive tower, in 1876-9.

HARBERTON (F10) is a large unspoilt village which takes its name from the Harbourne river. Harbertonford is another village within the parish, situated at the crossing of the Harbourne. The old name for the ford seems to have been Hernaford, now a farm to the S. A bridge was built here in the late 16th–early 17th cent. Harbertonford was made into a separate ecclesiastical parish in 1860, when the church of St. Peter was built. There is a large woollen mill here, and a little higher up the river an edge-tool factory in an old mill.

Harberton church (St. Andrew) is a splendid 14th and 15th-cent. building;

but it must have been still more exciting before the "restorations" of 1861 and 1871-2, which swept away a good deal of the old furniture and did barbaric things to the medieval rood-screen. The vaulting of the screen is perfect; the cornice enrichments very fine; but the top cresting is coarse modern work. At the "restoration" the whole screen was smothered with shiny paint, and the painted figures of saints on the lower panels covered up with tin-plate painted by an amateur with the figures of angels. Baring-Gould says (in his *Little Guide*) that these paintings were portraits of the young ladies of the congregation in 1870. As such, they have a certain melancholy interest. The pulpit is remarkably fine, with a good series of statuettes. It is 15th-cent. in date, and one of the best medieval stone pulpits in Devon. The font is very beautiful Norman work, of red sandstone, with almost pure Byzantine ornament.

There are a number of architecturally interesting houses in the parish. Beenleigh, beside the Harbourne river, is substantially a 15th-cent. "mansior," with a hall and primitive gatehouse. Luscombe, not far away, is an early 17th-cent. "mansion." Great Englebourne, NW. of Harbertonford, was a Domesday manor and has traces of the former manor house. Other Domesday manors were Hazard and East and West Leigh, now farmhouses. Hernaford, first recorded in 1285, was also a medieval "mansion." The Church House Inn at Harberton is a 16th-cent. building with an interesting interior.

Harberton parish is fertile and beautiful country. It seems likely that it once covered the whole enclave between the Dart and the Harbourne, and that it included the present parish of Ashprington and the site of the 10th-cent. borough of Totnes, which grew up at the extremity of the district and was in due course carved out of it.

HARFORD (E10) is identical as a name with Hereford, the first element being the OE word *here*, "army." But the history behind this "army ford" is quite lost. The church stands almost alone beside the Erme, where it leaves the Moor, and is indeed the gateway to one of the most interesting and beautiful parts of Dartmoor—the upper Erme valley. In this valley is to be found one of the densest concentrations of hut-circles, pounds, stone-rows, and other remains of the Bronze Age to be seen anywhere on the Moor. The exact sites will be found on the 2½-inch maps (sheets 20/65, 20/66). Piles Copse is a wood of stunted and contorted trees, somewhat similar to Wistman's Wood. Near it is a bee-hive hut; and another stands a little higher up the valley on the other side. These are medieval erections put up by tin-miners. Higher still up the valley are the remains of a blowing-house for tin. At this point the Bronze Age remains also are particularly concentrated.

The church is an attractive little moorstone building of late 15th-cent.-16th-cent. date. It is said to be dedicated to the Celtic St. Petrock, but Oliver gives no dedication, and Brooking-Rowe gives St. Patrick. The wagon-roofs have carved ribs and bosses. On the wall-plate on the N. side of the chancel is the inscription: *I.H.S. helpe us. Amen. Walter Hele p'son* 1539. *I.H.S. Salus.* Below this is the altar-tomb, with two brasses, of Thomas Williams (d. 1566) who was born at Stowford, in this parish, and became Speaker of the House of Commons in 1563. Stowford was practically rebuilt early in the 19th cent. but some portions of the 16th-cent. house remain. There

is also a brass to John and Agnes Prideaux, the parents of John Prideaux, rector of Exeter College, Oxford, and bishop of Worcester (1578-1650), who was also born at Stowford. Hall, ½ m. W. of the church, was the seat of Col. Thomas Chudleigh, father of Elizabeth Chudleigh, the notorious Duchess of Kingston (1720-88), who was born here. The manor house is now a farm-house. At Lukesland there are the remains of a "mansion."

Harford bridge existed in the 16th cent. Parts of the existing bridge of two semi-circular arches may be of that date.

HARPFORD (J6) lies astride the peaceful unspoilt Otter valley. The village contains some excellent houses (cob and thatch chiefly). Court Place, now a farmhouse, was once the manor house. The church (St. Gregory) has a fine 15th-cent. tower but the interior, grossly over-restored in 1884-5, is devoid of interest.

HARTLAND (A3) is a small town and an immense parish of some 17,900 acres occupying the peninsula in the extreme NW. corner of Devon. It contains the most impressive cliff scenery in England and Wales, above all the iron coast from Hartland Point southwards (plate 22), with its coastal waterfalls. The sea-scapes are superb, for there is no land between this coast and America:

Where on Hartland's tempest-furrowed shore
Breaks the long swell from farthest Labrador.

Inland the scenery is very Cornish in feeling: white farmhouses and cottages dotted about an immense grey land-scape, the clustered hamlets at intervals, grey stone and slate everywhere, even a Cornish name or two, like Trellick and Velly. One could write a chapter about this wide, buzzard-haunted countryside, so remote and withdrawn from the villainies of the human race, far from railways and the lunacies of the modern world. Buzzards sail slowly above the quiet combes, throwing their shadows on the sunlit slopes below, the wild bubbling cry of curlews is everywhere on the moory grounds above, swallows flash in and out of ancient slate-grey courtyards: it is a timeless scene.

Hartland means " stag-island," though the district is in fact a peninsula. There are earthworks—"cliff castles"—at Embury Beacon and Windbury Head, perhaps associated originally with the immense Early Iron Age hillfort of Clovelly Dykes. Tradition says there was a third of these "cliff castles" at Hartland Point, now undermined by the sea. On Bursdon Moor there are numerous round barrows, probably of Bronze Age date, the beginning of a long series which is scattered across North Devon to the very summit of Exmoor. Hartland enters history as a royal estate. In his will King Alfred left it to Edward, his elder son, and it remained a royal possession until the reign of Canute who apparently granted it to Gytha on her marriage to Godwin.[1] At the Norman Conquest it was seized by William, but soon after his death it was granted to one of the Dynham family (from Dinant in Brittany), in which family it descended until 1501. It was then divided among four co-heiresses, and the later history is somewhat complicated. Like so many ancient royal estates, Hartland gave its name to a hundred.

Oliver de Dynham created a borough at Hartland c. 1290, having obtained (in 1280) the grant of a market and a three-day fair at the feast of St. Nectan. The town was too far removed from trade-routes to come to anything much. In the 18th cent. it was described as being as depressed-looking as a Cornish borough. Its market ceased about 1780. Nevertheless, the town grew steadily in numbers until the 1840s, and then began to decline. Today it has about 1,300 people, not much more than half the size of a hundred years ago. It is a pleasant little town, mostly of one street, with a few solid 18th–early 19th-cent. houses of some character, and a number of old-fashioned shops. The nearest railway station is Bideford (13 m.) but buses now run through it on the Bideford-Bude route, a fine run for scenery.

The parish church (St. Nectan) is at Stoke, 2 m. W. It has a lofty 15th-cent. tower (128 ft.) visible far out at sea. A collegiate church was founded here by Gytha c. 1050, and dedicated to St. Nectan, as a thank-offering for the escape of her husband Earl Godwin from shipwreck. In 1066 there were twelve canons here. This college of secular canons was refounded by Geoffrey de Dynham in 1169 as an Arroasian monastery of regular canons on a new site in the valley below.[2] Nothing remains of Hartland Abbey to-day, except a fragment of the cloisters in the present house, which was rebuilt in 1779.

The parish church perpetuates the old site of Gytha's collegiate church. It is a splendid building, and of the highest interest. The rood-screen (c. 1470) is magnificent, extending nearly 48 ft. across nave and aisles, and in perfect condition. The cornices are particularly rich; but the whole screen calls for detailed study. Many other features of the church call for notice: a splendid Norman font, carved bench-ends (early 16th-cent.) in the N. transept, the roofs, especially that of the N. chancel aisle, the priest's chamber in which Parson Hawker wrote "The Bell by the Sea," and the numerous floor-slabs and monuments to the gentry of the parish.

The parish is dotted with interesting houses and most picturesque farmsteads, of which one can only recite a catalogue—South Hole, Docton, Eddistone, Milford, Long Furlong, and Blegberry, to name only a few. East Titchberry now belongs to the National Trust.

Hartland Point (350 ft.), one of the boldest headlands on the English coast, has generally been identified as the *Hercules Promontory* of Ptolemy's geography. A lighthouse was built here in 1874, and a powerful foghorn installed. The summit of the headland was reduced in area for the protection of the lighthouse, but it is still an impressive and savage piece of coast. Hartland is another of those Devonshire parishes in which one could happily spend a week in leisurely exploration, better still a fortnight, and best of all in the spring; and one would always wish to return to it. A very good book has been written about it — Chope's *Book of Hartland* (1940)—which is indispensable to the explorer.

HATHERLEIGH (D5), like so many of the inland market towns of Devon, has been declining in population since the middle of the 19th cent. It is a peaceful little place for those who like to absent themselves awhile from the felicities of modern science, for it has not changed much during the past century. The town contains much good domestic building in the local tradition, from the 16th cent. to the 19th. Some buildings may be older, behind their stucco and roughcast. The attractive George Hotel is probably 15th- and

early 16th-cent., and may have been the court-house of the abbots of Tavistock, who held the manor from the late 10th cent. until the Dissolution. The Old Church House is a medieval building. The London Inn looks pre-16th cent. in part. The town suffered severely from a great fire about 1840, after which many of the houses were rebuilt and the principal street widened.

It was part of the original endowment of Tavistock Abbey, founded about 974 by Ordulf, who had vast estates in North and West Devon. Some time in the 13th cent. it was made a borough and given certain modest liberties, including that of having a borough court, but it was never incorporated, and continued to be governed, as it is today, by a portreeve and other officers.

After the Dissolution, the manor and borough of Hatherleigh was sold by the Crown to the Arscotts, a rapidly rising family of gentry in West Devon. It never formed part of the vast block of Tavistock Abbey lands granted to John, Lord Russell, as Lysons surmises. At the beginning of the 19th cent. Hatherleigh was smaller than most of the old market towns, being in one of the poorest regions of Devon. Its woollen manufacture had also dwindled almost to nothing:

The people are poor as Hatherleigh Moor,
And so they have been for ever and ever.

Hatherleigh Moor, formerly a waste of 430 acres, was given to the inhabitants for grazing their cattle and cutting furze for fuel. There is no truth in the tradition that it was the gift of John of Gaunt, who is not known ever to have had any rights in Hatherleigh. It is much more likely to have been a gift of one of the abbots of Tavistock. On the moor is St. John's Well, a "holy well," the water from which was formerly used at baptisms.

Deckport, an Elizabethan house, was the home of John Lethbridge, gent., to whom there is a mural monument in Hatherleigh church (1706). Other houses and farmsteads on ancient sites are Essworthy, Fishleigh, Pulsworthy, Hannaborough, Passaford, Upcott, and Great Velliford. Jasper Mayne (1604-72), chaplain to Charles II, and a dramatist of some note in his early life, was born at Hatherleigh.

Hatherleigh church (St. John the Baptist) is mainly a 15th-cent. building, built of red sandstone and possessing a shingled spire. A few 16th-cent. carved benches remain, and an early 18th-cent. pulpit and altar rails. The war memorial bears many very characteristic West Devon surnames—Battishill, Collacott, Cory, Ellacott, Fishleigh, Meardon, and Medland, all the names of farms round about, and a reflection of the long stability of country life in these remoter parts.

HAWKCHURCH (M5) lies in attractive hilly country rising to the Dorset Border. The name means " Hafoc's church," indicating the presence of a church here in pre-Conquest times. The present church (St. John the Baptist) though drastically restored in 1862 (except the tower) is still of considerable interest, retaining much of its Norman interior. The N. arcade is 12th-cent.; that on the S. is somewhat later (c. 1200) with stiff foliage and quaint figures on the square caps. The tower is stately, rising in four stages and bearing the arms of Cerne Abbey. It shows strong Somerset influence. Wyld Court is a fine late 16th-cent. house with a much-gabled front and mullioned windows. It was formerly E-shaped but the W. wing has been pulled down.

Over the porch are the arms of Moore, which also occur on two overmantels. The builder was probably Robert Moore whose initials, with the date 1593, occur on a lead rainwater pipe. Lambert's Castle is a fine Iron Age hill-fort, commanding the Axe valley.

HEANTON PUNCHARDON (D2) lies on the seaward end of a sharp ridge, and commands very fine land and sea views. Chivenor, a 13th-cent. settlement, is now the site of a large aerodrome, chosen because it was one of the few level stretches of land in N. Devon.

The church (St. Augustine) is finely sited on the end of the ridge. It is almost entirely 15th–early 16th-cent. in date, with a graceful W. tower. Plastered and whitened throughout, well kept and wholly charming, it is a most "atmospheric" country church. The furniture is mostly inoffensive Victorian deal. Many coloured mural monuments hang on the plastered walls like pictures, as indeed they are: portraits of a vanished society. The rood-screen was taken away at the "restoration" and put back at another. Its 19tl.-cent. extension across the N. aisle is completely out of keeping with the old work. Beyond the screen, in the N. chancel aisle, are some interesting coloured mural monuments to the Bassets (who lived at Heanton Court) ranging in date from 1635 to 1686, and there are inscribed Basset slabs in the floor. The chancel is in excellent taste, with still more monuments and an elaborate canopied tomb, probably that of Richard Coffin (d. 1523) who desired in his will to be buried in Heanton church.

In the churchyard is the tomb of Edward Capern (1819-94), the so-called " Postman-poet," whom Landor oddly called " The Burns of Devon." Also buried in this beautiful churchyard are many airmen from the Dominions (Canada, Australia, and New Zealand), who were stationed at Chivenor during the war of 1939-45. Here, high up under a bright Attic sky, they look westwards down the placid Taw estuary as it opens silently out to the sea, homeward towards Canada where most of them belonged.

Heanton Court, beside the Taw estuary, was the seat of a younger branch of the Bassets from the 15th cent. down to 1802. It is now a farmhouse.

HEMPSTON, LITTLE (G9), has two exceptionally interesting buildings—the parish church and the medieval manor house. The former (St. John the Baptist) is an attractive building with a fine W. tower. The chancel and the font are 14th-cent., but the rest of the church is 15th-cent.[1] The window tracery was inserted in 1863. There is a 15th-cent. rood-screen, of which the loft and vaulting have disappeared, and parclose screens of the same date. In the window recesses of the S. aisle are three 14th-cent. effigies which are thought to represent members of the Arundell family, who possessed the manor from the time of Henry I.

The old manor house, one of the most perfectly preserved medieval buildings in England, has been continuously inhabited since it was built in the late 14th cent. The house was occupied as a parsonage from the middle of the 15th cent. until 1921, whence it acquired its name of the Old Parsonage. It consists of an outer courtyard 45 ft. square, and a tiny inner courtyard (only 20 ft. by 18 ft.) round which the house is built. The hall is small (2 bays) and perfect, with its original plaster to within four feet of the floor. At the far end is a fresco (c. 1450) of the Resurrection, in a remarkably good state of preservation. The primitive original screens remain. There is no trace of a fireplace; the presumption is that there was a central hearth. From the corner of the hall a circular stone staircase leads to the solar above, and the original kitchen lies behind this stair.[2]

HEMYOCK (K4) is a large, dull village at the end of the delightful Culm valley railway. The church (St. Mary) was enlarged and practically rebuilt in 1847, and is of no interest except for its Norman font. Near the church are the small remains of Hemyock Castle, probably a fortified house rather than a true castle, erected in the late 13th or the early 14th cent.

Culm Davey, a hamlet 1½ m. N., has an ancient chapel. A number of farms and hamlets are mentioned in Domesday Book—Culm Davey, Culm Pyne Barton, and Gorwell Farm.

HENNOCK (G7) is a wildish, hilly parish between the Teign and Bovey valleys, the village standing some 600 ft. above sea-level. The parish church (St. Mary) is a typical fully-aisled building of 15th-cent. date, with granite arcades. The plain, unbuttressed tower may be older. The font, with rude carvings, is probably early 13th-cent. in date. Some medieval glass remains, but much is said to have been carted away at the "restoration" of 1873-5, when the church was filled with bad Victorian woodwork. The rood-screen, of the ordinary 15th-cent. type, was spared. It extends across nave and aisles, and retains some of its ancient paintings. Vaultings and cornices have disappeared, but the enriched canopy of honour to the rood remains in the nave roof.

Warmhill, now a good early 17th-cent. farmhouse, was a Domesday manor. Chudleigh Knighton, at the S. end of the parish, was a separate Domesday manor. Longlands, in the village, is an interesting old house, probably of late 15th-cent. origin, altered in the early 17th cent. It seems to be a medieval hall-house, modernised just after 1600.

HIGHAMPTON (c5) stands on a conspicuous ridge from which there are splendid views, especially towards Dartmoor. The rounded mass of Cawsand Beacon dominates all views in this part of Devon. The church (Holy Cross) has a good Norman S. doorway, somewhat restored, and a graceful Norman font of which the base and shaft are modern. The body of the church (15th-cent.) was largely rebuilt in 1833 and again restored in 1876. It is of little interest.

Burdon was the home of the Burdons for about 650 years. The present farmhouse has substantial remains of a Tudor "mansion" at the rear, bearing the date 1569 and the initials EB: AB. The rest of the house was remodelled in the 18th cent. and is uninteresting.

Totleigh Barton, at the NE. end of the parish, is an ancient site. It was a seat in the 13th and 14th cents. of the Zouches and Fitzwarrens, and had a private chapel dedicated to St. Katherine, licensed in 1401. The present house appears to be a rebuilding of late 16th-cent. date. The moat W. and N. of the present house, of which there are distinct traces, almost certainly represents the site of the 13th-cent. Zouch manor house.

HIGHWEEK (see NEWTON ABBOT).

HITTISLEIGH (F6) is a small parish

in the wooded foothills of Dartmoor, with no village. The church (St. Andrew) is altogether charming, with its plastered and cream-washed walls, and ceiled roofs. The nave and chancel are probably 14th-cent. The N. aisle was added c. 1500, with a simple granite arcade. A W. tower was added about the same time. There are several 16th–17th-cent. granite floor-slabs to the yeomen of the parish. The wagon roof of the aisle has carved bosses, wall-plates, and ribs. The font is late Norman, of black marble, upon an early 13th-cent. base.

HOCKWORTHY (J4). The church (St. Simon and St. Jude) was rebuilt and restored, except for the tower, in 1865, and is of no interest except for the Norman font.

HOLBETON (E10) is a considerable village set back a little from the beautiful wooded shores of the Erme estuary, amid quite unspoiled country. The coastal scenery of the parish is also most attractive. The banks of the Erme are lined with country houses, of which the most notable is Flete, in a large park, formerly the seat of Lord Mildmay and now a Plymouth hospital. Flete owes its present character as a house to Norman Shaw who remodelled it extensively from 1878 onwards. He built the great tower on the N. front, rebuilt the NW. wing, and drastically altered the interior to put in "over-rich Tudor." The house had already been drastically remodelled in the Gothic style in 1835, and the front is all of this date.

Flete was a Saxon estate (it is recorded in Domesday). Other Saxon estates in the parish—all recorded in Domesday—were Battisborough, Lambside, and Membland.

Mothecombe, a beautiful site at the

mouth of the river, is first referred to in the early 13th cent. The present house was built about 1710. Membland was rebuilt in the 1780s. Pamflete is delightfully situated near the wooded shores of the Erme. The house has traces of old work.

The church (All Saints) has a dignified and spacious interior, with lofty granite arcades (early 16th-cent.), and shallow N. and S. transepts. The tower and spire are probably early 14th-cent. The church contains much excellent modern woodwork, notably the screens, benches and stalls. The modern chancel roof should also be noted. In the Hele chapel is a striking monument with 22 figures arranged in four steps or tiers, representing three generations of the Heles. The effigy in armour is that of Sir Thomas Hele of Flete (d. 1670). Above is his father, Thomas Hele (d. 1624) and family, and above him again Sir Thomas's grandfather, Thomas Hele of Exeter (d. 1613), and family.

HOLCOMBE BURNELL (G6) is in rolling green country S. of the Exeter-Okehampton road, a parish of scattered farms and no village. The church and the barton (formerly the manor house of Sir Thomas Dennis) stand alone, with superb views of combes and wooded hills S. from the sycamore-shaded churchyard.

The church (St. John the Baptist) was rebuilt, all but the tower, in 1843-4, but is still a pleasant country church in character. The 15th-cent. style was preserved, and there are traces of Norman work in the S. doorway. The rood-screen was used to make the pulpit, which has eight panels painted with the Madonna, Gabriel, and six saints. Apart from some small remains of medieval coloured glass, the church is excellently lit with clear glass. The

decent box-pews date from 1844. There are the usual floor-slabs, mostly 17th-cent., to local gentry and yeomen. The Easter sepulchre was used as the tomb of Sir Robert Dennis, 1592.

Holcombe Barton has much early Tudor work. It was built as a manor house in Henry VIII's reign by Sir Thomas Dennis (c. 1480-1561), a great power in Devon at this time. He was a privy councillor, chancellor of Anne of Cleves, custos rotulorum for Devon, frequently sheriff of the county between 1508 and 1556, and recorder of Exeter 1514-44.

HOLCOMBE ROGUS (J4) possesses what is perhaps the finest Tudor house in Devon, much more akin to Somerset than to the modest Devonshire houses of the period. The principal part of the house was built by Sir Roger Bluett (d. 1566), perhaps with the materials of an older house on the site. The fine hall and three-storied tower porch are of this period. Considerable alterations and additions were made by Richard Bluett, who succeeded to the estate in 1585. A handsome drawing-room was made in 1591 above the kitchen and its offices, but the panelling was done in the late 17th cent. The open roof of the Edwardian hall was hidden by a flat ceiling, and the space above made into a long gallery above the hall and drawing-room. Large additions were made to the house on the W. side during the third quarter of the 19th cent., and it now surrounds a small court, with the kitchen in the new wing. The ceiling, panelling, and screen of the hall are modern, as also is the present balcony opening from the drawing-room into the hall. The Bluetts sold the estate to the Rev. W. Rayer in 1858, so ending a stay of some 400 years; and a few years ago Holcombe Court was sold again to Mr. Fleetwood-Hesketh, of an old Lancashire family.

The near-by church (All Saints) is a 15th-cent. building. At the E. end of the N. aisle is the Bluett pew, enclosed by a large cinquecento screen which includes portions of the old rood-screen. The cornice is composed of a series of large medallions carved with scenes from the books of Genesis and Exodus. In the N. chapel are the Bluett monuments. Among these is a fine tomb with effigies of Richard Bluett (1615) and Mary Chichester his wife, with their eleven children, and another of Sir John Bluett (1634) and his wife Elizabeth Portman. There are very pleasing 18th-cent. mural monuments also, notably that to the Rev. Robert Bluett (1749).

At the entrance to the churchyard is the Church House (early 16th-cent.), a good example of its type with oak-mullioned windows. Kerswell Farm is recorded in Domesday Book: its name means "cress spring."

HOLLACOMBE (B5) is a tiny parish, with a pleasant but much over-restored church (1887), dedicated to St. Petrock. It was mainly an early 14th-cent. church before the restoration, with a saddleback tower, unusual for Devon.

HOLNE (F9) parish is romantically beautiful. In Holne Chase, commanding the Dart valley, is a perfect earthwork, roughly circular in shape, with a single rampart and ditch. It is probably of late Iron Age date. On the high moorland in the W. of the parish are hut-circles and tumuli. The farmstead of Stoke was a Domesday manor.

The Dart is crossed near Holne by two good medieval bridges. The present Holne Bridge was built after the destruction of an earlier bridge by a flood

in 1413; New Bridge, higher up the river, is of the same date.

Holne church (St. Mary) was originally a cruciform church, built c. 1300, with a W. tower and transepts. As at Ilsington, the church was enlarged about 1500 by the opening out of the transepts into aisles with granite arcades. The fine screen, with much good detail, has lost its vaulting and is otherwise mutilated. The carved pulpit is of the same date (early 16th cent.).

At the vicarage Charles Kingsley was born on 12 June 1819, while his father was curate-in-charge of Holne for a few months.

HOLSWORTHY (B5) is a small market town and a large parish in the bleak "yellow-clay" country of West Devon. Its market and fair were granted between 1155 and 1185, and St. Peter's Fair is still held on 9, 10 and 11 July.[1] It became a seignorial borough some time in the 13th cent., governed by a portreeve, an office which still survives. Like many of the inland towns of Devon, Holsworthy reached its maximum population in 1841 (1,857 people) and has declined slowly ever since. It is now the dullest town in Devon to look at, having scarcely a single building of the slightest architectural merit. The church (St. Peter and St. Paul) has a noble W. tower of granite, built c. 1500, but the rest of the church has been so restored that it is of little interest, except for the handsome organ, built by Renatus Harris.

Thorne, now a farmhouse, was a Domesday manor, and has some remains of a medieval chapel. Chilsworthy was a Domesday manor. Arscott (now called South Arscott) was the original home of the Arscotts, who began here in Henry III's time, and rose rapidly in the 16th cent., partly on a fortune made in the law. Soldon was a manor house of the Prideaux in the 17th cent. and contains a considerable amount of work of that date.

HONEYCHURCH   (see SAMPFORD COURTENAY).

HONITON (K5) is a cheerful little town, mostly of one long wide street, on the main London-Exeter road, which was its *raison d'être*. The original settlement of " Huna's farm " may have been on the hillside to the S. of the town where the former parish church of St. Michael now stands. The valley is dotted with old farmsteads linked by narrow winding lanes, of which Coomb-hayes Farm (*c.* 1600) and Higher Blannicombe are worth seeing. Near the Sidbury road is Heathfield Farm (16th-cent.).

The manor came to the Earls of Devon, and William de Vernon, the 5th earl, founded a borough here between 1194 and 1217. Until 1846 Honiton was governed by a portreeve. In that year it was incorporated, and became a "mayor town." It was a parliamentary borough from 1640 to 1868, with a singularly unsavoury reputation.

Honiton is said to have been the first town in Devon in which serges were made, and there was a flourishing woollen industry here in the 17th–18th cents. It was also notable from Elizabethan times for the manufacture of a fine lace, which became especially famous under royal patronage in the 19th cent. Like most inland market towns in Devon, Honiton reached its highest population in the 1840s, but its subsequent decline was not as drastic as most, and it is a busy little place today.

Fires devastated the town in 1672, 1747, 1754 and 1765 (when 115 houses were burnt down), so that it presents the appearance to-day of a late 18th–early 19th-cent. town for the most part. The High Street is typical of a late Georgian coaching town, with a good deal of decent 18th-cent. building. The oldest house in the town is Marwood House, at the NE. end of the High Street, built in 1619 by John Marwood, physician. He was the second son of Thomas Marwood, physician to Queen Elizabeth, who enjoyed great fame as a doctor, having cured the Earl of Essex in 1592 when the best London doctors had failed to do so.[1]

In the main street is Allhallows Chapel, used for nearly 300 years as a schoolroom. It has some 15th-cent. work, but was partly rebuilt in the 17th cent. and is now used as a local museum. The Congregational Chapel has its original 1774 building behind a later front. St. Paul's church was built 1835-8 in the Norman style by Charles Fowler.

The former parish church (St. Michael) stands on a steep hillside above the town. It is a distinguished building of late 15th–early 16th-cent. date, with large windows of clear glass, and something of the air of a cathedral. The chancel was probably rebuilt by John Takell (d. 1529) as is suggested by the inscription on two of the chancel piers. The interior was gutted by fire in 1911, when the splendid rood-screen perished, but a number of interesting memorials remain, including the tomb of Thomas Marwood the physician (d. 1617). There are fine views from the churchyard over the town to the Blackdown Hills.

On the Exeter road, about ¾ m. SW. of the town, is St. Margaret's Hospital, founded as a leper hospital at an unknown date and refounded and rebuilt *c.* 1530 by Thomas Chard as an alms-house. Some work of this period remains.

HORWOOD (D3).

The church (St. Michael) is beautifully situated, commanding fine views of the Taw and Torridge estuary. It is a delightful little building, mostly *c.* 1500 in date. An excellent N. arcade of five bays leads into the Pollard aisle. An inscription which formerly existed in one of the windows showed that the original aisle was built by John Pollard and his wife Emma, daughter and co-heir of John Doddescombe, probably *c.* 1400. The beautiful alabaster effigy in this aisle of a lady with a mitred or horned head-dress, and a rich robe in which three figures of children are enfolded, is said to be that of Emma Pollard.

The furniture of the church is interesting: a number of excellent carved bench-ends in the nave (early 16th-cent.); some plain bench-ends in the Pollard aisle which may well be older; a good pulpit (1635) and altar rails (17th-century). Some ancient glass remains in the E. window of the Pollard aisle, and a considerable number of late medieval tiles in the floor.

HUISH (D4)

is in beautiful country, running down to the wooded Torridge valley. Much of the parish is occupied by the park of Heanton Satchville, the principal residence of Lord Clinton. The house, built towards the end of the 18th cent., was gutted by fire in December 1932, and has been rebuilt. The church (St. James) was wholly rebuilt by G. E. Street in 1873, except the 15th-cent. tower. It contains a memorial to John Cunningham Saunders, the eminent eye-surgeon, who was born at Lovistone or Lovelstone in this parish in 1773. He took a prominent part in the founding of the first ophthalmic hospital (the Royal London) and discovered a new method of operating for cataract.

HUISH, NORTH (F10),

has a number of ancient estates and houses. Besides Huish itself, Broadley, Butterford and Lupridge were all Saxon estates and are described in Domesday Book. Broadley, in the Avon valley, is now substantially an Elizabethan mansion. Butterford was rebuilt as a mansion by the Palks about 1790. Black Hall and Norris also show traces of former mansions. Both Norris and Butterford gave their names to ancient families.

The parish church (dedication unknown but said to be St. Mary) was dedicated by Bishop Grandisson on 15 June 1336. Like Diptford, it has a medieval spire. The body of the church is probably early 14th-cent. work, enlarged in the 15th by the addition of a S. aisle. The granite font is dated 1662.

Bickham bridge is on the site of a very old crossing of the Avon. It is mentioned as a bridge in a charter of King Edgar dated 962 (*beoccan bricge*)[1] and appears to have joined two important ridgeways on the hills E. and W. of the Avon valley. The present bridge may well be of 16th-cent. date.

HUISH, SOUTH (E11),

lies in a beautiful valley opening on to Bigbury Bay. The parish church (St. Andrew) is now ruined. Its tower and walls appear to be of 13th-cent. date. In 1866 the old church was found to be hopelessly out of repair, and abandoned. The fine medieval chancel screen was rescued and set up in the private chapel of Bowringsleigh (see ALVINGTON WEST).

Hope, a picturesque fishing hamlet, was once a notable smuggling centre.

HUNTSHAM (H3). Huntsham Castle, on high ground bordering Tiverton parish, is a hill-fort of Iron Age date, and commands beautiful views. The church (All Saints) was enlarged and over-restored in 1856 and a N. aisle added 1871. It is of no interest. Huntsham Court was rebuilt in 1869-70.

HUNTSHAW (D3) church (St. Mary Magdalene) is partly an early 14th-cent. building, considerably reconstructed in the 15th, probably in and after 1439 when Bishop Lacy granted an indulgence in aid of the rebuilding of the fabric.[1] There are many late medieval tiles of Barnstaple manufacture in the chancel floor; but the church suffered somewhat from a complete restoration in 1862. Among the rectors was Blessed Cuthbert Mayne, instituted in 1561. He was born near Barnstaple and was the first seminary priest to suffer martyrdom. He was beatified by the Roman Catholic Church in 1886.

HUXHAM (H6) is a tiny parish in the Exe valley, with some attractive cottages near the church. The latter (St. Mary) is a small, plain building of early 14th-cent. date, but much rebuilt in 1865-71. The Norman font is a fine example of its period.

IDDESLEIGH (D5) is an excellent example of a cob and thatch village, most attractive to explore. The church (St. James) stands well, commanding splendid views of Dartmoor, including Cawsand Beacon, Yes Tor, and High Willhays. It is entirely 15th-cent., with excellent wagon-roofs to nave and N. aisle. In the N. chancel aisle is a noble recumbent effigy of a knight, c. 1250, probably a 13th-cent. squire of Iddesleigh and believed to be a Sully,

ancestor of the redoubtable Sir John Sully who is buried at Crediton.

Ash House is a very attractive house of the time of Charles II. When Sir Stafford Northcote (1818-87) was raised to the peerage in 1885 he took the title of Earl of Iddesleigh, a curious choice as his chief estates lay elsewhere.

IDE (G6) (pron. *Ede*) takes its name from St. Ida, to whom the church is dedicated.

The church, entirely rebuilt in 1834, is poor inside and out.

The vicarage, rebuilt about the same time as the church, is more attractive. Ide Bridge, over the little river Alphin, is mentioned as early as 1244.

IDEFORD (G8) lies in a beautiful hollow in the Haldon Hills. The church (St. Mary) is plain 15th-cent. and was excessively restored in 1852 and again in 1887-91. A Norman tympanum, discovered when the chancel was rebuilt in 1890, is built into the S. wall of the chancel (outside).

ILFRACOMBE (D1) is a seaside resort on the N. coast of Devon with distinctive and striking cliff scenery, arising from the slates which reach the sea in glistening rocks and reefs. Down to the end of the Napoleonic Wars it was simply a market town and fishing port, with a small overseas trade, but always overshadowed by Barnstaple and Bideford. By the time Lysons wrote it was "an agreeable summer residence" and was increasingly frequented as "a bathing-place." Herrings were, however, still more important than visitors. The population grew more rapidly during the 1830s, and there is a certain amount of attractive building of this period. The Bath House (1836) is a good Greek Revival building. Montpellier Place dates from the 1830s; Hillsborough Terrace is somewhat earlier, perhaps 1810-35. The most rapid growth took place between 1861 and 1891 when the population doubled (3851 to 7692), and the predominant architecture is therefore late Victorian. During the past fifty years Ilfracombe has hardly grown at all, in contrast to the rapid expansion of the S. coast resorts. It is exceedingly hilly, and has a more bracing climate than the S. coast. Moreover, the charms of its scenery are such as appeal to the few rather than the multitude.

There are few ancient buildings in the town. St. Nicholas's chapel on the Lantern Hill, at the entrance to the harbour, was a landmark for mariners and a votive chapel for fishermen and sailors like St. Michael's at Braunton. It is mainly a 15th-cent. building. Since the Reformation it has been used as a lighthouse. The parish church (Holy Trinity) is mostly 14th–15th-cent., with a Norman tower now half-enclosed within the N. aisle. The font is re-cut Norman, the pulpit Jacobean. Two of the windows have glass by Kempe.

Lee, about 3 m. W., contains a number of interesting cottages and farmhouses, some of 16th–17th-cent. date. The church (St. Matthew) was built in 1833, but many of the fittings are 17th-cent. The rock scenery of Lee Bay is very striking. 1½ m. farther W. is Bull Point, where the lighthouse was first lit in 1879.

The parish contains a number of fine old farmhouses, best of which is perhaps Damage Barton, once a medieval "mansion" and for long the seat of the Cutcliffes. It is a splendid example of a Devon *barton*, grouped around a courtyard, in part medieval but mostly 16th–17th-cent. It has its own mill, as at Westcott Barton in Marwood. Lin-

combe was a Domesday manor and a medieval mansion, and still retains much old work including oak-mullioned windows. Chambercombe Farm belonged to the Champernownes in the time of Henry II, and was a medieval mansion with a private chapel (licensed 1439). The present farmhouse is mainly 16th–17th-cent.

ILSINGTON (F8) is a large parish extending into the E. uplands of Dartmoor. It takes in Rippon Tor (1,564 ft.), Saddle Tor, and Hay Tor (1,490 ft.), and extends E. to the Bovey heath-country. The Hay Tor granite quarries are in this parish, and a good deal of the old Heytor railway (see ch. VIII).

Bagtor, Ingsdon, Sigford and Staplehill, were all small Domesday manors. Bagtor developed into a "mansion" and became the seat of John Ford in Henry VIII's time. John Ford, the dramatist, was born here and baptized in Ilsington church on 12 April 1586. The present house is apparently late 17th–early 18th-cent., but beside it is a good specimen of a 16th-cent. moorland farmhouse, with granite outbuildings, which may well be the Elizabethan house in which the dramatist was born.

Ilsington church (St. Michael) is an early 14th-cent. cruciform church, so commonly found in this part of Devon, enlarged in the late 15th cent. into a fully-aisled plan. Ashburton, Holne, and Widecombe show the same development in this district. At West Ogwell (q.v.), on the other hand, we find the original 14th-cent. cross-plan unaltered. Ilsington also received new roofs in the 15th-cent. reconstruction (note the carved bosses in the nave) and a richly carved rood-screen to nave and aisles. Some late detail on the screen suggests that it cannot be earlier than 1530.

INSTOW (C2) is now a small seaside

resort at the meeting of the Taw and Torridge in a beautiful estuary. The old village lies on the hillside above, commanding delightful views of Appledore and the bay beyond. The parish church (St. John the Baptist) is a pleasant building, with a 14th-cent. nave and chancel, and a N. aisle added by Richard Waterman and Emma his wife in 1547, as appears by an inscription on two capitals of the arcade. This aisle retains its original roof. The font and S. wall of the nave are Norman. In the S. transept is an attractive mural monument to a student—John Downe, son of the rector—who d. 1640 after two years at Oxford. His father was a nephew of Bishop Jewel, and wrote several religious tracts. Another mural monument (by Kendall of Exeter) commemorates Humphrey Sibthorpe (1797), who was Sherardian professor of botany at Oxford. His son John succeeded him in the chair, and endowed the chair of rural economy at Oxford.

The Sibthorpes lived at Fullingcott, a large farmhouse (formerly a mansion) built *c.* 1600. The country around it is very beautiful, with wide views of land and water. Bickleton and Worlington, now farms, are both recorded in Domesday Book.

INWARDLEIGH (D6) takes its name from Inwar, its Domesday owner. Other Domesday manors in this large parish were Curworthy, Oak, and Widefield.

The church (dedication unknown, but now attributed to St. Petrock) is a pleasant little 16th-cent. building, dulled internally by a too-thorough restoration in 1899. There is a fine Norman font, of an early cushion-bowl type, decorated with beautiful naturalistic sprays.

The Barton, beside the church, is on the site of the ancient mansion of the Coffins, who held the manor from the 12th cent. to the 14th, and contains some features of antiquarian interest.

IPPLEPEN (G9) is a grey and rather dismal village, with much bad modern building. The church (St. Andrew) stands well at the head of the village, and is almost entirely a 15th-cent. rebuilding. The Perpendicular windows of the nave are notably good. The font and rood-screen are said to be *c.* 1430-50. The pulpit is a magnificent specimen of 15th-cent. art, with canopied niches from which the statuettes have disappeared. There are also two parclose screens.

At Ipplepen was founded *c.* 1100 a dependent cell of the Augustinian abbey of St. Pierre at Fougères in Brittany. Remains of Ipplepen priory are said to be incorporated in a house now known as The Priory. Ambrook is first recorded in 1238, and was a medieval franklin's "mansion," of which traces survive in the present house of Great Ambrook.

Battleford, now a small farm, was a Domesday manor. So, too, was Combe Fishacre. Dainton, a hamlet with extensive quarries, is recorded in a Saxon charter of 956.

IVYBRIDGE (E10) is now a small market town. It was constituted a civil parish in 1894, formed out of parts of Ugborough and Ermington. The church (St. John) was built in 1882, but there was a chapel here as early as 1402. Ivybridge took its name from the ancient bridge over the Erme, which probably goes back to the early 13th cent. when the rise of Plymouth brought a great increase of traffic along this road. The present bridge is a single-arched structure of some age, difficult to date, and now by-passed by a modern bridge. The Erme valley above the town is romantically beautiful. There are grist and paper mills on the river. Woodland Farm is a 16th-cent. (and later) house.

JACOBSTOWE (D5) church (St. James) was over-restored in 1902, and is of no interest. Lower Cadham is an early 17th-cent. farmhouse on a much older site; and Broomford was a Domesday manor.

KELLY (B7) lies in pleasantly rolling and wooded country. The church (St. Mary) is in the usual local 15th-cent. style, especially noticeable in the bold W. tower with its massive pinnacles. Though the Kellys were established here at the Norman Conquest, being descended from Motbert who held the manor in 1086, there are no monuments of any note to them in the church. The Devonshire squires rarely went in for expensive marble monuments, and the Kellys were no exception. The family still survives, but Kelly House has been vacated and is now a guest-house. It is a Tudor house, remodelled in the 18th cent. These parishes where old families have ruled for centuries have a flavour all their own, even a characteristic smell of wet, decaying plantations.

KENN (H7) is a luxuriantly fertile parish on a deep red soil, with fine timber everywhere. The parish has or had a number of good parks and houses —notably Haldon, Trehill, Bickham, and Woodlands. Haldon House, superbly sited against the background of the wooded hills, was one of the most notable country houses in Devon (Plate 14). It was begun c. 1735 by Sir George Chudleigh, the 4th bart., upon a new site, and completed after his death in 1738. About 1770 it was purchased by Robert Palk who had made a fortune in India. He greatly enlarged the fine timbered park. The Palks (later Lords Haldon) lived here until 1892. The house is now mostly demolished, the small remains occupied as flats.

The Belvedere, on one of the highest points of Haldon, was erected about 1780 by Sir Robert Palk in memory of his great friend Stringer Lawrence, who had been Governor of Madras. Haldon Belvedere, as it is always called, is a landmark over a great part of Devon, and commands magnificent views. Trehill (early 19th cent.) is on the site of an older house. Bickham was the seat of the Shorts from Elizabethan days until recently.

The church (St. Andrew), beautifully situated and built of a deep-red sandstone from the Trehill quarry, is an interesting building. It is essentially an early 14th-cent. structure, enlarged and given new windows late in the 15th. There are early 15th-cent. bench-ends, and a Purbeck marble font (early 13th cent.). The rood-screen, extending the entire width of the church, is the usual 15th-cent. type. In 1889 the rood and its figures (carved at Ober Ammergau) were added, the first rood to be restored in Devon since the Reformation. The paintings of saints in the lower panels, done about 1500, form a singularly interesting series in their selection and arrangement: the male saints are all to the north of the central doorway, the female saints to the south: the only example in Devon of this correct arrangement. Notice also the canopy above the rood. There is a mural monument to Richard Waltham of Trehill (d. 1637), one-time recorder of Exeter.

KENNERLEIGH (G5) is a small village and parish in quite unspoiled country. The church (St. John the Baptist) was much restored about 1847 and partly rebuilt, but is not unattractive. Oliver says it was originally dedicated to St. Clement and that a chapel of St. Clement was first mentioned here in 1334, dependent on the mother-church of Crediton.

KENTISBEARE (J5) has a 15th–early 16th-cent. church (St. Mary) with a beautiful checkered tower and exceptionally interesting fittings, of which the rood-screen is the most striking. This extends in ten bays across the nave and S. aisle and is the model or prototype for a widespread class of screen which extends well into Somerset. The screen bears the arms of John Whytyng (d. 1530) whose altar-tomb is in the S. aisle. Until 1858 this bore the brass effigies of John Whytyng and his wife Anne. At the W. end of the church is a very fine Caroline gallery (1632) with an inscription. The S. arcade of Beer stone has some good carving: on one capital is a woolpack and a Tudor ship on the heraldic shield of the Merchant Adventurers of London, possibly a reference to the fortune of John Whytyng who built this aisle and probably gave the screen. In the aisle is the tomb of Mary (Wotton), great-aunt to Lady Jane Grey.

The ancient parish of Blackborough is now united with Kentisbeare for all purposes. The church (All Saints) was rebuilt in the Early English style in 1838 by the 4th and last Earl of Egremont, who also built Blackborough House (1838) in the Italianate style. This is now a training home for young wayfarers.

Kentisbeare parish lies in the fertile red-sandstone country and had no fewer than nine Domesday manors. Wood,

the seat of the Whytyngs from the 14th cent. to the 16th, and then the home of Sir Gawen Carew, has some medieval features.

Priesthill or Priesthall, adjoining Kentisbeare churchyard, is a medieval church-house, one of the most untouched examples of its kind with its original oaken screens, buttery hatches, minstrels' gallery, and oak-mullioned windows. Among the numerous farmhouses of the parish, those of Orway, Kingsford, Sainthill, Sowell, Aller. Court and Ponchidown are all worth seeing.

KENTISBURY (E1) is a parish without a village. The church (St. Thomas) has a fine late 15th-cent. tower built of the dark local slate, and a S. porch of the same period, but the restoration of 1874-5 was a disaster to the rest of the fabric. Breadwick and Patchole were Domesday estates. Kentisbury Down, rising to 1,105 ft. with fine views over Exmoor, has a number of barrows.

KENTON (H7) is a large and pleasant village in the luxuriant New Red Sandstone country between the Exe estuary and the Haldon Hills. The church (All Saints), built of red sandstone, is a fine example of the fully-aisled Devonshire plan, entirely of 15th-cent. date, with a handsome W. tower showing Somerset influence. The S. porch is singularly beautiful. Internally, the effect is one of great richness. The white Beer stone arcades have capitals carved with foliage of the local type and with a variety of figure-sculpture. The rood-screen (late 15th-cent.) is one of the finest in Devon. Like Kentisbeare and Dartmouth, it seems to be the prototype of many others, of massive and stately proportions and retaining much ancient colour and gilding. The lower panels have a remarkable series of paintings, chiefly of saints and apostles. The pulpit is a careful reconstruction by Herbert Read of the medieval one destroyed by the "restorer" (Ashworth of Exeter) in 1866. The reredos is a fine piece of work by Kempe. There are monuments to Sir Nicholas Martin of Oxton (1653), Elizabeth Martin (1695), and John Rashleigh of Menabilly (1651).

Mowlish Farm is recorded in Domesday Book, Cofford in a charter dated 1044. Oxton is an ancient estate, probably dating from the 12th cent., one of the many attractive small estates in the neighbourhood of Exeter which successful city merchants liked to buy. It belonged at different times to the Exeter merchant-families of Wilford, Hurst, and Martin, passing eventually to the Rev. John Swete who built the present house about 1789, and laid out the beautiful grounds. The house is now a girls' school.

Starcross is a large village in the parish, on the estuary of the Exe and the ancient landing-place for Kenton. There was an inn here (the Courtenay Arms) and "several neat buildings" by the time Polwhele wrote (1793), and the opening of the South Devon Railway in 1846 brought more people. Starcross never fulfilled expectations as a watering-place, being overshadowed by Dawlish, but it still wears, along the river front, a placid air of early Victorian days.

KERSWELL (see ABBOTS KERSWELL and KINGSKERSWELL).

KILMINGTON (L6) is chiefly interesting for Coryton, a handsome house built of brick with Portland stone dressings in 1754-6 by Benedictus Marwood Tucker, sheriff of Devon in 1763. Some remains of the older mansion may be seen at Old Coryton. The parish church (St. Giles) was rebuilt, except the tower, in 1862 and contains nothing of note except a large marble monument to Thomas Southcott of Dulshayes, erected in 1735.

KINGSBRIDGE (F11) is a small town on a steep hill which rises from the head of a beautiful, many-branched estuary. There was a bridge here in the 10th cent. (referred to in a charter of 962) linking two large royal estates—Alvington to the W. and Chillington to the E.: hence known as " King's bridge." The abbot of Buckfast obtained a market here in 1219, and the new town began to grow. By 1238 it was a borough, though it was never incorporated in later times. The neighbouring manor of Dodbrooke, now joined to Kingsbridge, and part of it for civil purposes, was granted a market in 1257 and reckoned to be a borough by 1319.[1] But it never grew to any size: in 1801 it had only 608 people.

Kingsbridge contains much good 18th–19th-cent. building. In the Fore Street are several modest late Georgian houses and inns. The Shambles (or Market Arcade) was rebuilt in 1796. It now extends over the pavement in six bays with granite piers, five of which are Elizabethan (1586). The Grammar School, founded and built by Thomas Crispin in 1670, contains a full-length portrait of him. On the Promenade is Pindar Lodge, the birthplace of John Wolcot (1738-1819), the satirist and poet who wrote under the name of Peter Pindar. He was educated at Kingsbridge Grammar School. His birthplace was largely rebuilt about 1800. William Cookworthy (1705-80), who discovered "china clay" in England and produced the first true English porcelain, was also born in Kingsbridge.

Kingsbridge church (St. Edmund) is mainly a 13th-cent. building, enlarged by the addition of aisles in the 15th. There is a Flaxman monument to the wife of Major Hawkins, and in the chancel a fine miserere.

Dodbrooke consists chiefly of one street, at the top of which is the uninteresting church of St. Thomas Becket. This is mostly 15th-cent. in date, too much restored. It has a fine rood-screen and parclose screen. Well House has some 16th-cent. work in a mainly Georgian house. Unlike most small Devon market towns, Dodbrooke grew throughout the 19th cent. By the 1880s it had twice as many people as in 1801 —a complete reversal of the usual trend. It had an active coasting trade, a shipbuilding yard, a tannery, two breweries, an agricultural implement works, and a great cattle market every month: a true local community solidly founded on its own resources and needs. The railway came in 1893, and almost immediately the population began to fall, as it did at Kingsbridge also. Since then they (particularly Kingsbridge) have risen to favour as a holiday centre, and have grown again.

KINGSKERSWELL (G9) is a large village, by reason of its nearness to Newton Abbot and Torquay. The church (St. Mary) is one of the common type in this part of Devon: an early 14th-cent. building (with a W. tower of that date), which was enlarged during the 15th cent. by the conversion of the transepts into full aisles. In the N. aisle are three mutilated recumbent effigies of the Dinhams who held the manor in the 14th–15th cents. They probably represent Sir John Dinham (d. 1428) and his two wives (*c.* 1394, *c.* 1410).

Near the church are the small re-mains of the fortified manor house of the Dinhams, described incorrectly on the map as a " Castle."

KING'S NYMPTON (E4) is a large village on the hills E. of the Taw valley. *Nemeton* is a sacred or consecrated place or grove. There can be little doubt that among the earliest places of Celtic worship were groves, some of which remained sacred after Christian churches were built. In these groves would have stood symbols or images of the Celtic gods and an altar. Caesar speaks of the "consecrated place" where the Druids met yearly. The Old Irish word *nemed* means "sacred grove."[1]

King's Nympton church (St. James) is mainly a 15th-cent. building, with a massive W. tower that may be older. All the roofs, including that of the porch, have remarkable carved bosses, portraying foliage and heads of men and women. The men are all grotesque and have mouth-foliage. The fittings of the church are interesting, most notable being a perfect rood-screen of unusual design, with tracery of the " Exe Valley " type, and fan-vaulting and cornices similar to those at Hartland and Burrington. The roof above the screen has a painted canopy of honour to the rood, similar to that at Lapford. There are box-pews, Jacobean altar-rails, and an 18th-cent. painted ceiling to the chancel, the latter a memorial to the Southcomb family.

King's Nympton Park was first enclosed by Sir Lewis Pollard, the judge (*c.* 1465-1540), who bought the manor and built a mansion here in Henry VII's time. The present house is an attractive early Georgian mansion in red brick, built by James Buller (d. 1765).

KINGSTEIGNTON (G8) is a large and unattractive village, with much yellow brick and cold grey limestone, but it has a long history. It was one of the early villages in the Saxon conquest, founded probably *c.* 700 or shortly afterwards, and was the head of a vast royal estate centred on the Teign estuary. The church (St. Michael) is a spacious building, entirely rebuilt in the 15th cent., with a good W. tower of Devonian limestone. The remainder of the church, except the S. porch, is of new red sandstone. The windows and font are excellent. The screen was cut down in 1801 as being "decayed and ruinous,"[1] but fourteen panels of the base remain on either side of the chancel, painted with figures of saints and bishops. There are many inscribed floor-slabs, memorials of the 17th-cent. gentry in the parish. Their houses, some of which retain old work, were Ware Barton, Whiteway Barton, Babcombe, Gappah and Bellamarsh. The parish has large modern potteries, based upon the excellent local clay, much of which is exported to other parts of the country.

KINGSTON (E11) village has many attractive old houses. The church (St. James the Less), built of the local slate, is mainly an early 14th-cent. building, probably cruciform originally, with N. and S. transepts. The N. transept was enlarged into an aisle, by a westward extension, in the 15th cent. At Wonwell and Langston are traces of former "mansions."

KINGSWEAR (G10) is a small town on the E. side of Dartmouth Harbour, about 1 m. from the mouth of the Dart. At the mouth is Kingswear Castle, erected in 1491-1502 as part of the defences of this important harbour (Frontispiece). It was so exposed to the elements that the iron guns had to be replaced by brass. Soon after 1643 the increasing range of guns on the Dartmouth side allowed it to be abandoned. It was held by Sir Henry Cary for the king during the Civil War, but he found it necessary to throw up additional defences on the brow of the hill, at what is now called Mount Ridley, which remains a good example of a Civil War redoubt. It was captured with the town by Sir Thomas Fairfax on 19 January 1646. Kingswear Castle remained in good repair and was converted into a summer dwelling for Mr. Seale Hayne in 1855.[2]

Kingswear itself contains little of interest except a number of very attractive early 19th-cent. "villas" overlooking the harbour, of which Brookhill, just SE. of the town, is perhaps the most notable.

Kingswear church (St. Thomas) was a daughter-church of Brixham in which parish and manor Kingswear formerly lay. The church was rebuilt, except the tower, in 1845, and is of little interest. A regular ferry has crossed the Dart from Kingswear to Dartmouth from time immemorial.

KNOWSTONE (G3) (pron. *Now-stone*). The 15th-cent. church (St. Peter) has a good tower, and a plain Norman S. doorway. The N. arcade, said to be Norman, is more probably a 17th-cent. rebuilding. There are good pews of late 18th-cent. or early 19th-cent. date, and mural monuments to Philip Shapcote (1690) and Joan Culme (1691). Sir John Berry (1635-90), a distinguished naval commander under Charles II, who was knighted for his bravery at the battle of Sole Bay in 1665, was born at the vicarage, his father Daniel then being vicar. Two Froudes were vicars here from 1767 to 1853, the second one being the infamous " Parson Froude " who held the living with that of Molland. This unspeakable oaf is buried at Knowstone. He left his two parishes, like himself, in a heathen and lawless condition. He is Parson Chowne in Blackmore's *Maid of Sker*.

Wadham was a Domesday estate and the original home of the Wadham family who founded the Oxford college of that name. The present farmhouse is of no architectural interest. Little Wadham, near by, is a good example of a farmhouse rebuilt *c.* 1600. Shapcott Barton, in the east of the parish, was also a Domesday estate, held by Algar in 1066 and retained by him after the Conquest. The Shapcotts may well descend from this 11th-cent. owner. The last of the Shapcotts died at Exeter about 1770, when the estate was sold for the first time. The present farmhouse is mainly Elizabethan, and in part medieval.

LAMERTON (c8) church (St. Peter) was burnt in 1877. It was rebuilt (except the tower) in the 15th-cent. style in 1879-80. It is a spacious church, with large Perpendicular windows filled with clear glass. There is a fine monument to the Tremayne family, erected in 1588, and there are some good incised slate tombstones in the churchyard. Opposite the church is the medieval priest's house, carefully restored in 1934. Chaddlehanger, a farmhouse, is 15th-cent. and later; Hurlditch Court is late 16th-cent. (rebuilt); and Collacombe is a notable Elizabethan mansion, the home of the Tremaynes from the 14th cent. to the end of the 17th when they moved to Sydenham, in Marystow (q.v.). The great hall (now divided) contains an enormous transomed window, and a plaster mantelpiece dated 1574. Collacombe was a Saxon estate. So, too, were Ottery and Willestrew.

LANDCROSS (c3) is the smallest parish in Devon, almost wholly contained within a beautiful sweep of the Torridge. The small church (Holy Trinity) was rebuilt in 1435,[1] and contains a Norman font from the older fabric, and a fine set of carved benchends (early 16th cent.). General Monk was baptized here 11 December 1608.

LANDKEY (D2) church (St. Paul) is most attractive, entirely a late 15thcent. building, except for the chancel which was rebuilt in 1870. It is plastered and whitened throughout, with ceiled and bossed roofs, and possesses an elegant early Perpendicular font *c.* 1400. The N. aisle contains three stone effigies of the Beaupels who held the manor of Landkey under the Bishop of Exeter. The small S. transept is the Acland chapel, and contains a fine coloured monument to Sir Arthur Acland (1610) and his wife.

The Aclands, one of the most notable of Devon families, originated at Acland Barton, from which they took their name in Henry II's time. They continued to own it until 1945, when Sir Richard Acland sold it to the tenant. The farmhouse is a very interesting example of a late 15th-cent. "mansion," remodelled internally in 1591, and again altered slightly in the 18th cent. (plate 35).[2]

LANGTREE (c4), like so many North Devon villages, stands high on a ridge, its bold church-tower a landmark for miles. The church (dedication unknown) is a 15th-cent. building, with a fine 17th-cent. pulpit.

LAPFORD (F5) is a pleasant village on the rising of a hill above the river Yeo. Bury was a Domesday manor, taking its name from the earthwork surrounding it and giving its name in turn to the Bury family who owned it for several centuries.[1] Their mansion, now a large farmhouse, is 16th–17th-cent. in date. Adjoining the barton is the detached ruin of the Burys' private chapel. It is one of the best-preserved buildings of its kind, and is undoubtedly the chapel of St. James licensed by Bishop Lacy in 1434. Several other farmhouses in the parish are good examples of 16th and 17th-cent. architecture. The village also has many ancient houses, including Court Barton, formerly a manor house.

The church (St. Thomas Becket) is almost entirely a 15th-cent. building, of no especial note, and badly restored. But few parish churches have such an array of ancient carved woodwork: bench-ends, roofs and rood-screen. The bench-ends are remarkable and varied, and are worth a close study. Most are c. 1530-40, with distinctively Renaissance designs. The wagon-roofs have carved cornices, wall-plates, and bosses. The rood-screen is exceptionally fine. In general treatment it is like that at Atherington, but the richly decorated cornices are more like those at Hartland. The vaulting of the screen is perfect, with enriched panels.

LEW, NORTH (D6), is a large village for these parts, full of character and good rural building. There are superb views of the N. and W. edge of Dartmoor from the lanes round about.

The church (St. Thomas Becket), though badly over-restored in 1885, is interesting for its fittings. It is mostly 15th-16th cent. in date, with granite N. and S. arcades. The principal features are the carved roofs of the aisles; the screen, which incorporates parts of the original rich 15th-cent. screen demolished during a "restoration"; and the boldly carved bench-ends, of which

a considerable number date from Henry VIII's reign. One is dated 1537, probably the date of all those that are not modern.

The parish contained several Domesday manors—Lew itself, Rutleigh (formerly Redcliff), Gorhuish, and East and West Kimber.

LEW TRENCHARD (c7) is chiefly notable as the parish of the Rev. Sabine Baring-Gould (1834-1924), one of the best known of all Devonshire parsons, who was rector here for 43 years. He was one of the last of the "squarsons," a hymn-writer, theologian, antiquary, novelist, and musician, who published over a hundred volumes. Among his many achievements he collected the old folk songs of Devon and (with Cecil Sharp) published them. His two volumes of *Reminiscences* are very readable.

The church (St. Peter) is mainly an over-restored 15th-cent. building. The woodwork is, however, notable. The medieval rood-screen was destroyed by Baring-Gould's grandfather in 1833, but Baring-Gould collected the fragments as a boy and had it reconstructed in 1899. It is a fine example of modern carving. The pulpit, modelled on the ancient pulpits of Kenton and Launceston, was added in 1900. The church contains some carved Tudor bench-ends, and many of good modern workmanship. There are several Gould memorials, mostly incised slate slabs from the early 17th cent. onwards. Lew House and estate were bought by the Goulds in 1625. The house is partly of that period, but was much restored by Baring-Gould out of the proceeds of his copious books. The Dower House by the river Lew is dated 1664.

LIFTON (B7) was undoubtedly one of

the earliest villages to be founded in West Devon by the Saxons, and was of considerable military importance, being within a mile of the Tamar and the Cornish frontier. It is the *Liwtune* referred to in King Alfred's will 880-5, and it also appears to be the *Leowtun* where Athelstan held his court in November 931.[1]

Ashleigh was a Domesday manor, later a medieval mansion, and now a farmhouse. Wortham was also a medieval mansion and remains substantially unchanged to this day. Part of it may date from the 14th cent., but it is mostly late 15th–early 16th-cent., reconstructed internally in the early 17th cent., as so often happened, when the medieval hall-house was converted into something warmer and more convenient. The house has recently been rescued from its decay as a farmhouse and well restored. Other ancient farms are Tinhay and Gatherley, both recorded before 1200. Lifton Park is comparatively modern, the house dating only from 1815 and later. It commands beautiful views of the Tamar valley and the Cornish hills. Smallacombe, now a farmhouse, has doorways of 15th-cent. granite. The house was modernised in the early 18th cent. (in brick) and "turned around" to face the other way.

The church (St. Mary) is a 15th-cent. building, badly restored in 1871. There are some traces of 14th-cent. work and there is a magnificent late 12th-cent. font. The monuments are interesting: (1) to John Dynham of Wortham (1641) and his wife Margaret (1649); (2) a splendid monument to the Harrises of Hayne, 1590, 1618, 1631, repaired and beautified by their descendants in the 18th cent.; (3) an incised brass to John Harris of Hayne, 1657.

LITTLEHAM (J7) has lost some of its rural charm since the rapid growth of Exmouth (*q.v.*) which now covers a good deal of the parish. The church (St. Margaret and St. Andrew) is mainly 15th–early 16th-cent in date, with a 13th-cent. chancel, the whole restored in 1884. The N. or Drake aisle was added in 1528, and has one window with contemporary glass. There are various memorials to the Drake family, who lived at Sprattshayes, now a farm. In the chantry chapel is a fine memorial by Turnerelli to Lady Nelson, the unhappy widow of the great admiral, who d. in London (1831), but is buried here in the SE. corner of the churchyard.

Sprattshayes is now a house of *c.* 1700, improved in the 19th cent. Green Farm, near by, is 17th–18th-cent.

LITTLEHAM (c3) lies in pleasant, wooded, and hilly country S. of Bideford. It has little of interest except the 15th-cent. church (St. Swithin). The original rood-screen was removed long ago, and the present screen and rood-loft are modern, designed by Mr. Temple Moore of London, who followed the general arrangement and style of those at Patricio in Monmouthshire. He also designed the striking tomb with alabaster effigy of General Crealock (1891). The original bench-ends (late Henry VIII) have been incorporated with the new seating. They are of a most interesting Renaissance type with grotesque heads, dolphins, etc., carved with great delicacy and imagination. There is some excellent stained glass by Kempe.

LODDISWELL (F11) is a large, untidy, and planless village. The church (St. Michael) is almost entirely a 14th-cent. cruciform church, enlarged in the 15th by the usual extension of the S. transept into a full aisle, and by the addition of chancel aisles or chapels on both sides. The font is Norman. The N. transept seems to have been the Woolston chapel, as it contains many memorials to the Wises of Woolston, and to earlier owners, the Furlongs.

Woolston is a 17th-cent. mansion, with the remains of a more ancient house near by. Hatch is a good example of an Elizabethan or early Jacobean farmstead. Hazelwood House was built in 1830 by Richard Peek, Esq., after retiring from business as a merchant in London.

Loddiswell Rings, or Blackdown Camp, commanding wide views of the South Hams, consists of a mount, with an inner bailey or courtyard of one acre, and an outer bailey of ten acres. It lies just E. of the great ridgeway from the Moor down to the sea, and seems to be a 12th-cent. castle site, of which there is no documentary record.

LOXBEARE (H4) has an interesting little church, and not much else. Leigh Barton was the Domesday manor of *Lega* and contains a certain amount of old work. The church (unknown dedication) is a 12th-cent. structure. The square and massive W. tower is probably Norman and contains its set of three medieval bells in their original cage. They are from the foundry of I.T. and are said to date from Henry VI's time. The 12th-cent. S. doorway is notable. Though the interior has been Victorianised, it is still pleasant. A fine pulpit and sounding board (*c.* 1700) remain, but much has gone. The screen was destroyed at the "restoration" of 1832. The royal arms over the S. door (1725) are rustic and pleasing.

LOXHORE (E2) church (St. Michael) is mainly 15th-cent. in date. It was over-restored in 1876-82, but has a number of things worth seeing: a N. arcade carried on two 15th-cent. oak piers, a font with a medieval carved cover, and some good Hammond monuments (1684, 1704, 1727).

LUFFINCOTT (B6) is a small, remote parish on the Cornish border, commanding fine views over the Tamar valley. The church (St. James) was over-restored in 1893 and is of no interest except for its bells, two of which are pre-Reformation. The tower was rebuilt in 1791.

LUNDY (A1), the only island of any size off the coast of Devon, lies 11 m. NNW. of Hartland Point, about 22 m. NW. of Instow with which there is a regular service by motor-boat, and in the entrance to the Bristol Channel. It is about 3 m. long, averages about ½ m. wide, and covers some 920 acres. It is composed mostly of granite, with slates at the S. end, and forms a tableland about 400 ft. above the sea. The highest point is at Beacon Hill (471 ft.), from which there are magnificent views of the Welsh coast one way, and the Devon and Cornish coasts the other. The name Lundy is derived from the Old Norse words *lundi*, "puffin," and *ey*, "island"; and puffins still nest on the island in large numbers. The island was well known to the Scandinavian pirates who harried the shores of Wales and Devon, and is indeed first mentioned by name in the Orkneyinga-saga in 1139-48.

Lundy was occupied in prehistoric times, for flint flakes and pottery have come from the small barrows that dot the surface of the island, but nothing is known of its history before the 12th cent. At that time it belonged to the turbulent family of the Mariscos, who became pirates and terrorised the neighbouring coasts until William de Marisco was caught and hanged in 1242.[1] In the early 17th cent. the island again became the haunt of pirates, and was frequently attacked by the Spanish and French. Lord Say and Sele obtained Lundy in 1656. He is said to have retired there during the Protectorate, and to be buried under the W. window of the old St. Helen's chapel. The island has frequently changed hands in recent times. In 1834 it was bought for 9,400 guineas by W. H. Heaven, who claimed it to be a "free island" and successfully resisted the jurisdiction of the mainland magistrates. Lundy was in consequence sometimes referred to as "the kingdom of Heaven." It belongs in fact to the county of Devon, and has always been part of the hundred of Braunton.

A lighthouse was erected in 1819 on the highest point of the island but experience showed that the light was frequently obscured by fog at that height, and in 1897 the North Light and South Light, at either end of the island, were substituted for it. The only landing place among the towering cliffs is at the SE. end, in the shelter of Rat Island. Above the landing place are the few houses on the island, and the new St. Helen's church (1889). The old church, used until about 1747, stood near the Old Lighthouse where some foundations are to be seen. Also at the SE. end of the island is the square keep of Marisco Castle (probably 13th cent.) now converted into cottages. It was re-fortified during the Civil Wars.

Lundy has long been notable for its multitude of rabbits and its colonies of puffins. It is also of particular interest to geologists and botanists. The cliff scenery is spectacularly wild. On the Shutter Rock, at the SW. point of the island, Charles Kingsley caused Don Guzman's great ship to be wrecked in *Westward Ho!*; and in 1906 H.M.S. *Montagu* was in fact wrecked here. Rat Island is one of the few remaining homes of the aboriginal black rat, now almost exterminated by the brown rat. The granite of Lundy was used for the Thames Embankment, and was long used for parish churches on the Devon mainland.

LUPPITT (K5) is a country of deep, winding lanes running from one ancient farmstead to another, haunted by buzzards in the valleys and by curlews on the heaths above, and full of flowers. One gets a wonderful view of this great field-patterned bowl on emerging from Honiton Tunnel, on the Southern Region line, going W. In the foreground of the view is the curious isolated knob of Dumpdon Hill (855 ft.), crowned by a fine kite-shaped earthwork, some 800 ft. long from N. to S. and 370 ft. wide at its broad N. end. On three sides the hill slopes precipitously; at the more level N. end are additional defences. The earthwork has never been scientifically excavated, but it is probably a hill-fort of late (pre-Roman) Iron Age date. The views from the summit are striking.

Luppitt itself is little more than a hamlet; the isolated farmstead is the characteristic dwelling. Of these, besides Luppitt itself, Greenway Farm, Mohuns Ottery, and Shapcombe, are all mentioned in Domesday Book. Moorland farm had a chapel in 1308.

Mohuns Ottery lies on the rising of a hill above the Otter valley, grey and fortress-like from a distance. By 1303 the Carews had succeeded the Mohuns here, and established a large house and a park. They lived here until the death of Sir Peter Carew in 1575, when the estate came to the Southcotts. In the

16th cent. the Carews were among the leading Protestants of the county and were implicated in Wyatt's Rebellion. Sir Peter Carew (1512-75) probably rebuilt the house: the initials P. C. appear in the spandrels of the front doorway. The mansion had become a farmhouse by Lysons's day and was reduced in size. It was mostly burnt down about 1868, but a considerable part of the gatehouse remains.

Luppitt church (St. Mary) is a 14th-cent. cruciform building with N. and S. transepts, restored in 1885-90 and again in 1923. The two remarkable features of the church are the sculptured font of the 10th cent., and the fine 14th-cent. cradle roof in the nave and transepts.

LUSTLEIGH (F7) is a picturesque village with a good deal of excellent domestic building in granite of 16th–18th-cent. date (plate 38), and also some "olde worlde" fabrications that followed the "discovery" of the village. The moorland scenery W. of the village is locally famous, especially at Lustleigh Cleave overhanging the beautiful little river Bovey. Becka Falls, also a famous beauty spot, are near by on the Becka Brook, though actually in Manaton parish.

The church (St. John the Baptist) is an attractive and interesting building, ranging in date from the 13th cent. to the early 16th. In the S. transept is the effigy of Sir William Prouz (1329), and in the N. aisle wall two other effigies, probably also Prouzes though sometimes erroneously called Dinhams.[1] The rood-screen is unique, being almost certainly a post-Reformation and coarse copy of the fine screen at Bridford. It bears the pomegranate badge of Katherine of Aragon, but a date in Mary's reign (1553-8) has been suggested for it.

The Rev. William Davy (1743-1826) was for many years curate of Lustleigh, and here he printed, at the rectory and on a printing-press constructed by himself, the 26 unreadable volumes of his *System of Divinity*, besides six volumes of his sermons on which he lost £100.

Just across the stream from Lustleigh village (though in Bovey Tracey parish) is Wreyland, where Cecil Torr wrote his delightful three volumes of *Small Talk at Wreyland*, of gossip and talk about this bit of Devonshire countryside during the space of a hundred years or so.

LYDFORD (D7) is a small village and a long-decayed borough on the NW. foothills of Dartmoor (plate 11), with a parish that takes in an enormous tract of the Moor and is reckoned at some 50,000 acres. The village stands on a narrow tongue of land above the Lyd, which enters a remarkable wooded gorge immediately below. There is no doubt that the site of Lydford was chosen for military reasons. It was one of the four *burhs* of Devon, set up by Alfred for defence against the Danes, and was one of the four Domesday boroughs two hundred years later. It was never a walled town, but was defended by a massive earthen rampart and stockade. This rampart, drawn across the neck of the promontory, is still clearly visible on either side of the road at the NE. end of the village.

At the SW. tip of the promontory a castle was probably thrown up between 1066 and 1086, as Domesday Book records of the royal borough of Lydford that "40 houses have been laid waste since King William has had England." It seems likely that the mount and ditch about 100 yds. SW. of the present stone keep represents the site of this 11th-cent. castle. In 1195 this was super-

seded by the great square stone keep, of
which the gutted shell still stands, built
expressly for the custody of offenders
against the forest and stannary laws.
By the early 12th cent. the military
importance of Lydford had passed away
to Launceston Castle, the key to the
whole of Cornwall, and to Okehampton
Castle.

Lydford was one of the four Saxon

lanes that cross the present street at
right angles inside the ramparted area.

The church (St. Petrock) stands near
the castle keep. It is a 15th-cent. building in granite, with a N. aisle added in
1890. There is an excellent modern
screen of the Devonshire type by Bligh
Bond (1904), and some finely carved
modern bench-ends. One window contains medieval glass brought from else-

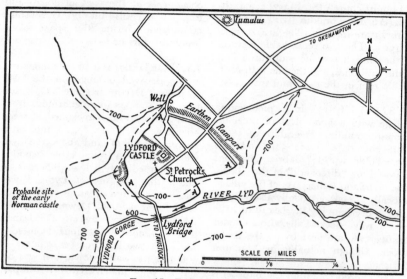

FIG. 15—EARLY LYDFORD

*The line marked A indicates the probable limit of the built-up area. The open fields
of Lydford lay to the N.E. of the town between the Rampart and Fernworthy Downs*

mints of Devon. Its coins are known
from the reign of Ethelred II (979-1016)
to that of Edward the Confessor (1042-
66).[1] But just as its military importance
passed away at an early date to Launceston and Okehampton, so its commercial life decayed also with the rise
of Tavistock and of Okehampton. One
can still trace the lines of the early
medieval streets, in the grass-grown

where. In the churchyard is an in-
genious epitaph to George Routleigh,
a local watchmaker. Lydford Gorge,
a remarkable place, is now National
Trust property.

Princetown is in the parish of Lydford, a grim little town some 1,400 ft.
above sea level, with an abominable
climate of fog, snow, wind, and more
than 80 in. of cold rain—sometimes

over 100. It stands on a *col* between the two Hessary Tors, exposed to the bitter N. and E. winds, the least suitable place that could ever have been chosen for a town. But the site was dictated by Sir Thomas Tyrwhitt so as to be near his granite quarries.

As early as 1780 a farm, named Prince Hall, was reclaimed on the site of an ancient tenement near Two Bridges, and in 1785 Mr. Tyrwhitt (later Sir Thomas), who had been appointed Lord Warden of the Stannaries, set about improving the moor at a place which he named Tor Royal, about ½ m. SE. of Princetown. Here he made a productive estate and built a house in 1798.[1] He was later instrumental in building the road from Tavistock to Princetown, and the other good roads that now cross the Moor and make it (or some of it) accessible to the motorist.

It was Sir Thomas Tyrwhitt who proposed that a prison be built on the Moor to house the thousands of captives of the Napoleonic Wars, who had become too numerous to lodge in the prisons and prison-ships at Plymouth. The site was given by the Prince of Wales, who held the lands of the Duchy of Cornwall to which all the Moor belonged: hence the name Princetown. The prison was built in 1806 (architect, Daniel Alexander) at a cost of £130,000 and at one time between seven and nine thousand prisoners were crammed into it.

A small town grew up near the prison. Two large inns were built during the war; one of them is the present Duchy Hotel. Many of the prisoners had prize-money to come from their own country; many others made their own in their hammocks at night, even forging Bank of England and local bank notes, which they passed off in the great daily market held in the prison. With the closing of the prison in 1816 the town almost collapsed, but the completion of the Dartmoor Railway in 1823 brought back many people to the granite quarries. The prison remained derelict until 1850, when it was reopened for prisoners serving long sentences. It has since been considerably extended.

The prehistoric antiquities of Dartmoor are too numerous to mention. Some are referred to in Part I, and all the more important are marked on the special map (Fig. 5). Reference should also be made to the other semi-moorland parishes, principally North Bovey, Chagford, Cornwood, Manaton, Walkhampton and Widecombe-in-the-Moor.

LYMPSTONE (H7) opens out between low sandstone cliffs on to the Exe estuary. The views from the shore across the river to the woods of Mamhead and Powderham and the Haldon skyline, are strikingly beautiful. The village is still unspoilt and has great character. It is full of pleasant cottages and villas of the period 1800-40, when it was thronged with summer visitors, who enjoyed the scenery and the rich smells of the estuary mud-flats.

The church (St. Mary) is a Perpendicular building, rebuilt in 1864 except for the tower, and enlarged in 1928.

LYNTON (F1) includes Lynmouth, at the foot of the tremendous hog-backed cliffs, which rise to over 1,000 ft. in places. The scenery of this parish, coast, moorland, and valley, is too well known to call for further description, beyond saying that it is spectacularly beautiful along the East Lyn river, in Lyn Cleave, and in the so-called Valley of the Rocks W. of the town.

The remote farms of Coffins Heanton and Ilkerton were Domesday manors. So, too, were East Lyn and West Lyn. At Lower East Lyn are the remains of the 17th-cent. manor house of the Pophams.

The town of Lynton itself has little to commend it. It is almost entirely late Victorian and Edwardian. Nor is the church (St. Mary) any better. Apart from its 13th-cent. tower, it has been rebuilt and enlarged so often that it is now a neat, dull Victorian.

Lynmouth is much more picturesque (in the proper sense of that word). It was "discovered" in the first decade of the 19th cent. when the Napoleonic Wars had closed the Continent to English visitors, two of the earliest visitors being Mr. Coutts the banker, and the Marchioness of Bute. Southey described it as "the finest spot, except Cintra and the Arrabida, that I ever saw" (plate 13). The Shelleys stayed here for nine weeks between June and August 1812 in a cottage belonging to a Mrs. Hooper. Two "cottages" claim to be, and call themselves, Shelley's Cottage. The actual cottage was burnt in 1907 and partly rebuilt.[1] The first hotel was built in 1807, but most visitors stayed in "cottages" of which there are many attractive examples dating from the 1830s and 1840s when the town began to develop steadily. The quay and pier were built in the 18th cent. for the herring fishery, which was once important, and a machicolated tower at the end added early in the 19th cent. by General Rawdon in imitation of the towers on the Rhine. By 1856 there were three hotels at Lynton, and Murray's *Handbook* in that year warns the visitor that "telescopes are employed at the rival houses for the prompt discovery of the approaching traveller. He had better, therefore, determine before-

hand on his inn, or he may become a bone of contention to a triad of post-boys, who wait with additional horses at the bottom of the hill to drag the carriage to its destination." Sir George Newnes, the publisher, lived at Lynton for many years and gave to the town the cliff-railway which makes the steep ascent from the shore up to Lynton town.

On the night of 15–16 August 1952, Lynmouth was overwhelmed by floods arising from torrential rain on Exmoor, and suffered great damage. 31 people lost their lives, 93 houses were destroyed or so damaged as to call for subsequent demolition, and 28 bridges in the district destroyed or damaged. Among the casualties was General Rawdon's tower (above).

Lee Abbey, now a hotel, is a misnomer. For centuries it was a farmhouse, glorified into a small manor house when Hugh Wichehalse of Barnstaple removed his family here in 1628 away from the plague and the uncongenial party strife of his native town. It remained the seat of the Wichehalses until 1713, when they lost their estates. The present house was built about 1850 and then christened Lee Abbey.

MALBOROUGH (F12) lies on a 400-ft. plateau in the extreme S. of the county. Within its boundaries is perhaps the grandest and most unspoiled cliff scenery on the S. Devon coast, a 4½-m. stretch from Bolt Head to Bolt Tail, most of which is now in the hands of the National Trust.

This piece of country was settled early, possibly by coastal immigrants. Alston, Ilton, Collaton, and Sewer were all Domesday manors. Hope is a fishing hamlet, first heard of in the 13th cent.

Malborough church (All Saints), with its slender broach spire, is a landmark over a wide landscape. It is a spacious church, with N. and S. aisles running the full length of its nave and chancel, and good 15th-cent. arcades of Beer stone. The fine rood-screen, which extended across the great width of the church, was destroyed at the "restoration" of 1870.

MAMHEAD (H7) is a small parish on the massive E. flank of the Haldon Hills, which rise to over 800 ft. Mamhead Park is exceedingly beautiful, with many noble trees, and views over a luxuriant landscape to the sea. The estate was sold by Sir Peter Carew to Giles Ball, whose son Sir Peter Ball (1598-1680) became attorney-general to Queen Henrietta Maria, and recorder of Exeter. He began the building of a mansion here, to replace an older house (which had been garrisoned for the king in the Civil War), which was completed by his son before 1718. His grandson Thomas Ball (1671-1749) was a merchant. When he succeeded to the estate about 1718 he brought back numerous exotic trees from his European journeys and planted extensively. It was he who erected the obelisk on the hill above the house in 1743 "out of a regard to the safety of such as might use to sail out of the Port of Exon [Exeter] or any others who might be driven on the coast."

In 1823 Mamhead was bought by Mr. Newman, whose family had been prosperous merchants at Dartmouth since Elizabethan times, and he completely rebuilt the house on a new site in 1830, to the designs of Salvin. Westley Farm was rebuilt by Salvin in 1833.

The church (St. Thomas the Apostle) stands in the park. It is in the main a 15th-cent. building. The chancel was rebuilt about 1830 by the Newmans, who also built the S. transept as the Mamhead pew. Among the rectors of Mamhead was William Johnstone Temple (rector 1766-77), grandfather of Archbishop Temple and a member of the company who gathered to hear Dr. Johnson talk. Temple and Boswell were fellow-students at Edinburgh, and Boswell visited his friend at Mamhead rectory just after Easter, 1775. The rector was a water-drinker, and it is said that under his influence Boswell made a vow under the branches of the great churchyard yew at Mamhead—still flourishing—never to get drunk again.

MANATON (F7) is a good moorland village, with fine views everywhere. The church (St. Winifred) has a typical granite interior of the late 15th cent., with wagon-roofs having carved bosses. The rood-screen (c. 1490) is very fine, with interesting detail. It is of eleven bays, extending across nave and both aisles, and retains much of its ancient colour and gilding.

The parish extends far into the Moor. 3 m. due W. of the church is Grimspound, one of the most remarkable antiquities on Dartmoor, a circular walled enclosure containing 24 Bronze Age hut-circles. The name Grim undoubtedly refers to the Devil. This is one of several well-known sites in England "where a large prehistoric work was associated by the Saxons with diabolic forces." There are a great number of hut-circles and other prehistoric remains scattered about the moorland end of the parish, the exact sites of which are best located on the 2½-inch Ordnance maps (20/77 and 20/78).

Langstone was a Domesday manor, together with Houndtor and Neadon. Wingstone, near the village, was the home for some years of John Galsworthy, the novelist and dramatist.

MARIANSLEIGH (F3) is a small cluster of houses on a high, exposed ridge. The church (St. Mary) was a 15th-cent. building with some ancient glass. It was destroyed by fire in 1932 and has since been rebuilt.

MARLDON (G9) possesses the best example of a fortified manor house left in the county—Compton Castle. An excellent guide to the building can be obtained at the house and a summary description is all that is necessary here. It is a building of early 14th–early 16th-cent. date. Of the early 14th-cent. building, erected c. 1330-40 by Geoffrey Gilbert, who had married the Compton heiress, the solar and the cellar remain, and some foundations of the great hall. The second building period, which brought about extensive changes, was 1450-75; much of the existing house dates from this time. Further large changes were made about 1520, when three of the five machicolated towers were added. The whole house, which is of outstanding interest, has been handed to the National Trust by Commander W. R. Gilbert, descendant of the Gilberts who built it. It was the home of Sir Humphrey Gilbert, the explorer and coloniser, and remained in the family until 1800, when it was sold. Commander Gilbert bought back the property, and has restored it carefully over a period of years. It is an astonishingly romantic place to come upon in a quiet Devonshire lane, bursting suddenly upon the eye without any warning.

Marldon church (St. John the Baptist) is entirely a 15th–early 16th-cent. building, the oldest part being the W. tower, c. 1400, and the latest the S. chancel aisle (the Compton chapel)

built c. 1520 by John Gilbert of Compton, whose shield of arms appears on the E. respond. On each side of the chancel is a small canopied cenotaph, commemorating Otho Gilbert and his wife, Elizabeth, who built most of the church c. 1450. There are a number of incised slate slabs to local families.

The Church House Inn contains some 15th-cent. work.

MARTINHOE (E1) parish contains some superb scenery, with tremendous hog-backed cliffs that are a feature of this coast. The church (St. Martin) has a charming exterior but was in fact murdered at the "restoration" of 1866-7, when, among other crimes, the old musicians' gallery was done away with. The N. aisle was added in 1867.

On the Beacon is a circular earthwork of the same size and type as that at Old Barrow in Countisbury (q.v.), which is known to have been a Roman signal station.[1] The Martinhoe site has recently been excavated and shown to be a Roman fortlet of the 1st cent. A.D., with a signal station, probably one of several set up to give warning of the approach of hostile craft to the Roman towns and villas of Somerset. The name of the Beacon suggests that it was used in later times, probably in the 16th cent., as a signal station.

Killington was a Domesday manor. Croscombe Barton is conceivably a Celtic homestead in origin: it means *Cradoc's combe*, and Cradoc is a British personal name.

MARWOOD (D2) is a large and beautiful parish, with wooded combes, open downland (rising at Hewish Down Beacon to 859 ft.), and a number of interesting farmhouses. A considerable number of farmsteads go back to Saxon times and are recorded in Domesday

Book. These are Marwood itself, Blakewell, Kingsheanton, Metcombe, Varley, Westcott Barton, Whiddon, and Whitefield Barton. Kennacott, another farm, is recorded as early as 1167. Westcott Barton, a home of the Chichesters in the 17th cent., is a very interesting example of a large Devon *barton* in site and layout, with its own small mill. It appears to be medieval in part, remodelled *c.* 1600.

The parish church (St. Michael) is excellently sited, looking down a wooded valley, and is of unusual interest for its fittings. It is mainly an early 14th-cent. cruciform church, of which the N. transept was enlarged into an aisle in the late 15th cent. It is plastered and whitewashed throughout, and is most attractive. The fittings include (1) a fine rood-screen to the N. aisle, with good Renaissance detail. It bears the name of Sir John Beaupel "parson of Marwood," fl. 1520, which is the period of the screen. The screen retains the carved E. back of the roodloft, but the remainder of the work was destroyed after 1852; (2) carved benchends in the nave; (3) a 17th-cent. pulpit; (4) royal arms of George III in plaster; (5) a number of pleasant monuments, esp. one to William and Anthony Peard, 1652; (6) carved ribs and bosses to N. aisle roof; (7) sundial by John Berry (1762) on the S. porch, showing the approximate time in the principal capitals of Europe and at Jerusalem. John Berry made many sundials in North Devon.

MARYSTOW (c7) is "the holy place of St. Mary," where the parish church now stands, but the Domesday manor was down at Sydenham in the wooded valley of the Lew. Raddon, a hamlet in the NE. of the parish, was also a Domesday manor.

The manor of Sydenham came to the Wises *temp.* Henry IV, and the present house was built by Sir Thomas Wise, who was knighted at the coronation of James I in 1603. It is one of the most beautiful Jacobean houses in Devon. Sir Edward Wise remodelled the interior of the house *c.* 1656. In 1675 Sydenham passed to the Tremaynes, who made it their principal residence. The ironwork of the gateway carries the Tremayne crest and the curious device of a Puritan hat.

In April 1937 the contents of the house, the accumulation of more than 300 years of uninterrupted ownership, were sold and dispersed, and the house has since been used as a school.

Marystow church (St. Mary) is largely a 12th-cent. structure, though much altered: the S. doorway and most of the S. wall of the nave may be dated *c.* 1160, and the font is a splendid example of late Norman workmanship, of the same design as Lifton. The chancel was rebuilt early in the 14th cent. (note the double sedilia and the tracery of the windows), and the W. tower added at the same time. The tower was largely rebuilt in granite in the early 16th cent. There is a splendid Renaissance monument to Sir Thomas Wise (1630). Despite the heavy hand of the restorer the church is most attractive.

MARYTAVY (d8) has an interesting mining history; many abandoned tin and copper mines will be found, especially the Devon Friendship Mine, just N. of the village, and Wheal Betsy below Kingsett Down. An old mine leat is now used to supply a large hydroelectric plant in the parish with motive power.

Besides Marytavy itself, Wringworthy, North and South Warne, and

Burntown were all Domesday manors. North Warne and Wringworthy are good examples of freeholders' "mansions." Marytavy church (St. Mary) is mostly a 15th–early 16th-cent. granite structure, drastically restored in 1878-9, but nevertheless pleasant in feeling.

MEAVY (D9) lies on the SW. edge of Dartmoor, and its uplands are scattered with hut-circles and other Bronze Age remains, especially on Wigford Down. The exact sites of these "antiquities" will be found on the 2½-inch map (sheet 20/56). At Brisworthy, a hamlet in the SE. of the parish, occurs the earliest specific reference to tin-working on Dartmoor, in 1168.[1]

The church (St. Peter) is of some interest. The N. pier of the chancel arch, carved with rams' heads, is a relic of an early Norman building, and the greater part of the N. wall is almost certainly Norman, but the remainder of the church is mostly early 16th cent.

A number of interesting houses are dotted about the parish. Near the church is a former mansion, now a farmhouse, of Elizabethan date. Goodameavy is a 16th-cent. (and later) house; Greenwell is 16th–17th-cent. Gratton and Callisham both have traces of their former status as "mansions." Marchant's Cross, ½ m. SE. of the village, is a fine example of a moorland wayside cross. It is referred to in a record of 1291.

MEETH (D5) stands high, with fine views over the Torridge valley. Hele, Stockleigh Barton, and Woolladon were all recorded in Domesday Book, as well as Meeth itself. Crocker's Hele and Friar's Hele are farmhouses of some antiquarian interest.

The church (St. Michael) contains some Norman work. The nave is pro-bably substantially 12th-cent. work; the chancel has been partly rebuilt. In the churchyard is a monument to John Lemprière, compiler of the famous classical dictionary, who was rector here from 1811.

MEMBURY (L5) takes its name from the hill-fort to the E. ("the stone fort"), probably of late Iron Age date, and a part of the frontier defences of the Dumnonii against the people of Dorset.

The church (St. John the Baptist) is interesting. The chancel is 13th-cent.; much of the remainder is 1400-1500. The S. or Yarty aisle contains a monument to Sir Shilston Calmady, who was killed in a skirmish near the village in February 1646, and was buried in the chancel. There are several monuments to the Frys of Yarty. The roof and screen should be noted. Yarty was rebuilt by Nicholas Fry, who was sheriff of Devon in 1626, and is a good E-shaped manor house of that period.

Waterhouse Farm is an attractive 16th-cent. house, built around a small courtyard. At Membury Court one room contains a fine oak ceiling of early 16th-cent. date. In the field just beyond a Roman villa was excavated in 1914.

MERTON (D4) village is unexciting; and the church of All Saints was grossly over-restored at great cost in 1875. Only the bold W. tower and the lofty N. arcade of granite (both 15th-cent.) remain of the old building.

Walter de Merton, founder of Merton College at Oxford, was born here. Other Domesday estates were Potheridge, Speccott, and Dunsbear, all of which have some interest. The Monks owned Great Potheridge as early as Henry II's time. George Monk, 1st Duke of Albemarle, was born here in 1608 and rebuilt the ancestral house on a grand scale *c.* 1660-70. This great house was almost entirely demolished after the death of the second duchess in 1734 but the splendid oak staircase remains, together with its painted and plastered ceiling, and a fine panelled room.

At Speccott Barton, about 1 m. SW. of Great Potheridge, the Speccotts lived from the 12th to the 17th cent. The present house was much rebuilt in the 19th cent.

MESHAW (F4) church (St. John the Baptist) was rebuilt in 1838. It contains a monument to James Courtenay (1683), in whose memory the tower was rebuilt in 1691. Irishcombe Farm was a Domesday manor.

MILTON ABBOT (c8) takes its name from the fact that it formed part of the original endowment of Tavistock Abbey *c.* 974. At the Dissolution it passed to John, Lord Russell, as part of an enormous grant of the Tavistock lands, and still belongs to his lineal descendant, the Duke of Bedford. The estate has therefore changed hands only once in a thousand years. In 1810 the then duke built a "cottage" at Endsleigh, overlooking the wooded Tamar valley, from the designs of Sir Jeffry Wyattville. A statue of the last abbot of Tavistock thoughtfully decorates one of the ornamental gables of the cottage.

Not far from Endsleigh is the original nest of another great family—the Mount Edgecumbes. They were freeholders at Edgecumbe in the 13th cent. and the senior branch resided here until the 1840s. The present Edgecumbe House is mainly late medieval in date, but was refronted in 1719. Leigh Barton was a Domesday manor.

The church (St. Constantine) is mostly a 15th-cent. building in the attractive green Hurdwick stone.

MILTON DAMAREL (B4) church (Holy Trinity) is an early 14th-cent. building, carefully restored in 1904. The windows retain their Decorated tracery, a rarity for Devon. A N. aisle of five bays was added early in the 16th cent. A royal coat-of-arms in plaster, dated 1664, perhaps marks the completion of much 17th-cent. restoration. There are medieval tiles in the nave, and a rustic pulpit *c.* 1700.

MILTON, SOUTH (F11), has an attractive church (All Saints), built of the local greenish slate. It is mostly a 14th-cent. building, though it retains a good Norman font, and a S. doorway of the same period. Part of the S. wall of the nave may be Norman also. A beautiful little screen (15th-cent.) spans the nave and N. aisle, with figure paintings in the lower panels. The parclose screen is also notable.

Collacott, due S. of the church, is a farmhouse of considerable age, possibly medieval in part. Out in the parish, Horswell House, Didwell, and Holwell, which all go back to the 13th cent. or earlier, retain traces of their former status as "mansions."

MODBURY (E10) is a pleasant little market town, with much good building of 18th–early 19th-cent. date, including many of the slate-hung houses which are characteristic of the South Devon towns between Exeter and Plymouth. At the W. end of the town are the slight remains of the Champernownes' mansion. They were lords of the manor and borough from the time of Edward II until 1700; in 1334 Richard Champernowne had a licence for castellating his mansion here. In February 1643 Sir Nicholas Slanning, who had entrenched himself at Modbury with 2,000 men, was defeated by the Devonshire clubmen.

Modbury was a borough before 1238, with a weekly market and two annual fairs. Down to the 1880s St. George's Fair was a great nine-day fair and a holiday for all the townspeople. The ten inns kept open all day long, the streets were filled with people and stalls and there was dancing at the inns after 6 o'clock each evening.[1] Now it lasts one day and is chiefly a cattle market, with a small pleasure-fair at the top of the town.

The church (St. George) is a spacious building, mainly of early 14th-cent. date, but enlarged in the 15th–early 16th cent. The N. transept was the Orcheton chapel and contains mutilated Prideaux effigies; in the S. transept (the Champernowne chapel) are Champernowne effigies. The church is unusual for Devon in having a medieval spire.

Scattered over the large and fertile parish are a number of ancient mansions, or remains of them. Just NE. of the town is Old Traine, a picturesque house partly 15th-cent. in date.

Great Orcheton was a Domesday manor. It was held by the Prideaux family in 1224 and they continued here for thirteen generations. Their mansion, now a farmhouse, retains some early work, notably a granite fireplace of 11 ft. span in the kitchen.

At Oldaport Farm, S. of Orcheton, are remains of buildings of unknown age on a tongue of land between two streams. They may represent a site of the late Roman period or of the succeeding Dark Ages; but only scientific excavation can give an answer. The present farmhouse appears to be chiefly of 16th-cent. date.

Whympston is interesting as the oldest known home of the Fortescues. It is said by Pole to have been granted to them by King John in 1209, but they were in this district c. 1140 when Ralph Fortescue of Modbury gave lands to Modbury priory at or soon after its foundation.[2] Nothing remains of their ancient house, and the estate now belongs to the Plymouth Co-operative Society. Shilston Barton, Spriddlescombe, and Leigh were all Domesday estates. There are remains of former mansions at Edmeston and Yarnicombe. Along the N. boundary of the parish runs one of the best examples of a prehistoric ridgeway in South Devon, commanding splendid views along its entire length of the Moor on one side and the South Hams on the other.

MOLLAND (G3) is a large parish in beautiful, unspoilt country, running N. from the Yeo valley up to Molland Common, over 1,200 ft. up on the S. edge of Exmoor. Beyond this great ridge Somerset begins. In the S. of the parish are many delightful wooded combes.

West Molland is an ancient mansion, now a farmhouse, with the Courtenay arms over the entrance. It is probably medieval in part, but visitors are discouraged. Champson is another ancient house, mainly 16th-cent., with some original windows and contemporary panelling. At Great Champson the Quartlys perfected the breed of red North Devon cattle in the late 18th cent., and kept a fine herd here for some generations.

Molland church (St. Mary) is of outstanding interest. It is a simple 15th–16th-cent. building, replacing an older structure of which the Norman font alone remains, together with two medieval bells. But it escaped the Victorian "restorer" and its atmosphere is wholly that of the 18th cent.—rustic, plastered and whitewashed throughout, with box-pews and canopied three-decker pulpit (plate 49), ceiled roofs, and leaning arcade, and a chancel completely enclosed (like Parracombe). The quasi-screen is of the same period as the pews, with folding gates and open framework on either side, surmounted by a plastered tympanum which completely fills the chancel opening. There is, too, a fine series of monuments to the 17th- and 18th-cent. Courtenays, together with a curious double heart-stone, railed off, a receptacle for the hearts of a Courtenay and his wife. In this delightful little church, in the foothills of the high wild moor, one breathes again the tranquil air of the Georgian countryside.

MOLTON, NORTH (F3), is an enormous parish (over 15,000 acres) extending well up on to Exmoor. At Five Barrows Hill it reaches a height of 1,617 ft. A number of barrows, probably all of Bronze Age date, lie on North Molton Ridge, at Two Barrows on Fyldon Common, and at Five Barrows on Western Common.

North Molton was formerly a royal manor and a separate hundred.

At some date it became a borough, though it was never incorporated. The "town" now has a decayed air. There was formerly a woollen industry here: in Polwhele's day the population were mostly combers and weavers, very poor but healthy. This trade vanished as a result of the Napoleonic Wars.

The parish also has a mining history, going back to Elizabethan days when German miners were brought over to develop English minerals. Westcote says that " Iron mines were sometimes wrought near North Molton and Molland " but had ceased work by his time. Iron-mining was resumed in the 18th and 19th cents. at Florence and Marcia Mines; the former was still being

worked in the 1890s, and a tramway had been cut down to the railway near South Molton station. The remains of this tramway can be seen above and below Brinsworthy bridge, and of a disused iron mine on Radworthy Down, about ½ m. SSE. of South Radworthy. There are adits in the hillside, on both flanks of the combe towards Tabor Hill, which may be the relics of the Elizabethan iron-workings.

The principal evidences of past working and mining are to be seen in the valley just above Heasley Mill. Copper was worked here in the 17th and early 18th cents. The mine was abandoned before 1778, but had been re-opened in Vancouver's day (1808) and was later abandoned again. About 1840 a very rich copper mine—Prince Albert's mine —was opened in the N. of the parish from which gold was also obtained. Copper-mining seems to have ceased in the 1880s.[1] Silver and lead have also been found in the parish.

The parish church (All Saints) is striking and its contents interesting. The massive tower (100 ft. high) is built of Pickwell Down sandstone, probably from the old quarry at Flitton. The rebuilding of the church was perhaps begun in the late 14th cent. A rector of North Molton, by will dated 1398, left 40s. towards "the making of the nave of my church."[2] On the S. side of the tower is a beautiful image of the Virgin and Child. The clearstoried nave is unusual for Devon. Internally the church has the usual Devon wagon-roofs with plastered panels; a beautiful 15th-cent. font; a good rood-screen and parclose screens; some oak panelling (1609) around the sanctuary walls; one of the finest medieval pulpits in Devon, with a singularly beautiful stem, and a carved early Hanoverian sounding-board; and two excellent monuments.

The Parkers, a local family who eventually became lords Boringdon (1784) and then earls of Morley (1815), owned and lived at the Court House immediately W. of the church. The Parker chapel contains some medieval glass. The Bampfylde chapel on the S. contains a striking alabaster monument to Sir Amyas Bampfylde (d. 1626) and his wife Elizabeth with their 12 sons and 5 daughters. The E. window of this chapel contains some coloured glass, c. 1500.

Court House, W. of the church, is a late 16th-cent. house. Court Hall, E. of the church, was and is the home of the Bampfyldes (created lords Poltimore in 1831). It is a Jacobean house much altered and enlarged about 1835.

MOLTON, SOUTH (F3), is a cheerful little market town on the main road from Barnstaple to Taunton. Broad Street is an unspoilt group of building set off by the excellent façade of the Town Hall, which is carried on a series of arches over the pavement. This building was begun in 1740, finished in 1743,[1] and carries a bust of Hugh Squier (1625-1710), "our great benefactor." He built and endowed a grammar school in 1686, afterwards known as Hugh Squier's school, which was amalgamated in 1877 with the Blue Coat Schools (1711) and the National Schools (1833) to form the South Molton United Schools.

The parish church (St. Mary Magdalene) is a spacious 15th-cent. building with an austere W. tower (1435). It was enlarged in 1820 and drastically restored in 1865. It has a beautiful medieval stone pulpit and a good font, both 15th-cent. By the act of 1534, when 26 suffragan bishops were to be created, South Molton was selected as one of the new sees, but nothing came of this.

South Molton originated as a large village early in the Saxon occupation, probably c. 700, and gave its name to a hundred. Gilbert de Turberville created the borough of South Molton c. 1150-70.[2] The borough was incorporated in 1590, and its charter renewed by Charles II in 1684. It sent two burgesses to the parliament of 1302, but afterwards petitioned to be exempted from this expensive privilege. The woollen industry flourished here from medieval times until the late 18th cent. and in a dwindling degree until the late 19th. The town grew in population down to 1851, but the coming of railways killed its busy coaching trade, and this, coupled with the ending of the old woollen manufacture, brought about a decline during the next century. The coming of railways not only killed the coaching trade and all its ancillaries—the grandfather of J. M. W. Turner, the painter, was a saddler at South Molton, and Turner himself only just missed being born here—but helped also to kill the prosperous and well-attended markets. The opening of the North Devon Railway in 1854 led to the establishment of a more convenient cattle market at Eggesford, and the opening of the Devon and Somerset Railway to a cattle market at Molland, the home of the famous North Devon breed.

The large parish (which is co-terminous with the borough) contains much beautiful scenery and some interesting houses. Bremridge, remotely situated in the N. of the parish, was a Domesday manor. It came eventually to Sir John Dodderidge, the judge, who rebuilt the house about 1622. Part of this house was pulled down about 1830, but a considerable portion with contemporary windows and chimney-stacks remains. West Clatworthy is a 17th-cent. farmhouse. Snurridge is an 18th-cent. brick house, unusual for Devon. Honiton Barton was a Saxon estate and is now an attractive farmhouse, c. 1600 in date, with some reconstruction in 1676 (plate 36). It came to the Southcombs of Rose Ash (q.v.) and in 1730 the Rev. Lewis Southcomb built here a chapel dedicated to the Trinity, on the site of an older chapel. He and his father were buried here. The building is now derelict.

Other Domesday manors were North and South Aller, Blackpool, and Hacche. Kingsland Barton is of some age.

MONKLEIGH (c3) is a pleasant village on high ground immediately W. of the Torridge valley. There are fine views all over the parish. The church (St. George) is an interesting building, restored in 1862-3, with a splendid tower that is a landmark for miles around. The fabric was being rebuilt in 1423 when Sir William Hankford of Annery made his will, leaving money for the completion and maintenance of the S. aisle on condition that he and his heirs should have a burial place there.[1]

A parclose screen, with late and rich detail, shuts off the Annery chapel from the rest of the S. aisle. Dame Anne St. Leger founded a chantry in this chapel after 1537 and the screen may date from then. There are a number of well-carved bench-ends in the Annery aisle, bearing the emblems of the Passion and the arms of Annery families; and a considerable number of late medieval tiles in both the nave and the aisle.

Among the various mural monuments and brasses in the church is one in the chancel to James Coffin, Esq., 1566, represented by a brass effigy of a man in armour kneeling, which came from a high tomb now destroyed. There is also a brass in the Annery aisle to Sir James St. Leger, 1509. More important is the canopied altar-tomb which is that of Sir William Hankford, chief justice of the King's Bench, who acquired Annery and other substantial estates.

Annery stands in a fine timbered park, commanding the Torridge valley. It came to the Stapeldons before 1260, in which year Walter de Stapeldon, Bishop of Exeter 1307-26, and lord treasurer under Edward II, was born here.[2] By Polwhele's time the old house was in decay, and about the year 1800 it was drastically altered and modernised, as we see it to-day.

MONK OKEHAMPTON (D5) church (All Saints) was rebuilt, all but the tower, in 1855. The E. window of the church was shown in the Great Exhibition of 1851.

MONKTON (K5) church (St. Mary Magdalene) contains nothing of interest, except the E. window, and the windows of the N. and S. walls, which are by Burne-Jones. It was wholly rebuilt in 1862, except for the tower.

MORCHARD BISHOP (F5) is a large and pleasant village on the old turnpike road from Crediton to Barnstaple. The Bishop of Exeter bought the manor in 1165. In 1548 the then bishop was obliged by Edward VI to part with it to Sir Thomas Darcy, after which it changed hands several times.[3] The making of the new turnpike road to Barnstaple along the valley in the 1820s gave the village a heavy blow. In 1831 it had 2,000 people; by 1901 the population had halved, and it has continued to fall since then.

The church (St. Mary) is entirely a

15th–early 16th-cent. structure, except the plastered and panelled chancel which was rebuilt in the 18th cent. and has a reredos and altar-rails of that period. There is also a two-decker pulpit with canopy. The church was in process of being built in 1451, when Bishop Lacy granted an indulgence to all who should contribute to the work or the furnishings.[1] In the S. aisle, formerly known as the Easton aisle, are the recumbent effigies of a Devonshire franklin and his wife, in civilian dress. These are almost certainly the effigies of William Easton (d. 1505) and his wife who paid for the completion of the aisle (plate 16).

Easton Barton, the home of the Eastons from the 13th cent. to the 17th., is a notably good example of a late-medieval "mansion," built *c.* 1500 and practically unaltered since.

MOREBATH (H3) church (St. George) is 15th-cent., badly over-restored in 1874-5. The N. aisle, however, retains a good wagon roof, and there is a 13th-cent. saddleback tower. The church-wardens' accounts for 1520-73 have been printed. (See pp. 231, 235, 562.) Timewell is mainly a 16th-cent. house.

MORELEIGH (F10) lies in plateau country with far views towards the Salcombe estuary. The church (All Saints) is a delightful little building, mainly early 14th-cent. in date. The church was "restored" in the 17th cent. and has some pleasant work of that period, including a plaster ceiling and the pulpit. The reading-desk incorporates parts of the ancient screen.

Place Barton, beside the church, has some remains of the former manor house.

MORETONHAMPSTEAD (F7) is a small market town on the edge of Dartmoor, originally called simply *Morton,* "moor farm." On Mardon Down, NE. of the town, the hills rise to 1,170 ft. In the NW. of the parish, Cranbrook Castle (1,103 ft.) is an impressive Iron Age hill-fort (1st cent. B.C.), commanding the deep gorge of the wooded Teign valley, and looking across to its companion Prestonbury Castle, on the N. side of the valley. Wooston Castle, about 2 m. E. of Cranbrook, is an earthwork of similar age and type.

Wray Barton, in the beautiful valley of the Wray Brook below the town, was a Domesday manor, and became a "mansion." The present house is mostly Tudor. The farmstead of Lowton, W. of the town, was also recorded in Domesday. At Great Doccombe, beside the hilly road to Exeter, are the remains of another medieval mansion.

Moretonhampstead church (St. Andrew) is almost entirely a 15th–early 16th-cent. structure, one of the most spacious and impressive of the granite churches. The W. tower is granite Gothic at its finest—almost megalithic. We know that it was under construction in 1418.[2] The almshouses (dated 1637) are another delightful little building in granite (plate 39).

George Parker Bidder (1806–78), the famous "calculating boy," was born here, but his birthplace was destroyed by fire in 1926. He became a civil engineer, was associated with Robert Stephenson in the London and Birmingham railway project (1834), helped to found the Electric Telegraph Company, and constructed the Victoria Docks, London.

MORTEHOE (C1) is a coastal parish with striking cliff scenery. The so-called Morte Slates give a very distinctive type of cliff and rock, with razor edges and glistening surfaces. The jagged reefs and stacks of Morte Point are particularly impressive, running out to the deadly Morte Stone on which no fewer than five ships went down in one winter (1852). All the land on Morte Point now belongs to the National Trust. Bull Point is also in this parish, with a lighthouse first lit in 1879 and a powerful fog-signal which warns vessels away from this deadly coast.

Woolacombe, now a developing seaside resort, with the finest beach in N. Devon, was a Domesday manor. The farms of Oussaborough, Roadway, and Spreacombe, are all recorded in Domesday Book.

The church (St. Mary) is one of the most interesting in N. Devon, for it has been largely spared by the "restorer." A small Norman church (of which there are traces) seems to have been enlarged *c.* 1300, producing a cruciform church with N. and S. transepts, and a N. tower. The early 14th-cent. tomb in the S. transept is probably that of the rector, William de Tracey (d. 1322), as it bears on the top the incised figure of a priest in full vestments holding a chalice. The N. transept (if such there was) was enlarged into a short aisle about 1540. The long wagon-roof of the nave is a fine example of a 15th-cent. open-timbered roof. In the nave is a series of carved bench-ends, *temp.* Henry VIII, some bearing the initials of donors, others the emblems of the Crucifixion, and yet others grotesque sea monsters.

MUSBURY (L6), in delightful country on the margin of the Axe valley, takes its name from the Iron Age hill-fort which crowns the hill above the village. The church (St. Michael) is a 15th-cent. structure, devastatingly restored by Hayward of Exeter, and much rebuilt.

The chancel was rebuilt in 1865, the N. aisle in 1875. There is much other poor Victorian work. The only notable feature of the church is the Drake monument, erected in 1611 and extended by a bay *c.* 1646.

Ashe, about 1 m. N., came about 1415 to John Drake of Exmouth, whose descendants held it until 1793. The present Ashe House is that rebuilt by Sir John Drake, 2nd bart., *c.* 1670-80, though there are slight traces of its 15th-cent. predecessor. The detached chapel, on the site of one licensed in 1387, was also rebuilt in the 17th cent. It is most unlikely that John Churchill, afterwards Duke of Marlborough, was born here, as is so often said, as the house was burnt and uninhabitable from 1644. It is almost certain that he was born at Great Trill, not far away, in the parish of Axminster.

NETHEREXE (H5) has a small church away in the fields by itself (dedication unknown). It is a rectangular building of Thorverton stone, apparently largely rebuilt, in the 15th-cent. style. It has a Norman font, all that remains of the first church on the site.

NEWTON ABBOT (G8), at the head of the Teign estuary, is a flourishing market town of some 19,000 people. A hundred years ago it had barely 4,000. During Queen Victoria's reign it trebled its numbers, and this growth has determined its architectural character to-day. It is, nevertheless, a town of considerable antiquity, taking its rise in the early 13th cent. on the waste land along the valley of the river Lemon which enters the Teign just below the town.

In 1196 the manor of Wolborough was given by William Brewer to his foundation of Torre Abbey, and we hear of a *Nova Villa,* a small settlement, along the S. bank of the Lemon by about 1200. For a time this "new town" was called Shireborne Newton, but before the end of the 13th cent. the form Newton Abbot established itself. Meanwhile, the lord of the manor of Teignwick or Highweek, Sir Theobald de Englishville, obtained a market and fair for his "new town" on the N. side of the Lemon and established a borough here in 1246,[1] which became known as Newton Bushel after the later manorial lords. In the course of time the two small boroughs coalesced and the name Newton Abbot is now applied to both.

When the South Devon Railway reached Newton Abbot in 1846, it had about 4,000 people. Because of its geographical position, at the head of an estuary, at the meeting place of several valleys, and with the moorland behind, the town soon became a focus for railways, and is now an important railway junction. From 1846 onwards considerable building took place, largely under the direction of the Courtenays, who owned most of the site. Courtenay Park was laid out with detached and semi-detached villas, mostly Italianate in style, with wide roads and open spaces; Devon Square is of the same date and style. To some degree Newton Abbot is a "railway town," but not noticeably so, for it has retained and improved its old character as a good market and shopping town. The older buildings may be found in East Street, Highweek Street, and Wolborough Street. St. Leonard's Tower is all that is left of a 14th–15th-cent. church, demolished in 1836. The churches of the town are all modern, that of St. Mary (in Abbotsbury, NW. of the centre) being by E. H. Sedding (1904-6).

Wolborough parish contains two in-teresting buildings. The parish church (St. Mary) is of 15th–early 16th-cent. date, standing on a hill commanding a view of the Teign estuary. It has a remarkable series of screens: a very good rood-screen of early 16th-cent. date, N. and S. parclose screens, and small screens fencing two chantries or chapels. The whole of the screenwork is richly coloured, with 66 panel paintings that call for detailed study. In the chancel is some 17th-cent. furniture; and there is a large monument (1633) to Sir Richard Reynell of Ford, Kt., and Lucy his wife. The church also contains a good pulpit and modern glass, a pre-Reformation bell in the nave (made by John Bird, 1390), a restored Norman font; a medieval brass lectern (15th cent.) and some 15th-cent. glass.

Ford House, on the E. edge of the town, is a good example of a Jacobean mansion, built in 1610 by Sir Richard Reynell, who had just bought the old Torre abbey manor of Wolborough from the Crown. Here he entertained Charles I and the Duke of Buckingham in September 1625. In November 1688 the Prince of Orange stayed here for a short time, after landing at Brixham, and before advancing on Exeter. Ford was bought from the Earl of Devon in 1936 by the Newton Abbot U.D.C. It still retains seven remarkable plaster ceilings of early 17th-cent. date, some of the best in Devon.

Highweek parish also has a remarkable house—Bradley Manor, to the SW. of the town in the Lemon valley. It is a good example of a 15th-cent. manor house, of the small West Country type, containing a great hall, screens, passage, buttery, solar and chapel. It was probably built by Richard Yarde immediately after marrying the heiress in 1419, and remodelled about 1495, the date of the present E. front. The chapel is dated about 1428. The house now belongs to the National Trust, and is open at certain times to the public.

The parish church (All Saints) is mainly 15th-cent., with a 14th-cent. W. tower, and granite arcades. It has been heavily Victorianised and is of no great interest, but the views from the churchyard are worth seeing.

NEWTON AND NOSS (D11) lie opposite each other on a creek of the beautiful wooded estuary of the Yealm. Their full names are Newton Ferrers and Noss Mayo. Newton church (Holy Cross) is mainly 15th-cent., with a 13th-cent. chancel. There are monuments to the Potters and the Yonges of Puslinch.

Puslinch, at the head of the Yealm estuary, was built by James Yonge about 1720, a perfect "Queen Anne" house. It is still owned by the Yonges. Architecturally it belongs to the Plymouth group, which includes Antony (1721) and Plympton. The architect of these three houses is not known: probably he was a Plymouth mason who had worked under Wren as his style closely resembles that of Wren and his school in the Home Counties twenty years earlier.[1] 200 yds. W. is the older Puslinch, now a farm, which was a small late 15th-cent. manor house of the Devonshire type.

Noss Mayo is in the ancient ecclesiastical parish of Revelstoke. The church at Noss (St. Peter) was built by St. Aubyn in 1882, but the ancient parish church (also St. Peter) lies 1½ m. SE. on the cliffside near Stoke Point. As at Wembury, the church was built far from any settlement, probably as a landmark for shipping on this dangerous coast. The old church was abandoned during the 1870s, and it has become a remote and beautiful ruin, well worth a visit. It was an early 14th-cent. cruciform church with transepts and a N. tower, to which a S. aisle and porch were added in the 15th cent. The coastal scenery around here is superb, above all the massive slates of Stoke Point.

NEWTON POPPLEFORD (J7), stretched along the main Exeter-Sidmouth road, contains much decent building in cob and thatch. The church of St. Luke was erected in 1897.

NEWTON ST. CYRES (G6) is an attractive village of coloured cob and thatch, with an interesting church. The S. part of the parish is hilly, rising to over 700 ft., and is finely wooded.

The church (St. Julitta and St. Cyriac) is entirely an early 15th-cent. rebuilding, in Posbury stone, with a good Beer stone arcade. The pulpit and canopy are late 17th-cent. work; the seating is modern, plain and good, but the old box-pews looked even better forty years ago. The church was restored in 1914-21 with great taste and restraint.

The monuments are numerous and interesting. Those of the Quickes run from the 17th cent. to the 20th. The Quickes still live at Newton House, a stuccoed Georgian house of c. 1780.

The Northcote monuments are also striking, especially that of John Northcote of Hayne (1570-1632), with medallion portraits of his father and grandfather (both of whom were serge merchants of Crediton) and of his two wives on either side of the central figure of the warrior. The Northcotes made their fortune in the Crediton woollen trade, bought lands all round the town, and settled at Hayne in Newton St. Cyres, which came to them by marriage with a Drewe heiress in 1585. Hayne is now a plain farmhouse, c. 1800 in date.

Bidwell, for centuries the home of the Bidwells, is now a large farmhouse with an Elizabethan look about it. At Sweetham is a most attractive old bridge over the Creedy.

NEWTON ST. PETROCK (C4) has a pleasant little church (St. Petrock), mostly of 14th and 15th-cent. date, with a rude Norman font of polyphant stone and a number of well-carved bench-ends (16th cent.).

NEWTON TRACEY (D3) church (St. Thomas Becket) is pleasant outside but was made hideous internally in 1868 to a degree unusual even for Victorian restorers. The N. aisle was added at that date. The only thing of interest to-day is the Norman font. Ravens and buzzards haunt the beautiful country all around.

NORTHAM (C3) includes Appledore and Westward Ho, and fills the peninsula between the Torridge estuary and Barnstaple Bay. The village occupies the top of a hill overlooking what was once a supremely beautiful scene, now ruined by power-lines, pylons, masts, ill-placed bungalows, and much local white brick. It is an outstanding example of what unplanned "development" can do. Yet there are still fine views in the parish and much of historical interest. Northam itself contains little worth looking at. The parish church (St. Margaret) stands well on the edge of a bluff overlooking the Burrows and the bay. Its tall tower has been for centuries a landmark for shipping crossing the dangerous bar at the entrance to the estuary. The church is better outside than in, having been thoroughly restored in 1849-65. The

memorials to the Leighs and other local families were either swept away or buried out of sight, and the ancient plate melted down. Risdon says "the well-disposed people have twice enlarged their church" and the N. aisle bears the date 1593. These were the great days in this estuary. Burrough, a little SE. of the village, was the ancestral home of Stephen and William Burrough or Borough, the notable 16th-cent. navigators. Kingsley made Burrough the centre of his epic *Westward Ho!*, which is saturated with scenes from this corner of Devon. No Amyas Leigh ever lived here; but all the same, one cannot stand unmoved in the churchyard of Northam, looking westwards over the foaming bar, remembering how Mrs. Leigh hurried out of the house to this spot and how she stood here to see her son's ship home again after all those silent years. A barbarian pulled down in 1868 the old house that Kingsley knew and built two semi-detached houses on the site.

Kenwith Castle is an earthwork which has been identified with *Arx Cynuit*, the scene of a decisive Danish defeat in 878, now believed, however, to have taken place at Combwich in Somerset. The general configuration of Kenwith rather suggests an early medieval site. About 350 yds. E. is a linear earthwork of unknown purpose.

Appledore is a delightful unspoilt village at the meeting place of the beautiful Taw and Torridge estuaries. The delicate colouring of the estuary, of the Braunton Burrows, and of the hills beyond, is matched by the colour-wash everywhere in the village. The streets are narrow, many of the houses old; some are certainly Elizabethan. The church (St. Mary) was built in 1838 and is dull: everything else in Appledore is fascinating. There is little doubt that a village called Tawmouth existed here in the 11th cent. It seems to be identical with the *Tawmutha* referred to in the Anglo-Saxon Chronicle under 1068 (actually 1069) when Harold's three illegitimate sons crossed from Ireland with 64 ships, landed here and were beaten off with great losses. The scene of this battle may be *Bloody Corner*, just below Northam, where human bones and coins are said to have been found. This site is marked on the O.S. map as the scene of the battle of 878 but there is no authority for this identification.

The name Appledore first occurs in the grant of a shop or a stall (*seld*) "next the strand ate Apildore" in 1335, but it seems to have decayed almost to nothing during the 15th cent. if Westcote's statement *c.* 1630 is correct. He says, speaking of Northam: "This parish is grown very populous lately, for in the memory of man, at a place called Appledore . . . stood but two poor houses; and now for fair buildings and multiplicity of inhabitants, and houses, it doth equal divers market towns, and is furnished with many good and skilful mariners." On the other hand, Leland, writing about 1540, calls Appledore "a good Village" and it is plainly marked on Saxton's map of 1575. It certainly became a populous place in Elizabethan days, rising with Bideford, having the advantage of being the first place within the bar where ships could lie up.

On Staddon Hill, the summit W. of the village, is an earthwork, thrown up during the Civil War, which commanded the two estuaries and commands to-day a magnificent view towards Exmoor and Dartmoor. In Ogilby's day (1675) the main road from Bideford to Ilfracombe passed over Staddon Hill, crossed the estuary by a ferry to St. Ann's chapel (now gone), and continued across the Braunton Burrows. A small shipbuilding industry is still carried on at Appledore, which has two dry docks. The salmon fishery in the estuary has been carried on continuously since Saxon days. In 1086 the abbot of Caen had a fishery in the manor of Northam (probably here at Appledore) worth 30 pence yearly.

Westward Ho is an entirely modern settlement. Following the publication of Kingsley's book in 1855, a company was formed to develop this site as a watering place. The Westward Ho Hotel was built, a church (Holy Trinity) followed in 1870, and by 1872 there were two or three rows of terraces, many scattered villas, and a single line of shops. A golf course was laid out on the Burrows which became known as one of the finest in England. The United Services College for the sons of officers was opened in 1874, and is the *mise en scène* of Kipling's *Stalky & Co.* Within the next thirty years much more building took place in a planless way, but worse came in the 20th cent. To-day Westward Ho is a sad spectacle of what uncontrolled speculative building can do with a fine site. Many of the buildings are alien to Devon, and most of them could be anywhere else. The golf course remains superb. The Pebble Ridge is a remarkable natural phenomenon nearly 2 m. long, about 50 ft. wide, and 20 ft. high.

NORTHCOTT (B6) is a hamlet of the Cornish parish of Boyton, across the Tamar, but is constituted as a separate civil parish in Devon.

NORTHLEIGH (K6) lies remote among the luxuriant valley scenery of East Devon. The church (St. Giles), built largely of local flints in the 14th and early 16th cents., was too well restored in 1869; the chancel rebuilt about 1858. The font and S. doorway are Norman. A fine series of carved bench-ends, and the chancel screen, date from the early 16th cent., and there is a good Caroline pulpit. Smallicomb farm is recorded in Domesday.

NYMET ROWLAND (F5) is a tiny parish with a rustic 15th-cent. church (St. Bartholomew). Traces of the 12th-cent. church remain in the S. doorway, and the crude font. Internally, the most remarkable feature is the oaken arcade to the N. aisle (the only other in Devon is at Dowland), which dates from the 15th cent. and is treated exactly like stone. The W. arch is propped by a massive oak post, inserted about 1636 when much restoration work was done (plate 52). Notice the bosses of the N. aisle roof. Some complete benches of 15th-cent. date remain in the church.

Pitt Court, SE. of the church, has traces of a 15th-cent. building.

OAKFORD (H3) church (St. Peter) dominates the village from an eminence. It was rebuilt in 1838-9, except for the 15th-cent. tower, with a spacious nave and short chancel. Spurway Barton lies remote above a wooded combe and was a Domesday manor. The Spurways were already settled here in 1244 and continued to own it until recently. Other farms mentioned in Domesday are Bickham Barton, Mildon, Woodburn and East and West Tapps.

OFFWELL (K6) has a 15th-cent. church (St. Mary), much restored by Edward Copleston (1776-1849), bishop of Llandaff and dean of St. Paul's, who was born at the rectory. The Coplestons have been rectors without a break from 1773 to the present day, and have

produced a number of distinguished churchmen. Edward Copleston was a great builder. He built Offwell House (1828), the rectory (1845), and the tower on Honiton Hill (1843) from which there are magnificent views. Colwell Barton, Culbeer, and Wilmington were all Domesday manors, and Glanvill Barton occurs as early as 1173-5.

OGWELL (G8) is a union of two ancient parishes (E. and W. Ogwell) which were joined in 1881. East Ogwell has a 14th-cent. cruciform church (St. Bartholomew). In the 15th cent. the N. transept was enlarged into a full aisle; the S. transept was left untouched. It contains the canopied Elizabethan altar-tomb of Richard Reynell, Sheriff of Devon (d. 1585), and of his wife Agnes. The chancel screen is of an early square-headed type, probably early 15th-cent. A Jacobean screen spans the tower arch. Note also the fine octagonal 14th-cent. font, and some ancient glass in the vestry window.

Holbeam was a Domesday manor, and was the home of the Holbeams for at least twelve generations.

West Ogwell consists only of the "big house" and a delightful little church (dedication unknown) in the park. The latter is interesting as having an unaltered early 14th-cent. cruciform plan, with N. and S. transepts. The interior is completely charming: plastered and whitened walls and roofs, clear glass, high box-pews, bowed altar rails of early 19th-cent. date, and a Jacobean pulpit. West Ogwell is one of the half-dozen most appealing country churches in Devon.

West Ogwell House was built in 1790, and is now a Diocesan House for retreats and conferences.

OKEHAMPTON (D6) is surrounded by a large parish known as Okehampton Hamlets, of which Kigbeare and Chichacott were Domesday manors, and Meldon occurs in the 12th cent. The parish rises S. to the high moorland of Dartmoor and includes its two highest points—High Willhays (2,039 ft.) and Yes Tor (2,028 ft.). Yes Tor, probably the name originally given to the whole hill of which High Willhays is part, is recorded as *Ernestorre* and *Yernestorre* in a 13th-cent. perambulation of the Moor, meaning "eagles' tor." The military have had their grip on this part of the Moor for fifty years or more, but one may on occasions gain access to the summit of Yes Tor, from which there is an extraordinary view: N. over most of Devon, W. as far as Bodmin Moor, S. a vast, awe-inspiring, and desolate prospect into the deepest recesses of the Moor.

Okehampton town was founded by Baldwin de Brionne, the Norman sheriff of Devon, shortly before 1086, on a new wedge-like site between the East Okement and West Okement rivers, and the Saxon site was gradually abandoned except for the church (All Saints), which now stands alone. The 15th-cent. church was entirely destroyed by fire in 1842, except the fine granite tower. It was rebuilt by Hayward of Exeter in 1843-4. Because of the distance of the parish church from the new town, a chantry chapel of St. James was erected in the town. This was rebuilt in 1862, except the 15th-cent. granite tower. Okehampton is a singularly dull town, with very little to look at. The only building of any merit is the Town Hall, a handsome structure erected in 1685 by John Northmore as a town house, and converted to its present use in 1821. Just outside the town, to the N., is Oaklands, a mansion

erected in 1820-2 by C. Vokins for Albany Saville, who had bought the castle and manor of Okehampton from Henry Holland.

Okehampton was incorporated in 1623. From 1640 to 1832, when it was disfranchised, it regularly returned two members to Parliament.

About 1 m. SW. of the town, on a commanding site above the West Okement river, is the castle, of which there are substantial remains. A strong site was made even stronger by an artificial cut on the W. side, above which towers the square keep. The keep may be late Norman in date, but the other buildings represent mostly a rebuilding of *c.* 1300. On the N. side of the bailey are the remains of the great hall and buttery, stores, and the kitchen with its two ovens; on the S. side the lodge, ward-rooms, and a very picturesque chapel. The whole site is romantically beautiful.[1] The position of the castle, beside the main road from Exeter into Cornwall, probably accounts for its building and early importance.

At Brightley, about 2 m. N. of the town, is an ancient house, and the remains of a chapel, now used as a barn. Here Richard fitz Baldwin founded a religious house in 1133, and on 3 May 1136 a superior and twelve monks arrived from Waverley Abbey to build a new monastery. They abandoned Brightley in 1141 and were given a new site at Ford in East Devon, which subsequently became Ford Abbey.

At Meldon, about 2½ m. SW. of the town, are great quarries of limestone. Meldon Viaduct, near by, is a notable piece of railway engineering, carrying the railway over a deep ravine at a height of 160 ft. The scenery around here is of striking beauty. Between Meldon and Okehampton, on the hillside below the military camp, is the site of Okehampton Park, the chase of the medieval Courtenays, now a wild spot covered with ancient hawthorns, holly trees, and great furze bushes.

OTTERTON (J7) is a large, pleasant village with much good building in cob and thatch, and the local red sandstone. A good house in the main street is dated 1627, and there are others of the same period. The church (St. Michael) was rebuilt in 1871 (Benjamin Ferrey), except the tower, and turned into a suburban edifice.

Otterton priory, founded *temp.* William II, was a dependent of Mont St. Michel in Normandy. It was suppressed as an alien priory in 1414 and its endowments granted to Syon Abbey in Middlesex. At the dissolution of Syon in 1539, Richard Duke (who was clerk of the Court of Augmentations, handling the disposal of monastic property) immediately bought the manor of Otterton. He converted part of the monastic buildings into a mansion, which still stands by the church, and is now divided internally and occupied by several cottagers. The manorial mills, recorded in Domesday Book, are still working.

Pinn farmhouse has a good deal of 16th-cent. work. Ladram Bay is a much-visited "beauty-spot" on the red-sandstone coast of this parish.

OTTERY ST. MARY (K6) is a pleasant little town set in the midst of a large, fertile, and beautiful parish. The parish occupies mainly the valley of the Otter, from which it takes its name, but it reaches both E. and W. to high ridges from which there are superb views over a luxuriant countryside.

Edward the Confessor gave the manor and hundred to the cathedral church of St. Mary at Rouen. Bishop Grandisson of Exeter procured it by exchange in 1334, and in 1337 he founded a college of secular priests, with 40 members in all, endowing it with the manor and hundred, and the tithes of the whole parish. The college was suppressed by Henry VIII in 1545, when the fabric of the church, and a small residue of the collegiate property, were transferred to a body of four governors, to whom Edward VI added eight assistants in 1552. These are still the legal owners and guardians of the church and churchyard. Among the property so transferred was the school-house of Grandisson's foundation, which was re-founded as "The King's New Grammar School" and continues to the present day. John Coleridge (1719-81) was vicar of Ottery and master of the grammar school, and his son Samuel Taylor Coleridge, the poet and philosopher, and perhaps the only literary genius that Devon has produced, received his earliest schooling here. Ottery is the Clavering St. Mary of *Pendennis*, by W. M. Thackeray, who used to spend his vacations from Charterhouse (1825-28) at Larkbeare, near by; and William Browne, the author of *Britannia's Pastorals*, lived here for many years and died here in 1645.

Although swept by great fires in 1767 and 1866, Ottery retains many good Georgian houses, especially in the neighbourhood of the church; but it is the latter (St. Mary) which is the glory of the town. It is perhaps the finest church in Devon other than Exeter Cathedral, upon which it was closely modelled by Bishop Grandisson when he greatly enlarged and beautified the existing church for his college of canons. It is a 13th-cent. church, reconstructed in 1338-42, added to c. 1520 by the Dorset Aisle, and restored by Butterfield in 1849-50.

Among the notable features of the church are (1) the 14th-cent. clock (*c.* 1340) in the S. transept, with its original works, though no longer working; (2) the canopied tombs in the nave of Sir Otho de Grandisson (1358), brother of the bishop, and Lady Beatrice, his wife (1374); (3) the tomb of John Haydon of Cadhay (1588) in the chancel; (4) the monument, in the N. aisle, with full-length standing figure, to John Coke of Thorne (1632); (5) the 14th-cent. choir stalls, altar screen, and sedilia; (6) the minstrels' gallery, stalls, and gilded wooden eagle, all in the Lady Chapel, the latter given to the church by Grandisson himself; (7) the fine pulpit (1722), carved by a parishioner, and the bronze lectern copied from that at St. Nicholas, King's Lynn; (8) the eight coloured bosses in the roof, extending from the middle of the nave to the E. end of the Lady Chapel, the W. boss depicting Bishop Grandisson in his episcopal robes, the others a summary of Our Lord's life and works; (9) the carved exterior of the N. porch; (10) in the S. transept the recumbent effigy by Thrupp of Jane, Lady Coleridge (1878).

Ottery has subsisted for a thousand years as a market town for a fertile countryside. It formerly had a considerable woollen manufacture, and still had in Lysons's day "a large manufactory for spinning wool." The old mill near the station was probably this manufactory. In the parish are a number of interesting houses, of which Cadhay, 1 m. NW., is the most notable. This is a fine Tudor mansion, built by John Haydon (d. 1588), a successful Devon lawyer who married the Cadhay heiress. There is a quadrangle known as " The Court of the Kings," with an entrance in the centre of each side, above which are the figures of Henry VIII and his three "sovereign" children.

Knightstone, SE. of the town, is substantially a medieval hall-house, remodelled in the 16th cent. It belonged for a time to the Bonvilles and the Greys, and then to the Shermans, a local family, for several generations. Other " mansions" in the parish were Thorne, Holcombe, Ash (Elizabethan), and Bishop's Court, said to have been the seat of Bishop Grandisson.

PAIGNTON (G9), a flourishing seaside-town on the shores of Tor Bay, has trebled in size since 1900 and now has some 25,000 people. A hundred years ago it was described in *White's Directory* as "a neat and improving village and *bathing place,*" which had "risen into notice as a place of resort for invalids during the last fifteen years, and is capable of being made a first-rate watering place . . ." But it was still chiefly a farming parish, noted for the excellence of its cider of which great quantities were shipped to London and elsewhere, and for its very large and sweet cabbages, called " Paignton cabbages" which were sent all over the county. The real rise of the town as a seaside resort dates from late Victorian times. The railway reached the village in 1859; and in the last 40 years of the century the population trebled (8,385 in 1901).

Paignton was an ancient village, founded about ½ m. inland from the shore, possibly by Saxon colonists who arrived by sea. Before the Norman Conquest the large and fertile manor had come into the possession of the bishops of Exeter. They had a palace here, of which some small remains of 14th-cent. date may be seen near the church.

Under the bishops of Exeter, Paignton acquired in 1295 a weekly market and a three-day fair at the festival of the Holy Trinity; and a borough appears to have been set up about the same time. Much of the old village remains around the parish church, chiefly Church St., Kirkham St., Well St., and Winner St., in all of which 16th–18th-cent. cottages may be seen.

The parish church (St. John) was the mother-church of a large district which formerly included the parishes of Marldon and Stoke Gabriel. There are considerable remains of the 12th-cent. church, chiefly the N. and S. rubble walls of the chancel, the red sandstone font, and the W. doorway of the tower. This doorway is, however, not in its original position. The church was almost entirely rebuilt in red sandstone in the early 15th cent., possibly during the episcopate of Lacy (1420-55), whose arms appear in the painted glass of the N. aisle. It contains a late medieval stone pulpit, richly carved.

The stone screen to the Kirkham chapel in the S. transept has been barbarously mutilated but is still beautiful. It was erected c. 1526 by the Kirkhams of Blagdon, and is elaborately canopied. The interior ceiling is particularly notable, with its "exquisite vine-leaf enrichment whose fragile beauty is a masterpiece of execution." The sculptured panels are also noteworthy.

Oldway, a mansion of 115 rooms, was built for Singer, the sewing-machine millionaire, in 1874 at a cost of over £100,000 (architect, G. S. Bridgeman). The family ceased to live there in 1914 and after being put to various uses the house and grounds were bought by the town in 1945 for £45,000. It only remains to add that this palatial and opulent house was called The Wigwam when it was first built.

Blagdon Barton, 2 m. W. of Paignton, was the seat of the Kirkhams from the reign of Edward I until the 17th cent. It is one of the most interesting of the smaller medieval "mansions" of Devon, retaining as it does its 14th-cent. hall, screen, etc. The house was remodelled in 1567 and again early in the 18th cent.[1] The adjoining farm has tremendous cathedral-like barns and other buildings around a courtyard, as befitted a former estate of more than 1,000 acres.

PANCRASWEEK (A5) consists of an isolated church and scattered farmsteads. The original Domesday settlements were as Dunsdon, Hamsworthy, and Virworthy. The present church (St. Pancras) is largely 15th-cent. in date, though there are traces of original Norman work in the nave walls. The plain W. tower has fine crocketed pinnacles of the W. Devon type. There is a Jacobean pulpit and a good granite S. arcade. At Lana, 1 m. N., is an attractive roadside Methodist chapel (1838).

PARKHAM (B3) contains a number of former "mansions." Halsbury was the home of the Halsbury family in Henry II's time, but passed to the Giffards by marriage temp. Edward I. In 1885 Mr. H. S. Giffard, Q.C., was raised to the peerage as Lord Chancellor and took the title of Baron Halsbury of Halsbury. The present house, a large stone-built barton, is of 16th- and 17th-cent. date. A record of 1560 speaks of it as a "new dwelling house,"[2] which fixes the date of the older parts as mid-16th-cent. There are some good panelled rooms. Bableigh was a home of the Risdons from the 15th cent. until 1760, but the rebuilt farmhouse is uninteresting. West Goldworthy was a "mansion" and retains some evidence of its former status. Stone was a house of some consequence in the 18th cent.

Parkham church (St. James) is mainly a 15th-cent. structure, with early 16th-cent. aisles. It has a fine late Norman S. doorway (*c.* 1160-70), and a Norman font surrounded by some excellent medieval tiles. The N. aisle was erected by the Risdons. The S. aisle is of the same date, and may have been erected by the Giffards of Halsbury. There are inscriptions to the Giffards of Halsbury from 1595 to 1712.

PARRACOMBE (E1) is a small village in a fold of Exmoor, which rises to 1,575 ft. at the SE. end of the parish. There are barrows on Parracombe Common, probably of Bronze Age date, and a number of other small earthworks dotted about the parish. Rowley Barton ("rough clearing") was a Domesday manor; so, too, were East and West Middleton.

The parish is chiefly remarkable for its old church, which stands on the moorside high above the village. It was proposed to pull it down in the 1870s, but an agitation, in which John Ruskin played a leading part, saved it from destruction. A new church was built down in the village in 1878, and the old church, which has a completely unspoiled Georgian interior, is now used only occasionally in summer. It is dedicated to St. Petrock and is undoubtedly a very ancient foundation, but the present building is largely the result of an early 16th-cent. reconstruction. The chancel, however, was not rebuilt at this date, but is early 13th-cent. work; so, too, is the lower part of the small, square W. tower. The interior is plastered and whitewashed; everything is irregular and leans in different directions. There are 18th-cent. box-pews; an 18th-cent. screen with a wooden tympanum above it; a Georgian pulpit; and a number of early 16th-

cent. benches also survive. At the back of the church is the old musicians' gallery. On the walls are the wooden hat-pegs of the Georgian church, and oval plaques inscribed with suitable texts, such as " Let all things be done decently and in order." There are mural tablets to the old yeoman family of Lock (1667-1803) who still farm in the parish. All the roofs are ceiled and whitewashed. It is an enchanting example of an unspoilt Georgian interior, though now in need of careful repair, and is by far the most interesting of all the churches in this part of Devon.

PAYHEMBURY (J5) church (St. Mary) is chiefly 15th-cent., with all the usual features: a Beer stone arcade with well-carved capitals bearing shields of arms (including the arms of Courtenay), a good rood-screen (*c.* 1450), some ancient carved bench-ends, and Queen Anne altar-rails and pulpit with sounding-board. There is some medieval glass in the N. aisle, and a splendid panelled and coloured roof with bosses.

Higher and Lower Cheriton represent the Domesday manor of *Cherleton*, and Tale the manor of *Tala*. Uggaton, a large farmhouse of late 17th-cent. date, is mentioned as early as 1196. Leyhill Farm was rebuilt in 1657 and much altered in Queen Anne's time.

PETERS MARLAND (c4) lies in dullish country. The church (St. Peter) stands high and commands superb views of Dartmoor. It was, however, rebuilt in 1865, and is entirely without interest. Twigbear, Week, Winswell, and Winscott were all pre-Conquest estates.

PETERTAVY (D8) church (St. Peter) is mainly a building of *c.* 1500, abominably restored. Portions of the medieval rood-screen, which was chopped up at the "restoration," are fastened to a wall. The remains of a fine carved pew, also chopped up, were put across the tower arch. There are, however, several interesting secular buildings in the village and outlying parts of the parish. The Petertavy Inn is probably early 17th-cent. Coxtor is a good example of a moorland yeoman's dwelling of the same date. Willsworthy, far up the infant Tavy, was a Saxon farmstead, held by Siward in 1066. It had a chapel in medieval times. It is now a somewhat altered 16th-cent. farmhouse. Wapsworthy, recorded in 1230, has a ruined 16th-cent. farmstead. Bagga Tor, recorded in 1238, is a remote moorland farmstead built into the side of a hill, of considerable interest to the student of English peasant building. Nat Tor (1340) is another primitive farmstead. At Cudlipptown, behind Edgecombe Farm, a 15th-cent. farmstead, now abandoned as a dwelling, survives largely intact.

The moorland in the parish is thickly sprinkled with hut-circles, cairns, stone rows and circles, and other Bronze Age remains, which can be best located on the 2½-inch maps (sheets 20/57, 20/58). On Standon Down is a remarkable collection of more than 70 hut-circles representing an unenclosed Bronze Age village, one of the most important sites on the Moor. It lies at the S. end of Tavy Cleave, a romantically beautiful gorge where the Tavy breaks out of the Moor. One must beware of the military's firing activities around here, but adequate notice is given. The visitor should not be deterred from seeing this most interesting and beautiful place. Along the Tavy near Cudlipptown are disused tin and copper mines.

PETHERWIN, NORTH (A7), occupies the extreme W. end of the great tongue of Devon which thrusts into Cornwall. The church (St. Paternus), on an ancient Celtic site, is an imposing building, quite Cornish in feeling. The N. arcade has three massive early Norman piers rising abruptly from their square foundations, without any moulded base, like those at St. Breward. Elaborate mouldings are dispensed with: everything is left simple and plain. The original Norman arches were replaced in the 14th cent., when other structural changes were made, but the most substantial enlargement came in the 15th cent. when the S. aisle and the W. tower were added. The granite S. arcade is particularly graceful. The chancel, S. aisle, and S. porch, have their original cradle roofs. The modern S. porch door has splendid wrought-iron hinges (15th-cent.); those on the N. porch door are a good modern imitation. In the tower arch are the Jacobean altar rails dated 1685, of excellent country workmanship. There are no monuments of any note, but the lettering on the incised slate-slabs of the 18th cent. (e.g. to the Pedlars of Win) is worth inspection. All the farm and hamlet names of this large parish are English, whereas those across the river Ottery almost immediately change to Cornish, strongly suggesting that the Ottery was a racial frontier for a considerable period.

PETROCKSTOW (D5) means "holy place of St. Petrock," to whom the church is dedicated. The church was rebuilt, except the tower and 14th-cent. N. arcade, in 1870-80, and is dull. It retains its ancient font (c. 1300) with a 16th-cent. cover, and some medieval glass in the vestry. A brass commemorates Henry Rolle and Margaret, his wife (d. 1591). They lived at Heanton

Barton in this parish. Allisland, Heanton, Hele, Little Marland, and Varleys were all Domesday manors.

PILTON (D2), now mostly incorporated in the borough of Barnstaple, was one of the four *burhs* of Devon in Alfred's reign, keeping guard over Barnstaple Bay. By the end of the 10th cent. it had been superseded by Barnstaple, which has now swallowed up its parent. There was a small priory at Pilton, founded in the 12th cent. as a cell of Malmesbury, and dissolved in 1536. The site of the priory was on the N. side of the parish church.

The church (St. Mary) was the priory church until 1536. It was a 13th-cent. building (cf. the N. aisle and lower part of the tower), but the nave and chancel were reconstructed *c.* 1320 and the S. aisle of nave and chancel added in the early 16th cent. But the real interest of the church lies in its splendid woodwork and monuments. The rood-screen may be dated *c.* 1420-50, and is of a rare and beautiful type. The rich S. parclose screen to the Chichester chapel is later in date. Over the font is a carved medieval cover, and above that a remarkable tester or canopy of 16th-cent. date. The stone pulpit is also 16th-cent., with an Elizabethan canopy above it and an hourglass attached to it. Stretching across the chancel and S. aisle is a fine Elizabethan altar rail; and the altar table also appears to be Elizabethan. The church seems to have been much "done up" by the Chichesters of Raleigh, who acquired the site of the priory and the manor soon after the Dissolution. There is a good Renaissance monument in Beer stone to Sir John Chichester (1569), who was twice sheriff of Devon and twice represented the county in Parliament, and his wife, Gertrude (Courtenay), who d. 1566. There are also monuments to Sir Robert Chichester (1627), and to Christopher Lethbridge of Westaway (1713), and there are two small brasses in the chancel aisle to Robert and Alexander Bret.

A few interesting houses remain in the town, of which Broadgate House (18th-cent.) and Bull House (partly medieval) are the most notable.

PINHOE (H6) church (St. Michael) is beautifully placed on a hill with fine views S. to the sea. The adjoining vicarage is Queen Anne red brick, with a massive red sandstone chimney stack at the back (plate 10).

The church, almost entirely a 15th-cent. building of local red sandstone, contains much that is interesting. The screen is perfect. It retains its vaulting and cornices with their enrichments and its proportions are singularly good. The pulpit is carved and is of the same date as the screen (late 15th-cent.). The nave roof retains some of its original bosses and colour. The font is curious: the bowl is certainly Norman, but the lower half may be Anglo-Saxon. A modern brass tablet commemorates John Reynolds, D.D. (1549-1607), who was President of Corpus Christi College, Oxford, and tutor to Richard Hooker. A curious figure of a parish beadle (1700) surmounts an alms-box.

The parish was the site of a battle in 1001, in which the Saxons were defeated by the Danes. The actual site is said to be in or near Mincimore copse. Pinhoe village has been suburbanised by its contact with Exeter.

PLYMOUTH (C10) is a city of some 239,000 people, by far the largest town in Devon, extending for about 4 m. from W. to E. across the peninsula between the estuaries of Tamar and Plym. To the S. lies the Sound, a magnificent deep-water anchorage, and one of the finest harbour views in Europe. Inland, the city boundaries reach Tamerton Lake to the NW. and include the rural parish of Egg Buckland on the NE., taking in altogether an area of 13,136 acres, or rather more than 20 sq. miles. The city is essentially a union of the three towns of Plymouth on the E., Devonport on the W., and Stonehouse

pendent centres. Few cities, if any, in Britain have such a superb site, with the blue edge of Dartmoor in full view to the NE., the Cornish hills and the noble estuary of the Tamar to the W., and the Sound in front enclosed between fine headlands, and dotted with shipping.

The old town of Plymouth lay in a hollow behind a limestone cliff-wall, which stretched from the Tamar to the Plym and continued beyond the Plym in the heights of Oreston and Mount

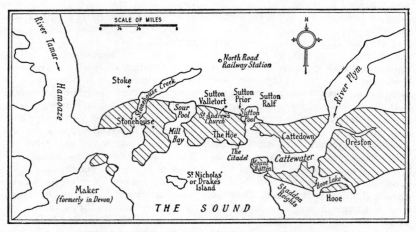

FIG. 16—THE SITE OF EARLY PLYMOUTH

The limestone area is shaded. A few modern landmarks are shown for guidance

between them. Though the three towns had coalesced long before, they were not united under one authority—the borough of Plymouth—until 1914. In 1928 the borough was made a city by royal charter, and is now headed by a lord mayor.

The topography of Plymouth is complex, with its numerous inlets of tidal water, the undulating and broken character of the peninsula itself, and the fact of its growth from three independent

Batten. The central section of this limestone wall forms to-day the famous Hoe. Three deep inlets breached the wall— Sutton Pool, Mill Bay (with Sour Pool), and Stonehouse Creek, of which the last two originally extended much farther inland than they do to-day. Around Sutton Pool, or more precisely a little NW. of it, in the region of Old Town Street to-day, lay the Saxon germ of this great city—the hamlet of Sutton or " South *tun*." Where Devonport now stands was a bird-haunted waste of marsh and mud along the Tamar mouth. The sketch-map shows the elements of Plymouth topography.

The hamlet of Sutton was part of a royal estate in Saxon times. Much of this royal estate (the manors of Sutton, King's Tamerton, and Maker) was granted away by Henry I to the Valletorts, who in turn gave part of the manor of Sutton to Plympton Priory, not far away. The monastic half of the manor became known as Sutton Prior; to the N. and W. of it lay Sutton Valletort (or Vautort).

Until the latter part of the 12th cent., Sutton Prior remained a small agricultural and fishing village. With the acquisition of the provinces of SW. France by Henry II, the harbour was increasingly used by military and commercial shipping, though always overshadowed by Dartmouth which had a more sheltered anchorage. The great defect of Plymouth Sound was that it lay wide open to the prevailing SW. winds, and it could become a prison for sailing ships.

The priors of Plympton created a borough on the shores of Sutton Pool, probably about the middle of the 13th cent.,[1] and the name Plymouth began to be used of the port proper. By the late 13th cent. the harbour was being used increasingly as a place of assembly for military expeditions and for ships engaged in the French wine trade, and Plymouth became second only to Exeter in population and wealth.[2]

In its early days, Plymouth was held back by the close control exercised over the borough by the priors of Plympton. After a prolonged struggle the town shook itself free of its maternal parent and was incorporated by act of parliament in 1439. By this charter the three Suttons (Sutton Prior, Sutton Vautort,

and Sutton Ralf) were amalgamated, and a mayor and corporation set up for the enlarged borough.

Although Plymouth merchants were considerable men in the early 16th cent. —old William Hawkins, the father of Sir John, being the most notable—the town did not achieve any national importance until the latter part of the cent. when it became the principal naval base in the war against Spain. It became a clearing-house for prizes taken at sea, a starting point for voyages of exploration and colonisation, and a port of assembly for the navy. The choice of Plymouth, rather than Dartmouth, as the naval base was largely due to Sir Francis Drake, whose home port was Plymouth, and to Sir John Hawkins, a native of the town, who was treasurer of the navy 1578-89, and comptroller 1589-95. It was from Plymouth that Drake sailed on 19 July 1588 to attack and defeat the Armada, and it was on Plymouth Hoe that he played his famous game of bowls. This traditional story is almost certainly true. It first appeared in print in 1624, within living memory of the event;[3] and there are certain other details as to tides and winds which make the story highly probable.

Plymouth rose with the Spanish menace and fell away with its removal in the early 17th cent. The population nearly doubled in the war town of 1580-1600. We hear of new streets being built all round Sutton Pool at this date. " Sperke's new streete " named after a big merchant (and called New Street to-day) is first recorded in 1584; Treville Street is named after the Elizabethan merchant Richard Treville; Southside Street appears in 1591, Looe Street in 1588. This is now the oldest and most historic part of the town, where several 16th–17th-cent. merchants' houses remain. The most notable example is No. 32 New Street, which dates from *c.* 1590. It now belongs to the Plymouth corporation and is open for inspection. New Street itself retains much of its old character, narrow and winding, and paved with granite cobbles.

As the Spanish threat to England lessened in the 17th century, Plymouth lost much of its importance as a naval base. It remained the second town of Devon, stinking, sprawling, and full of poverty-stricken fishermen, carrying on also a considerable trade with the New England colonies. The next great impetus to its growth came with the rise of France as the national enemy, and hence the renewed necessity for a western naval base. Dartmouth and Falmouth were considered and rejected, and the site for the new naval dockyards was fixed, not at Plymouth itself, but on the unpeopled marshes and meadows along the edge of the Tamar. By 1696 the naval base of Dock had come into being. The incessant wars of the 18th cent. nourished the new town to such effect that within a hundred years it had surpassed Plymouth, and the rivalry between the two was intense. By 1815 Dock had some 32,000 people against Plymouth's 22,000. Stonehouse, which lay between them, had grown to about 6,000 with the overflow of naval buildings from Dock, but the three towns were still separate entities. In 1824 Dock was granted the more dignified name of Devonport and Foulston's fine column (which still stands) went up to commemorate the event. Devonport achieved complete recognition as a separate town when it was incorporated in 1837.

With the end of the long wars, Devonport's growth slowed up, and Plymouth forged ahead as a fishing port and a growing commercial harbour. The construction of the Breakwater by Rennie (1812-40) gave the port one of the largest and safest harbours in Britain. By 1881 Plymouth had 74,000 people, Devonport rather less than 49,000, Stonehouse some 15,000—a total of about 138,000 in the Three Towns, as they were now habitually called. They were now one continuous mass of building and their unification under one authority was inevitable. This came in 1914, when the whole borough took the name of Plymouth, though each town retains its own distinctive character. Plymouth flourished as a great naval base during the war of 1914-18: "Upon the British coast what ship yet ever came that not of Plymouth hears, where the brave navies lie?" said Drayton long ago in his *Polyolbion.*

But the Second German War reached it as the First had not done. From 1940 to 1943, and above all in the terrible spring of 1941, the city was pounded from the air by the missionaries of 20th-cent. civilisation, and suffered vast damage and casualties. About 1,000 people were killed, 5,000 injured, 10,000 houses destroyed, and some 70,000 more damaged. The whole centre of the city was wiped out, but the congested area around Sutton Pool largely escaped and represents all that is left of old Plymouth. Now the new city has risen from the ruins but it is too soon to pass judgement upon the result. Old Plymothians look sadly upon it.

Of medieval Plymouth, very little remains. The fine 15th-cent. parish church of St. Andrew was gutted by fire in the 1941 raids. The tower and walls stood, and it has now been well rebuilt. Chantrey's marble bust of Zachariah Mudge, a great Plymouth

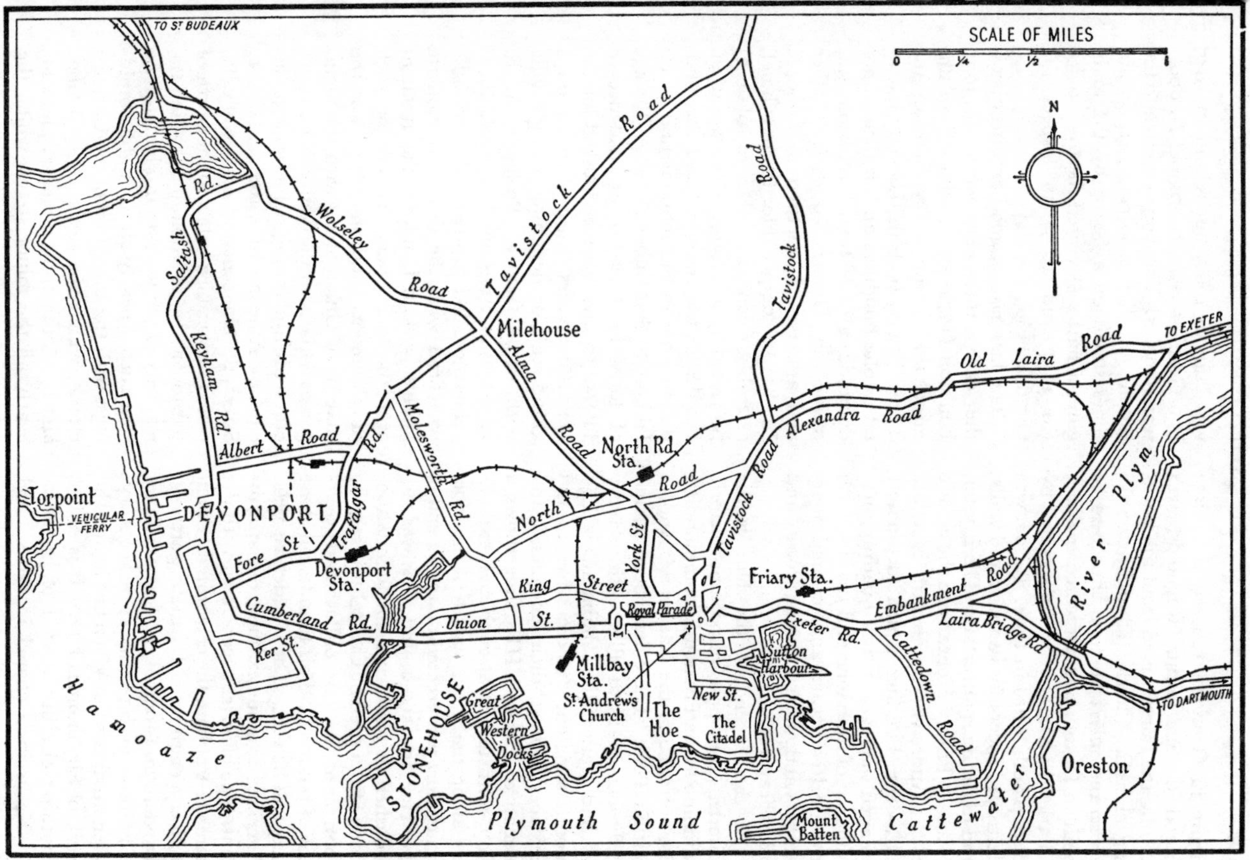

FIG. 17—MODERN PLYMOUTH

figure in Georgian times and a close friend of Sir Joshua Reynolds, was among the things saved from the burning church. Charles Church, not far away, the only 17th-cent. church to be built in Devon, was dedicated to King Charles the Martyr, and consecrated by Bishop Seth Ward in 1664. It, too, was destroyed except for its tower and walls, and its future is uncertain. The Prysten House ("Priests' House") on the S. side of St. Andrew's churchyard, is a late 15th-cent. building which fortunately escaped damage. It is a quadrangular building of limestone and granite, with a central courtyard and original doorways, windows, staircases, roofs, and other features.[1]

At the E. end of the Hoe is the Citadel, the most important historic building left in Plymouth, commanding the entrance to the Cattewater and to Sutton Pool. There had been earlier defensive works at Plymouth. Henry IV had granted the inhabitants of Plymouth a patent "to erect towers and defences against their enemies," and a map of Henry VIII's time shows a wall, with towers at each end, extending along the whole length of the Hoe. A new fort was erected on the E. end of the Hoe in 1590-2, but this was demolished in 1666 when the foundation-stone of the present Citadel was laid by John Grenville, Earl of Bath and governor of the town. This foundation-stone may still be seen. The Citadel has been described as a fine example of the 17th-cent. type of fortress associated with the name of Vauban, the celebrated French military engineer. Its main gateway, dated 1670, is one of the best examples of baroque architecture in this country, often attributed to Wren but in fact the work of Sir Thomas Fitz.[2] It is unlike anything else in the west of England. St. Katherine's chapel in the Citadel

was built in 1668, but rebuilt in 1845 in a Gothic style. Its original N. doorway remains. The chapel is open to the public for divine worship at certain times stated on a board by the main gate. Charles II visited the town twice (in 1671 and 1677) to inspect the Citadel.

The last gasp of good architecture is the early 19th-cent. work of John Foulston (1772-1842), who left an unmistakable stamp everywhere in the Three Towns, both in their monumental public buildings and in their minor domestic architecture. Foulston was trained in Thomas Hardwick's office and apparently practised in London. In 1811 he competed for the new hotel, assembly rooms, and theatre (plate 2) projected by the Plymouth corporation. His design was accepted and the foundation stone of this monumental group laid on 10 September 1811. At the age of forty he took up his residence in Plymouth and here he worked for the next thirty years, town-planning on a grand scale or designing a single villa with equal facility. Professor A. E. Richardson sums up his work thus: " Foulston, like Granger of Newcastle, was fired with the desire to emulate Nash's work in London; the moment and the man had arrived for such developments, and the result was the shaping of Union Street with the Octagon as a hiatus at the centre. Foulston's other town-planning achievements included Athenaeum Street, Lockyer Street, the Crescent and a range of villas called Devonshire Villas to the north of the town. In addition to designing the majority of the terraces in Plymouth he constructed nearly all the public buildings, with the exception of the Customs House, which was designed by Laing; and he at this time prepared plans for nearly all the minor streets which the speculative builders of the day were eager to proceed with. Plymouth in the early 'twenties was a forest of scaffold poles, soon to be cleared to reveal the stuccoed conventions in Greek taste devised by this architect. It is, of course, burking the question to assume that Foulston designed every house, but his personality is stamped on the doors, windows and iron gates, while it is clear the builders of the time were sworn to allegiance, for they caught the spirit of his manner and faithfully obeyed his orders. At Stoke Damarel, Foulston's hand is to be seen in the composition of the stately façade forming St. Michael's Terrace, as well as in the unique Albemarle Villas which are contiguous (plate 5). His work at Devonport included the civic centre, the Naval Column and many other works."[1] Towards the end of his life, Foulston took into partnership George Wightwick, who did much good building in Plymouth and Devonport in the 1850s. But after 1860 the Foulston tradition was lost and new building in the Three Towns became as commonplace as anywhere else.

Of Foulston's great civic centre in Plymouth, most is gone. The Theatre was destroyed before 1939 to make room for a gigantic cinema which might just as well be in the outer suburbs of London (it survived the air-raids), and the Royal Hotel and Assembly Rooms perished in the raids of 1941. The Athenaeum, built next to the theatre by Foulston in 1818-19, is also gone. The Proprietary library (1812) in Cornwall Street, was destroyed in the war of 1939-45. The Royal Union Baths (1828), in Foulston's best classical style, were pulled down as early as 1849 to make room for the new Millbay railway terminus. One of the few public buildings by Foulston left in

Plymouth was St. Catherine's Church in Lockyer Street, built in 1823 but this too was pulled down in recent years.

At Devonport most of Foulston's civic centre in Ker Street survives; the Town Hall (plate 3), a handsome classical building modelled on the Parthenon, finished in 1823, the Column commemorating the new name of Devonport (1824), and the Civil and Military Library (1823). The Column was origi nally intended to have a colossal statue of George IV on the top, but the necessary funds were never forthcoming. The Civil and Military Library was built in the Egyptian style one of Foulston's few eccentric buildings. It is now a Christian Scientist church and exceedingly shabby. The Mount Zion chapel, now destroyed, formed part of this civic centre. It was built for the Calvinists in a vaguely Mohammedan style. Foulston calls this extraordinary collection of buildings "an experimental group." His own opinion was that it was a strange but picturesque combination.[2]

Among the numerous 19th-cent. churches of Devonport, a number were designed by J. P. St. Aubyn, including St. Paul's (1849), St. Mary's (1850), St. James the Great at Keyham (1849-51), and St. Stephen's (1852). St. Aubyn's Church was built in 1771, St. John's (Duke Street) in 1779. The ancient parish church of Stoke Damarel (St. Andrew) is of little interest. It was a 15th-cent. church, but has been so enlarged and altered as to have little character left.

The monumental architecture of the Dockyard and the other naval establishments in Devonport and Stonehouse is of much more importance. Sir John Rennie's Royal William Victualling Yard at Stonehouse (1826-35) is one of the grandest monuments of the 19th

2H

cent. in England. It is a vast conception, of Spartan severity: an engineer's architecture suitable in every way for naval affairs and designed down to the detail of the lamp-posts. Less exciting are the Royal Naval Hospital at Stonehouse (1762 onwards) and the Royal Marine Barracks (1784 and later). The two dockyards that constitute the Naval Dockyard front the mouth of the Tamar—here called the Hamoaze—for some 2 m. and cover together 243 acres. Visitors of British nationality may be conducted around them on application at the main (Keyham) gate at any time during ordinary working hours. The two yards are separated by the Gun Wharf, built in 1718-25 by Vanburgh.

St. Budeaux, N. of Devonport, is now completely engulfed in suburban Plymouth. The parish church (St. Budoc) was rebuilt in 1563 in the Gothic style on a new site which commands fine views of the river and the Cornish bank. The old site was somewhere by the shore of the creek near Budshead, and was perhaps the landing place of the Celtic saint Budoc in the 6th or 7th cent. There are considerable traces of the old mansion of the Budsheads here. The whole creek is beautiful and full of feeling, associated as it is with many of the early saints, Indract, Dominic, Budoc, and all their company (see TAMERTON FOLIOT also). The present church is chiefly of interest for its associations with Sir Francis Drake who was married here to Mary Newman in 1569, and with Sir Ferdinando Gorges (1566?-1647). He was governor of Plymouth, became interested in colonisation, and formed two companies which received grants of land in New England. He founded the settlement of New Plymouth in 1628, and was appointed first governor of Maine in 1635. He died

in 1647 and his table monument is here.

Egg Buckland parish on the NE. side of Plymouth is partly occupied by the military defences of the town and port. The church (St. Erasmus) has a good 14th-cent. tower and S. porch, but was otherwise rebuilt in 1864. Widey Court, about ½ m. NW., was the headquarters of Prince Maurice when he besieged Plymouth in 1643, and was visited by the king in September 1644. The house is now neglected and dilapidated.

In the middle of Plymouth Sound lies Drake's Island, formerly called St. Nicholas's Island from the chapel that stood on it. It is fortified and garrisoned, and was formerly a State prison. The republican general Lambert died a prisoner here in 1683, after sixteen years' confinement which he passed chiefly in painting flowers and working out problems in algebra. For a time he had as a fellow-prisoner James Harington, the political theorist and author of *The Commonwealth of Oceana.* Harington was afterwards allowed to live in Plymouth for his health's sake, and eventually died in London in 1677. Several adherents of the parliamentarian cause were confined on the island after 1660, as well as dissenting ministers after the act of 1662.[1] The chapel of St. Nicholas, which stood on the summit of the island, was demolished in 1548 to make room for the fortifications. The island now belongs to the War Department and is not normally open to the public.

Beyond the island lies the Breakwater, begun in 1812 and finished by Sir John Rennie in 1840. It lies 2 m. from the Hoe, is about a mile long, and required about 4,500,000 tons of limestone for its construction. The lighthouse on the end was first lit in 1844. In the centre is a large fort, which is actually a separate structure.

Fourteen miles from the Hoe, from which it is visible on clear days, is the famous Eddystone lighthouse, the fourth on the site. The first structure was Winstanley's (1696), swept away in the great storm of 1703. Rudyerd's lighthouse (1706) was burnt down in 1755. Smeaton's (1759) was only superseded in 1882 because the rock on which it stood was being undermined by the sea. It was taken down and re-erected on Plymouth Hoe. The present lighthouse was built by Sir J. N. Douglass and lit in 1882. It rises 133 ft. above high-water mark. It is built of granite blocks, weighing in all 4,668 tons, and has been the model for most lighthouses since built in similar situations on isolated reefs.

Plymouth has given its name to some forty Plymouths all over the English-speaking world. What greater testimony is needed to the affection that it has inspired for the past 400 years? It is the mother of all Plymouths everywhere.

PLYMPTON EARL (or PLYMPTON ST. MAURICE) (D10) lies on a by-road ½ m. S. of the busy main road from Plymouth to Exeter. Those who have a special feeling for the small, ancient, and decayed boroughs of England will be delighted with Plympton. It has been left on one side in the past two hundred years or so, and one smells cow-dung in the streets instead of petrol fumes: the immemorial life-giving smell of the land from which the little town took its birth in the 12th cent.

The manor and honour of Plympton were granted by Henry I to Richard de Redvers before 1107. He built the castle on his demesne land, on the S.

side of which there grew up a small community of traders and farmers. His descendant, William de Vernon, 5th Earl of Devon, made a borough of it in 1194, with a market and fair; and unlike so many of the seignorial boroughs of Devon Plympton grew into a town, though never of any great size. It was one of the few "regular boroughs" of Devon, returning members of Parliament without a break from 1295 until it was disfranchised in 1832; and it was incorporated in 1602 and had a mayor and corporation from then until 1859. In 1328 it was made one of the four stannary towns. By Elizabeth's time the town had a weekly market and no fewer than four annual fairs; and the charter of William and Mary added two more fairs, making six in all. The decay of the castle and the dissolution of the priory did not affect the life of the little town unduly. Even if we did not know this from the records, the architectural evidence from the 16th to the 18th cents. would reveal the prosperity of the place. Plympton carried on wool-combing, tanning and brewing, coopering and hat-making. All these trades died for one reason or another, and at the first census (1801) the borough had only 604 people. It grew slowly during the 19th cent., mostly at the perimeter and not in the old town itself. But it still has only some 1,200 people, and the town keeps its ancient atmosphere. Some recent growth is due to the influence of Plymouth.

The disfranchisement of the borough in 1832 gave it a mortal blow, for the close corporation depended on its patron and recorder (the Earl of Mount Edgcumbe) for meeting the greater part of its annual expenditure.[1] With the abolition of the parliamentary borough, the patron withdrew the favour of his countenance and his cash. It was this that led the desperate corporation to start selling their pictures, including Sir Joshua Reynolds's self-portrait. The Guildhall is an interesting building in the local slate and granite, dated 1688-96. It is now occupied by the Plympton St. Maurice parish council, who succeeded the old corporation after an interval. The corporation allowed its charter to lapse in 1859, when the last mayor was elected; and the ancient borough, so long enfeebled, passed quietly away in its sleep.

The castle, built by Richard de Redvers, was surrendered during the rebellion of his son Baldwin in Stephen's reign, and is said to have been razed. The ruins of the stone keep date from this time. The earthworks of the castle, including the motte, are substantially intact and make a promenade from which one gets a good view over the roof-tops of the little town.

The grammar school, built about 1664 in a Jacobean Gothic and restored in 1870, is famous for its associations with Sir Joshua Reynolds, whose father was master here. Much of the original building remains, including the schoolroom and the granite arcade or cloister, the subject of one of Reynolds's earliest drawings. Here also were educated Northcote, Haydon and Eastlake; Haydon was at the head of the school in 1801. Few schools in England can have such rich associations in the history of painting, but few towns in England can have been so unaware of their greatest son. Plympton pulled down the birthplace of the greatest portrait painter the country has produced; there was not even a memorial to Reynolds until a tablet was placed in the church in 1904.

The parish church (St. Maurice) was formerly dedicated to St. Thomas of Canterbury, this dedication being changed in the time of Henry VIII.

It is an unexciting building of 14th-15th-cent. date, restored in 1879.

Many old houses survive in the grey streets of Plympton. Plympton House, now a mental hospital, was begun in 1700 by Sir George Treby, Lord Chief Justice, and finished by his son, George Treby, in 1720. It has a perfect Queen Anne front, and retains complete and intact its contemporary gardens.

PLYMPTON ST. MARY (D10) is a vast parish, covering well over 10,000 acres, with an ancient village on the main road from Plymouth to Exeter. To-day the village is almost a suburb of Plymouth, and has doubled its numbers since 1900.

An Augustinian priory was founded at Plympton St. Mary in 1121, but a collegiate church of St. Peter and St. Paul had existed here from the time of Alfred. Plympton priory became the second richest monastery in Devon and Cornwall, exceeded only by Tavistock Abbey, but scarcely a vestige of this great house remains to-day. Such small fragments as remain lie to the S. of Plympton Parish Church. Among its property was the site of Plymouth, a town which owes its origin to the priory.

Plympton church (St. Mary) stood in the churchyard of the conventual church: hence its comparative isolation from the village to-day. It now stands in a lawn-like churchyard, a handsome building of early 14th- and 15th-cent. date, built largely of granite. The granite tower (108 ft.) is notably good. Among the features of the interior are the Strode monuments (1460, 1637), some ancient heraldic glass, the mutilated canopied tomb of a Courtenay (15th-cent.), the handsome triple sedilia and piscina in the chancel, and the good modern parclose screens.

The fertile countryside of Plympton

had no fewer than thirteen lesser Domesday manors besides the royal manor. All these ancient estates survive to-day (except the lost Walford), most as farmhouses, some as country houses. The Domesday manors were Baccamoor, Battisford, Bickford Town, Challonsleigh, Elfordleigh, Hemerdon, Holland, Langage, Loughtor Mills, Torridge, Woodford, Walford (lost), and Yealmpstone. Sparkwell appears by 1167, Saltram by 1249, Boringdon by 1279, Newnham by 1292.

Boringdon came to the Parkers in the time of Elizabeth. They rebuilt it on a substantial scale and made it their principal residence until they moved to Saltram after 1712. The house has been half-demolished, but there are considerable remains of the Elizabethan house, including the great hall.

Saltram, on a fine site overlooking the Plym estuary, is the largest house in Devon. In the reign of Charles I it was the seat of Sir James Bagg of Plymouth, and was then a substantial Tudor mansion. John Parker married Lady Catherine Powlett and it was they who built Saltram much as we see it to-day: a house of George II's time. It has been altered and added to three or four times, and is now rich in all that the 18th-cent. architects and craftsmen could effect.[1] In 1768 the lower rooms were superbly decorated by Adam, notably the saloon and the dining-room. The former is a double cube, and is said by Polwhele to have cost at least £10,000. The ceilings of these rooms were painted by Zucchi. Among the art treasures of this great house, the collection of English and French furniture, and the pictures, are equally outstanding. The furniture includes a superb writing-table which formerly belonged to Louis XIV. The pictures are undoubtedly the finest collection in Devon. They include a considerable number of the works of Sir Joshua Reynolds, who was a friend of the Parkers and often stayed at Saltram, and the fine Italian pictures collected from 1751 onwards on the advice of Reynolds. Saltram is one of the three great houses still kept up in Devon. The other two are Powderham (the Earl of Devon) and Castle Hill (Earl Fortescue).

Newnham Park is the seat of the Strodes, who originated at Strode in Ermington, and moved to Newnham in the 15th cent. Their old house is now a farmhouse (Old Newnham) with many traces of the former "mansion," but about 1700 they built their present house in a large park.

On the NE. side of the parish, on the high foothills of the Moor, are extensive china-clay works. The scenery of the parish is beautiful and varied, especially in the wooded valley of the Plym. Plym Bridge is the most interesting and picturesque on the Plym. A bridge existed here as early as 1238, on the important main road from Tavistock to Plympton.

PLYMSTOCK (D10) is now swamped by suburban Plymouth. The church (formerly All Saints, now St. Mary and All Saints), is essentially a 14th-cent. building enlarged in the 15th, when the fine bold W. tower was added. There are two excellent granite arcades, of differing styles, and a handsome rood-screen of the same period (15th-cent.). The pulpit is late 17th-cent., with contemporary stairs and sounding-board. In the S. chancel aisle, which was the chapel of Harris of Radford, are some good 17th- and 18th-cent. mural monuments of the family.

Radford, the seat of the Harrises from Edward IV's time (1461-83), was demolished in 1937 to make way for a building estate. An account of the house will be found in DA **77** (1944), 149-55. A number of small manors existed here as early as the Norman Conquest—Goosewell, Hooe, Staddiscombe and Staddon.

Oreston, now a populous suburb, has extensive quarries of limestone from which the stone for Plymouth breakwater (1812-41) was taken—4½ million tons in all. At Mount Batten, now a seaplane station, considerable discoveries of burials, pottery, coins, and other evidence, show that a native trading settlement existed on the S. shore of the Cattewater throughout the greater part of the Roman period. The coin sequence runs, with slight breaks, from Nero (54-68) to Honorius (433).[1] During excavations for the present Stamford Fort in 1864, a late Celtic cemetery was discovered on the hillside a little SW. of the fort.[2]

Stamford Fort occupies the site of defences thrown up in 1643 by the inhabitants of Plymouth in preparation for the royalist siege, and is named after the parliamentarian commander, the Earl of Stamford.

PLYMTREE (J5) is a small parish set in a fertile red sandstone country of rich dairy pastures, magnificent oak timber, and orchards that produce some of the best cider in Devon. It contains a number of interesting houses. Fordmoor, formerly called simply Ford, is said by Lysons to have been the home of the Fords from Henry II's time until 1702. It is a fine Elizabethan house. Woodbeer passed through a succession of families from Domesday onwards. The present house (Woodbeer Court) is a medieval hall-house, with walls 4 ft. thick. It was reconstructed internally at a later date, like so many medieval mansions in Devon, to make more

convenient rooms. Hayne House is early Georgian. Greenend was the manor house and was for long the residence of the Pratts, ancestors of Earl Camden.

The parish church (St. John the Baptist) is a 14th-cent. building, with a S. aisle and W. tower added in the 15th cent. There are 15th-cent. carved bench-ends, and some interesting church plate, but the glory of the church is the rood-screen. This is a very beautiful example of the fan-vaulted Devonshire screens, dating in all probability from just after 1470. The painted figures on the lower panels of the screen rank as one of the most perfect sets yet remaining; most of them keep their ancient colour. The four panels representing the Adoration of the Magi are particularly notable; but there is no basis for the assertion that the three Kings portray Cardinal Morton, Henry VII, and Prince Arthur.

Thomas Mozley, who was rector 1868-80, was for many years a leader-writer to *The Times* and author of *Reminiscences of Oriel College and the Oxford Movement.* He used to walk or drive every afternoon to Ottery Road station (now Sidmouth Junction) where he had a room at the Railway Hotel. Here he found the subject on which he was to write his leader, sent down from London by telegraph, and his article would be despatched to *The Times* by the late afternoon train.

POLTIMORE (H6) gives its name to the barony of Poltimore, created 1831. The manor came to the Bampfyldes soon after 1303 and has remained with them to the present day. Their house, a plain square mansion in a dull park, was probably rebuilt by Sir Coplestone Bampfylde, the 2nd baronet (1636-91). The date 1681 appears on the stone gate-piers at the main entrance to the park and may indicate the date of completion of the house, which was altered in the 1840s by the first Lord Poltimore. A new wing was added in 1909. The house is now a private hospital.

The church (St. Mary) was rather heavily restored by Medley Fulford in 1878-84 when a number of drastic changes were made, but it retains some interesting features, including a fine chancel screen. This has its ancient tracery, with beautiful Renaissance detail of late date in the vaulting (c. 1520-30). The 18th-cent. Bampfylde pew is a good specimen of its kind with a fireplace. In the south transept is the tomb with recumbent figures of Richard Bampfylde (d. 1594) and Elizabeth, his wife (d. 1599).

POOL, SOUTH (FII), lies at the head of a long creek of the Kingsbridge estuary and is one of the most attractive and unspoilt villages in Devon. The fine church (St. Nicholas and St. Cyriacus) is of considerable interest. It is built entirely of local slates, the tower being a notable example of building in this stone. The present fabric is mainly late 15th-cent. in date, but the core of the church may be that of the building consecrated by Bishop Stapeldon on 24 August 1318. The rood-screen, a fine example, is probably c. 1500 or a little later, and is similar to that of Dartmouth. In the S. transept is a female effigy (early 14th-cent.), either a Courtenay or a Chichester. The Easter sepulchre is occupied by the tomb and effigy of Thomas Briant, rector of S. Pool and Portlemouth (living 1536). At the back of the recess is a carving of the Resurrection. There are monuments to Leonard Darre, Esquire, and his wife (1608, 1615), and a splendid Norman font.

PORTLEMOUTH (FI2) faces Salcombe (to which there is a ferry) across the mouth of the Kingsbridge estuary. From the hillside just below the parish church is seen one of the most beautiful estuary views in England, looking N. to Kingsbridge and the distant Moor. The coastal scenery is also very beautiful; most of the cliffs belong to the National Trust. The church (St. Winwaloe) suffered a thorough restoration in 1881 when the floor-levels were radically altered. All the window-tracery, roofs, and seating were modernised at the same time. The rood-screen (c. 1500), of the Dartmouth type, probably marks the completion of the new fabric. The lower panels have a fine series of figure paintings, the figure holding a church being St. Winwaloe.

POUGHILL (G5) (pron. Poil) is in the remote, hilly country between the Exe and Taw valleys. The church (St. Michael) was heavily restored in 1855-6 and is consequently of little interest.

POWDERHAM (H7) consists of little more than the red sandstone church, familiar to all who travel on the Great Western Railway beyond Exeter, and the castle and park of the Earl of Devon. The church (St. Clement) is entirely a 15th-cent. building with the usual Beer stone arcades. Margaret Courtenay says in her will (1487) that she and her husband had made the new aisle and the body of the church at their own cost "except that I had of the parish to the help of the said building 8d."[1] They were both buried here, almost certainly under a fine tomb as the builders of the church; but not a single Courtenay monument remains to-day except that of Elizabeth, Countess of Devon (1867), hidden behind the organ.

On the N. side of the chancel is the

cenotaph of a lady who is probably Elizabeth de Bohun, daughter of Edward I, and mother of Margaret de Bohun who married Hugh Courtenay, 2nd Earl of Devon. Powderham then belonged to the Bohuns and Margaret brought it with her as her marriage portion. By her will dated 1390 she bequeathed it to her fourth son, Sir Philip Courtenay. So began the long line of the Courtenays of Powderham, who are still there, though Powderham did not become their principal home until after the attainder of Henry Courtenay, Marquess of Exeter, and the forfeiture of all his lands to the crown in 1539.

Sir Philip Courtenay, Lord Lieutenant of Ireland (d. 1406), began the building of Powderham. There is no evidence that a castle existed here before his time.

Sir Philip Courtenay's building must be regarded as a strongly fortified manor house (like Compton Castle in Marldon) rather than as a true castle, but the site was much stronger than appears to-day as one steams by the placid and almost level park, catching a fleeting glimpse of the battlemented towers of the castle between the trees. Until the late 18th cent. the Exe spread its waters almost to the E. walls of the castle, and its tributary the Kenn almost washed the S. walls.

The original building comprised a hall, kitchen, and other offices, strengthened by four angle-towers and an entrance tower facing the Exe. This building can still be traced, though swamped by later alterations. Leland describes Powderham as a strong castle, with a bulwark or barbican to protect the haven here. This would be the small harbour of Kenton. By the attainder of Henry, Marquess of Exeter, all the great estates of the elder branch of the Courtenays were lost for ever. Though Edward Courtenay, son of the Marquess, was recreated Earl of Devon by Mary in 1553, the family did not recover their ancient honours and castles; and from this date onwards Powderham became their principal residence.

In the Civil War, Powderham was garrisoned for the king. Fairfax, in the final campaign in the west, sent a party to attack it on 14 December 1645. Meeting with unexpectedly strong resistance they fell back and took possession of Powderham church, which was then attacked by a royalist detachment from Exeter, during which handgrenades were thrown into the church. No doubt the Courtenay monuments suffered severely on that occasion. The next day Sir Hardress Waller relieved the parliamentary garrison in the church. The castle surrendered a few weeks later (25 January 1646).

In the 18th cent. the medieval house was transformed by a series of large-scale alterations, beginning in 1717 when the chapel was built, together with the library above. The major reconstruction took place when the 2nd Viscount Courtenay succeeded to the estates, particularly between 1770 and 1788. The great hall was divided into two parts, one of which was transformed by the insertion of a grand staircase. The park was improved by the making of an embankment along the Exe estuary, and extensively planted with fine trees, and the Belvedere was built (1773) on the ridge NW. of the castle.

Other internal changes were made under the direction of James Wyatt, and a further extensive remodelling of the whole building was carried out by the 10th earl, who ruled from 1835 to 1859. Among other changes he rebuilt the W. front (except the centre tower) and made it the principal entrance, instead of the E. front as hitherto. The latter now (after 1846) faced the South Devon Railway and the fine river view had been shut off. Thus Powderham is to-day a house of the period 1760-1860, with a medieval core (plate 31).[1]

Among the pictures at Powderham are a full-length of the Duchess of Suffolk, attributed to Holbein; General Monk by J. M. Wright; Lady Honeywood and her son by Sir Joshua Reynolds; Lady Frances Courtenay by Hudson; the 2nd viscount with his wife and family by Hudson; and some full-size portraits by Cosway of the 9th earl and six of his sisters. There is also a fine portrait of Louis XVI, attributed to Callet. A history of the Courtenays, the most eminent and distinguished family in Devon, is in course of preparation. The present earl, the 17th from the re-creation of 1553, resides at Powderham.

PRINCETOWN (see LYDFORD).

PUDDINGTON (G4) church (St. Thomas à Becket) was vigorously restored in 1837-8, but there remain 23 carved bench-ends.

PUTFORD, EAST (B4) is a pleasant little place among trees, with good quiet views and some picturesque stone-built farmhouses, probably of Elizabethan date. The church (dedication unknown) was almost wholly rebuilt in 1882. It contains an elegant 12th-cent. font, some late medieval tiles in the south porch, and a pulpit made out of a medieval rood-screen.

Among the farms of the parish, Mambury and Winslade are interesting. Mambury, approached by a long avenue of beeches, was a freehold estate from its beginning in the 12th or 13th cent.

Winslade lies in remote country, below the topmost point of Melbury Hill (709 ft.). It gave its name to the Wynslade (sometimes Wydeslade) family, who were long seated here. John Wynslade and his son William took a prominent part in the Western Rebellion of 1549; the former was executed for his share in the rising and all his estates were forfeited to Edward VI. The present farmhouse contains a good deal of the early 16th-cent. mansion.

PUTFORD, WEST (B4,) lies on the W. slopes of the upper Torridge valley. Kismeldon Bridge, a mile upstream, is the first important bridge over the youthful Torridge and is mentioned in 1279. The name is interesting, for it goes back to an early Christian cross in this lonely country (cristelmael, "cross, crucifix") which may have marked a ford at this point.

The church (dedication unknown: believed to be St. Stephen) is well sited on an eminence and is one of the most attractive churches in North Devon. Almost completely untouched by the Victorian restorer, it is spotlessly clean and well preserved: the walls are plain, plastered and whitewashed. It is a pleasure, not merely to the antiquary, but to all who see it. It is a cruciform building of the early 14th cent., with a W. tower added c. 1500. The font is Norman. The chancel is entirely floored with late medieval tiles, and there are modest mural monuments and inscriptions to local families of the late 17th and early 18th cents.

Cory Barton, half a mile N. of the church, is a good Elizabethan farm-house, possibly with even older portions.

Churston House (a corruption of "church-town") stands near the church and is an attractive Elizabethan manor house in the unsophisticated style of rural Devon at that period.

PYWORTHY (B5) has a large church (St. Swithin) for a small village, with fine views from the churchyard. Although rather over-restored, it is an interesting building structurally, being almost entirely a rebuilding of 1300-30. The S. aisle retains its 15th-cent. wagon roof with carved bosses and wall-plates. Pyworthy is exceptional in Devon in having a clearstory. Bradford was a Domesday estate.

QUEENS NYMPTON (F3) was formerly a detached part of the borough of South Molton, and was formed into a separate civil parish in 1900.

RACKENFORD (G4) lies high and remote. The church (All Saints) is a small, late 15th-cent. building, over-restored, and contains nothing of interest. Rackenford Manor, formerly called Cruwyshaye, is on the site of the old manor house. It is a mid-18th-cent. house, enlarged in 1928-32. Backstone, Bulworthy, Sideham, and Worthy Farm were all Domesday estates.

RATTERY (F9) church (St. Mary) is essentially a cruciform building of the 13th cent., remodelled in the 15th by the enlargement of the transepts into aisles both eastwards and westwards. The font is Norman, of red sandstone, with ornament like that at South Pool. The W. tower is a plain 13th-cent. structure. The 15th-cent rood-screen and parclose screens remain.

Luscombe was a Domesday manor. Velwell is first mentioned in 1249. It was a medieval "mansion" with a chapel licensed in 1417. Willing, now a farmhouse, was an old seat of the Savery family. Marley House has been known as Syon Abbey since 1935, when a community of Bridgettine nuns removed here after being at Chudleigh for nearly forty years. It is the only English community which can show an unbroken continuity from pre-Reformation days. Syon was founded in 1415 at Isleworth in Middlesex and had much property in East Devon. The community maintained an unbroken succession of English nuns during its long wanderings on the Continent after the Dissolution, and returned to England in 1861, Spettisbury in Dorset being its first home.

REVELSTOKE (see NEWTON and Noss).

REWE (H6) church (St. Mary) is a pleasant 15th-cent. building. The chancel screen is 15th-cent. work, modernised and newly coloured; some of the bench-ends are old and well carved.

Upexe, a Domesday estate, had an ancient chapel (dedication unknown), which was rebuilt in 1888. Rudway is another Domesday estate.

RINGMORE (E11), a very attractive village with much good building of 16th–18th-cent. date, is worth a careful exploration. The coastal scenery is also beautiful. The church (All Saints), though heavily restored in 1862-3, and lavishly coloured in the best Victorian manner, is worth inspection. It appears to be c. 1300 in date, but the N. transept contains Norman work from an earlier church.

At Okenbury, a Domesday manor, are substantial remains of the former medieval mansion.

ROBOROUGH (D4) church (St. Peter) was of 15th-cent. date, but the restoration in 1868 left a heavy mark. Coombe Barton is an early 16th-cent. farmhouse, with some contemporary doorways and windows. Owlacombe, Villavin, and Barlington were Domesday manors.

ROCKBEARE (J6) Manor is a perfect Regency house—straight out of Jane Austen. The original house was built *c.* 1760-70 and owned by Sir John Duntze, the wealthy Exeter woollen merchant and banker. About 1820 the house was remodelled with complete simplicity and refinement, possibly by Kendall of Exeter "who gave Plymouth and Exeter so many scholarly buildings between 1820 and 1840."[1] Rockbeare Court, beside the church, is a plain stuccoed late Georgian mansion. The church (St. Mary) is a melancholy exhibition of "restoration": it was almost entirely rebuilt in 1888 and is devoid of interest.

ROMANSLEIGH (F3) took its distinctive name from the dedication of the church to the Celtic saint Rumon. The present church was rebuilt in 1868 and is of no interest. The parish is hilly and commands fine views, especially towards Exmoor.

ROSE ASH (F3) lies on the back of a long ridge, nearly 800 ft. up, which is traversed by a prehistoric ridgeway. Much of the parish is wild, moory ground from which there are superb views of Exmoor and Dartmoor. The church (St. Peter) is a small 15th–16th-cent. building, entirely rebuilt (except for the tower) in 1888-92. The chancel screen is of plain Perpendicular character; the N. aisle screen is Jacobean, dated 1618, and carries the arms of James I, Anne of Denmark, and Prince Charles. The parclose screen, enclosing

the Southcomb chapel, is of the same date and design.

The Southcombs were rectors here without a break for eight generations from 1675 to 1948. An only son, the eleventh generation to live at Rose Ash, was killed in France in 1917. The present rectory was rebuilt in 1718 by the fourth Southcomb rector. Yard was a Domesday estate.

ROUSDON (*see* COMBPYNE).

ST. BUDEAUX (*see* PLYMOUTH).

ST. GILES-IN-THE-HEATH (B6) gave rise to the great Devonshire family of Cary who originated here in the 12th cent. at Carey Barton; but the present house is of no note. West Panson was a Domesday estate and has some old work. The church (St. Giles) is a plain little building with a low W. tower, a Norman font, and a mural monument to the Carys (1565).

ST. GILES-IN-THE-WOOD (D4) is a large parish with a number of hamlets, the greater part of which formerly belonged to the Rolle estate, centred at Stevenstone. George Rolle, one of the many successful Tudor lawyers, bought the Stevenstone estate shortly before 1524, and built himself "a right fair house of brick" (Leland) which was probably completed by 1539 when we find him writing to Lady Lisle from "my poor house" of Stevenstone. This Tudor house was rebuilt or remodelled some time in the 18th cent., but in 1868-72 the Hon. Mark Rolle rebuilt the house again in the worst style of the time. The richest man in Devon built himself the ugliest house. This is now being allowed to fall into ruin, but the attractive out-buildings of the 18th-cent. house (which were left standing) have been converted into flats. The Deer Park of 370 acres, once finely timbered, is now naked and devastated of its trees.

The church (St. Giles) was "restored" in 1863, with further alterations in 1879, by the Hon. Mark Rolle who spared no expense to make it as ugly as his own house. There remain, however, a number of brasses, as follows:

(1) Recumbent effigy and brass (1648) of Thomas Chafe, Esq., of Dodscott, now pushed into the tower, and dirty and neglected;

(2) a brass effigy of Elinor, wife of John Pollard of Way (1430), in the S. aisle, mutilated;

(3) a brass with effigies of a lady and ten children, of Margaret, the wife of John Rolle, Esq., of Stevenstone (1592), in the S. aisle;

(4) a brass effigy of Joan, the wife of William Risdon of Winscott, gent. (1610);

(5) a brass of John Rolle of Stevenstone, Esq. (1570).

The parish contains a number of interesting farmhouses, some of them formerly "mansions." Way is interesting as the *fons et origo* of the mighty tribe of Pollard, who bought it from the Ways before 1242, and who flowered forth in such profusion in the 16th–17th cents. It is now a farmhouse, but contains considerable traces of 16th-cent. and perhaps earlier work.

Winscott Barton came eventually to Tristram Risdon, the antiquary, who wrote here his *Chorographical Description or Survey of the County of Devon* between 1605 and 1630. The present farmhouse is a late 18th-cent. house. Kingscott is an attractive hamlet with several 16th–17th-cent. farmhouses. Whitsleigh Barton was a Domesday manor.

ST. MARYCHURCH (*see* Torquay).

ST. NICHOLAS (H8) consists of the two old villages of Ringmore and Shaldon, which were annexed to Teignmouth for urban purposes in 1881. They are attractively situated on the S. bank of the Teign estuary, and connected with Teignmouth by a ferry and by Shaldon Bridge, opened in 1827. The original wooden bridge has been largely replaced by iron as it now carries the main Exeter-Torquay road.

Ringmore church (St. Nicholas) was thoroughly restored in 1896. Apart from a Norman font, it contains nothing of note. Shaldon church (St. Peter), at the end of the bridge, was built 1893-1902.

Shaldon village is very pleasing. It contains much late Georgian stucco, especially in the Fore Street and the Strand, and is a good place in which to idle away a summer morning.

SALCOMBE (F12) is a small seaport and holiday town on the W. side of the Kingsbridge estuary and about 1 m. from its mouth. The climate is perhaps the mildest in Devon, and the scenery of extreme beauty. It began to attract residents in the later years of the 18th cent., The Moult (the house of the historian Froude) being the first of the "villas" to be built, in 1764. Woodville (now Woodcot), where Froude died, was built in 1797. The Grange is also a late 18th-cent. house. Such houses were rare, however, for even in 1822 Lysons describes Salcombe as "a fishing town" with three shipwrights' yards, and a Whitsuntide fair for trinkets, sweetmeats, etc. It began to grow more rapidly in the 1840s, especially after the opening of the railway at Kingsbridge in 1893. It is now chiefly a yachting and fishing centre and offers little to day-visitors.

The church (Holy Trinity) was built in 1843-4, enlarged in 1889, and calls for no comment. Salcombe Castle (Fort Charles) was erected by Henry VIII as part of the defences of the southern coast of England, and withstood sieges during the Civil War. The remains consist chiefly of one tower.

Batson is an attractive hamlet at the head of a creek. Batson Hall, an old farmhouse, was formerly a "mansion" and is recorded in Domesday Book. Ilbertstow, farther down the creek on the N. side, has some medieval work, and an E. wing added in 1784.

SALCOMBE REGIS (K7) is a delightful little place. The coastal scenery of the parish is very striking, with red sandstone cliffs rising to more than 500 ft. on either side of the Salcombe valley. The Norman Lockyer Observatory, opened in 1913, stands on the top of the W. hill. It is a privately endowed observatory, and is mainly concerned with the chemistry of the stars and their classification.

The village is situated in a warm and fertile combe facing S., about a mile back from the sea. The church (St. Peter) was originally a 12th-cent. building with a N. aisle. About 1300 the chancel was lengthened, a S. aisle added, and the arches of the N. arcade remodelled, leaving the Norman pillars. About 1430 the aisles were widened, and given new windows, and the W. tower added. The church possesses an eagle lectern of 15th-cent. date, carved from a single block of wood.

Thorn is an interesting old farmhouse, possibly 15th-cent. in part, and was farmed by the Hoopers for about 400 years from 1355. At Dunscombe are the remains of a former mansion, occupied by a branch of the Drakes of Ashe, and disused quarries of good

building stone, some of which went to Exeter Cathedral in the 14th and 15th cents.

SAMPFORD COURTENAY (E5) is a large parish on the N. side of Dartmoor, of which there are fine views. It now includes the ancient ecclesiastical parish of Honeychurch, about 1½ m. N.

The village is cheerful, neat, and clean with much whitewashed cob and good thatching. It was the scene of the beginning of the Western or Prayer-Book Rebellion of 1549. The 16th-cent. Church House retains its original interior and furniture.

The church (St. Andrew) is exceedingly attractive both inside and out: granite building at its most elegant. The lofty pinnacles of the W. tower are stained by an orange lichen, so that they glow perpetually with colour. The interior is spacious and light and well kept, with graceful arcades. The S. arcade is of two dates and two different stones: the four W. bays are of polyphant, a singularly beautiful dove-grey stone from Cornwall, and the two bays beyond the screen are early 16th-cent. granite. The carved bosses and wallplates of the roofs should be studied. The font is Norman, on a modern stem.

Honeychurch church (St. Mary) is charming: very small, very remote, and completely unsophisticated. It is an almost untouched 12th-cent. building, to which a W. tower and S. porch were added late in the 15th cent. In the tower are the three medieval bells in their original cage. The chancel arch was also re-made at that date, the roof renewed, and Perpendicular windows inserted in the old walls. The fittings are in keeping with the building: an excellent Norman font beneath a rustic Jacobean cover, a rustic Elizabethan pulpit, a complete set of late medieval benches (some with carved ends, but most of plain unvarnished oak), a crude wall painting in the nave (possibly the Royal Arms of Elizabeth), altar rails of simple country carpentry: all as well kept as the mother-church at Sampford. Honeychurch has one of the simplest and most appealing interiors of all English country churches. It lives up to its delightful name in a way that so rarely happens, and just to see it on a fine morning puts one in a good humour for the rest of the day.

There are a number of ancient farmsteads in this very attractive parish, of which Reddaway is particularly interesting. It was held by the Reddaways before 1240, and a Reddaway still owns and farms it. Halford and Rowden are also worth visiting. Sticklepath is a small village on the main Exeter-Okehampton road. The good old blacksmith's forge here gets its power from a water-wheel behind.

SAMPFORD PEVERELL (J4) was formerly regarded as a "borough" on the strength of its two-day fair and weekly market.

The church (St. John the Baptist) is mainly 15th-cent. but was badly over-restored in 1863-4. The font is late 12th-cent.; there are considerable traces of 13th-cent. work in the nave and chancel.

SAMPFORD SPINEY (D8) is a moorland hamlet. The church (St. Mary) was probably a 14th-cent. cruciform building, enlarged to its present size in the early 16th cent. Hall Farm, beside the church, was the manor house. It was rebuilt in 1607 and is a good example of its kind. The whole scene is remote and boulder-strewn. Easton Town is a 17th-cent. farmhouse, and behind it is Warne's Kitchen, c. 1600 in

date, one of the best examples to be found of the old Dartmoor type of farmhouse in which there was direct communication between the living-room and the cattle-shippen. It retains its primitive porch and original circular stone staircase in a curious "turret." Woodtown, in the picturesque valley of the Walkham, is a 17th-cent. farmhouse. Huckworthy bridge over the Walkham is of uncertain age.

SANDFORD (G5) is a large, unspoiled village, with some good farmhouse and cottage architecture, of which Town Barton (late 16th-cent.) is a fine example. Sandford School (1825) is a large classical building, erected by Sir Humphrey Phineas Davie, 10th and last baronet, of Creedy Park.

The church (St. Swithin) is disappointing externally, but has much to commend it within. It was largely rebuilt in 1523-4, and was restored and enlarged in 1847-8, when the clearstory was added. There is a fine W. gallery (1657) with an elaborately carved front, erected by the second Sir John Davie of Creedy; and many vigorously carved bench-ends, with medallion busts of men and women, which are probably contemporary with the rebuilding of the fabric. There are various monuments and mural tablets to the Davies, from 1627 to 1846; and a fine brass in the N. aisle to Mary Carew, sister of George Carew (first and only Earl of Totnes) and widow of Walter Dowrich of Dowrich in this parish (1604).

The parish is exceptionally interesting for its houses. Creedy Park is still the seat of the Davies, who descend from John Davie, a successful Exeter merchant. He built the first house here about 1600, which was called Newhouse alias Creedy. This house, much altered since it was first built, was entirely burnt down in 1915, and has been rebuilt in the Tudor style. It stands in a fine park of 370 acres.

Dowrich is a far older house, though much restored in part. It was the home of the Dowrich family from *c.* 1200 until 1717. There are substantial remains of a 15th-cent. gatehouse, which formerly opened into a court-yard. The house itself has some 15th-cent. work, but was much restored early in the 19th cent. Dodderidge was the home of the family of that name from the 13th cent. until 1746. Prowse, formerly called Higher Dodderidge, appears an ordinary thatched farm-house, but internally it keeps much of of its ancient plan. The central passage has a fine carved oak roof (*c.* 1500) with a coat-of-arms, probably that of the builder, and a contemporary oak screen to the hall. Bremridge, now a farmhouse also, was the home of the Bremridges from about the time of King John until the late 18th cent.

Ruxford Barton is mentioned in a charter of 930, granting a large estate in Sandford to the canons of Crediton. The present farmhouse was largely re-built *c.* 1608, the date given on the plaster coat-of-arms in the principal bedroom.

SATTERLEIGH AND WARK-LEIGH (E3), originally two small

parishes in the hills between Taw and Mole, are now united for all purposes. Satterleigh church (St. Peter) is small, simple, and charming. It is essentially a 15th-cent. building, with a wooden bell-cote. The Exeter episcopal re-gisters show that it was being rebuilt in 1435. It is probable that the chancel was once completely shut off from the nave as at Molland and Parracombe. The division between the two is formed by a partition on which are painted the Lord's Prayer and the Creed, and the rood-screen must have filled the space to the bottom of this partition. The altar is surrounded on three sides by railings. On the N. and S. sides are seats for the communicants, with pegs above for their hats.

Warkleigh church (St. John) is a 15th—early 16th-cent. building but over-restored and dull. In the chancel is the Warkleigh Tabernacle, a receptacle for the reservation of the Blessed Sacra-ment, made of oak and originally richly coloured (15th-cent.).

SEATON (L6) is a small seaside town on the W. side of the mouth of the Axe. The old village was about ½ m. inland, near the parish church. The latter (St. Gregory) is a much restored and rather shapeless building. It was originally a cruciform building of early 14th-cent. date. Later additions and alterations, including a fine W. tower (15th-cent.), have produced the present perplexing plan. The restoration of 1866 (at which the old screen disappeared) has left us nothing but poor Victorian furnishings.

Seaton developed late among the sea-side resorts of Devon. In the 1850s it had barely 800 people, living chiefly by fishing. A branch line of the L. & S. W. R. reached Seaton in 1868 and stimulated its growth, but at the end of the century it still had only 1,300 people. It is mostly a town of common-place late Victorian and Edwardian building, completely different in archi-tectural character and social history from Sidmouth, just along the coast. The cliff scenery of Seaton is striking, especially its varied colouring.

SHALDON (*see* ST. NICHOLAS).

SHAUGH PRIOR (D9) consists largely

of moorland, rising to over 1,500 ft. in places and thickly dotted with remains of the Bronze Age. The upper Plym valley has a greater density of hut-circles than any other part of the Moor. Trowlesworthy Warren, about 2 m. NE. of Shaugh church, has the most important group of prehistoric monuments: numerous enclosures, hut-circles, a stone circle, and a stone row. Another important group lies on Hentor Warren. On Lee Moor is the only example yet found on Dartmoor of a chambered hut of pre-Roman Iron Age date, a type of dwelling which is better known in Cornwall. The O.S. 2½-inch map (sheet 20/56) is necessary for the successful location of these and numerous other prehistoric antiquities in the parish.

The parish is bounded on N. and W. by the picturesque Plym valley, especially beautiful at Shaugh Bridge and in Bickleigh Vale. There are extensive china-clay deposits in the parish, which have been worked since the 1840s, and are now the most important source of the mineral in Devon.

The small village of Shaugh is singularly picturesque, and commands fine views down to Plymouth Sound and across to Cornwall. The church (St. Edward, King and Martyr) is a 15th-cent. granite building with a fine W. tower. The remarkable 15th-cent. font cover was rescued from a linhay in the 1870s and restored. A number of ancient farms are scattered about the parish, of which Brixton Barton, Coldstone, Fernhill, Pethill, and Lee are all recorded in Domesday. Coldstone to-day is a good example of a gentleman's house of 16th- and 17th-cent date.

SHEBBEAR (c5) is a nondescript collection of houses around a large square, the most interesting being the 17th-cent.

New Inn. The church (St. Michael) contains some Norman work, including a good S. doorway, c. 1180. The S. aisle is said by Risdon to have been built by the lady (of Ladford in this parish) whose recumbent effigy is in the S. wall. The nave and chancel are early 14th-cent. in date, but the window tracery has been restored. An evangelical curate ripped out the chancel screen in 1812, but the parish got rid of him in turn. There is now a good modern screen. The pulpit and reading-desk are Jacobean, the grotesque figures on the former being worth close examination.

Ladford, now a farmhouse, was formerly a mansion. Lovacott is recorded in Domesday. South Furze, Badworthy, Binworthy, and Worden all existed by 1167. At Allacott was a private chapel (St. Stephen), licensed by the bishop in 1409. The house, now a farmhouse, was then described as a "mansion." Durpley Castle, 1 m. N. of Ladford, is a small Norman castle-site with a motte and bailey surrounded by a ditch, covering about an acre.

SHEEPSTOR (D9) is a mere hamlet at the foot of the Tor from which it took its name in the 12th cent (plate 37). It has a typical little moorstone church (dedication unknown) of the Dartmoor type, mostly an early 16th-cent. re-building. The windows are cut in the more tractable Roborough stone. A good medieval rood-screen was destroyed by Sir Massey Lopes at the "restoration" of 1862. Enough fragments were found to enable it to be reconstructed in an exact copy in 1914. There are also good modern carved bench-ends. Near the church is a 15th-cent. priest's house.

Sheepstor is associated with that remarkable man, Rajah Brooke, who bought an estate at Burrator about 1858. He died there in 1868 and is buried on the N. side of Sheepstor church under a massive tomb of red Aberdeen granite (but why not the Dartmoor granite?) His nephew succeeded him as Rajah of Sarawak, and is also buried here.

The Burrator reservoir, which supplies Plymouth, was made in 1891. In 1928 it was enlarged from a capacity of 668 million gallons to 1026 million. It now covers 150 acres, and is surely one of the most beautiful reservoirs in England, among the folds of the Moor. The parish is rich in Bronze Age remains (see 2½-inch sheet 20/56), the most notable being those along the N. bank of the Plym at Legis Tor and Ditsworthy Warren.

SHEEPWASH (c5) church (St. Lawrence) was rebuilt in 1880 and is dull. Newcourt Barton is a late 16th-cent. house, remodelled in the early 18th cent. and later.

SHELDON (k5) is a remote parish in the Blackdown Hills. The small church (St. James) was entirely rebuilt in 1871, except for the tower, and contains nothing of interest except the Norman font.

SHERFORD (f11), situated in a pleasant valley, has some good groups of vernacular building. The church (St. Martin) is wholly built of Charlton slate inside and out, even to the piers and capitals of the two arcades. The W. tower is a bold early 15th-cent. structure, but most of the church is somewhat earlier, the unusual star-shaped tracery of the aisle windows suggesting late 14th-cent. work. The rood-screen is a fine example, with tracery of the Dartmouth and Portle-

mouth type and considerable traces of ancient colour.

Keynedon, Malston, and Stancombe were Domesday estates. Keynedon, in a beautiful valley running down to Frogmore creek, was the residence of the Hals family in the early 15th cent. John Hals (justice of the Common Pleas, 1423) lived here, and his son John (Bishop of Coventry and Lichfield 1459-90) was born here. The early 15th-cent. gate-tower of their house was demolished about a century ago, but much of the early Tudor house remains. Malston was the principal seat of the Reynells from Richard II's time onwards and contains some 15th-cent. and later work.

SHILLINGFORD (h7) church (St. George) is a small 15th-cent. building of red sandstone, over-restored internally in 1856, but containing a good brass (on the N. side of the chancel) to Sir William Huddesfield (d. 1499) and his wife Katherine Courtenay, with three children.

SHIRWELL (d2) is an old village, which gave its name to a hundred. The church (St. Peter) is a much-restored 15th-cent. building. In the chancel is an effigy, believed to be that of Blanche St. Leger, da. of William Bourchier, Lord Fitzwarren (d. 1483). Above this tomb is a monument to Anne Lady Chichester (1723). A branch of the Chichesters lived at Youlston from Henry VII's time to the early 20th-cent.

Youlston is an 18th-cent. house. Youlston Old Park, 1 m. S. of the village, is presumably the site of an earlier house. Plaistow Barton was a Domesday manor.

SHOBROOKE (g5) lies in quiet, unspoilt country, with many fertile "red-land" farms. It formerly had several prosperous gentry and yeomen. The church (St. Swithin) was drastically restored and enlarged in 1879-80, when the S. aisle was added. There is, however, a good Norman S. doorway (c. 1160) in Thorverton stone. Shobrooke Park was formerly called (Little) Fulford. It was bought by Sir William Periam (1535-1605), Chief Baron of the Exchequer, who built a house here. This was pulled down c. 1820 and a new house built (by Hakewill) called Shobrooke Park. The house became a school, was gutted by fire in 1947, and is now desolate.

West Raddon was one of several good houses in this parish. It was a Domesday manor, and in Henry VIII's time was bought by the Westcotes. Thomas Westcote, the antiquary, was born here in 1567, and wrote his *View of Devonshire* here. A good deal of Westcote's house remains, the W. wing being largely 15th-cent. work, the rest rebuilt in the 18th cent. Raddon Top (772 ft.) is a landmark for 20 m. around. Westcote tells us there was an earthwork on the summit, practically ploughed down even in his day. The views from here are superb, even for Devon.

SHUTE (L6) was the home of the Bonvilles, the powerful antagonists of the Courtenays during a considerable part of the 15th cent. It eventually came to Sir William Petre, principal secretary of state to Mary. His descendant, Lord Petre, sold it in 1787 to Sir John Pole, Bart., who signalised his purchase by building Shute House in 1787-90. This house, with fine rooms of the period, is now a girls' school.

The Poles had, however, been in possession of Shute under long leases since about the middle of the 16th cent. The arms of William Pole, who was buried at Shute in 1587, appear on the gate-house of the old mansion. This house, now known as Shute Barton, was partly demolished in 1787, but much early work remains, including the fine gatehouse, c. 1550.

Shute church (St. Michael) was originally an early 13th-cent. cruciform building, with N. and S. transepts and a central tower, and much work of this period has survived. In the 15th cent. the N. transept was extended to form a complete aisle to nave and chancel, and the S. transept widened. The fittings of the church are all commonplace Victorian. In the N. chancel aisle (the Pole chapel) is a fine marble statue of Sir William Pole (d. 1741) in the costume of Master of the Household to Queen Anne. Other Pole memorials are in the S. transept. Some good armorial glass (dated 1673, 1808) is to be seen in the N. aisle.

SIDBURY (K6) is a large village in warm and fertile country. From the hills on three sides of the village magnificent views are to be had, especially over the sea from Portland Bill to beyond Berry Head, and far into Dorset. Roncombe Gate, formerly a meeting place for the smuggling traffic from Beer, Branscombe, and Salcombe, is one such viewpoint.

The village takes its name from the early Iron Age hill-fort to the SW., now known as Sidbury Castle. It is a kite-shaped earthwork, with a double rampart and ditch, and an entrance at the narrow NW. end. 1,300 ft. long internally, and 400 ft. wide at the maximum, it is the largest earthwork in the district.

Sidbury church (St. Giles) is one of the most interesting in Devon. Restoration work on the chancel in 1898-9 revealed a Saxon crypt underneath, the precise date of which is unknown. The structural history of the Norman and later church may be summarised as follows: (a) an early 12th-cent. church of nave and chancel only, of which considerable parts remain; (b) a W. tower and N. and S. aisles added late in the 12th cent.; (c) the chancel lengthened c. 1260-80, and N. and S. transepts either added or remodelled; (d) a substantial reconstruction in the mid-15th cent, in which the aisles were rebuilt, the walls of the nave raised and fine wagon roofs inserted throughout the church, new windows inserted at various points in the church and a new font put in. Some extensive repair work was carried out early in the 17th cent. by John Stone, freemason (probably the father of the famous Nicholas Stone), whose tomb dated 1617 is in the S. wall (outside) of the chancel. In 1843-5 the Norman tower was taken down and rebuilt to the old design; the spire was added in 1895.

There are several interesting buildings in the parish. The Porch House in Sidford is dated 1574, and there are other houses worth looking for in this village, and on the road to Sidbury village. Manstone Farm has some considerable remains of old work, some of medieval date. Sand Barton, 1 m. NE. of the church, is first mentioned c. 1175. The present house was built by Rowland Huyshe in 1594-1600 and is a good example of a late Tudor mansion. Court Hall has some Elizabethan work. Buckton and Harcombe farms are both mentioned c. 1200 in the dean and chapter archives at Exeter.

SIDMOUTH (K7) is one of the most attractive seaside towns on the S. coast of England, framed in a narrow valley opening on to the sea, and sheltered E. and W. by tremendous red sandstone cliffs that rise to over 500 ft.

For centuries it was a small market and fishing town. Risdon, in the early 17th cent., calls it "one of the especialest fisher towns of the shire," but the fishery had much declined by the early 19th cent. Fortunately, visitors had begun to discover the mildness of its climate and its beautiful scenery, and from the 1780s onwards it was increasingly patronised, even during the winter. The Napoleonic Wars gave a great stimulus to the town by closing the Continent to the upper and upper-middle classes, who began to settle at Sidmouth and to build themselves "cottages" in every sheltered spot. These "cottages"—now frequently converted into hotels—are a delightful feature of Sidmouth architecture. Sidmouth remained "select" throughout the 19th cent. Its shingle beach did not attract families with children, it did not set out to offer other "attractions"; the railway came late (1874) and even then stopped far short of the town. For all these reasons Sidmouth has preserved its early 19th-cent. character to a high degree.

Knowle Cottage (now the Knowle Hotel) was typical of the kind of building that created modern Sidmouth, though more opulent than most. It was built by Lord le Despencer in 1805, a thatched building of about 40 rooms, in ten acres of ornamental grounds, with a suite of drawing-rooms nearly 100 ft. long.[1] Woodlands Hotel was built as a "cottage" by Lord Gwydir, Salcombe House was occupied by the Marquess of Bute, and Woolbrook Glen (now the Royal Glen Hotel) was occupied during the winter of 1819-20 by the Duke and Duchess of Kent and their infant daughter Victoria. Sid Abbey is early 19th-cent. Gothic.

Besides these and numerous other "cottages" scattered about the vale, a number of terraces of lodging-houses were built between 1800 and 1820, when the population of the town more than doubled. Fortfield Terrace, Clifton Place, York Terrace, and Elysian Fields are characteristic of this period.

In the old town are Georgian houses and shops. The Unitarian chapel in the High Street retains its 18th-cent. pulpit with sounding-board, gallery front, and clock. Among the ancient buildings of the parish are Woolcombe House (now the Sidmouth Museum), which has a medieval hall with an open timber roof; and Manstone, which is substantially a 15th-cent. stone house altered in 1589.

The sea-wall was first built in 1835-8: before that there was simply a paved walk along the shore; but attempts to make a harbour at the same time failed. After 1840 Sidmouth grew much more slowly: possibly Torquay was becoming the more fashionable in mid-Victorian years. Sidmouth is thus not much disfigured by late Victorian brickwork. In recent years it has attracted wider attention as a holiday centre and as a place to retire to, and is now growing perceptibly. As a contrast to the aristocratic and genteel history of Sidmouth in the 19th cent. one might read Stephen Reynolds's *A Poor Man's House* (1908), a faithful picture of a Sidmouth fisherman's household and life, and of the life of ancient native Sidmouth, persisting beneath the veneer that has been imposed on it during the past 150 years. The atmosphere and feeling of the book are, to a Devonian, absolutely right.

The parish church (St. Giles or St. Nicholas) was rebuilt, except the arcades and the 15th-cent. tower, in 1859-60, and is devoid of interest. All Saints' church was built 1837-40. St. Francis's church at Woolbrook, consecrated in 1938, is one of the last works of Caroe whose most notable work is perhaps St. David's, at Exeter. The Old Chancel, near the parish church, was erected in the 1860s by the local antiquary P. O. Hutchinson from the demolished materials of the parish church, which he tried in vain to save from "restoration." He wrote a valuable history of Sidmouth in six MSS. volumes, now in the Exeter City Library.

SILVERTON (H5) is a large and very pleasant village, containing much domestic building in cob and thatch ranging in date from the 16th cent. to the 19th. The whole parish is very beautiful, diversified and undulating, and one could walk its roads and lanes and fields for days on end to enjoy its richness.

The village is one of the oldest in Devon, dating from the first years of the Saxon occupation, and like most of these ancient primary settlements was a royal manor before the Conquest and gave its name to a hundred (later changed to Hayridge Hundred). It formerly had a market and a fair, and was reckoned to be a "borough."

The church (St. Mary) is mostly a 15th–early 16th-cent. building, built of the local volcanic stone. The chancel-pier on the N. side bears the date 1503. The chancel was rebuilt on a mean scale in 1863, spoiling an otherwise handsome interior, and the old screen (which was probably Jacobean, and contemporary with the W. gallery) was taken out and chopped up for firewood.

About 1 m. E. of the village is Silverton Park, where the 4th and last Earl of Egremont (d. 1845) built a large mansion, of which nothing is now left except the "Classical" stables. The farms of Greenslinch, Yard, and Burn are all recorded in Domesday Book. Of these, Greenslinch is still substantially a 15th-cent. house. Dunsmoor occurs as early as 1211, and part of the present house is Tudor in date. At Great Pitt Farm, just NW. of the village, is a very interesting 17th-cent. ceiling, depicting sporting subjects.

SLAPTON (G11) is set a little way back from the remarkable fresh-water lake known as Slapton Ley, which is separated from the sea by a raised bank of sand and shingle. In 1943-4 the American armed forces took over the whole of the country behind this beach and practised amphibious landings in preparation for the attack on the Normandy beaches in June 1944. An obelisk to commemorate this piece of history now stands in the middle of the long beach.

The church (St. James the Greater) has a medieval spire, and is 14th–15th-cent. in date. In 1373 Sir Guy de Brian, standard-bearer to Edward III and lord of the manor, founded a collegiate chantry here, of which the great tower, 80 ft. high and built of Charleton slate, is the boldest feature of the village as one enters it.

SOURTON (D6) takes in a piece of the NW. edge of Dartmoor, rising at Sourton Tor to 1,447 ft. The church (St. Thomas Becket) is a 14th–16th-cent. building, mainly of moorstone.

Lake is a fine old farmstead, in part 16th-cent. or older. Collaven, N. of Lake, is another ancient farmstead.

SOUTHLEIGH (L6) is a scattered village among the wooded hills S. of the Coly valley. The church (St. Lawrence), attractively situated on the edge of a small combe, is built of flints and much restored. It was probably an early 13th-cent. church. The south aisle was added in 1821, and the chancel rebuilt

in 1854. Wiscombe lies in a romantic situation among finely wooded hills. It belonged in the 13th cent. to the great Bonvill family, who made a deer park here. The old house was pulled down, and the present one built in the Gothic style in 1826.

Blackbury Castle (i.e. "black earthwork") is a large Iron Age hill-fort on a commanding ridge S. of Wiscombe. It is roughly oval in shape, with a remarkable inturned entrance on the S. side. The other entrances are probably modern.

SOWTON (H6) church (St. Michael) was wholly rebuilt in 1845, and is quite dull. Bishop's Court was formerly a palace of the Bishops of Exeter (called *Clyst*). Bishop Bronescombe bought the estate and had erected a palace and chapel here before 1276. Much medieval work remains, including the chapel (*c.* 1270) and 15th-cent. barns and stables, but the house itself was "altered and improved" about 1863.

SPREYTON (E6) stands high (750 ft.) in the rolling foothills N. of Dartmoor.

The church (St. Michael) is a 15th-cent. building in granite, with a fine, dignified tower that is a landmark for some miles. It is approached by an avenue of lime-trees planted in 1802. A Latin inscription in the chancel roof suggests that the church was completed in 1451. The nave and N. aisle roofs are ceiled and have excellent carved bosses, ribs, and wall-plates. In the churchyard is a headstone to Thomas Cobley, gent., of Butsford in the neighbouring parish of Colebrooke, d. 1844, aged 82. He was the nephew of the famous "Uncle Tom Cobley," who also lies buried in this churchyard. "Uncle Tom" was a substantial yeoman of Spreyton, who died at the end of the

18th cent. at a great age. His companions on the famous ride to Widecombe Fair all came from this district. He disinherited his son Thomas for being too free with the girls and left his considerable estate to this nephew who, however, does not seem to have put up so much as a headstone to the old man.

Spreyton Barton, near the church, is probably a 17th-cent. farmhouse, the seat of the Battishills for a time.

STAVERTON (H7) rises in billowy country from the Dart valley above Totnes, and has long been famous for its cider. Staverton bridge, over the Dart, is one of the best medieval bridges surviving in Devon, probably built in 1413.

The church (St. Paul) is mostly an early 14th-cent. building, with a plain, battered W. tower from the 13th-cent. church. When Bishop Stapeldon visited Staverton in 1314 he gave directions for a larger church to be built, and the present church is the result. The excellent 15th-cent. rood-screen, which was dilapidated, was almost rebuilt by Bligh Bond in 1891. There are good parclose screens of the same date, a Georgian pulpit, and a reading-desk formed of carved Jacobean panelling from the old clerk's pew removed many years ago.

Among the interesting houses of the parish are Pridhamsleigh, Sparkwell, and Blackler. The former is medieval in part. Kingston House was rebuilt by John Rowe after a fire in 1744. The Rowes were a Catholic family, and the house possessed a private chapel, of which part remains.

STOCKLAND (L5) is a pleasant village with some interesting houses. Near the church is a farmhouse dated 1602. The parish has many scattered farmsteads, joined by narrow winding lanes, and is a good example of land cleared piecemeal and directly from the forest. The church (St. Michael) is a 14th-cent. building, altered and enlarged in the 15th.

On the hill SW. of the village is Stockland Great Camp, 667 ft. above sea level, of which only the N. half remains. It was a hill-fort of great strength, probably of late Iron Age date, and may have been constructed by the Dumnonii on their frontier against the Durotriges (of Dorset). The single vallum is still over 40 ft. high in places.

STOCKLEIGH ENGLISH (G5) is a small parish in beautiful unspoiled country with fine views every few minutes for the walker. Externally the 15th-cent. church (St. Mary) is small and pleasant; internally it has been ruined by a dreadful restoration (1878-83), and everything in it is mean, dark and ugly. Stockleigh Court was the home of the Bellews from Elizabethan until recent times.

STOCKLEIGH POMEROY (G5) lies in remote and beautiful red-earth country at the foot of the Raddon Hills. The church (St. Mary) has a Norman S. doorway (c. 1160), but the rest of the church was rebuilt in Bishop Lacy's time (1420-55). The chancel was rebuilt again about 1840. A considerable number of well-carved bench-ends remain, together with a medieval pulpit, and some medieval glass in the N. aisle. The climb to the top of Raddon is worth making for the magnificent views over Devon at its most luxuriant.

STOKE CANON (H6) contains several pleasant old farmhouses and cottages, but the church (St. Mary Magdalene) was wholly rebuilt in 1836 except for the W. tower. It contains a remarkable font of Norman date, made from a single block of lava, and a number of 17th-cent. floor slabs to local families. Stoke Canon bridge, over two arms of the Culm, was already built in the late 13th cent. Bishop Stapeldon left money in his will (1326) for its upkeep. It contains some old work but has been much widened to carry the main road.

STOKE DAMAREL (see PLYMOUTH).

STOKE FLEMING (G11) church (St. Peter) stands boldly on a hill and has been a landmark from the sea for centuries It may possibly have been put here for that reason, like Wembury. But it was grossly restored in 1871, and is of no interest except for a fine brass to John Corp (1350) and his grand-daughter, Eleanor (1391), and a brass to Elias Newcomen (1614), great-grandfather of Thomas Newcomen of Dartmouth, inventor of the steam engine. Under the tower arch is a good effigy, said to be that of Eleanor Mohun, c. 1300.

At the charming cove of Blackpool a Breton force which had landed at Slapton in 1404 to attack Dartmouth was decisively defeated by the Dartmouth men, a victory for which Henry IV ordered a *Te Deum* to be sung in Westminster Abbey.

STOKE GABRIEL (G10) church (St. Gabriel) has a plain W. tower (13th cent.); the remainder of the church was rebuilt during the 15th cent. on a typical fully-aisled plan. The church has been much restored and its levels altered. The 15th-cent. rood-screen, spanning nave and aisles, retains a series of painted panels, representing

apostles and prophets alternately, but other panels have been repainted in a poor, conventional fashion. The medieval pulpit, of the same date as the screen, is covered with modern paint. On the S. side is the Sandridge chapel, with a curious slate tablet to the wife of Roger Pomeroy of Sandridge (1660).

The village is romantically situated at the head of a creek of the Dart estuary, and is now the chief scene of the Dart salmon fishery. Sandridge, on high ground commanding a wonderful view of the estuary, was held by the Sandridges under the Bishop of Exeter in Henry II's reign. The present house was built by John Nash in 1805 in an Italianate style. It is now (1951) un-occupied, the park ragged and decaying. John Davis, the great navigator and explorer, was probably born at Sandridge Barton, a little below the mansion, in 1543. Waddeton Court was a house of similar status to Sandridge. The present house is an early 19th-cent. mansion in the Elizabethan style, erected near the remains of the medieval house. From the sandstone quarries on the edge of Galmpton Creek came the stone for the beautiful tower of Totnes church.

STOKE RIVERS (E2) church (St. Bartholomew) is mainly 15th-cent. in style, but sadly altered. According to Davidson it was almost entirely rebuilt in 1832. It is a lamentable sight to-day, damp and decay everywhere. There is a good inscribed slate slab near the S. porch to the wife of a local yeoman (1705).

STOKE-IN-TEIGNHEAD (H8) is a small village clustered in a combe 1 m. S. of the Teign estuary. The church (St. Andrew) was originally a cruciform building with N. and S. transepts, pro-

bably of early 14th-cent. date, enlarged in the 15th cent. The sculpture of the Beer stone capitals of the arcades is worth special notice. The rood-screen (*c.* 1400) is of unusual character, square-headed and early in type. Inside the altar rails is a fine brass, of a priest in vestments, to John Symon, canon of Exeter and rector of this parish (d. 1497).

STOKENHAM (G11) is called Stoke in Hamme in the 13th cent., to distinguish it from other Stokes. The scenery of the parish, both inland and coastal, is most beautiful and unspoilt. It includes some miles of the Start Bay coastline and the striking headland of the Start, where there is a lighthouse erected in 1836, a period piece internally. Start means "tail" from the shape of the headland (O.E. *steort*).

Torcross takes its name from the *tor* or great rock which terminates the S. end of the long raised beach. The whereabouts of the cross is not known: possibly one stood on the summit of the rock as a mark for shipping. The hamlet probably originated as a small fishing settlement, like Beesands and Hallsands to the S. All were noted for their fine crabs in the 19th cent. which were esteemed in the London market. Torcross is described in 1850 as "a pretty little bathing place, with several lodging-houses for visitors." It is much the same to-day. Beesands was bombed in 1943 when several people were killed and much damage done. Hallsands has suffered greatly from the sea. The storm of January 1917 especially did great damage and much of the hamlet had to be rebuilt in a safer place. The ruins of the older houses by the sea may be seen.

The parish church (St. Michael and All Angels) seems to have been dedi-cated originally to St. Humbert the Confessor (d. 1188).[1] It is a fine, bold 15th or early 16th-cent. building in local slate, with a good tower of a common S. Devon type. The rood-screen (15th- cent.) occupies the full width of the church.

The village and its hamlets contain much good building in local slate and reed-thatch. Widdicombe House was rebuilt *c.* 1725 and enlarged *c.* 1820. Slapton Ley extends into Stokenham and is notable for its fishing and its rare wild birds.

STONEHOUSE (*see* PLYMOUTH).

STOODLEIGH (H4) lies in high country, broken up by beautiful, wooded valleys. From Stoodleigh Beacon (987 ft.), the highest point between Exmoor and Dartmoor, there are wonderful views in all directions. On this hill, says Risdon, a beacon was set up by order of Edward II "when he doubted of the landing of his queen Isabel." The lonely farms of War-brightsleigh Barton, West Whitnole, and Rifton were all Domesday estates, as well as Stoodleigh itself. The church (St. Margaret) is mostly 15th-cent. with a Norman font. Stoodleigh Court is now a school.

STOWFORD (C7) church (St. John) has a most attractive interior, although restored by Sir Gilbert Scott in 1874, when the N. aisle was added. The woodwork was all done at this time, but, being copied from older work by local craftsmen, is excellent. The roofs of the S. aisle, S. chancel aisle, and S. porch are the original, and are notably carved. There are several good 18th-cent. monuments to the Harrises of Hayne, especially one to Christopher Harris, 1718. John Harris of Hayne was Master of the Household to George II and George III. In the S. chancel aisle are the tabard, helmet, and gauntlet of Harris. An Ogham stone—an early Christian monument to one Gunglei—stands at the churchyard gate.

Hayne itself was rebuilt by Wyatville in 1810 in what Baring-Gould dismisses forthwith as "cockney Gothic," but it is good of its kind. It was the seat of the Harrises from Henry VIII's reign until 1864. Milford and Sprytown, now farmhouses, were Domesday manors. Shepherds is a good 16th-cent. farmhouse.

STRETE (G11) was formed into an ecclesiastical parish out of Blackawton in 1881. The church (St. Michael) was built in 1836.

SUTCOMBE (B4) is a remote parish with an interesting church (St. Andrew). It has retained a simple 12th-cent. S. doorway, but the building is otherwise entirely of late 15th- to early 16th-cent. date, with a certain amount of alteration, especially to the windows, in the 17th cent. There are a considerable number of late medieval floor-tiles, a 16th-cent. pulpit, and an exceptionally good collection of well-carved 16th-cent. bench-ends, chiefly heraldic. The granite arcade, c. 1500, is graceful. The rood-screen is well restored, with portions of the original screen in the lower panels; and there is some medieval glass in the E. window of the Thuborough aisle. The whole church is attractive and well cared for, and is full of atmosphere: granite and oak give the feeling of the interior.

Thuborough was a Domesday estate: the name means "thieves' hill." It came to a branch of the numerous family of Prideaux about 1500, who made it their mansion throughout the 16th and 17th cents. The present farm-house still bears evidence of its former status.

SWIMBRIDGE (E3) lies on the main road from Barnstaple to South Molton. The church (St. James) is a 15th-cent. rebuilding, except the tower and lead-covered broach spire, which remain from the early 14th-cent. church. The spire is one of three medieval spires in this district, the other two being at Braunton and Barnstaple. The fittings of the church are of exceptional interest, most notable being the stone pulpit (c. 1490) which retains some of its original colour and is freely and beautifully carved and ornamented. The rood-screen, well restored by Pearson in the 1880s, is of about the same date, and is singularly fine and perfect. The font cover is a good example of Renaissance carving of early 16th-cent. date, and above this is a richly decorated tester or canopy.

Notice the monument to Charles son of John Cutcliffe of Damage (1670), surmounted by a beautiful oval portrait in oils, which has been attributed to Lely but is more probably the work of James Gandy (1619-89), a pupil of Vandyke.

Hearson, Stowford, and Marsh were formerly "mansions." Stowford is the traditional birthplace—and there is no reason to doubt the tradition—of St. Urith, who was martyred at Chittlehampton in the 8th cent. The present house is in part medieval. Ernesborough was an ancient freehold estate, first recorded in 1175, and taking its name from the "eagles' hill" (earnbeorh). There are considerable traces of antiquity in the present house.

SYDENHAM DAMAREL (c8) lies in attractive country, sloping down to the Tamar, well wooded with oak and beech. The church (St. Mary) is beautifully situated, and has a fine W. tower of granite. It is entirely a 15th-cent. building, and retains its original wagon roofs and some medieval glass in the N. aisle. There is a good incised slate monument to John Richards (1634).

TALATON (J6) lies in a neat, park-like landscape. The church (St. James) was rebuilt, except the tower, porch, E. wall, and vestry in 1859-60, but is still worth seeing. The W. tower is good. There are excellent wagon roofs with carved ribs and bosses, a few medieval bench-ends, and a fine 15th-cent. screen.

Escot, first recorded in 1227, is built on the site of Sir Walter Yonge's mansion, finished c. 1688. There is a tradition that John Locke, the philosopher, often visited Yonge at Escot, and that he planted certain clumps of beeches in the park. The present house was built about 1810. Escot was formed into a separate ecclesiastical parish in 1840. The parish church (St. Philip and St. James) was built at the cost of Sir John Kennaway in 1838.

TAMERTON FOLIOT (C9) is a large village at the head of Tamerton Lake, a creek two miles long which opens into the Tamar. Although one can reach it by one of the frequent Plymouth Corporation buses, and it is steadily being approached by the suburbs of the city, it is a place of great interest and much beautiful scenery.

The Celtic saints Indract and Dominic, and all their company, landed in the closing years of the 6th cent. at a port called *Tamerunta*, which can only be Tamerton Foliot. St. Budoc, too, landed in the same creek, and founded a church at Budshead (now in St. Budeaux).

The manor of Tamerton had come to the Foliots by King Stephen's time (1135-54), according to Risdon, when Sampson Foliot made his dwelling at Warleigh, close to the confluence of Tavy and Tamar. Warleigh may have been a watch-place (OE *weard*), when Cornwall was still unconquered, Warleigh Point being admirably suited to that purpose. It came to the Coplestones by marriage in 1472. At some time in the 16th cent. the Coplestones left their ancestral home of Coplestone, near Crediton, preferring to live in this beautiful spot by the tidal waters of the Tavy, and here they rebuilt the ancient Foliot house towards the end of the century. The S. (principal) front of the house still keeps in the main its Elizabethan elevation, but the house was extensively remodelled in the late 18th cent. and early 19th, and part of it is in a Strawberry Hill Gothic style. It is now a hospital. Warleigh possesses one of the few dovecotes to be found in Devon, a circular structure of brick with over 500 nest-holes, c. 1600 in date.

Blaxton or Blackstone was a Domesday manor. The ferry across the Tavy, from here to Bere Ferrers, is referred to as early as 1263.

Maristow, now a large mansion in a park, was originally "Martin's-stow." There was a quay here in the 13th cent. We read in 1294 of silver being shipped here, from the Bere Ferrers mines over the river, up to London. The present house dates mainly from 1740. The Maristow estate was bought for £65,000 by Sir Manasseh Lopes in 1798 from the Heywood heiresses, and has continued in the Lopes family (Lords Roborough) since. The house, in exceedingly beautiful grounds, is now a home for aged clergy.

Ashleigh Barton is a late 15th cent.– 17th-cent. farmhouse. It has a plaster overmantel depicting the sacrifice of Isaac, similar to the one at Alston (in Malborough).

Tamerton Foliot church (St. Mary) is chiefly 15th-cent., much rebuilt. There are some interesting monuments. That to a Gorges of Warleigh and his wife is 14th-cent., with two good effigies. The monument to John Coplestone of Warleigh and his wife, erected 1617, depicts two kneeling figures facing each other, with their ten children kneeling below.

Gilbert Foliot, Bishop of London (1163-87) and the great opponent of Becket, was probably born at Warleigh. He exercised great influence over Henry II until his death in 1187.

TAVISTOCK (c8) is the most delightful town in West Devon, and perhaps the most attractive of all the inland towns of the county. Much of it is built of a green volcanic ash from quarries at Hurdwick, about 1½ m. N. of the town, a stone which also appears frequently in the medieval churches of the surrounding countryside. The town stands mostly on the N. side of the river Tavy, itself a decorative feature of the town-scene, and at the E. end of a large parish—known as Tavistock Hamlets—which extends all the way to the Tamar. The scenery of the parish is of great variety and beauty, not excluding the abandoned mining landscape at Blanchdown on the W., above the Tamar. This is another of those great Devonshire parishes, so full of views, attractive old houses, and fascinating history, in which one can happily spend a week of exploration. Tavistock has, too, been fortunate in its historians. Few aspects of its varied history have not been adequately dealt with (see the Bibliography).

The town is essentially the product of its two owners: Tavistock Abbey from the 10th cent. to the 16th, and the earls and dukes of Bedford from the 16th cent. to the 20th. The abbey created the town; the Russells gave it its present appearance and character. Between them they owned the town from 974 until 1911.

A small community existed here before the abbey came. On the hillside about 1 m. NE. of the town is an irregular earthwork known as the Trendle, which has yielded evidence of a late Celtic settlement. Later, possibly in the early 8th cent., the Saxons occupied the lower ground beside the brawling Tavy, and founded the *stoc* that gives the place its name. By the time the Benedictine Abbey was founded about the year 974, a hamlet existed at Tavistock, with its own chapel, which stood near the NW. corner of the present inner market.

The establishment of the abbey, which became the largest and wealthiest in the South-West, naturally gave a great impetus to the village. In 1105 the abbot obtained for it a weekly market, which is still held on Fridays, and in 1116 a three-day fair was added, on the eve, feast, and morrow of St. Rumon (29-31 August). Some time before 1185, probably during the abbacy of Walter (1155-68), the final step was taken of detaching an area of some 325 acres from the vast rural manor in order to set up a borough. The immediate stimulus to the creation of a borough was almost certainly the "tin rush" of these years when the virgin deposits on the SW. edge of Dartmoor, not many miles away, proved to be the largest European source of tin. So began the borough of Tavistock which continued uninterruptedly until it was deprived of its municipal status in 1885, and so began its equally long, but considerably more interrupted, mining history. For a very short period (1682-8), Tavistock was an incorporated borough with a mayor.

From 1295 down to 1868, with occasional interruptions, Tavistock was also a parliamentary borough, represented by two members. In 1868 the two were reduced to one, and in 1885 the borough was disfranchised and merged with a county division. The Russells (earls, and later dukes, of Bedford) had acquired the borough, together with a vast estate round about, at the Dissolution of the abbey in 1539. From the beginning they exerted a strong political influence. The local man who had sat for the medieval borough gave way to relatives, personal friends, or political associates of the noble patrons; but not until the 1730s did the Russell influence become paramount and the town a true pocket borough. The long dominance of the Russells in the Whig influence is apparent down to the present day in the continuing Liberal tradition of the constituency, though the strong force of Devon nonconformity has also been a considerable factor.[1]

Tavistock was interested in tin-mining from the 12th cent. onwards. In 1305 it was established, or re-established, as one of the three stannary towns (Ashburton and Chagford being the other two) where all tin raised in Devon was to be weighed, stamped, and put on sale. The Devonshire tin trade had practically disappeared by the early 17th cent., but by then the ancient cloth industry of the town had become considerable and decay was averted. When in turn the cloth trade decayed, from the early 18th cent. onwards, copper-mining developed opportunely to take its place. Though there had been earlier attempts, mining

began in earnest in the 1790s and reached its peak in the early 1860s when the famous Devon Great Consols mine at Blanchdown was at the peak of its production as one of the richest copper mines in the world. This mine closed down in 1901. It has left behind a vast, broken landscape, extending for some 2 m. along and above the Tamar. The site, together with that of other mines in the district, will be found on the 2½-inch map (sheet 20/47), and should be explored for its fantastic and desolate beauty, the silent haunt of buzzards, foxes and grass-snakes. In its later days the Devon Great Consols concentrated on the production of arsenic, for which the ovens and long ducts remain. Only Graham Sutherland or John Piper could do justice to this romantic scene, quite unlike anything else in Devon.

In order to convey the copper ore cheaply from the Mary Tavy mines and others, a 4-m. canal was constructed from Tavistock to a point 240 ft. above Morwellham quay, which was then reached by an inclined plane. The canal barges were loaded on to trolleys, which ran down the grooved rails of the plane, controlled by a windlass and chain, to the quay on the Tamar where ships of 200 tons could lie. The cutting of the canal was done largely by the labour of French prisoners of war, and involved the driving of a tunnel nearly 2 m. long through the heart of Morwell Down. The canal was opened in 1817, carried a great traffic for many years, but went out of use by the 1890s. Mining had largely ceased by then, and such traffic as there was went by rail. The canal lies silent but not useless, for in 1933-4 it was cleaned out to provide power for supplying electricity to the neighbourhood. It now makes a delightful summer evening's walk as far as the mouth of the tunnel. The deserted Morwellham quay, once the scene of so much activity, is also a picturesque spot for a visit, and a picnic among the ruins.

Tavistock itself, apart from the fragmentary remains of the abbey, and the medieval parish church, is almost entirely a 19th-cent. town, and largely the result—in one way or another—of the mining prosperity of the years down to 1870. Between 1801 and 1861 the population nearly trebled (3,420 to 8,965). In the following twenty years it fell by over 2,000, owing to the closing of many of the copper mines. Miners and their families left for the north of England coalfields, or emigrated to the mines of America and Australia. By 1931 the population of the town was smaller than it had been a hundred years earlier, but it is by no means decayed. It is a cheerful little market town, far enough from Plymouth to have a life and character of its own, and serving its original purpose as a market for a wide countryside around. It is curious to reflect that it is substantially a 19th-cent. mining town: such words conjure up visions of Barnsley or Wigan. But copper and tin did not blacken the landscape as coal would have done, and the dukes of Bedford, with their almost complete ownership of the town and district, ensured the neat and orderly expansion of housing. At the S. end of the town, along the Yelverton road, the Duke of Bedford laid out in the late 1840s and early 1850s a hundred miners' houses, an object lesson to speculative builders and central planners alike.

The Duke also remodelled the centre of the town during the 1840s, largely over the abbey site. He erected the guildhall (1848) in the Gothic style, and laid out the new Plymouth road from the Guildhall Square to Fitzford. He also Gothicised the Bedford Hotel which had been built as a private dwelling house c. 1725 by Jacob Saunders, a rich Presbyterian merchant, on the site of the abbey frater or refectory. Saunders' house was turned into an inn early in the 19th cent., but a good deal remains of his "pompous dwelling house" (as his enemies described it), notably the fine dining-room of the present hotel.

The fate of the abbey buildings after 1539 has been described by Mr. Finberg in his *Tavistock Abbey*. Very little remains of this once-splendid Benedictine house, but the accurate reconstruction shown in Plate 15 reveals what it was once like and where the buildings lay. The abbey-site lay between the parish church on the NW. and the Tavy on the SE. The visible remains may be summarised as follows: (1) a late 13th-cent. wall in the parish churchyard, representing the NW. corner of the cloister, the longer wall being that of the abbey church; (2) Betsy Grimbal's tower (so called) in the vicarage garden, which represents the W. gatehouse of the abbey and part of the abbot's lodging (15th-cent.); (3) the still-house and abbey precinct wall along the Tavy; (4) Court Gate in Guildhall Square, the main gateway of the abbey, late 12th-cent., remodelled in the 15th cent. and altered and restored by John Foulston in 1824. Since 1829 it has housed the Tavistock Library; (5) the misericord, a dining-hall reserved originally for the use of the sick, survives intact as the Unitarian chapel to-day, though the E. entrance dates only from 1845. From 1691 it has been used continuously as a place of worship, at first by the Presbyterians and later by the Unitarians. The coved plaster ceiling dates from 1755, the

original timber roof surviving underneath; (6) the porch to the misericord
survives at the back of the Bedford
Hotel, and is now used as a dairy. It
was the original N. entrance to the
misericord and has a vaulted roof with
bosses (early 16th cent.); (7) the
police station and sergeant's house, in
Guildhall Square, incorporate some
remains of the abbey. All these remains
should be studied with the aid of the
reconstruction of the site already
referred to.

The parish church has the rare dedication to St. Eustace, found in only two
other English parishes. It was first
founded, in all probability, in the early
13th cent., and rebuilt and enlarged
shortly before 1318 when Bishop Stapeldon dedicated it. Very little remains
of the 14th-cent. building, for between
1425 and 1450 the church was further
enlarged and rebuilt. The second S.
aisle, known as the Clothworker's Aisle,
was built in 1445 by the gift of Con-
stance, widow of John Wyse. Notice its
fine wagon roof with carved bosses.
The arcade leading into this aisle is of
granite but the other arcades and
interior stonework are of Roborough
elvan. The external walls are of the
green Hurdwick stone. Among the
noteworthy contents of the church are
the organ, the original specification for
which was drawn up by Samuel
Wesley, organist here for a time; the
early 15th-cent. Italian picture in the
chapel; the remarkably fine tomb of
Sir John Glanville (1600), who was born
at Tavistock and was the first attorney
to reach the judicial bench; the William
Morris window near the warshrine, and
the Kempe window in the N. choir aisle.
The churchwardens' accounts are
among the earliest in England, beginning in 1385-6, though the series is
very imperfect down to 1535-6.

In the vicarage garden are preserved
three inscribed stones, probably funerary monuments of the 6th cent. Two
were found at Buckland Monachorum
and one in Tavistock. All have Latin
inscriptions. One of the Buckland
stones is also carved with Ogham
characters, a script invented in S. Ireland and brought by Irish invaders to
the W. of England. The vicarage itself
is a pleasant early 19th-cent. building
in Hurdwick stone.

There is much other decent early
19th-cent. building in the town, including the Corn Market (1835), now a
cinema, and the workhouse on the N.
side of the town, erected in 1837, and
attributed to Sir Gilbert Scott. Fitzford
church, large and gaunt, was built in
the Italian Gothic style in 1866-7.
After being disused for many years, it
was taken over by the Roman Catholics
in 1951 as a place of worship.

The Abbey Bridge was built in 1764
and widened in 1859-60. Vigo Bridge,
also over the Tavy, dates from 1773.
Near here the beautiful Quaker
Cemetery should be noticed, with its
clipped cypresses, rhododendrons, weep-
ing willows, and great copper beeches.
At the S. entrance to the town stands a
fine statue to Sir Francis Drake (c.
1540-96), by Boehm. The better-known
statue on Plymouth Hoe is a replica of
this original. Drake was almost certainly born at Crowndale Farm,
about 1 m. S. of the town, but nothing remains of the farmhouse of his
date.

Tavistock was described by Fuller as
"that fruitful seed-plot of eminent and
famous men." Besides Drake, there
were Sir John Glanville, William
Browne, the poet and author of
Britannia's Pastorals (much of his poetry
is about the beautiful Tavistock
country), and Sir John Maynard (1602-

90), who sat in the Short and Long Parliaments and framed Strafford's impeachment.

In the parish are a number of interesting houses. Morwell was a country seat of the abbots of Tavistock, and is a perfect little 15th-cent. house on a quadrangular plan. Kilworthy lies secluded at the end of a long lane. It was the home of the Glanvilles in the 16th cent. but the present house was rebuilt *c.* 1800. The Elizabethan walled garden and terraces, however, remain unchanged. Of the ancient house of the Fitz family at Fitzford (now at the S. end of the town) nothing is left but the rebuilt gatehouse.

TAWSTOCK (D2), a large parish in singularly beautiful country W. of the lower Taw valley, was the seat of the Bourchiers, Lords Fitzwarren and Earls of Bath, from the 15th cent. to the 17th, when their heiress carried it to the Wreys. The Bourchiers were created earls of Bath in 1536 and were one of the most powerful families in Devon in their time. Their great mansion was burnt down in 1787. Only the splendid gatehouse survives, dated 1574. The house was rebuilt by Sir Bourchier Wrey in 1787, to his own "Gothick" design, and is remarkably ugly. It is now a school.

Below it lies the church (St. Peter) which contains the finest collection of monuments in Devon, and one of the most notable in England. It is beautifully situated in the timbered park, on a hillside falling gently to the Taw, and is externally one of the most attractive churches in the county (plate 30). Cruciform in plan, with a central tower, it is almost purely early 14th-cent. in date, itself an unusual feature in Devon churches. The fittings and monuments in the church are of the highest interest:

an entire half-day should be allowed for their inspection.

The N. transept has a ceiling of Italian plaster-work, and medieval glass in the window. A beautiful late 16th-cent. gallery leads to the belfry. This may possibly have been the minstrels' gallery, rescued from the old house in 1787. The Wrey manorial pew is French Renaissance work, perhaps the finest example of its kind in Devon, and has some excellent carved bench-ends near it, *temp.* Henry VIII. The transept contains a considerable number of monuments, including a beautiful one to Mrs. Ann Chilcot (1758).

In the chancel is a beautiful little mural monument, with a kneeling figure, to Mary St. John (1631), and beyond that the oldest of the Tawstock monuments, a 14th-cent. effigy in oak of an unknown lady. Inside the altar rails is the magnificent tomb, with recumbent life-size effigies, of William Bourchier, 5th Baron Fitzwarren and 3rd Earl of Bath (d. 1623) and Elizabeth, his wife, daughter of Francis, Earl of Bedford. Both are portrayed in their full robes of the peerage, and the earl is coroneted. At either end of the tomb are ranged the kneeling sons and daughters of this noble pair. The whole tomb is sumptuously coloured.

In the S. chancel aisle, which was added about 1540, and has a fine open cradle-roof of that date, the monuments are overwhelming. The sculptured standing figure of Rachel, Countess of Bath (d. 1680), is by Balthasar Burman, and is a replica of the statue of the Countess of Shrewsbury at St. John's College, Cambridge, done by his father in 1672.

Near her is the massive and ugly table-tomb of her husband, Henry, the 5th and last Earl of Bath. Against the S. wall is the tomb of Frances, Lady

Fitzwarren (d. 1586), erected in 1589, every detail of which is worthy of study. Her effigy is most beautifully and delicately sculptured. Finally, in this aisle, are two mural monuments to officers of the Earl of Bath's household—Thomas Hinson and William Skippon.

In the S. transept, which has a plaster ceiling similar to that in the N. transept, are numerous Wrey monuments and memorials of 18th–20th-cent. date, and many hatchments.

Leaving this remarkable church, we return through the park to the village, which has a good deal of attractive building and, some little way beyond, a handsome late Georgian rectory as befitted a rich family living. There are a number of interesting farmhouses scattered about the parish, which the visitor to Tawstock, exhausted by this prolonged contact with nobility, will find for himself in the lanes and byways.

TAWTON, NORTH .(E5) is one of those ancient, decayed market towns, of which there are so many in Devon. We find it called *Cheping Tawton* as early as 1199 (OE. *cieping* = market). At some date also it was made a borough, governed by a portreeve elected annually, an office which lasted until the end of the 19th cent. The town formerly had a considerable woollen industry which greatly declined, as it did all over Devon, in the second half of the 18th cent. Nevertheless, one woollen mill (at Taw Bridge) survived and gave considerable employment to the townspeople until recent years.

The railway did not reach North Tawton until 1865, and then had its inevitable effect on the economy of the town. The almost simultaneous closing of the woollen mill and the flour mills, which used to employ most of the people, gave the death-blow in recent

years. There are fewer people in North Tawton to-day than there were in the 18th cent.

The town has suffered greatly from extensive fires and is now mostly a rather drab collection of mid- and late-19th-cent. houses, coated with a grey roughcast. There are a few more pleasing houses, the most interesting being a late 15th-cent. building of some pretensions in the Square, probably a small manor house originally. The church (St. Peter) is quite unexciting, with a squat W. tower (13th cent.) capped by a shingled spire (rebuilt, 1900). The rest of the church is 15th–early 16th–cent. with lofty granite arcades, and an inadequate, much-restored chancel. Nearly all the fittings are Victorian, except a few vigorously carved 16th-cent. bench-ends in the nave.

There are a number of interesting houses in the parish. Ashridge was a medieval "mansion" and shows some remains of this and of a chapel. Cottle's Barton, near the Taw, is an attractive stone-built Elizabethan "mansion," built in 1567 and somewhat restored (but not spoilt) in 1866.

At Nichols Nymet, which was a Domesday manor, are the remains of an old *barton*; and Crooke, which was also a Domesday manor, has the remains of a manor house and a medieval chapel. Greenslade, now a farmhouse, was a Domesday estate also.

North Tawton now includes, for civil purposes, the ancient parish of Broad Nymet which covered only 52 acres. The present barton has a plain front of *c.* 1800 but is substantially a late 16th–early 17th-cent. building which originally faced the other way. The church (dedication unknown) is one of the rare ruined parish churches of Devon and is worth a pilgrimage to this rather remote spot. It is a late 13th-cent. building, to which a S. porch was added in the 17th cent. It became a sinecure rectory, and the church fell into disuse. It is an interesting little building and should be rescued from its desecration, but no one seems to care about its fate.

TAWTON, SOUTH (E6) includes Cawsand Beacon (1,789 ft.), one of the most conspicuous landmarks on Dartmoor from its vast rounded shape. From the summit one gets an amazing view, ranging from the Atlantic near Bude to the English Channel between Teignmouth and the Start, and S. over Dartmoor at its wildest and most impressive. On the flanks of the hill are Bronze Age kists (burial chambers), barrows, hut-circles, and stone rows, and just S. of Sticklepath the remains of abandoned copper mines. The 2½-inch Ordnance map, sheet 20/69, is invaluable for the detailed exploration of this interesting parish.

The parish abounds in interesting houses, the "mansions" of moorland gentry. Oxenham was the seat of the Oxenhams from the time of Henry III until 1814. The present house was built in 1714. Wickington is largely 15th–cent. in date., with a tower-porch. North Wyke is 15th–cent. and 17th-cent., very picturesque but much restored. West Week, the home of the Battishills, is dated 1656. Other ancient farmhouses are Powlesland, c. 1600 or a little earlier, with some 15th-cent. work in the barn behind. Sessland, another remote farmhouse, is Elizabethan: much dilapidated but an interesting survival of its age. A branch of the Oxenhams lived here from the 16th to 18th cent. The student of old peasant building, and of social history, could profitably spend a week or more in this unspoilt countryside.

At South Zeal, on the old line of the Exeter-Okehampton road, the Oxenham Arms is a good early 16th-cent. granite building; but the medieval chapel, rebuilt in 1713 and restored in 1877, is dull.

The parish church (St. Andrew) is a handsome 15th-cent. building, mostly of granite, with a particularly fine W. tower. Notice the carved roof bosses, especially in the nave roof, and the fine monument with effigy in armour to John Wyke of North Wyke (1592). The Church House (c. 1500), near the church, is one of the best examples of its kind, and is still used for parochial purposes.

TEDBURN ST. MARY (G6) lies in beautiful, billowy country, full of colour at any time of the year. The church (St. Mary) is mainly a 15th-cent. building, with considerable traces of earlier work, as in the S. transept. The whole church was greatly altered inside in the 17th cent. and again in the Victorian restoration. Great Hackworthy, now a farmhouse, was a Domesday manor; so, too, were Melhuish Barton and Upcott.

TEIGNGRACE (G8) church (St. Peter and St. Paul) was rebuilt by the Templers in 1787, and, though restored in 1872, retains some of its original interest as an early specimen of Strawberry Hill Gothic. Over the altar is a large painting by James Barry, R.A., a copy of the famous *Pieta* by Vandyke in the Antwerp museum. There are several mural monuments to the Templers of 18th- and early 19th-cent. date, and a handsome cenotaph to Nelson. Stover House, now a school, was built in 1776-81.

TEIGNMOUTH (H8) is, except for Exmouth, the oldest seaside resort in

Devon. It began to attract summer visitors as early as the middle of the 18th cent. and remained, like Exmouth, a fashionable resort until after the coming of the railway in 1846. It has, however, a much longer history as a small seaport, fishing town, and market town. The present town is the result of the union of two parishes, East and West Teignmouth, each with a distinct history, which were separated by a stream called the Tame, now covered in and forgotten.

For centuries both towns had a considerable inshore fishery. They carried on an active trade with Newfoundland throughout the 18th cent., and also had a particularly flourishing trade in the 18th–early 19th cents. in local granite, pipe-clay, manganese, timber, etc. In 1821 George Templer of Stover built the New Quay for the shipment of granite from his Hey Tor quarries. There is a long tradition of shipbuilding here also, from at least the 17th cent., down to the present day. Many beautiful yachts have been built in the Teignmouth yard since the days of the sailing ships ended.

In 1340 the port of Teignmouth was burnt by the French, but the worst catastrophe occurred on 13 July 1690 when the French, under de Tourville, bombarded and fired the town without opposition.

Teignmouth was a fashionable seaside resort in the late 18th–early 19th cent. Both Keats and Fanny Burney stayed here, among other notable people. The town retains a good deal of pleasant late Georgian and early Victorian architecture, particularly along the open space known as the Den and in the adjoining streets. On the Den were built the Assembly Rooms (1826, by Andrew Patey of Exeter), now a cinema. Northumber-

land Place is a late Georgian street: at No. 20 Keats stayed in 1818. Teign Street is of the same period. In this street Thomas Luny, the painter, built "Meadcombe" for his own occupation.

St. Scholastica's Abbey, on the Dawlish road, is a notable Gothic Revival building (1864) by Henry Woodyer, a pupil of Butterfield. The Roman Catholic Church (1878), also on the Dawlish road, is a late work of Hansom, the inventor of the hansom cab and an architect of some note.

The two parish churches of Teignmouth are dull, though that at West Teignmouth (St. James) is something of a curiosity. It was rebuilt about 1820, except the medieval tower. Internally, the slender cast-iron pillars supporting the vaulted roof make a striking composition. St. Michael's at East Teignmouth is an ancient foundation: it is mentioned in a Saxon charter of 1044. But the present church is entirely late Victorian.

Teignmouth suffered severely in the Second German War of 1939-45. It was repeatedly bombed in "tip-and-run" air-raids between 1940 and 1943, in which 79 people were killed and 151 wounded (a proportion of 3 in 100 of the wartime population). The port of Teignmouth is more active to-day than it has perhaps ever been, chiefly in the export of ball and fire clays to all the countries between Finland and Italy. These clays come from the mines of the lower Teign valley, where they have been worked for at least two hundred years.

TEMPLETON (G4) church (St. Margaret) was rebuilt in 1876, except the tower, and is of little interest.

TETCOTT (B6) consists of little more than the old Arscott mansion and the parish church (plate 24). The latter (Holy Cross) is mostly a 13th-cent. building. Some alterations were made in the early 16th cent., when the tower was added. The font is Norman. There are a few old benches in the nave; the Arscott pew in the S. chapel is vigorously carved, as befitted such a robust family. The chapel contains a good mural monument to John Arscott (1675) and Gertrude his wife (1699), and a tablet to the last of the Arscotts of Tetcott (John Arscott, 1718-88), a wonderful old character who is described in R. S. Hawker's *Footprints of Former Men in Cornwall* and in Baring-Gould's *Devonshire Characters and Strange Events* (*First Series*). He kept a dwarf jester, known as Black John, as remarkable a character as his master: they were both survivors out of the Middle Ages.

A junior branch of the Arscotts settled at Tetcott about 1550. In 1603 Arthur Arscott built the low, rambling mansion we still see. In the time of Anne, the house was enlarged and to some extent remodelled, and the outbuildings rebuilt in brick, most unusual in this remote part of Devon. Tetcott is altogether an atmospheric place, with its mixture of rustic Elizabethan and equally rustic Queen Anne. Here, more even than in most places in Devon, we feel

Impalpable impressions on the air—
A sense of something moving to and fro.

There are magical overtones in the very words Arscott of Tetcott. They epitomise all the ancient Devonshire squires and their homes: the wind-flung rooks on December afternoons, branch-strewn parks emerging from curtains of fine rain, rambling, echoing stone-flagged houses set all alone at the end of muddy lanes, darkened by beeches and sycamores. Even the historian feels his reason wavering as the *genius loci* takes possession of his senses, and is prepared to believe almost anything of such a place, even to see John Arscott appear on Black-bird across the deserted park,

and hear in full cry,
The pack from Pencarrow to Dazzard go by.

THELBRIDGE (F4) church (St. David) is a landmark for some miles around and is an attractive little building externally, built in the warm brown dunstone. It was, however, rebuilt in 1871-4 and is devoid of all interest except for a good 18th-cent. organ. Middlewick Barton was a Domesday manor.

THORNBURY (C5) gets its name from some earthwork of which there is now no trace. Of the scattered farms Wonford and North Week were Domesday manors, and Bagbeare gave its name to a family who lived here for some centuries.

The church (St. Peter) is one of a group in this district retaining much 14th-cent. work. There is a good Norman S. doorway (*c.* 1150), all that remains of the 12th-cent. church which was rebuilt *c.* 1330. A heavy-handed restoration in 1876 (when the tower was raised by 5 ft.) has obscured much of the original work. There is a fine altar tomb with recumbent effigies in alabaster to Sir John Specott (d. 1641) and Elizabeth his wife.

THORVERTON (H5) is a large and ancient village with much interesting building in cob, local stone, and thatch. The well-known Thorverton stone was quarried from the 12th cent. onwards at Raddon, 1 m. W. of the village, where the abandoned workings may be seen.

Among the buildings may be noticed particularly a butcher's shop in the local style (1763); the Dolphin Hotel (18th-cent.), dating from the days when Thorverton was on a busy cross-road; and several good 18th- and 19th-cent. houses along the station road. The main streets are followed by a channelled stream, characteristic of several E. Devon villages.

The church (St. Thomas Becket) was rebuilt in the late 15th–early 16th cent., and satisfactorily restored about 1834, when the nave was rebuilt. There are slate floor-slabs to the Tuckfields of East Raddon, but no other monuments of any note.

The parish contains much beautiful hill scenery. It consists largely of a fertile red earth, excellent for wheat, barley, and apples; but the apricots for which the village has long been famous are no more.

There are several ancient farms in the parish. Raddon Court, 1½ m. W. of the village, takes its name from the prominent range of hills near by ("red hill") and was a Saxon estate. Other old farms are Upcott, Bidwell, and Lynch. Traymill, in the N. of the parish, on the Exe, is substantially a small medieval manor house, built c. 1400, with some traceried windows, arched doorways, and its original hall roof.

Thorverton Bridge, over the Exe, is a modern concrete structure, the successor of several earlier bridges. In 1307 the first bridge was "newly built," probably of timber. Both Thorverton mill (still working) and Traymill were Domesday water-mills, serving the large manor of Silverton.

THROWLEIGH (E6) is a remote parish on the NE. edge of Dartmoor, much of it running far up into the high moorland. Numerous hut-circles are to be found on Throwleigh Common.

The church (St. Mary the Virgin) is most attractive: rebuilt of granite in the 15th cent. with a N. aisle added early in the 16th. The dignified granite tower was added c. 1500. Notice the fine priest's doorway, the 15th-cent. pulpit incorporating fragments of the rood-screen, and the E. window by Comper.

The parish contains a number of fine old moorland farmhouses, lying down in the sheltered hollows below the intricate lanes. Most notable of these are North Wonson (a fine specimen of an early 16th-cent. granite farmhouse), Wonson Manor (17th-cent.) near the remains of an older house, and Shilston (16th–17th cent.). In the "village" are the 15th-cent. Church House, and some other houses and cottages of 16th- and 17th-cent date. This is an unspoiled piece of country, in which the student of English peasant building will find much to please and interest him.

THRUSHELTON (c7) lies in the unknown country falling from Lewdon to the river Thrushel. The river gets its name from the O.E. word for "thrush" (cf. "throstle" to-day), the bird that most haunted its banks, just as the Yarty in E. Devon is named after the water-wagtails (earte) that flickered up and down its stones. The parish church (St. George), beautifully sited, has a delightful unsophisticated country interior: oil lamps, rough plastered walls, everything simple and plain. It is substantially a 14th-cent. building, enlarged in the 15th. Orchard was the seat of the Woods from the 16th to the 18th cent., and is now a much-altered farmhouse.

THURLESTONE (E11) takes its name

from the pierced ("thirled") stone, just off the shore, which is mentioned as a boundary point in a Saxon charter of 845. The village is attractive, with several old cottages. Much modern building has been done since this remote coast was "discovered," but the village remains one of the most pleasing on the S. coast, except for the large hotel which is more appropriate to the suburbs of London. Buckland, now two farms N. of the church, was a Domesday manor.

The church (All Saints) is built of the dark grey local slate. The chancel is early 13th-cent.; the remainder of the church 15th–16th-cent. Notice the fine Norman font, the bosses and wall-plates of the chancel, and some pleasant 17th-cent. mural monuments.

TIVERTON (H4), a bright and bustling town of some 10,000 people, occupies a wedge-like site between the Exe on the W. and the Loman on the E. The rivers join just below the town. In King Alfred's will (880-5) Tiverton is referred to as *Twyfyrde*, i.e. "double ford," the place being reached by a ford over each river. It was founded early in the Saxon settlement, probably *c.* 650, gave its name to a hundred from the 10th cent. onwards, and was a royal estate from the beginning. Henry I gave the large and valuable manor in 1106 to Richard de Redvers, whose son Baldwin was created Earl of Devon.

Tiverton Castle was built by Richard de Redvers and became the principal residence of the Courtenays until 1539. A borough was founded at Tiverton by William de Vernon, 5th Earl of Devon, some time between 1193 and 1217. It remained an unimportant place, however, until the establishment of the kersey manufacture in the late 15th cent. This new industry, which grew rapidly in the hands of merchants like John Greenway, John Waldron, Peter Blundell (all of whom have left their physical mark upon the town)—coupled with the downfall of the feudal house of Courtenay—liberated the little agricultural township from its economic bondage. It quickly developed a suburb on the far side of the Exe (we hear of West Exe for the first time in 1504) and it had galloped ahead of all other woollen towns in Devon by the end of the 16th cent. During the 17th–18th cents. it was the most considerable industrial town in Devon, taking the high place that Totnes had occupied in the early 1500s. One of the last of the woollen mills was taken over in 1816 by John Heathcoat, a lace manufacturer of Loughborough in Leicestershire, who was driven out of the Midlands by the Luddite machine-breakers. His factory still goes on, making much else besides lace to-day, and a great part of the life of modern Tiverton revolves around it. The old mill was destroyed by fire 1936 and replaced by a modern building.

Tiverton was incorporated in 1615 and at the same time made a parliamentary borough with two representatives. Members were first elected in 1620. It continued to return members until disfranchised in 1885, when it was merged with a county division. The most notable of all Tiverton members was Lord Palmerston, who represented the borough continuously from 1835 until his death in 1865.

The town has a remarkable number of charities and benefactions, as might be expected from its generations of prosperity as a textile centre. The water that runs through the principal streets was given to his borough by one of the earls of Devon in the time of Henry III, and has run ever since. Greenway's Almshouses, in Gold Street, founded in

1529, have been several times repaired and enlarged. They were almost entirely rebuilt in 1732, but the little chapel is Tudor in date. Waldron's Almshouses in Welbrook Street were founded in 1579. The present building bears the date 1597. There is a chapel similar to that in Greenway's Almshouses. Slee's Almshouses in St. Peter's Street, founded in 1610, are less attractive. The other great benefaction of a Tiverton clothier—perhaps the greatest—is Blundell's School, founded in 1599. The Old School, built in 1604, still stands near the Loman bridge at the SE. end of the town, but was converted into dwelling houses in 1880 when new and larger premises were taken over. Among the notable men who received their schooling at Blundell's were Archbishop Temple, R. D. Blackmore (who puts John Ridd to school here in *Lorna Doone*), and Bampfylde Moore Carew. Another school was founded by Robert Chilcott, Blundell's nephew. This was built in St. Peter's Street in 1611, and has fortunately escaped all the disastrous fires that mark the history of the town.

The castle and parish church form an attractive group at the NW. end of the town, on a cliff overlooking the river. The former was dismantled after its capture by Fairfax in October 1645 and is now a dwelling house. The remains of the castle, which are 14th-cent. in date, consist of the great gateway, a round tower, part of the chapel, and a large square building of which the upper part is said to have been the banqueting hall.

The church (St. Peter) is a large, dignified 15th-cent. structure, to which was added in 1517 Greenway's chapel and S. porch (plate 9). The whole S. side of the church was rebuilt by Greenway and is lavishly carved with all manner of decoration, including ships, wool-packs, staple-marks, coats-of-arms, and figures of men, children and horses. On the corbel line of the chapel are represented events in the life of Christ, beginning with the flight into Egypt and ending with the Ascension. The W. tower belongs to the Somerset class, of which Chittlehampton is the finest example in Devon. The interior is disappointing, having been in great part rebuilt in 1853-5 (by Ashworth of Exeter). Notice the memorial brasses of John and Joan Greenway (1529), the tombs of the merchants John Waldron and George Slee, and a picture presented in 1784 by Richard Cosway (who was a native of the town) depicting " St. Peter delivered out of Prison by the Angel." Another picture, " The Adoration of the Magi " by Gaspar de Crayer, a contemporary of Rubens, hangs over the Norman N. door.

There are in the principal streets of the town a number of attractive 18th- and early 19th-cent. houses, some of them built after the great fire of 1731. Few houses survived this fire, but one, in St. Peter's Street, is a good late 17th-cent. merchant's house. St. George's church, in the middle of the town, was built in 1714-30 and is the only notable Georgian church in Devon. It retains its original ceilings, galleries, and other fittings, but the seating, pulpit, and font are Victorian intrusions. In the churchyard lies buried Hannah Cowley (1743-1809), a native of Tiverton who was a dramatist of some contemporary fame. Her best-known play was *The Belle's Stratagem*. At the N. edge of the town is the workhouse, of the early Union type, built in 1836-7 and attributed to Gilbert Scott.

A number of hamlets and farmsteads in the parish (which is extensive) are recorded in Domesday: Bolham, Bradley, Chettiscombe, Chevithorne, Craze Loman, Patcott, and Peadhill. Chevithorne Barton, 3 m. NE. of the town, is mainly a Tudor house still. The chapel at Chevithorne was built in 1843 (Benjamin Ferrey). That at Withleigh, 3 m. W. of the town, was built in 1846 upon the site of a medieval chapel. Cove chapel was also rebuilt in 1846 on the old site.

Collipriest, S. of the town, is an attractive late 18th-cent. house. It was for many years the seat of the Blundell family. On the hill above is Cranmore Castle, an extensive but weak earthwork of unknown age. In 1549 some of the insurgents in the Prayer-Book Rebellion made a stand here but were defeated by the King's troops.

Knightshayes Court, N. of the town, is the seat of the Heathcoat-Amorys. The house (1869) stands in a wooded park of 200 acres which was formerly part of the demesne of the earls of Devon.

About ½ m. SE. of the town is the termination of the derelict Grand Western Canal, constructed under an act of 1796. Its towpath now makes a pleasant summer evening walk.

TOPSHAM (H7) is one of those ancient, decayed estuary-ports which are perhaps the most fascinating kind of town that England can show, with their colour, smells, and strong sense of past life everywhere in the streets and alleys and along the water-fronts. It consisted formerly of one long main street with a number of short streets running at right angles to it down to the foreshore of the Exe, where its life and navigation lay.

It is possible that a native Celtic trading settlement existed on this site, comparable with the Mount Batten site on Plymouth Sound, but the evidence of prehistoric occupation is so far slight. What is undoubted is that a Roman port grew up here about the middle of the 1st cent. A.D. to serve *Isca Dumnoniorum* (Exeter), with which it was connected by a straight road 3 m. long leading directly to the forum of the tribal capital. This is the present Topsham Road along which the Exeter buses now travel. The port was active throughout the Romano-British period down to about A.D. 400.

Whether or not Topsham survived after the Roman withdrawal from Britain, we do not know. The depopulation of the Celtic kingdom of Dumnonia in the late 5th–6th cent. may have produced economic changes leading to its collapse as a river port, but there was no reason why a small agricultural community should not have continued on these fertile light soils that are noted to this day for their market-gardening.

However this may be, the Saxon occupation of East Devon during the 7th cent. brought important changes. A considerable village was planted on or near the old site, with its own open fields. Athelstan gave it in 937 to the monastery of St. Mary and St. Peter at Exeter, a gift which was later confirmed to Bishop Leofric. By 1066 Harold had unjustly seized the estate from the Church (as he had seized other estates elsewhere) and at the Conquest it was taken back into the royal demesne. Henry I parted with it to Richard de Redvers, whose son Baldwin founded St. James's Priory, between Topsham and Exeter, in 1141 and endowed it *inter alia* with half the tithes of his fishery at Topsham. The fishery would have been a salmon fishery, which is still carried on in a small way (plate 54).

The most important event in the medieval history of Topsham was the closing of the Exe by the Courtenays, who by building weirs across the river between here and Exeter prevented ships from reaching the city, and so forced merchants to land their goods at Topsham. Although the city took legal proceedings, the weirs remained, and Topsham became a flourishing port. All goods had to be unloaded here and carried on to Exeter by road. The construction of the Exeter ship canal in 1564-7 restored some trade to the city, but for various reasons the canal was not entirely satisfactory and Topsham remained in fact the outport for the greater part of the vast Exeter trade in woollens throughout the 16th-18th cents. Its prosperity, throughout this period, and well into the 19th cent., is well evidenced by the architecture of the town, which contains some notable merchants' houses. In the Strand are the beautiful " Dutch " houses, with delightful small courtyards, which were built *c.* 1700-25 by Topsham merchants from Dutch brick brought back as ballast, and obviously with Dutch architecture in mind (plate 41). Holland was then the largest customer for Devonshire serges, and these were the greatest days of the port.

The buildings of Topsham, from the 16th cent. to the 19th, are so varied, numerous, and individual, that one cannot even begin to catalogue them. It is quite the most rewarding small town in Devon for the student of local styles in building, and probably one of the most interesting in England. The whole feeling of the water-front is remarkable: the decaying shipyards, the rotting hulks on the river mud, the derelict warehouses, nail factories, and quays, the multitudinous cats, the wonderful river views across to the Exminster marshes and down to the sea, with the woods of Haldon closing the western horizon. No wonder Topsham has been a favourite walk for Exeter people since the 18th cent., for Polwhele tells us they were accustomed to stroll down by the canal banks on summer evenings in the 1780s, and probably before that. The view from the churchyard, set on a small cliff overhanging the river, is incomparably beautiful when the evening tide is coming in. Poor harassed George Gissing, who had so little peace in his life, used to walk here from Exeter, where he lived for a couple of years (1891-3), and remembered it when he poured out his heart in *The Private Papers of Henry Ryecroft*. " A whole day's walk yesterday with no plan; just a long ramble hour after hour, entirely enjoyable. It ended at Topsham, where I sat on the little churchyard terrace, and watched the evening tide come up the broad estuary. I have a great liking for Topsham, and that churchyard, overlooking what is not quite sea, yet more than river, is one of the most restful spots I know."

The collapse of the Devonshire woollen industry at the end of the 18th cent. greatly injured the trade of Topsham, but the little town had many irons in the fire and it continued to grow throughout the first half of the 19th cent. It had a considerable shipbuilding industry, which had probably taken root in the 16th cent., and also an important salmon and herring fishery. Shipbuilding also meant nail, chain, and rope factories, and a number of other subsidiary trades.

The inns and taverns of Topsham are as varied and excellent as those of any old river-port. Best of all is the *Salutation* (1720) with its former Assembly Room, Bowling Green, and all the other attributes of a good 18th-cent. inn. The *Globe* is also notable. Nor should the visitor fail to visit the *Passage House Inn,* the *Steam Packet Inn*, the *Lighter Inn*, the *Lord Nelson Inn*, and the *Bridge Inn*. The last named is particularly fascinating. It stands away from the old town, facing the Clyst, and is said to be of 16th-cent. date.

After the middle of the 19th cent. the town lost many of its ancient trades and crafts, but in the past 30 years it has developed rapidly as a dormitory for the city of Exeter and now has almost as many people as it had a hundred years ago. Fortunately, the new housing has been forced to develop on the farther side of the town, away from the water-front, and the old town remains almost completely unchanged and unspoiled. May it long remain so, for it has an incomparable charm and quality that the muddy fingers of the 20th cent. could only soil.

Of all the buildings of the town, the parish church (St. Margaret) is the least interesting. It was rebuilt in 1876-8, except for its medieval red sandstone tower, and utterly ruined. It does contain, however, two monuments by Chantrey to the Duckworths. These, and its superb site on a bluff above the estuary, save it from complete nonentity.

TORBRYAN (G9) possesses what is perhaps the most uniformly attractive village church in Devon (Holy Trinity). It is entirely an early 15th-cent. building with an imposing, severely plain W. tower. The interior is completely characteristic of a Devon country church in its plan and fittings. The white Beer stone arcades, the plastered walls and ceilings, and the uninterrupted light coming through the large windows of clear glass (except some coloured medieval glass in the traceried heads) make a perfect foil for the vivid polychrome of the screen, pulpit, and

altar table. It is all highly "atmospheric."

The rood-screen (*c.* 1430) has lost its vaulting, and has been in places cheaply restored; the carved woodwork of the altar table is of exceptional beauty and merit. It is made up of woodwork taken from the original medieval pulpit and is so well put together as to have the appearance of an original medieval composition. The present pulpit is in turn made up from the pier-casings of the rood-screen. The 15th-cent. seating is preserved, encased within early 18th-cent. box-pews which all have brass candle-holders. The four bells are the original medieval bells, said to have been cast at Exeter *temp.* Henry VI.

The Church House Inn, *c.* 1500 in date, was formerly the Church House. At Tornewton was born Sir William Petre (?1505-72) the son of an ancient franklin family. He became Secretary of State to four monarchs, profited greatly by monastic spoils, and founded a great new family of which Lord Petre (the 17th) is the present representative

1½ m. N. of Torbryan is Denbury, now united with it for civil purposes. Denbury is an ancient village, taking its name from the strong earthwork which crowns a lofty igneous rock to the SW. It is "the fort of the men of Devon" (*Defnas burh*), a name which may well commemorate a stronghold where the Dumnonii held out for a time against a Saxon advance from the head of the Teign estuary. The fort consists of an elliptical, ramparted area, with an outer court on the W. side, and with two large mounds in the main camp.[1] It has never been excavated and its date is unknown: it may conceivably be of two distinct periods.

Denbury belonged to Tavistock Abbey in 1086 and possibly earlier. It was granted a market in 1286, and given the status of a borough with a portreeve some time in the 14th cent.[1] but never became more than a village. The church (St. Mary) is a cruciform building with a battered tower, all of early 14th-cent. date and pretty certainly the church dedicated by Bishop Stapeldon in 1318.[2] The fine 12th-cent. font remains from an earlier church.

Denbury House is an Elizabethan mansion. There is some good 16th–17th cent. building in the village; several houses have massive chimney-breasts on the street, a characteristic feature of certain Devon villages.

TORQUAY (H9), the best known of all the Devon seaside resorts, occupies a superb position on the N. promontory of Tor Bay, completely sheltered by higher ground from the N. and E. winds. It is a town almost entirely of 19th-cent. growth, but a hamlet probably stood near the shore from medieval times. Torre Abbey, near by, built a small quay here. During the 17th–18th cents. the English fleet frequently lay up in Tor Bay in preference to Plymouth Sound. The bay was large enough to take the whole fleet comfortably, and sheltered from all but E. and SE. winds. During the Napoleonic Wars, too, the fleet anchored here for long periods, so that officers had their wives and families brought down and found accommodation ashore for them at Tor Quay. The hamlet had indeed begun to attract attention as a summer watering place before the war, but the first real impetus to growth came with the fleet, and possibly also the civilian visitors who were debarred from the Continent. Still, there were fewer than 2,000 people in 1821. Then it was found that the town, besides being suited to summer visitors, also had a mild winter

climate, and doctors despatched their consumptive patients to Torquay in great numbers. By 1841 there were nearly 6,000 people, and some elegant terraces were being built of which Hesketh Crescent to-day is perhaps the best example. The atmosphere of these years is well conveyed in a charming book : A Panorama of Torquay, by Octavian Blewitt, published in 1832. He tells us, among other things, that those who wished to avoid the fatigue of the long coach journey from London, travelled to Portsmouth by coach and there took the Brunswick—"a steam vessel of considerable power"—direct to Torquay. All this was immensely simplified by the coming of the railway in 1848, which led to even more rapid growth. By 1850 the town was calling itself "the Queen of Watering Places" and " the Montpellier of England," and its terraces and suburban villas extended for more than a mile along the N. shore of the bay. The period of most rapid growth was between 1841 and 1871, when the population rose by over 5,000 in each decade; and this has stamped Torquay architecturally as a mid-Victorian town. The layout of the town, as seen from the Bay, is a remarkably fine piece of planning, with wooded drives and terraces following the contours of the hill in sweeping convolutions. Much of this excellent planning was due to the Palks and the Carys who, between them, owned the greater part of the site, especially to Sir Lawrence Palk who set out to develop his property for an upper-class clientèle. Among other improvements he enlarged and partly rebuilt the Royal Hotel (in 1828) and adapted it " for the reception of families of the first distinction." He also began the construction of the present Inner Harbour, and built terraces of lodging-houses for genteel families.

The Mallocks of Cockington, who were the other considerable landowners, resisted these changes for a long time. They did not want a town on their rural property, and they threw away a fortune rather than have it. Not until 1865 did one of them consent to grant a building lease, and that only to a family connection.[1] Growth slowed up in the 1870s and 1880s, mainly because the well-to-do, for whom Torquay catered to the exclusion of all others, now began to take their summer and winter holidays abroad. Meanwhile, the adjacent parish of St. Marychurch, on the N., had taken the overflow of Torquay, and had grown from 800 people at the beginning of the century to nearly 7,000 at the end. In the same period, Cockington had been transformed, in a milder degree, from a deep country parish to a villa-strewn suburb, though the old village remained untouched. In 1892 Torquay was incorporated as a municipal borough; in 1900 its boundaries were extended to take in Babbacombe, Chelston, Ilsham, and St. Marychurch; and in 1923 the parishes of Tormohun and St. Marychurch were united to form the new parish of Torquay. The village and parish of Cockington were taken in in 1928. To-day the borough has rather more than 53,000 people. It extends 5 m. northwards almost to the mouth of the Teign, and includes 6,244 acres. The social and economic changes of the last generation have had their effects on Torquay. The winter visitors and the retired class are still an important element in the economy of the town, but the summer holiday trade is considerably more important than it ever was before and the town sets out to attract it in a restrained fashion. Torquay is losing, perhaps has already lost, its exclusive Victorian and Edwardian flavour and is falling more into line with the changed national economy; but whatever happens it can never become quite like other places, if only because of the unrivalled beauty of its site and its layout, and the lingering flavour of the large stuccoed villas and the winding tree-shaded drives. Here one will find for a long time to come the haunting memories of Victorian peace, security, and comfort, that world that has vanished so completely from our ken almost everywhere else.

Historically, Torquay consists of three ancient parishes—Tor Mohun, St. Marychurch, and Cockington. Tor Mohun takes its name from the *tor* or conspicuous hill known as Tor Hill to-day, and its suffix from the Mohuns who acquired the manor from the Brewers in the 13th cent. The village lay about a mile inland from the shore of the bay, which was named after it. Tor Mohun church (St. Saviour) is an undistinguished 15th-cent. building, with a plain 14th-cent. tower. It has been much altered and restored to meet the needs of the rising population of Torquay, but retains a strong early Victorian flavour. There is an imposing early 17th-cent. monument erected by Sir Thomas Ridgeway to the memory of his father Thomas and his grandfather John (d. 1560). In the sanctuary is a brass to Wilmot, the wife of Sir George Cary (d. 1581). Near by is the tomb of Sir Thomas Cary, father of Sir George (d. 1567).

Torre Abbey was founded near the shore of the bay in 1196, and was at the Dissolution the richest Premonstratensian house in England. Considerable remains of the monastic buildings are to be seen, including the late 12th-cent. entrance to the chapter house, the early 14th-cent. gatehouse, the guest hall, and the great barn. The present house of Torre Abbey is 17th- and 18th-cent. in date. The Abbey site was bought in 1599 by Thomas Ridgeway, ancestor of the earls of Londonderry. The Ridgeways held it only until 1653, when they sold it to Sir John Stowell, who re-sold it in 1662 to Sir George Cary. The Carys remained at Torre Abbey until very recently, and when they sold out the Torquay Corporation acquired the house and site as a museum. The Carys were one of the few great Catholic families of Devon, and converted the guest-hall of the abbey into a chapel for Catholic worship, which was so used from 1779 until 1854. Torre Abbey was built as a country house by the Carys, for the Ridgeways had built themselves a house at Torwood in 1579, since demolished and replaced by a Victorian manor house of 1862, though some traces of the Elizabethan house remain. At Ilsham Manor (so styled) is another relic of the abbey—part of its medieval grange, embedded in Victorian surroundings.

The manor of Torwood was distinct from that of Torre, and was bought in 1768 by Sir Robert Palk, an Ashburton man who had made a great fortune in India and returned to his native Devon as a country gentleman. His purchase of the manor was momentous for the later development of Torquay, and for his descendants' fortunes, for on this land and that of the Carys of Torre Abbey the town was systematically and carefully "developed." The Palks made a second great fortune, this time out of an English town, and dominated the town as long as they retained their interests here, which they did until 1914. Though the Carys went on a little longer, and lived in Torquay all the time (which the Palks did not) they had far less influence on the town's history. It was the Palks who really

created Torquay and gave it its distinctive appearance and social flavour.

The churches of Torquay deserve some special attention. St. John's on a remarkable site cut into the hillside, is the most notable. It was first built in 1823, but rebuilt on a larger scale by G. E. Street in 1861-7. It has some fine qualities and there are those who greatly admire it; but others may find the total effect of the internal decoration somewhat restless and fussy. It has always been the " high church " and has a stormy if short history, being the scene of the first of the 19th-cent. " ritual prosecutions." Those who find these things entertaining (and anything connected with the formidable Bishop Phillpotts has its fascination) will find a good history of the church by Preb. J. S. Boggis, and an excellent smaller guide on the spot.

All Saints' Church at Babbacombe is by Butterfield (1867); the Catholic church at St. Marychurch by Hansom. The ancient parish church of St. Marychurch (St. Mary) was rebuilt in 1861, except the tower. The latter was rebuilt in 1872 as a memorial to Bishop Phillpotts (1778-1869) who is buried in the churchyard. Phillpotts had built himself a palace at Torquay, where he preferred to live, which he called Bishopstowe (now the Palace Hotel). The church at St. Marychurch was greatly damaged during the 1939-45 war by enemy aircraft.

The little village of Cockington still stands unspoilt, beyond the suburbs of Torquay, and is famous even among Devon villages for its beauty. Cockington Court is a house of 16th- and 17th-cent. date, delightfully placed in a small park. It was the home of the Carys from the time of Richard II until they were forced to sell out to the Mallocks in 1654. It continued with the Mallocks down to 1927. W. H. Mallock's *Memoirs of Life and Literature* has some good pages on life here in his early days. The mansion and park were acquired by the Torquay Corporation in 1935 for the sum of £50,000.

The church (St. George and St. Mary) is a charming building, mainly of 14th- and 15th-cent. date; the tower is chiefly 13th-cent. The pulpit came from Tor Mohun church, where it was rescued from destruction in 1825. Other features of the church are the fine restored rood-screen, the 15th-cent. font with its enriched Jacobean cover, the carved bench-ends under the tower and two 15th-cent. stalls with misereres in the chancel, and a certain amount of medieval glass in two windows.

TORRINGTON, BLACK (c5) is a small, nondescript village. The parish church (St. Mary) is entirely 15th-cent., well restored and well kept. It has some good modern woodwork, and a fine wagon roof to the S. aisle, with carved ribs and bosses.

TORRINGTON, GREAT (c4), is one of the most finely sited towns in Devon, on the top of a cliff rising steeply from the meadows of the Torridge. Indeed, the best things about the town are the distant views of it from the adjacent hills, and the exceedingly beautiful views from it, especially of the deep wooded valleys of the Torridge and its tributaries as seen from the bowling-green where the castle formerly stood. It is in itself a dull town with little architectural merit about it.

Palmer House, in New Street, was built in 1752 by Mr. John Palmer, who married Sir Joshua Reynolds's sister Mary. Sir Joshua occasionally visited her at Torrington, and was accompanied on one visit (1762) by Dr. Johnson, so that two of the greatest men in England once stayed in this stylish house. Mary Palmer's portrait, painted by Sir Joshua, may be seen in the Cottonian Library at Plymouth.

Another sister of Sir Joshua, Elizabeth, married William Johnson of Great Torrington, whose great-nephew was William Johnson (1823-92), better known as William Johnson Cory, the poet.

Another good house is No. 28 South Street, built in 1701. The interior has been much altered, but contains one exceptionally fine ceiling, depicting fiddles and other musical instruments. Fore Street and High Street have a certain degree of Georgian feeling, and the Market Place is Georgian in scale and atmosphere. The Black Horse Inn is 1681 and earlier, much restored, and the Torridge Inn is probably 17th-cent.

The parish church (St. Michael) was blown up in February 1646, while some 200 royalist prisoners lay inside after the defeat of Lord Hopton by Fairfax. It was substantially rebuilt in 1651, but the whole building was drastically restored in 1864 and has lost all its former character. The pulpit is good late 17th-cent.; and there are some early Georgian monuments.

A castle was first built, on a site dominating the narrow valley of the Torridge, early in the 13th cent. A bowling-green occupies the E. end of the site to-day.

Torrington as a borough dates from the late 12th cent., possibly founded by William, baron of Torrington (c. 1135-94) who is traditionally said to have given the common pasture of Torrington to the burgesses. These commons still belong to the town. In its early days the town flourished on its markets and fairs, and was reckoned by Hooker to be the best market town in the shire

except perhaps Honiton. It was one of
the earliest towns in Devon to receive a
charter of incorporation, coming fourth
after Plymouth, Totnes, and Exeter, in
1554.

Like most towns, Torrington had a
number of small industries based on
local materials. It had the usual woollen
industry, and was also notable for glove-
making. The town is described in 1801
as rich, populous, and "spirited." None
of these adjectives would apply to-day,
least of all the last-named. It now has
fewer people than it had in the 1820s
and is the only town in North Devon to
show an actual fall in population over
the past 20 years.

Rothern Bridge, over the Torridge,
is a 15th-cent. structure. It has been
widened on both sides but the original
medieval bridge remains. Taddiport
Bridge, also over the Torridge, may be
late 17th cent., widened later. It formerly carried the main road S. out of
Torrington, but this is now carried by
New Bridge (1843). The Town Mills,
beside this bridge, are of the same date,
and make an attractive group.

In 1823-4 Lord Rolle constructed
a 5-m. canal from Torrington to the
navigable part of the Torridge below
Wear Giffard. At one point this was
carried across the valley by a lofty stone
aqueduct (engineer, James Green),
which still stands though the canal has
since been filled in.

TORRINGTON, LITTLE (c4), stands
high and commands fine views of the
Torridge valley. The church (St. Giles)
is dull, mostly rebuilt and enlarged in
1857 and later. The parish contains a
number of interesting farmhouses.
Frizenham, Hollam, and Smytham, are
all mentioned in Domesday Book
(1086). Woodland, the home of a
branch of the Copplestones from the

late 15th cent. until the end of the 18th,
is essentially a medieval hall-house, remodelled in the late 16th cent. It is a
good example of a small squire's house,
and is of considerable antiquarian
interest.

Taddiport is a hamlet beside the
Torridge, which is here crossed by a
massive three-arched bridge, possibly of
17th-cent. date. A chapel, attached to
a leper hospital founded in the 13th
cent., still remains, though considerably
altered.

TOTNES (G9) is, next to Exeter and
Plymouth, the most interesting town in
Devon, a lively little place of some
5,500 people on a hill rising from the W.
bank of the Dart. Part of the town
extends across the river into the suburb
of Bridgetown, which was incorporated
in the borough in 1835.

Totnes does not appear in history
until the reign of Edgar (959-75), and
then it is the evidence of coins minted
here. It is possible, indeed likely, that
a small settlement existed here before
a *burh* was set up about the middle of
the 10th cent., but of this we have
no record. Totnes coins were minted
intermittently between the reigns of
Edgar and William Rufus.

The limits of the Saxon *burh* are probably represented by the lines of the
medieval walls. This small area, about
10 acres in all, was surrounded at first
by an earthen rampart, which was replaced by stone walls in the 12th cent.[1]
The ridge on which the *burh* was founded
rises sharply to 100 ft. above the river
at its highest point, where the Norman
castle was built. By the end of the 12th
cent. it is likely that the built-up area
had extended down the hill from the E.
gate to the river's edge, where the first
bridge is said to have been built by the
time of John (before 1216).

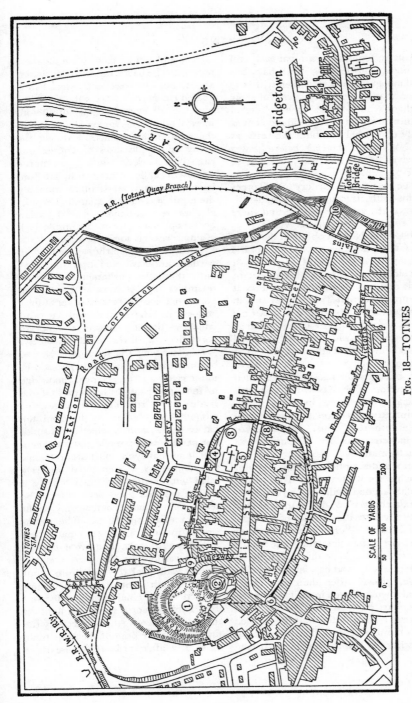

FIG. 18—TOTNES

The line of the medieval town-walls is shown by a continuous black line, the destroyed portions by a broken line.

1. *Totnes Castle (inner bailey).* 2. *The Keep.* 3. *Benedictine Priory (site).* 4. *Guildhall.* 5. *Parish church of St. Mary.* 6. *West Gate (site).* 7. *South Gate (site).* 8. *East Gate.* 9. *North Gate (site).* 10. *Town Quay.* 11. *Bridgetown church.*

Totnes, founded as a royal *burh*, still belonged to the king in 1066; but William granted it, together with 107 other manors in Devon, to Juhel or Judhael, who took the name of Juhel of Totnes from his chief residence. It is likely that Juhel first built the castle at the NW. end of the *burh*, before he was deprived of his lands for rebellion in 1088-9.

The economic history of Totnes begins with its coins in the mid-10th cent., when we may assume that there was some overseas trade. As early as 1130 Guy de Nonant obtained the grant of a fair for the town, at the feast of the Assumption of the B.V.M. (15 August). The cloth trade was the most important single industry from the start, and it was upon this that Totnes grew rich in later centuries. By Henry VIII's time it was second only to Exeter in merchant-wealth. This prosperity lasted throughout Elizabethan times and probably down to the eve of the Civil War, but for some reason Totnes failed to develop the " New Draperies," especially the serge industry which dominated the Devon textile industry of the 17th-18th cents. By the 1660s the industrial history of Totnes was virtually ended.

Defoe's description in the reign of Anne makes it clear that Totnes had become a good country market town again, a cheap place to live in, and that it already had the flavour of a "residential" town—"especially for such as have large families and but small estates." It has kept this character to the present day, and has, largely for this reason, grown faster than any other inland town in Devon in the past twenty years. It has excellent shops and markets, especially for country people, and a number of small flourishing local industries, of which the large bacon factory and a cider factory are the most notable. The bacon one can only dream about, but the excellent cider, like a golden *vin du pays*, solaces the historical traveller all over this part of Devon, most of all at the Warren House Inn in the middle of Dartmoor. Among the many minor pleasures of Totnes, one can still embark at Totnes Quay on the steam-packet for Dartmouth, an 8-m. journey down what is unquestionably the loveliest river in England. There is, alas, no second-hand and antiquarian bookshop in the town, a notable lack of enterprise on someone's part.

Totnes was regularly represented in parliament by two members from 1295 until 1868. Its parliamentary history resembles that of most of the Devon boroughs: local representatives at first, eminent merchants and such-like, and later the development of the pocket borough with all the usual attributes.

In describing the town it is best to begin at the top end, and to proceed E. to the river, and thence over the bridge to the suburb of Bridgetown. Of the castle there remains the motte or mound, rising about 55 ft. from the bailey below, and crowned by a small but perfect example of a circular keep. The inner bailey or court also remains, surrounded by a deep moat formerly filled with water and encircled by a wall of which a good deal can still be seen. Of the outer bailey only slight traces remain on the N. The earthworks (mound, moat, etc.) date from the late 11th cent. and were part of Juhel's castle, but the keep and the curtain walls probably date from about the mid-12th cent. when they supplanted the original timber defences.[1] The Totnes records throw no light on this development. Almost certainly the town walls were built at the same time, or shortly afterwards. Of these there are substantial remains, especially on the E. and S. sides (see Map). Of the gates, that on the N. still stands fairly perfect, though the roadway has been lowered; and the East Gate still picturesquely bridges the High Street. It appears to have been rebuilt early in the 16th cent.

Proceeding down the High Street from the castle, notice the covered walk or piazza on the N. side, formed by carrying the overhanging storeys of the houses on pillars. On the S. side of the street, the house-fronts are slate-hung to keep out the rain, as in many South Devon towns between Exeter and Plymouth. A number of 16th–17th-cent. houses line the street, the oldest dated (1585) example being No. 16, which was the residence of Nicholas Ball, who represented Totnes in parliament in 1584. The decorated plaster ceilings of this house, and of Nos. 10 and 32, are remarkable. No. 64 in Fore Street, and other Totnes houses, also have these rich ceilings, which were once numerous in Dartmouth also, and suggest a late 16th–early 17th-cent. school of plasterers at Totnes equal in reputation to those of Barnstaple.

On the N. side of the High Street stands the fine parish church (St. Mary), and behind it the Guildhall. St. Mary's Church was wholly rebuilt between 1432 and 1460. The nave was constructed between 1432 and 1444, the chancel 1445-48, and the handsome red sandstone tower, 1449-59. The magnificent rood-screen of Beer stone was erected in 1459-60 by order of the corporation, who directed that the chancel should be separated from the body of the church by a stone screen as in Exeter Cathedral[1] (plate 8). The stone pulpit is of the same date as the screen; so, too, are the fine doors of the church. The Scott restoration

destroyed a good deal of the atmosphere of the church, but could not wholly disguise its structural beauty, especially the lofty arcades with their capitals and piers of unusual design. The corporation pews (restored) are of Caroline date, perhaps 1636 when the royal arms were put up.

On the N. side of the church stood Totnes priory, founded c. 1088 by Juhel of Totnes as a cell of St. Nicholas's Abbey at Angers. Its buildings were demolished soon after the Dissolution, for the present Guildhall, which is of 16th- and 17th-cent. date, is built on part of the site. The older part of this picturesque little building dates from 1553, the main doorway and the Court Room being of this period (plate 40). The Council Chamber is dated 1624, and has a fine plaster frieze.

The Fore Street contains much interesting building, including a number of slate-hung 17th-cent. houses and some pleasant 18th- and early 19th-cent. building of which the Royal Seven Stars Hotel will serve as example. On the Plains, at the foot of the hill, stands a memorial to William John Wills (1834-61), a native of Totnes, who was the first man, with Burke, to cross the Australian continent and who perished of starvation on the return journey. Other eminent natives of the town were William Brockedon (1787-1854), the painter (of whom there is a fine self-portrait in the Guildhall); and Benjamin Kennicott (1718-83), the Hebrew scholar.

Totnes bridge, a handsome structure, was rebuilt in 1828 by Charles Fowler, the Devon-born architect. Beyond the bridge is Bridgetown, once a borough on its own. The borough of " Bridge" was set up by the Pomeroys early in the 13th cent. but derived its importance from Totnes and was absorbed into it in 1835. The church (St. John the Evangelist) was built in 1835, and is the usual decent building of its period.

TRENTISHOE (E1), exceedingly remote at the end of a rough lane, has a small church (St. Peter), rebuilt in 1861. Externally it is charming; internally it has been over-restored and filled with bad Victorian woodwork. Heddon's Mouth is a fine piece of coastal scenery, but the hills on all the approach roads are formidable. Tattiscombe was a Domesday manor.

TRUSHAM (G7), in the broken western foothills of Haldon where they fall to the Teign valley, has an attractive little early 15th-cent. church (St. Michael). There is a curious monument, with portraits, to John Stooke and his wife (1697), and a monument to Hugh Staplehill and his family (1583) painted on wood.

TWITCHEN (F2) church (St. Peter) was entirely rebuilt in 1844, except for the tower, but still retains its original Norman font.

Praunsley and Pulham farms are recorded in Domesday.

UFFCULME (J4) is a large village on the upper reaches of the Culm. It was an early and important village which gave its name to a hundred in Domesday Book, and it continued to be important throughout medieval times. A considerable woollen industry developed here in the 16th cent., reaching its height about the middle of the 18th cent. when large quantities of Uffculme serges were exported to Holland by the Tiverton merchants.

The church (St. Mary) is mainly 15th-cent., with some earlier and later work. The tower and spire were re-

built about 1845, and a second S. aisle added in 1846. There is a good deal of 17th-cent. woodwork in the church. The Bradfield chapel has been much mutilated but it still contains the Walrond monuments, including an extraordinary one to Sir William Walrond (1663) with rustic coloured portraits. The fine medieval rood-screen has been much rebuilt; it is earlier in date than most in Devon (possibly *c.* 1400), more massive and with plainer detail.

Bradfield, 2 m. SSW., has belonged to the Walronds since the reign of John. The present house—now a public institution—dates mainly from the time of Elizabeth and James I. The whole house was well restored about 1860, when the S. and N. walls were rebuilt and some alterations made. Externally, there may be more beautiful houses in Devon, but the interior of Bradfield is matchless. The hall, with its minstrels' gallery, is an exquisite example of early Tudor work, with a magnificent hammer-beam roof and much linenfold panelling. The drawing-room is of extraordinary beauty—"full of the character of English domestic life of the seventeenth century." The ceiling is richly and elaborately decorated; the walls panelled with carved and moulded oak; the chimney-piece a splendid example of its time (*c.* 1600), the upper part coloured and gilded. The angledoor, of the drawing-room, really an internal porch or lobby, is a masterpiece of enriched carving.

UGBOROUGH (E10) is a large compact village, and an extensive parish, rising to more than 1,500 ft. above sea level at Quickbeam Hill and Three Barrows. There are Bronze Age barrows and hut-circles on the moorland, and a stone row running N. from

Butterdon Hill. The views of the South Hams from Western Beacon and Ugborough Beacon are extensive.

Ugborough village is built around a large open square, with the church on an eminence at the S. end. The latter (St. Peter) is said to stand inside an earlier earthwork, and is approached by a lofty flight of steps. It is a building of early 14th- to early 16th-cent. in date, of great length (131 ft.), with a fine W. tower (94 ft.). The high altar was dedicated by Bishop Stapeldon in 1311, the whole church in 1323. This 14th-cent. church probably had N. and S. transepts which in the 15th cent. were opened out into the present aisles. The curious granite arcades should be noticed. The tower was completed in the early 16th cent. (said to be 1520).

The features of the church are: (1) the timber roof of the N. aisle with its remarkable large carved bosses, of which one represents St. Brannoc's white sow and her litter of eight, and another St. Loye, the patron saint of metal-workers; (2) the cut-down roodscreen with its 32 painted panels and the parclose screens; (3) the unusual 17th-cent. stone pulpit, and (4) the splendid (but mutilated) late Norman font. It must originally have been one of the finest examples of its type.

There were several manors in the parish: besides Ugborough itself we find Broadaford, Langford Barton, Ludbrook, Peek, and Venn, all in Domesday Book. Fowellscombe was the medieval mansion of the Fowells at an early date. They were said to have been here before the Norman Conquest, but a 12th-cent. origin is perhaps more likely.

Fowellscombe is now a romantic ruin, alone in the fields, with ivy falling in cascades down its Tudor walls. It was built in 1537 by Sir Thomas Fowell, on the rising tide of the family fortunes, and enlarged in the 18th cent. Fillham, for long a medieval mansion, is now an 18th-cent. and later house, with the remains of a chapel (St. Andrew), to which is attached a lofty 18th-cent. "gaze-tower."

Witchcombe, now a farmhouse, has remains of a former mansion where Sir John Kempthorn, the eminent naval commander, was born in 1620. West Peek and Whitehouse Farm have some interesting 17th-cent. work.

UPLOWMAN (J4) church (St. Peter) is said to have been built *c.* 1500 by Margaret Beaufort, Countess of Richmond and mother of Henry VII. It was over-restored in 1864. Besides Uplowman itself, Chieflowman, Coombe, Kidwell, Murley, and Whitnage were all Domesday estates. Spalsbury Farm is a very interesting example of a 15th-cent. franklin's house.

UPLYME (M6) was given to Glastonbury Abbey by King Cynewulf in 774 and held by the abbey until the Dissolution. It was then bought from the Crown by John Drake whose descendants sold it in 1775: the manor had thus changed hands only once in a thousand years. Shapwick ("sheep farm") is first mentioned in 1167. It became a grange of Newenham Abbey, near Axminster, and in 1670 was in the hands of Solomon Andrew, a rich merchant of Lyme Regis, whose granddaughter and heiress—Sarah Andrew —attracted Henry Fielding. Her guardian disapproved of his suit and removed her elsewhere. She is supposed to be the model for Sophia Western in *Tom Jones*.[1] The church (St. Peter and St. Paul) was so badly over-restored in 1876 that it has lost all interest. In 1850 a Roman villa was discovered at Uplyme.

UPOTTERY (L5) lies high up the beautiful, pastoral Otter valley, between two great fingers of the Blackdown Hills. The manor, together with that of Rawridge across the river, was bought by Dr. John Addington of London in the later years of the 18th cent. His son, Henry Addington, Speaker of the House of Commons, Prime Minister 1801-4, and later 1st Viscount Sidmouth, built a mansion and occasionally resided here. One cannot imagine a more complete change than this from the cares of London and the political world. The present Manor House was built about 1845.

The church (St. Mary) is a much-restored 15th-cent. building, of little interest internally. Rawridge was a Domesday manor.

UPTON HELLIONS (G5) is a small parish on the E. slopes of the Creedy valley, seeming much more remote than the map suggests. There is no village.

The church (St. Mary) stands boldly on the side of a hill. Its gaunt, rough-cast W. tower is built of Thorverton or Posbury stone, as also is the Norman S. doorway (c. 1160-70). The masonry of the building consists mostly of small rubble, probably of 12th-cent. date, in which 15th-cent. windows have been inserted. It is essentially a Norman church, with a S. aisle added just after 1500. Upton Hellions has a delightful, unsophisticated air: small, plastered, and whitewashed: restored conservatively and gently. It retains its 15th-cent. wagon roofs, a simple early 18th-cent. pulpit, and some good carved bench-ends (c. 1500) at the back of the church. In the chancel is a curious, country-made monument with the

kneeling figures of a man and a woman on either side of a prayer-desk. There is no inscription, but the figures are said to represent Richard Reynell of Creedy Wiger (d. 1631), and Mary, his wife. Creedy Wiger (called Lower Creedy to-day) is of some architectural interest. Upton Hellions Barton has some 16th-cent. work. Both were Tudor "mansions" of the small Devonshire type.

UPTON PYNE (H6), is a small unspoilt village of thatched and whitewashed cottages, on the N. slope of the wooded clump of Pynes Hill. The churchyard looks N. to the hills of Raddon, Cadbury, and Christ Cross, over a placid countryside of the fertile Red Sandstones. At any time of the year this is one of the most satisfying views in all Devon. This piece of country between Pynes Hill and Raddon must have been open in the Bronze Age, as four barrows of that period are found in it, three near Stevenstone farm and one at No Man's Cross.

The manor came to the Pynes in the time of Henry I. They held it for ten generations, followed by the Larders for five. Early in the 18th cent. the heiress of Stafford of Pynes married her neighbour Sir Henry Northcote, 5th bart., and took the manor to him. The Northcotes still live here. Sir Henry probably built the present Pynes, a typical Queen Anne house, enlarged in 1851 without spoiling its formal beauty.

Cowley is a hamlet of Upton Pyne, chiefly notable for a fine bridge of classical design, built over the Creedy in 1813-14 by James Green, pupil of Rennie and surveyor to the county of Devon. Although so recent in date, the bridge has been scheduled as an ancient monument. Cowley church was built in 1866, and is decent.

Upton Pyne church (St. Mary) is

singularly attractive externally. It is built of the local volcanic stone, and has a particularly beautiful tower, with figures of the four evangelists at its corners and that of Christ in Benediction on its W. face. The chancel has some early 14th-cent. work; the W. tower and S. aisle were probably added about 1400, the N. aisle in 1833. The altar-piece is a painting of the Last Supper by an unknown hand, brought from Italy by one of the Northcotes about 1710. There is an altar-tomb to Humphrey Larder (d. 1588), another with a recumbent effigy of Edmund Larder (d. 1521), and several monuments to the Northcotes of Pynes, later Earls of Iddesleigh.

Dr. John Walker, author of *The Sufferings of the Clergy*, was rector here 1720-47, and is buried on the N. side of the churchyard.

VENN OTTERY (J6) church (St. Gregory) was rebuilt in 1882, except the tower, and has nothing of interest except a few carved bench-ends.

VIRGINSTOW (B6) church (St. Bridget the Virgin) is well sited on a ridge, commanding far views of Cornwall. Only the font now remains of the 12th-cent. church, which was entirely rebuilt in 1851-2. The farms of Bradaford and Telleslow were Domesday estates.

WALKHAMPTON (D8) church (dedication unknown) stands well outside the village on a hill, its slender tower a landmark for miles. It is a 15th–16th-cent. building of no great interest. It fell into ruin after the Reformation, and about 1600 the S. aisle was rebuilt. The 16th-cent. Church House stands near by. On the Moor are numerous hut-circles, etc., the exact site of which can be found on the 2½-inch map, sheet 20/57. There are also remains of old blowing-houses in the parish where tin was smelted in Elizabethan times.

WARKLEIGH (*see* SATTERLEIGH).

WASHFIELD (H4) lies on the hills NW. of Tiverton in beautiful country, overlooking the wooded valley of the Exe. The parish includes the estate of Worth which was a Domesday manor and the home of the Worths from the 12th cent. until 1880. The present Worth House, in a small park, was rebuilt about the time of Anne but has been altered within recent years. Among the farmhouses of the parish, Brook Farm and Hatherland are worth visiting. The former has some late medieval work, and bears a date 1564; the latter is said to have had a chapel dedicated to St. Michael as late as 1554 (now gone) and has an interesting interior.

The church (St. Mary) is mostly a 15th-cent. structure. Its most remarkable feature is the Jacobean screen crossing the chancel and N. aisle, made in 1624 by one Bernard Serridge, with rich and beautiful detail. There are some Worth monuments and brasses.

WASHFORD PYNE (G4) church (St. Peter) was wholly rebuilt in 1883-7 and is of no interest.

WEAR GIFFARD (C3) (pron. *Jifford*) lies in the wooded Torridge valley and makes a highly attractive picture with its 15th-cent. manor house, built by the Fortescues when they acquired the estate in 1454. The wall of the outer courtyard was partly demolished in the Civil War, but the gatehouse remains. The great hall (with a splendid hammerbeam roof) and other rooms of the original house survive. Details of the masonry and of the woodwork confirm the tradition that the house was rebuilt by Martin Fortescue (d. 1472) and finished in the time of his son John. The panelling of the hall is local work of the time of Henry VIII. Other rooms contain fine woodwork of Tudor and Jacobean date.

Near by is the parish church (Holy Trinity), which has a 14th-cent. nave and chancel, and a S. aisle and W. tower added in the 15th cent. The chancel has a very fine 15th-cent. roof, possibly done by the craftsmen who built the hall roof in the manor house. The contents of the church are varied and interesting. There are some excellent heraldic bench-ends; some 15th-cent. glass (in the E. window of the S. aisle especially); a good medieval wall-painting in the S. aisle, supposed to represent the martyrdom of St. Edmund; and two 13th-cent. Giffard effigies. There are also Fortescue monuments, including a fine one to Hugh Fortescue and his wife (1661). Huxhill and Little Weare were Domesday manors.

WELCOMBE (A4) means "spring-valley," the spring being in all probability St. Nectan's Well or Holy Well, near the church, which is dedicated to the same saint. There is no doubt that the 6th-cent. Irish missionary-saint walked these hills and valleys in North-Western Devon. St. Nectan's Chapel was one of the many medieval chapels in the vast parish of Hartland. It lies in unspoiled country, altogether Cornish in appearance and feeling, with views down the combes to the Atlantic. Welcombe was raised to parochial status in 1508, when the church was enlarged by the addition of N. and S. transepts. The square-headed screen (early 14th-cent.) is of unique interest.

It is, except for its cornice, which is later and much resembles that at Hartland, by far the earliest remaining screen in Devon. The lectern and pulpit are notable, the former Jacobean, the latter restored Tudor. There are the usual floor-slabs to local families. These slabs often act as a guide to the interesting houses of the parish wherever one may be in Devon. Over the arches of the transepts is some carved oak work, representing the Fruitful Vine and Barren Fig-Tree.

The coastal scenery is wild and impressive. Hawker, the Cornish poet and antiquary, was curate here for thirty years, and held the living in conjunction with Morwenstow from 1851.

WEMBURY (D11) lies between the estuary of the Yealm and Plymouth Sound, on a wild coast. The church (St. Werburgh) stands alone on the edge of the cliff and has long been a landmark for mariners making for Plymouth harbour. It has a striking W. tower of 14th-cent. date; the rest of the building is 15th- to early 16th-cent. with granite arcades. There is much excellent modern woodwork, and a magnificent Jacobean monument to Sir John Hele (1608), with recumbent figures of Sir John and his wife, and their ten children below. There are monuments to the Calmadys of Langdon Court, including a large tomb of Lady Narborough, daughter of Josias Calmady, who died aged 20 in 1678: " Mightily afflicted with a cough & Bigge with child." Wembury church is the little grey church by the sea, which Galsworthy describes in *Swan Song*, the scene of Soames Forsyte's pilgrimage to the home of his ancestors.[1]

Langdon was a Domesday manor. In 1555 Vincent Calmady, a lawyer, purchased it from the crown and rebuilt the medieval house about 1577. Josias Calmady remodelled it in 1707. The present house, which has four fronts enclosing a quadrangular court in the centre, is of these two dates. The Calmadys sold Langdon in 1875, after a stay of 320 years.

Wembury House was built in 1803 on the site of the great mansion of Sir John Hele which was then demolished. He bought the estate in 1592 and built a new house which was esteemed the most magnificent mansion in the county at a cost (says Prince) of more than £20,000. Even the gatehouse was fit for the accommodation of "a large and genteel family." At Wembury are the Hele Almshouses (1682), the gift of Sir Warwick Hele. The little chapel in the centre of the block is charming.

WEMBWORTHY (E5) village is small, with good cob and thatch building. The church (St. Michael) is decent but of little antiquarian interest, having been almost rebuilt in 1868 and restored again in 1902. The low tower was rebuilt in 1626. The three original medieval bells remain.

Rashleigh, now a farmhouse, was a Domesday manor and gave its name to the Rashleigh family from the 13th cent. onwards. Thomas Clotworthy of Clotworthy married the heiress cf Rashleigh about 1535 and his descendants occupied Rashleigh until 1682, when their heiress in turn carried it by marriage to the Tremaynes who still owned it in 1935.

The present house was probably built by Thomas Clotworthy, son of the Rashleigh heiress, as the Clotworthy arms appear (above a modern doorway) quartered with Rashleigh and not impaled. These arms are repeated on the plaster and woodwork inside; the house may therefore be dated as *c.* 1600. The

interior, though somewhat altered, contains much work of this date. Especially notable are the plaster ceilings and friezes of the "summer parlour" and of the two upper rooms in the N. wing, which are amongst the finest of their kind in Devon. The house contains also a good deal of contemporary woodwork, including the wainscoting and chimney-piece of the small "winter parlour" to the S. of the main entrance, and a staircase with an early 17th-cent. dog-gate.

Eggesford House occupies a commanding site among extensive woods. Built in 1832 by the Hon. Newton Fellowes to replace the old house near Eggesford church, it is already a romantic ruin in a desolate park. Heywood Wood, to the N. of the house, contains two interesting earthworks of the mount and bailey type.

WERRINGTON (B7) was given by Gytha, mother of Harold, to Tavistock Abbey in 1066-8, and was among the vast estate of monastic lands granted to John, Lord Russell, in 1540. In 1651 Sir William Morice, afterwards Secretary of State to Charles II, bought the estate and lived here. The present house was built by a Morice, perhaps in the 1730s, and the architect may well have been William Kent himself,[1] who was building Castle Hill and laying out its park at this date (*see* FILLEIGH). At Werrington, as at Castle Hill, the medieval church had to be demolished and rebuilt on a new site, as it stood in the way of the grand scheme. The estate was bought by the Duke of Northumberland in 1775, who continued the superb decoration of the interior, and occasionally resided here. The park of 355 acres, one of the most beautiful in the West Country, extends across the river Ottery into Cornwall.

The church (St. Martin and St. Giles) is a disappointing building. What must have been an extremely interesting church of 1742 was so rebuilt and altered in 1891 that it has almost entirely lost its original character. Externally, it retains some of the features of the 18th-cent. church. Baring-Gould approved of the changes of 1891: "the church has undergone alteration for the better, and is less like a conventicle than it was."

WESTLEIGH (c3) is a village on the E. slopes of the Torridge estuary. Both East and West Leigh were Domesday manors. So, too, was Tapeley, which is now a Georgian mansion in a large park. Eastleigh, now a farmhouse, was the Berry mansion from about 1500 to 1802. Southcott Barton is a good example of an Elizabethan "mansion," with decorative plaster ceilings in some of the rooms and other contemporary features.

The church (St. Peter), at the head of the village, was built c. 1300 with a wide nave and chancel. Aisles were added c. 1500. A number of excellent carved bench-ends of this date remain in the nave. There are monuments to the Clevlands of Tapeley.

WESTWARD HO (see NORTHAM).

WHIMPLE (j6) lies in placid, tidy country largely given over to cider-orchards. The church (St. Mary) was enlarged and rebuilt, except the tower, in 1845, and contains nothing of interest. Larkbeare Court has associations with Thackeray, who stayed here often as a schoolboy.

WHITCHURCH (c8) means "white church." There must have been a church here as early as the 11th cent., probably built of the white elvan found on Roborough Down only two or three miles away. The present church (St. Andrew) is mainly a 15th-cent. building, of elvan and granite. There are a number of interesting memorials in the church, including a well-carved early 17th-cent. slate slab to the Mooringes of Moortown, and a good monument to Francis Pengelly (1722) by John Weston of Exeter, showing a sort of celestial ballet on a medallion.

The parish has a considerable number of interesting houses. The so-called Priory, near the church, is a 19th-cent. granite building incorporating a square 14th-cent. entrance tower of an earlier structure. Walreddon is an attractive Elizabethan house, altered to some extent in the 18th cent. It was the home of a younger branch of the Courtenays in the 18th and early 19th cents.

Sortridge was built c. 1640. Moortown, 800 ft. up on the flank of Whitchurch Common, was the home of the Mooringe or Morwen family from at least the early 14th cent., and probably much earlier.

Holwell was the ancient seat of the Glanvilles from the late 14th cent. until about 1700; there are remains of the Glanville mansion. At Lower Collaton the farmhouse is of some antiquity.

Horrabridge takes its name from the *Horebridge* ("boundary bridge") over the Walkham. The present structure may well be 14th-cent. in date.

WHITESTONE (G6) is very hilly and beautiful, with fine woods along its N. slopes. There are magnificent views in all directions, especially from Waddlesdown (815 ft.).

Several of the farmsteads and hamlets of the parish date from pre-Conquest times (e.g. Oldridge, Whitestone, Heath Barton, Halsford, Rowhorne, and West

Town), and most of the rest from the period of forest-clearing in the 13th cent. At the remote hamlet of Oldridge the medieval chapel was rebuilt in 1789 and again in 1842. It is a plain, not unpleasing little building, amid beautiful scenery.

Whitestone church (St. Catherine of Alexandria) stands high. Its tower has been for centuries a landmark for mariners entering Exmouth haven, 15 m. away. The church is attractive, mostly a 15th-cent. reconstruction of an earlier building, much restored again early in the 17th cent., probably about 1621 when the W. gallery was put in. Only the front of the gallery now remains, the rest having been taken down in 1912. Some medieval glass remains in two windows. Near the church is the former rectory (private), partly good medieval, partly Georgian.

WIDECOMBE-IN-THE-MOOR (F8)

is an immense parish, covering nearly 11,000 acres, of which some 4,000 acres are wild moorland. The village lies in the broad valley of the East Webburn river which is bounded by high granite-strewn ridges reaching 1,500 ft. Hamel-down Beacon (1,697 ft.) was a beacon in Elizabethan times. On the moors are many hut-circles, barrows, and kists (burial-chambers or "chests") of Bronze Age date. Hamel Down has a number of barrows, and also two of those mysterious raised trackways known as *reaves*. The late Mr. Hansford Worth, after studying Dartmoor for some sixty years, could come to no conclusion about their purpose or their date. At Foales Arrishes is a group of hut-circles, which are important as having produced early Iron Age pottery, evidence of a longer occupation of Dartmoor than had hitherto been suspected.

Natsworthy and Dunstone were both Domesday manors, the former the highest in Devon (1,200 ft.). On the marginal slopes we also find Dewdon (now part of Blackslade Farm), Spitchwick, and Scobitor, all in being by the late 11th cent. Bittleford is named in a Saxon charter of 956. Several fine old moorland farmhouses survive in the parish, of which Corndon, Chittleford, and Lower Tor (or Tarr) are examples. Lizwell was a "mansion" in the 17th and 18th cents. With the aid of the 2½-inch maps (sheets 20/67, 20/77) the reader should explore the parish on foot, when he will make his own discoveries.

Widecombe church (St. Pancras) is sometimes called "the cathedral of the moor" (plate 29). It is essentially a cruciform 14th-cent. church, reconstructed and enlarged in the late 15th–early 16th cent. The granite tower is noble, combining grace with strength, and is one of the finest in the west of England. The massive crocketed pinnacles are very characteristic of church towers around Dartmoor, especially W. and NW. of the Moor. The rood-screen had been cut down before 1822, but the remains are interesting, exhibiting a fine series of 32 paintings of saints, apostles, and the four Latin Doctors. The church was struck by lightning, during the Sunday afternoon service, on 21 October 1638. Four people were killed and 62 injured. The rustic verses in the N. aisle commemorate the event. The Church House (c. 1500), a fine example of a moorstone building, now belongs to the National Trust.

The well-known Widecombe Fair is held on the second Tuesday in September. Formerly great numbers of cattle, sheep and Dartmoor ponies were sold, but the modern fair is largely a "pleasure fair" and is highly commercialised. It became popular with the spread of the ballad of that name, which is inevitably sung at all village concerts in Devon, and was sung by the men of the Devon Regiment in the South African War.

WIDWORTHY (L6) lies among beautiful hills and combes: East Devon at its best. The church (St. Cuthbert) is delightfully situated beside the barton-farm and is a small cruciform building of the 14th cent. with N. and S. transepts and no aisles. There are a number of good monuments to the Marwoods, and a notable recumbent effigy in the N. transept believed to be that of Sir Hugh Prouz, c. 1340.

Widworthy Barton is a good specimen of an Elizabethan manor house. The hall retains its screens, and an upper room has a plaster mantelpiece dated 1591. There is other plasterwork of the same period. Sutton Barton is a late 17th-cent. house, and was a Domesday manor. NW. of the house are the Sutton quarries, now disused, which produced a fine freestone similar to that at Beer. Cookshays is an attractive 16th-cent. house, remodelled in the time of Anne. Widworthy Court, in a small park, was built c. 1840 by Sir Edward Marwood Elton.

WILLAND (J4) is a messy, built-over landscape, too near to Tiverton Junction. The church (St. Mary) is entirely 15th-cent. The interior was thoroughly Victorianised in 1863, but the beautiful rood-screen was spared.

WINKLEIGH (E5) is an ancient village on a lofty hill. It was one of the nucleated villages founded in the early days of the Saxon occupation of Devon, and gave its name to a hundred.

Court Castle seems to have been a small Norman castle-site. At the SW' end of Castle Street is a smaller mount known as Croft Castle, which probably served a similar purpose. The buildings may have been fortified manor houses rather than true castles.

Winkleigh had the only park recorded in the Devon Domesday. It also had a 500-acre wood of which the present Winkleigh Wood is probably a remnant.

At some unknown date, Winkleigh acquired a fair and a market and became one of the numerous seignorial boroughs of Devon. Its borough court sat until 1848. The hamlet of Hollocombe, 2½ m. N., also had a medieval market and fair.

Winkleigh remained an important local centre for its remote district until late Victorian times. It reached its maximum size in the 1840s, and thereafter began to decline. By 1931 it was little more than half the size it had been ninety years earlier.

Winkleigh village contains few houses of any individual interest: it is mostly the typical Devon market town, stucco and rough cast. The church (All Saints) is a 15th-cent. building, over-restored in 1873 at great cost. It retains, however, its richly carved wagon roofs, a good 15th-cent. font, and some medieval glass in the W. window of the S. transept. Loosedon was a Domesday manor, and later a medieval mansion.

Court Barton was the seat of the Keynes manor, where their manor courts were held. Southcott was the seat of the Southcotts, probably from the 12th cent. onwards, from whom "a great kindred" sprang and dispersed all over the county. The present farmhouse shows some traces of the former mansion, which had a chapel in 1427.

WITHERIDGE (G4) is a large compact village in the upland country between Tiverton and South Molton, roughly equidistant from each. It was the earliest settlement in the district and gave its name to an ancient hundred. Much of the parish consists of wet moors rising to 700-800 ft. which were, however, occupied in the Bronze Age, as witness the numerous barrows on Witheridge Moor and Dart Raffe Moor. Berry Castle, on a ridge between two headstreams of the Little Dart, is a small quadrangular fortification, surrounded by a rampart and ditch. Queen Dart, near by, was a small Domesday manor. Other Domesday estates, besides Witheridge itself, were Adworthy, Bradford Barton, Dart Raffe, and Drayford. In 1248 Robertson of Pagan (Fitzpaine), Lord of Witheridge, was granted a weekly market on Wednesdays and a three-day fair on the eve, feast, and morrow of the Nativity of St. John the Baptist, the dedication festival of the parish church (June 24). In 1890 the village had two fairs and three great cattle markets annually.

The parish church (St. John the Baptist) is built of the local brown dunstone. The chancel is early 14th-cent. in date, but the remainder of the church was rebuilt during the 15th cent., and restored in 1876 and later. As a whole, the church is unexciting, but it has some fine points. Notice the excellent 15th-cent. font and the fine medieval stone pulpit. The village to-day is large and cheerful, with some interesting native Devon architecture. After a long decline in the 19th cent., it has now revived with the establishment of bus services to and from neighbouring towns.

WITHYCOMBE RALEIGH (J7) now includes half of Exmouth (q.v.). The original parish church (St. John-in-the-Wilderness) stands 1½ m. farther on.

It was a 15th-cent. building which was allowed to fall into ruin, possibly because it was so remote. Between 1926 and 1937 it was rebuilt and restored to use. There are good 15th-cent. windows in the N. aisle, and monuments to the Drakes and Raleighs who formerly lived here.

The church of St. John the Evangelist in the village was built in 1864 at great cost, largely met by Lady Rolle. The Rolles uglified nearly everything they touched. This replaced a church of classical design, erected in 1722 and pulled down in 1865, only because it was "too small."

A-la-Ronde is in this parish, a house of unique design erected in 1795 by the Misses Parminter. Point-in-View, near by, was finished in 1811, a group of almshouses surrounding a tiny chapel, erected by the same ladies. All this is well worth seeing as a charming period example of eccentricity.

WOLBOROUGH (see Newton Abbot)

WOODBURY (J7) takes its name from the earthwork known as Woodbury Castle on the summit of the sandy ridge to the E. This was "the wooden fort" or "the fort in the woods." It is eccentric in shape, with very strong defences nearly ½ m. around; mostly surrounded by two great ramparts with a ditch between them more than 20 ft. deep. The site commands the whole of the Exe estuary, and must have been of considerable importance. The "camp" has never been scientifically excavated but presumably was constructed in the late Iron Age, perhaps in the century before the coming of the Romans. An ancient ridgeway passes through the middle of the earthwork. Because of its command of the mouth of the Exe it

was occupied as a camp between 1798 and 1803, during the Napoleonic Wars.

The village lies in the centre of the parish and is larger than most in Devon: it is certainly ancient, founded perhaps in the late 7th cent. when the Saxons began to colonise East Devon. It was important enough to have a parish gild in the 11th cent., and was a royal manor.

The church (St. Swithin) was rebuilt and reconsecrated in 1409,[1] but was ruinously "restored" by a Victorian parson, the Rev. J. Loveband Fulford, who was vicar here 1846-98. He eviscerated the medieval rood-screen so that the parishioners should see and hear him better, and painted it himself with the muddy colours we see to-day. He carved the monstrous poppy-head stalls in the choir, laid with his own hands " Th' encaustic tile" in the sanctuary, painted the walls of the church, and put in most of the dreadful glass.

Nutwell Court is a small and demure country house of the Jane Austen period (1810), overlooking the Exe estuary. It was a Domesday manor, later a medieval fortified house of the Dinhams. It came to the Drakes, descendants of Sir Francis Drake's brother Thomas (Sir Francis himself died without issue), in 1731. The 5th baronet wrecked the fine medieval house with his "improvements," demolishing the two-storied gatehouse with great difficulty in 1755-6 and cutting through the timbered roof of the 14th-cent. chapel to make a plaster ceiling. The present house is perhaps some justification for all this destruction.

WOODLAND (F9)

WOODLAND (F9) was formerly in the parish of Ipplepen. There was a chapel here in 1424, licensed by Bishop Lacy. In 1536 it was elevated to parochial status and rebuilt. The present church (St. John the Baptist) is entirely of early 16th-cent. date. About ½ m. NW. of the church, near Wickeridge, are large, disused quarries which formerly produced valuable green and purple slates.

WOODLEIGH (F11)

WOODLEIGH (F11) church (St. Mary) consists of nave and chancel, with small N. and S. transepts. It is mainly 14th-cent. but looks much rebuilt. It suffered a "thorough restoration" in 1891, which left little of interest except the Easter sepulchre erected by Thomas Smyth, rector of Woodleigh 1492-1527.

Wood Barton, 1 m. N., is an attractive "mansion" of 15th and 16th-cent. date, with farm buildings of the same period. It was a home of a branch of the Fortescues. The extensive modern buildings near the Barton are those of a Cistercian monastery which settled here from France in 1902. The war of 1914-18 depleted their numbers and in 1921 the monastery was abandoned.

Grimpstonsleigh, now a farmhouse, was a Domesday estate.

WOOLFARDISWORTHY (G5) (pron. Woolsery), near Crediton

WOOLFARDISWORTHY (G5) (pron. Woolsery), near Crediton, is a parish of hilly, fertile land, with attractive wooded combes. The church (Holy Trinity) was entirely rebuilt in the local brown dunstone in 1845. It is a not unpleasing building externally, situated in a pretty churchyard which commands wide views of a billowy landscape, well wooded and placid.

WOOLFARDISWORTHY (B3) (pron. Woolsery), near Hartland

WOOLFARDISWORTHY (B3) (pron. Woolsery), near Hartland, is a parish with much lonely marsh and moorland. The small village is rather untidy but at West Town is a pleasant group of old farmsteads, one of which is probably 16th-cent. There are many remote farms, of which Ashmansworthy and Almiston are mentioned in Domesday.

So also is Woolfardisworthy itself and the very attractive little fishing hamlet of Bucks Mills. This small settlement lived for centuries mainly by fishing, like Clovelly a little farther W. The parish church (dedication unknown) is interesting. It is mainly a 15th-cent. rebuilding in the purplish local stone, but a fine late 12th-cent. S. doorway has been preserved from an earlier building, together with a 13th-cent. font. Several excellently carved bench-ends (c. 1500) survive, and a Jacobean altar-table. There are Prust memorials (17th- to 19th-cent.), a fine monumental effigy to Richard Cole (1614), and a monument to John Whitlocke, Esq., of Lincoln's Inn (1750).

WORLINGTON, EAST (F4), in the remote upland country between Withe-ridge and Chulmleigh, includes the ancient parishes of East and West Worlington and Affeton. Pedley Barton and Ruston were both Domesday estates, besides Worlington itself, and Cobley appears before 1200. In the extreme N. of the parish the small farm of Blagrove was also a Domesday manor.

About the middle of the 12th cent. the parishes of East and West Worlington were formed and two churches built, both dedicated to the Virgin Mary. On the W. side another parish was created at Affeton, probably in the 13th cent. Affeton was always small and poor and by the middle of the 15th cent. was absorbed again into West Worlington. There is no trace of a church here to-day. East and West Worlington were united for civil and ecclesiastical purposes in 1885.

Affeton Castle is a restored 15th-cent. gate-tower. The castellated building to which it gave entrance was probably erected by the Affetons in the 13th or 14th cent. and was a fortified manor house rather than a true castle.

East Worlington village has some old buildings, notably the rectory and the early 17th-cent. Church House, but the church (St. Mary) was almost rebuilt in 1879 and spoilt.

West Worlington church (St. Mary) is much more attractive. It has a twisted spire of wooden shingles above a late 13th-cent. tower, possibly rebuilt in the 17th cent. The body of the church is built of the local brown dunstone, with a 14th-cent. chancel and 15th-cent. nave and S. aisle. There are carved bench-ends of unusual design (possibly 16th-cent.) and a screen of late type (c. 1500) across the E. end of the aisle enclosing the chapel of the Stucleys, who lived at Affeton. Notice the carved roof bosses.

YARCOMBE (L5), enclosed by the bleak plateau of the Blackdown Hills, was very remote until the new main road from Honiton to Chard was cut early in the 19th cent. The church (St. John the Baptist) is mostly a 15th-cent. structure, with a few earlier traces, badly restored in 1889-91, when the chancel was rebuilt.

The manor was acquired by Sir Francis Drake whose descendants still own it. Sheafhayne House, reputedly the manor house, is an Elizabethan building, enlarged and modernised in 1925. Dennington, now a farmhouse, was a Domesday manor. The Yar-combe Inn was almost certainly the Church House at one time.

YARNSCOMBE (D3) Church (St. Andrew) is entirely 15th-cent. and is pleasant but of no great interest. Some medieval tiles and glass remain in the S. aisle. The altar-tomb on the N. side of the chancel is that of John or Nicholas Cockworthy and his wife (15th cent.).

Their estate passed by marriage to a branch of the Trevelyans before 1522, who lived in some style at Court Barton, now a farmhouse.

Delley was a Saxon estate, and later the site of a medieval mansion of which some traces remain in a modernised house. Langley Barton was a home of the Pollards for some centuries. It belonged to Richard Pollard in Richard II's time. A Pollard of Langley was usher to Queen Elizabeth and James I. He married a sister of " Bess of Hardwick," Countess of Shrewsbury. The present house is externally a good 18th-cent. farmhouse, but contains traces of older work.

YEALMPTON (D10) (pron. *Yampton*) stands just above the head of the Yealm estuary. The church (St. Bartholomew) was rebuilt by Butterfield, in 1850, in the Decorated style. Mr. John Betjeman considers it "the most amazing" Victorian church in Devon. The walls are inlaid with a variety of local marbles (polished limestones), and in the pillars a black and a grey marble alternate. There are a number of memorials to local families, notably a good brass to Sir John Crocker of Lyneham (1508).

Kitley is the most interesting house in the district. The estate came in the reign of Henry VIII to the Pollexfens, who built a considerable house here. In 1710 the property passed to Pollexfen Bastard, whose father had married the Pollexfen heiress, and he reconstructed the house. The fine early Georgian staircase of this house survives. In 1820-25 Kitley was again remodelled by G. S. Repton in the "Gothic Revival" style to express the antiquity of the Bastard family. The interior of the house (except the staircase hall) is entirely Late Regency, the library being an especially notable example of untouched decoration of this period. There are some fine portraits in the house.

The library at Kitley possesses the only known copy of the first edition of the Mother Hubbard rhymes (1805), which were written here by Sarah Martin. Her sister had married squire Bastard, and Sarah lived with them for a time. Mother Hubbard is said to have been the housekeeper at Kitley.

Of the other houses in the parish, Lyneham was the seat of the ancient family of Crocker, Bowden the seat of a branch of the Coplestones for several generations, and Treby the original home of the family of that name who became prominent in Plympton politics in the 18th cent.

ZEAL MONACHORUM (F5) is a small cob and thatch village in unfrequented country. The church (St. Peter) was much restored in 1913 when a chancel screen of cast iron and bad design was put in; but it had already been devastated in 1854 by the then parson who removed the medieval screen and the box-pews. The fabric is mainly 14th-cent. in date, with a 15th-cent. S. aisle. Loosebeare and Lower Newton were Domesday manors.

ILLUSTRATIONS

1. Chittlehampton : the west tower is of the Somerset type and is the finest tower in Devon

*2. The Royal Theatre and Athenaeum (1811-19) : two of John
Foulston's public buildings in Plymouth, now destroyed*

*3. The Town Hall, the Column, the Mount Zion Chapel (now gone)
and the Civil and Military Library : the 'civic centre' of
Devonport built by John Foulston between 1821 and 1824*

4. The Dockyard and Harbour at Devonport about 1829

*5. Albemarle Villas at Stoke Damarel (1828-30) by John Foulston,
with Stonehouse in the distance and Plymouth Sound beyond*

6. Dawlish Beach and Public Baths about 1830, before the coming of the railway

7. The Atmospheric Railway at Dawlish (1846) from a contemporary print, showing one of the engine-houses

8. Totnes Church about 1842, showing the interior before its drastic restoration by Gilbert Scott

9. Tiverton Church about 1842

10. *Pinhoe Church and the Queen Anne vicarage*

11. Lydford in 1820. This view shows the parish church, the castle or stannary
prison, and Dartmoor in the background

12. Appledore in 1819 from the Instow shore

13. *Lynmouth in 1831, very much as Southey and Shelley would have seen it*

14. *Haldon House, begun by Sir George Chudleigh about 1735 and modelled on Buckingham House London. On the hill above is Sir Robert Palk's memorial (c. 1780) to his friend Stringer Lawrence*

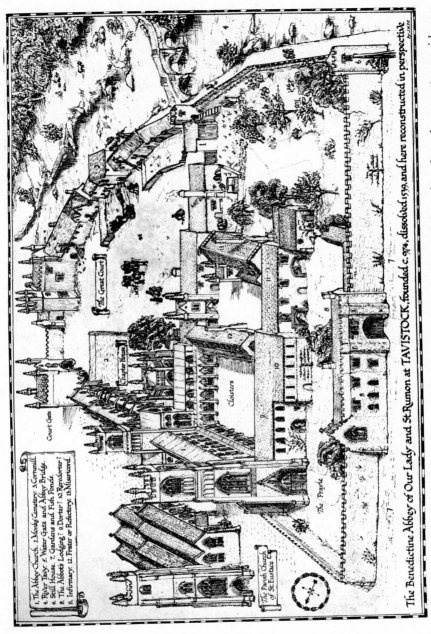

1. The Abbey Church. 2. Monks' Cemetery. 3. Cornwall
4. River Tavy 5. Water Gate and Abbey Bridge.
6. Still House. 7. Gardens and Fish Ponds.
8. The Abbots' Lodging? 9. Dorter? 10. Reredorter?
11. Infirmary. 12. Frater or Refectory. 13. Misericord.

The Court Gate

The Great Court

Chapter house

Cloisters

The Frayle

The Parish Church of St Eustace

The Benedictine Abbey of Our Lady and St Rumon at TAVISTOCK, founded c. 974, dissolved 1539, and here reconstructed in perspective

15. Tavistock Abbey as it was : a reconstruction by Mrs. J. H. P. Finberg based on documentary evidence

16. A Devonshire Franklin and his wife : probably the effigies of
William Easton of Easton (died 1485) and Joan his wife in Morchard
Bishop church (drawn by M. Meredith-Williams)

ÆTATIS SVÆ LVIII
Aᶯ Dᶯi 1591

*17. A Devonshire Sea-Captain : Sir John Hawkins (1532-95).
A portrait painted in 1591 and attributed to Zucchero*

18. A Devonshire Lawyer : William Fortescue (1687-1749), Justice of the Common Pleas and Master of the Rolls, from an engraving of the portrait painted by Thomas Hudson

19. *A Devonshire Painter : a self-portrait of Sir Joshua Reynolds (1723-92)*

20. Slapton Ley : a remarkable fresh-water lake separated from the sea by a raised bank of shingle, and notable for its fishing and wild birds

21. Bideford Quay and the estuary of the Torridge, looking down to Appledore

22. The Atlantic coast south of Hartland Point : the medieval chapel of St. Catherine stood on the summit of this cliff

23. *The pastoral Lyd valley near Coryton : a characteristic west Devon landscape*

24. *Tetcott : a typical grouping in a countryside of isolated farms and hamlets*

Crown Copyright

25. *Postbridge : this bridge over the East Dart river is constructed of massive granite slabs. Though of primitive construction, it is probably thirteenth-century in date*

26. *The china-clay workings at Lee Moor near Shaugh Prior : another aspect of the Dartmoor granite, here altered (kaolinized) to form a valuable clay for pottery and other uses*

Western Morning News

27. *Haytor from Hound Tor, on the eastern side of Dartmoor, showing characteristic granite*

A. Vincent Bibbings

28. *Bennett's Cross on Dartmoor : a number of these rough-hewn granite crosses are found on the Moor and its fringes. They served the purpose of guide-posts and are probably thirteenth-century in date for the most part*

A. Vincent Bibbings

29. Widecombe-in-the-Moor : one of the most graceful of the granite church towers. The building of this tower is traditionally attributed to the tinners of Widecombe who were prosperous in the early sixteenth century

R. L. Knight

30. Tawstock : a fourteenth-century cruciform church, of a type that is rare in Devon, set in the former park of the Earls of Bath

31. *Powderham Castle : the seat of the Earls of Devon. The present house is mostly the result of reconstructions between 1760 and 1860 around a medieval core*

32. Great Fulford: the home of the Fulfords since at least the twelfth century. The present mansion is an early Tudor rebuilding around a courtyard, remodelled externally about 1780

33. Canonteign Barton or Old Canonteign : an Elizabethan squire's mansion in decay. It was abandoned as a manor-house when the present Canonteign House was built on a new site about 1820

34. *Bradley near Newton Abbot : a good example of a small fifteenth-century manor-house of the South-West of England type. The private chapel (1428) is on the right*

35. *Acland Barton near Landkey : the late medieval wing of the ancestral home of the Aclands who originated here in the twelfth century*

36. *Honiton Barton near South Molton : a seventeenth-century rebuilding upon the site of an isolated farmstead recorded in Domesday Book*

Val Doone

37. *Sheepstor : a granite church and village. The pinnacled church-tower is of a type common in west Devon*

38. *Granite cottages at Lustleigh*

Travel Association

39. The almshouses at Moretonhampstead (1637), a remarkable building in granite

40. The Guildhall at Totnes (mainly sixteenth and seventeenth centuries) showing the slate-hanging that is characteristic of the south Devon towns

41. Topsham : one of the so-called Dutch houses in the Strand. This house was probably built by a Topsham merchant in that trade

42. Exmouth: the upper part of Beacon Hill, on which building was begun in 1792 when the resort was becoming fashionable. The house on the right was the home of Lady Nelson after her estrangement from her husband

Reece Winstone

43. *Brixham and its Harbour: once the largest fishing-port in Devon but now sadly diminished*

44. *Plymouth : part of the central area destroyed in the air-raids of the spring of 1941. In the background are the towers of the parish church of St. Andrew (left) and of the Victorian Guildhall (right)*

45. Plymouth : the rebuilding as it was in 1952, showing the Royal Parade, the centre of the replanned area. On the left is St. Andrew's church, temporarily repaired

Aerofilms Ltd.

46. Combe Martin: an early village, founded well inland, which has straggled down the narrow valley to the sea. The fields show distinct traces of former open fields on both sides of the valley.

47. *Cultivation-terraces or lynchets on the E. side of Challacombe Common, Dartmoor, of unknown date but possibly Celtic*

48. *Cullompton: the interior of a large Devon church of a fully-aisled plan (early sixteenth century) with Beer stone arcades, a magnificent coloured wagon-roof, and a coloured roodscreen across the entire width of the church*

49. Molland: an unspoiled early Georgian interior

50. *Tawstock: the monument of William, third Earl of Bath (died 1623)
and Elizabeth his wife, daughter of the Earl of Bedford*

Reece Winstone

51. Dittisham: the late medieval stone pulpit with crude carved
figures and vine-leaf enrichment

52. *Nymet Rowland: an unsophisticated country interior with a fifteenth-century oak arcade (the baluster-post is a Jacobean repair)*

53. *Bridford: the richly carved and coloured roodscreen given by an early sixteenth-century rector. Notice the charming small figures in the panels instead of the conventional painted ones*

54. Topsham: salmon fishermen drying their nets beside the Exe estuary. There has been a
salmon fishery here since the twelfth century

Western Morning News

Picture Post

55. *A Devonshire lane in winter: near Liddaton in west Devon, with Dartmoor in the background*

56. *Chillaton: a roadside hamlet in west Devon*

Picture Post

57. *Fingle Bridge over the Teign. It is probably Elizabethan or slightly later in date, and is built of granite like all those on or near the Moor*

58. *Clovelly: the Harbour at low tide. The massive pier on the right was built by George Cary, the Elizabethan squire of Clovelly*

TABLE OF POPULATION

It should be observed that few parishes in Devon escaped more or less substantial changes during the period 1801–1971, and that the individual parish figures must be interpreted in the light of these changes. Major changes of boundary have been indicated in footnotes, but it is impossible to list the others in any abbreviated form. In particular there were great changes following the act of 1894 setting up parish government, and again in 1935. There were also important boundary changes from 1961 onwards, chiefly affecting Plymouth, Exeter, and the new county borough of Torbay.

The latest population figure for most places is the census figure for 1961. For the cities, boroughs, and urban districts, however, the preliminary 1971 census figures are available. These are indicated by a dagger wherever they are used. For the details of recent boundary changes, the County Planning Department at Exeter should be consulted. Some boundary changes are indicated in the 1961 column by *.

	1801	1851	1901	1931	1961
ABBOTS BICKINGTON	68	80	61	46	22
ABBOTSHAM	313	361	451	384	287
ABBOTS KERSWELL[1]	389	460	457	642	3,729
ALLINGTON, EAST	468	640	396	389	418
ALPHINGTON	845	1,293	1,113	1,280	2,085
ALVERDISCOT	278	340	241	222	231
ALVINGTON, WEST	655	1,008	940	437	476
ALWINGTON	310	374	316	309	319
ANSTEY, EAST	165	225	216	207	206
ANSTEY, WEST	215	302	192	167	128
APPLEDORE (see NORTHAM)					
ARLINGTON	207	209	217	159	121
ASHBURTON	3,080	3,432	2,628	2,505	3,495†
ASHBURY	41	70	83	48	51
ASHCOMBE	280	242	125	144	126
ASHFORD	73	191	148	152	192
ASHPRINGTON	509	609	479	383	327
ASHREIGNEY	756	989	540	459	421
ASHTON	176	360	150	166	156
ASHWATER	643	929	758	664	569
ATHERINGTON	484	599	453	443	360
AVETON GIFFARD	746	979	657	563	599
AWLISCOMBE	426	594	464	424	429
AXMINSTER[2]	2,154	2,746	2,933	2,326	2,656*
AXMOUTH	375	680	643	641	484
AYLESBEARE	687	953	225	307	392
BAMPTON	1,361	2,102	1,657	1,392	1,517
BARNSTAPLE	3,748	8,667	9,698	14,700	17,342†
BEAFORD	516	666	428	379	303
BEAWORTHY	218	357	246	243	240
BEER[3]	—	1,281	1,118	1,266	1,453

[1] *The 1961 figure is the combined total for Abbots Kerswell and Kingskerswell, now united as Kerswell.*

[2] *Includes Axminster Hamlets down to 1901.*

[3] *The Beer figure for 1801 is included in Seaton.*

	1801	1851	1901	1931	1961
BELSTONE	137	181	236	321	316
BERE FERRERS	1,110	3,401	1,955	1,888	1,976
BERRYNARBOR	532	854	589	561	626
BERRY POMEROY	1,124	1,038	1,193	381	366
BICKINGTON	237	359	215	210	250
BICKINGTON, HIGH	693	851	539	507	410
BICKLEIGH (nr. Tiverton)	297	280	207	200	217
BICKLEIGH (nr. Plymouth) ...	264	403	296	272	957
BIDEFORD	2,987	5,775	8,754	8,778	11,766†
BIGBURY	430	583	260	424	458
BISHOPS NYMPTON	902	1,246	893	847	708
BISHOPS TAWTON	747	2,004	2,632	827	1,056
BISHOPS TEIGNTON	673	1,119	1,076	1,176	1,451
BITTADON	24	67	54	31	45
BLACKAWTON	1,019	1,360	946	869	489
BONDELEIGH	286	294	143	126	102
BOVEY, NORTH	519	600	418	378	391
BOVEY TRACEY	1,431	2,086	2,658	3,053	3,357
BOW	677	994	660	650	608
BRADFORD	352	490	280	329	296
BRADNICH	1,187	1,834	1,521	1,592	1,663
BRADSTONE	105	157	105	83	57
BRADWORTHY	634	1,071	847	775	697
BRAMPFORD SPEKE	273	432	374	276	289
BRANSCOMBE	603	1,017	627	538	626
BRATTON CLOVELLY	548	696	499	457	373
BRATTON FLEMING	406	700	511	442	488
BRAUNTON	1,296	2,364	2,135	3,019	4,303
BRAY, HIGH	264	323	219	175	150
BRENDON	260	265	262	283	213
BRENT, SOUTH	1,032	1,203	1,360	1,550	1,803
BRENT TOR	108	161	105	475	448
BRIDESTOWE	581	1,049	457	540	505
BRIDFORD	444	609	404	455	436
BRIDGERULE	332	428	375	407	366
BRIXHAM[3a]	3,671	5,936	8,092	8,145	10,721*
BRIXTON	635	777	652	669	1,048
BROAD CLYST	1,540	2,450	1,900	1,904	2,043
BROADHEMBURY	780	884	554	586	556
BROADHEMPSTON	667	754	441	410	467
BROADWOOD KELLY	311	376	222	201	181
BROADWOODWIDGER	586	890	593	682	589
BRUSHFORD	146	132	59	55	53
BUCKERELL	280	343	240	224	195
BUCKFASTLEIGH	1,525	2,613	2,781	2,410	2,657†
BUCKLAND BREWER	872	977	644	526	515
BUCKLAND, EAST	138	149	96	86	70
BUCKLAND FILLEIGHT	252	267	182	175	150
BUCKLAND-IN-THE-MOOR	106	141	87	76	48

[3a] *Now absorbed in the county borough of Torbay (see* Torquay).

	1801	1851	1901	1931	1961
BUCKLAND MONACHORUM	918	1,548	1,717	2,617	2,687
BUCKLAND TOUT SAINTS	9	48	37	191	155
BUCKLAND, WEST	257	279	277	322	251
BUDLEIGH, EAST	1,014	2,447	2,653	768	673
BUDLEIGH SALTERTON[4]	—	—	—	3,162	4,139†
BULKWORTHY	110	179	92	86	83
BURLSECOMBE	853	911	684	637	725
BURRINGTON	755	1,001	669	516	444
BUTTERLEIGH	125	160	83	96	79
CADBURY	238	264	187	157	134
CADELEIGH	226	410	228	162	142
CALVERLEIGH[5]	70	95	69	—	—
CHAGFORD	1,115	1,557	1,397	1,584	1,346
CHALLACOMBE	158	289	195	181	153
CHARDSTOCK[6]	—	—	—	935	1,065
CHARLES	217	344	220	215	203
CHARLETON	522	652	455	221	289
CHAWLEIGH	755	833	649	556	488
CHELDON	91	78	46	55	32
CHERITON BISHOP	604	806	455	432	521
CHERITON FITZPAINE	884	1,207	678	530	545
CHITTLEHAMHOLT[7]	—	—	—	215	190
CHITTLEHAMPTON	1,406	1,886	1,342	778	713
CHIVELSTONE	562	571	385	433	349
CHRISTOW	422	863	520	611	607
CHUDLEIGH	1,786	2,401	1,820	1,944	2,053
CHUMLEIGH	1,333	1,771	1,158	1,165	960
CHURCHSTOW	219	559	311	329	313
CHURSTON FERRERS	663	786	532	656	1,582
CLANNABOROUGH	59	62	42	75	57
CLAWTON	383	573	389	362	303
CLAYHANGER	213	289	149	136	144
CLAYHIDON	690	798	481	433	428
CLOVELLY	714	937	621	528	445
CLYST HONITON	348	422	262	300	350
CLYST HYDON	257	342	286	260	286
CLYST ST. GEORGE	249	370	241	210	260
CLYST ST. LAWRENCE	156	184	113	94	110
CLYST ST. MARY	97	197	157	140	225
COCKINGTON[8]	294	171	2,669	—	—
COFFINSWELL	261	214	201	174	173
COLATION RALEIGH	627	851	474	519	509

[4] *Until 1894 Budleigh Salterton was part of East Budleigh, and its population figures are included in that parish in 1801, 1851, and 1901.*
[5] *Calverleigh was united with Loxbeare for civil purposes in 1885 and the figures for 1931 and 1961 will be found under that parish.*
[6] *Transferred from Dorset to Devon in 1896.*
[7] *Chittlehamhol was separated from Chittlehampton and constituted a separate civil parish in 1885.*
[8] *Now included in Torquay.*

	1801	1851	1901	1931	1961
COLDRIDGE ...	697	607	374	324	294
COLEBROOKE	762	871	650	508	425
COLYTON	1,641	2,504	1,982	2,040	1,922
COMBE-IN-TEIGNHEAD[9]	505	435	415	364	398
COMBE MARTIN	819	1,441	1,521	1,920	2,228
COMBE RALEIGH	237	289	223	188	187
COMBPYNE[10]	141	138	101	83	268
COMPTON GIFFORD[11]	92	391	6,282	692	—
COOKBURY ...	261	280	146	137	89
CORNWOOD ...	745	1,034	1,115	972	813
CORNWORTHY	468	567	329	321	292
CORYTON ...	154	311	205	136	111
COTLEIGH ...	214	245	186	167	189
COUNTISBURY	120	174	279	317	80
CREACOMBE	29	35	57	48	52
CREDITON ...	4,929	6,000	5,266	3,490	5,144†
CRUWYS MORCHARD	556	732	523	463	427
CULLOMPTON	3,138	3,655	2,922	2,973	3,415
CULMSTOCK ...	1,496	1,224	766	775	692
DALWOOD[12]	430	537	346	335	403
DARTINGTON	486	660	627	692	1,183
DARTMOUTH[13]	2,398	3,147	3,702	6,708	5,696†
DAWLISH ...	1,424	3,546	4,584	5,425	9,505†
DEAN PRIOR	495	507	259	238	305
DENBURY[14] ...	330	406	303	—	—
DEVONPORT (see Stoke Damarel and Stonehouse, East)					
DIPTFORD ...	578	747	502	393	318
DITTISHAM ...	639	755	549	572	508
DODBROOKE[15]	608	1,302	1,183	—	—
DODDISCOMBSLEIGH	317	386	210	228	169
DOLTON ...	582	926	621	517	415
DOWLAND ...	184	208	119	103	83
DOWN, EAST	311	455	326	249	213
DOWN ST. MARY ...	313	402	337	310	323
DOWN, WEST	257	587	553	473	514
DREWSTEIGNTON	959	1,232	693	674	625
DUNCHIDEOCK	183	178	134	145	98
DUNKESWELL	393	579	288	278	352
DUNSFORD ...	661	977	633	547	572
DUNTERTON	129	170	100	83	59
EGG BUCKLAND[16] ...	711	1,415	2,689	2,494	—

[9] *Combe-in-Teignhead includes the parish of Haccombe throughout.*
[10] *The 1961 figure includes Rousdon.*
[11] *Now included in Plymouth.*
[12] *Transferred from Dorset in 1842.*
[13] *The 1931 and 1971 figures include Townstall, united with Dartmouth in 1891.*
[14] *Now united with Torbryan, q.v.*
[15] *Later figures included under Kingsbridge.*
[16] *Included Laira Green in 1801. Now part of Plymouth.*

				1801	1851	1901	1931	1961
EGGESFORD ...	...	...	...	173	138	126	80	89
ERMINGTON[17]	...	...	...	917	1,423	2,034	805	1,245
EXBOURNE ...	...	...	...	421	525	382	306	282
EXETER ...	...	...	...	17,398	32,823	47,185	66,029	95,598†*
EXMINSTER ...	...	...	...	795	1,623	2,560	2,807	3,302
EXMOUTH[18] ...	...	...	...	—	—	10,485	14,591	25,815†
FARRINGDON	...	...	...	293	395	216	196	251
FARWAY ...	...	...	...	287	380	233	253	198
FENITON ...	...	...	...	252	366	387	344	320
FILLEIGH ...	...	...	...	220	367	319	284	209
FREMINGTON	...	...	...	875	1,350	1,194	1,172	4,409
FRITHELSTOCK	...	...	...	479	610	429	360	297
GEORGEHAM	...	...	...	627	971	698	834	1,018
GEORGENYMPTON	...	...	...	237	292	170	143	181
GERMANSWEEK	...	...	...	133	318	204	151	130
GIDLEIGH ...	...	...	...	125	166	121	143	117
GITTISHAM ...	...	...	...	459	384	314	312	262
GOODLEIGH ...	...	...	...	248	294	253	223	219
HACCOMBE (included in Combe-in-Teignhead)								
HALBERTON	...	...	...	1,436	1,745	1,238	1,202	1,268
HALWELL ...	...	...	...	358	411	246	275	219
HALWILL ...	...	...	...	156	284	434	370	407
HARBERTON	...	...	...	1,138	1,324	1,170	1,041	897
HARFORD ...	...	...	...	142	139	198	121	115
HARPFORD[19]	...	...	...	190	253	213	303	1,021
HARTLAND ...	...	...	...	1,546	2,183	1,634	1,385	1,326
HATHERLEIGH	...	...	...	1,218	1,710	1,293	1,130	984
HAWKCHURCH[20]	...	...	...	—	—	—	490	539
HEANTON PUNCHARDON	...	...	418	576	404	369	931
HEAVITREE[21]	...	...	...	833	3,112	7,529	—	—
HEMPSTON, LITTLE	...	...	...	266	259	182	159	203
HEMYOCK ...	...	...	...	1,020	1,185	806	857	1,063
HENNOCK[22] ...	...	...	...	537	894	746	1,046	954
HIGHAMPTON	...	...	...	204	388	219	207	170
HIGHWEEK[23]	...	...	...	777	1,398	2,709	—	—
HITTISLEIGH	...	...	...	124	185	107	131	111
HOCKWORTHY	...	...	...	283	382	244	201	192
HOLBETON ...	...	...	...	869	1,029	850	699	598
HOLCOMBE BURNELL	...	...	...	176	289	167	165	180

[17] *Part annexed to Ivybridge in 1904.*
[18] *Exmouth Urban District was formed out of the parishes of Littleham and Withycombe Raleigh in 1895.*
[19] *The 1961 figure includes Venn Ottery.*
[20] *Transferred from Dorset 1896.*
[21] *Now included in Exeter.*
[22] *Includes Chudleigh Knighton.*
[23] *Now included in Newton Abbot.*

				1801	1851	1901	1931	1961
HOLCOMBE ROGUS	...	...	...	662	759	607	478	483
HOLLACOMBE	...	...	...	74	103	69	62	63
HOLNE	...	...	...	359	386	273	301	348
HOLSWORTHY	...	...	...	1,045	1,833	2,076	1,403	1,618*
HONEYCHURCH[24]	...	...	...	66	59	44	—	—
HONITON	...	...	...	2,377	3,427	3,271	3,008	5,058†
HORWOOD	...	...	...	103	105	102	68	79
HUISH	...	...	...	97	161	86	107	60
HUISH, NORTH	...	...	...	380	464	317	223	355
HUISH, SOUTH	...	...	...	286	382	227	405	472
HUNTSHAM	...	...	...	158	170	222	183	132
HUNTSHAW	...	...	...	212	266	143	111	117
HUXHAM	...	...	...	135	156	136	135	90
IDDESLEIGH	...	...	...	441	518	335	272	227
IDE	...	...	...	507	694	681	629	598
IDEFORD	...	...	...	339	319	254	235	274
ILFRACOMBE	...	...	...	1,838	3,677	8,557	9,175	9,846†
ILSINGTON	...	...	...	866	1,214	886	1,135	1,384
INSTOW	...	...	...	341	626	634	646	782
INWARDLEIGH	...	...	...	384	693	421	412	418
IPPLEPEN	...	...	...	821	833	813	845	1,128
IVYBRIDGE[25]	...	...	...	—	—	—	1,609	1,753
JACOBSTOWE	...	...	...	193	255	229	173	171
KELLY	...	...	...	201	208	167	152	121
KENN	...	...	...	818	1,098	781	770	959
KENNERLEIGH	...	...	...	94	115	80	48	44
KENTISBEARE	...	...	...	1,042	1,104	733	714	692
KENTISBURY	...	...	...	241	424	304	290	270
KENTON[26]	...	...	...	1,639	2,082	1,723	1,837	2,055
KILMINGTON	...	...	...	444	533	523	521	562
KINGSBRIDGE[27]	...	...	...	1,117	1,679	1,413	2,978	3,535†
KINGSKERSWELL[28]	...	...	...	532	959	1,027	1,405	3,729
KINGSNYMPTON	...	...	...	510	719	502	452	350
KINGSTEIGNTON	...	...	...	856	1,658	1,942	3,157	4,833
KINGSTON	...	...	...	354	523	399	311	303
KINGSWEAR	...	...	...	300	315	841	809	696
KNOWSTONE	...	...	...	427	517	343	271	212
LAMERTON	...	...	...	722	1,510	1,028	557	591
LANDCROSS	...	...	...	50	124	58	71	71
LANDKEY	...	...	...	607	758	621	558	824
LANGTREE	...	...	...	583	878	613	504	463
LAPFORD	...	...	...	587	766	528	507	612
LEW, NORTH	...	...	...	638	1,047	629	569	499

[24] *Now included in Sampford Courtney.*
[25] *Civil parish formed 1894.*
[26] *Includes Starcross.*
[27] *The 1931 and 1971 figures include Dodbrooke.*
[28] *The 1961 figure includes Abbots Kerswell.*

	1801	1851	1901	1931	1961
LEW TRENCHARD	154	436	257	216	167
LIFTON	843	1,667	942	860	841
LITTLEHAM (nr. Exmouth)[29] ...	1,909	4,150	5,793	6,371	—
LITTLEHAM (nr. Bideford)	292	413	302	267	266
LODDISWELL	608	949	650	672	637
LOXBEARE[30]	132	129	100	159	162
LOXHORE	209	317	202	168	141
LUFFINCOTT	76	96	62	68	69
LUNDY	—	—	—	21	32
LUPPITT	675	761	467	401	442
LUSTLEIGH	246	367	394	439	590
LYDFORD[31]	422	1,968	2,812	2,218	2,059
LYMPSTONE	883	1,107	1,012	1,042	1,620
LYNTON (with Lynmouth) ...	481	1,059	1,641	2,011	1,981†
MALBOROUGH[31a]	1,056	2,354	2,167	615	793
MAMHEAD	230	252	178	127	148
MANATON	348	442	315	370	424
MARIANSLEIGH	199	334	205	223	153
MARLDON	364	514	506	520	1,179
MARTINHOE	165	216	174	175	149
MARWOOD	632	1,054	681	612	584
MARYSTOW	297	570	255	222	193
MARYTAVY	376	1,367	717	680	763
MEAVY	239	294	261	389	527
MEETH	257	333	203	206	133
MEMBURY	709	793	603	555	491
MERTON	689.	790	507	423	292
MESHAW	135	297	181	157	118
MILTON ABBOT	862	1,242	719	649	614
MILTON DAMEREL	469	734	442	427	388
MILTON, SOUTH	302	414	287	378	324
MODBURY	1,813	1,858	1,330	1,110	1,077
MOLLAND	473	602	397	320	242
MOLTON, NORTH	1,541	1,982	1,069	938	855
MOLTON, SOUTH	2,753	4,482	2,892	2,832	2,993
MONKLEIGH	379	600	358	335	323
MONK OKEHAMPTON	182	270	177	149	120
MONKTON	121	121	106	140	233
MORCHARD BISHOP	1,698	1,854	985	829	780
MOREBATH	420	514	424	403	399
MORELEIGH	127	158	104	94	102
MORETON HAMPSTEAD	1,768	1,858	1,527	1,587	1,541
MORTEHOE	254	387	788	1,164	1,289
MUSBURY	280	506	422	392	477

[29] *Now included in Exmouth.*
[30] *The 1931 and 1961 figures include Calverleigh also.*
[31] *Includes the Forest of Dartmoor and Princetown.*
[31a] *Down to 1901 the figures include Salcombe, now separate.*

				1801	1851	1901	1931	1961
NETHEREXE	...	...	...	86	103	60	75	56
NEWTON ABBOT[32]	...	...	...	—	—	—	15,010	19,367†
NEWTON FERRERS[33]		...	...	590	749	611	884	1,842
NEWTON POPPLEFORD[34]		...	...	—	—	441	447	—
NEWTON ST. CRYES...		...	...	867	1,144	700	670	758
NEWTON ST. PETROCK		...	...	215	272	179	177	143
NEWTON TRACEY	...		...	86	143	127	110	92
NORTHAM[35]	...	...	...	2,054	3,680	5,355	5,563	8,082†
NORTHCOTT	...	...	...	71	115	60	52	22
NORTHLEIGH	...	...	...	180	290	161	139	121
NYMET ROWLAND	...		...	76	99	67	66	111
NYMET TRACEY (see Bow)								
OAKFORD	...	...	...	480	625	484	444	316
OFFWELL	...	...	...	302	389	304	301	453
OGWELL, EAST	...	...		256	316	219	326	508
OGWELL, WEST	...		...	53	51	27	—	—
OKEHAMPTON	...	...	...	1,500	2,165	3,223	3,352	3,908†
OTTERTON	...	...	...	920	1,231	622	599	611
OTTERY ST. MARY		...	...	2,415	4,421	3,495	3,713	5,824†
PAIGNTON[35a]	...	...	...	1,575	2,746	8,385	18,414	*
PANCRASWEEK	...	...	...	330	460	277	289	209
PARKHAM	...	...	...	584	951	786	614	568
PARRACOMBE	...	...	...	322	460	315	329	309
PAYHEMBURY	...	...	...	416	544	415	406	443
PETERS MARLAND	...	...	...	289	292	286	280	253
PETERTAVY	...	...	...	291	561	293	366	291
PETHERWIN, NORTH[35b]		...	...	672	942	682	568	537
PETROCKSTOW	...	...	...	467	574	385	381	305
PILTON[36]	...	...	...	831	1,813	2,238	2,669	126
PINHOE	...	...	...	353	527	952	1,653	3,431
PLYMOUTH[37]	...	...	...	16,378	52,933	107,636	208,182	239,314†*
PLYMPTON EARL or								
PLYMPTON ST. MAURICE			...	604	833	1,117	1,075	1,796
PLYMPTON ST. MARY		...	...	1,562	2,815	3,837	5,077	10,600
PLYMSTOCK	...		...	...	1,633	3,302	3,195	7,057	14,700
PLYMTREE	...	...	...	375	468	359	327	305
POLTIMORE	...	...	...	250	281	298	246	311
POOL, SOUTH	...	...	...	412	486	296	247	237
PORTLEMOUTH, EAST		...	...	298	461	264	259	239
POUGHILL	...	...	...	274	350	222	165	176

[32] Urban district created 1894-1901.
[33] The 1961 figure includes Revelstoke (Noss Mayo).
[34] Separated from Aylesbeare 1896.
[35] Includes Appledore and Westward Ho.
[35a] Now in county borough of Torbay.
[35b] Now transferred to Cornwall.
[36] 1961 figure for West Pilton only. East Pilton is now included in Barnstaple.
[37] In 1914 Devonport and Stonehouse were absorbed into Plymouth. Further boundary changes since 1961.

	1801	1851	1901	1931	1961
POWDERHAM	175	294	238	156	98
PRINCETOWN (included in Lydford)					
PUDDINGTON	135	215	173	155	126
PUTFORD, EAST	139	194	125	116	102
PUTFORD, WEST	274	424	216	206	185
PYWORTHY	499	663	429	436	467
QUEENSNYMPTON[38]	—	—	—	34	26
RACKENFORD	340	473	302	317	291
RATTERY	451	413	347	345	371
REVELSTOKE[39]	417	510	405	347	—
REWE	195	289	237	230	320
RINGMORE	309	337	204	146	201
ROBOROUGH	461	518	312	252	208
ROCKBEARE	419	477	404	491	553
ROMANSLEIGH	156	246	155	109	103
ROSE ASH	397	587	439	340	268
ROUSDON[40]	—	10	46	41	—
ST. BUDEAUX[41]	544	1,096	6,291	1,819	—
ST. GILES-IN-THE-WOOD	547	964	623	492	414
ST. GILES-ON-THE-HEATH	187	354	258	237	252
ST. LEONARD (Exeter)[42]	133	1,499	2,598	—	—
ST. MARY CHURCH[43]	801	2,293	6,748	—	—
ST. NICHOLAS (see Shaldon)					
ST. THOMAS (Exeter)[44]	2,189	4,577	9,560	15,421	—
SALCOMBE[45]	—	—	—	2,384	2,471†
SALCOMBE REGIS[46]	300	476	635	775	—
SAMPFORD COURTENHAY[47] ...	960	1,084	758	693	707
SAMPFORD PEVERELL	763	855	612	630	711
SAMPFORD SPINEY	205	522	478	381	124
SANDFORD	1,742	1,970	1,248	1,034	982
SATTERLEIGH[48]	64	57	55	240	175
SEATON[49]	1,497	766	2,443	2,349	4,134†
SHALDON[50]	585	1,297	1,121	1,209	—
SHAUGH PRIOR	480	554	783	864	959
SHEBBEAR	744	1,151	840	656	589

[38] Constituted a separate civil parish in 1900.
[39] Now included in Newton Ferrers under the name of Newton and Noss.
[40] 1961 figure included in Combpyne.
[41] Now wholly included in Plymouth.
[42] Now in Exeter.
[43] Now in Torquay.
[44] Now in Exeter.
[45] Civil parish formed in 1894. Earlier figures under Malborough.
[46] Now under Sidmouth.
[47] Includes Honeychurch since 1894.
[48] Satterleigh is now united with Warkleigh. The 1931 and 1961 figures are for the combined parishes.
[49] The 1801 figure includes Beer.
[50] Now included in Teignmouth.

				1801	1851	1901	1931	1961
SHEEPSTOR ...	...	...	...	99	126	95	77	53
SHEEPWASH	...	...	...	348	525	326	273	240
SHELDON ...	...	...	...	128	177	120	109	109
SHERFORD ...	...	...	...	380	523	342	268	258
SHILLINGFORD	...	...	...	71	69	63	72	212
SHIRWELL ...	...	...	...	513	725	338	294	359
SHOBROOKE	...	...	...	686	812	557	498	375
SHUTE ...	...	...	...	558	597	461	428	590
SIDBURY[51] ...	...	...	...	1,233	1,872	1,076	1,595	—
SIDMOUTH[52]	...	...	...	1,252	3,441	4,033	6,126	12,039†
SILVERTON ...	...	...	...	1,236	1,376	1,188	1,129	1,248
SLAPTON ...	...	...	...	558	706	527	443	460
SOURTON ...	...	...	...	450	615	403	400	408
SOUTHLEIGH	...	...	...	237	321	157	159	167
SOWTON ...	...	...	...	318	361	374	431	425
SPREYTON ...	...	...	...	333	384	360	287	267
STARCROSS (see Kenton)								
STAVERTON ...	...	...	...	1,053	1,152	663	629	612
STOCKLAND[53]	...	...	...	988	1,164	772	684	625
STOCKLEIGH ENGLISH	...	...	116	126	50	53	44	
STOCKLEIGH POMEROY	...	...	196	221	164	118	105	
STOKE CANON	...	...	...	254	480	383	366	336
STOKE DAMAREL[54] ...	...	...	23,747	38,180	63,917	—	—	
STOKE FLEMMING ...	...	...	578	707	708	630	683	
STOKE GABRIEL ...	...	...	531	718	565	699	967	
STOKE RIVERS ...	...	...	225	276	174	154	128	
STOKE-IN-TEIGNHEAD	...	...	574	633	614	574	511	
STOKENHAM ...	...	...	...	1,301	1,603	1,403	1,217	1,314
STONEHOUSE, EAST[55]	...	...	3,407	11,979	15,111	—	—	
STOODLEIGH	...	...	...	355	499	381	300	278
STOWFORD ...	...	...	...	235	576	323	289	266
SUTCOMBE ...	...	...	...	330	488	351	280	245
SWIMBRIDGE	...	...	...	1,082	1,738	1,106	961	910
SYDENHAM DAMAREL	...	...	199	466	312	221	168	
TALATON ...	...	...	...	393	443	415	447	369
TAMERTON FOLIOT[55a]	...	...	747	1,147	1,102	1,232	—	
TAVISTOCK ...	...	...	...	3,420	8,147	5,841	4,471	6,088
TAWSTOCK ...	...	...	...	1,131	1,383	1,241	819	1,285
TAWTON, NORTH ...	...	...	1,436	1,906	1,529	1,280	1,098	
TAWTON, SOUTH ...	...	...	1,538	1,758	1,079	1,182	1,260	
TEDBURN ST. MARY	...	...	527	861	475	458	559	
TEIGNGRACE	...	...	...	133	187	190	122	201
TEIGNMOUTH[55b]	...	...	...	2,012	5,149	7,366	8,723	12,554†

[51] *Now under Sidmouth.*
[52] *The 1971 figure includes Salcombe Regis and Sidbury.*
[53] *Transferred from Dorset 1842.*
[54] *In 1914 Stoke Damarel (Devonport) was absorbed into Plymouth.*
[55] *In 1914 Stonehouse was absorbed into Plymouth.*
[55a] *Now in Plymouth.*
[55b] *Boundary changes since 1961.*

	1801	1851	1901	1931	1961
TEMPLETON	200	218	175	155	128
TETCOTT	166	289	220	140	141
THELBRIDGE	155	260	186	295	260
THORNBURY	330	489	291	306	223
THORVERTON	1,168	1,511	813	717	674
THROWLEIGH	331	395	241	331	272
THRUSHELTON	417	535	307	263	257
THURLESTONE	356	460	354	635	685
TIVERTON	6,505	11,144	10,382	9,610	15,548†
TOPSHAM	2,749	3,377	2,790	3,437	3,963
TORBRYAN[56]	258	229	164	443	500
TORMOHUN[57]	838	11,474	24,473	—	—
TORQUAY[58]	—	—	—	46,165	108,888†*
TORRINGTON, BLACK	706	1,115	652	541	429
TORRINGTON, GREAT	2,044	3,308	3,241	2,913	3,536†
TORRINGTON, LITTLE	449	623	407	311	281
TOTNES	2,503	3,828	3,116	4,526	5,771††
TOWNSTALL[59]	1,014	1,303	2,726	—	—
TRENTISHOE	128	129	68	60	47
TRUSHAM	135	205	173	138	138
TWITCHEN	145	203	163	117	81
UFFCULME	1,837	2,098	1,704	1,672	1,663
UGBOROUGH	956	1,463	1,610	1,845	2,051
UPLOWMAN	360	386	357	316	272
UPLYME	549	1,032	798	1,005	1,243
UPOTTERY	795	1,042	666	518	450
UPTON HELLIONS	136	137	109	105	76
UPTON PYNE	409	491	355	398	417
VENN OTTERY[60]	127	105	111	66	—
VIRGINSTOW	101	173	115	90	96
WALKHAMPTON	336	751	584	673	577
WARKLEIGH[61]	291	337	220	240	175
WASHFIELD	422	452	332	315	323
WASHFORD PYNE	109	192	150	104	79
WEAR GIFFARD	419	551	317	297	275
WELCOMBE	220	234	150	132	117
WEMBURY	390	577	501	596	1,423
WEMBWORTHY	323	444	315	228	210
WERRINGTON[61a]	489	657	632	548	533
WESTLEIGH	408	508	401	403	380

[56] *The 1931 and 1961 figures include Denbury.*

[57] *Now included in Torquay.*

[58] *The earlier figures for Torquay are chiefly included in St. Marychurch and Tormohun. The 1971 figure is for the new county borough of Torbay, formed in 1968 out of Torquay, Paignton and Brixham.*

[59] *Now included in Dartmouth.*

[60] *Now included in Harpford.*

[61] *Warkleigh is now united with Satterleigh. The 1931 and 1961 figures are for the combined parishes.*

[61a] *Now transferred to Cornwall.*

	1801	1851	1901	1931	1961
WESTWARD HO (see Northam)					
WHIMPLE	483	704	680	775	885
WHITCHURCH	478	1,156	1,508	1,411	463
WHITESTONE	471	624	409	538	750
WIDECOMBE-IN-THE-MOOR ...	843	974	657	704	557
WIDWORTHY	245	192	148	138	202
WILLAND	255	398	418	566	963
WINKLEIGH	1,214	1,554	1,079	881	934
WITHERIDGE	875	1,309	1,024	743	699
WITHYCOMBE RALEIGH[62]	692	1,811	4,690	—	—
WOLBOROUGH[63]	1,623	3,227	9,720	—	—
WOODBURY	1,286	2,014	1,527	1,637	2,736
WOODLAND	212	188	170	107	101
WOODLEIGH	240	233	183	188	163
WOOLFARDISWORTHY (nr. Crediton)	131	208	170	155	163
WOOLFARDISWORTHY (nr. Hartland)	591	824	648	591	505
WORLINGTON, EAST[64]	196	277	173 }	294 }	260
WORLINGTON, WEST	158	229	154 }		
YARCOMBE	740	780	561	519	451
YARNSCOMBE	358	479	273	231	203
YEALMPTON	993	1,155	937	869	1,060
YELVERTON (see Buckland Monachorum)					
ZEAL MONACHORUM	622	578	316	321	263
ZEAL, SOUTH (see Tawton, South)					

[62] *Now absorbed into Exmouth.*
[63] *Now included in Newton Abbot.*
[64] *East and West Worlington are now united as East Worlington.*

To the above list should be added the following civil parishes with their 1961 populations:

BICTON	191
HORRABRIDGE	1,397
STRETE	346
WEST BUCKFASTLEIGH	284
AXMINSTER HAMLETS	1,629
CREDITON HAMLETS	1,082
HOLSWORTHY HAMLETS	630
OKEHAMPTON HAMLETS	992
TAVISTOCK HAMLETS	699

It must be emphasised once again that though the larger boundary changes have been noticed in the above table, the County Planning Department should be consulted for a considerable number of minor changes which affect the latest figures in various parishes.

LIST OF ABBREVIATIONS
USED IN NOTES

B.M.	British Museum.
D.A.	*Transactions of the Devonshire Association.*
D.A.E.S.	*Devon Archaeological Exploration Society.*
D. & C. MSS.	MSS. of the Dean and Chapter of Exeter.
D.C.N.Q.	*Devon and Cornwall Notes and Queries.*
D.C.R.S.	Devon and Cornwall Record Society.
D.S.	W. G. Hoskins and H. P. R. Finberg, *Devonshire Studies.*
Early Tours.	*Early Tours in Devon and Cornwall,* ed. R. Pearse Chope.
E.D.R.	Exeter Diocesan Registry.
E.H.R.	*English Historical Review.*
Ekwall	E. Ekwall, *The Concise Oxford Dictionary of English Place-Names.*
H.M.C.	Reports of the Historical MSS. Commission.
H.M.S.O.	Her Majesty's Stationery Office.
I.P.M.	Inquisitio post mortem.
Lysons	D. and S. Lysons, *Magna Britannia,* vol. vi.
P.N.D.	*The Place-Names of Devon* (English Place-Name Society).
Pole	Sir W. Pole, *Collections for a History of Devon.*
Polwhele	R. Polwhele, *History of Devonshire.*
Prince	J. Prince, *Worthies of Devon* (1810 ed.)
P.R.O.	Public Record Office.
Reg.	Episcopal Register.
R.H.	O. J. Reichel, *The Hundreds of Devon.*
V.C.H.	*Victoria History of the County of Devon,* vol. i.
Westcote	T. Westcote, *A View of Devonshire.*

NOTES

PAGE

9   [1] Ekwall, 137, and Introd., **xi**.
     [2] *D.A.* **79** (1947), 16.
     [3] *P.N.D.*, Introd., xiv note.

10   [1] *D.A.* **53** (1921), 175 and *D.A.* **65** (1933), 140.
     [2] *P.N.D.*, Introd., xiii.
     [3] Kelly, *Directory of Devonshire* (1935), 1.
     [4] For a detailed study of this boundary see *D.S.*, 19-39.
     [5] *P.N.D.*, Introd., xiii.
     [6] For what follows see *D.S.*, 19-39.

12   [1] Ekwall, 355; *Studies in English Place-Names*, 79-80.

14   [1] For the possible glaciation of Dartmoor, see Col. Ransom Pickard's Presidential address to the Devonshire Association in D.A. **75** (1943), 25-52.

19   [1] So called from the sooty, soft coal which they sometimes contain, known locally as culm. The word is derived from the Latin *culmus*, "stem of a plant."

24   [1] *V.C.H.*, 341-3, gives the fullest account of the excavations and finds in Kent's Cavern.
     [2] *V.C.H.*, loc. cit.; Hawkes, *Prehistoric Britain*, 219.

25   [1] *V.C.H.*, 344-6. Worth, " Prehistoric Plymouth," in *Trans. Plymouth Institution* (1931).
     [2] The richest deposits at Broom are just on the Dorset side of the border. See *D.A.E.S.*, **2** (1936), 264-75. For the Seaton-Beer road finds, ibid., 275-82.
     [3] The intervening mesolithic culture is represented at Westward Ho and at Yelland, on the south bank of the Taw estuary. *D.A.E.S.* **3** (1946), 109-35.
     [4] *D.A.E.S.* **2** (1935), 135-75, gives a full account of the excavations at Hembury Fort in 1934-35. For a summary of the neolithic material, see 161-3.

PAGE

25   [5] The Haldon site is fully reported on in *D.A.E.S.* **2** (1936), 244-63; and *D.A.E.S.* **3** (1937), 33-43. The exact site is 150 yards N. of Haldon Belvedere.

26   [1] Another is at Coringdon Ball, near South Brent. It is possible that these megalithic monuments belong to the earliest phase of the Bronze Age.
     [2] The following pages on Dartmoor are based upon J. W. Brailsford, " The Bronze Age Stone Monuments of Dartmoor," in *Antiquity* **12** (1938), 444-63, and R. Hansford Worth, " The Dartmoor Hut-circles," in *D.A.* **77** (1945), 225-56.

28   [1] See Curwen, *Air-Photography and the Evolution of the Cornfield* (1938 ed.), for details, esp. 8-11 and 29. Good examples are to be seen ½ m. SE. of Trowlesworthy Warren House in Shaugh Prior parish, and at Standon Down, near Petertavy.
     [2] The earliest evidence of tin-streaming on Dartmoor comes from the middle of the 12th century (see Ch. VII).
     [3] Alignments are absent from the east Cornish moors, and the Cornish stone circles are also of a rather different type: Brailsford, loc. cit., 461.

29   [1] For a plan and fuller description of this important prehistoric village see *V.C.H.*, 355-6, and *D.A.* **34** (1902), 160-3.
     [2] Curwen, op. cit., 9, 10, 29.
     [3] R. Hansford Worth, " The Prehistoric Pounds of Dartmoor," in *D.A.* **75** (1943), 282. Brailsford, 455, gives the area as 12 acres.

30   [1] See the distribution-map in *D.A.* **77** (1945), 226.
     [2] Information from Mr. A. H. Shorter, of University College, Exeter.

31   [1] A detailed account of the con-

31 struction of the huts is given by Worth,
D.A. **77**, 229-37.

² See Worth, " Retaining-Circles
associated with Stone Rows, Dartmoor," in *D.A.* **73** (1941), 227-38.
Brailsford, loc. cit., 444-7.

³ *D.A.* **24** (1892), 387 ff.

⁴ Dartmoor Schedule of Ancient
Monuments, prepared by the County
Planning Department, Devon County
Council, 1947. I am indebted to the
Department for the loan of this
schedule.

32 ¹ Possibly datable at the 3rd century
B.C. If so, the occupation of the Moor
went on considerably longer than has
hitherto been supposed.

² *D.A.E.S.* **4** (1948), 1-19: " The
Broad Down (Farway) Necropolis and
the Wessex Culture in Devon."

33 ¹ *D.A.E.S.* **3** (1947), 150-63.

² *V.C.H.*, 354.

³ Ralegh Radford, " The Dumnonii," *D.A.* **79** (1947), 15-30.

34 ¹ These Iron Age hill-forts frequently
go by the name of "castle" in south-
western England.

² *D.A.* **33** (1901), 129; *V.C.H.*, 365.

³ *D.A.E.S.* **2** (1935), 164-5.

35 ¹ *D.A.E.S.*, Interim Report on . . .
Milber Down Camp (1938).

² Lady (Aileen) Fox, " Roman
Objects from Cadbury Castle", in
D.A. **84** (1952), 105-14.

³ Radford, " The Dumnonii " (*D.A.*
79), for all references to the Dumnonii before and after the Roman
Conquest.

36 ¹ Radford, 21.

37 ¹ *D.A.* **54** (1922), 66-8. One Seaton
villa was excavated about 1865, the
other was found in 1921. *D.A.* **60**
(1928), 169, says the Membury villa
was excavated in 1914, but I cannot
find that any report on it was ever
published.

² Radford, 24.

³ *D.A.E.S.* **3** (1937), 6-23, on which
these and the following remarks about
Topsham are based.

38 ¹ ibid., 10.

38 ² *D.A.E.S.* **3** (1938), 67-82.

39 ¹ Tansley, *Britain's Green Mantle*, 97.

² *P.N.D.*, 8.

40 ¹ Collingwood and Myres, *Roman
Britain and the English Settlements*, 312.
The migration was strong between
450 and 550, but had begun earlier.
Also Stenton, *Anglo-Saxon England*,
5n.

41 ¹ Stenton, 63. Stenton takes the
view that this victory carried the
Saxons "at least as far as the hills
which form the natural boundary
between Somerset and Devon."

² Alexander identifies *Hehil* as near
the Camel estuary, about half-way
down the north coast of Cornwall
(*D.A.* **64** (1932), 171), but Stenton
places it on the Hayle, 36 miles farther
on.

³ *D.A.* **71** (1939), 113.

42 ¹ J. J. Alexander, esp. in *D.A.* **64**
(1932), 75-112 and **71** (1939), 112-16.

² *D.A.* **64** (1932), 170-1.

³ ibid., 91, 103-4.

⁴ *P.N.D.*, xvii.

44 ¹ *D.A.* **71** (1939), 115. A "minster"
was established at Crediton in 739.

² William of Malmesbury, *De Antiquitate Glastoniensis Ecclesiae* (printed in
Hearne's edition of Adam of Domer-
ham, 1727), 52, 97.

³ Cf. Stenton, *Anglo-Saxon England*,
233.

45 ¹ *D.A.* **54** (1922), 193-6.

² The authority for this grant is
William of Malmesbury, op. cit., 68,
98.

47 ¹ *P.N.D.*, xxiii, 248; Finberg,
Tavistock Abbey, 31-2.

² Crooke is from the British *cruc*, "a
hill," but the settlements themselves
are low-lying.

³ See Fleure, *The Races of England
and Wales*, 54-5, 102.

48 ¹ Cf. Fleure, illust., 104-5.

² Beddoe, *The Races of Britain*. 258.

³ Cf. *Domesday Book and Beyond*, 15.

⁴ See *D.S.*, 300-10, for a fuller discussion of the early Saxon villages in
Devon.

PAGE

49 [1] See *D.S.*, 265-88.

[2] ibid., 312-14.

50 [1] See above, p. 44. The Burghal Hidage, probably drawn up between 911 and 919, suggests that a portion of Cornwall was included in Devon. *D.A.* **56** (1924), 271-2.

[2] Stenton, *Anglo-Saxon England*, 289. The evolution of the hundred in Devon is discussed by Alexander in *D.A.* **71** (1939), 117-18.

[3] Stenton, 295.

[4] Alexander, loc. cit., 118.

52 [1] A *regio* based on Crediton, far greater than the hundred of Crediton that was subsequently created, can be discerned. Another *regio*, extending all the way from the Dart to the Plym, was known as *Homme* and was the subject of a charter by Ethelwulf, king of the West Saxons, in 846. There was also a *regio* of Lifton, which included a good deal of land on the Cornish side of the Tamar. See *D.A.* **74** (1942), 237-61 (Crediton); *D.A.* **61** (1929), 249-80 (Homme); and *D.A.* **78** (1946), 268-9 (Lifton).

[2] See *D.A.* **56** (1924), 264-5. Mrs. Rose-Troup's later suggestion of Wiggaton, a hamlet in Ottery St. Mary, accompanied by much circumstantial detail about the battle, may be safely dismissed. *D.A.* **71** (1939), 216-18.

[3] Stenton, *Anglo-Saxon England*, 370.

53 [1] One chronicler says they entered the mouth of the Exe. As they were making for Exeter in the first place, they may have landed at Topsham which was joined by a Roman road to the city.

54 [1] *P.N.D.*, xxvii.

[2] *D.A.* **72** (1940), 305-31.

55 [1] Alexander, " The Saxon Conquest and Settlement," *D.A.* **64** (1932), 94.

58 [1] See Buckatzsch, " The Geographical Distribution of Wealth in England, 1086-1843," in *Economic History Review*, Second Series **3** (1950), 186.

59 [1] For a detailed list see Finberg,

PAGE

59 " The Boroughs of Devon," in *D.C.N.Q.* **24** (1951), 203-9.

[2] There were 36 such "boroughs" in Cornwall: Henderson, *Essays in Cornish History*, 22.

60 [1] See the map of medieval markets and fairs in *D.S.*, facing p. 224.

61 [1] Buckatzsch, loc. cit., 186-7.

64 [1] Figures calculated from the P.R.O. Lay Subsidies for Devon (hundreds of Fremington, Colyton, East Budleigh, and Axminster, and the boroughs of Exeter, Plymouth and Plympton.)

65 [1] The figures are given in Polwhele, iii, 495n.

[2] These figures are calculated from the Devon hearth tax returns at the P.R.O., mainly from those for 1674.

66 [1] For the technical differences between kerseys (an " Old Drapery ") and serges (a " New Drapery ") see Lipson, *History of the English Woollen and Worsted Industries*, esp. 21-6, 130. Briefly, kerseys were a coarse cloth, serges a cloth of fine texture.

[2] Westcote, 60-1, writing about 1630, says that " the late made stuff of serges, or perpetuanos, is now in great use and request with us." For Tiverton, see Dunsford, *Historical Memoirs of Tiverton*, 201-2.

69 [1] According to Polwhele there were reckoned to be 1733 villages—by which he means hamlets also—in Devon in his day (*Hist. Devon*, i, 312).

70 [1] *D.S.*, 317-18.

[2] ibid., 316.

[3] In *D.S.*, 322-3, I have expressed the view that in many instances the creation of new farms in the "waste" may have meant in practice the permanent occupation, in severalty, of outfield which had long been intermittently occupied and tilled.

71 [1] " Studies in Family History: Sokespitch," *D.S.*, 105-19.

73 [1] *D.S.*, 328-9.

[2] *General View of the County of Devon*, 65.

[3] *D.S.*, 332-3.

74 [1] Fraser, *General View of the County of Devon*, 16-20.

[2] B.M. Add. MS. 9427, fol. 96. Lysons Correspondence.

[3] *White's Directory* (1850) says "about 8000 freeholders" were entitled to vote. Polwhele's figure (i, 312) of 18,000 seems to be a misprint.

75 [1] Vivian, *Visitations of Devon*, 243. Reginald died in 1194 and was buried at Ford Abbey.

76 [1] The earliest spellings of Cruwys are always *de Crues*, and the likeliest place of origin is *Cruys-straete*, in Nord department to-day, but formerly in Flanders. For the Norman homes of Devon landowners see *D.A.* **71** (1939), 283-7 (and map).

[2] Finberg, *Tavistock Abbey*, 63-4.

77 [1] ibid., 8-9.

[2] The Fulfords paid, until recent years, ten shillings a year rent to the Earl of Devon (Courtenay) for Fulford, in lieu of all service.

78 [1] For Bremridge: Polwhele, ii, 89 n.; Lysons, clxxxvi. For Dowrish: *R.H.*, 82; Pole, 226.

[2] *Devon Fines*, nos. 281, 323, 677.

79 [1] E.g. Chilton, near Thorverton, nearly 700 acres, contained 88 acres of demesne in 1317 and the rest was divided among the ten free tenants. P.R.O., C. 134. File 58/17 (John de Furneaux). Matford, near Alphington, had nine free tenants in 1301, and no others.

[2] Extracts from the MS. were given in *D.A.* **26** (1894), " Furse of Moreshead." The MS. is now lost, and all my efforts to find it have failed.

81 [1] B.M. Add. Ch. 13178. Accounts of officers of the Marquess of Exeter, 28 Henry VIII [1536-7].

[2] I.P.M. Henry, Marquess of Exeter, 13 March 1538-39. Transcript in *D.C.R.S.* library, Exeter.

[3] *Valor Eccles.*, ii, 289-91 (Bishop); 292-5 (Dean and Chapter).

[4] These figures represent the gross value of their Devonshire properties alone.

82 [1] The earliest record of the Dinhams in Devon is a charter of 1122. See *D.A.* **50** (1918), 431-92, " The Last of the Dynhams."

[2] *P.R.O.*, Lay Subsidies, E. 179, 97/186, 99/307, 100/342.

83 [1] I am indebted to Miss Joyce Youings for these figures, taken from her thesis, " The Disposal of Monastic Property in Land in Devon, 1536-58." The Devon monasteries include Ford Abbey in this instance, now in Dorset but then in Devon.

84 [1] I.P.M. George Rolle, 1553. Transcript in the *D.C.R.S.* Library, Exeter.

[2] Prince, 632. The Petres had strong Catholic affinities in the 17th century.

[3] *Letters and Papers of Henry VIII*, *passim*.

85 [1] Westcote, 119, 435.

[2] Prince, 652.

86 [1] *Early Tours*, 105 (Tour of the Grand Duke of Tuscany in 1669).

[2] Watkin, *The House of Stuart and the Cary Family*, 1-13.

[3] *Calendar of Committee for Compounding, passim*. It is not clear from the calendar what fine Sir Thomas Hele eventually paid, as one-quarter was later added to it because of his slowness in paying. He was also ordered to pay interest on the whole from the date of its being fixed.

87 [1] Lysons, lxxxii b.

[2] See the list of gentry and their residences given in the appendix to Risdon's *Survey of Devon*, 1811 edn., 19-22.

88 [1] These are the revised figures in Bateman, *Great Landowners of Great Britain* (1883), 385, but the 1873 return gave 45,088 acres worth £70,586 p.a.

[2] The 1873 return gave 17,047 acres for Lord Poltimore. It gave 16,904 acres for Mr. F. L. Knight but Bateman's revised figure for his Devonshire lands is only 5,721.

[3] The figures are given to the nearest thousand acres. A closer approxima-

88 tion is impossible because of the nature of the return.

90 [1] *P.R.O.*, various Devon rentals and surveys.

[2] Finberg, *Tavistock Abbey*, 252.

[3] *P.R.O.*, Rentals and Surveys. S.C. 11, Roll 168 (Stokenham); Woburn MSS., rental of 1588 (Bishops Clyst).

91 [1] Cathedral Library, Exeter. D. & C. MSS. No. 1902 (1661 Survey), No. 1889 (1675 note).

[2] Bedford Estate Office, Tavistock. Various surveys, 1726.

[3] For fuller details of these changes see my note on The Occupation of Land in Devonshire, 1650-1800, in *D.C.N.Q.* **21** (1940-1), 2-12.

[4] Exeter City Library. Survey of the estates of John Courtenay of Molland, Esq., 1740. Fines for other farms on the Courtenay estate varied from ten to fourteen times the annual value according to the particular circumstances of the farm.

92 [1] Vancouver, 82. The entry fine had risen on the Duke of Bedford's estates also, from 12 years' purchase in 1726 to 18 years' in 1804. Bedford Papers, loc. cit.

[2] Cash Book of Sir Courtenay Pole, 1658-65 (in my possession), fol. 71.

[3] For the general rebuilding of farmhouses and buildings between 1570 and 1640, see Ch. XIV.

93 [1] F. W. Morgan " Domesday Geography of Devon," *D.A.* **72** (maps). The densities for cattle, sheep, etc., are of demesne animals only. We have no information about the peasants' livestock.

[2] Morgan, 322-3.

[3] The figures are calculated from the *Valor Ecclesiasticus* for the parishes of Uplyme, Combpyne, Rousdon, Musbury, and Branscombe. The total corn tithe was valued at £24 15s. 4d., and the wool and lamb tithes at £22 13s. 4d.

[4] Finberg, *Tavistock Abbey*, esp. 113-15.

94 [1] *P.R.O.*, Assize roll, Devon, 1249, m. 29.

[2] Finberg, 89-91.

[3] *P.R.O.*, Ministers' Accounts, Earldom of Devon, S.C. 6. Bdle. 827, No. 39, Michaelmas 15 Edward I.

[4] Finberg, *Tavistock Abbey*, 138.

95 [1] Finberg, *Tavistock Abbey*, 158, on which the substance of this paragraph is based.

[2] *D.A.* **47** (1915), 346-7.

[3] ibid., 344.

[4] This often-quoted remark was heard by Aubrey. It may be found in the Bodleian MS. Aubrey 2, fol. 83. But Cromwell had actually seen little of Devon, and that mainly the best parts around Crediton and Exeter.

[5] See Finberg, 91-4, 107-9.

96 [1] Hooker, loc. cit.

98 [1] For this and certain other information I am indebted to a valuable paper on " Four Centuries of Farming Systems in Devon : 1500-1900," by G. E. Fussell, *D.A.* **83** (1951), 179-204.

[2] Devon county records, The Castle, Exeter. Land tax assessments, 1780-1832.

99 [1] Tanner, *Journal of Royal Agric. Soc. of England*, 1848; Caird, *English Agriculture in 1850-51*, 48-56.

[2] I have attempted a history, from the limited materials that are available, in *D.S.*, 419-41, " The Farm Labourer through Four Centuries."

[3] Heath, *The English Peasantry*, has a chapter on " The Work of Canon Girdlestone."

100 [1] For the condition of labourers at Halberton in these years, see Heath, 162 *seq.*

[2] Heath, *British Rural Life and Labour*, 295-7.

101 [1] See Appendix I to the *Land Utilisation Survey, Part 92, Devonshire*. The arable acreage given on p. 488 of the report (742,115 acres), is an error.

[2] ibid., 490.

[3] ibid., 492-3.

[4] *Rural England*, i, 175-217.

102 [1] ibid., 192.

102   ² Land Util. Survey, Devon, Appendix I.

103   ¹ For the position of Devon farming to-day, see Ch. XVI, 302-4. This account of wartime changes is based on the annual agricultural returns of the Ministry of Agriculture and Fisheries, supplied to me by the Devon County Planning Department.

104   ¹ *D.A.* **65** (1933), 140.

105   ¹ See Finberg, " The Boroughs of Devon," *D.C.N.Q.* **24** (1951), 203-9.

107   ¹ For details of the 15th-century towns see *D.S.*, 229-31.

108   ¹ P.R.O. Lay Subsidies, E. 179. 97/186 and 99/307.

      ² If we include the suburban parishes of St. Edmund and St. Leonard there were 64 payers in Exeter, with a total assessment of £6,800.

109   ¹ Russell, *Dartmouth* (1950), 61. Figure based on the port-books for 1565 at the P.R.O.

110   ¹ Philip Bere, the squire, was assessed at £40. The Beres had been squires here since the beginning of the 14th century.

111   ¹ Quoted in Weinbaum, *The Incorporation of Boroughs*, 8-9.

      ² Weinbaum, *British Borough Charters*, 1307-1660, 27-8.

      ³ Weinbaum, *The Incorporation of Boroughs*, 127-30. Bideford has always been given as 1574 hitherto, but Weinbaum shows (*British Borough Charters*, 22-3) that it should be 1573.

112   ¹ Weinbaum's lists in *The Incorporation of Boroughs*. Incorporations after 1700 are not included.

113   ¹ Caldwell, " Devonshire from the accession of Queen Elizabeth until the English Civil War " (MS. thesis, Yale University Library). I am indebted to the University for permission to see this thesis.

      ² *Exeter City Records*, 376; Rogers, *Ships and Shipyards of Bideford*, 21.

114   ¹ I have used *Early Tours* as the source for all quotations from these writings.

115   ¹ The change in the respective

115   standing of the two ports must have come about since 1667, when Barnstaple's taxable capacity was practically twice that of Bideford.

117   ¹ Polwhele, ii, 215; Sheldon, *From Trackway to Turnpike*, 117.

      ² Sheldon, loc. cit.

      ³ *Early Tours*, 237.

118   ¹ *Early Tours*, 241.

      ² Lysons, 289.

119   ¹ Chanter, *Lynton and Countisbury*, 31.

121   ¹ *White's Directory*, 1890.

122   ¹ See Walling, *Story of Plymouth*, 197-8.

124   ¹ See Chapter XIV on Building and Building Materials.

      ² *Pipe Roll Society* **51** (New Series **13**), xx.

      ³ *Cal. Close Rolls*, 1253-4, 176. The Totnes records throw no earlier light on this industry, though the name of Thomas le fulur occurs in the earliest Totnes Guild Roll about this time. Watkin, i, 67.

      ⁴ Carus-Wilson, "An Industrial Revolution of the Thirteenth Century," *Econ. Hist. Rev.* **11** (1941), 39 *seq.*

125   ¹ *D.A.* **44** (1912), 569; *Econ. Hist. Rev.* **11** (1941), 49; *Barnstaple Records*, i, 110, 115. The Honiton and Tiverton references are in extents of Baldwin de Redvers' lands at the P.R.O. (C. 132/3/10).

      ² Some of the Devon aulnage accounts were examined by Chanter, " The Aulnager in Devon," *D.A.* **44** (1912), 568-96. These accounts have been criticised by Miss Carus-Wilson in *Econ. Hist. Review* **2** (1929), 114 *seq.* Some of them were undoubtedly faked by the officials concerned. The Devon accounts need re-examination in the light of this criticism.

      ³ *D.A.* **44** (1912), 581.

126   ¹ Strictly speaking, the founder of the Creedy Park family was John Davie, fourth son of Robert, who was an Exeter merchant and three times mayor of the city (1584, 1594, 1604). But he owed his start to his father's Crediton fortune. Gilbert, second son

126 of Robert, founded another landed family at Canonteign, in Christow parish.

² Chanter, 586; Heaton, *Yorkshire Woollen and Worsted Industries*, 85.

³ Schanz, *Englische Handelspolitik gegen Ende des Mittelalters* (1881), from tables based on the Enrolled Customs Accounts in the P.R.O. The port of Exeter-Dartmouth included all the Devon ports except Plymouth at this date.

⁴ Plymouth-Fowey included all the Cornish ports besides Plymouth, but almost the whole of the cloth trade from this group of ports centred on Plymouth, which was the outlet for the Tavistock district.

127 ¹ Dunsford, *Historical Memoirs of Tiverton*, 346-50.

128 ¹ Dunsford, 201-2. The last kersey was made about 1710.

² For a fuller account, see my *Industry, Trade, and People in Exeter*, 1688-1800, esp. 30-61, 66-74.

³ ibid., 74.

129 ¹ Dunsford, 235-6, note 165.

² Dunsford, 230-2. This was in 1749.

³ Dunsford, 460-1. The poor rate in 1720 was £946 4s. 11½d., in 1780 £2,274 6s. 10d. In 1788 the poor rates totalled £3,394 9s. 2d.

⁴ Bodleian Library, MS. Top. Devon. b. 1-2 (Milles MSS.).

130 ¹ Hoskins, *Industry, Trade, etc.*, 82-6.

² *White's Directory* (1850), 44.

³ Information from the Devon County Planning Department, Exeter, based on a survey of 1948.

131 ¹ Finberg, "The Stannary of Tavistock," in *D.A.* **81** (1949), 155-84.

² It has been suggested that the Jews may have taken the initiative in this new industry. The old smelting-houses on Dartmoor were traditionally known as "Jews' Houses." (ibid., 157-8).

³ A thousandweight was 1,200 lb.

⁴ Lewis, *The Stannaries*, app. J, gives

131 figures of tin production for Devon and Cornwall from 1156 to 1806.

132 ¹ The parish gild of St. Pancras of Widecombe either received gifts of metal or invested funds in the tin-works (*D.A.* **81** (1949), 172, 174, 178). It appears in the Coinage Roll of 1523 together with a number of men whom one recognises as Widecombe men.

² Lysons, cclxxxi.

133 ¹ Westcote, 53.

² Cf. *Early Tours in Devon and Cornwall*, 25, 53; but neither of these references relates to Devon. Salzman (*English Industries of the Middle Ages*, 66n.) quotes an example of a deep tin mine near Truro in the first quarter of the 16th century.

³ *D.A.* **72** (1940), 201-50. Lysons, cclxxxi, gives a list of 25 abandoned tin mines.

⁴ See the account of lode-mining in Carew's *Survey of Cornwall* (1602), 8-11.

134 ¹ Pipe Roll Society **44** (New Series **6**), 126.

² *D.A.* **81** (1949), 19. Finberg, *Tavistock Abbey*, 183-4.

135 ¹ The roll is given in full by Finberg, *D.A.* **81** (1949), 173-82.

² Lewis, *The Stannaries*, 77, 88, 192.

136 ¹ Salzman, *English Industries of the Middle Ages*, 56-7; Lewis, 192-4.

² Salzman, 52.

³ Lewis, 195-6.

⁴ Nor does Leland mention them, though he speaks of Bere. He could hardly have failed to do so had they been working.

⁵ *White's Directory* (1890), 78.

137 ¹ *D.C.N.Q.* **7** (1912-13), 54-5, from an account written by Stephen Atkinson in 1619. He had been employed by Sir Bevis Bulmer in refining silver at Combe Martin and had had access to an old account-book at Bere Ferrers for the period 1485-90.

² *Letters and Papers of Henry VIII*, vol. xii, part ii, 354.

³ *D.A.* **2** (1867-8), 194, gives the date as 1593. Jewitt and Hope's *Corporation Plate* gives 1594. The London

PAGE

137 cup was melted down in 1643 and made into three tankards, which still survive though they were re-made in 1731-2.

138 [1] Lysons, cclxxxvii; *D.C.N.Q.* **9** (1916-17), 128.

[2] Lysons, cclxxxiii.

139 [1] Bedford estate papers, Tavistock. Mining account, 1845-78.

[2] Mackail, *The Life of William Morris* (World's Classics ed.), 14-15.

[3] *White's Directory*, 1890, 76-7.

[4] *D.A.* **77** (1945), 169; *D.A.* **46** (1914), 263.

140 [1] Westcote, 65.

[2] White, loc. cit.

[3] Lysons, cclxxxix-ccxc.

[4] Hoskins, *Industry, Trade, etc.*, 49-50; Lysons, ccxcii.

[5] Robert Sture of Bovey Tracey "collyor" is referred to in an enrolled deed of 1541. Celia Fiennes mentions Bovey "coal" in 1698.

[6] Fishing is treated in Chapter XI under Maritime History. I am indebted to the Institute of Historical Research for the loan of unpublished Victoria County History material on the lace, carpet, and pottery industries, to which I have added material of my own.

141 [1] Moore, *History of Devonshire*, i, 564-6.

[2] *Report on the Honiton Lace Industry*, 1887.

142 [1] Moore, i, 568n.

[2] See the autobiography of Thomas Whitty in *D.A.* **21** (1889), 331-7.

[3] Moore, i, 562.

[4] This account of the paper industry in Devon is based on two articles by A. H. Shorter in *D.C.N.Q.* **23** (1948), 97-103, 193-8.

143 [1] "Notes on North Devon Pottery." *D.A.* **38** (1906), 255-60.

[2] Lysons, ccxci.

[3] *White's Directory*, 1890, 564.

144 [1] See *Econ. Hist. Review*, Second Series **1** (1948), 20-33, and *D.A.* **44** (1912), 382-93, " Plymouth China."

PAGE

144 [2] Honey, *English Pottery and Porcelain*, 196-7.

[3] *Devon and Cornwall: Preliminary Survey*, 97-8.

145 [1] The highway returns of 1814 show that there were then 6,712 miles of road for wheeled carriages. In 1839 money was expended for the maintenance and repair of 6,898 miles of road. (*White's Directory*, 1890, 18.)

[2] "Ancient Highways of Devon." *Archaeological Journal* **98** (1941), 131-64.

147 [1] For the dating of bridges, I have used Henderson's *Old Devon Bridges*, supplemented by *Place-Names of Devon*.

[2] For Teignbridge as a hundred name in 1086, see *The Devonshire Domesday*, vol. i, p. xii. Davidson, " Remarks on Old Teign Bridge," in *D.A.* **16** (1884), 444-52, gives details of the discoveries of 1815. There are difficulties about accepting the oldest bridge as Roman, but the subject as a whole needs careful re-examination.

148 [1] Sheldon, *From Trackway to Turnpike*, 50; *Letters of John Shillingford*, ed. Stuart Moore, Camden Society, New Series **2** (1871), 67.

[2] See, for example, the remarkable tour of Bishop Bronescombe in the autumn of 1259. In the space of thirty days he dedicated no fewer than twenty-one churches all over Cornwall. (*Reg. Bronescombe, Quivil, and Bytton*, xi-xii.) Stapeldon's diocesan journeys between 1307 and 1326 are also illuminating (*Reg. Stapeldon*, 547-60).

150 [1] Quoted by Sheldon, op. cit., from Baring-Gould, *Old Country Life*, 215.

[2] *D.N.Q.* **2** (1902-03), 120.

[3] Sheldon, 78-9, 101-2.

[4] Sheldon, 83. In 1635 the London-Plymouth road had been established as one of the eight main running post roads. The 1672 Act established a riding-post over the same road. It now took only 4-6 days to send a letter from Plymouth to London and get a reply.

151   [1] Sheldon, 149-50, quoting Cary's *Coach Directory* (1819).

152   [1] For the Plymouth roads, see Worth, 335-8. The Barnstaple turnpike trust (1763-1880) is dealt with in *D.A.* **74** (1942), 139-67. A good account of the Exeter trust (1753-1884) is given by Buckingham, *A Turnpike Key.* Okehampton trust, *D.A.* **68** (1936), 307-23.

[2] In 1829 the Barnstaple and Exeter trusts agreed to make the new valley road between them, meeting at Eggesford. The Exeter portion was opened in 1831 (Buckingham, 28, 30).

[3] S. and B. Webb, *The King's Highway*, 225.

[4] Carrington, " Parochiales Bridfordii ": MS. in City Library, Exeter, written about 1840.

153   [1] Sheldon, 170.

[2] *Kelly's Directory*, 1935, 236, 514.

154   [1] *H.M.C. City of Exeter Records*, 289; Hooker, *History of Exeter*, 757-8.

[2] Delderfield, *Exmouth Milestones*, 91.

[3] *Earldom of Cornwall Accounts*, 1296-7 (Camden Soc. 3rd Series **68**), ii, 216; B.M. Harleian MS. 6126, inquisition on the lands of Edmund, Earl of Cornwall, 1300.

155   [1] *Early Tours*, 222.

[2] ibid., 155.

[3] Whitfield, *Plymouth and Devonport in Times of War and Peace*, 370.

156   [1] This account of the canals is based largely on Lysons, cclx-cclxi.

[2] *White's Directory*, 1850, 398.

[3] *D.A.* **78** (1946), 153-60, " The Old Heytor Granite Railway."

157   [1] MacDermot, *History of the Great Western Railway*, ii, 166.

[2] Details of these abortive schemes are given in Vancouver, *General View of the Agriculture of Devon*, 372-83.

[3] Parts of the Exeter-Crediton canal were cut, and may still be seen, but it never came into use.

[4] For this canal see Leeson Day, *Holsworthy*, 37-8.

158   [1] This account is based on Worth,

158   *History of Plymouth*, 338, and Moore, *History of Devonshire*, i, 488-9.

[2] Worth, 338.

159   [1] For the details of the route, see the O.S. 2½-inch maps, sheets 20/55 and 20/56.

[2] A full account of the proceedings in connection with this railway is given in *D.A.* **34** (1902), 168-200.

160   [1] Except where otherwise stated, the following pages are based on MacDermot's *History of the Great Western Railway.*

[2] MacDermot, ii, 195.

162   [1] The Millbay terminus involved the demolition of the Royal Union Baths, a valuable amenity to the town, built in 1828.

[2] For the mechanical details of this extraordinary idea, see MacDermot, ii, 199 ff.

[3] A list is given by MacDermot, ii, 211.

[4] The somewhat complicated details of these manoeuvres are given by MacDermot, ii, 145-51.

164   [1] See MacDermot, ii, 348-50.

[2] The South Western was bound by an agreement of October 1862 not to promote or assist any new line in the South Devon's territory, which was defined by a line running roughly east-west immediately south of Okehampton.

[3] C. F. D. Marshall, *History of the Southern Railway*, 157.

[4] So says *White's Directory* for 1890, but Marshall (op. cit., 174) says that the whole line from Lydford to Devonport was opened in 1890.

166   [1] Ellis, *General Introduction to Domesday Book* (1833); Burnard, *D.A.* **39** (1907), 202-3.

167   [1] Russell, *British Medieval Population*, 313.

168   [1] F. W. Morgan in *D.A.* **72** (1940), 305-31.

[2] ibid, 316. Morgan has calculated all his figures per thousand acres in order to maintain uniformity with similar studies in other counties.   I

PAGE

168 have not attempted to translate his figures back into square miles.

169 [1] P.R.O., Enrolled Accounts, E. 359/8.

[2] Russell, op. cit., 139.

[3] Coulton, *Medieval Panorama*, 496; Pickard, *Population and Epidemics of Exeter*, 22-8.

[4] *Reg. Lacy*, ii, 780-7. These depositions are summarised in Oliver, *Eccles. Antiq.*, i, 103-5.

170 [1] *Dartmoor Preservation Association Publications*, i, 21; Lewis, *The Stannaries*, 156, 253.

[2] Rich, "The Population of Elizabethan England," *Econ. Hist. Review*, Second Series, 2 (1950), 247-65. Mr. Rich prints a total of 13,610 (loc. cit., 254) but this seems to be a slip for 14,610, the "sum total" entered at the end of the record. The muster, a very full one with names, will be found at the P.R.O., S.P. 12/57/1.

[3] I am indebted to Mr. G. Poole for arriving at this figure for me.

171 [1] The figures I have given for these parishes are taken from transcripts of Devon parish registers in the D.C.R.S. library, Exeter.

172 [1] The Protestation Returns are in the House of Lords Library. They are nearly complete for Devon, the largest gap being for East Budleigh hundred. The Hearth-Tax Returns are in the Public Record Office.

[2] I owe these figures to the kindness of Mr. C. A. F. Meekings of the P.R.O., who has made a special study of the Hearth-Tax Returns.

173 [1] Branscombe, 40 per cent.; Clyst St. George, 61 per cent.; Hemyock, 65 per cent.; Huntsham, 53 per cent.; Lustleigh, 72 per cent.; Parkham, 60 per cent.; Parracombe, 51 per cent.

174 [1] The contemporary return gives 58,106 inhabited houses and 343,076 people, but these figures were corrected later.

[2] The census figure of 6,505 includes the large rural parish also. In 1790

PAGE

174 the town alone had 5,343 people: Dunsford, *Historical Memoirs of Tiverton*, 298.

175 [1] *D.A.* **34** (1902), 49.

[2] Hattersley, *The British Settlement of Natal* (1950), 171-3. Altogether, 235 persons embarked at Plymouth for Natal in the three years 1849-51.

177 [1] *Devon and Cornwall: a Preliminary Survey*, 17.

178 [1] *D.A.* **72** (1940), 118; *D.A.* **65** (1933), 143-4.

179 [1] *D.A.* **62** (1930), 159-60.

[2] ibid., 159. The six are Lydford, South Molton, Crediton, Bradninch, Fremington, and Modbury. The solitary return for Fremington (1332) is in any event dubious.

[3] *D.A.* **72** (1940), 120.

[4] *D.A.* **69** (1937), 159-60.

180 [1] ibid., 161, 173, 175. The only exception to the rule at Totnes was Sir Lewis Pollard, the judge, whose home was at King's Nympton in north Devon.

[2] *D.A.* **32** (1900), 438-9 (Totnes); **72** (1940), 251-7 (Barnstaple).

[3] For the county names from 1529 to 1601, see *D.A.* **47** (1915), 365-71.

[4] Neale, *The Elizabethan House of Commons*, 143-4. *D.A.* **41** (1909), 152-78, gives an account of Bere Alston's parliamentary history.

[5] See the map at the end of Neale, op. cit.

181 [1] Neale, 196-7.

[2] Neale, 201. The earl was recorder of the borough, and very much on the spot.

[3] *D.A.* **19** (1887), 649-74. There is still room, however, for a more thorough inquiry into the parliamentary history of Plympton.

[4] *D.A.* **32** (1900), 439-440.

182 [1] Dunsford, 453-4; *D.A.* **67** (1935), 315-47, for Tiverton members, 1620-1832.

[2] This section on the county 1603-1832 is based on J. J. Alexander's articles on the Devon members in *D.A.* **48, 49,** and **50.**

183   [1] Alexander, in *D.A.* **49** (1917), 368.

184   [1] Russell, *Dartmouth*, 138-9; *D.A.* **43** (1911), 353-7.

    [2] *D.A.* loc. cit., 356.

    [3] *Report of the Comm. on Municipal Corporations*, 1835, under Dartmouth.

185   [1] *D.A.* loc. cit., 357

186   [1] *D.A.* **28** (1896), 227.

    [2] Hoskins, *Industry, Trade, and People in Exeter*, 44-5; Dunsford, *Historical Memoirs of Tiverton*, 451 n.

    [3] Some valuable material from the Harrowby (Ryder) papers was printed in *Notes and Queries*, Jan.-April 1936, under the heading of " Tiverton Letters and Papers, 1724-1843."

187   [1] *D.A.* **66** (1934), 253-78, for Honiton's political history.

    [2] ibid., 254.

188   [1] *D.A.* **66** (1934), 258-9, 269-71.

    [2] Walling, *Story of Plymouth*, 216-7. Also, Select Ctee. on Plymouth Election Petition, 1853, Minutes of Evidence. Totnes was a fitting scene for the Man in the Moon's activities, as corrupt a borough as could still be found. There is a report from a Select Committee on the Totnes election of 1852 also.

189   [1] I am indebted to Mr. G. Poole for preparing for me all the data of Devon election results since 1832, on which this section is based.

    [2] The Conservative figure includes, however, Mr. C. J. Mare who was unseated for corrupt practices. A Liberal-Conservative was elected in his place in 1853.

192   [1] Will of Sir John Fulford, P.C.C. Alen 10, dated 11 July 1544.

    [2] The lists will be found in the published *Patent Rolls*, from which I have derived these names and numbers.

    [3] For the list see *D.A.* **8** (1876), 521-5.

193   [1] Some of the judicial activities of the quarter sessions are discussed below in Chapter XIII on Social History.

    [2] Hamilton, 114-15.

194   [1] Unpublished thesis, " The De-

194   velopment of Quarter Sessions Government in Devon in the Nineteenth Century and the Transition to County Council Government " (Univ. of London Library).

    [2] Tucker, 6.

    [3] Tucker, 171-7.

    [4] Tucker, 180, quoting *The Flying Post*, 28 June 1882.

195   [1] Simmons, " The Civil War in the West," in *The West in English History*, ed. A. L. Rowse, 84-5.

196   [1] Coate, *Cornwall in the Civil War*, 33.

    [2] The accounts are transcribed in *D.A.* **17** (1885), 215-39.

197   [1] Sprigg (1854 edn.), 157-8.

    [2] For the details, see Sprigg, 192 *seq.*

198   [1] Hamilton, 141.

    [2] Walling, 275-82.

199   [1] For fuller accounts of the Devonshire Regiment see chiefly Jeremy Taylor, *The Devons* (Bristol, 1951), *The Bloody Eleventh* (*Histories of the Regiments of the British Army*, ed. Wolmer White, London, n.d.) and Cannon, *Historical Records of the British Army* (*11th Foot*) (London, 1845). Also to the point are Walrond, *Historical Records of the 1st Devon Militia* (London, 1897) and Benson Freeman, *The Yeomanry of Devon* (London, 1927).

201   [1] Oliver, *Monasticon*, 40b.

    [2] Another version gives Dartmouth 357 men, instead of 757, and yet another version gives Exmouth 293 men. The copy of the roll at Cruwys Morchard House also inserts Ilfracombe, 8 ships, 62 men.

202   [1] *D.S.*, 222-5.

    [2] Russell, *Dartmouth*, **17**. The London ships numbered 13, Hull 11, Bristol 9.

    [3] Russell, 18. For piracy, see Kingsford, *Prejudice and Promise in Fifteenth-Century England*, essay on West-country Piracy.

203   [1] *D.S.*, 230-1.

    [2] The detailed statistics are given in Schanz, *Englische Handelspolitik gegen Ende des Mittelalters*, 2 vols. (1881).

    [3] B. M. Harl. MS. 306, ff. 32-6.

I have rounded off the figures to the nearest £ in the text.

⁴ P.R.O., State Papers Domestic, S.P. 12/30/8. Customs and subsidies on woollen cloths and wines, 1559-63.

204 ¹ P.R.O., Exchequer Special Commissions, E. 178/2880. 8 Eliz. (1565).

² These and subsequent figures are taken from unpublished V.C.H. material on the Maritime History of Devon, by M. Oppenheim.

205 ¹H.M.C. Exeter City Records, 376. The J. W. referred to is possibly John Wolcott, merchant, who was mayor in 1565.

² Oppenheim, loc. cit.

207 ¹ D.A. 33 (1901), 41.

² ibid., 46-7.

³ D.A. 46 (1914), 325.

⁴ " Sir John Davie, 5th Baronet of Creedy ": D.A. 36 (1904), 116-22.

208 ¹ For further details, see my Industry, Trade, and People in Exeter, esp. 90-1, 161-2.

² Russell, 82, 95 ff. The Butterwalk was badly bombed in 1943, but is to be rebuilt in its former style.

³ For a brief survey of the trade of the Devonshire ports in 1714-17, see D.S. 405-8. For an account of the Customs receipts from the Devon ports in 1761-3, see D.C.N.Q. 25 (1953), 39-40. Plymouth had become by far the largest port by this date.

210 ¹ Dartmouth was rejected in 1689 mainly because of the hazards of entering. Falmouth was not surveyed until 1693, but was found to be clogged with shoals and sudden soundings.

² D.S., 104-5.

212 ¹ The foundation charter of Torre Abbey speaks of net-fishing in Tor Bay as early as the 12th cent.

213 ¹ Lysons, ccxcv-ccxcvi, and under the names of the various places; and unpublished V.C.H. material.

214 ¹ V.C.H. Devon, unpub. material; White's Directory, 1850.

² Devon and Cornwall Survey (1939), 141-2.

215 ¹ ibid., 131. The figures are averages for the period 1919-38.

215 ² Finberg, Tavistock Abbey, 159-66.

216 ¹ Hearne, De Antiquitate Glastoniensis Ecclesiae, 69, 70, 99. I owe this reference to Mr. Finberg.

² Oliver, Monasticon, 192.

³ Early Tours, 115.

⁴ Finberg, 161.

217 ¹ Information from the Fisheries Department, Ministry of Agriculture and Fisheries, London.

² Fish entering English ports were exempted from customs duty from 1563, so that one does not get a complete list of the ships in the Newfoundland trade. Only those carrying other cargo as well (such as train oil) would appear in the records.

³ Harte, " Some Evidence of Trade between Exeter and Newfoundland to 1600," D.A., 64 (1932), 475-84. See also Russell, Dartmouth.

⁴ Russell, 71-2. The same system of sharing apparently obtained at Plymouth. (Plymouth Municipal Records, ed. Worth, 6-7.)

218 ¹ Watkins, History of Bideford, 60-1.

² The New England fishermen, on the American side, were exempt from naval service and were thus able to capture a large part of the market for cod while the West Country fishermen were fighting (Russell, 121).

³ Watkins, 68-70.

219 ¹ D.A. 79 (1947), 45.

² Radford, D.A. 79 (1947), 25-6; D.A. 81 (1949), 15-16.

220 ¹ Doble, Four Saints of the Fal (Cornish Saints Series, No. 20), 27-30. St. Kea and St. Fili are closely associated in Cornwall and Brittany also. Ekwall and PND derive Filleigh as a name from topographical sources, overlooking this other possibility. Ide, just outside Exeter, is similarly named after the Celtic saint Ida, to whom the church is still dedicated, and not (as Ekwall and PND both say) after some lost stream-name.

² Chanter, The Church of St. Brannock, Braunton (1934), 4-6.

221 ¹ The subject of church dedications

221 in Devon requires a careful examination afresh. It is full of pitfalls, and only a minute re-examination of the early evidence will be of any value.

² For further evidence, which is not easy to extract, see Canon Doble's *Cornish Saints Series*, especially *St. Petrock* (No. 11), *St. Nectan* (No. 25), *St. Budoc* (No. 3), and *St. Indract and St. Dominic* (No. 48).

222 ¹ The authority for this is a life of St. Indract, printed by Canon Doble in *St. Indract and St. Dominic* (loc. cit.).

² *D.S.*, 29, where the exact date of Lyfing's dual appointment is discussed.

³ The Bishop's Tawton story originates with Hooker in the late 16th cent. See his *Description of the Citie of Excester*, (*D.C.R.S.*, 1919), Pt. II, 223-4. The evidence is critically examined by Chanter, " The First Saxon Bishopric of Exeter," in *D.A.* **7** (1875), 179-96.

223 ¹ For St. Urith see *D.A.* **46** (1914), 290-308. She was born and martyred at Chittlehampton, probably in the early 8th cent.

² The Devon figures are Reichel's calculations in *D.A.* **30** (1898), 279-80. They are based on certain assumptions about the area of the plough-land and cannot be regarded as mathematically accurate, but they reveal the orders of magnitude well enough. My Cornish figures are taken from *The Cornwall Domesday* (*V.C.H.* edn., 1924). Here the bishop is credited with 301 ploughlands out of a total of 2,572, and the ploughland is reckoned at the uniform figure of 120 acres (ibid. 51, 56).

³ Hughes, *The Reformation in England*, i, 31n. Exeter was taxed at 6,000 crowns by the Roman curia, Lincoln and Norwich at 5,000 each.

224 ¹ For the foundation dates of the religious houses, I have followed Knowles, *The Religious Houses of Medieval England* (1940).

² For details, see Ch. XIV on Building and Building Materials.

226 ¹ *Dict. of English Church History*, art. " Exeter, See of."

227 ¹ *Reg. Bronescombe*, 212 (Trusehara, 1272) and *Reg. Quivil*, 364 (Boswythgy, 1283).

228 ¹ *Reg. Stapeldon*, 300-1.

229 ¹ For these and other details see Boggis, *History of the Diocese of Exeter*, 177-8, and *passim*.

230 ¹ Boggis, 160, for these and the following figures.

² Boggis, 167-9.

³ Russell, *British Medieval Population*, 134. Throughout the whole diocese the proportion was 1 in 62: 2,001 clerks to 124,000 lay people.

231 ¹ *The Accounts of the Wardens of the Parish of Morebath, Devon*, 1520-73, transcribed by Rev. J. Erskine Binney (Exeter, 1904).

232 ¹ Finberg, *Tavistock Abbey*, 267n.

234 ¹ Rowse, *Tudor Cornwall*, 282.

² Boggis, 341.

235 ¹ Hooker, 87, says that a thousand were killed on Clyst Heath, but this is certainly an exaggeration.

² *Morebath Accounts*, 185.

236 ¹ *D.S.*, 366-7.

² Oliver, *Collections Illustrative of the Catholic Religion*, 17-19.

³ House of Lords MSS., Devon Protestation returns.

⁴ *Catholic Record Society*, **18** (1916), 36; Polwhele, ii, 44.

⁵ House of Lords MSS., Return of Papists or reputed Papists, 1767.

237 ¹ *D.A.* **9** (1877), 250-91. Worth, " Puritanism in Devon and the Exeter Assembly," from which much of the following account is drawn.

238 ¹ Worth, loc. cit., 264-5. Worth estimates the number actually ejected in Devon at 128.

² Worth, 266.

³ Worth, 269, 276-8.

⁴ For the Bartlets see Wickham, " Early Nonconformity in Bideford," *D.A.* **34** (1902), 410-7.

239 ¹ See principally *D.A.*, esp. **9, 16, 17, 19, 21, 28, 32, 34, 78.**

² *Early Tours*, 157.

³ Boggis, *History of the Diocese of Exeter*, 449-50.

PAGE

239   ⁴ Boggis, 461-2.
240   ¹ Boggis, 477-81.
      ² Boggis, 501.
      ³ For a more sympathetic account of Phillpotts than is usually given, see Boggis, op. cit., 490-515.
241   ¹ For some remarkable stories of Froude, and his nephew Radford, see Boggis, *I Remember* (1947), 178-9. Blackmore, who knew them, painted their portraits in *The Maid of Sker* as Parson Chown and Parson Rambone.
245   ¹ Dunsford, *Historical Memoirs of Tiverton*, 106-67.
246   ¹ *Report of the Charity Commissioners*, iii (1830), 91.
247   ¹ Vincent, *The State and School Education*, 1640-60, 122, gives a list of 29 places in Devon that had schools, to which it is possible to add Okehampton, where a grammar school is known to have existed in 1610 (*D.A.* **57** (1925), 213).
      ² Leach, *The Schools of Medieval England*, 193, 194, 197, 327.
      ³ Finberg, *Tavistock Abbey*, 274-5.
      ⁴ Jones, *The Charity School Movement* (1938), 333-7, 352, gives these numbers, classified by decades for the period 1698-1800.
248   ¹ Diocesan Registry, Exeter, Petitions for Licences.
249   ¹ *Charity Comm.*, i, 13.
      ² *Parliamentary Papers*, 1867-8, xxviii, esp. Part I, Schools Enquiry Commission.
      ³ J. Brooking Rowe, *History of Plympton Erle*, 344.
250   ¹ Vincent, 9-10.
      ² *D.A.* **17** (1885), 246-65.
251   ¹ Hamilton, *Quarter Sessions from Queen Elizabeth to Queen Anne*, 30-1.
      ² ibid., 33-4.
252   ¹ ibid., 113.
      ² ibid., 28-9.
253   ¹ *D.S.*, 436.
      ² See Hamilton, 177-82, 221.
      ³ B.M. Add. MS. 30,077.
254   ¹ Hamilton, 227-40, quotes from MS. letters written by Mr. Northmore to Richard Coffin, the sheriff. These

PAGE

254   letters were then preserved at Portledge.
      ² Dunsford, *Historical Memoirs of Tiverton*, 57-9.
255   ¹ Polwhele, ii, 216n.
      ² Delderfield, *Exmouth Milestones*, 35-41.
      ³ ibid., 39.
256   ¹ Walling, *Story of Plymouth*, 181-2.
      ² Walling, 180. For a further discussion of the Plymouth painters see Ch. XV.
      ³ ibid., 186-7.
259   ¹ I am indebted to my friend Mr. A. W. Everett for this information. The west doorway of the Saxon church of St. George in Exeter (revealed by the air raid of 1942) was made up of pieces of Beer stone from a Roman building.
      ² Howe, *Geology of Building Stones* (1910), 262-3.
260   ¹ Oliver, *Lives of the Bishops of Exeter*, 390.
261   ¹ *Report on the Geology of Cornwall, Devon, etc.*, 487-8.
      ² " The Quarries of Salcombe Regis," *D.C.N.Q.* **17** (1933).
      ³ Oliver, 384, 387, citing the Fabric Rolls of the cathedral.
262   ¹ Oliver, *History of Exeter*, 1861 edn., 86n.
263   ¹ Some account of these " Devonshire marbles " is given in *D.A.* **7** (1878), 217-19, 236-8.
      ² Westcote, 66-7.
      ³ *D.A.* **57** (1925), 282.
      ⁴ I.P.M. Richard de Bello Campo. D.C.R.S. Library, Exeter.
264   ¹ Lysons, ccxciv.
265   ¹ The late Mr. Hansford Worth in " The Moorstone Age," Part I, *D.A.* **81** (1949), 311, says that moorstone " cut and dressed from surface blocks " was in use before the Norman Conquest," but does not state where, and for what purpose.
      ² *D.A.* **81, 82** (1949, 1950).
266   ¹ *Early Tours*, 1.
      ² *Early Tours*, 7.
      ³ Carew, *Survey of Cornwall*, 1602 ed., 53.

PAGE

267 [1] Stephens, "Plymouth Dock" (University of London thesis, unpublished).

[2] For photographs and other details of early brick houses in Devon see Richardson and Gill, *Regional Architecture of the West of England*.

[3] Other examples of early brick-building will be found in *D.C.N.Q.* **11** (1921), 55-6, 100-1, 140-1.

268 [1] Torr, *Small Talk at Wreyland* (1932 ed.), 150-1.

[2] Cf. Innocent, *The Development of English Building Construction*, 134-5.

[3] ibid., 134.

[4] See *D.A.* **52** (1920), 179-82, for a good modern account of cob construction.

269 [1] A. Hamilton Thompson, "Church Architecture in Devon," *Archaeological Journal*, **70** (1913), 457.

270 [1] ibid., 464.

271 [1] ibid., 453.

[2] See Cave, *Roof Bosses in Medieval Churches* (1948).

[3] For a general survey see Cox, *Bench-Ends in English Churches* (1916), 74-90.

272 [1] P.R.O. Early Chancery Proceedings, 1544-7. C.I. 1116/49 (bill of complaint only).

[2] D.C.R.S. Library. Transcript of Winkleigh Churchwardens' accounts, 1512-1647.

274 [1] *Archaeological Journal*, **70** (1913), 164.

281 [1] Finberg, *Tavistock Abbey*, 290; *D.A.* **60** (1928), 73-4.

[2] Finberg, op. cit., 293.

[3] Worth, "Notes on the History of Printing in Devon," in *D.A.* **11** (1879), 497-515, on which the following section is based.

[4] *The Times Handlist of English and Welsh Newspapers*, 1620-1920 (1920).

[5] Worth, loc. cit., 507.

282 [1] ibid., 503-4.

284 [1] "Miss Burney in Devonshire": *D.A.* **59** (1927), 279-88.

[2] *The Letters of George Gissing to his Family* (1927), 311-32.

PAGE

286 [1] Pycroft, *Art in Devonshire*, **2**, on which this section is largely based throughout.

[2] For a comprehensive account of the Devon paintings, see Bond and Camm, ii, 209-53.

[3] See Baker and James, *British Painting*, 38.

287 [1] Pycroft, 46, quoting William Jackson's *Essays*, published 1798.

[2] *D.A.* **16** (1884), 157-9, gives further details of these portraits.

288 [1] For the Saltram portraits see *D.A.* **19** (1887), 86-91.

291 [1] *Catalogue of Exhibition of Pictures by Richard Wilson and his Circle* (Tate Gallery, 1949), 13-14. For Powderham, see Part II.

[2] See Mayne, *Thomas Girtin* (1949), for the details of these drawings.

[3] A. J. Finberg, *Life of J. M. W. Turner* (1939), 182.

[4] See *Journeys in England*, ed. J. Simmons (1951), 213-15. I am indebted to Professor Simmons for the suggestion about the scene of the painting.

[5] Baker and James, op. cit., 177.

294 [1] *Census 1951 England and Wales, Preliminary Report* (1951) forms the basis for the section which follows.

[2] ibid., 45. The estimated population in mid-1939 was 220,800. The 1951 figure is 208,985.

299 [1] See above, 110.

301 [1] My figures are taken from the *Exeter Diocesan Directory* (1951).

302 [1] Personal information from the Congregational Union of England and Wales.

[2] *Catholic Directory*, 1950. Separate county totals are not given.

303 [1] *National Farm Survey*, 1941-3.

[2] In 1868 the average farm in Devon was one of 60 acres. *Parliamentary Papers*, 1867-8, lxx, Agricultural Returns for 1868.

[3] Figures supplied by the secretary of the National Farmers' Union, Devon County Branch, Exeter.

[4] June 1950 figures from the

PAGE

303 Ministry of Agriculture and Fisheries' Agricultural Returns. The 1938 figures are those of the Ministry also, taken from the *Land Utilisation Survey of Devon*.

304 [1] These and the following figures are taken from Mr. Amery Adams's presidential address to the D.A. *D.A.* **82** (1950), 36-9.
[2] Information from the County Planning Department, Exeter.

305 [1] Raleigh Radford, Memorandum to Dartmoor Enquiry, 1950.

306 [1] See H. G. Nicholas, *The British General Election of* 1950, map facing p. 316.

307 [1] Lysons, xxxiv.

308 [1] An excellent analysis of the Devonshire towns and their hinterlands will be found in *Devon and Cornwall: a Preliminary Survey*, 42-60. I have drawn almost exclusively upon this account for this discussion of the Devon towns, though I have supplemented it by my personal observations of all of them during the years 1947-51.

320 [1] *D.A.* **56** (1924), 53-4, 94-6.

322 [1] *D.A.* **82** (1950), 209; *D.C.N.Q.* **23** (1948), 98.

324 [1] *D.A.* **67** (1935), 306-7.

326 [1] Pulman, *Book of the Axe*, 869-70.
[2] An essay on Axmouth and Bindon will be found in Rogers, *Memorials of the West*.

328 [1] *R.H.*, 416.
[2] Oliver, *Mon.*, 198b; Wainwright, *Barnstaple Records*, ii, 261-2.

329 [1] Gribble, *Memorials of Barnstaple*, 197, 371.
[2] For an account, inadequate in some respects, of Barnstaple members down to 1832 see *D.A.* **71** (1939), 249-65; *D.A.* **72** (1940), 251-64; and *D.A.* **73** (1941), 181-94.
[3] *D.A.* **16** (1884), 157-9.
[4] *Reg. Stapeldon*, 137; Hussell, *North Devon Churches*, 1.

330 [1] *D.A.* **70** (1938), 190-7.

334 [1] So Worthy, *Devonshire Parishes*, i, 19. But Kelly's Directory (1935) says the church was rebuilt to the design of Fowler of London in 1838 and restored in 1882.

336 [1] Whiting, *The Long Bridge of Bideford*, 18-19.
[2] *R.H.*, 559; Lysons, 51.
[3] *D.C.N.Q.* **24** (1951), 204.

337 [1] White's *Directory* (1850), 757-8.
[2] *D.A.* **34** (1902), 226-8.

338 [1] Prince, *Worthies of Devon*, 641.

341 [1] Lysons, 364-5. Lysons gives 1258 as the date of the grant, but it should be 1259.
[2] *D.C.N.Q.* **24** (1951), 205.

342 [1] *D.C.R.S.*, I. P. M. Humphrey Arscott, 1580.
[2] Lysons, 58; Vivian, *Visitations of Devon*, 18.
[3] *D.A.* **24** (1951), 204.

343 [1] Croslegh, *History of Bradninch*, 312.

344 [1] See *V.C.H.* Devon, 575, for a brief description.

346 [1] Round, *E.H.R.* **31** (1916), 586 ff.

348 [1] *E.H.R.* **62** (1947), 357.
[2] *Reg. Stapeldon*, 137.
[3] *D.A.* **46** (1914), 235.

349 [1] *D.A.* **18** (1886), 199.
[2] Hencken, *Archaeology of Cornwall and Scilly*, 124-5; Chope, *Story of Hartland*, 8.

350 [1] See the map facing *D.S.* 308. For the open fields, ibid., 277-8.
[2] Oliver, *Mon.*, 172b.

354 [1] For the possibility of an earlier date, see Stéphan, *Historical Guide to Buckfast Abbey*, 2-3. The suggestion of a Celtic foundation must be received with caution.

355 [1] *D.S.*, 95-102.

356 [1] *R.H.*, 427.

359 [1] Oliver, *Mon.*, 224; Stéphan, 69.

360 [1] Davidson, MS. Church Notes, *sub* Calverleigh.

361 [1] Baring-Gould, *A Book of Dartmoor*, 160.
[2] *D.C.N.Q.* **23** (1947), 21.

362 [1] *V.C.H.* Devon, 595-6.

364 [1] So Kelly, 1935; but Oliver, *Mon.*, 446, leaves the dedication blank.
[2] For Radford, see *D.A.* **35** (1903), 251-78; for Upcott, see *D.S.*, 147-52.

364   [3] For all that is known of St. Urith, see *D.A.* **46** (1914), 290-308.

365   [1] *Reg.* Lacy, ii, 442, 523. The chapel existed in the 1420s.

371   [1] For the history of the Sokespitches see *D.S.*, 105-19.

376   [1] For the Dartmoor blowing-houses in general, see *D.A.* **72** (1940), 201-50 and *D.A.* **78** (1946), 281-4.

     [2] For the history of this family and of Cholwich Town see *D.S.*, 78-94.

377   [1] *D.A.* **75** (1943), 94.

     [2] *D.A.* **70** (1938), 158-9.

379   [1] BM., Add. MS. 9,426 (Lysons Correspondence), fol. 246.

381   [1] Oliver, *Eccl. Antiquities*, i, 109.

383   [1] A fuller account of the topography of Dartmouth will be found in Russell, *Dartmouth*, 21-6.

     [2] *D.A.* **82** (1950), 282.

384   [1] *D.S.*, 223-5.

     [2]ibid., 231-2. The fall of Bordeaux in 1453 hit Dartmouth's trade severely.

     [3] Watkins, *Dartmouth*, 38n.

     [4] *D.A.* **82** (1950), 281-90: " The New Quay at Dartmouth, 1584-1640."

385   [1] Russell, 159-60.

     [2] For its parliamentary history, see *D.A.* **43** (1911), 350-70, and *D.A.* **61** (1929), 217-8.

     [3] " Dartmouth Castle and other Defences of Dartmouth Haven " in *Archaeologia* **85** (1935), 129-57.

387   [1] Richardson and Gill, *Regional Architecture*, 127, 133.

388   [1] Details of the glass will be found in Cresswell, *Notes on the Churches of the Deanery of Kenn*, 72-3.

390   [1] See *Country Life*, **98** (1945), 200-3, 244-7, for further details of the house.

391   [1] *Reg. Stafford*, 88.

396   [1]Delderfield,*ExmouthMilestones*,83-4.

398   [1] This account is based mainly upon *Country Life* **75** (1934), 272-7, 300-5, and **84** (1938), 426-30.

     [2] E.D.R., Patent Books, Vol. I (1628-1733), fol. 148. Petition dated 15 January 1694.

399   [1] Fortescue, *A Chronicle of Castle Hill*, I, 4.

399   [2] *Notes and Queries* **164** (1933), 279.

400   [1] *D.A.* **57** (1925), 267-71.

     [2] *D.A.* **79** (1947), 103.

405   [1] Chope, *The Book of Hartland*, 19.

     [2] Chope, 54-5. The Arroasians were a reformed branch of Austin Canons, founded at Arouaise, near Bapaume. They were absorbed into the Augustinian order before 1470.

408   [1] Oliver, *Mon.*, 449, citing Bishop Lacy's register, vol. iii, fol. 198, says it was rebuilt in 1439 but there is no entry to this effect in the register.

     [2] For a fuller account of the house, see *Country Life*, **74** (1933), 120-6.

411   [1] Leeson Day, *Holsworthy*, 8-9.

412   [1] Coxhead, *Honiton and the Vale of Otter*, 32.

413   [1] *D.A.* **61** (1929), 251.

414   [1] *Reg. Lacy*, ii, 742.

419   [1] *D.A.* **45** (1913), 145; *D.C.N.Q.* **24** (1951), 205, 206.

420   [1] MacCulloch, *The Celtic and Scandinavian Religions*, 62-3.

421   [1] E.D.R., Faculty Registers, vol. iv, fol. 189.

     [2] Russell, *Dartmouth*, 54-5; Lysons, 548-9.

422   [1] *Reg. Lacy*, ii, 634.

     [2] For a fuller account, see *D.S.*, 140-2.

423   [1] *D.S.*, 145-7.

424   [1] *P.N.D.*, 188n. Also *D.A.* **63** (1931) 354-6.

426   [1] For the 13th-cent. Mariscos, see " The Murder of Henry Clement " in Powicke, *King Henry III and the Lord Edward* (Oxford, 1947).

427   [1] Hamilton Rogers, *Effigies and Monuments of Devon*, 33-4.

428   [1] *D.A.* **65** (1933), 140.

429   [1] Rowe, *Perambulation of Dartmoor*, 255.

430   [1] *Daily Graphic*, 30 April 1907; *Daily Telegraph*, 21 May 1907.

432   [1] *Jour. Roman Studies*, **22** (1932), 71-2.

434   [1] Finberg, *Tavistock Abbey*, 170.

436   [1] For reminiscences of St. George's Fair at Modbury, see *D.A.* **65** (1933), 128-30.

     [2] I owe this information to Mr. Noel

PAGE

436 Blakiston of the P.R.O., who has transcribed the early 14th-cent. cartulary of the priory now in the possession of Eton College.

437 [1] *D.A.* **70** (1938), 217; *White's Directory*, 1890.
 [2] Oliver, *Mon.*, 451.

438 [1] *Records of the Borough of South Molton*, ed. Cock (1893), 54-5.
 [2] Worth, *Early Days in South Molton*, *D.A.* **26** (1894), 122-32. I date the original charter from the fact that Pagan de Turberville, the son of the first Gilbert, was alive in Devon in 1199 (Pipe Rolls).

439 [1] The complete will is given in *The Register of Henry Chichele* (ed. Jacob, 1938), ii, 290-3.
 [2] Oliver, *Lives of Bishops of Exeter*, 55.
 [3] *D.A.* **33** (1901), 391; *Patent Rolls, Edw. VI*, iv, 18.

440 [1] Oliver, *Eccl. Ant.*, iii, 47.
 [2] *Reg. Stafford*, 420.

442 [1] *D.A.* **18** (1886), 223-4.

443 [1] *Country Life*, **74** (1933), 524-9.

447 [1] For a fuller description of the castle, see Young, *Okehampton*, 35-8.

450 [1] A detailed architectural account of Blagdon will be found in *D.A.* **69** (1937), 479-82.
 [2] D.C.R.S., Enrolled Deed, No. 513.

455 [1] The prior of Plympton was granted a market and fair at Sutton in 1253. A borough may have been set up forthwith. There was certainly one by 1275 (Hundred Rolls).
 [2] *D.S.*, 223-4.
 [3] Bracken, *History of Plymouth*, 91-3.

458 [1] For fuller details see Judge, *The Story of the Prysten House, Plymouth*.
 [2] Copeland, *The Royal Citadel, Plymouth*, 9. I am indebted to this admirable booklet for the details of the Citadel.

459 [1] Richardson and Gill, *Regional Architecture of the West of England*, 54.
 [2] Foulston, *The Public Buildings in the West of England as designed by John Foulston*, 63.

460 [1] Mowan, *A Brief History of Drake's Island*, 12.

PAGE

461 [1] *Report of the Commission on Municipal Corporations*, 1835 (Plympton).

463 [1] *Country Life*, **59** (1926), 160-70; *Tourists' Companion to Plymouth, etc.*, 289.

464 [1] For the details of these and other discoveries, see Worth, " Prehistoric Plymouth," in the *Trans. Plymouth Institution* for 1931, 1944.
 [2] A full account of the discovery is given in *Archaeologia*, **40** (1866), 500-10, and a short account in *V.C.H.*, 367-8.

465 [1] Cresswell, *Churches of the Deanery of Kenn*, 131.

467 [1] This account of the structural history of Powderham Castle is based on *Trans. Exeter Diocesan Archit. Soc.*, Second Series (1867), i, 170-83; *Archaeological Journal* **70** (1913), 531-2; and Polwhele, ii, 158, 169-70.

469 [1] *Country Life*, 19 April 1930.

477 [1] Mogridge, *A Descriptive Sketch of Sidmouth* (*c.* 1836), 45-6.

482 [1] *Cal. Inq.*, viii, 348 (No. 476). Inquisition taken 1343-44.

486 [1] See *D.A.* **42** (1910), 258-77; **43** (1911), 371-402; **69** (1937), 260-4.

499 [1] See *V.C.H.*, 589-90, for a fuller description.

500 [1] Finberg, *Tavistock Abbey*, 4; *D.C. N.Q.* **24** (1951), 206.
 [2] *Reg. Stapeldon*, 137.

501 [1] Mallock, *Memoirs of Life and Literature*, 10.

504 [1] A Totnes Priory deed (n.d. but before 1205) makes it clear there were walls at that date (Watkin, *Hist. of Totnes Priory and Medieval Town*, 97).

506 [1] At Berkhampstead castle the stone shell keep and curtain walls of the bailey supplanted the timber defences in 1155; at Hertford castle in 1170.

507 [1] Watkin, *passim*, prints many documents dealing with this rebuilding.

509 [1] Davidson, *Newenham Abbey*, 166; Hutchins, *History of Dorset* (3rd ed., 1863), 78.

512 [1] *D.S.*, 94-5.

513 [1] I owe this suggestion to Prof. N. Pevsner.

518 [1] *Reg. Stafford*, **371**.

BIBLIOGRAPHY

A COMPLETE bibliography of the sources for Devonshire history would by itself fill a substantial volume, and a complete account of the manuscript sources for such a history is nearly impossible to compile. The following lists must therefore be highly selective. In the section on manuscript sources I have confined myself to those records which I have used extensively in preparing this book, whether or not they are referred to specifically in the text. In the section on printed materials I have listed only the more valuable publications, so far as they are known to me. Useful bibliographies of Devonshire history will also be found in Hoskins and Finberg, *Devonshire Studies* (London, 1952), and in Finberg, *Tavistock Abbey* (Cambridge, 1951).

A. MANUSCRIPT SOURCES

BEDFORD OFFICE, TAVISTOCK
Surveys, rentals.
BODLEIAN LIBRARY, OXFORD
Milles MSS. (Devon Topography).
BRITISH MUSEUM, LONDON
Additional Charters.
Additional Manuscripts.
Harleian Manuscripts.
CRUWYS MORCHARD HOUSE, TIVERTON
Surveys, rentals, leases, and other estate papers.
EXETER CASTLE
Quarter Sessions records, 1592 onwards (Sessions Books and Depositions).
Calendar of Enrolled Deeds, 1536-1763 (4 vols. typescript).
Land Tax Assessments, 1780-1832.
Enclosure Awards, 1802-74.
EXETER CATHEDRAL LIBRARY
Dean and Chapter surveys, rentals, and deeds.
EXETER CITY LIBRARY
Manorial surveys, court rolls, and rentals.
Deeds.
Burnet Morris, MS. Index to Devon Places and People.
Davidson. Church Notes (compiled mainly in the 1840s).
Parish registers, churchwardens' accounts, and overseers' rate-books.
Various parish histories and memoranda (typescript).
Various family histories and memoranda.
EXETER DIOCESAN REGISTRY
Episcopal Registers (1257 onwards). These registers have been printed down to 1441. See Hingeston-Randolph, below (Section B, under " Ecclesiastical History ").

Act Books, 1568-1734 (9 vols.).
Patent Books, 1628-1805 (2 vols.).
Faculty Books, 1737-1863 (6 vols.).
Bishops' Transcripts of Parish Registers (late 16th cent. onwards).
Tithe awards and maps, 1838-47.

EXETER PROBATE REGISTRY
Wills and inventories (now destroyed).

HOUSE OF LORDS LIBRARY, LONDON
Devon Protestation Returns, 1642. A nearly complete return for Devon of all who took the oath of protestation.
Return of Papists and reputed Papists, 1767.

PUBLIC RECORD OFFICE, LONDON
Census Schedules, 1841, 1851.
Chancery Proceedings.
Committee for Compounding, Papers.
Court of Requests Proceedings.
Court of Wards (Feodaries' Surveys).
Enrolled Accounts.
Exchequer, Depositions by Commission.
Exchequer, Special Commissions.
Feet of Fines.
Hearth Tax Returns.
Inquisitions post-mortem and extents.
Lay subsidy rolls.
Miscellaneous Inquisitions.
Rentals and Surveys.
Star Chamber Proceedings.
State Papers Domestic (Elizabeth).

B. GENERAL TOPOGRAPHICAL WORKS

THE only bibliography relating solely to Devon was published a hundred years ago, when James Davidson produced his *Bibliotheca Devoniensis: a Catalogue of the Printed Books relating to the County of Devon* (Exeter, 1852). He later published a Supplement (Exeter, 1862), the two together forming an invaluable work of reference for local historians. J. P. Anderson, *The Book of British Topography* (London, 1881) is useful as a brief guide to Devon topographical literature, but is necessarily highly selective. A. L. Humphreys, *A Handbook of County Bibliography* (1917) is a bibliography of bibliographies relating to the counties and towns of the British Isles, and is valuable. The amount of printed matter relating to Devon is probably greater than that devoted to any other English county. A good deal published in this century is worthless: topographical writing at its slushiest. A complete bibliography of Devonshire topography and local history down to the present day is being prepared in the Exeter City Library.

The earliest topographical account of Devon was written by John Hooker (1525-1601), who was Chamberlain of the city of Exeter, and an antiquary of considerable reputation. His Synopsis Chorographical of Devonshire was written about 1599, but was never printed. It is now in the British Museum (Harleian MS. 5827), a manuscript volume of 171 pages. Extracts from this were printed in *D.A.* **47** (1915), 334-48. Both Thomas Westcote and Tristram Risdon borrowed freely from Hooker's manuscript for their respective county topographies. Westcote's *View of Devonshire in 1630* was not published until 1845. Risdon's *Chorographical Description or Survey of the County of Devon,* begun in 1605 and finished in 1630, was not published *in extenso* until 1811 (London), though a pirated and mangled edition had been published by Curll as far back as 1714. Westcote and Risdon are both useful, but are almost entirely concerned with the descents of families and estates, like so many of the early topographers, and their books do not compare in value as portraits of the county with Richard Carew's delightful *Survey of Cornwall* (1602). Sir William Pole (1561-1635), the antiquary, left large manuscript collections for the history and antiquities of Devon, most of which perished during the Civil War. The surviving papers were published in 1791 (London) as *Collections towards a Description of the County of Devon*, an invaluable work, for it was based throughout upon manuscript records, many of which have since been lost.

William Chapple began a *Review of Risdon's Survey of Devon*, but the work was stopped by the death of the author and part only was published (Exeter, 1785). Shortly afterwards, the Rev. Richard Polwhele published the most ambitious *History of Devonshire* yet attempted (3 vols. Exeter, 1793-1806), but it is an incomplete and rather ramshackle production. The general historical chapters are nearly valueless. It is most useful for its parochial descriptions in Vols. 2 and 3, but even these tail off badly towards the end and the work is brought to an abrupt close. A more significant contribution to Devonshire topography was made in 1809, when the 1st edition of the Ordnance Survey appeared, on a scale of one inch to the mile.

Not until 1822 did Devon get a history worthy of the name, when the Rev. Daniel Lysons published his *Topographical and Historical Account of Devonshire*, being the sixth and last volume of the *Magna Britannia* projected by his brother and himself. Lysons almost decided to give up the preparation of the Devonshire volume on the death of his brother in 1819. Fortunately, he changed his mind (though Devon was the last county to be published), for upon Lysons nearly all subsequent writers have largely based their work.

The Rev. T. Moore published his *History of Devonshire* in 3 vols. (London, 1829-36), again an incomplete work, for none of the intended Parochial History appeared. Thereafter no county histories appeared, though several were projected. As time went on, and the record material accumulated, it was felt that even the history of one county was a matter for a committee rather than an individual. R. N. Worth, it is true, published *A History of Devonshire* in the Popular County Histories series (London, 1886), but—though readable and still useful—it is not what we should call a history to-day. Finally, in 1906, the Victoria County History Committee published the first volume of *A History of the County of Devon*. Considerable progress was made in the preparation of volume ii, but it never appeared, and there the *Victoria County History of Devon* rests. The fact is that, apart from Lysons—and he is a topographer rather than an historian—there is as yet not a single comprehensive history of Devon.

Nevertheless, the materials for a history have piled up at a formidable rate. The Devonshire Association was founded in 1862, and between 1863 and 1952 published 84 volumes of *Transactions*, mainly historical in nature. These volumes are uneven in quality, like those of all local societies, but they contain a mass of valuable papers on nearly every aspect of local history. Without these *Transactions*, my own book could never have been written. Other valuable general series are:

Devon and Cornwall Notes and Gleanings (5 vols. in 3. Exeter, 1888-92).
Devon and Cornwall Notes and Queries (24 vols. In progress. Exeter, 1900——).
Devon and Cornwall Record Society (30 vols. In progress. Exeter 1905——).
Transactions of the Plymouth Institution (21 vols. In progress. Plymouth, 1865——).
Transactions of the Torquay Natural History Society (In progress. Torquay, 1909——).

In 1850 appeared the first county directory of any real historical value: William White's *History, Gazetteer, and Directory of Devonshire*. The second edition appeared in 1878, the third and last in 1890. Kelly's *Directory of Devonshire* first appeared in 1856. The 21st edition (and the last) appeared in 1939. For early town directories (before 1856) reference should be made to the *Guide to Directories*, No. 5 of the Royal Historical Society Guides and Handbooks (London, 1950).

In 1850 also appeared the first edition of Murray's famous *Handbook for Devon and Cornwall*. Down to 1872 (8th edn.) Devon and Cornwall appeared together. In 1879 (9th edn.) *Devon* was treated separately. The 11th and last edn. of the *Handbook for Devon* appeared in 1895. These handbooks are now of considerable value for 19th-cent. history. In 1907, *Devon* was first published in the " Little Guides " (London), written by Baring-Gould. This was a highly characteristic production: " his personality stamped all over it." It was abominably " revised " in 1950.

R. P. Chope (ed.), *Early Tours in Devon and Cornwall* (Exeter, 1918) is a useful reprint of Devonshire material from Leland to Southey.

For biographies of eminent Devonians there is, apart from *D.N.B.*, John Prince's *Worthies of Devon* (Exeter, 1701). A new and fuller edn. appeared in London, 1810. Of quite a different flavour is S. Baring-Gould's *Devonshire Characters and Strange Events* (2 vols. London, 1908). Charles Worthy's *Devonshire Wills* (London and Derby, 1896) is useful, but on Devon family histories is unreliable at times.

The following are the principal printed sources used in each chapter of Part I:

GENERAL DESCRIPTION

On Geology, Sir Henry de la Beche's *Report on the Geology of Cornwall, Devon, and West Somerset* (London, 1839) was a pioneer work and may still be read with profit. The various memoirs of the Geological Survey of Great Britain (London, 1902 onwards) are useful to the historian, especially the sections on Superficial Geology, Water Supplies, and Economic Geology. For a general view, there is H. Dewey, *British Regional Geology: South-West England* (2nd edn. H.M.S.O. London, 1948).

The Land Utilisation Survey of Britain: Part 92, Devon (London, 1941) has a useful survey of Devon geology and climate. Dr. Thomas Shapter's *Climate of the South of Devon* (2nd edn. London, 1862) is still valuable.

The scenery of Devon has attracted a vast literature, most of it bad. Among the best, A. W. Clayden, *The History of Devonshire Scenery* (Exeter, 1906) is concerned with the physical geography. W. H. Thompson and G. G. Clark, *The Devon Landscape* (London, 1934) is the best short survey of the county that has been written. On a larger scale is the C.P.R.E. *Devon Survey* (London 1932). J. A. Steers, *The Coastline of England and Wales* (Cambridge, 1946) discusses the two coasts of Devon in some detail. *Devonshire Scenery*, ed. Rev. W. Everitt (Exeter, 1884), is an anthology of prose and verse on the subject. J. L. W. Page, *The Rivers of Devon* (London, 1893), is pleasant reading. In the early 19th cent. F. C. Lewis produced three books of engravings of the scenery of Devonshire rivers: the Dart (1821), the Tamar and Tavy (London, 1823), the Exe (London, 1827), and on Devon rivers generally (London, 1843). Books on *Dartmoor* are referred to among the " regional " books at the end of this bibliography.

PREHISTORIC AND CELTIC DEVON

W. T. P. Shortt, *Collectanea Curiosa Antiquae Dumnoniae* (Exeter, 1841) is still a useful source-book.

Victoria County History of Devon, vol. i (all published) (London, 1906) contains a chapter on Early Man, and a short section on Anglo-Saxon remains. Prof. F. Haverfield was to have written the chapter on Roman Devon, but did not succeed in doing so. The most valuable section of the *V.C.H.* for the early history of Devon is that on Ancient Earthworks, which I have consulted throughout the writing of this book. The *Proceedings of the Devon Archaeological Exploration Society* (1929 onwards, in progress) contain the most valuable material for Devon pre-history and the Romano-British period; and there is much (of uneven value) in the *D.A. Transactions,* and to a lesser extent in the *Transactions of the Plymouth Institution.* There is great need for an authoritative history of early Devon, comparable with Hencken's admirable *Archaeology of Cornwall and Scilly.*

A recent scholarly study, covering Devon archaeology, is Aileen Fox's *South West England* (London, 1964).

THE ENGLISH SETTLEMENT.

The Place-Names of Devon, ed. J. E. B. Gover, A. Mawer, and F. M. Stenton (2 vols. Cambridge, 1931-2), is quite indispensable for the Anglo-Saxon period. There is also much useful material on Celtic place-names. I have supplemented this by E. Ekwall's *Oxford Dictionary of English Place-Names* (Oxford, 1947) and his *Studies in English Place-Names* (Stockholm, 1936).

The Devonshire Domesday and Geld Inquest (2 vols. Plymouth, 1884-92) is the most valuable of all the Devonshire Association's publications. It gives the Latin texts (with translations) of both the Exchequer Domesday and the fuller Exon Domesday. There is much work still to be done on Domesday for Devon, but the greatest need of all is for a collected edition of the Anglo-Saxon charters relating to Devon, of which there appear to be some seventy known. These are at present scattered about in various more or less inaccessible printed works. Pending such an edition, H. P. R. Finberg's *Early Charters of Devon and Cornwall* (Leicester, 1953) helps to fill the bill.

Several essays in W. G. Hoskins and H. P. R. Finberg, *Devonshire Studies* (London, 1952) relate to the Anglo Saxon period, and should be consulted. W. G. Hoskins in *The Westward Expansion of Wessex* (Leicester, 1960) presents a new chronology for the Saxon conquest which generally supersedes that discussed on pages 42-4 of this book.

THE ECONOMIC BACKGROUND

See the sources for the Land, the Towns, Industry and Trade, Communications, and Population.

THE LAND

For medieval manorial and family history, O. J. Reichel, *The Hundreds of Devon* (issued in ten parts by the Devonshire Association, 1928-38, with index volume 1942), is an inexhaustible mine of information. I have relied on it for any manorial history discussed in Part II of this book.

The printed public records used for this chapter are too numerous to catalogue here. Among the more important for local medieval history are *The Red Book of the Exchequer* (ed. Hubert Hall), the Book of Fees, the Pipe Rolls, Feudal Aids, Calendars of Inquisitions Post Mortem and Miscellaneous Inquisitions, the Close Rolls, and the Patent Rolls. The list of sources in *Devonshire Studies* gives bibliographical details of all these except Hall's edition of *The Red Book of the Exchequer* (London, Rolls Series, 1896).

Of family histories, the following may be consulted:

F. Harrison, *The Devon Carys* (2 vols. New York, 1920).
E. Drake, *The Family of Chichester* (——, 1887?).

Lord Coleridge, *The Story of a Devonshire House* (London, 1905) deals with the Coleridge family, mainly 18th and 19th cent.

Lady Elliott-Drake, *The Family and Heirs of Sir Francis Drake* (2 vols. London, 1911).

Lord Clermont, *History of the Family of Fortescue* (London, 1869).

C. H. Fulford, *The Fulfords of Great Fulford, Devon* (typescript, 1937).

R. Granville, *The History of the Granville Family* (Exeter, 1895).

E. P. Powley, *The House of de la Pomerai* (Liverpool, 1944).
A good modern study of the great medieval family of Pomeroy.

C. Walrond, *The Walrond Papers* (London, 1913).

J. L. Vivian, *The Visitations of the County of Devon* (Exeter, 1895).
The standard work on the pedigrees of the Devonshire peerage and gentry.

There is no good modern history of the Courtenays, though *The Complete Peerage* (ed. G.E.C.) under DEVON supplies some of this great deficiency. Nor is there any history of the Aclands, the Bampfyldes, the Parkers, or the Rolles, all of them important in Devon history. Most of the family histories that have been done are inadequate by modern standards.

On the agriculture of Devon, the literature is considerable. H. P. R. Finberg, *Tavistock Abbey* (Cambridge, 1951) is a scholarly study of monastic farming in the medieval period. In *D.A.* **83** (1951) G. E. Fussell surveys Four Centuries of Farming Systems in Devon, 1500-1900, on the basis of printed sources only. The best of the 18th and 19th-cent. authorities are: R. Fraser, *General View of the County of Devon* (London, 1794); W. Marshall, *The Rural Economy of the West of England* (2 vols. London, 1796); C. Vancouver, *General View of the Agriculture of Devon* (London, 1808); H. Rider Haggard, *Rural England* (2 vols. London, 1902). For the 20th cent., the *Land Utilisation Survey of Britain, Part* 92, *Devon* (London, 1941) is indispensable.

Three valuable papers on "The Old Devon Farm-House," by C. H. Laycock, appeared in *D.A.* **52** (1920), **54** (1922), and **55** (1923). These deal with the exterior construction, interior plan and furnishings, and the domestic economy. R. P. Chope deals with "Some Old Farm Implements and Operations" in *D.A.* **50** (1918).

Other works which have been drawn upon for this chapter include:

Valor Ecclesiasticus (Record Commission edn. 6 vols. London, 1810-34).

Return of the Owners of Land in 1873 *in England and Wales* (2 vols. London, 1875).

B.H. Williams, *Ancient West Country Families*, vol. i. (all published). (Penzance 1916).

J. Bateman, *Great Landowners of Great Britain and Ireland* (4th edn. London,1883).

W. G. Hoskins, " The Ownership and Occupation of the Land in Devonshire, 1650-1800 (unpublished thesis, 1936, University of London Library).

J. Youings, " The Disposal of Monastic Property in Land . . . in Devon, with special reference to the period 1536-58" (unpublished thesis, 1950, University of London Library).

THE TOWNS

For separate town histories see the special bibliography (below) relating to particular places.

Hoskins and Finberg, *Devonshire Studies* (loc. cit.) should be consulted for the medieval towns, especially the essays on the Borough of Tavistock and the Wealth of Medieval Devon. For a preliminary list of all the seignorial and other boroughs of medieval Devon, see H. P. R. Finberg, " The Boroughs of Devon " in *D.C.N.Q.* **24** (1951), 203-9. On borough charters and incorporations there is much Devonshire material in:

A Ballard (ed.), *British Borough Charters*, 1042-1216 (Cambridge, 1913).

A. Ballard and J. Tait (eds.), *British Borough Charters*, 1216-1307 (Cambridge, 1923).

M. Weinbaum, *British Borough Charters*, 1307-1660 (Cambridge, 1943).

M. Weinbaum, *The Incorporation of Boroughs* (Manchester, 1937).

Early Tours in Devon and Cornwall (loc. cit.) is useful for contemporary descriptions of towns from John Leland to Robert Southey. White's *Directories* for 1850, 1878 and 1890 are invaluable for 19th-cent. town history. The *Report of the Commissioners on Municipal Corporations* (1835) contains a good deal of material on the twelve incorporated boroughs of Devon, with particular reference to local politics and finances. The *Report on the Boundaries of Municipal Corporations* (1837) is also valuable. Each borough report is accompanied by a map, sometimes the best early map that is available.

For the towns to-day, the best general survey is in *Devon and Cornwall: a Preliminary Survey* (Exeter, 1947).

INDUSTRY AND TRADE

(a) Cloth Trade

The history of the medieval and Tudor cloth trade in Devon has yet to be written. Finberg, *Tavistock Abbey*, has a little to say about it. For the later period, W. G. Hoskins, *Industry, Trade, and People in Exeter*, 1688-1800 (Manchester, 1935), deals with the Devonshire woollen industry as a whole. Fuller details of the county industry will be found in the same author's " Rise and Decline of the Serge Industry in the South-West of England" (unpublished thesis, 1929, University of London Library).

M. Dunsford's *Historical Memoirs of Tiverton* (Exeter, 1790) is especially valuable for the Tiverton trade.

Hooker's " Synopsis Chorographical of Devonshire " (B. M. Harl. MS. 5,827) contains some material for the Elizabethan trade. F. A. Mace, " The Trade and Industry of Devonshire in the later Middle Ages " (unpublished thesis, 1925, University of London Library) is generally valuable.

(b) Mining

The standard work on the tin industry is G. R. Lewis, *The Stannaries* (Cambridge, Mass., 1924), which covers both Devon and Cornwall. H. P. R. Finberg, " The Stannary of Tavistock," in *D.A.* **81** (1949), is an important supplement to Lewis.

The history of the lead and silver mines of Devon has not yet been written. L. F. Salzman's *English Industries of the Middle Ages* (Cambridge, 1913) contains some medieval material for such a history. For the later period, the introduction to Lysons's *Magna Britannia* is very useful. So, too, is De la Beche's *Report on the Geology*, etc. (loc. cit.) and J. H. Collins's *Observations on the West of England Mining Region* (Plymouth, 1912). A good book is waiting to be written on the whole history of mining in Devonshire.

(c) Other industries

Various papers in *D.A.* and *D.C.N.Q.* deal with the carpet, paper, and pottery industries. Again, the long introduction to Lysons is valuable for early 19th-cent. material. The East Devon lace industry was reported on by a parliamentary committee in 1887. Modern industry is surveyed in *Devon and Cornwall: a Preliminary Survey*, already cited.

COMMUNICATIONS

Apart from the standard histories of the Great Western Railway and the Southern

Railway, there are L. T. Catchpole, *The Lynton and Barnstaple Railway* (South Godstone, Surrey, 1936), and papers on the projected Okehampton-Bideford Railway and the Heytor Granite Railway, in *D.A.* **34** (1902) and **78** (1946). There is a considerable amount of information about the early Plymouth-Dartmoor railway scattered about in various local periodicals and books.

On canals, there is no important Devonshire literature.

For roads, apart from the general sources, there is an excellent monograph by G. Sheldon, *From Trackway to Turnpike* (Oxford, 1928), dealing with the history of roads and road traffic in East Devon. C. Henderson and E. Jervoise, *Old Devon Bridges* (Exeter, 1938) is the standard book on this subject. Davidson's *Bibliotheca Devoniensis* gives a useful list of acts of parliament relating to Devonshire roads (210-12). Various turnpike trusts are dealt with in papers in *D.A.*

POPULATION

Apart from the record material in the P.R.O. (already listed) and the printed Census Reports from 1801 to 1951, there is little of value on the subject of Devonshire population. J. C. Russell's *British Medieval Population* (Albuquerque, New Mexico, 1948) is unreliable and inadequate when examined closely for this county. R. Pickard, *The Population and Epidemics of Exeter in Pre-Census Times* (Exeter, 1947) is a valuable monograph, but contains little about the county. The pre-census population of Devon is a subject awaiting a courageous research student.

POLITICAL AND MILITARY HISTORY

The various borough histories are listed in the next section of this bibliography. Those for Dartmouth, Plymouth, Plympton, and Tiverton proved to be the most useful. The history of the parliamentary representation of the county and of the various boroughs has been dealt with in a number of papers (mainly by J. J. Alexander) in *D.A.* Sufficient reference to these has been given in the footnotes to Chapter X of Part I. It is very desirable that Mr. Alexander's scholarly papers on this subject should be collected together.

The *Report of the Commissioners on Municipal Corporations*, 1835 (already cited) is a valuable source. There are several petitions and reports of committees relating to electoral corruption in Devon after 1832. These all need listing and examining: yet another task for the local historian.

The files of the local newspapers are, of course, invaluable for the later 18th cent. and onwards, particularly the *Exeter Mercury* from September 1763, later the *Exeter Flying Post*.

On county government there is A. H. A. Hamilton, *Quarter Sessions from Queen Elizabeth to Queen Anne* (London, 1878), which is based almost entirely on the Devon quarter sessions records, and D. R. Tucker, " The Development of Quarter Sessions Government in Devon in the Nineteenth Century, and the Transition to County Council Government " (unpublished M.A. thesis, 1939, University of London Library).

For military history the only important source is Sprigg's *England's Recovery* (1854 edn.), which deals fully with the final campaign of the Civil War in the West. For the regimental histories see page 199, note 1.

MARITIME HISTORY

An unpublished article by M. Oppenheim on the Maritime History of Devon, prepared for vol. ii of the *V.C.H.* for Devon (still incomplete), was the main source for this chapter, together with certain town histories, chiefly those of Barnstaple, Bideford, Dartmouth,

Exeter, and Plymouth. The record material in the P.R.O. and the B.M. has already been listed, but only the surface of this immense field has been scratched. My own *Industry, Trade, and People in Exeter* (loc. cit.) is useful for the 18th century.

For Devon fishing, an important industry since the 15th cent., there is still no standard history. P. Russell, " Some Historical Notes on the Brixham Fisheries," in *D.A.* **83** (1951), is an introduction to the subject; and the introduction to Lysons is useful for the late 18th–early 19th cent.

ECCLESIASTICAL HISTORY

For the obscure Celtic period there is Canon G. H. Doble's *Cornish Saints* series, now almost unobtainable. Most useful for Devon were *St. Budoc* (No. 3), *St. Petrock* (No. 11), *Four Saints of the Fal* (No. 20), *St. Nectan* (No. 25), *St. Patern* (No. 43), and *St. Indract and St. Dominic* (No. 48). Canon T. Taylor, *The Celtic Christianity of Cornwall* (London, 1916) is also valuable.

On the religious houses, I have followed D. Knowles, *The Religious Houses of Medieval England* (Cambridge, 1940) for dates of foundation. Specialist Devonshire works are J. Brooking Rowe, *The Cistercian Houses of Devon* (Plymouth, 1878); and H. P. R. Finberg, *Tavistock Abbey* (1951), mainly economic. G. Oliver, *Monasticon Diœcesis Exoniensis* (Exeter and London, 1846), is a great work of scholarship. It is indispensable for the study of monastic houses in Devon and Cornwall.

Almost on the same level as Oliver are the *Episcopal Registers of the Diocese of Exeter* ed. by F. C. Hingeston-Randolph in 10 vols. (London and Exeter, 1886-1915). These cover the period 1257-1441, Lacy's register (1420-55) being so far incompletely published. For the history of the diocese as a whole, there is R. J. E. Boggis, *History of the Diocese of Exeter* (Exeter, 1922). In a lighter vein is the same author's *I Remember* (Exeter, 1947). Other personal recollections of the 19th-cent diocese are contained in W. H. Thornton's *Reminiscences of an Old West-Country Clergyman* (2 vols. Torquay, 1897-9) and S. Baring-Gould's *Early Reminiscences* and *Further Reminiscences* (London, 1923-5).

Other works which I have consulted with profit are: J. E. Binney (ed.), *Accounts of the Wardens of the parish of Morebath,* 1520-73 (Exeter, 1904) and R. Cornish (ed.), *Kilmington Church Wardens' Accounts,* 1555-1608 (Exeter, 1901). G. Oliver's *Collections Illustrative of the Catholic Religion* (London, 1857) is the only book dealing with the post-Reformation Catholics in Devon, an important subject about which too little is known. F. Rose-Troup, *The Western Rebellion of* 1549 (London, 1913) is useful but unreliable in matters of detail. G. W. Copeland, " Ancient Chapels and Oratories in Devon," in the *Transactions of the Plymouth Institution* **21** (1948-9) is valuable.

SOCIAL HISTORY

White's *Directories* for 1850, 1878 and 1890, and the files of old newspapers, are good sources for 19th-cent. history. Most town and parish histories yield some material, especially those written in the late 18th and early 19th cents. The *Report of the Commissioners concerning Charities (Devon)* (3 vols. in 2, Exeter, 1826-32) contains a vast amount of social history, not least on schools. The *Report of the Schools Inquiry Commission* (1868) contains much material on the Devonshire endowed schools. The general sources for the history of schools are sufficiently indicated in the references to Chapter XIII. Hamilton, *Quarter Sessions, etc.* (loc. cit.) is valuable on crime and punishment. Much good material for social history lies buried in the collection of typescript and manuscript parish histories in the Exeter city library, some of which I have used. C. Torr, *Small Talk at Wreyland* (3 vols. Cambridge, 1918-23) is in effect a delightful social history of a small district during a period of 120 years.

BUILDING AND BUILDING MATERIALS

On building materials in Devon, the various Geological Memoirs already cited provide a useful starting point. So, too, does De la Beche's *Report on the Geology, etc.* (see under GENERAL DESCRIPTION for these references). On granite in particular there are R. H. Worth's two papers on The Moorstone Age in *D.A.* **81** and **82** (1949-50). On cob-building there is an extensive literature, mostly in the form of articles in *D.A.* Particular reference may be made to *D.A.* **52** (1920), 179-82, for a concise account. There is no good account of the important Beer quarries, and the use of Beer stone in building.

On churches in Devon: G. Oliver, *Ecclesiastical Antiquities in Devon* (3 vols. Exeter, 1840-42) is valuable for its " pre-restoration " descriptions. W. Spreat, *Picturesque Sketches of the Churches of Devon* (Exeter, 1842) is equally valuable for its views of unrestored interiors. J. Davidson, " Church Notes " (5 MS. vols. in Exeter city library), mostly made in the 1840s, is useful. Sir Stephen Glynne's Church Notes for Devon—made mostly in the 1840s and 1850s—were reprinted by T. Cann Hughes in *Notes and Queries*, vols. 163-6 (1932-34). Also useful are J. Stabb's *Some Old Devon Churches* (3 vols., London, 1908-16) and his *Devon Church Antiquities*, vol. i (all published) (London, 1909). A. Hamilton Thompson, " Church Architecture in Devon," in the *Archaeological Journal* **70** (1913), is the best survey of the medieval churches of the county. C. F. Cornelius deals with the medieval churches of the Newton Abbot district in *D.A.* **78, 79** and **83.** The last of these papers deals with effigies, brasses and monuments. The Patent Books and Faculty Books in the Exeter diocesan registry contain much useful material for the 17th to 19th cents. On screens and rood-lofts the standard work is F. B. Bond and B. Camm, *Roodscreens and Roodlofts* (2 vols., London, 1909). Vol. ii deals in detail with Devon, and I have used this throughout for the description and dating of screens in Part II of this book. Medieval effigies and monuments are described in W. H. H. Rogers, *The Ancient Sepulchral Effigies . . . of Devon* (Exeter, 1877).

On domestic architecture in Devon, the volumes of *Country Life* are my main source for the larger houses. Avray Tipping's *English Homes* also deals with many of the more well-known houses. For the smaller houses, A. E. Richardson and C. L. Gill, *Regional Architecture of the West of England* (London, 1924) is a valuable work, dealing mostly with the towns. There is as yet no book on the minor rural architecture of Devon. R. H. Worth, " The Dartmoor House," in the Torquay Natural History Society's *Transactions* for 1934-35, is a good pioneer study of peasant building in Devon. The various papers by G. W. Copeland in the *Transactions of the Plymouth Institution* (esp. **18**) are also noteworthy.

LITERATURE AND THE ARTS

Most of my material comes from general histories and other sources which cannot be listed here. For local newspapers, the *Times Handlist of English and Welsh Newspapers*, 1620-1920, has been my chief source, supplemented by Willing's *Press Guide* (current vol.). G. Pycroft's *Art in Devonshire* (Exeter, 1883) is the best local book on Devon painters, musicians, etc., with brief biographies, but there are some important omissions, notably John Foulston, the Plymouth architect. On John Downman, see G. C. Williamson's *John Downman, A.R.A.* (London, 1907), but there is room for a fresh biography of Downman and for a new catalogue of his works. E. D. Martin, *Wayfarer's Guide to Eight Picture Galleries in South-West England* (Oxford, 1940) deals with the Exeter and Plymouth galleries, where there are important collections of the work of Devon painters.

There is no good book on the writers and literary associations of Devon, nor is there anything like an adequate list of the pictures in the Devon country houses. The compilation of such a list ought to be undertaken without delay by the Devonshire Association.

THE COUNTY TO-DAY

Among the major printed sources that were used are: *Census* 1951, *England and Wales: Preliminary Report* (London, 1951); *Devon and Cornwall: a Preliminary Survey* (Exeter, 1947); *Exeter Diocesan Directory*, 1951 (Exeter, 1951); the *Catholic Directory*, 1950 (London, 1950); *National Farm Survey*, 1941-43 (London, 1946); the Agricultural Returns for 1951 (Ministry of Agriculture and Fisheries); and the *National Trust: List of Properties* (London, 1951).

Most of the information in this chapter has been gathered from personal sources, and from my own travels in the county between 1947 and 1952.

C. BOOKS ON PARTICULAR PLACES AND DISTRICTS

IN the following list, guides to particular churches have necessarily been omitted for reasons of space. These, if in print, will generally be found in the building to which they refer. Occasionally, however, I have listed an exceptionally good church guide.

ASHBURTON

There is no adequate history of Ashburton, but J. S. Amery's Presidential Address to the Devonshire Association in *D.A.* **56** (1924), 43-102, is an excellent survey of the subject.

The Parish of Ashburton in the 15th and 16th Centuries, published anonymously (London, 1870), is based entirely upon the earliest book of churchwardens' accounts, 1479-1580.

AXMINSTER

James Davidson, *Axminster during the Civil War* (1851).

James Davidson, *History of Newenham Abbey* (London, 1843).

Davidson's history of Axminster was prepared for publication in 1832, but never published. He also compiled Collections for Axminster. Both these MS. volumes are in the Exeter City Library.

W. H. Wilkin's Notes on Axminster, which together make a considerable contribution to a history of Axminster, will be found in *D.A.* **65, 66, 67** and **68.**

BARNSTAPLE

J. B. Gribble, *Memorials of Barnstaple* (Barnstaple, 1830).

Barnstaple Bribery Commission. Report of the Proceedings of the Royal Commission on corrupt practices at the Barnstaple election, 1852 (reprinted from the *North Devon Journal*, Barnstaple, 1853).

C. Wills, *A Short Historical Sketch of the Town of Barnstaple* (Barnstaple, 1855).

J. R. Chanter, *Memorials of St. Peter's Church, Barnstaple* (Barnstaple, 1882).

J. R. Chanter, *Sketches of the Literary History of Barnstaple* (Barnstaple, 1886).

R. W. Cotton, *Barnstaple during the Civil War* (London, 1889). Deals with North Devon generally also.

W. F. Gardiner, *Barnstaple: 1837-97* (Barnstaple, 1897). A detailed and valuable work for the 19th century.

J. R. Chanter and T. Wainwright, *Reprint of the Barnstaple Records*, 2 vols. (Barnstaple, 1900). An inadequate compilation, but useful in default of anything else.

T. Wainwright, *Barnstaple Parish Register*, 1538-1812 (Exeter, 1903).

R. J. E. Boggis, *History of the Parish and Church of St. Mary Magdalene, Barnstaple* (Canterbury, 1915).

Barnstaple members of parliament 1295-1832 are dealt with in *D.A.* **71, 72, 73,** and **74.**

B. W. Oliver deals with the history of Barnstaple Bridge in *D.A.* **70** and **78.**

BERRY POMEROY

E. B. Powley, *Berry Pomeroy Castle* (Liverpool, 1947).

See also Powley, *History of the De la Pomerai Family* (Liverpool, 1944).

BIDEFORD

J. Watkins, *A History of Bideford* (Exeter, 1792).

A. G. Duncan, *The Long Bridge of Bideford and Bideford under the Restored Monarchy* (Bideford, 1930).

F. E. Whiting, *The Long Bridge of Bideford* (Bideford, 1945).

I. Rogers, *Ships and Shipyards of Bideford, 1568 to 1938* (Bideford, 1947).

BOVEY TRACEY

C. Torr (ed.), *Wreyland Documents* (privately printed, Cambridge, 1910).

Notes on Wreyland (reprint of part of Introduction to *Wreyland Documents*, Lustleigh, 1910).

BRADNINCH

F. C. Croslegh, *History of Bradninch* (London, 1911).

BRANSCOMBE

F. C. Butters, *Branscombe: the Parish and the Church* (Exeter, 1949).

BRAUNTON

There is no history of this interesting parish, but J. F. Chanter, *The Church of St. Brannock, Braunton* (Exeter, 1934) fills one gap.

BRIXHAM

There is no history of the town, but a number of articles are valuable. Among these are P. Varwell, Notes on the Ancient Parish of Brixham, in *D.A.* **18** (1886).

P. Russell, Some historical notes on the Brixham Fisheries; and C. E. Hicks, Early Banking in Brixham, both in *D.A.* **83** (1952).

BUCKFASTLEIGH

Dom A. Hamilton, *History of Buckfast Abbey* (Buckfastleigh, 1907).

See also J. B. Rowe, *Cistercian Houses of Devon* (Plymouth, 1878).

Dom J. Stéphan, *Historical Guide to Buckfast Abbey* (Exeter, n.d.).

BUCKLAND BREWER

W. H. Rogers, *Buckland Brewer* (Bideford, n.d.).

A good example of a parish history.

BUDLEIGH SALTERTON

W. Baker, *Budleigh Salterton and its Vicinity* (Budleigh Salterton, 3rd edn., about 1860).

CHUDLEIGH

M. Jones, *The History of Chudleigh . . . with a Description of the Surrounding Scenery, Seats, Families, etc.* 2nd edn. revised and corrected by W. W. Snell (Exeter, 1875).

CLAWTON

H. H. Harvey, *History of Clawton* (Exeter, 1939).

CLYST ST. GEORGE

H. T. Ellacombe, *The History and Antiquities of Clyst St. George* (Exeter, 1865).

COMBE MARTIN

K. M. Toms, *Notes on Combe Martin* (Barnstaple, 1902).

COUNTISBURY (see LYNTON)

CREDITON

Very little has been written on this town. *D.A.* **54** (1922) contains four articles on different aspects of the town's history.

W. Pope, *Glimpses of the Past in and around Crediton* (Tiverton, 1927) is full of interesting reminiscences of the recent past, and makes pleasant reading.

CRUWYS MORCHARD

M. C. S. Cruwys, *A Cruwys Morchard Notebook*, 1066-1874 (Exeter, 1939). An account of one of Devon's oldest families, and of their parish, based on the family muniments and the parish records.

DARTINGTON

A Short History of Dartington Hall, with Architectural Notes (5th edn. Dartington, 1942).

Dartington Hall (Totnes, 1947).

DARTMOUTH

V. Butteris, *Butteris's Guide to the Dart, Dartmouth, and the Neighbourhood* (Dartmouth, 1852).

H. R. Watkin, *Dartmouth: Pre-Reformation* (Exeter, 1935). Vol. i (all published) is the best compilation of borough and church records for any town in Devon, but it is not a history in the proper sense. Invaluable as a source-book down to the 16th cent.

P. Russell, *Dartmouth* (London, 1950). A useful and readable history down to the present day.

DAWLISH

S., R. S. *Cornelius's Guide, Dawlish: historical and topographical* (Dawlish, 1869).

DEAN PRIOR

C. J. Perry Keene, *Herrick's Parish: Dean Prior* (Plymouth, c. 1927). Anecdotal and good reading.

DEVONPORT (*see* PLYMOUTH)

EXMOUTH

E. J. Brabazon, *Exmouth and its Environs* (Exmouth, 1866).

Exmouth Ancient and Modern (Exmouth, 1868).

W. Webb, *Memorials of Exmouth* (Exmouth, 1872).

E. R. Delderfield, *Exmouth Milestones* (Exmouth, 1948). Excellent on the social history of the 19th and 20th cents., based on newspapers, directories, etc. Perhaps the best of Devonshire town histories.

FILLEIGH

Earl Fortescue, *A Chronicle of Castle Hill*, 1454-1918 (privately printed, London, 1929).

FRITHELSTOCK

R. P. Chope, *Frithelstock Priory*, (Torquay, 1929).

HARTLAND

R. P. Chope, *The Book of Hartland* (Torquay, 1940). An almost model history of an exceptionally interesting parish. Deals fully with the abbey.

Hartland Parish Register, 1558-1837 (Exeter, 1930-4).

I. L. Gregory (ed.) *Hartland Church Accounts*, 1597-1706 (——, 1950).

HATHERLEIGH

J. Manaton, *Hatherleigh History in Brief* (Exeter, 1951).

HOLCOMBE ROGUS

Holcombe Court is dealt with in *Country Life* 37; in Avray Tipping, *English Homes*, ii, 1558-1649; and in the *Archaeological Journal*, 70 (1913).

HOLSWORTHY

W. I. Leeson Day, *Holsworthy* (Torquay, 1934). A useful compilation.

HONITON

A Farquharson, *History of Honiton* (Exeter, 1868).

J. R. W. Coxhead, *Honiton and the Vale of Otter* (Exmouth, 1949).

Deals with several surrounding parishes, and devotes some attention to the interesting farmhouses, etc., of the district.

W. H. Wilkin, " Notes on the members for Honiton, 1640-1868," in *D.A.* **66** (1934) covers the whole period of Honiton's parliamentary history.

ILFRACOMBE
D. W. Bowring, *Ilfracombe through the Ages* (Exeter, 1931).
F. Nesbitt, *Ilfracombe Parish Church* (3rd edn. Ilfracombe, 1937).

INSTOW
A. E. Blackwell, *The Charm and History of Instow* (*with Lundy Island*) (Bideford, 1948). An excellent little guide to the parish, its history and its buildings.

IPPLEPEN
R. D. Cooke, *Notes on the Churches and Parishes of Ipplepen and Torbryan* (3rd edn. Newton Abbot, 1941). Deals with the interesting houses of the parishes also.

KENN
F. W. Vining, *Kenn: Our Home*, 1086-1910 (Exeter, 1910).

KENTISBEARE
E. S. Chalk, *Kentisbeare and Blackborough* (——, 1934).

KINGSBRIDGE
Kingsbridge and Salcombe. . . . Historically and topographically depicted (Kingsbridge, 1819).
S. P. Fox, *Kingsbridge Estuary with Rambles in the Neighbourhood* (Kingsbridge, 1864).
S. P. Fox, *Kingsbridge and its Surroundings* (2nd edn. of above, Plymouth, 1874).

LAPFORD
N. J. Drake, *A North Devon Village* (Lapford) (Taunton, 1950). An account of the social and economic changes in one village during the last two generations.

LITTLEHAM (*see* Exmouth)

LUNDY
J. R. Chanter, *Lundy Island: a monograph descriptive and historical* (London, 1877).
L. R. W. Loyd, *Lundy: its History and Natural History* (London, 1925).
R. Perry, *Lundy: Isle of Puffins* (London, 1940).
P. T. Etherton and V. Barlow, *Tempestuous Isle: the story of Lundy* (London, 1950).

LYDFORD
Dartmoor Preservation Association Publications, I. A Short History of the Rights of Common upon the Forest of Dartmoor and the Commons of Devon (Plymouth, 1890) contains a good deal on Lydford. A valuable and scarce book, printing many Dartmoor documents.

LYNTON
J. F. Chanter, *Lynton and Countisbury* (Exeter, 1907).
A good history of the two parishes, based on original records.

MARLDON
Compton Castle is described in a good guide with plan and drawings (Paignton, n.d.).

MODBURY
G. A. Cawse, *Modbury* (London, 1860).

MOLTON, SOUTH
J. Cock (ed.), *Records of the Borough of South Molton* (South Molton, 1893). A very useful account of a small market town, especially for the 18th and 19th cents.

NEWTON ABBOT
A. J. Rhodes, *Newton Abbot: its History and Development* (Newton Abbot, *c.* 1904). Useful for the 19th-cent. development of the town.

OKEHAMPTON
W. H. K. Wright (ed.), *History of Okehampton* (Tiverton, 1889).

E. H. Young, *Okehampton* (——, 1931). The first of the Parochial Histories of Devonshire, published by the Devonshire Association.

OTTERY ST. MARY

C. D. and M. Whetham, *A Manor Book of Ottery St. Mary* (London, 1913). A valuable 17th-cent. survey of a large manor.

J. N. Dalton, *The Collegiate Church of Ottery St. Mary* (Cambridge, 1917). A standard work.

Ottery St. Mary Parish Register, 1601-1837 (2 vols., Exeter, 1908-29).

PLYMOUTH

The picture of Plymouth; being a correct guide to the public establishments . . . (Plymouth, 1812).

A View of Plymouth Dock, Plymouth, and the adjacent country (Plymouth-Dock, 1812).

Samuel Rowe, *The panorama of Plymouth* (Plymouth, 1821).

The Tourist's Companion, being a Guide to the Towns of Plymouth, Plymouth-Dock, Stonehouse, Morice-Town, Stoke, and their Vicinities (London, 1823). A contemporary guide and directory to Plymouth, etc., in its most formative architectural period.

The Stranger's Handbook to the Western Metropolis; containing a concise and familiar description of Plymouth, Devonport, Stonehouse, etc. (Devonport, 1841. 7th edn., 1855).

Sir J. Rennie, *An historical, practical, and theoretical account of the Breakwater in Plymouth Sound* (London, 1848).

Views of Plymouth and the Neighbourhood (London, 1860).

R. N. Worth, *History of the Town and Borough of Devonport* (Plymouth, 1870). Still the standard history.

R. N. Worth, *A History of Plymouth* (Plymouth, 1872).

L. Jewitt, *A History of Plymouth* (London, 1873).
These two histories appeared almost simultaneously and caused some heart-burning. Both are valuable.

R. N. Worth, *The Three Towns Bibliotheca* (Plymouth, 1873). A catalogue of books, pamphlets, papers, etc., written by natives of Plymouth, Stonehouse, and Devonport, or published therein, or related thereto, with brief biographical particulars.

R. N. Worth (ed.), *Calendar of Plymouth Municipal Records* (Plymouth, 1893). A rather unsatisfactory book, scrappy and unreliable in detail.

H. F. Whitfeld, *Plymouth and Devonport in War and Peace* (Plymouth, 1900). Excellent on the 18th and 19th cents.

E. Eldred and W. H. K. Wright, *Streets of Old Plymouth* (Plymouth, 1901). A valuable record of the old buildings, many now gone.

C. W. Bracken, *A History of Plymouth and her Neighbours* (Plymouth, 1931). Based on newspaper articles, and somewhat scrappy, but still useful.

C. Gill, *Plymouth: a New History* (Newton Abbot, 1966) goes as far as the Elizabethan period.

H. P. Twyford, *It Came to our Door: Plymouth in the World War* (Plymouth, 1946). Account of the great air-raids on Plymouth.

R. A. J. Walling, *The Story of Plymouth* (London, 1950). The most readable history of Plymouth, especially valuable for the 18th and 19th cents. Like all the histories of Plymouth, it is weak on the medieval period.

PLYMPTON EARL (or ERLE)

J. Brooking Rowe, *A History of Plympton Erle* (Exeter, 1906). One of the best of the older town histories.

PLYMPTON ST. MARY

Saltram is described in *Country Life*, 59 (1926).

SALCOMBE (*see also* KINGSBRIDGE)

    J. Fairweather, *Salcombe, Kingsbridge, and Neighbourhood* (2nd edn. Salcombe and Kingsbridge, *c.* 1897).

SIDBURY

    D. C. A. Cave and C. H. Blakiston, *A Short History of Sidbury Church* (Exeter, 1930).

SIDMOUTH

    E. Butcher, *The Beauties of Sidmouth* (4th edn. Exeter, 1830). Illustrates the formative period of Sidmouth architecture.

    T. H. Mogridge, *A Descriptive Sketch of Sidmouth* (Sidmouth, *c.* 1836). Valuable for its contemporary information.

    P. O. Hutchinson, *A Guide to the Town and Neighbourhood of Sidmouth* (Sidmouth, 1865. 8th edn. Sidmouth, 1894).

    V. Cornish, *The Scenery of Sidmouth* (Cambridge, 1940). An interesting essay in the aesthetics of scenery, with particular reference to the Sidmouth and Salcombe Regis district.

    P. O. Hutchinson (1810-97) was an eminent local antiquary. His MS. History of Sidmouth in six folio vols. (illustrated) is now in the Exeter City Library.

STAVERTON

    E. D. Drake-Brockman, *Staverton on the Dart* (Exeter, 1947).

SUTCOMBE

    E. K. Prideaux, *Sutcombe Church and its Builders* (Exeter, 1913). A model account of the development of a village church and its contents.

SWIMBRIDGE

    J. F. Chanter, *The Church of St. James, Swimbridge* (Exeter, n.d.).

TAVISTOCK

    R. Evans, *Home Scenes: or Tavistock and its Vicinity* (London, 1846).

    R. N. Worth (ed.), *Tavistock Parish Records* (Plymouth, 1887). Unsatisfactory but still useful. The remarkable collection of churchwardens' accounts (from 1385-6) is too selectively transcribed.

    J. J. Alexander, *Tavistock Parish Church* (Gloucester, n.d.). The new edition, revised, and largely rewritten by H. P. R. Finberg (Gloucester, 1951) is a model account of the church and the early history of the town.

    Lady Radford, *Tavistock Abbey* (Exeter, 1929).

    H. P. R. Finberg, *Tavistock Abbey: A Study in the Social and Economic History of Devon* (Cambridge, 1951). The definitive account of the most important monastic house in Devon and Cornwall, and the most notable contribution to the medieval economic history of Devon that has yet been made.

    H. P. R. Finberg, " The Borough of Tavistock," in *Devonshire Studies* (*q.v.*) deals with the origin and early history of the town.

TAWSTOCK

    F. and C. Wrey, *A Guide to Tawstock Church* (3rd edn. Barnstaple, 1938). Tawstock is the most important church in Devon for its monuments and other fittings. A good guide.

TEIGNMOUTH

    The Teignmouth Guide, containing a description of the town (Teignmouth, 1840).

    The Teignmouth Guide and complete Handbook to the Town and Neighbourhood (Teignmouth, 1875).

THROWLEIGH

    E. Varwell, *Throwleigh: the story of a Dartmoor Village* (Exeter, 1938).

THURLESTONE

    F. E. Coope, *Thurlestone Church and Parish* (2nd edn. Thurlestone n.d.).

TIVERTON

M. Dunsford, *Historical Memoirs of the Town and Parish of Tiverton* (Exeter, 1790). Still valuable, especially for the 18th cent.

W. Harding, *The History of Tiverton* (2 vols. Tiverton, 1845-7).

F. J. Snell, *Chronicles of Twyford* (Tiverton, 1892).

F. J. Snell, *Palmerston's Borough: a budget of electioneering anecdotes, etc.* (Tiverton, 1894).

E. S. Chalk, *History of St. Peter's Church, Tiverton* (Tiverton, 1905). A full description and history of the church, with a catalogue of the vestry library.

E. K. Prideaux, *The Late Medieval Sculpture from the Church of St. Peter's, Tiverton,* reprinted from the *Archaeological Journal* **75** (1918).

TORBRYAN (see IPPLEPEN)

TORQUAY

O. Blewitt, *The Panorama of Torquay: a Description and Historical Sketch of the district comprised between the Dart and the Teign* (2nd ed. London, 1832). A valuable and charming account of Torquay at that date.

E. Cockrem, *Cockrem's Tourist's Guide to Torquay and its Neighbourhood* (Torquay, 1856).

J. T. White, *The History of Torquay* (Torquay, 1878).

H. R. Watkin, *A Short Description of Torre Abbey* (Torquay, 1909). The best architectural account of the Abbey and of the country house that succeeded it.

A. C. Ellis, *An Historical Survey of Torquay* (Torquay, 1930). The fullest history of the town so far.

Percy Russell, *A History of Torquay* (Torquay, 1960). Accurate and readable.

TORRINGTON, GREAT

J. J. Alexander and W. J. Hooper, *The History of Great Torrington* (Sutton, Surrey, 1948). A good modern town history, though weak on the medieval period (as so often).

TOTNES

Percy Russell, *The Good Town of Totnes* (Exeter, 1964): An excellent short history for the general reader.

W. Cotton, *A graphic and historical sketch of the Antiquities of Totnes* (London, 1850). A trifle, of no great value, which fetches an absurd price.

H. R. Watkin, *The History of Totnes Priory and Medieval Town* (2 vols. and index. Torquay, 1914-17). Like the same author's *Dartmouth,* this is a valuable and accurate compilation of original records, and not a history. But it breaks the back of the task for the medieval period when the historian of the town appears.

WASHFIELD

J. M. Turner, *Washfield: the Story of a Devonshire Village* (Tiverton, 1947).

WIDECOMBE-IN-THE-MOOR

R. Dymond, *Widecombe-in-the-Moor* (Torquay, 1876).

J. B. Rowe, *The Two Widecombe Tracts, 1638, giving a Contemporary Account of the Great Storm* (reprinted with an introduction, Exeter, 1905).

BIBLIOGRAPHY 571

In addition to the works listed above, certain districts have been well covered
by local histories and topographies, most notably DARTMOOR, which has
attracted a considerable literature. The following is a select list of these
regional works:

DARTMOOR

S. Rowe, *A Perambulation of the Ancient and Royal Forest of Dartmoor* (3rd edn.
Exeter and London, 1896). The first edition of this standard work, still the
most comprehensive book on Dartmoor, was published in 1848.

R. J. King, *The Forest of Dartmoor and its Borders* (London, 1856).

J. L. W. Page, *An Exploration of Dartmoor and its Antiquities* (London, 1889). Still
the best detailed guide to the Moor. The 4th edn. appeared by 1895.

R. Hansford Worth (1868-1950) made a life-long study of Dartmoor in all its
aspects. His valuable papers will be found in the *Transactions of the Devonshire
Association* from 1897 onwards. Much of his best work was collected in
Worth's Dartmoor, originally published 1953. The latest edn. was published
recently (Newton Abbot, 1970). See also *Dartmoor: a New Study* ed. by
Crispin Gill (Newton Abbot, 1970).

EXMOOR

E. T. MacDermot, *The History of the Forest of Exmoor* (Taunton, 1911). A first-
class piece of local history, mainly concerned with the Somerset side but
with some Devon material.

C. S. Orwin, *The Reclamation of Exmoor Forest* (Oxford, 1929). Also a first-class
study, covering the period 1815–1928. New edn. (Newton Abbot, 1970).

NORTH DEVON

L. V. Grinsell, *The Archaeology of Exmoor* (Newton Abbot, 1970) is a valuable
study, the first of its kind, which contains much material relating to North
Devon generally.

J. W. Fortescue, *My Native Devon* (London, 1924). A very " atmospheric " book
on the North and West Devon country.

EAST DEVON

G. P. R. Pulman, *The Book of the Axe* (4th and best edn. London, 1875). A good
study of the topography and history of the Axe valley.

W. H. H. Rogers, *Memorials of the West: historical and descriptive* (Exeter, 1888).
Pleasant antiquarian essays with an old-fashioned flavour.

E. R. Delderfield, *The Raleigh Country* (Exmouth, 1950). Deals with the country
between Topsham and Sidmouth. Good on the 19th cent. and present day.

SOUTH DEVON

W. Hyett, *A description of the watering-places on the South-East coast of Devon from
the river Exe to the Dart inclusive* (Exeter, 1805).

S. Heath, *The South Devon and Dorset Coast* (London, 1910).

E. R. Delderfield, *Cradle of the Sea-Dogs* (Exmouth, 1951).

E. R. Delderfield, *Torbay Story* (Exmouth, 1951).

The two latter cover the country between the estuaries of the Dart and the
Exe, and give a good deal of unusual information.

WEST DEVON

A. E. Bray (Mrs.), *The Borders of the Tamar and the Tavy* (new edn. 2 vols. London,
1879). First published in 3 vols. in 1838 in the form of a series of letters to
Robert Southey. Good reading.

C. Worthy. *Devonshire Parishes* (2 vols. Exeter, 1887-9). Antiquarian studies of
28 parishes in West and South Devon, with special reference to their churches.

ACKNOWLEDGMENTS

IT is impossible to acknowledge individually the help of all those who have made my task easier and more pleasant than one might have expected even in Devon. I must, however, refer particularly to a few who have helped me substantially, above all to the City Librarian of Exeter (Mr. N. S. E. Pugsley) for long continued assistance in a wide variety of ways; and to the City Librarian of Plymouth (Mr. W. Best Harris) for valuable information about various Plymouth matters. The County Planning Department of the Devon County Council, through the good offices of the Director of Planning (Mr. Geoffrey Clark), has answered all my many requests for information, some of them entailing much work, and my book owes much to this help for the modern period. I need hardly say that where I have used information and statistics from this Department, as from other official bodies (such as the National Farmers' Union), the conclusions I have drawn are my own, and these authorities are in no way responsible for them or for the manner of their expression.

I have to thank also the Central Committee of the Victoria History of the Counties of England for permission, readily given, to make use of their unpublished Devon material, above all the population tables (1801-1901) and a valuable chapter by M. Oppenheim on the maritime history of the county. My chapter on Building and Building Materials, together with much factual information in Part II, owes a great deal to my expert friends, Mr. G. W. Copeland of Plymouth and Mr. A. W. Everett of Exeter. Both have corresponded liberally with me for years, and have helped me immeasurably.

The valuable map of the prehistoric antiquities of Dartmoor was specially drawn for me by Mr. C. A. Ralegh Radford, whose unrivalled archaeological knowledge of South-Western England has been freely placed at my disposal. On this subject I have learnt much also from Lady (Aileen) Fox; but neither is responsible for any errors there may be in my account of this phase of Devonshire history.

The officials of the Public Record Office, the British Museum, and the Library of the House of Lords have been as helpful as always, and I wish it were possible to thank at least some of them by name here.

My illustrations have also gained from the generous help of friends. Mr. M. Meredith Williams of Bathe Barton allowed me to choose freely from his admirable drawings of Devonshire effigies and monuments. It is a matter for regret that considerations of space forced me to select only one drawing, that of the effigies of William Easton of Morchard Bishop and his wife. Mr. A. J. West of Dawlish generously lent me a rare print of Brunel's atmospheric railway, and Mr. J. Sands of Dawlish gave his services in photographing it for reproduction.

The thanks of the editor and publishers, as well as of the author, are due to Mr. J. F. Trotter for the line maps and diagrams in the text of the book ; to Mr. F. L. Attenborough for the photographs which appear as Nos. 22, 24, 32, 33, 35, 36, 41, 48, 49, 52, 53; to Mr. Reece Winstone for Nos. 28, 40, 42, 43, 51 ; to the Central Office of Information (Crown copyright reserved) for Nos. 21, 23, 25, 44 ; to Mr. Vincent Bibbings for the Frontispiece and Nos. 27 and 29 ; to the British Travel and Holidays

Association for Nos. 37, 57, 58 ; to *The Times* for Nos. 34, 39, 45 ; to Aerofilms, Ltd. for Nos. 31 and 46 ; to the *Western Morning News* for Nos. 26 and 54 ; to *Picture Post* for Nos. 55 and 56 ; to Mrs. Finberg for No. 15 ; to Mr. J. Allan Cash for No. 20 ; to R. L. Knight, Ltd. for No. 30; to Val Doone, Ltd. for No. 38; to the National Buildings Record for No. 50 ; and to Dr. J. K. St. Joseph and the Cambridge University Collection of Air Photographs (Crown copyright reserved) for No. 47. For permission to reproduce the portraits on plates 17, 18 and 19, their thanks are due to the Plymouth Art Gallery, the British Museum and the Trustees of the National Gallery.

Old prints reproduced among the illustrations came from the following sources: Nos. 1, 8, 9 and 10 from Spreat, *Picturesque Sketches of the Churches of Devon* (1832) ; Nos. 2, 3, 4, 5, 6, 13 and 14 from Britton and Brayley, *Devon and Cornwall Illustrated* (1832) ; and Nos. 11 and 12 from water-colour drawings by George Shepherd, now in the Sutherland Collection at the Ashmolean Museum.

Acknowledgment is made of permission given by the Controller of Her Majesty's Stationery Office for the use of maps in official publications as a basis for maps and diagrams in the text.

Of all the others who have helped me—the country gentry, the clergy in scores of parishes, farmers all over the county, and my personal friends in Devon—I can say little here beyond thanking them collectively for their hospitality and many kindnesses. Though my immediate task is accomplished, for better or worse, I retain the liveliest recollections of their conversation and good company. The kindliness for which Devonshire people have long been known is in no way diminished. All that Hooker said on this subject 350 years ago I can truthfully repeat even in these hard times.

INDEX

INDEX